Shattered Resolve
A Redemption Novel

Elizabeth Morquecho

Shattered Resolve
Copyright © 2025 All rights reserved.
ALL RIGHTS RESERVED: No part of this book may be reproduced, stored, or transmitted, in any form, without the express and prior permission in writing of Crossroads Publishing, LLC. This book may not be circulated in any form of binding or cover other than that in which it is currently published. This book is licensed for personal enjoyment only. All rights are reserved. Crossroads Publishing, LLC does not grant you rights to resell or distribute this book without prior written consent of both Crossroads Publishing, LLC and the copyright owner of this book. This book must not be copied, transferred, sold or distributed in any way.
Disclaimer: Neither Crossroads Publishing, LLC, or our authors will be responsible for repercussions to anyone who utilizes the subject of this book for illegal, immoral or unethical use.
This book is a work of fiction. Names, characters, businesses, organizations, places, events, and incidents either are the product of the author's imagination or are used fictitiously. Any resemblance to actual people, living or dead, events or locations is entirely coincidental. The views expressed herein do not necessarily reflect that of the publisher. This book or part thereof may not be reproduced in any form, stored in a retrieval system, or transmitted in any form by any means-electronic, mechanical, photocopy, recording or otherwise- without prior written consent of the publisher, except as provided by United States of America copyright law. This book is authentically written and designed. The author approved the final PDF of this book. This book may not be used for anything to do with AI, training, creating, etc.
Scripture Works Cited: The ESV Study Bible: English Version; Crossway Bibles: Wheaton, Ill, 2008.
Crossroads Publishing, LLC—620-204-1710
www.crossroadspublishingllc.com
ISBN: 979-8-9905820-9-5
Author Elizabeth Morquecho
Cover Illustration by Tristen Dulany
Edited by Elizabeth Morquecho and Tonya Andrews
Shattered Resolve Copyright: TXu 2-473-242

Forward

I don't even remember how or when I met "Mizz Liz" because she seems to have always been around my life in some form or another. She is an accomplished pianist and singer, an incredible mother, grandmother, teacher, strong wife, a thorough, dedicated editor, and passionate writer. She is also passionate in her zest and love for her God and Father.

"Mizz Liz," as I call her, took it upon herself to edit my book in exchange for me reading, critiquing, improving upon (rarely), and clarifying parts of the novel she was crafting. Her love for her Lord shows out in nearly every line, every hand-crafted word, every dosage of emotion she injects into her characters. She met them where they lived and brought the written word and created persons to life.

There were times when I would offer guidance on a legal matter and explain the best the most realistic way for her to write the scene. Any time my advice was given, she put her writer's ego into the back of the closet and really listened and took to heart my suggestions. Of course, the Quid Pro Quo happened when she did the same with me for my book.

In true Scriptural manner, her children rise up and bless her, and her husband calls her blessed (Proverbs 31:28-31). Even in times when inspiration couldn't be found, "Mizz Liz" girded her loins and remembered God was still on His throne.

I was pleased to be introduced to the main characters: Josh, Jordan, Rhea, Nichole, and Garrett. The true heart of Christ is on full display here, as His redeeming and relentless love shines through the lives of the people "Mizz Liz" has so realistically crafted. "Shattered Resolve" is the first of a series and a breath of gritty salvation for even the hardest hearts.

"Mizz Liz," if you are wondering if this book will be the witness for Christ you hope it will be, I have one thing to say:

Indubitably, "Mizz Liz." Indubitably.

Scott Morales
Author of "Strawberry Concrete"

You may find Scott Morales, author of "Strawberry Concrete," on any of these platforms:

WEBSITE:
https://authorscottmorales.com/

FACEBOOK:
https://www.facebook.com/search/top?q=author%20scott%20morales

X:
https://x.com/morales1496?s=11

INSTAGRAM:
https://www.instagram.com/writerscottmoralesigsh=dmxwN2h0azRwMWxw

TIKTOK:
https://www.tiktok.com/@scott.morales1701?_t=ZT-8sz3w1gKZBL&_r=1

Endorsement

As an author myself, I could only hope and pray my writings could be this Holy Spirit led. This is the start of an intriguing series that will leave you turning the pages to find out what happens next. You might not be able to put this book down, so please consider planning some time to read it. You also might want something to write some notes on. There is sure to be some guiding of revelation. Mrs. Morquecho's ability to weave the love and mercy of God throughout this story is nothing short of phenomenal. The story takes you on a journey through the life of a young gentleman who has made some mistakes. Through her Holy Spirit led writing, Mrs. Morquecho allows the reader to not only see no one is perfect, but also gives the opportunity for the reader to see a path to their own redemption. There are so many that need this message of forgiveness in the safety and shelter of God's love.

I absolutely could not stop reading the book until I knew what happened, and how the characters saw the love of God at work in their own lives. This book will definitely pull your heart strings, and you will want to share it with others who may just need a touch of God's grace and mercy.

I cannot wait to see what happens in the other books of the series. Thank you, Mrs. Morquecho, for following God's plan for you.

Pastor Tonya Andrews

Acknowledgments

Words cannot express my gratitude for those who came alongside me during this journey. I have been writing books since childhood, and my siblings were always there to cheer me on and push me forward. Though each of them has impacted my writing, it is you, Rachel, who shoved me out of my comfort zone the most. I have admired your thirst for reading since we were kids and never thought I'd attain the reading stats you have (I probably still haven't!)—but look who now has two bookshelves stuffed to the max! Thank you, sis, for being such an inspiration, for being my sounding board, my critique partner, my beta reader, and one of my biggest fans. I will forever be grateful for your impact on this book—and for the inspiration you gave me for the character named after you! You are both full of feistiness and spunk, adding richly to the world around you.

Much to my heartache, my next acknowledgment goes out to my aunt and best friend, Mica, whom God deemed fit to take home in March of 2024. From "Aunt Mica" to "best friend," this woman was there for me at every turn. She would have been thrilled to see my books published, but there is no thrill like the thrill of being in the arms of Jesus! A writer, herself, I regret the fact that her books were never published. The world would be a better place if it had access to the words written from Mica's heart. I will forever be grateful to you. For our laughter, our tears, and our inside jokes that earned us stares from all around... Mica, I butt you. Always and forever.

Kerrie! The Viking Queen! The craziest of crazies! Another of my best friends in the universe! You have been my biggest fan and supporter through this. You have pushed me for years to leap into publishing, telling me these books are too good to sit on my hard drive. You have read every word I've ever written and have loved it from the start. You fell in love with the characters right alongside me and took me down the river when I threw a plot twist into their stories you didn't see coming. (Sorry, not sorry!) You have listened to me talk endlessly about plot lines, character arcs, writer's block and never once told me to take a hike. I cannot thank you enough for your awesome input, your crazy ideas, and your love and laughter along the way. Viking Queen! Be a Jordan, not a Josh!

Mama, sweet Mama. It took me forever to get brave enough to show you this book. Something is intimidating about showing the one who birthed you the books you write! But you were thrilled to read "Shattered Resolve," and you have cheered me on every step of the way, always begging for the next chapter. When I told you I had a chance to become a published author, you were so excited and told me you knew I could do it! Thank you for reading my work, Mom, and thanks for not disowning me as you followed the MC's character arc! I love you!

To all my beta readers–you guys rock! Anna Lissiman, thank you for your amazing input and honesty. You taught me so much during our time writing together! You are why I hurdled the obstacle of "show, don't tell." Antoinette and Lori, it took so much courage for me to ask ya'll to read this–after all, who asks their coworkers to critique their books? –but I have no regrets! You both had such an impact on me as you read "Shattered Resolve", and I will always appreciate you! Chris Murphy, fellow writer and critique partner–thank you for your constant encouragement and wisdom during this journey. And for the many beta readers I have had along the way, thank you. A million times, thank you.

My husband and children–you have put up with my moodiness as I wrote, revised, edited, screamed, and repeated. You have been in my corner from day one, cheering me to the finish line. You have all read with me, listened to the scenes I wrote and recorded, critiqued me, gave me input, and loved me when I felt like quitting. Anthony, I will never forget how God used "Shattered Resolve" to show me you were the one I was to marry. I stand by my original statement–I wrote about you years before ever laying eyes on you. We serve the most amazing God! I am so blessed to be called yours!

Mr. Scott! How do I even start with my thanks to you? God has worked in the most intricate, surprising ways since that first day you messaged me about my book. Never in my wildest dreams would I have anticipated a stranger being so involved in my writing process. You will forever be known to me as my "Cop-Writer, Adopted Dad, Friend, and Writing Partner." You gave me the sense of realism I desperately needed to pull off the legal aspects of my novels. I never would have understood the ins and outs of Josh's journey through the system had it not been for you. Thank you for helping me with the scenes on all things law, for reading "Shattered Resolve" and forme an honest critique. Thank you for walking this journey with me and cheering me along without asking for anything in return. It is an honor to know you, and an even greater honor to have you in my corner! Had it not been for God using you in my life, I would have never branched out into editing for other writers, and I certainly wouldn't have been connected to a publisher! Thank you, thank you, a million times thank you!

The most important acknowledgment I could ever give is to the One Who saved me. The One Who never gives up on me, no matter what. Jesus Christ, my best friend yesterday, today, forever. Lord, You have shown so much mercy and grace toward me throughout this journey. Convicted me when I wrote scenes displeasing to You, showed me how to write Josh's story in a way that honors You, and been patient with me as I stumbled my way through. Thank You, Jesus, for the blood You shed for me. Thank You for always being my shelter. I am forever indebted to You.

Nothing between my soul and my Savior.

Chapter 1

"My son, be attentive to my wisdom; incline your ear to my understanding, that you may keep discretion, and your lips may guard knowledge."
~Proverbs 5:1-2~

"Trouble on deck, boss! We need you right away." The distressed crewman rushed back to the main deck with Titus Delancey, the ship's authority, hot on his heels. The adrenaline rushed through Titus' veins at the sound of a high-pitched scream. Had someone been injured? His pace quickened as he took the stairs three at a time. Another shriek resonated in his ears, and he pushed through the crowd just in time to witness one of his divers towering over a shaken guest.

"Take another step and I'll have your job." The short, rounded man had both arms flung before him as he fended off his attacker. His beady eyes were huge in his pale face; his balding head sporting a fresh sunburn.

"It's people like you who give common sense a bad name. You could've gotten us both killed!" Joshua Cameron towered above the small man, fury burning in his eyes. "I have never come across a man as stupid as you. If all the idiots in the world were standing in front of me right now you would be more stupid than all of them combined."

"How dare you talk to me like that? I am a guest on this ship and I deserve to be treated with respect. I demand to see your manager this very minute!" With outstretched limbs, he shrieked again and leaped back to evade Josh's advance but wasn't so lucky.

Titus watched in horror as Josh shoved the guest and sent him flying into the crowd.

"How about the owner? Will he do? 'Cause I'll go get him!" Josh shouted.

"Josh!" Titus' deep voice resounded as he closed the gap between his maintenance diver and himself. Grabbing his forearm and yanking him back, he leveled him with a look. Josh jerked away from him, glaring with disgust before he turned and stormed away.

"I want that man fired!" the guest screamed, scrambling to his feet and pulling at his wet suit in an attempt to cover his protruding belly.

Titus scanned the faces, his heart sinking as several people stepped forward in shock to check on the man. Forcing a smile, he parted the crowd and placed a hand on the man's back. "Let's talk about this in my office. After you, Mr. ...?"

"Hubert. Felix Hubert." He allowed Titus to lead him away, glancing at him as they walked. Noting the set line of Titus' jaw, he moaned as his stubby legs worked to match the taller man's stride. "My blood pressure must be skyrocketing. My head is pounding. And oh! My back! Ohhh..."

Titus clenched his jaw, praying he wasn't facing another lawsuit. Opening the door to his cabin, he moved aside, allowing Felix to enter. "Have a seat." He nodded toward a chair and closed the door. Once seated behind his desk, he prepared to smooth talk his guest into letting the incident go. "Would you like some water?"

Felix shook his head. "I can't drink anything right now! I'm far too upset."

"Please, tell me what happened."

"That diver of yours is a jerk. Did you see what he did to me?" he whined; his voice high-pitched.

Titus focused his dark eyes on his hands and summoned his calm. "Start at the beginning."

Felix brought one thick hand to the back of his head and smoothed down the last patch of black hair that still clung. "Well, I went for a dive and—"

"Alone?" Alarm registered on Titus' face.

"I am a skilled diver, sir!"

"Yes, but—"

"I was minding my business when this ball of rage jerked me by the collar of my wet suit and hauled me up to the surface!"

Titus' eyes narrowed as he listened.

Felix shifted beneath his stare. "After that, he started shouting profanities at me!"

"We have a policy on the Tourista II—we don't allow guests to dive without a guide. Josh takes the safety of our guests seriously. I'm sure it frightened him to find you down there alone."

"Are you excusing his behavior?"

"No, I'm just—"

"You heard the way he talked to me out there. He attacked me! Ask the guests who were on deck; they saw the whole thing. You're his manager. Are you going to let him get away with treating me this way? I'd hate to involve my lawyers," Felix threatened.

Anger burned in his chest. "Mr. Hubert, you have my sincerest apologies for my diver. You're right—his behavior was unacceptable. Let me make it up to you. How do two free nights and a complimentary dinner sound to you? The Tourista II has an excellent dining room I'm sure you will be pleased with."

Felix raised his double chin. "Okay, but keep that jerk away from me or I'll report him to the owner."

"I'll be here if you need me," Titus assured.

His eyes grew large. "You're the owner?"

"Yes, I am. Now, is there anything else I can do for you?"

"No. I'll see myself out." Standing, his eyes darted to Titus as he walked out the door.

Titus sighed, though the relief was short-lived. Josh had pushed him to his breaking point. Something had to be done while his anger toward him was still white-hot.

JOSH

Crisp, ocean air slapped Josh in the face as he made his way to the sun deck. With a glance around him, he picked the lock on the maintenance shed and went inside. Not bothering with the light, he stepped to the middle of the shed and yanked the string that popped the ceiling hatch. Pulling himself through, he walked to his favorite spot and settled his back against the wall.

Looking out at the ocean, he took a deep breath as he worked to calm his restless spirit. Titus' anger hung over him like an ominous cloud waiting to pour down its wrath. There wasn't a doubt in his mind that he was in for it the next time he crossed paths with his boss. Emptiness swirled in his soul and he reached into his pocket for his wallet, searching for the one thing that could make him feel whole. He stared at the face of the girl who'd captured his heart in high school. The picture was worn and faded from years of handling, but it was still her. Where was she now? Was she happy? Had she moved on after he'd run away from home or was there a chance she was longing for him, too? His gaze drifted back to the water, and he leaned his head back, his thumb caressing the picture as he thought back on the promise he'd made her. "I'll come back for you."

After four years of waiting, she'd probably given up on him and moved on to someone else. The thought was a punch to the gut. If only she knew how often he'd tried to convince himself to go back for her, only to give into the terror of his past and abandon his feat. Would she forgive him if she understood the torment in his soul? Would she accuse him of abandoning her? Hadn't he abandoned her?

Josh's right hand opened and shut as he worked out the tension in his muscles. He ached with the memory of her lips on his the night he'd run away. As he stared at her bright, green eyes he knew it didn't matter if she'd moved on without him–his heart would never let him move on from her.

"Yo, Cameron!"

Josh's head snapped up and he groaned, spotting his roommate on the deck below.

"Boss is looking for you. Seems mad," Nate called up to him.

Sighing, Josh closed the picture in his hand before

bringing it to his lips and returning it to his wallet. Dreading this impromptu meeting with his boss, he rolled his eyes and jumped through the hatch, closing it behind him.

TITUS

The knock on his door came before he was ready. Steeling himself, Titus prayed for wisdom before calling for Josh to enter.

"You wanted to see me?" Josh asked, hovering near the door.

"Sit." Titus focused on his face, reading every emotion as it flashed in his eyes only to vanish as quickly as it appeared.

Josh obeyed. Though his gaze remained fixed on his boss, his stomach lurched from anticipation of what was coming.

The older man's thoughts betrayed him as he battled memories of the scared, outcast kid from three years back. He could still see him clearly perched atop a diner barstool; his hooded sweatshirt cinched tight to keep out the world.

"Man, that storm's relentless." Titus slid into the seat beside the stranger, chanced a glance, and found himself drilled to the core by the kid's cold glare. *That's some real torment right there...* He cleared his throat, determined to press on. "Where you headed on a night like this?"

The kid's face twisted in disgust. "Isn't there some other punk around here you can play daddy to?"

"You just gonna stare at me?" Titus' mind snapped back to the present, and he forced himself to remember why he'd called Josh in. "Your actions today were unprofessional and appalling."

"Not as appalling as that guy's gut in a wetsuit," Josh quipped.

"He is a guest!" Titus gaped.

"He almost got me killed! What was I supposed to do, hug him?"

"Well, you for sure weren't supposed to assault him!"

"He was swimming straight for the rudders!"

"The entire deck witnessed you put your hands on that man!"

"The current was sucking us in, and that idiot fought me!"

"You're the professional!" Titus slammed a hand on his desk, his eyes flashing fire.

Josh's right hand opened and closed repeatedly as he worked his jaw, fighting the anger brewing in his bones. "What about all those safety precautions you have the guides drill into the guests at every tour? Are those just, what, formalities? Empty words?"

"You're homeless, aren't you?" Titus delivered his observation with measured calm, stopping the teen in his tracks. His eyes remained focused on the boy as he turned to face him. A desperate hollowness had replaced the cold glare, confirming his suspicions.

"Man, you don't know me," the kid spat in a poor attempt to cover the weakness he'd shown.

"No. I don't know you. But I know someone like you, and I know what it took for this person to let his guard down and accept the help he needed."

Titus' heart pounded as his spirit warred with his flesh. God… his soul wailed. He needed the Creator to make this right. To turn the clock back and give Josh another chance. The truth was, the kid was all out of chances in his book. If he allowed his behavior to continue, he'd lose his business; he could not let that happen. "You never learn. I've tried and tried, teaching the same lessons over again. Instead of improving, you've gotten worse. Last month it was the fight in the cabins with one of the tour guides. The month before, you threatened a guest with a free trip to the infirmary if he didn't change how he spoke to you. The incidents just keep rolling in."

He took a deep breath, noting the storm brewing across Josh's features. "You've forced my hand this time, son. I can't cover for you anymore. You're fired."

Josh blinked hard and squeezed his eyes shut, working

to process what Titus had just said. This couldn't be happening. Titus, his mentor, confidant, friend–firing him? The words had been spoken with such calmness, as though Titus didn't care that they'd slammed his chest like the anchor of the Tourista II. Josh swirled in a black ocean of fear as the waves began to pull him under.

Fired.

Fired.

Fired.

The word pummeled his thoughts like a machine gun. "Titus." His voice sounded weak in his ears. "I have nowhere to go if I leave the Tourista."

Guilt slammed Titus' gut and his mouth twitched. It was true. Before his employment on the ship, Josh had lived with him. Back when Titus had hope for the kid who'd lost his way. Despite this, he had to be held accountable for his actions. Hardening his heart, he dropped his eyes to the paperwork on his desk and picked up a pen. "Not my problem. I suggest you find a counselor to help you work through your issues, but you'll probably ignore my advice and do what you want like you always do." Glancing up, he was unnerved by the sudden change transforming the young man's face.

Josh stood, staring down at him as rejection laced its black cords in and out of his soul. Once it had taken root in every recess, it began the game it loved.

"I wish your mother had aborted you. You'll never amount to anything; you're a waste of time. Don't bother me anymore."

He heard his father's words and felt the slap on his cheek as though he was still that timid eight-year-old boy. All he'd ever wanted was to be loved by his dad, but that had been too much to ask. Instead of love, he'd only received his father's hateful wrath. The memories washed through his mind until they were all he could see. He swallowed the bitter taste in his mouth and backed his way to the door as his hand fumbled for the knob, his eyes fixed on Titus. "You're no different." His voice was flat.

"All this talk about me being like a son to you. It's all a lie. You're no better than my father. The only difference between you two is he hides behind the bottle, and you hide behind the Bible." The knob twisted in his hand, and he was gone.

JOSH

Within two hours, Josh had every possession he owned shoved into three duffel bags tossed atop his bunk bed. He sat on the floor with his back against the wall, elbows resting on his knees as the ocean carried him closer to the terrors that haunted him. He couldn't focus, but needed to. In less than half an hour, the ship would dock, and he'd be forced to return to the land–and he had no idea what to do once he got there. He had nothing. Titus had paid him well, but with no house, car, or girl, he'd had no reason to save and had blown through each paycheck every time the ship docked for a night or two to swap out passengers. He'd had everything he'd needed right here on the ocean. The one thing he'd never anticipated was the ocean spewing him back onto land to face his past—alone, and with no green lining his pockets.

Ping!

Glancing down at the glow of his cell phone, Josh scooped it up to read the text that had just intruded into his thoughts.

Hey, Josh, it's Jordan. Please text me back, man...please...

His heart stopped in his chest. Nobody from Highshore knew where he was or had his number. There was no way this was real. He stared at the screen a second time, sure he'd misread. The words continued to stare back at him. He dropped the phone as though it had burned him. He'd made it four years without being tracked down by anyone from his past. It made sense that the one to find him would be Jordan–he'd always been a tech nerd–but why now? Why wait four years to search him out? He made a fist and squeezed it tight. He missed his friend. The two had been inseparable for ten years. Leaving Jordan behind had been almost as painful for Josh as leaving his mother.

The ship's horn sounded, arresting his attention. He threw his duffel bags over his shoulder and scooped up the phone, shoving it into his back pocket. He could not focus on the mystery of that text right now—it was time to face his fate head-on. He wasn't surprised to find Titus waiting for him on deck. Shame colored his cheeks and Josh dropped his gaze, letting the silence hang between them. Fishing inside his pocket, he withdrew a cigarette and lit it, breathing the nicotine deep into his lungs and willing it to calm the tension in his muscles.

Titus cleared his throat and stared out at the land drawing near. "Pretty day," he commented stupidly. He was losing his boy, choosing his career over a relationship with him. Guilt stabbed at his heart.

Josh raised a brow in mock acknowledgment. The sight of the shoreline was anything but pretty to him. It twisted the knife in his chest, taking the life from his soul. Out of the corner of his eye, he watched as Titus extended his arm, a Book in his hand. Josh felt the tease of curiosity in his soul, yet stared in indecision.

"Take it," Titus urged quietly. "You never know when it will come in handy."

He studied the title, then fixed his boss with a confused stare. "Since when have you known me to be a Bible thumper?"

Titus' lips pressed into a thin line. Never. No matter how many times Titus had presented it to him, Josh had never paid attention to the Bible. "Josh, there's stuff you don't know...about me." He paused as uneasiness teased. "I've tried so many times to tell you, but have always failed. Everything I need to say is in that Book." When Josh said nothing, he extended it to him again, relieved when he took it and shoved it into his bag

"There's something else I want to give you."

Josh's eyes met his and his brows furrowed in confusion when Titus withdrew a gold pocket watch and pressed it into his hand. His stomach sank at the familiar weight of the metal. The watch had belonged to Titus' father. He knew, because he'd stolen it from Titus' home safe during the first week of his stay. Why was he doing this to him? "Titus, I–"

The older man shook his head. "Keep it. Let it be a reminder of grace to you."

"But, Titus–"

"About earlier," Titus interrupted. He glanced at Josh and found him watching him. "I am so sorry, kid. I never wanted this to happen. I pray that someday you see why I had to let you go. You've got to wrestle those demons to get the peace you're searching for."

Josh dropped his gaze to the deck. His conscience pricked his chest, and he felt compelled to confess something to his boss. He forced himself to meet the older man's gaze, though his eyes were drawn like magnets to anything but. "All I've ever known is anger," he said, his voice thin and strained. "It's the only emotion my father ever gave me. Peace is like an unreachable dream for me." He gave a shuddering breath, his eyes drawn back to Titus'. "Don't you see? I'm not like you. I'll never have the strength it takes to wrestle my demons and win this war."

Before Titus could respond, Josh gripped his bags tight and lost himself in the crowd of passengers exiting the ship. Titus squeezed his eyes shut, his heart ripping in two. Josh had been the closest he'd ever been to having a son. As much as it hurt, he knew the only way to find healing was for Josh to face what he was running from–and he couldn't do that while sailing the ocean on the Tourista II.

Chapter 2

"Whoever trusts in his own mind is a fool, but he who walks in wisdom will be delivered."
~Proverbs 28:26~

RHEA

Rhea Romans stepped back and stared at the wall she'd been painting, the wet brush dripping from her hand as she admired her work. "It's perfect," she breathed, a smile on her lips. Glancing at the time, she rushed the paintbrush to the sink and wiped her hands on her jeans. "Sterling!" she called into the empty room. "Sterling, come quick!"

"What? What happened?" His voice preceded him as he pounded down the stairs and stopped at the sight of his girlfriend's face. "Rhea, I thought something hap—"

"Isn't it beautiful?" She beamed, twirling in the middle of the floor, arms spread wide.

Shaking his head, Sterling laughed as he went to her and wrapped his arms around her waist, kissing her lips. "You're crazy, you know that?"

Rhea scrunched her nose and cast him a mischievous smile as she swiped a finger down his cheek. "But you love me."

"That, I do." He clasped her hand in his and turned to observe his kitchen. "Wow. Looks like a new room, Nic."

Her smile faltered at the nickname but was back in place before he glanced back down at her. "You like it? It's not too…bright?"

"No, love. It's beautiful." He pulled her close. "Like you."

His lips were inches from hers when she remembered the time. "I have to go!"

Disappointment clouded Sterling's features as she spun from his grasp and pulled the bandana from her hair. "You don't have to…" His eyes followed her as she rushed to the sink to scrub the paint from her arms.

Sighing, Rhea scraped her nails across a stubborn paint

spot. "We've been through this, Sterling. I love my job at the diner. I can't leave it." She grabbed a towel and turned to face him, wishing he understood. "And Chloe?"

The corners of his mouth twitched. "You could still see them all, Rhea. Quitting the diner doesn't mean you have to abandon those you love. It just gives you extra time to do the things you love most…like…redecorating my entire house," he teased, hoping to erase the worry in her eyes.

He'd give anything to know the reason for the worry in her eyes. Why did she cling so tightly to her minimum-wage job?

Rhea's eyes dimmed. "You hate it."

Surprised, Sterling glanced at the walls. "No! I told you—I love it. I meant what I said, Nic. I want you to make my house your home. This is our house now. I'd let you paint the walls pink if it meant having you here with me."

Laughing, she tossed the towel at him and headed for the stairs. "Good thing I hate the color pink. Though purple might be on the table before I come home tonight," she teased.

He followed her as she climbed the stairs. "What time should I expect you? Are you working double today?" He hated when she worked doubles, but she was insistent on filling in when needed.

"I'll be home by eight. I'll bring dinner," Rhea called from the bathroom.

"Can't wait. Seeing you is going to be a light to a dreary day. I have to meet my father to discuss that new account he's considering taking on. I think he's crazy to consider it, but he's determined."

Sterling pilfered through his closet for a shirt, settling on a black long-sleeved button-down.

"Who's the account for?"

"Some hotshot who thinks we all should worship the ground she walks on. Talking like she wants to buy up the whole city of Highshore."

Applying her lipstick in the bathroom mirror, Rhea

checked her reflection before grabbing her purse and walking back into their room.

Sterling's eyes fell on her waitressing uniform and he grinned. "Remind Samson you're taken."

She grinned. "He's harmless. Only comes to the diner to avoid Maebell's chore list." Going on tiptoe, she kissed him. "See you tonight—don't be too hard on your father. He may see something you don't."

"And yet again, you defend him." He smiled as she walked out the door, leaving him to prepare for his day.

"Rhea, table six!"

Rhea adjusted her apron in the mirror at the back of the employee lounge and tied it around her waist. Four hours into her shift, it had already proven to be a crazy one from Ted Baker cursing them all out because his bacon wasn't cooked right, to their cook quitting because Ted Baker had cursed them all out. She was supposed to be on break, but Izaak had asked her to jump back on the clock after only ten minutes.

"Rhea!" her manager yelled a second time.

"Coming!" Rhea grabbed her purse and shoved it into her locker, pausing when a picture fell onto the floor.

"I've got you." Chloe Daultry snatched up the photo and moved to hand it back, but paused, staring. "Ooohh! He's cute, Rae! Who is he?"

Blushing, Rhea snatched the picture away from her best friend and shoved it into her purse. "Nobody." Slamming her locker, she glanced at Chloe and groaned at the look on her face. There was no way she was letting this go....

"Come on, bestie! Dish! Is he into you? Is he available?" She gasped. "Does Sterling know?"

Rhea sighed. "Chloe..."

"Look, I just wanna know two things. Number one, are you and the King of Hot in any trouble I should know about? And two, where can I find this cutie, if you're not into him?"

"Ray-UH!" Izaak's shouting intensified, and Rhea

glanced at Chloe before rushing for the door.

"I have to go, Chloe!"

"Later!" she called after her. "We gonna finish this later, Miss Thang."

Rhea rushed by Izaak and mumbled an apology as she headed to the floor to bus tables. She could feel her friend watching her from the cash register and wished she'd let the matter drop. There was no way she was giving out information about that picture, but that wouldn't stop Chloe from trying to force her hand.

"I need more ice water. Hello?"

She glanced at the customer hollering from across the room and forced herself to smile in his direction. "Yes, sir. Right away." Racing to his table, she snatched his glass and refilled it, aware of three more orders being shouted at her from around the diner. As the orders poured in, she entertained the thought of quitting, knowing Sterling would be thrilled. But she wouldn't do that—no matter how demanding her job became. With renewed determination, Rhea delivered the meals and greeted her guests with a smile.

"Bless you, child. Here's yourself a dollar. Buy a nice cup of coffee." An elderly woman stretched out a shaky hand, extending a dollar bill in Rhea's direction.

"Thank you," Rhea smiled, accepting the tip as she cleared the dirty dishes. "Have a good night."

It was an hour until closing time by the time the diner died down and Rhea could take a moment to rest. Catching Chloe's eye, she grinned as she watched her friend dance around the kitchen with two sundaes in her hands, mouthing the word "sit." Obeying, she slid into a booth and closed her eyes, only for them to fly open again as Chloe plopped across from her.

"Sundae for your thoughts?" Chloe teased, handing the treat to her friend.

Grateful, Rhea reached for it but paused when Chloe pulled back and made a face.

"Oh, no you don't! Who's the guy you're carrying

around in that purse of yours?"

Rhea rolled her eyes. "Chloe, I'm dying over here. Please. Let me eat before I faint on the floor."

"Gimme a name."

"Chloe," Rhea groaned.

"Bob. No…Jeremy. Wait, wait…Pierre."

Rhea's brows shot up. "Pierre?"

"What? It could happen." Chloe pulled a face.

"I won't tell you his name, so you can give up now."

"Well, is he available, then?"

Rhea's hand shot up and grabbed the sundae from Chloe. Taking a big bite, she closed her eyes, ignoring her friend's protest.

"Okay, now you owe me an answer. Come on, Rae, give a sister something!"

With a sigh, Rhea stared at her. "I don't know if he's available, because I don't know where he is. But, if you find him, you're more than welcome to ask."

Chloe fell silent as she thought about her answer. "He hurt you."

Finishing the last bites of her sundae, Rhea rolled her eyes as she stood. "It doesn't matter. He's ancient history. Come on. Izaak's waiting.

"What a day." Sterling collapsed onto the couch, leaning his head back and closing his eyes.

Rhea smiled as she finished laying out their dinner in the kitchen. "Well, dinner from Theresa's African Cuisine should make it all better."

Sterling laughed. "Another new restaurant, babe? The food poisoning that seafood place gave us last week didn't teach you anything, did it?"

"Not a thing." She grinned. "Besides, this is Chloe's favorite restaurant. Says it reminds her of home."

Sterling rolled his eyes. "Chloe is an African American woman who has never set foot in Africa. That girl is more dramatic than a box of used tissues."

"You love her, and you know it. Besides, she refers to

you as 'The King of Hot.' Now hush." Rhea tossed a napkin at him.

"The what...?" His cheeks flamed.

Ignoring him, she handed him a plate. "Make yourself useful and help me carry the plates to the couch."

"The couch?" Sterling raised a brow.

"The couch. My feet are screaming after the day I had. Guess who quit today?"

"Who?" Setting the plates on the coffee table, he turned to grab the glasses.

"Elliot Fisher."

"The baker?"

"The cook!"

"Oh, snap. I bet Izaak popped a blood vessel."

"It was intense." Rhea glanced at his face, trying to read him as they sat on the couch for dinner. "He's asked me to pull doubles until he hires a new cook."

Sterling scoffed. "Of course, you told him no."

She only stared.

His face fell. "Rhea, you can't work doubles. I don't want you working there at all."

"It's not your choice," she whispered.

Frustrated, he ran a hand through his hair and sat on the edge of the couch. "So, I have no say in this at all? We're not in a relationship? We don't live together?"

"Yes, of course, but–"

"We don't need the money. I can take care of us!"

"I don't want you to take care of us!" Rhea's eyes shimmered with tears, and she gasped when she realized what she'd just said.

Working his jaw, Sterling's gaze locked onto hers. "Why are you afraid of me?"

"I-I'm not," she protested, though her heart resonated with the truth.

Shaking his head, he stood and walked up the stairs, leaving her alone with the dinner meant for two.

Chapter 3

"There is a way that seems right to a man, its end is the way to death."
~Proverbs 14:12~

JOSH

The crowd on the loading dock buzzed with excitement. A little girl bounced around her mother, tugging at her shirt and whining, "Let's go!" The mother remained too engrossed in her phone to notice. The straps on the duffel bags dug into the groove of Josh's collarbone, yet he did nothing to ease his discomfort as he scanned his surroundings. The pain served as the reminder he needed that this was not a dream. He'd been beached, and now he had to figure out his next move. His eyes returned to the whining child who'd now launched herself into a full-blown fit, tossing her small body onto the dock and demanding her mother's attention. A mixture of sympathy and irritation swirled in his chest as the mother yanked her daughter to her feet and shouted, "I. Am. On. The. Phone. Adeline!" Josh pulled his gaze away and forced his feet to move.

Don't do it. Don't do it, man.

Despite his stern warning, he turned, his bright blue eyes dimming to match the fierce waves of the ocean as he took one last look at the ship he loved. He snapped his head back around, anger and sorrow vying for his attention.

Shoving a cigarette between his lips, he lit it and walked off the dock. He was a man whose stride spoke of purpose and intent to the outsider, but he knew the truth. He was a man without a plan, aware of the sunset looming in the distance and that he had no place to rest his head for the night. He gripped the straps on his shoulder tighter. A passerby waved and tossed a "Hello" in his direction, but he kept his eyes forward, his gaze growing colder with each step.

Titus hadn't been wrong in letting him go—Josh knew that. But he couldn't ignore the betrayal he felt at having been discarded by him. He'd thought their bond had been stronger. Titus had seen him at his worst, so why ditch him now? Josh had made no pretense of his character. He'd been true to his nature right down to the ugly fact that he was a cold-hearted thief without an ounce of love for another person in this miserable world.

Breathing in the smoke from his cigarette, Josh allowed it to fill his lungs with its cancerous toxins.

"No matter what you do, Joshua, don't mess with drugs. They will never hold the answers you seek."

His mother's words, spoken throughout the years, floated through his mind, her sweet voice lingering with the comfort she'd always given. Somehow, by the skin of his teeth, he'd managed to heed her advice. But cigarettes…ah, now that was something he couldn't do without.

"Sorry, Mom," he said around the filthy thing between his lips. He came to a stop in the street, noting a quaint diner. As though on cue, his stomach grumbled and he realized he hadn't eaten today. Glancing at the sunset painting the sky, he sighed and turned for the diner, pulling the door open and stepping inside as he tossed his cigarette outside.

The smell of coffee hung with the heavy film of grease in the air. As he walked to the counter, Josh took a mental tally of how much he could spare for a meal. He could swing three, maybe four bucks, but that was it. He perused the menu, aware that the girl behind the counter was staring at him with interest.

"Hey there, what can I get for you?" She batted her eyes as she waited for his response.

Josh stared hard. What was she, sixteen? He rolled his eyes and settled on a plain burger and water. Pulling cash from his pocket, he handed it to the girl, returning her flirtatious smile with a tight one. Beside him, a little girl pulled at her father's hand as she begged him for a meal with a toy. Josh ignored the rush of pain shooting through his heart and gave the girl a forced smile as she looked up at him.

Accepting his order tray, he turned to find a semi-secluded booth, settling in to enjoy his food. The meat was dry and tasteless, but Josh was determined to savor every bite. He wasn't sure when his next meal would be and had no plans to rush through this one. Fishing his phone from the pocket of his jeans, he tossed it onto the tabletop. Spinning the device as he ate, he stared vacantly as it spun.

"Hey, Josh…It's Jordan. Please text me back, man…please…"

The text played on repeat in his mind as the phone spun faster. More than anything, he wanted to reply, but did he dare? The phone spiraled out of control, ricocheting off the wall next to the booth and back to the center of the table. Josh slapped his hand on top of the device and swallowed the last bite of his dinner, drowning the dryness of the meat with one large gulp of water.

He missed his friend and longed to hear his voice; to tell him all that had happened since he'd run away from home—and to ask about his girl. In the past, Josh hadn't kept much from Jordan. The two had told each other almost everything, swearing the other to secrecy with burdens too heavy to bear on their own. If only he could just pick up the phone and call him. If only he could reopen that door to his past and walk back in. If only his father hadn't remained in Highshore working his magic on all those ignorant enough to buy his perfect facade. If only, if only. But "if only" wasn't for him. No, that was a sacred idea for people who deserve good things to happen to them. Not one meant to be thrown at the feet of society's disappointments. Not one meant for the heathen of Highshore.

Josh lost himself in thought, forgetting about time and the people around him. His mind betrayed him–offering itself as a playground for painful memories to dance to the beat of his bleeding heart. He could see Jordan and himself plain as day in his mind's eye. Just a couple of twelve-year-old kids messing around, stirring up childish trouble…

Josh dropped his skateboard to the pavement and pushed off, adrenaline shooting through his veins as he aimed for the ramp.

Jordan held his breath, eyes transfixed on his friend.

Josh swooped down the ramp, came up on the other side, flipped, and nailed a perfect landing on the platform. A grin exploded across his face as he picked the board up and shoved it high above his head, a victory whoop emitting from his lips.

"You have got to start wearing protective gear, man. One of these days you'll snap that cocky little neck of yours." Jordan joined his friend on the platform, his board in his hands.

"And chance looking like you? Look at yourself, J, with your helmet, elbow pads, knee pads, and…what is tied to your butt? A pillow?!" Josh teased, ducking Jordan's shove and cursing into the air.

"Watch your mouth! You'll end up in the front of the church again if they hear," Jordan warned. A glance at his watch told him they'd both be in trouble if they didn't hurry home. "Hey, it's seven. We gotta scram."

"Who gives a crap about curfews? I'm going again."

Jordan raised his hand to protest, but Josh was already headed for the ramp. "Josh, I gotta get home. You know my dad threatened to ground me if I got into trouble with you one more time!"

"So, go. Be a slave to The Man," Josh teased as he swooshed down the ramp and landed his flip with dramatic flair. He groaned at the uncertain expression pulling at his friend's face. "You're such a pansy, J."

"Last time I checked, we were twelve, not twenty," Jordan grumbled, shifting his board to his other arm. "You coming with me, or not?"

Josh sighed and rolled his eyes, knowing if he didn't give in, then the idiot in front of him would get himself into trouble waiting for him instead of going home. He grabbed his board and began to walk. "Feels weird going home before the streetlights are out. All the guys are gonna think we're pansies!" he complained, throwing a sideways glance at his buddy.

Jordan stood an inch taller than Josh, although he was several months younger. Despite his height advantage, he never could keep up with his friend's stride. He jogged forward a few paces to catch up. "Well, like you always say, we're nerds. We're not like them."

Josh's eyes doubled in size, shocked at the statement.

"You're a lying liar who lies. I never say we're nerds. I say you are a nerd." He reached out and shoved Jordan's shoulder, laughing when he almost fell.

"You're a real prick," Jordan grumbled, catching himself with his board.

"Watch your mouth or it'll be you they stand at the front of the church," Josh laughed. "See you tomorrow, J," he called over his shoulder as he ducked into the woods that would lead him home.

"Later, Josh." Jordan waved and disappeared down the opposite wooded path.

Josh took his time going through the woods, pausing to skip stones across the stream that separated his family's property from the Hendricks's. It had been the best day. His mom had awakened him with an upbeat rendition of "Happy Birthday" and led him down the stairs to the birthday cake she'd worked hours on the night before. She was bursting at the seams to have him open his gift, and he'd torn through the wrapper to reveal the board he now gripped in his hands. It was the best on the market—expensive, for sure—and he'd been begging for it all year. To top matters off, his father had been away on business for the past few days and wasn't due back until tomorrow. Nothing could be better than a birthday without his father around.

Noting the darkening sky around him, he decided it was in his best interest to hurry home before his mom came looking. He broke into a run, bursting through the edge of the woods that lined his backyard, and then screeched to a stop, his heart in his throat. No, that's not right…it couldn't be!

But it was.

His father's car was parked in the driveway. His mother's car was nowhere to be found.

Josh stood frozen to the ground, unsure of his next move. Walking up to that house on his birthday was a death sentence. Every birthday from his past had been marked with punishment inflicted by his grieving, drunken father who refused to put the past behind him. It was inescapable. He was destined to be the brunt of his father's pain.

Not today. Josh's features darkened. He would sneak to the barn and stay there all night. Most likely, his father was too drunk to notice his absence anyway. His chances were good. Moving forward with caution, he kept his eyes peeled on the house. His fingers were pale from the intense grip on his board as he stole past the side of the house. Yes! Once past the back door, he broke into a run, a grin spreading across his face at the luck of his success.

He never saw it coming.

Mid-run, and not even four strides from the barn, Josh's shirt collar was yanked by what seemed to be an invisible force. He was jerked into the air and felt his sneakers dangling at least a foot off the ground. He gasped for air, his shirt threatening to cut off his life supply. His board fell to the ground as he grappled with the collar twisting tighter around his neck.

"Just where do you think you're going?"

Tears burst to the surface of his eyelids, his nose stinging from the stench of alcohol on his father's breath. Josh managed to work his fingers between the collar and his neck, allowing himself a gulp of air. He fell to the ground in a heap, and his heart plummeted as Garrett snatched up his new skateboard. He forced himself not to cry out in protest. If his father so much as detected an attachment to the board, he'd never see it again.

"Where did you get this? You steal it?" Garrett slurred, shoving it into his son's face.

Josh swallowed hard. His blond head slowly indicated he hadn't, but he knew his father wouldn't believe him.

"I won't have…a thief…for a son." He breathed heavily over Josh as he dragged him to his feet, the board clutched in his hand. "Get to the barn and take what you have comin'."

Josh fell forward from his father's shove and scrambled to right himself. Ordering his feet to move took all the courage he could muster. His birthday was ruined—doomed to meet the fate of years of birthdays before it. As Garrett marched him toward the barn, his eyes frantically searched for signs of his mother. She should be here. She was supposed to be here! Where had she gone? Why wasn't she here to rescue him from his father's grief?

Please, Mama.

Please.

Please.

Mama…

Garrett yanked the barn door open and threw his son inside. The doors clattered with a resounding echo throughout the empty barn. He picked up a half-drunk bottle of beer and took a long swig, aware that Josh's eyes were glued to him. Grinning, he threw the bottle against the wall, the shards ricocheting.

Josh screamed; his left shoulder embedded with glass. Pain tore through him like an electric shock as scarlet blood began to stain his white t-shirt. He stared in horror as the crimson stain expanded along his shirt sleeve. His tear-streaked face turned to his father who wasted no time popping open another bottle. Josh calculated the distance between himself and the door, measured the position of the drunk in front of him, and tried to think through the pain that was suffocating him. He had to do it. His life depended on it. Before he could talk himself out of it, he was on his feet and scrambling toward his escape.

Run.

Run.

RUN!

His shoulder pounded, the shards of glass digging deeper as he ran. Fear shot messages of urgency to his feet and legs. His father had put the bottle down long enough to notice what he was up to—and he looked mad. No, mad wasn't the word. He was furious, and Josh regretted his choice to run. Refusing to give up on his attempted escape, he raced straight toward him and bolted between his legs. A high-pitched scream came from somewhere, but Josh couldn't tell from where. Maybe it was his own, though he didn't recognize his voice. He'd been caught. Large hands grabbed him, dragged him back to the middle of the barn, and stood him against the center pole.

"Excuse me, sir?"

Josh jumped to his feet, one fist gripping the collar of the man in front of him, the other cocked in mid-air. Eyes wild, he stared into the terror-stricken face of an older man and realized what he'd done. His hand released the man's collar as though an electric current radiated from his body. His fist fell to his side, and he jumped backward, fumbling over his chair. "I'm sorry." He gasped. "I'm so sorry!"

"I-I think it's time for you to go." The small voice squeaked past his lips as the owner of the diner trembled beside the table.

Josh stared at him a moment, swallowing hard. His eyes scanned the room of those trying to enjoy a peaceful meal, their calm disturbed by his unexpected outburst. "I'm so sorry," he whispered as he grabbed his phone from the table and lifted his bags, the weight of their stares following as he rushed out the door.

Five blocks away from the diner, Josh collapsed onto a bench. His chest heaved as he tried to breathe through tight lungs. He dropped his face into his hands, panic forcing tears through eyelids squeezed tight. "Breathe," he ordered his body. "Just breathe." He rocked himself, arms locked across his chest as his fingers dug into his skin. He looked up, dread filling his bones to find the sun sinking beneath the earth.

Sudden exhaustion overtook him, and he knew he needed to find a place to stretch out and sleep for a few hours. Hoisting his bags to his shoulder, Josh lit a cigarette and shoved it between his tight lips, his features once again drawn into a mask of hardened strength. Determination drove him forward in confident strides, his entire being putting out an aura that warned others to keep their distance.

Reaching into his back pocket and withdrawing his phone, he thumbed through his iTunes until he came to Green Day's "Boulevard of Broken Dreams" and hit play. Turning the volume up, he continued down the street in search of the perfect spot—secluded, unnoticed. He wandered into a public park marked with "No Loitering After Dark" signs and made his way toward the playground. The city hadn't bothered with streetlights in the park; an effort to keep out the after-dark loiterers, Josh assumed, but that only helped his cause, not deterred it. He surveyed his surroundings, noted a tunneled bridge, and dismissed it. It would leave him too vulnerable if someone wanted to jump him. He needed a place he could escape from if needed.

There.

His gaze fixed on a swinging bridge that dipped in the middle. It was out in the open, but the darkness created a shield for his presence. Yeah, that would do. He headed for the bridge and unloaded his duffel bags, breathing a sigh of relief.

For a while, Josh just sat on the bridge, dangling his legs over the side and swinging it back and forth as the music blared in his ears. The lyrics were a reflection of his current state and his mouth curled in a tight smile around the cigarette. Lonely roads had defined his life. Nothing could describe the emptiness in his soul at being separated from those he loved.

Memories of Jordan played in his mind. The town had a

saying about the two friends: "The saint can't save the heathen." But it had never mattered how they'd seen him, because Jordan had never cared what they'd said. He'd defended Josh countless times, even though Josh was usually guilty of whatever they'd accused him of. Graffiti, vandalism, car thefts, armed robberies... He'd dragged Jordan right along with him, but his friend had rarely taken part in his heathen ways. Instead, Jordan had been his lookout. Not by Josh's choosing, but by his own. Jordan would rather risk getting himself into trouble than leave Josh in a vulnerable state, regardless of his stupidity. Maybe Jordan still felt that way. Would he be there for him if he reached out? He sighed and pulled his phone out, swiping until he saw Jordan's text. Staring down at the words, his chest tightened as he considered giving in and calling the number taunting him on the screen. It would be so easy. So...easy...

Before his mind could cast logic on his heart Josh hit "send," and the shrill ringing in his ears sent panic through his veins. He refused to relent. He missed his friend and trusted Jordan to keep his secrets. Jordan would never betray him by telling his fa—

"Hello?"

JORDAN

"Hello...?" Jordan Hendricks asked a second time. When there was still no answer, he glanced at the number on his screen. He didn't have it saved in his contacts and didn't recognize it. About to disconnect the call, his heart skipped a beat and pounded in his chest. Wait a second...was this the number he'd texted in hopes of reaching Josh? His breath came in excited gasps as he managed his friend's name.

"Josh? Josh, is that you? Josh, if it's you, please answer. Please." Jordan held his breath and begged God to give Josh the courage to answer him.

"It's me."

Tears sprang to Jordan's eyes. He couldn't believe his

luck. After years of putting his nerdy tech tricks into place to try and track his friend, Josh sat on the other line waiting for him to say something. Say something! Oh, snap… "Josh? Josh Cameron?" he confirmed.

A sigh crossed the distance. "Yeah."

"Joshua Taylor Cameron?"

Josh cursed. "Cut the crap, J. It's me, okay?"

Jordan sat frozen on his couch; the book he'd been engrossed in discarded beside him. "I've searched everywhere, man. I've exhausted every idea in my head trying to find you."

"I know."

Jordan searched his mind for something to say that would keep his friend talking. "So um, w-where are you? Or ignore that question if it's not okay to ask."

Josh's gaze roamed his surroundings. "At the park," he answered bitterly. He didn't know what to say. Words, sentences, paragraphs—books—threatened to spill from his lips. It took every fiber of his being to hold himself back.

"Aren't you a little old to be doing graffiti?" Jordan hoped it sounded like the teasing he'd meant it to be.

Josh tightened his grip on the phone, a smile tugging at his lips. "I'm not doing graffiti."

Okay, so Josh was not going to make this easy. But that was alright with Jordan. He'd always been driven by a challenge.

"So why the park? It's almost midnight." When it occurred to him that Josh might be in trouble, his body went cold. "You're not hiding out, are you? If you are, just turn yourself in, man. You know you always get into less trouble if you just—"

"I'm not in trouble, J. At least, not in that kind of trouble. I'm at the park because I have no place else to go." The admission was a blow to his pride.

Jordan's heart seized in his chest. This was not the news he'd hoped to hear, though it didn't surprise him. Josh had always been a wanderer. Jordan pondered the question on the tip of his tongue, testing it in his mind before asking. "You still in Cali?"

Josh laughed and shoved a hand through his thick, blond hair. "You're kidding, right? I was free of California the night I ran. No way I'd still be in the same state as that man."

Jordan's eyes slid shut. If only he knew. "I miss you, Josh. It hasn't been the same since you left."

Josh sighed and leaned his back against a post supporting the bridge. Kicking the ground with the toe of his sneaker, he sent the bridge into a soothing sway. "I know what you mean." He took a draw on his cigarette, welcoming the tar into his lungs before blowing the smoke into the air. "I'm not okay, J." His voice caught and he gasped, shocked at the words that had tumbled from his lips.

Jordan sat straight up on the couch, his muscles tense. "Talk to me, man."

Josh pulled his left knee into his chest, his right sneaker still shoving the ground. He hated himself for the weakness he'd let slip. Calling Jordan had been a stupid move. "I lost my job, Jordan. I had it made. I was on the ocean all the time. I only stepped foot on land when we docked in port to pick up passengers. I'd go ashore, blow some money, take a long walk, and then go back to the ship and sail back out into nothingness. Out on the ocean I was free, J. Here on land, I'm...scared."

Jordan held his breath, afraid if he breathed Josh would stop talking. He sat in the silence hanging between them, knowing Josh just needed him to be there. He counted to one hundred before breaking the silence. "When did this happen?"

Josh kicked the ground harder, the bridge creaking in protest.

"Today. I'm such an idiot, Jordan. I never saved my money. I didn't have any reason to. I just...I never thought I'd be in this position. Tonight, I'm sleeping in the park on a bridge. Tomorrow, I have to walk the streets looking for work, pretending I'm not the homeless bum I am and hope somebody takes pity and gives me a job." He took a shuddering breath. "I'm a felon, dude. I'm so screwed."

"That's not true, Josh. Lots of felons find jobs. You're no different, and you're not someone who gives up. I mean...you're only twenty-one. Your record isn't that extensive."

Josh let out a bitter laugh. "It's cute you think my criminal days stayed behind me in Cali."

Jordan felt a blow to his gut. Things were not looking good for his friend, and his heart hurt over the realization.

"Josh, I don't know what has gone down since you left, but it doesn't have to be this way. We all miss you, man. You have people who love you here in Highshore. Just come home. I'll even come get you if you'll tell me where you are."

Silence.

Jordan winced, praying he hadn't blown his chance at further communication. "You wouldn't even have to see him, Josh. You could stay with me. I have my own apartment. It's not much, but it's big enough for us both if you're interested."

Josh ground the cigarette between his teeth, immediately regretting the subconscious decision. Spitting on the ground, he flicked the cigarette into the mulch. "I will never live in the same state as that monster ever again. Tomorrow I'm going to look for work, land a job, and work my tail off until everything's okay again."

"I'll come get you. You won't even have to pay rent. You can just find a job and stay with me and then you can foc—"

"I said 'No,' Jordan." Josh's tone was threatening. Moving back to Highshore could not be an option. He had to squash this idea fast. "I have to go."

Desperate, Jordan panicked. Would Josh keep in touch with him or disappear like the ghost he'd become?

"Josh, if you'd just listen, I think we could—"

"No, you listen, Jordan. I'm not going back. You have

to swear to me you won't tell anyone I called. And don't give out this number. I don't know how you found me, and I really don't give a crap, but if California numbers start calling my phone, I swear I'll never speak to you again."

"Josh…"

"Swear it, Jordan."

Jordan breathed a resigned sigh. "Okay. I swear I won't tell anyone or give out your number. Is it okay if I contact you again?"

The line went dead.

Chapter 4

"The heart of man plans his way, but the LORD establishes his steps."
~Proverbs 16:9~

DREW

Drew Randall paced the alley behind the bar where he'd just slammed three beers in a row. He'd rather smash his hand with a hammer than call this in, but hiding the latest events would mean dire consequences. He gripped the phone, a heavy sigh escaping his lips as he hit "send" and raised it to his ear. Shuffling his shoes in the dirt, he kicked a beer can and sent it flying.

"What." The voice on the other end of the line was clipped.

"The kid is in Panama. Docked last night."

"And?"

Drew stared at a cockroach scurrying toward a dark corner. "The ship left without him."

"What do you mean it left without him?"

Beads of sweat broke across his brow. "Nate says he was fired." Without giving a chance for a reply, he rushed on. "I don't think we have anything to worry about, though. I made sure he blew his paycheck every time he was in port. There's no way he has cash on him. He called me this morning. Said he slept in the city park last night."

"Idiot! Josh is resourceful. He'll get money, even if he has to steal it. Does Nate suspect you?"

"No. Nate is convinced he's just gossiping to a friend. He's got no clue who I am. I couldn't believe our luck when he told me who his roommate was." Pride welled in Drew's chest as he reminded his boss he'd been the one to find Joshua Cameron.

The man cursed. "None of that matters now, does it? The kid is back on land. I told you not to let this happen!"

Drew's injured pride roared, but it was useless to explain how irrational his boss's expectations were. "I know where he is…" he protested weakly.

"Yeah? Know how to keep him out of California? Because that's the only thing that'll save you from paying for your mistakes. If that boy takes two steps toward Highshore, you're finished. I don't care what you do, just keep him far away from home."

Drew shoved a hand into his back pocket. "I don't know why we're wasting our time. Josh doesn't want to go back, so why tail him?"

"I don't pay you to think, Drew. The less you know, the better. Stay on his trail and call me the second you see something that doesn't add up. Can you do that, cupcake?"

Drew bristled. "You know I can."

"Good. And don't get drunk on the job, idiot. You're no good to me with beer in your belly."

JOSH

Josh woke to the sound of children playing. The excited shrieks drew closer, and he groaned as he shifted his body. Ouch. Everything hurt. Why did everything hurt?

"Mommy, Mommy! There's a man on the bridge! Look, see? There!"

Josh ran a hand down his face to clear the fog of sleep clouding his brain. Glancing up, he squinted as a sunbeam shone into his eyes. Why was the sun looking at him? Where was he?

"Ew, don't touch him, Lilith! Don't go over there, baby. Come back to Mommy."

Oh yeah. Everything made sense now. He'd slept in the park last night. Sitting up, he cursed as his body protested. He hoped he wouldn't have to sleep on a bridge again that night.

"I'm calling the police. How dare he just crash out on a children's playground like this? He's probably drunk. The audacity of these stupid homeless bums!" a second female spoke.

Josh bristled at being called a drunk, but he couldn't focus on that. He had to leave this park before the police showed up—he wanted nothing to do with the law. Grabbing the straps on his duffel bags, he shoved himself off the bridge.

"Hey, mister, are you homeless?"

His eyes snapped to the little girl who'd appeared beside him. He resisted the urge to spew curses at her mother's ignorance. "Your mom is waiting," he said, careful not to allow any part of himself to touch the kid.

"Get away from her!" The assuming mother raced toward them, pepper spray in hand. "Lilith, run!"

Josh rolled his eyes and shot her the finger before taking off in a run toward the street. He made sure to run down several streets in case the cops decided to search for him. The last thing he needed today was an encounter with the police.

Once he'd put a good six or seven blocks between him and Crazy Park Lady, he slowed to a walk. Fishing in his pocket, he pulled out a smoke and lit it. That's better. Inhaling, he looked around and blew the smoke out through his nose. He needed a plan. He hated making uncalculated decisions, but in situations such as his, there didn't seem to be much room for choice.

Spotting a newsstand on the sidewalk, he swiped a job search ad and settled on a nearby bench to peruse the listings. After reading each one, he lowered the paper to his jean-clad legs and thought about his options. Most of the work required certain skills he didn't possess. Some he could do, but they wouldn't touch him with a ten-foot pole considering the felonies hanging over his head. That narrowed it down to four or five options.

He needed a pen.

Josh scanned the crowd and spotted a businessman carrying a briefcase and ordering coffee from one of those free-standing locations on the sidewalk. Leaving his bags behind, he walked to the coffee stand and purposefully bumped into the businessman.

"Hey! Watch where you're going!" the man shouted, extending his arms as though Josh were the dumbest person on Earth.

"Sorry. Didn't see you there." His fingers dipped into an opening in the briefcase, lifted a pen, and slid it into his waistband as he spun away from the man.

He returned to the bench and withdrew the stolen pen as though it was normal to take from random people on the street. Circling the listings he thought he had a shot at, he latched the pen to his belt loop.

There. He had a plan. Now he needed to go to each one and inquire about their ad. He studied the addresses, comparing them to where he was now. Assessing the time it might take him to walk to each one, he cursed. He had to hurry if he was going to hit each one today.

Determination energized him as he snatched up his bags and tossed them across his shoulders. One job listed was close enough that he could walk to it in fifteen minutes. The exercise would do him good—he needed time to think. For the millionth time since leaving the ship, he kicked himself for losing his cool with that guest. The prick had deserved it, though. He'd gotten off easy. He'd needed his liver handed to him, but Josh had more important things to focus on. With sheer luck, he'd land the first job he came to—maybe even be allowed to start immediately.

The clock was ticking, and he knew there was no time to take it easy. Until he earned enough money for a motel room, his bed would consist of random benches or hideaways he might find. He could fall back on old habits and break into an abandoned building for the night, but he was not excited about the idea of getting tossed back into a jail cell. He was sick to death of being arrested.

Jordan's words from years before came to mind: "Josh, you are the definition of insanity. You do the same thing over and over and expect different results every time. Why don't you change it up and try obeying the law for a change?"

Josh sighed. He knew in his gut that if he'd only listened to more of Jordan's advice in the past, he wouldn't be in this position.

A sign loomed up ahead announcing his destination. Feeling a spark of hope as he walked up to the gas station, he tossed his cigarette and went inside. His hope grew when the clerk behind the counter announced he was the manager and needed help immediately, would Josh like an application? Eagerly, he accepted and found a spot to fill out the questions on the app. Gritting his teeth through some questions, he forced himself to be transparent on the form and handed the paper back to the manager, who began to read.

His eyes were glued to the man, anticipation etched onto his features. His excitement dimmed when the manager began to shake his head. Anger stirred within him as he began to laugh and handed the form back to Josh.

"So much jail!" His Indian accent was heavy, as he mocked. "You want me hire you, but you thief! No. Go. Get out of my store."

Resentment burned in his chest. "I'm not a thief," Josh protested as the stolen pen burned a hole in his skin, but the man waved him away. "I mean, I was, but I don't do that mess anymore. Please give me a chance," he pleaded.

"No! You go. Go now before I have more jail for you!" The man came around the counter and shooed Josh out the door, locking it behind him.

Tossed onto the sidewalk like a stray dog, Josh stared at the closed door in disbelief as a cold realization settled over him. No one out here was going to treat him the way Titus had.

Titus was rare. He wore his heart on his sleeve and showed compassion for any man in sight. He was a risk-taker and was unafraid of failure—even less afraid of being taken advantage of by those he tried to help. He knew all about Josh's run-ins with the law, and he'd still taken him in as his own. Josh had blown any chance of having a friend like Titus again.

As he stared at that door, he knew there was no going back. Titus' words came back to him, and he shuddered at the thought of warring with the demons that haunted him. Lighting another cigarette, he walked to the location of the second ad in the paper. This job had to be different. It was a lumber yard. Those were full of people with rough backgrounds—right?

The ten-mile walk took him a little over two hours. By the time he reached the office, it was after one. Sighing, he wished he had the money for a cab to cover more ground. Josh paused to catch his breath and tossed his cigarette before walking in and asking about the job posting.

"Ah, yeah sure, man. Fill out this app and we'll see what we can do." The clerk handed him the form and returned to work, leaving Josh alone.

He took extra time with his answers, careful not to give unnecessary information while remaining honest. It wouldn't do him any good to be caught fabricating. Josh handed the form to the clerk, his eyes roaming the room as he waited for the manager. The smell of fresh-cut wood comforted him, reminding him of when he and Jordan used to pass the time by playing in Levi's shop while he worked on his boat. Jordan's dad had been the calmest guy Josh had known growing up. The way he spoke in a level tone with his son, even when angered, had always awed him. He'd longed to be Levi's son instead of Garrett Cameron's.

Titus often reminded him of Levi. This was the main reason Josh had allowed his guard to fall at times with his boss. There was something about that level-headed confidence that put him more at ease. He admired both men's faith in something bigger than themselves, even though he didn't understand it.

"Hi, you're Joshua?"

Josh's mind snapped back to reality as memory lane shut down, and he watched a man approach him with an outstretched hand. He stood a little taller as he shook his hand, a farce of confidence in the smile he pinned on his face. "I am. Heard you needed some help. I'm in the market for an immediate job."

"Mm-hmm." The manager looked over the application, his glasses slipping to the end of his sharp nose. "Looks good, looks good. No lumber yard experience, though."

"I'm a quick learner. I do what I'm told," Josh interjected, hoping the man would be as gracious as Titus. He held his breath.

The manager looked down at the paper again and made a face like he'd tasted something sour. "Eh...that's quite the record you have." He glanced up, meeting Josh's eyes. "And it's only been two years since your last release?"

"Three," Josh stated firmly, ignoring that Titus could have had him jailed several times over in the years he'd known him. "I don't mess around anymore. That life is behind me." Liar. His conscience pricked. "Listen, I work hard, and I just need a job. Everyone needs to make a living, right?"

The man's eyes narrowed. "At my company's expense I'm just not sure, son. I have to protect my assets. I don't take risks. Look, I know you deserve another chance, but this is just not the place. I'm sorry."

When his application was thrust back at him, rage threatened to ignite in his veins. An idea sparked, and he decided to try and prove he was worth the risk. Quickly, he reached into his back pocket and withdrew his wallet. "Wait. Just take a look at this." Opening the wallet, he held it out for inspection. "I have a valid driver's license. I earned it back after my revocation. I'm a certified divemaster, trusted with the safety of hundreds of lives. I have a job right now—I just needed a break from the water for a while. I am worth the risk. Please. Just give me a chance; I won't let you down." His eyes pleaded with the man, hope hanging between them.

"Look, kid, I'm sorry. I'm glad you're gettin' your life together and all, but I'm responsible for this company. If it goes down, I go down. Get it? Now I gotta get back to work."

Defeat pulled at Josh's muscles, and his arms dropped to his sides, his wallet dangling from his fingertips. "I'm a hard worker. I'll show up early every day and leave late without complaint. I'll work extra days if needed. I'll even take less pay than the average worker just please, give me a job." He followed him past a line of forklifts.

"You've got guts, kid, I'll give you that." The manager called over his shoulder as he walked out to the lumber yard. "It's just not gonna work." He stopped abruptly and turned to face Josh. "Go home. There's nothing for you here."

Josh's eyes locked with his, and his jaw clenched tight. The manager gave a nod of dismissal and turned and walked away, leaving him standing alone. Spinning on his heel, Josh slammed a fist into a pile of lumber, scattering it on the floor. Ignoring the shouts of protest from the workers, his stride announced his anger to all who observed his exit.

Fresh air smacked him in the face as he stormed outside and down the road, shouting curses into the wind.

"Young man," gasped an elderly woman passing on the sidewalk, her eyes wide with alarm.

"Oh, go read a Bible," he snapped as he continued past her. Hot tears boiled behind his eyes; his fists clenched at his sides. Time slipped between his fingers, and the sun crept higher in the sky. He checked the next listing location and stopped mid-stride, shoving a hand through his hair. Fifteen miles. It would take him a little over three hours to walk fifteen miles. By that time, it would be almost six o'clock. The business would be closing. With a sigh, he lit a cigarette, shoved it between his lips, and walked on.

TITUS

It had been a long day, and it wasn't over yet. Titus sat behind his desk, the door to his office locked. He'd ordered his staff not to disturb him unless it was an emergency. He needed a moment to collect his thoughts and pray, and to mull over all that felt so wrong. Things hadn't been the same since he'd fired Josh. He missed him and the long conversations that happened out of nowhere at the most random of times. During these times, Josh had allowed him a glimpse into his heart to see what drove all the anger and bitterness eating his soul.

Titus knew one thing for sure: Josh hated his father. What he didn't know was why. He'd learned to gauge his reactions and interpret the storm behind each one. Any time Titus became irritated with him, Josh tossed up a wall to protect his heart. Titus' calm was met with sarcasm or anger, which had bewildered him until he'd realized the sarcasm was a deflection, and the anger stemmed from Josh not knowing what to do with someone who remained calm amid conflict. The kid reeked of the damage done to him by his father, and the fact pained the older man to his core.

Absentmindedly, he ran a finger across his desk, tracing meaningless lines in the dust gathering from neglect. Josh was a damaged soul, full of fear and trusting no one. Titus had given in to his anger and turned his back on him, tossing him aside like all the others who had broken his heart in the past. He squeezed his eyes shut as Josh's heartbreaking words came back to him.

"You're no better than my father…"

He sighed, worry gnawing at his stomach. For the millionth time since Josh had left, he considered calling him to see how he was managing. When he'd brought Josh on board the Tourista II, he'd been living with him for about six months and was on the streets before that. He wondered where Josh was staying now that he was back on land. He'd paid him plenty, and the boy hadn't had any bills he'd known of, so he should have had a good amount of money saved up. He should at least be able to rent a motel while he figured things out. He'd be okay, Titus assured himself.

But what if he wasn't okay? What if he needed help, and no one was there? Grabbing his hair in his hands, Titus turned to God. "Lord, wherever he's at, give him peace and let him know it's okay. Tell him there's still hope, God. Send someone in his path to shake him up and get a hold of his heart. Please, God…protect my boy…"

JOSH

Something cold and wet slapped Josh in the face as he walked. His progress had been slow, the weight of his bags beginning to wear on him, and now it was raining. His shoulders slumped beneath his black t-shirt as a realization weighed on him.

God hated him and wanted him to die alone. But that was okay with him, because he hated God, too. Any God Who would allow a little boy to endure years of beatings at the hands of his drunken father was no God he wanted any part of. He'd rather take his chances out on his own.

Thoughts of God reminded Josh of the Bible Titus had given him and, as the rain began to pelt the sidewalk, his curiosity was piqued at what he might have written inside its pages.

"Everything you need to know is written in this Book."

Titus' words came to mind, and he wished he had time to stop and pull out the Bible to search out his handwriting and get a look at his mysterious past, but he couldn't stop– not with the clouds threatening to unleash their wrath on him.

Josh pushed himself to walk faster. He was still ten miles away from his destination. At the rate he was walking, he knew he wouldn't make it in time to talk to the manager about the job listing. He told himself to keep his eyes peeled for any possibilities for work along his route, but the hope in his heart was washed away by the drops of rain that had now unleashed their fury in a solid sheet of downpour. In a matter of seconds, he was soaked through, his t-shirt a sticky mess against his skin. He needed to find shelter, and fast.

Spotting a coffee shop, he ducked inside, doing his best to shake the water from his body before walking to a nearby table and collapsing into a chair. Releasing his shoulders of their burden, he set his bags on the floor beside him.

As he watched the sheets of water blanketing the earth outside, he decided it was the perfect time to pull out the Bible and look inside.

He wondered at the excitement shooting through him as he unzipped the duffel hiding the Book. Maybe it was the knowledge that both he and Titus had endured dark pasts. Or that both had secrets they couldn't tell another soul. His fingers found the Bible, and he reverently pulled it from the mound of clothes inside. Laying it on the table, Josh stared at its closed cover, afraid of what he might find inside.

The cover was brown and well-worn—the leather bent and cracked from obvious years of use. Titus' name was inscribed in gold at the bottom; Josh traced the letters with his forefinger, stalling himself from opening the Book.

"Can I get you something?"

His eyes jerked up to find a barista standing by him, pad and pencil in hand. "Uh…sure." He thought fast. What could he get for a dollar fifty? "Can I have a cup of hot tea?"

"Large?" she suggested, pencil poised to jot down his request.

"Small." His answer was too quick and abrupt.

She watched him for a moment too long before scribbling on the pad. Raising her eyes to meet his, her gaze fell to the bags at his feet. "You're welcome to use the restroom to change into some dry clothes." Her smile was warm and tender with her suggestion.

His pulse quickened, her kindness eliciting a strange stirring within his soul. Her face looked wise beyond her years. She probably had a family back home and was working her butt off every day to make ends meet. He pictured her as a loving wife and mother with a husband and kids who adored her. Realizing he'd been staring, Josh snapped his eyes from hers and busied himself by flicking a piece of dust off the cover of the Bible.

"Uh, yeah. I'll do that."

She smiled and rushed to fill his order, probably hoping for the tip he couldn't give her. Josh watched her go before taking her up on her offer to change into dry clothes. Maybe he'd wait out the storm in the coffee shop and remain dry as he searched for a place to crash for the night.

The thought of sleeping on the cold, wet ground made him sick. Pushing the thought away, he grabbed his bags, secured the Bible under his arm, and stood. Locating the men's room, he went inside and peeled off his wet clothes. His body began to warm as he pulled on some dry jeans. Digging through the duffel, he pulled out a long-sleeved shirt and slipped it over his head, pulling it down over the artwork that covered his back—tattoos he'd gotten to hide years of scars he'd received at the hand of his father, ever since he was just five years old.

He stared at his reflection in the mirror as he ran a hand through his hair, spiking it in random bursts all over his head. Wringing his wet clothes into the sink before wrapping them in bunches of paper towels and shoving them into his bag, he zipped it before heading for the door.

As he walked back to his table, he stared in confusion. Instead of the single napkin he'd left there, his table was spread in a full-blown meal, complete with soda and hot tea.

Had the barista given his table away to someone else?

With a sigh of irritation, he turned to find another table but caught the barista's eye as she dried a cup from behind the counter. Was she winking at him? The barista stared hard then mouthed the word "sit," motioning with her head to the table spread with food. He faltered as he turned to the table, slowly lowering himself into the chair and staring at the food. His stomach roared, and he glanced back at her. Receiving a nod and a smile, Josh mouthed his thanks before picking up his fork and eating.

It was just what he'd needed after the day he'd had, and he savored every bite. The biscuits melted in his mouth, the mashed potatoes and gravy warming his stomach as he ate.

When only his drinks were left, Josh picked up the Bible and opened the cover. Written in a shaky scrawl, Titus had written a confession of prayer. One that chilled him to his bones.

"Dear God, how can You ever forgive me? I've killed someone. I am now a murderer. A murderer on the run…"

Chapter 5

"Wisdom cries aloud in the streets…"
~Proverbs 1:20~

DREW

The TV blared an old MTV broadcast, filling the small living room with beats loud enough to strip the paint from the walls. Drew mindlessly stared at the screen, weary from working to think up a plan to keep Josh nearby. He was out of ideas. It wasn't like he and Josh were close friends—he had no leverage to make him stay in town. They'd met at a local hangout before Josh had taken the job on the Tourista II. From Josh's perspective, their meeting had been by chance. But Drew knew better. He'd been sent to befriend him, with the ulterior motive of keeping close tabs on his whereabouts.

A commercial interrupted the broadcast, and children's laughter replaced the filthy music. Drew sat up as he watched the kids running around a playground and threw his empty beer bottle into the wall. "That's it!" Grabbing his phone, he scrolled through his contacts until he found Josh's number and dialed.

His fingers drummed the crude coffee table as the line rang. "Come on, come on, come on…"

"This isn't a good time," Josh clipped.

Drew grinned as he listened to the pounding rain on Josh's end. "Yo, bro, just checkin' to make sure you found a place to crash tonight, with this storm and all."

"Nah, I'm takin' shelter in a doorway right now."

"Straight up? Where you gonna sleep?"

"Don't know."

"Let me scoop you up. I'm just chillin' at the house." Drew snatched a rubber ball from the floor and bounced it on the tabletop. Though Josh took a while to answer, Drew was confident he'd say yes.

"Uh, yeah, man. That'd be great. I'm at the corner of Dodge and Treadwell."

"That's like fifteen minutes from me. Sit tight—I'll be right there." He hung up and laughed, chunking the ball into the corner of the room. Josh was less than five minutes away from him—but he had to prepare for his arrival before he could pick him up.

Standing, he snatched up his phone and dialed.

"Yo, Drew."

"What's up, cuz? I need a favor…"

"Thanks for letting me crash, man. I'm soaked—mind if I shower?" Josh followed Drew into the small house, his eyes stinging as the stench of beer hit his nose.

"Yeah, sure. You can take the first room on the left. Shower's across the hall." Drew watched him disappear into the room before grabbing the remote and flicking on the TV. When he heard the bathroom door close, he leapt up and darted into the guestroom, his eyes scanning for Josh's belongings.

"You smart little devil." Drew laughed when he found the room empty. "Can't outsmart me, though."

Pulling out his phone, he dialed a friend and walked to his bedroom, closing and locking the door behind him.

"'Sup, homie?"

"Hey, Ezekiel, you down to hang a while? My place—I've got some beers." Moving to his closet, Drew shoved his arm to the end of the rack and dug his hand into the pocket of his trench coat, withdrawing a small baggie.

Ezekiel cursed. "I'll be there in ten. You got some good?"

Drew rolled his eyes. Ezekiel was such a moocher. "Yeah, man. Come on."

He hung up and grinned, staring down at the white powder in the bag as he thought out his next move. Cameron was smart—and suspicious of everyone. It wouldn't be easy to pin something on him, but Drew felt confident he'd be able to pull it off with Ezekiel's help.

Lying back on the bed, he clasped the bag in his palm, thinking out the scenario from start to finish. He played it back in his head until he'd eliminated every flaw.

Josh didn't stand a chance against what was about to hit him.

JOSH

"Nate says you got fired 'cause you decked a guy. Any truth to that?" Drew fought a smile as he watched Josh tense his jaw.

"Nate's got a big mouth."

"So, it's true."

"What if it is?" Josh challenged, his eyes darkening.

"I'm just saying…seems like it could've been avoided, that's all." Drew ducked his head, watching the storm billowing across Josh's features out of the corner of his eye.

"And you're, what, an expert on my life all of a sudden?"

"Hey, I don't mean any disrespect." He held up his hands in surrender. "I just know how much that job meant to you. Nate said Titus was furious."

Josh shot him a glare. "Look, man, I didn't come here for this. You keep my business out of your mouth, you hear me?"

"It's a shame, that's all. I mean, Nate really likes Titus. Says he treated you real fair. Why would you do him like that?" Though he'd been waiting for the eruption, Drew tensed when Josh leaped to his feet.

"Watch your step, bro," Josh warned, anger pulsing through his veins.

Drew stood but was careful to keep his distance. Headlights bounced up the driveway, and he knew he had to escalate this before his window of opportunity closed. "Nate said you–"

Josh swung, connecting with Drew's jaw before he could finish his statement. "You've got no right to talk about me with Nate," he spat as he stormed toward the guestroom.

Hearing the car door shut outside, Drew raced after

Josh and followed him into the room. "Where are you going?"

"Back to the streets. They gossip less than you do," Josh said through his teeth as he scooped up his bags.

The front door opened, and Drew screamed, "Josh, put the gun down, you coked up freak!"

Josh's features clouded with confusion as Drew pulled a pistol from his pocket. His eyes widened when Drew aimed at the wall and pulled the trigger, and a scream came from the living room. "What did you do?!" Josh asked, shocked when a grin spread across Drew's face, and he put his phone to his ear.

"Someone's been shot! Hurry!"

"Drew!" Josh shouted when he'd hung up. Instead of answering, Drew raced from the room, closing Josh in the bedroom.

"Oh, Drew, I'm shot!" a man screamed.

"I'm so sorry, man! My friend just went crazy on me." Drew's voice was panicked.

Josh's blood ran cold as sirens sounded in the distance. There was no time to figure out Drew's motives. He had to get out of there. Racing to the window, he worked the stubborn locks, frustration mounting when he realized the window had been painted shut and refused to budge. Curses flew from his lips as police sirens drew nearer.

He was running out of time.

Squeezing his eyes shut, Josh slammed his fist through the window, shards of glass ripping through his hand before shattering to the ground. Tossing his bags outside, he scrambled to pull himself through the window, his hand searing in pain. He was cut badly and knew he needed medical attention, but there was no time for that. Dropping to the ground below, he grabbed his bags. His eyes fell on a vehicle parked on the street and he dashed toward it as the first squad car rounded the corner.

Noticing a small crack in the driver's side window, Josh slipped his fingers inside and shoved down hard, biting back the scream in his throat as the pain in his hand shot up his arm. Reaching over the bloody mess he'd left on the window, he popped the lock and flicked open his pocket knife, sticking it into the cowling around the steering column and breaking it off before tossing it to the floor. Pulling out the lever and starting the car, he gritted his teeth and yanked down hard on the steering wheel. Pressing his foot onto the brake, he broke the steering wheel lock as the first officer arrived.

"Don't let him get away! He just shot my friend!" Drew bolted from the house, nearly slamming into the cop headed his way.

The cop's head whipped around, eyes locking with Josh's. "Hey! Hey, you, stop!" His hand went for his gun, uncertainty written on his face as Josh peeled away from the curb.

Blood poured from Josh's hand as rubber screamed beneath him, the tires hot on the pavement as he tore from the scene. A glance in the rear-view mirror left his stomach lurching. Three cop cars were behind him and, for a split second, he wondered if his chances may have been better off back there.

"Too late now," he muttered as he sped down the narrow two-lane road. Whipping around a car blocking his path, he barely missed it as he jerked back into the lane, the cops shadowing his every movement. The pavement wound sharply to the right, and his blood became his downfall, slicking up the steering wheel until he realized with sickening dread that he could no longer maintain a grip. Josh saw the tree and terror seized his body.

This was it. He was going to die—and he wasn't ready.

The terrifying sound of rubber screaming against the blacktop mixed with metal wrapping itself around wood, and his world went black.

DREW

"I have good news," Drew announced, grinning into the phone as he scrubbed the blood from his carpet.

"I'll be the judge of that. Tell me what happened." The

voice on the other line was clipped.

"Cameron's been busted."

The statement was met with a long pause as the recipient mulled this over. "You're sure?"

Drew's grin spread so wide it hurt. "Positive. My cousin's the one who snapped the cuffs on his wrists."

"The gringo?"

Drew bristled. "Tristan. His name is Tristan. He picked him up for shooting a guy at my place."

"He shot somebody?"

"No." Drew scrubbed harder at the stain. "I did. But the cops don't know that."

"They're gonna find out, you idiot!"

"My prints aren't on the gun–I used gloves," Drew defended.

"Did you kill the guy?"

"Nah, man."

"Blasted idiot. He's gonna talk to the cops!"

Drew bristled. "He didn't see the shooter. The bullet came from the next room. He's convinced Josh was hopped up on coke and went nuts. That's exactly what we told the cops, too. And if that's not enough for you, check this out. Josh stole my car when trying to escape and crashed it down the street. They had to use the Jaws of Life to remove him. When Tristan nailed him, he planted a bag of coke on him while he was unconscious. He'll be going to prison for a long time with all they have against him. We won't have to worry about him for a while."

"I'm impressed," the man said. "Congratulations. You're one up from being an idiot."

Drew beamed as the line went dead.

ASHER

Asher Holmes had a headache. Not the type that annoyingly pokes at your head. This headache had a name. He pressed his fingers into his temples and rubbed in circular motions, eyes closed. He could smell the heat from his coffee and tried to convince himself he wanted the cup he'd just poured.

Things were looking up—he shouldn't be worried. So, why was he? Boisterous laughter rose from beyond his closed door, and he squeezed his eyes tighter to erase the crowd of detectives joking with one another as though his world wasn't falling apart.

Something was wrong. This was too easy. She wouldn't be satisfied with this solution. His intercom buzzed and he cringed at the sound of Milly's wrinkled voice over the wire. "Captain, you have a visitor."

"No visitors," he clipped, his brown eyes flying open as he told himself to focus. He would not allow her to control every aspect of his being. Here, he was the one in charge—not her.

Asher grabbed the stack of case files still waiting to be assigned. Thanks to her, he was several days behind, and his detectives were starting to notice. He'd allowed her to completely side-track him and was now kicking himself for it.

If only Josh Cameron hadn't been fired from the ship. If he still floated around on the ocean, then the wicked witch wouldn't have reappeared in his life.

Picking a file from the top of the stack and opening it, he began to read. Someone's kid had run away, and the mother wanted to list him missing. He sighed. What was wrong with kids these days? Didn't they realize they were better off with their parents than wandering the streets with other idiots like themselves? He checked the timeline listed on the paperwork: missing for eight hours. He rolled his eyes. The kid wasn't missing. He just didn't want to obey Mama. He tossed the file to the side and snatched up another. This one grabbed his attention. CPS had reported a father for beating his kid.

Asher lowered the case file and sipped the coffee that had grown cold beneath the air conditioner.

He wasn't a good guy. Sure, to the observer he was okay, maybe. As captain of the Detective Bureau, he'd earned the respect of his squad, but that was because they didn't know him. Despite the evil running through his veins, he had a firm line drawn in the sand for the bad guys he chased.

You don't hit kids.

The second some prick chose to raise a hand to a defenseless child, he was right there to hunt him down like the animal he was. That's one mistake he would never be guilty of again—not after all he'd been through.

He stretched out a bony finger and stabbed the intercom button.

"Milly, send me Trivett, Lawson, and Myles. Tell 'em to make it quick."

He scribbled some notes on the case file, intending to have this scum locked away before day's end.

A shrill ring jolted him, and his hand jerked the pen across the page, smearing ink over what he'd just written. Shouting curses into the air, his heart pounded in his ears as the ring sounded again, and he squeezed his eyes tight, popped them back open, and stared at the wall across from him.

He hated this woman and all that she stood for. He hated her very soul.

A third ring demanded his response. His hand fumbled for his jeans pocket and gripped the burner phone hiding there.

"What." He knew he was playing with fire, but he could not keep the edge from his voice.

"Well, aren't you a dose of cheer and joy this morning." Her voice dripped with an air that forced him to remember his place. "I want an update, Asher. You were supposed to have called last night. You didn't. Don't think I won't remember that."

Panic split his thoughts. The team he'd ordered was at his door, staring through the window with arms thrown in the air, exasperated at being summoned only to be ignored. He held up a finger, angered by the tremor he saw there.

"It's handled." *Please be satisfied with that answer...*

"Handled how? Do not play coy with me—it won't

help your cause."

"The kid got himself busted. My last update from Drew informed me that he'd been in a bad car wreck—wrapped the car around a tree."

Her irritation sparked across the miles. "He got busted for what? You are not very forthcoming today, and, I must say, it is not putting me at ease. I'll beg you to remember that your life is on the line here, Asher. One phone call. One fax. You're history. Got it? Now tell me everything."

Deciding to feed her the lie Drew had concocted, he dove in. "He crashed at Drew's last night, got into a fight, and shot a guy. When the police came, the kid stole Drew's car and split. He wrapped the car around a tree and, when the cops searched him, they found dope on him. I'm sure he has a long list of other charges, such as evading arrest, taking the cops on a high-speed chase, reckless driving… The point is, Cameron should be locked up for a long time and you should have nothing to worry about." He hoped his explanation put her hound dog instincts to rest.

She paused for a moment too long for his liking.

"Drugs," she mulled, her voice quiet. "No. That's not right. You've missed something, Holmes. Josh won't touch drugs. How could you be so stupid as to buy this story from your ignorant informant? How do you know he didn't let Cameron slip through his fingers and is selling you this story to keep you off his back?"

His hand rubbed his forehead, and his eyes snapped to the window where his team was still waiting.

He couldn't do this.

Asher leaped up, sending his rolling desk chair into the wall. He strode to his door and flicked the blinds closed with determination. The last thing he needed was an audience for his demise.

"Asher!"

His veins went cold. He hated himself. Such a tough guy in the streets and on the force. And here this woman had him by his balls. Through gritted teeth, he gave his response. "The drugs were planted."

"Planted?"

Asher waited her out, feeling the wheels in her brain spinning their evil plot.

The calm before the storm, her voice was drawn out and saccharine. "Yes…this could work." And then the bombshell. "You had better make sure this plays out in our favor and those charges stick. Cameron is to remain imprisoned. Do not disappoint me, Asher. I'm sure Bridget and Ty would appreciate your attention to detail in this matter."

Asher bristled at the mention of his wife and son, and it took everything in his power to keep from throwing the phone into the wall, shattering her voice in a thousand pieces.

He swallowed hard, hot tears piercing his eyes. It wasn't the first time his family's names had been on those evil lips. He knew her all too well. She was crazy enough to follow through on that unspoken threat. She'd have access to his family over his dead body. He had to move them—again.

"I'll make sure. Don't worry. I have everything under control. Cameron isn't going anywhere."

"Your life—and theirs—depends on it."

And with a brisk click of the line, evil receded over the wires and disappeared from his office. But the effects of evil remained, and so would remain.

In his heart, Asher knew there was no end to the blackmail this woman held over him.

Chapter 6

"Hear, my son, your father's instruction, and forsake not your mother's teaching.
~Proverbs 1:8~

RHEA

Rhea swiped a cloth over the last bit of dust on the antique dresser and stepped back to observe her work. A smile tugged at the corners of her mouth as she tucked a stray wisp of dirty-blond hair behind her ear, her eyes sweeping the room she now shared with Sterling. True to his word, he'd given her free reign over his home to do with as she pleased. At his urging, she'd traded his hunting decor for a soft, neutral look and had hung floating bookshelves around the walls, giving the room a literary look instead of a wild one.

Giving into the thirst that had plagued her for the last hour, she placed the cloth and dust spray on the dresser and headed for the bathroom. Splashing water on her sweaty face, she reveled in its coolness, not bothering to dry off before filling a glass and drinking large gulps. When her thirst was satisfied, she pulled her hair free from the bandana and brushed her fingers through it before twisting it back up.

"She's unreasonable, Dad. You need to walk away from this one. Why won't you listen to me?"

Rhea froze at Sterling's voice as he entered their bedroom. She hadn't expected him for a few hours and worried he wouldn't like the changes she'd made today.

"No amount of money is worth allowing someone to treat you like crap. Did you hear the way she talked down to you?..... This is ridiculous. I can't–how can you ask me to–but, Dad..."

She watched him through the mirror, concerned by the stress lines on Sterling's features. She'd never seen him turn down a client before. What could this client have done to sour his taste for her in the brief time Sterling had worked with her?

"Dad, please. Cut your losses and walk!" Sterling pulled off his tie and tossed it onto the bed before lying on his back. Throwing a hand over his eyes, he groaned. "Alright. …. I said alright! If you insist on working for her, so be it. I'll advise you. But don't say I didn't warn you."

Rhea watched him toss the phone, then turned and walked into the room, leaning against the door jamb. "Hey, handsome."

His eyes flew to hers, shock registering as he quickly sat up. "Rhea. baby, I'm sorry, I didn't realize–"

"Don't be silly," she scolded, pushing off the frame and joining him on the bed.

He shoved his hands into his hair and hung his head. "He won't listen to me. He's making a huge mistake and is too blinded by greed to see it."

Rhea was quiet for a moment, trying to understand. "You seem…threatened by this client."

His gray eyes met hers. "Two minutes with her and I'd already pegged her character. She's a manipulative control freak and expects to own my father in this business deal. He doesn't even care."

"What property does she have her sights set on?"

Sterling cut his eyes to hers. "The largest home in the city. And she can totally afford it, don't get me wrong, but that's not all she wants. She wants to buy out businesses all around town. I'm talking Mom and Pop businesses. She has ulterior motives. It's just all-around suspicious, and I don't like it. My father is soaking her up, Nic."

She tensed. "Maybe he'll eventually see but, baby, just because he takes her on doesn't mean you have to…"

"Oh, no." Sterling waved a hand in the air. "I'm not leaving him without legal counsel on this. She'd chew him up and spit him out before he even saw her coming."

Wanting to ease his stress, Rhea posed an idea. "Well, what's her name? I'll research her and see what I can dig up."

He considered her, but his eyes widened as he noticed the room. "Rhea…baby…? What…happened in here?"

"Oh, gosh, you hate it," she groaned.

"No…I don't. If you love it, I love it."

"Sterling, don't lie," Rhea warned, regretting her decision to redo the room.

He shook his head. "I'm not. I swear. Now, back to you researching this client…" He grinned and nudged her, his heart pained at the worry he read on her face.

"Give me a name, and I'll get you whatever you want."

"Nichole Sherard."

Rhea's face blanched white and she gasped.

"Rhea? Are you alright?" Sterling moved to wrap her in his arms, but she ducked away from him.

"I'm going to be sick!"

Shocked, he stared after her as she bolted for the bathroom and slammed the door.

JORDAN

"And then what did he say?" Jordan stared at the little girl on his lap.

Large, green eyes stared up at him. "He pinched me! See? Right there!" She pointed to a mark on her arm, barely visible to the naked eye, expecting Jordan to examine the injustice.

"I see that. That wasn't very nice of him, was it, Nevaeh?"

She scrunched her nose, her dimples exploding across her soft cheeks as she crossed her arms. "No, it was not very nice of him!"

Jordan bit his lip to keep from offending her with a laugh. "Well, what did you do when he pinched you?"

Nevaeh pulled a face. "I pinched him right back and then I telled his mommy!"

Jordan chanced a glance at her dad and the two exchanged grins. "You pinched him back? You didn't like it when he did that to you, Nevaeh…why did you pinch him?"

She became busy with the buttons on her dress, her gaze focused on her lap. The feeling she'd been scolded was evidenced in her quiet response. "He pinched me first, Jordan." Her eyes met his, tears threatening to spill. "I didn't wanna cry; I had to pinch him back! Don't you see?"

Jordan choked on his laughter and kissed her golden curls, his thumb brushing at a tear that escaped her eyelid.

"Why don't you play 'til dinner, Nevaeh? You'll forget all about your day. Sound good?" Her little head bobbed up and down as she slid off his knee and ran to her room.

The moment she'd gone, Jordan burst into laughter. "How do you stand it?"

A smile flourished across Garrett Cameron's features, his eyes following his daughter as she bounced up the stairs. "She's a rare gem, that's for sure." His blue eyes grew dark as he studied the younger man's face. Something was wrong. He read the trouble in the way Jordan wouldn't look him in the eyes, wasn't talking ninety miles an hour, and his signature move—the hyperactive tap of his foot against the floor any time he was seated—was absent. "Want to talk about it, son?"

Jordan's eyes shot to his, hands gripping his knees. "Talk about what? I'm cool, everything's cool. It's all cool." He shrugged his shoulders but the boulder that hung there remained. "How 'bout a game of chess?" *Please don't pry it out of me...please, oh please...* Keeping Josh's call a secret from his parents was sucking every ounce of energy from his body. He wished he could blurt the secret, but he didn't dare.

Garrett studied him a moment longer but let the matter drop.

"Alright, we'll play. But be prepared to lose." He grabbed the chessboard from the end table and placed it on the coffee table between them. Chess had become a regular activity for Jordan and himself. Sometime over the years, as time passed and God began to heal the brokenness, Jordan became like a second son to him. He treasured their relationship and considered it an honor to be involved in his life. But their relationship never erased the longing he had in his heart for his son. He dreamed of being as close to Josh one day as he was to Jordan–if not closer.

Jordan raised his brow. "Lose? To you? Are you feeling ok? Because that was a very disillusioned statement, sir. You know I beat you every time—I've been trained by the best. They don't call Dad 'chess master' for nothing."

"Hey, I've been studying technique, and I'm more than ready to wipe the floor with you this time—watch." Garrett grinned as he laid out the pieces on the board.

"'Pride goes before a fall.'" Jordan laughed as he edged closer to the board.

"Actually, the verse reads: 'Pride goeth before destruction and a haughty spirit before a fall,'" Garrett teased. "Proverbs 16:18-20. And here I thought you were versed in the Scripture!"

The game kept the two enraptured until Nevaeh wandered in, bouncing around Garret until he gave her his attention. "What is it, princess?"

"Mommy says come eat or she'll give it to the dog." She nuzzled his arm with her cheek and hugged him.

"Sounds serious…we can't let a perfectly good lasagna go to waste. Wanna pause the game?" Jordan asked, not taking his eyes off his opponent.

"I think we'd better, but I'm watching you. Don't sneak in here and change the layout like you did last time, Jordan." Garrett frowned as he stood to his feet.

"Me?" He held a hand to his chest, feigning shock. "Never." Jordan grinned and swung Nevaeh onto his shoulders, placing her into her chair before finding his seat at the table.

"Let's pray," Nevaeh suggested, extending her small hands out at each side, staring expectantly at those around her. When they'd joined hands, each hiding their smiles, she began. "Lort…Lort thank You for the 'sagna. It looks goot, an' I want to eat it. Amen." Laughter danced across the room, earning a troubled glare from the little girl. "Mrs. Maddison says you shouldn't laugh at people. You're not being nice."

"Oh, sweetie, we're not laughing at you. You are just so darn cute." Elysia smiled and mussed her daughter's curls. "Now you eat that "sagna" right up, and don't get your dress yucky."

"Okay, Mommy." Nevaeh wasted no time in grabbing her fork and shoving her mouth full of dinner.

Ready to dive into his meal, Jordan's fork was mid-air when his phone rang. His cheeks flamed as he glanced in Elysia's direction and pulled out the device to silence the Maroon 5 ringtone. Glancing at the caller's ID, his heart lurched to a stop before beating against his chest in rapid time.

"No 'lectronics at the table, Jordan… Mommy says so."

The little girl's chiding faded into the recesses of his mind as Florida Call flashed across his iPhone's screen. "I, um…I have to take this." Jordan leaped to his feet, his thumb slamming Accept as he slipped out the patio door, closing it behind him. "Yo, Jordan here," he answered with more confidence than he felt, his voice low as he checked over his shoulder to ensure he was alone. Expecting Josh's voice to greet him, he was caught off guard when a woman answered.

"Jordan? It's Serenity Blake. Are you still searching for your friend, Josh Cameron?"

His heart flipped with excitement. He and Serenity had interned together at the Highshore Tribune before she'd moved to Florida. He'd put feelers out through all his reporter contacts over the years and had asked each one to notify him if they ever came across news of Josh. "Yes, I am. What did you find?"

"He was big news this morning. He got into a wreck and wrapped his car around a tree. He's in the Panama City Hospital now, but that's all I know."

Jordan's pulse pounded in his temples. "You're sure that's all you have? You're an investigative journalist!

Can't you get me something?"

Serenity sighed. "In training. Besides, his story seems to be real hush-hush. No one's talking."

"You're sure it's him?"

"Positive, but the hospital isn't giving out any info."

"Thanks, Serenity. Thank you!" Hanging up, Jordan wasted no time looking up the hospital's number. They wouldn't talk to Serenity, but he'd give them no choice but to talk to him.

"Panama City Hospital, Amber speaking, how may I help you?"

"Hi, I'm calling to check the status of a patient by the name of Joshua Cameron."

"One moment, please."

He waited impatiently while she tapped on her keyboard.

"I'm sorry, I don't have a patient here by that name."

"Check again. Joshua Cameron. C-a-m—"

"Sir," she interrupted, her voice clipped. "As I stated, I don't have anyone here by that name. Now, if there's nothing else I can do for you…"

Frustration mounted as Jordan disconnected the call. Serenity wouldn't have told him about Josh if it wasn't true. Determined to get answers, he called her back.

"What'd you find out?" Serenity asked.

"Nothing. Receptionist stonewalled me!"

"Crap. Um…let me call in a favor. Give me ten."

"Thanks." He hung up, gripping his phone as he leaned against the cool concrete pillar on the patio. How was he going to deal with this on his own? If he hadn't sworn to Josh, he could just tell Garrett what had happened. But there was no way he was breaking Josh's trust like that. His gaze was pulled to the glass patio doors where he watched Garrett and Elysia laugh over their daughter's antics. He swallowed hard and squeezed his eyes shut, playing Serenity's words over in his mind.

"…wrapped his car around a tree…big news…

His imagination ran rampant with images of Josh's

banged-up body, eliciting bile from his sour stomach.

He was grateful when Serenity's call interrupted his thoughts, and the images vanished. He didn't want to think about Josh being vulnerable and alone. "Get anywhere?"

"Yep. A cop I know owed me one. I asked him where they took that guy from the news article, and he confirmed he's in the hospital. He said it's bad, Jordan."

"How so?" He fought to keep down his rising panic.

"Reynolds heard he has a concussion, some fractured ribs, and numerous cuts and bruises. The first officer on the scene said they had to cut him out of what was left of the car. But that's not all…"

"Just tell me," Jordan weakly urged.

"He's in police custody. Being held in the prison ward at the hospital."

Jordan squeezed his eyes shut and banged his fist against the pillar. "Do you know his charges?"

She sighed. "Sure you wanna know?"

"Serenity, my heart's in my throat over here."

"Sorry. He's looking at possession of a firearm, attempted murder, auto theft, possession of cocaine—"

"Wait, what?" Jordan's eyes flew open. "There's no way Josh had coke on him. He's never touched drugs!"

"Hey, Straight Shooter, don't shoot the messenger. Shall I continue…?"

"Yes." A stirring began to rise in his soul—a longing to be there for his best friend and make up for four years without him. *Don't do it, Jordan…*

He glanced at the window again but quickly looked away when he found Garrett watching him intently.

"—resisting law enforcement by fleeing in a vehicle, and a slew of traffic charges." Serenity read back over her notes, wanting to cover everything for her old friend. "That's a grand total of five felonies and a couple of misdemeanors."

Jordan gritted his teeth. *Tell Garrett! Don't get involved! He needs his father!* He ignored the wisdom in his heart. Shifted on his feet. *His father is right there. Go* get him! He shook his head to clear his mind. God, forgive me...

And just like that, a split-second decision was made. A really, really stupid decision.

"I gotta go. Thanks, Serenity. I owe you one!"

"You bet."

He clicked off the line, his mind racing with all he needed to handle before he could run to Josh's rescue. Sliding his phone into his back pocket, he glanced at the window and caught Garrett watching him. He looked away, knowing it made him appear guilty of some deep sin.

The LORD detests lying lips, but He delights in trustworthy people.

The Proverb ate at his soul as he paced the patio. He couldn't just waltz back in and have dinner with them–not with news of their son weighing on his chest. No, he'd have to make up an excuse to leave. Another lie. He ran a hand through his hair and exhaled sharply.

A faithful witness does not lie.

Jordan kicked a rock. "I know, I know!" he yelled, willing wisdom to shut up.

"Son, are you okay?" Garrett appeared at the door, his broad frame filling the space, concern etched on his face.

Jordan spun to face him, guilt radiating from his soul.

Tell him. Tell him!

"I have to go." With eyes downcast, he rushed past Garrett and through the gate, unable to bear facing Elysia with what he'd just learned buried deep in his heart.

Jet lag. What a beast. Jordan stood at the front desk of the hospital lobby and fought the sleep pulling at his eyes as he waited for the receptionist's attention.

"May I help you?"

"I'm looking for my friend, Joshua Cameron. I was told he was admitted due to an accident. He's in the prison ward." He leaned on the counter as she clicked at her keys, telling himself to stay awake.

"Hmm." She pulled a face, making his stomach tighten. "There's no one here by that name."

Jordan's mouth set in a straight line. There was no use arguing with her. He needed another plan.

"Thanks, anyway," he muttered. Turning away from the desk, his mind went into overdrive as his reporter instincts took over, devising a plan to obtain the unobtainable. Sitting in the lobby, he bided his time as he watched for the perfect nurse to approach.

He didn't have to wait long.

"Lacey Anne! Lacey Anne! You left your clipboard in room 103 again! Don't you fear HIPPA in the slightest?" An older nurse hissed as she thrust a clipboard into the hands of the younger woman.

"Oh, dear! It won't happen again, Regina. I can promise you that!"

Jordan watched her features bounce back to a cheerful grin as she walked down the hallway. Perfect. Jumping up, he fell into stride beside her, winking when she glanced up at him.

"Oh!" she exclaimed, coming to an abrupt stop. "Can I help you?"

"You sure can." Jordan flashed a smile he knew made his dimple pop. Girls went wild for that dimple. "I'm trying to find some information about my friend. Can you tell me anything about Joshua Cameron?"

"What a small world! I'm headed up to his room right now!" She gushed. "Oh!" She grasped his arm, lowering her tone. "But they're not letting him have any visitors."

"That's a shame," Jordan answered. "Well, thanks for letting me know."

"Oh, sure! See you!" She waved and headed for the elevator.

Jordan paced the lobby before stepping outside and taking a walk to think out his next move. The need to retain a lawyer for his friend pressed on his mind but the way he was feeling, he needed a moment to compose himself before taking on that task. It pained him to think of the condition Josh was in, and he prayed God would use this to bring his friend back home.

That is…if God was in the mood to throw a blessing in the direction of a liar.

His eyes roamed the scenery, and he mused that Josh couldn't have picked a prettier place to run to. Josh was notorious for running, and Jordan couldn't blame him. Not a summer went by when his friend hadn't made a break for it. Often, Jordan had helped plot his escape, though he'd never understood why Josh was so desperate to get away.

As best friends, they'd told each other almost everything, but Jordan had always known there was a big part of Josh's life he would never be privy to. He would never forget the day Josh had darted into his family's kitchen, shaking from head to toe and screaming hysterically, a deep gash in his upper arm. Jordan remembered his mother begging Josh to tell her what had happened, but he'd refused. It wasn't until years later, when Garrett confessed to breaking a beer bottle on his son, that Jordan learned the truth about that day.

There was a lot he hadn't known. Back then, Josh's parents seemed so cool and involved. Garrett had wanted every detail of where the two boys were going and what they were up to. It had seemed like normal parenting to Jordan, but now he knew better. It had been a show for the town, telling tales of a model father in tune with his son. It was the perfect facade to hide the unspeakable abuse that went on in the family's two-story home.

Tears clouded his vision as he wondered how many signs they'd been given throughout the years. Instead of realizing what was behind the scenes, his family—and the community—had bought the web of lies spun from the mouth of a deceitful lawyer.

A lawyer who was only known for doing good in the community. One who fought for justice and threw the book at the bad guys.

No one had suspected Garrett was the bad guy.

No one had any clue about the pain Josh had endured

from this man whom Jordan's parents had trusted enough to allow inside their home. They'd shared meals with him and let Jordan spend the night under his roof. If only they had known... It was no wonder Josh had run from Highshore and all the memories it held. He now understood why their hometown felt like death to his friend.

Running a hand down his face, Jordan steeled himself for what he was about to do. Josh needed a lawyer, and Jordan had to call his father for help. Normally, this would be a piece of cake, but because he'd fled the state without a word of explanation, it would be a challenge.

He sighed, kicking himself for not giving his father a reason for rushing off to Florida. When Levi had asked his son where he was going—and why—Jordan had avoided the question, responding only by asking his dad to ensure his apartment was okay while he was gone. His father had since called a couple of times, both of which he'd sent to voicemail, and now Jordan needed his help.

He pulled his phone from his pocket, found his father's name, and hit send.

"When're you coming back?"

Jordan tensed. He hated that he couldn't just explain himself to him like always. "Not any time soon. Listen, I need your help. I don't have much time, and I can't explain anything. I'm really sorry for that, but I need you to just trust me, okay?"

A pause. "Are you in trouble, son?" Levi's voice dripped with concern.

"Not me. Someone...else. I need a lawyer."

"What! For what?"

"Dad."

Levi groaned in his ear.

"Jordan, you take off on a plane, don't tell us where you're headed, don't explain why, and now you want me to get you a lawyer without any explanation?"

"Not for me," he repeated, as though that made all the difference. "For someone else."

"Yeah, I heard. But I can't just…"

"Sure, you can, Dad. Just pay for the retainer and get me the info. I can take care of everything else on my end. I'll pay it back—I swear."

"Don't swear."

"Sorry."

Levi sighed. "Son, this is a huge leap of faith."

"You're good at leaps of faith. And I've never proven myself untrustworthy to you. I know this doesn't make sense and it's a huge request, but I wouldn't ask if I didn't need your help. Please. This person's future depends on your decision. I need a lawyer now, Dad. There's no time to waste."

"Where are you?"

"Florida."

"Son…"

"Dad, please."

Another sigh. "I'll make the arrangements."

"I knew I could count on you. Thank you. Trust me—you won't regret this."

"Just don't do anything stupid, Jordan."

"Me? Never. Gotta go."

Chapter 7

"Hope deferred makes the heart sick, but a desire fulfilled is a tree of life."
~Proverbs 13:12~

GARRETT

Garrett paced the length of his office, his black dress shoes imprinting the thick, royal blue carpet with each step he took. He could feel Eunice's eyes on him as he paced, her tension mounting each time he passed her desk.

His secretary shuffled a stack of papers on her desktop, banging the edges on the wooden surface to capture his attention and stop the insanity. No matter how much he knew his actions made her wrinkly skin crawl, he could not make it stop. The blood pumping through his veins was charged with a nervous energy that refused to be contained. "Tell me the client's name again." His deep voice was thick, and he coughed to clear the tears in his throat.

Eunice breathed a sigh as she lifted the notepad to her face for the tenth time since she'd taken the message, then slipped her large-framed glasses onto the bridge of her pointed nose.

"Joshua Cameron, age twenty-one." Studying her boss, she noted his shoulders tensed tighter at the sound of the name. She squinted her gaze and wrinkled her nose, attempting to lock her glasses into place. "I told you he'd come back," she said quietly.

Garrett cast her a nervous glance and ran a hand along the gray stubble of his beard. Eunice knew very little about his relationship with his son and all that had transpired between them. From her understanding, Josh had been a rebellious kid, seeking his thrill when he'd run away. She'd always told him to let him sow his wild oats and watch him come home with shame wrapped around his shoulders. Now she sat with contempt in her eyes, sure she'd been right, with no clue how wrong her assumptions had been.

"I need to hear everything again."

"Garrett Cameron." She stared at him above her horn-rimmed glasses. "How many times are we going to go over this?"

"Humor me, will you, Uni?"

Her grunt of disapproval informed him of her grave irritation, nonetheless, Eunice complied. "Earlier today I received a phone call from Jordan Hendricks. He was a young one—maybe around twenty or so. Had a sexy voice," she added with a wry smile. "He told me his dad had referred him to us, and claims to know you personally. But he's not the potential client—your son is."

Garrett nodded slowly. "What else did Jordan say?"

"He said Josh had shot a man and fled the scene in a stolen car, then led police on a high-speed chase until he crashed into a tree. Mr. Hendricks stated someone planted cocaine on Josh's person and framed him for possession. He's asking that you investigate the charges and get his friend off the hook." Raising a brow, she frowned. "Good luck with that one."

Garrett stared at the floor. His son had shot someone and been caught with drugs? The burden of Josh's troubles pulled at his shoulders. Placing his palms on Eunice's desk, he leaned forward. Something wasn't right. "Can I see the message?"

She rolled her eyes and passed him the note. "If you want my opinion, you've got yourself all tense for nothing. Call the boy and tell him you're on your way to bail him out. He'll be glad to find out his dad is coming—they always are."

Garrett's eyes locked on her stern grandmotherly features. If only she knew…

Quickly, he grasped the note and opened it. His slogan shouted at him in bold letters—NEVER BE FOUND GUILTY AGAIN! It was both a hook and a promise. He was the best in the business within at least a hundred miles—and Highshore's most trusted defense attorney. His reputation preceded him wherever he went: ruthless, cut-throat, unafraid to get his hands dirty. But as he gripped the message within his trembling hands, he may as well have been a child pretending to play law.

"Uni, I need your help." He swallowed the lump in his throat. It was now or never. Eunice focused on him, the intensity of her gaze making him feel small. "I need you to dial this number for me. Put it on speakerphone and take detailed notes."

She folded her hands across her chest. He was so strange today. "Since when do you need me to hold your hand when calling a client?"

"Humor me?"

Eunice sighed. He'd always been an odd boss. Such drastic changes over the past few years. She had a soft spot for him though, and knew she couldn't deny him. "You're the boss."

"Yes, I am." He stared blankly at the wall and told himself to breathe. "Okay, Uni. Now." He watched as she picked up the office phone and began to dial. Panic seized him and he lurched forward, yanking it from her hands. "Wait! I'm not ready." He buried his face in his hands.

"Garrett, rip the Band-Aid off." Eunice placed a thin, weathered hand on his arm and gently patted him. When he didn't respond, she slapped him across his shoulder.

Surprised, he raised his head and stared. "You hit me."

She raised her chin and snatched the phone from his hands. "Call your son before you talk yourself out of it."

She had a point. Garrett sat up straight in the chair and took a deep breath. "Okay, now."

Eunice gave him a hard stare and dialed.

"Stop!"

Eunice sighed. Hung up. And stared.

Garrett ran his hands through his hair, eyes shut. "What if he won't let me help? What if he won't believe I can't represent him myself because I'm not licensed in Florida? What if he thinks I don't want to help him and refuses to let Brische represent him?"

She frowned. "Stop stalling!"

He bit his lip and nodded as she dialed the number, placed the call on speaker, and grabbed her pen and legal pad. Garrett sat with bated breath, terror pulsing through him.

"This is Jordan."

Tears flooded his eyes. It all made sense now–Jordan rushing out of dinner, refusing to look at him. He'd found Josh and had kept it a secret from him.

Eunice remained quiet, watching the emotions flash across his face.

"Tell me everything." Garrett's voice was thick, and he pressed two fingers into the corners of his eyes to stop the tears.

Jordan breathed a sigh that spoke of his exhaustion. "I'm not gonna lie, Mr. C. It's a mess." He launched into what he knew about Josh's charges and physical condition. "...but because he's in the prison ward, they won't even let me ask about him. How is he supposed to talk to you if the hospital's pretending he's not here?"

"Here's what we're gonna do." Garrett leaned forward, resting an elbow on his knee. "I can't represent him in Florida, but I have a good friend out there who can. He's the best I know in that area, and I'm confident he'll let me counsel him on how to proceed. His name is Brische. I'm going to call him immediately. If he's free, he'll show up at the hospital and speak with the detective in charge. He'll tell them that he's Josh's lawyer and demands to speak with him, but that he wants to take his assistant with him to take notes. That's you—go with him, Jordan. Check on my boy. I'll call you once I hear back from Brische, and we'll go from there."

"Okay. I'll be waiting."

"Jordan?"

"Yeah?"

"Why didn't you tell me, son?"

Jordan hesitated. "He made me swear I wouldn't tell anyone I'd found him. I'm really sorry, Mr. C. In hindsight, I see I should've told you anyway."

"No," Garrett answered quietly. "He would never have forgiven you if you had. You did the right thing. Now let's work on getting him out of there."

JORDAN

"What's your name, boy?"

Jordan stared through sleep-filled eyes at the white-haired man. Dressed in a neon green suit, bright orange tie, and brown dress shirt, the guy looked like he'd just stepped out of a comic strip. "Jordan..."

"No sleeping on the job. Let's go," the man prodded, turning his back and walking toward the elevator.

"Wait," Jordan called, leaping up and wiping the sleep from his eyes. "Who are you?"

The man frowned as he called the elevator and waited for the doors to open. "He said you were young—not dense."

Understanding dawned as the doors slid open, and they stepped inside. "You're Brische," he said, eyeing the older man with interest.

"What was your first clue?" Brische stabbed the floor number and perused a stack of notes in his hands. "You're my assistant. You go up, stand there, and stay out of my way. Understand?"

Jordan gaped at him. Garrett approved of this guy? "Um...how much did Mr. Cameron tell you about Josh?"

Brische's frown deepened. "Are you going to be a problem?"

Jordan's brows rose. "Um, no, but he might be. You can't take that attitude with him. He'll chew you up, spit you out, and walk himself to the jail."

"What are you, his mother?" Brische snapped, stepping into the hallway the second the doors opened.

Opening his mouth, Jordan shut it again, deciding to let the lawyer find out for himself. As he followed him down the hall, his phone vibrated, alerting him to a text.

Mr. C: Call me when you're in his room—don't say

anything. Just let me listen in on the interrogation. Brische already knows.

Jordan: K, but have you met this guy in person?!

Mr. C: Ha! He's all bark.

Jordan: Hope he's ready for a fight when your son gets a whiff of his attitude.

"Who's in charge here?"

Jordan raised his eyes to find Brische standing off with the guard at the prison ward.

"St. Patrick."

"Bring him out."

"Who're you?" The cop raised his chin.

"The man who's about to shove the law where the sun don't shine if you don't bring out St. Patrick."

His face blanched white as he keyed up his radio and called for his supervisor. "It'll be a moment. He's with a prisoner."

"We'll wait right here." Brische gripped his briefcase and stared the man down.

Nervously, the cop keyed for his supervisor again. "Just a moment…"

Five minutes after his call, the double doors barreled open behind him, and an agitated officer stepped out. "The heck is your problem, Victor? Got a kid flippin' his crap back there, and you're over here demanding my attention. What do you want?!"

"Are you St. Patrick?" Brische asked, staring him down.

"Who are you?"

"Brische. I'm Cameron's lawyer, and I demand to see him."

The officer laughed, and Jordan raised a brow. "Please do! Maybe you can get the kid to accept that nobody's removing that cuff from his wrist! Dude's crazy as they come. Follow me."

Nerves threatened to eject the coffee Jordan had chugged an hour before as he followed the men down the hall.

"Sir, sir! You need to lie down. You cannot get out of the bed. Sir!"

The voices behind the closed door spoke of war, and Jordan cringed at the sound of Josh cursing the nurse out. The door swung open and she rushed out, wiping her tears. "I can't handle him." She cried as she brushed past them.

The officer grinned and shot Brische a condescending look. "Looks like you're up."

"Let me go," Jordan blurted, his heart thundering. "He knows me–I can calm him down so he'll speak to you."

St. Patrick looked at Brische, who nodded his approval. "Alright, but I have to pat you down first. He just woke up after being sedated, so he's pretty out of it. Empty your pockets on that table." He nodded toward a small table, and Jordan obeyed. St. Patrick quickly patted him down, and Jordan collected his things. Taking a deep breath, he opened the door and stepped inside, aware of St. Patrick's presence behind him.

The room was dim as Jordan walked to Josh's bed. What had been interpreted as anger by the officers and nurses was obvious panic to Jordan–he knew that wild look all too well. Josh yanked against the handcuff clinging to his wrist, his eyes manic.

"Whoa, whoa, whoa," Jordan gently called out to him.

Josh stopped fighting for his freedom and stared blankly back at him. "J...what're you doin' here?" His gaze swept the room. "What am I doin' here? Where am I?" Cursing, he yanked his wrist, his panic mounting. "Am I in Highshore? Tell me I'm not in Highshore. I will kill you, Jordan!"

Behind him, Jordan felt St. Patrick inching forward. "I can handle him, thanks," he called.

"What is this? What's going on? Why am I cuffed, Jordan? Tell me why I'm cuffed!" A pathetic whimper escaped his throat as he tried to shift in the bed. He closed his eyes, squeezing until they hurt.

Jordan stepped closer, pain stabbing his chest at Josh's panic. "Breathe," he soothed. "You're in the hospital. You were in a bad accident."

Josh's chest heaved as his eyes darted off the walls, and he raised his left hand to rub his battered face. The memories of the night before came flooding back, assailing his senses with their harsh reality. Drew had a gun, and some guy had been shot. Drew blamed him for the shooting. He remembered panicking that the cops would find him and arrest him. He then remembered breaking through the window to make his escape. His eyes slid shut, hands balling into fists. He'd stolen a car to get away. They'd chased him… "What kind of accident?" he whispered.

"You wrapped a car around a tree. You should be dead right now."

"What are the charges?" Josh's voice was flat—dread seeping into each word.

Jordan sighed. Where did he begin? "Assault with a deadly weapon, attempted murder, felon in possession of a handgun, auto theft, resisting arrest, a slew of traffic charges and…" he took a deep breath, watching the color in Josh's face grow paler with each charge, "…possession of cocaine."

Josh's eyes flew to him. "What? I didn't…I-I've never…" Tears pooled. "Jordan, I didn't have drugs on me, man! You know I didn't!"

Jordan nodded. "Yeah, Josh. I know."

Josh desperately needed to shift his body. Everything hurt. His back spasmed, and his face twisted from the pain. "Jordan…" he cried, relieved when Jordan gently adjusted him.

"Okay, now that you're calm…" He watched Josh's face. "I have a lawyer here with me. Would you like to speak to him?"

Josh frowned. "Where'd you get him from?"

"My dad called in a favor." He stepped back, ensuring he was outside of Josh's reach.

A storm billowed behind Josh's eyes. "You called your dad? Does he know you found me? Does he know you're here? Does he know where I am?" His voice rose with each staccato word.

Jordan held up his hands in defense. "No. Nothing like that. Just hear me out before you go crazy on me, okay?"

Josh forced his thoughts into submission and reminded himself that he trusted Jordan. Taking a deep breath, he nodded.

"No one knows I'm here. No one even knows you called me. I kept my word, Josh. My dad only knows I had to leave town and won't be back for a while. I called him this morning and told him I needed a lawyer for a friend. I asked him to trust me and not to ask questions. He called a lawyer, who's outside waiting to speak with you." He watched as relief chased away the panic from his friend's face.

A smile tugged at the corner of Josh's mouth. "You called in a lawyer?" Maybe he wasn't as screwed as he'd thought.

Jordan grinned and forced himself to relax. "Of course. I couldn't just sit back and watch my best friend get tossed in the crowbar hotel now, could I?"

Josh laughed at the reference to their childhood. It was so good to have his friend back. At that moment, as they laughed together like old times, it didn't matter to him that he should be furious Jordan had come. His questions could wait. All that mattered was Jordan still cared enough to sit in his misery with him. A flicker of hope sparked in his dark soul.

"Gimme a minute, bro. I'm gonna go talk to him." Stepping into the hall, Jordan closed the door to speak to Brische. "I get that you know what you're doing, but I'm letting you know right now—if you tell him that Garrett sent you, or even mention his name, he's going to jail. Do you understand? He will not speak to you if he knows his father is behind this."

Brische stared at him for a moment, then nodded. "We won't tell him."

"Good. Let's go."

Chapter 8

"Fear not, for I am with you; be not dismayed, for I am your God; I will strengthen you, I will help you, I will uphold you with my righteous right hand."
~Isaiah 41:10~

GARRETT

"How'd you get into this mess, boy?"
"God hates me."
"Pity isn't pretty."
"Neither is your face, but you don't hear me complaining."
He paused the recording of Brische's interview with Josh and fought the urge to throw up. Gone was the scared, rebellious teen who'd fled his home. The voice on the recording was that of a man, hardened and cold. His son. He wiped his eyes and forced himself to continue transcribing the recording.
"The clock is ticking, kid. Each second brings you closer to a judge, so if I were you, I'd start talking." Brische's tone displayed his impatience.
"How much are you paying this fool?" Josh asked.
"The important thing is that you're not paying him, so do what he told you to do, Josh," Jordan admonished.
"Start at the beginning and tell me what happened. Don't skip any details, even if you're guilty. I have to know the whole story." Brische pushed.
He winced when Josh groaned, his pain evident over the speakers. He listened as his son recounted his story, paying close attention as he told what he remembered of the shooting.
 "It was like Drew was picking a fight with me, but I don't know why. We don't have any beef, but he started dragging up some crap about me getting fired from my job, and he wouldn't let up. He made me mad, and I punched him. Then I went to grab my bags so I could get outta there, but he followed me. Next thing I know, he pulls a pistol and starts screaming at me to put the gun

down and calling me a 'coked up freak.' I was shocked, but not as shocked as when he aimed at the wall and pulled the trigger. He hit some guy in the next room, then called 911 and told them I was the shooter."

"How do you know this 'Drew' character?" Brische asked.

"Met him at a party when I first got to Florida. I was only there to pick pockets, but I left with a friend—if you could call him that. We hit it off okay and would hang out whenever my ship was in port."

"What does he know about you?"

"Next to nothing. Just my name and that I worked on a cruise ship. Never told him where I lived on shore or anything about my past."

"What could be his motive for staging all this mess?" Brische sounded doubtful, and Garrett clicked his pen nervously when Josh picked up on his tone and cursed.

"You callin' me a liar, prick?"

"Don't get your panties in a wad. I have to investigate all angles to help you. Now, be straight with me, boy. You a felon?"

Josh didn't answer right away, and Garrett wondered if he would.

"My priors have nothing to do with what happened yesterday," Josh bit.

"So, you are a felon. You got yourself into a position with someone who had a gun and drugs, and want me to believe you're innocent?"

Metal clanged over the recording, and Garrett's mind raced to interpret all he was hearing.

"Hold it, killer," Jordan's firm tone cut through the noise, and all was quiet. "Brische, he is innocent. At least of the drug charges. Josh has never messed with anything that would alter his thinking. He doesn't do drugs, and he doesn't touch alcohol. He's got deeply seated reasons for this. You can trust him. There is no way he's guilty of possession."

Garrett set his jaw, fighting back the pain Jordan's

words incited in his chest.

Brische sighed. "Okay, but if I find out you're lying to me, it's your butt on the line."

The recording beeped, and Garrett wasted no time in calling Brische to set things in motion.

JORDAN

Exhaustion had finally overcome Jordan. After Brische had left the hospital to work on Josh's case, he'd sought out a corner of the lobby and stretched out across two chairs. He pulled his baseball cap low over his eyes and gave in to sleep. He wasn't sure how long he'd slept before he was rudely awakened—he just knew he was rudely awakened.

"Wake up, kid." Brische kicked Jordan's feet off the chair he'd propped them on and crossed his arms while Jordan fought to keep himself from sliding onto the floor.

"Did no one teach you manners, Brische?" he grumbled as he pulled the cap off his head and shoved a hand through his hair. Shooting him a look, he growled. "You'd better have release papers in your hand after waking me like you just did."

Brische's only response was to whack him over the head with the stack of papers in his hand and turn on his heel. "Up and at 'em, Sleeping Beauty. We've got a big fish to fry."

"Don't even give a guy a chance to grab some coffee," Jordan mumbled as he followed him to the elevator.

"You want this kid released or not?" Brische stabbed the button for Josh's floor.

Jordan rubbed at his eyes, wishing the pounding in his head would subside. "So, he's free?"

Brische threw him a look. "No, he's upstairs chained to a bed. But he will be free once I throw this evidence in St. Patrick's face. Dirty cop planted the coke on him, and the idiot forgot to turn off his body cam."

Jordan's jaw dropped. "What?! Why would he do that?"

Brische threw him another look. "Garrett said you're smart, but you're challenging that statement. Money. The world works off bribes and manipulation. Learn that now before you start running with the big boys."

Jordan's response was cut off by the opening of the elevator doors. Brische was in a rush, so Jordan quickly fell into step beside him.

"St. Patrick!" Brische yelled down the hall, causing Jordan's face to flush red.

St. Patrick glanced up from his desk and frowned as Brische stormed into his office, Jordan in tow. "I've got patients sleeping, Brische. Think you could be any louder?"

"Let them wake! Let them all hear of the injustices that were forced upon an innocent citizen of this good city!"

St. Patrick rolled his eyes. "I don't have time for this. I have a job to do." Moving to sit back down, he froze when Brische shoved a manila envelope in his face. "What's this?" he asked, hesitantly taking it into his hands and sitting down.

"That, my friend, is proof that this case was a setup. My client is an innocent man and is being illegally held, in direct violation of his Fourth Amendment rights." Perching on the edge of his desk, Brische grinned down at St. Patrick, his arrogance brighter than his neon tie. "Now, my suggestion to you is that you get your commander down here before I turn you into exhibit 'A' in the Civil Lawsuit I'm contemplating filing."

Swallowing hard, St. Patrick began to sweat as memories of a prior investigation into his office resurfaced. He was not going down that road again. "I, um, I'm gonna need a minute."

"Sure thing." Brische winked and jumped to the floor, nodding for Jordan to follow him into the hall. "These chairs right here," he urged, excitement charging his words. Making a big show of sitting and crossing one leg over the other, the lawyer stared through the glass walls of St. Patrick's office and watched as he picked up the phone and dialed. When the officer noticed him watching, he frowned and crossed the room, yanking the blinds down over the windows.

Jordan jumped at the sudden outburst of laughter beside him. "Wanna clue me in?"

"Nope. You don't learn anything that way. Get quiet and sit tight for a minute. Watch the big leagues battle for a bit."

Jordan fell asleep waiting but regretted the fact when he woke to Brische knocking his elbows off the chair arms. "Doggone it, boy, quit sleeping on the job! Here come the big boys!"

Jordan watched in silence as a bulky man stepped up to Brische and shook his hand. "Mr. Brische, I'm Chief Deputy Santiago. I've been informed of some type of police setup with your client. Care to explain?"

"Don't have to. Your idiot cop will take care of that for me. Jordan," he turned and snapped at him, motioning for his briefcase. "Assist!" When Jordan handed it to him, he pulled out his laptop and shoved a jump drive into the device, pulling up the footage of Josh's arrest. "As you will see, my client has indeed been set up."

Drawn by his curiosity, Jordan stood and inched closer to the screen, immediately angered by what he saw. While his friend was unconscious, lying in pools of his own blood, the arresting officer quickly shoved a bag of white powder into the front pocket of Josh's jeans.

Santiago's face was three shades of red as he watched. "May I borrow this drive, please?"

"Of course." Brische grinned, pulling it free and handing it off to him. "I've got three copies. We'll just be right here while you work on that release."

Frowning, Santiago moved down the hall and disappeared into St. Patrick's office.

Jordan watched in confusion as Brische sat back in his chair, pulled out his phone, and began a game of Sudoku. "What's going to happen now? Are they going to release him?"

Brische looked at him over the top of his glasses, his brows raised. "Remind me to tell Garrett that my fees are higher when working with children. I swear, boy, you're worse than an eight-year-old with all these questions. Just let the powers that be work on their mess! Not our problem. Your friend will be released without a doubt within the next couple of hours, so hold your tongue. Go get some of that disgusting coffee you've been craving, and leave me to my game. It's riveting, actually, and I'm determined to win this time."

Jordan stared as Brische lost himself in the game once more. Shaking his head, he took him up on his suggestion for coffee and called Garrett while he was at it. The line only had to ring once before it was answered.

"Do you have good news for me yet?"

"Uh…yeah. At least, I think so. Brische has evidence that the cop who arrested Josh planted the coke on him."

"Yeah, he told me. I couldn't be happier! Are they releasing him now?"

Stirring creamer into his fresh cup of coffee, Jordan took a sip and nearly spewed it out. This was the worst cup of coffee he'd ever had. Forcing himself to swallow, he answered. "Brische says they're working on it. This guy's a trip—you know that, right?"

Garrett laughed. "We graduated together. He's always been eccentric and brash, but he's sharp as a whip. What are your plans once Josh is freed?" Jordan picked up on the serious shift in his tone. "Uh, I'm not sure yet. I don't even know if he's processed the fact that I'm here. We've only seen each other for a total of twenty minutes, if that. I haven't had a chance to get a feel of where his head's at. I'd love to convince him to come home, but—"

"—we both know that will never happen," Garrett interrupted. "Aim lower, but please don't leave him in a vulnerable state. If you have to leave, call me first."

"I'm not going anywhere. Just please," he closed his eyes, "let me be the one to tell my dad, okay? He's gonna flip his crap on me, and I can't deal with that right now."

"You got it. Keep me posted—I'll be near my phone." Jordan hung up and wandered back to where he'd left Brische, but the older man was gone. Furrowing his brow, he turned his head at the sound of raised voices down the hall.

"Minor inconvenience? Minor inconvenience?! You owe him a heck of a lot more than that sorry excuse of an apology! Do it right or I'll pursue the suit."

Jordan rushed to the open door and stepped inside, relief flooding him to see Santiago removing the cuff from Josh's wrist. Catching Josh's eye, he raised a brow and grinned, knowing Josh was enjoying watching the deputy squirm.

"I truly am sorry, sir," he repeated to Josh, backing away from him. "St. Patrick, see that Mr. Cameron is transferred to a room downstairs immediately."

"Will do." As Santiago rushed from the room and St. Patrick called for transportation, Brische danced a victory dance at Josh's bedside.

"Told you I'd handle it, baby! You're outta here!" He waltzed to the door and clapped Jordan on the shoulder. "Never stop asking questions, kid. The squeaky wheel gets the grease."

With a wink, he was gone, leaving Jordan alone with Josh.

Chapter 9

"Not only so, but we also glory in our sufferings, we know that suffering produces perseverance."
~Romans 5:3~

JORDAN

"He looks like an Oompa Loompa."

"Say what?" Jordan glanced at him and took a swig from his water bottle.

Josh cocked his head to the side. "Brische. He looks like an Oompa Loompa."

Jordan spewed water from his mouth, directly into Josh's face, laughter erupting from his soul at Josh's accurate depiction of the lawyer. "I'm s-sorry, man, I didn't mean to spit at you."

Josh stared as the water dripped down his face onto the white hospital blanket surrounding him. "You just spat in my face."

"Here," Jordan tossed him a towel. "Wipe up. I didn't mean to spit at you, I swear."

"Don't swear," Josh muttered, wiping the towel down his chin.

Jordan smiled at the reference to his dad. He and Josh had received that phrase no less than a zillion times. It was one of his father's pet peeves. He hated swearing and had never let the boys get away with it in front of him. "So, you think Brische looks like a character from a movie."

"You do, too. You're just afraid to say it." Josh tried to shift but failed. Desperate for comfort, he yelled in frustration, startling Jordan upright in his chair. "Doesn't matter if the guy looks ridiculous—I'm just glad he got that bracelet off me."

"See where a little faith takes you?" Jordan grinned.

"Faith." Josh gave him a bored look. "You're still with that, huh?"

Jordan smiled. Faith, and anything else having to do with God, had always been their most heated topic. "I'll always be 'with that,' Josh. I've seen too much not to be. I wouldn't be where I am without God. And you? You'd be dead." He cut his eyes upward as he thought about what he'd just said. "Probably several times over."

Josh grunted at him. "God isn't why I'm still here. Street smarts have me where I am today."

"I won't steal your breath with an argument, but you're wrong." He grinned as Josh scowled at him. His phone pinged, and he glanced down, brow furrowed as he stared at the name. Looking at Josh, he found him focusing on an old episode of Nash Bridges. Taking advantage of his distraction, Jordan opened the message.

Mr. C: Now that things have calmed down, how is he? So many questions…

Jordan sighed. There was no point in holding back now. Pushing aside the fear of Josh finding him out, he answered.

Jordan: Not so great. He's pretty busted up from that wreck. Nothing life-threatening, thank God, but he'll probably be here for a good week or so. He calmed down when they got him out of the prison ward, but he's still testy. I'll answer any questions you have, and again—I'm sorry it went down like it did. Please forgive me for keeping this from you.

He gripped the phone tighter, his eyes focused on Josh. There was so much to say and ask him, but Josh had been like a closed book since he'd arrived. He hadn't even asked Jordan how he'd found him. Was he calm because of the meds he was on? Or was this the new Josh? The Josh he knew would have been demanding answers at the first sight of him, and yet, he lay in his hospital bed without one question on his lips. Jordan's phone pinged again, drawing his attention to the screen.

Mr. C: Don't be sorry. I understand. You've always been a good friend to him. I'd be lying if I said I wasn't jealous that you're there with him. I'd give anything just to see his face again. Have you found out anything about him from these last four years?

"She must be hot."

"What?" Jordan's head snapped up, and he found Josh staring at him.

"The girl you're fixating on."

"I, um, I'm not fixating on a girl." Jordan dropped his gaze to the floor as his cheeks flamed. "Just some guy I know who needed to ask me something."

Josh's eyes bore into his. "You're lying. I know that look. But whatever." He shrugged.

Tension pulled at Jordan's features. Even after four years of not one word between them, Josh still knew him so well. "You hungry?"

Josh held his gaze a moment longer before shaking his head. "No."

He studied his face, nervous energy tickling his spine as he watched Josh's features shift.

"Why are you here?"

Jordan swallowed. "You needed me."

"I don't need anyone."

Arching a brow, a twinge of irritation sparked in his veins at Josh's unceasing arrogance. "You're right. Forgive me. You have it all together, don't you? Everything in your life is all hunky-dory, isn't it?"

"I would have been fine," he answered quietly. His mind wandered to his arrest—his eyes speaking volumes about the amount of bull he'd just voiced. A heavy sigh escaped his lips. "I didn't do anything wrong in that house, J."

Jordan held onto his response for a moment. "I know, Josh." His voice was equally quiet, the solemnity of Josh's situation weighing on his heart. "They know, too, or they wouldn't have let you go."

"I'm not going back."

Confused, Jordan furrowed his brow. "I know. They released you, remember? It's done. They can't lock you up now."

"I'm not talking about the iron house, J." He met his eyes, darkness billowing across his features. "I'm not going back to Cali. Not now, not ever."

Jordan swallowed hard, shifting beneath Josh's intense stare. "So, what's your plan, then? I can't move out here, Josh."

"Who asked you to? Who asked you to come here? I told you—I don't need you or anyone else. I can make it just fine on my own."

Anger burned in Jordan's flesh, and he cursed. "Unless I'm blind, you're pretty messed up right now."

Josh whistled. "Look at the straight shooter cursing like the big boys. What would the church say?"

"Man, forget you!" Jordan seethed through grit teeth. "I dropped everything to come save your stupid butt, just like every time in the past, Taylor. And this is your thanks? You insult me and poke fun at my faith? Why did I even bother?"

"Hey, no low-blowing!" Josh growled, ignoring the pain shooting through his ribs.

"You think I'm low-blowing? You're the one with the low blows, Josh. Insulting my faith is going too far, man. Too. Far!"

"You used my middle name." Josh sulked. "Middle names aren't allowed, remember?"

Jordan slammed back into his chair and crossed his arms over his chest. What were they, twelve? He rolled his eyes to the ceiling and rested his dark head on the headrest. "You make it impossible to help you, Josh. Why are you so stupid-stubborn?" When no answer came, he sat up and looked at his friend.

Josh sat in silence, picking at a stray thread on the blanket. "I don't know," he whispered. "All I know is that I can't go back to Highshore. I won't do it, and you can't make me."

Jordan said nothing, but the words were loud and clear inside his head: Yeah, we'll see about that...

The silence lagged between them, each wrestling with their thoughts. When Jordan looked up again, Josh was asleep. Relief washed over him. He was glad for a chance to process all that had happened that day.

Ping!

He glanced at his phone and saw another text from Garrett.

Mr. C: You left me on "read," kid...

Jordan sighed and typed out his response.

Jordan: I don't know much yet. He won't open up to me. I know he lost his job and is homeless. He has nothing but a couple of duffel bags the paramedics pulled from the wreckage. He's in a mess, Mr. C. He refuses to come home–won't even discuss it. I keep waiting for him to demand that I leave, but he hasn't. His anger comes in waves, followed by calm and reason. IDK, man...but I won't give up. I promise. I will bring him home.

GARRETT

Garrett lay beside his wife in their queen-sized bed and watched her sleep. She was so beautiful with chestnut hair sprawled all over her pillow and stray wisps across her smooth cheek. He gently swiped the hair from her face, wondering at the peace that spread across her features at his touch. Though their marriage was well into the healing years, he lived in disbelief and awe that she'd stayed by his side through it all. He was so blessed to have this woman walk through life with him. He softly kissed her temple, relishing in her warmth as she sidled into his bare chest. He pulled her tighter into him and he lay still, breathing in the scent of her shampoo.

Oh, Elysia. What am I going to do? His thoughts weighed on his mind as he watched the sun peak above the earth. He'd been awake for two hours with no chance of going back to sleep. Thoughts of his son consumed him, and he had to fight the urge to run to him. Josh would never accept his help.

His wife stirred, and he squeezed back the tears as his secret burned in his chest. He could only pray that she would forgive him for not telling her about Josh. He'd pondered the issue well into the night but had decided against letting her know, out of allegiance to Jordan and his boy. It wasn't like Josh would be coming home once freed. That was just foolish dreaming, he knew. It was best Elysia didn't know. He was determined to protect her from that heartache.

Giving up on rest, Garrett gently moved Elysia off his arm and climbed from the bed. Pulling on a shirt, he quietly left the room. What was he moping for? Didn't God just free his son from police custody?

"Thank You, Jesus," he whispered in the hallway. Overcome with gratitude for his King, he dropped to his knees and threw his hands into the air, face lifted to the ceiling. "Thank You, God. Thank You!" His right fist pumped the air with his praise, and tears stained his cheeks.

"Daddy, why are you punching God?"

He froze at the sound of his daughter's voice. Looking at her, he smiled. Her mess of blond curls tangled into waterfalls down her back, Teddy dangling in one hand as her emerald, green eyes implored. "Hi, love bug. What're you doing up so early?"

"I heared you punching God and I comed to see why," she stated. "I don't think that's a very good choice, Daddy."

Garrett scooped her into his arms and squeezed her tight. "I love you, my baby. To the—"

"—angels above and the stars in the night sky." Her voice lilted in his ear as she snuggled into his neck. "Daddy?"

"Mm?"

"I'm hungry. Can you be Mommy today?"

He grinned against her hair. "Daddies can feed their babies, too."

"Not you. You don't know how—Mommy said so."

"Well, I'll have to have a talk with Mommy about her opinion." He laughed. "Let's go downstairs—real quiet, okay? Let's let Mommy sleep."

"Okay!"

He carried her down the stairs and rocket-shipped her into her chair at the table before grabbing a bowl and the cereal from the cupboard. After ensuring she was engrossed in a cartoon, he wandered into the living room to text Jordan.

Garrett: How's my boy?

Garrett settled into his recliner and rested his eyes while he waited for Jordan's response. He didn't have long to wait.

Jordan: Josh is high as a kite right now. He had a bad episode about two hours ago. It was awful. A team of nurses swarmed in like he was dying. He was screaming so much. They've got him doped up now, and he keeps demanding I get him out of here. When I refuse, he yells at his nurse: "HEY FATSO, LEMME OUTTA HERE BEFORE I BEAT THE CRAP OUTTA YOU!" So, yeah…I'm over here praying he doesn't get his stubborn self into more trouble while we wait… *facepalm*

Garrett laughed, running a hand across his stubbed jaw.

Garrett: Hang in there, son. Won't be long now. I'm sorry you're having to deal with Josh's anger. Any idea what he'll do once freed? Is the hospital talking about release yet?

"Daddy, can I go see Mommy?" Nevaeh bounced into the room, Teddy dragging the floor behind her.

"Let her sleep, baby pie. That way, when she wakes up, she won't be so grumpy, huh?" Garrett tweaked the little girl's nose, his heart warming at her lilting laughter.

"Who's grumpy?"

Garrett turned at Elysia's voice and offered a sheepish smile. "I was just trying to keep Nevaeh from waking you."

Smiling, she approached him from behind and rubbed his shoulders. She bent and kissed his temple as he received another text. "Who are you texting so early?" Her eyes drifted to his screen, surprise registering when he turned the phone away. The fleeting expression of hurt vanished as quickly as it had appeared.

His heart pounded as he gave a small shrug. "Sorry, babe. Attorney-client privilege."

She nodded and scooped Nevaeh into her arms. "Come on, you, let's see what kind of trouble we can get into today."

Garrett sighed. He'd been unable to read his wife's reaction. The two were careful to remain open about everything in their marriage. And he'd told the truth…mostly. He only hoped she believed him. Lifting the phone, he read Jordan's response:

Jordan: Doc says if he goes home with someone, he can get him out within the week. If he has no one to care for him, he'll have to keep him for another two. Josh doesn't know yet—I'll let you know what he says. I have no idea what he'll do once he's out of here. He's stupid-stubborn, you know? He insists he would've been fine without me. I'm not done trying to convince him to let me help.

Garrett reread the last three lines, trying to get inside his son's head. Josh always had been "stupid-stubborn." But how could he not have been, with a father such as himself? He closed his eyes, then made a decision he prayed he wouldn't regret. He was going to have so much to explain to Elysia…

Garrett: See if he'll let you take him to a hotel when he gets released. Don't worry about the cost. I'll front the bill—just let me know where you'll be staying, and I'll set it all up.

Across the miles, in the stuffy hospital room, Jordan read the text and smiled, wishing he could tell Josh about his father's generosity. But no, the truth would have to remain on the back burner for now. After screaming at the nurses for the tenth time that morning, Josh finally fell into a restless sleep. Jordan was exhausted from his long night of sleeping next to Josh's bed. Between the hard couch and Josh's pain-filled screams that jarred him awake any time he'd drifted off to sleep, Jordan had only managed two hours the entire night.

"I'll make sure he's okay if you wanna get some sleep,

son."

Jordan glanced up at the nurse who'd just walked in. He liked this guy more than the others. He was far more patient and understanding. But still, he couldn't fall asleep now. There was too much at stake.

"I'm straight, man. Thanks." He knew his weary tone was unconvincing, but he couldn't afford to care.

The nurse shrugged. "Suit yourself. I'm gonna go grab a coffee." He paused at the door, then turned back to Jordan. "Want one?"

Jordan thought back to the dirt-sprinkled-with-unicorn-poo coffee he'd suffered through the morning before and shook his head. "No thanks. I'm good." He watched him shrug and walk out the door, thinking he'd give his right arm for a Starbucks coffee. A moan drew his gaze to Josh's bed. He watched as Josh's eyes flickered open and attempted to focus on him.

"Hey, man."

"I'm gonna kick your butt," Josh muttered.

Here we go again…

"Look, dude, I cannot get you out of here. I'm sorry, okay? I wish I could, but I just can't."

Josh looked around the room as if noticing where he was for the first time, then looked back at Jordan.

"What, this? Nah, that ain't nothin'. I'm gonna kick your butt for scratching up the paint on my '95 Camero." Jordan's brow wrinkled in confusion.

"I didn't scratch your…Oh…"

"Yeah, 'oh.' I haven't forgotten what you did."

"Wait a minute, that wasn't even your car! You stole it!"

"Yes. Yes, I did. And you scratched the mess out of it because you were mad I took it, but you know as well as I do that Caleb Thomas had it comin'."

Jordan rolled his eyes. "For the last time, I tripped and fell into it, and my keys scraped the side as I fell."

"Yeah, well, your little accident cost me big. Never did get around to pummeling you for it, either. Can't remember why..."

Jordan smiled at the memory. "Rhea."

The name was a whisper, but Josh heard. The Camero forgotten, he hung his head and focused on a spot on the blanket. "Have you seen her?"

"No," he answered, searching Josh's face. "Not for a couple of years. They say she moved out of town, but I don't know where. The day you ran off she, um..." He glanced away, not wanting to upset his friend.

"Just tell me, J."

"She came to my house in a panic, asking if I'd seen or heard from you. I said no and asked her what had happened. She said you'd come to her window and begged her to run away with you, but she'd turned you down and hadn't heard from you since."

Josh remained still, the memory carrying him to some distant time and version of himself he no longer recognized. He could still see her in the window. Her golden-brown curls hanging down to her waist...

A calm wind blew through the open window and teased the curtains. The serenity of the night was a cruel joke to the girl trapped inside her bedroom. From where he hid in the bushes, Josh watched her as she sat at the window seat, her bathrobe drawn around her like a cocoon shielding her from the angry shouts coming from someplace deep inside the house. He watched as she wiped at a stray tear sliding down her cheek. She squeezed her knees into her chest and stared into the night. He could see the disturbance in her eyes—the conflict battling across her features. The wind shifted, and he could hear her mother's screeching in the background.

"What will the gossips say about me now, Lance? My daughter is a slut! A whore! She has ruined me!"

Josh gritted his teeth, his fists tight balls at his sides. What a witch. Rhea's mother was such a dramatic little Barbie. He hated her. He heard Rhea's exaggerated sigh and tried to read her thoughts. Was she buying into this crap? Did she believe her mother's words? He studied her face and saw the eye roll. No, she was too smart for that.

"Just send her away to boarding school."

Josh watched Rhea raise her head at her stepfather's voice. He sounded dull, bored even. He'd never seen him take any interest in Rhea—he'd probably be happy to send her away.

"I can't send her to boarding school," Nichole shrieked. "There would be too many questions! How would we explain her absence? That's not the answer. We have to get rid of that awful, heathen boy."

No worries there, lady, Josh thought. Pain stabbed his heart as he watched Rhea tense in the window.

"That won't be an easy task. You know his father and I depend on each other in the politics of this town. You cannot upset him—you'll ruin me, Nichole. Get rid of the girl. I'll make sure no one questions you."

"All you think about is yourself, Lance! What about me? She is my daughter. What will people think when I send my child away?"

Josh watched as Rhea squeezed her eyes shut, her hands pressed to her ears to block out her idiot parents. Enough. Anger burned as he emerged from his hiding place and crept to her window.

"Rhea," he whispered.

She stifled a scream and jumped up, her eyes darting to his.

"Josh! You can't be here—leave now!" Rhea returned to the window and crouched on her knees, her fingers gripping the windowsill.

"They're plotting to get rid of you—or me—right now. Can't you hear Mother yelling at Lance?!"

He heard. A smile stretched across his tight features. Rhea was so cute when she panicked. Focus. "Let them plot. We don't need them. We don't need anybody. We'll do them all a favor and give them what they want. Come with me."

Rhea stared at him, reading the tension on his face. Her eyes dropped to the bag on the ground beside him, and her heart raced as fear gripped her chest. He was leaving. She shook her head, a fresh spark of tears in her eyes.

"No, Josh. You can't leave me here with them—please!"

He placed his hands on hers and caressed her skin.

"Didn't you hear me? We can run together—just you and me."

She squeezed her eyes shut, aware of the increasing energy down the hall. "I can't. I can't just leave school…and my mom? I can't abandon her."

Josh stared, confusion clouding his eyes. "Why would you ever want to stay here with her? She treats you like a doormat, Rhea! She's a monster, and you know it. Come with me—please. You know I'll take care of you—you know I will!"

"She needs me, Josh. She'll die without me here." Rhea withdrew her hands, uncertainty lacing her brow.

A storm billowed across his face. His lips tightened into a thin line as he watched the girl he loved shrivel into her shell.

"That's bull, and you know it. That's what she wants you to believe. Can't you see that? It's all part of this sick manipulation game she plays with you. Break the spell, Rhea! Run with me! Please, baby, please!"

She raised her eyes to his, alarmed by his tears. Why couldn't she go with him? What was keeping her here? She hated her life in this house, always being under the careful watch of her controlling mother. What was wrong with her? Why was she so afraid of everything?!

She'll die without you.

Rhea sniffed and ran a hand through her hair. "I need you—" her voice broke, "—to understand. If I leave her, she'll die. Or kill herself. Or blow somebody up. She's crazy! You know that. I can't go with you, Josh. I just can't!"

Josh tensed his jaw. "Can't? No, Rhea. You won't."

What am I going to do? I can't leave her, but I can't stay!

His heart was grieved with indecision.

"Rhea, I don't know where I'm going but I know it's far away from here." He stepped closer to the window, grief clutching at his face. "I don't know what I'm gonna do without you. I need you!" He sniffed and cursed. "I've never needed anyone before. This is killing me—please just take my hand and go. Just do it, without thinking about it. Trust me. Please."

Josh held out his hand, eyes pleading with her to lower herself into his arms.

"Josh, I c—"

"Rhea? Who are you talking to? Who's out there?!"

The bedroom door burst open, and her mother raced through the door. Her eyes fell to the open window—and the boy lingering just outside. "Lance, call the cops! He's here! Lance!"

"Mother, no! He's leaving. Let him go, please!" Rhea leaped to her feet and grabbed her mother's forearm.

"Get off me, child!"

From where he hid, Josh watched the woman he hated slap the girl he loved. His muscles went rigid from the anger coursing through his veins and it took all his might to stop himself from charging through the window and beating her senseless. In the background, he heard Lance talking with the police, and knew he only had seconds to escape before all this blew up in his face and his plans were ruined. Pain ripped his heart in two as he tore his eyes from Rhea's form. Hot tears burned his eyes as he slipped into the street and took off at a run.

Chapter 10

"Trust in the LORD with all your heart, and do not lean on your own understanding. In all your ways acknowledge him, and he will make straight your."
~Proverbs 3:5-6~

STERLING

"My father won't be signing this." Sterling slid the document back across the table and leveled the woman with a stare. It was the fourth contract he'd rejected, yet she continued to push the boundaries he'd laid.

Nichole Sherard's red-stained lips curved into a condescending smile. "It's cute how you think you can push me into a corner," she replied, folding her hands on the table and matching his stare.

"You're not being pushed into a corner. Play within the legal guidelines, and your real estate will be set into motion. But I won't tolerate any more of this nonsense, Mrs. Sherard. It's insulting."

Beside him, his father sulked but Sterling refused to see him walk into ruin. Though his eyes remained locked with Nichole's, his mind was on Rhea. He was worried about her. Her face had been ashen when he'd told her this client's name, yet she'd refused to tell him why. She'd brushed off her reaction, but he knew better. She was scared. And he was determined to find out the reason.

"What a lovely couple."

His train of thought shattered, Sterling blinked at her before following her gaze to a picture of Rhea and himself. He fought the urge to snatch up the picture and shove it into a drawer. She had no right to look at his girl. Clearing his throat, he forced a smile. "Yes. My girlfriend."

"She has a beautiful name," Nichole commented, her gaze drifting to Sterling.

Shifting, Sterling clasped his hands on his desk. "Mrs. Sherard, we aren't here for you to admire my family. You have twenty-four hours to bring me a legal contract, or the deal's off. Good day."

His father's eyes tripled in size as he gaped at his son. "Sterling," he croaked. "Seal the deal before she walks!"

"Let her walk. Right out the way she came." He stood and went to the door. Pulling it open, he stared at Nichole until she grabbed her purse and headed toward him.

"You can't stop me," she hissed, pausing in front of him.

"I just did."

She cocked her head and looked up at him, a smile cracking the mask of makeup on her face. "I'd keep a close eye on that 'family' of yours. You'd be surprised how quickly life can change."

Sterling bristled, and his neck hairs stood on end. Had she just threatened him? "Get out."

When she'd gone, he slammed the door behind her.

JOSH

The morning of Josh's hospital discharge brought hope and a promise. After the doctor had questioned Josh about where he would be headed once released, Josh assured him he would let Jordan take him to a hotel to recover. Satisfied, the doctor signed the release forms and left Jordan with instructions on medical care. When the nurse brought in a wheelchair, Josh declined but thought better of it when pain seared through his ribs after only three steps.

Jordan talked non-stop as the nurse wheeled Josh to the elevator. "As soon as we get to the hotel, I'll get you settled in and then order you the biggest meal room service has to offer. You'll be fat full, man. Fat. Full. You'll never want to eat another bite."

Josh groaned. He wished Jordan would shut up so he could think. The hospital stay was behind him—his arrest a mere memory to bury in the vault with the others. The only thing spreading like an obstacle course before him was his recovery. That—and Jordan. It wouldn't be long before Jordan realized he'd been full of crap about his promise to go with him. He had no intention of going to a hotel with Jordan. He couldn't chance being talked into returning to Highshore, which meant he had to execute one of the plans bouncing around in his aching skull. First plan: ditch Jordan.

When the nurse wheeled him outside, Josh breathed in the breeze that slapped him in the face. He'd been trapped inside a stuffy room without access to fresh air for more than a week and now he couldn't get enough. The wheelchair came to a stop, and Jordan rushed to hail a cab.

"Why don't you wait here while he gets the car ready?" the nurse suggested, but he wasn't listening.

"Nah, I'm good. Thanks." He accepted her help as she pulled him to his feet, surprising her by asking for his bags.

"Why don't I just take them to the young man who's getting the car—"

"No. Just put them across my shoulders. Please." His eyes met hers, silencing any argument on her tongue. As she raised the straps, Josh braced himself, wincing as the weight of the bags rested across his chest.

"I really don't mind waiting with you." She tried again as he began to limp down the sidewalk.

Josh didn't answer as he focused all his energy on walking in the opposite direction. He'd made it only a few feet when he heard Jordan rushing behind him.

"Josh, where you goin', man? The cab's over here." Jordan placed a hand on Josh's arm to stop him.

"Let go of me, Jordan." Josh glared at the hand gripping his arm, his breaths rapid gasps.

Jordan's face was a mask of confusion as his mind battled to make sense of the scene. The realization that Josh had lied to the doctor and himself set into his mind, and he struggled to keep his patience. Why couldn't Josh just accept his help? "No, Josh. Come to the hotel with me. The doctor said it could be weeks before you're back to yourself, remember? You have to rest!"

Josh jerked out of his grasp, uninterested in what he had

to say. "I've done everything but beat the ever-loving crap out of you, J. Do not tempt me! For the last time, I am not going with you." His eyes warned of trouble if Jordan pressed him. His ribs were killing him, and his head felt no better. He was desperate to sit down but couldn't reveal that need to Jordan. He had to appear competent and intimidating.

Jordan wasn't a fool. He saw right through the bravado and quickly thought of a new approach while mentally cursing his friend for his stubbornness. "Man, I bet those ribs have you in a world of pain right about now. And those splitting headaches that had you screaming in the hospital…that's gonna be rough when they hit again." He stepped back to observe. "How far are you planning on going? I bet you'll make it one…maybe two blocks before your body gives out on you."

Josh's determination faltered and he shrugged. "I've got my prescription. Pop a few pills and I'll be good to go." A triumphant smile burst across Jordan's face, and he saw a flash of panic in Josh's eyes. "Uh-huh. How you gonna pay for it?"

He had him with that one.

"You just gonna ignore all that pain? What happens if the dizziness hits again? The nausea? Man, you sure were a mess the other night, weren't you?"

Josh eyed him warily. There was no way he wanted to go through all that again. He'd had a hard enough time coping with his pain meds, much less without. "You don't play fair, Blayze." He spat the middle name, sending a clear message to Jordan: This means war.

Jordan grinned shamelessly and stepped towards the cab. "After you."

"I can still kick your butt," Josh reminded him as he climbed into the car.

Jordan laughed to himself and scored one for winning another battle against Josh's foolish pride.

ASHER

"You're where?"

"I've been locked up." Drew's confession was barely audible.

Asher pinched the bridge of his nose and squeezed his eyes shut. "How could you let this happen?" he hissed, his eyes darting around Alabama Street where he stood. "I swear, Drew, there's no one as inept as you!"

Drew was silent before forcing the words past his tight throat. "My cousin got caught planting the dope on Cameron. He sold me out. I need you to post bail."

Asher laughed. "Oh, no. I'm not cleaning up your mess. I want no part of what you've done."

"I did this for you!"

"Did you? Did you really? Got any proof?"

"We're brothers, Ash. You can't just leave me like this," Drew pleaded. "Cameron's in custody because of me. You owe me!"

"I owe you nothing. And we're half-brothers, you inbred freak. You mean nothing to me. I hate your dad, and I hate you. I'm glad to be rid of you. Now get off my line so I can clean up your mess."

Asher hung up and ran a hand through his long beard, tugging hard to remind himself there was still life in his veins. He had to call her. If she found out from another source there would be hell to pay. But first—a cigarette. He lit up and walked around the block to clear his head. He should've known better than to trust Drew. He was too green behind the ears. Too eager. But there was no time for regrets. He had to act quickly to stay ahead of her. With a drawn-out sigh, he pulled out his burner phone. The cigarette still shoved between his lips; he dialed the only number listed.

"Good news?" she clipped.

"Drew got busted."

"I warned you not to let this happen, Asher. If Drew rats me out, I will end you. Do I make myself clear?"

"You think he knows about you? Think I'm stupid? Come on, it's me you're talkin' to." There was no hiding his irritation.

She laughed, dark and foreboding. "Oh, I know exactly who I'm talking to. I'm talking to the same idiot who allowed himself to fall into a blackmail scheme and has no way of digging himself out of trouble. The same imbecile whose family is now in grave danger due to his stupidity." Asher swallowed hard. He would have to check on Bridget and Ty. "Drew doesn't know anything about you, I swear. I have never mentioned you or why I need Cameron off the streets."

"Speaking of Cameron... I assume he's still behind bars, yes?"

Asher squeezed his eyes shut, praying he spoke the truth. "Of course he is. Didn't I tell you I'd make sure he stayed there?"

She laughed that evil laugh again and a chill shot down his spine.

"You exude confidence, yet your defenses give you away. I suggest you search for humility while you're looking for your balls."

The line went dead. Wasting no time, he traded the burner for his other cell and dialed Bridget, his fingers shaking with each press of the keys.

"Where are you? You missed another game." Her irritation warmed his soul and tears threatened.

"Oh, baby..."

JORDAN

Jordan lay across the plush hotel bed and absentmindedly stared at the television as he waited for Josh to finish his shower, his ears tuned for signs of distress. His eyelids threatened to give in to the sleep he so desperately needed, but he wanted to jump up at a moment's notice should Josh need him. Beside him, his phone buzzed, announcing his father's third attempt to reach him that day. He slid the icon to the right, rejecting the call. The phone beeped with a new voicemail, inciting yet another lecture from his conscience. He couldn't do it.

He just could not handle lying to his father any more than he had to. His phone pinged and he glanced at the screen:

    Pops: Just let me know you're okay and I'll leave you alone, kid.

Jordan sighed. The answer to that was complicated. He was not okay. He was exhausted, his emotions were shot, and he was tired of fighting Josh, but he would not relent. Somehow, he had to find a way to get his friend back home without getting himself murdered in the process. He picked up the phone.

    Jordan: "Okay" is relative, Dad. But yeah, it's all good. Hoping to be home soon, but no promises. It's taking a lot longer than I anticipated to help out my buddy. Sorry I haven't answered—I'm beat.

The phone pinged a second time, and he applauded his father's quick response.

    Everything went smoothly during your transition to the hotel? Did Josh settle in okay?

Jordan blinked, then blinked again. How had his dad found out about Josh? Oh, wait… he checked the contact. "Mr. C" flashed across the screen.

    Jordan: With all due respect, your son is an idiot. He fought me on coming here and actually thought he was gonna walk his injured butt to who-knows-where instead of just getting in the danged cab and coming with me. I think he has it in his head that I'm gonna force him on a plane and take him back home against his will or something. The dude's been trippin', major. I think he's starting to chill out, though.

A thud sounded from the bathroom. Jordan dropped the phone and leaped to his feet. "Hey, man, you okay in there?" he called through the door. A groan came from within. Worried, Jordan tested the knob and opened the door to find Josh on his knees, leaning against the counter with an open pill bottle in his hand. He'd managed to pull on his sweatpants, but his t-shirt lay discarded at his feet. His chest was a mess of fading black and blue bruises, and Jordan thanked God for the millionth time for saving Josh from death. "Whoa, dude. Come on, let me help you to bed." He pried the bottle from Josh's fingers and placed it on the counter, then wrapped an arm around his waist and began to lift him, freezing when Josh cried out.

"I c-I can't, J, I can't," he whimpered, his hands gripping Jordan's forearms. "Don't move me, Jordan! Please."

"You can do this—just hold onto me and let me do all the work, okay? On the count of three: one…two…three…"

Drawing in a breath as best as he could, Josh allowed himself to be pulled to his feet, gritting his teeth against the pain. He leaned all his weight on Jordan as they struggled to the bed nearest the bathroom. Relief flooded him when Jordan lowered him onto the thick mattress, and it enveloped his aching body in its warm embrace. The room was spinning. No, the whole world was spinning. Why wouldn't everything just hold still? He was vaguely aware of Jordan helping him settle into bed. He felt the pillows being arranged just right so that his ribs had a soft cushion around them. He heard Jordan settle into the bed across from his, and he let out a low moan.

From where he lay on his side, Jordan studied Josh's features and tried not to worry at the paleness of his face. The doctors had warned him the recovery would be a painful one. All he had to do was help him through it—and make sure he didn't do anything stupid to hurt himself worse. An argument escalated in the background on the TV, and Jordan clicked it off. "Hungry?"

Josh moaned a reply, his eyes squeezed shut against a sudden onslaught of dizziness. He shifted amongst the pillows, frustrated that even an inch of movement sent searing pain throughout his body. At last, the dizziness eased, calming the churning of his stomach. He heard Jordan humming—nerd—and asked the question plaguing him since his arrival.   "Why'd you really come out here, J?"

The humming stopped. Caught off guard by the

question, Jordan waited a moment before answering. Wasn't it obvious? "You're my best friend. When I got that call, I had to come. You'd have done the same for me."

Surprise sparked in Josh's eyes, and he contemplated Jordan's answer. "You really believe I'd go back to Highshore if you needed help?"

Jordan thought for a moment, then smiled. "Sure, you would have. Very covertly." He laughed. "You would've planned your entrance, and about a hundred escape routes should you need them, but you would have come. No doubt."

Josh remained quiet as he studied the confidence on Jordan's face, wrestling with what he'd said. Was it true? Would he face Highshore to rescue his friend? "What makes you so sure?"

Jordan smiled. "Remember in eighth grade when I got tired of everyone treating me like a nerd?"
Josh grinned and rolled his eyes. "Jordan, you are a nerd. You tracked me down using your tech judo." He leveled him with a pointed stare.

"I take offense to that." Jordan feigned a fierce frown.

"Anyway, eighth grade. The last straw was when Billy Andrews swiped my laptop, changed all my settings, and told me to 'nerd up' and fix it."

"I remember."

"So, I decided I needed an image change and started trying to act like you. You were cool and popular. The problem was, I didn't think that through too well and would've been expelled for hacking into the school computers and messing up all their programs if—"

"—I didn't save your butt." Josh picked at a loose string on his blanket. "I stepped in 'cause no one would've raised an eyebrow if it had been me who'd taken the fall, but it would've ruined you through high school." He laughed at the thought, as though hit with a realization. "You know, if Principal O'Neil was half as bright as he claimed to be, he would have figured me out. There ain't no way I could ever figure out how to hack into a computer and mess with the programs." The two shared a laugh at the thought before growing silent.

Jordan's features clouded as he thought over the past. "Josh, you've saved my butt more times than I can count. You've always been there for me. There's no way I could let you go through this alone. I must've texted and called a thousand numbers over the past four years looking for you. Numbers from all over the country, man. I couldn't handle the thought that you'd be out here just…lost. Forever."

Jordan's words struck him in the heart. He stared at his hands as memories flashed through his mind of his endless days with Jordan. "Thank you," he whispered. His eyes met Jordan's. "I'm really glad you found me, J. It scares the crap outta me, but I'm really glad. You've always been the only one I could really count on. You're an idiot for sticking with me though, since I always get you into trouble." He laughed.

Jordan smiled and hung his head. "Tell me about the last four years. I can't believe we've been apart that long."

Josh sighed, his mind working to answer the question and ignore the pain. "I had a killer job, J. It was perfect. Months of nothin' but ocean and diving." He smiled. "We'd stay out for a week, dock for a day, maybe two, browsing the land and wasting our paychecks, then we'd head back out again and leave all our cares behind us. There was nothing like it." The smile on his face faltered, and his eyes grew dim. "I really screwed up, J. I had it made. A boss who was more like…" his voice became a whisper as his mind wandered, "…a father to me. I mean, what I assume a father should be."

Jordan listened without comment, knowing Josh wasn't talking to him as much as he was trying to process the past month. He wondered at his obvious connection to this boss he spoke of. It took a special person to penetrate the walls in Josh's heart. Had this person succeeded in the monumental task?

"I was awful to him, Jordan." Josh let out a mournful

laugh and cursed. "Our relationship started out with me stealing from the man. For reasons I still can't understand, this guy brought me to his house, gave me a room, and required zero rent. Then one day, when he was out buying me dinner..." He stopped, rolling his eyes at his foolishness. "I found his safe. I broke in and stole some jewelry—his dead mother's jewelry. And you know what he did, J?"

Jordan waited, captivated by Josh's story.

"He forgave me. It's all still so...surreal, you know? I can still see him standing there. The betrayal was all over his face. Normally, that's part of the thrill—seeing the reaction of the one I'd just robbed blind. But for some reason this time was different. It hurt to see his face. But at the same time, I still had to be the one on top, you know? I had to be the one callin' the shots. He scared the crap outta me, Jordan. When he found me in front of his safe—his mom's jewelry in my hands—I just knew he was gonna call the cops. But he didn't. He just...stood there and told me to go eat my burger before it got cold."

Jordan blew out his breath and whistled.

Josh raised a brow. "I know. It was crazy. He sent me to the kitchen to eat—I could barely force down two bites—and stayed to clean up the mess I'd made in his hallway. For a while, he didn't say anything, and I started getting really nervous. I tried to tell him I was gonna pack my bags and leave, but he told me to sit down and shut up."

"What'd you do?" Jordan imagined Josh losing his cool and cursing the guy out.

Josh stared at him, wide-eyed. "I sat down and shut up."

"You didn't..."

"I did. And then he ordered me to go pack my bag."

"But he'd just told you to—"

"I know. I said the same thing. He told me to pack my bag and be ready to leave with him the next morning. So, by this point, I'm convinced this guy has lost his marbles and wants to get me off to some isolated place and let me have it or something. But, no. He told me I was going to work for him—for free—for an entire month. I told him no way was I goin' anywhere with him, and I was definitely not workin' for free. So, then he picked up his phone and dialed without saying a word to me—just looked at me the whole time. By this time, I was super scared, man. I had no idea what he was up to, and I didn't like that, so I asked him who he was calling. He calmly told me he was calling the police... and asked me if I had a problem with that. He looked right at me and said, 'Don't you think you need to be held responsible for what you've done here?' And then he said, 'You won't do it my way, so I'll do it yours.'"

"Man, he's good..." Jordan breathed.

"You have no idea." Josh grinned. "I was scared to my core and begged him to hang up the phone. Told him I'd go anywhere he wanted me to go, just please don't tell the police what I did. So, he hung up, told me to pack, and left the table. I got up to go pack my bags, but I saw his phone on the table. The screen was still lit, so I glanced at it and saw the most recent call. J, it was his mom. His dead mom. He never called the cops. I went to work with him the next day and have been working there ever since. Well," his eyes drifted, "until he fired me."

Jordan teased with the question on his lips before testing the waters. "Why'd he fire you?"

Josh closed his eyes. Why are we spinning again? He breathed through the nausea, fighting the urge to throw up.

"Too many complaints. I tend to get angry over very stupid people." He opened his eyes and fixed his gaze on Jordan. His eyes began to droop and he forced them open, his mouth spreading into a lazy grin. "Enough about me. Tell me about you. What was graduation like without me there to pull the senior prank? Did you follow through with the plan?"

Jordan cut him a look. "What do you think, Josh? Have you ever seen me execute an illegal plan without you there to drag me through it?"

"Awww don't tell me you bailed? You are such a spaz, Jordan. We had it planned perfectly, man! Principal O'Neil would've been trippin' major!"

"I have never in my life stolen a vehicle, and I wasn't gonna start my life of crime with the principal, dude. Nah, that's all you." Jordan grinned, but worry creased his brow at the look on Josh's face. "Yo, bro, what's wrong?" Nausea gripped Josh's stomach as he tried to focus on Jordan's voice. "Jordan," he called weakly. His head felt heavy, his body almost foreign. "Jordan, quit…quit spinning."

Jordan kept his eyes glued to Josh's face. He knew the dizzy spells were just a side effect of Josh's head injury but that didn't ease his apprehension over the fact. He sat on the edge of his bed, ready to run to Josh's aid.

Josh took three deep breaths, his brow trickling with sweat. "Jordan…"

"Right here. Just breathe. It's gonna be okay. Need some water?"

"No," he moaned. "Agh! Yes!" He threw his arm over his eyes and gritted his teeth.

Jordan leaped up and grabbed a bottle of water from the mini fridge. When he turned back to Josh, he found him drifting off to sleep. He placed the bottle by his bed and checked him for a fever. Satisfied to find none, he returned to his bed and fell asleep while his eyes were glued on his friend.

They'd been asleep for two hours when Jordan woke to gasps from Josh's bed. Leaping up, he noted his pale features and clammy forehead and grabbed the trash can just in time. Josh gripped the bin and hurled, his body shaking. When he'd finished, he lay back on his pillows, exhausted, while Jordan raced for cold, wet paper towels to help clean him up.

"Here, man. Wash your face." He handed the towels to Josh and dumped the trash can into the toilet, washed it out, and returned it to Josh's side. "You okay?" His voice was quiet as he watched Josh's face.

Josh's features crumpled as he grappled to stop the new wave of dizziness. Wiping a hand across his forehead, he focused a single spot across the room, willing his head to stay still. Once the dizziness had subsided, he lay quiet and still, vaguely aware of Jordan's presence at his side.

"Hey, man, you good?" Jordan crouched down on his haunches, his eyes never leaving Josh's face.

Josh slowly shook his head and closed his eyes. "No, man. I'm not."

Pulling up a chair, Jordan placed it beside Josh's bed and watched as he fell back into a fitful sleep. He spent the next couple of hours seeing Josh through several more episodes of nausea and dizziness, sleeping in between each one. He was in a deep sleep—stretched out on the floor by Josh's bed with a pillow under his head—when Josh cried out again. Jumping up, Jordan stood at his side and checked again for a fever. Finding none, he sat back in the chair and watched, knowing he could do nothing for the dizziness overtaking his friend.

Remembering the doctor had said his symptoms could last for weeks, Jordan breathed a frustrated sigh. What was he going to do? He had to ensure his friend was okay, but he couldn't stay in Florida forever. He wasn't sure if it was determination, exhaustion, or stupidity that pushed him to say his next words. All he knew was that there was no stopping him. "I'm taking you home with me."

"Mmkay."

Jordan stared at Josh's closed eyes. Had he heard him? Frowning, he said it again—louder and with added force.

"Did you hear me? I said 'I'm taking you home with me.' To Highshore. Where you belong."

Nausea teased Josh again, accompanied by violent spinning. "Agh!" he cried out, holding one hand to his head while pressing the other to his stomach.

Jordan's heart raced. If he was going to pull this off, he had to do it before Josh regained his rationale. Jumping off the bed, he grabbed Josh's things and tossed them into his duffel. He watched Josh as he worked, his worry growing heavier as his friend grew paler. How would he get him on a plane like this? Was he heartless to even consider it?

"What're you...doing?" Josh asked, his face pinched with pain.

Jordan threw a pair of jeans into Josh's duffel, then reached for his hairbrush and dropped it inside. "Told you. We're going home."

Panic seized Josh's senses, but nausea took his mind captive. He had to fight this. Had to overcome his body's weaknesses. Jordan was talking crazy, and he needed to think in order to outwit him. Opening his mouth to speak, he immediately snapped it shut again when bile pushed up his throat. "Jordan," he managed, but Jordan wasn't in a listening mood.

"Save your strength. You're gonna need it when we get on a plane." Jordan packed his bag and then disappeared into the bathroom to grab the remainder of their things. He stopped when his eyes fell on the medicine bottle with its open lid. Picking it up, he screwed the lid back on and shoved the bottle into his pocket. He would need them handy on the plane.

Where had he placed those sleep meds the doctor prescribed?

His scheme was picking up momentum as he rushed to pack everything. Finding the bottle of sleep medication, he shoved it into his other pocket.

Armed with medicine for Josh's pain, plus meds to knock him out in the air, Jordan felt confident his plan would bring them both back to Highshore.

Of course, there was one giant obstacle standing in his way. Once they landed and Josh found out where they were, he'd never speak to Jordan again.

He was dangling their friendship over the fire and tempting the flames with lighter fluid.

Chapter 11

"I acknowledged my sin to You, and my iniquity I have not hidden. I said, 'I will confess my transgressions to the Lord,' and You forgave the iniquity of my sin."
~Psalm 32:5~

GARRETT

It was quiet. Too quiet for his current state of mind, yet he welcomed its blanket of embrace. Garrett pushed his foot against the floor, sending his mother's rocking chair into a creaking rhythm. Against his chest, his daughter's heart beat a gentle rhythm, her warm breath creating a broken breeze along his neckline. He wrapped his arms around Nevaeh a little tighter as he glanced down at her sleeping features. She was so peaceful and calm, not a care in the world. Dressed in footy pajamas, he'd read her favorite story and sung her three songs as he'd rocked her to sleep. He knew he should be carting her off to bed, yet he sat in the silence and clung to her a little longer.

Upstairs, Elysia was taking the opportunity to grab some time alone. While Nevaeh had been busy with her breakfast, Garrett had run his wife a hot bath with rose-scented bubbles. He wished she would let him pour her a glass of the red wine he knew she wanted, but he knew better. Ever since he'd embarked on his journey towards sobriety, Elysia had refused to drink a drop of alcohol. This both warmed his heart and burdened it, knowing how much she used to enjoy a warm bath with a glass of wine and a good book. He'd settled her into the tub with lingering kisses and promised to get Nevaeh to bed. As he rocked his sleeping girl, he was grateful for the peace his wife and daughter were resting in and found himself longing for that peace, but he knew it was just a dream.

Something was wrong. He could feel it deep inside his bones. He'd texted Jordan three times this evening and had gotten no response. He didn't dare call, for fear it would draw Josh's attention to the phone and he'd be found out.

Worry gripped his chest. Nevaeh stirred in his arms, and he kissed her blond curls, checking his phone for the tenth time to see if Jordan had responded.

He hadn't.

Garrett sighed. *God, take care of my boys, okay? Please keep them safe.* His foot continued to rock the squeaking chair, and he hummed to the sleeping girl in his arms.

Guilt slammed his gut, but he continued humming. Guilt was a constant companion of his. Many times, a welcome friend, while other times it left him begging God to release him from its weight. Release from guilt would never be a reality for him. How could it, when Nevaeh sat safe and warm in his arms each night, listening to a story read by a daddy who loved her, while his son had no memory of one story read? Guilt threw itself at him wherever his gaze landed.

Garrett glanced up at a corner of the room where Elysia had placed a decorative table. Instead of the table, with all its pleasantries, he saw his little boy, only five years old, cowering in the corner with his little hands on top of his head to shield himself from his father's blows. He closed his eyes against the reminder. Opened them to a new spot in the room…and sighed. His terrified ten-year-old threw something across the room to try and stop his angry father from catching him. Garrett gently rubbed Nevaeh's back. He knew by now that the flashbacks would never fade. He was destined to relive the monster he'd been over and over and over again. Destined to hear those screams and see the terror haunting Josh's eyes.

"Yes, Jesus loves me…yes, Jesus loves me…yes, Jesus loves me…the Bible tells me so." He sang quietly, knowing Nevaeh was long past hearing. The children's song was more for his heart than hers, anyway. He'd found that if he could focus on something positive, the flashbacks would recede into the shadows—at least for a little while. And so, he continued singing. "Jesus loves me, this I know…" Josh's blue eyes looked up at him. "…for the Bible tells me so…"

"Please, Daddy, please…"

"…little ones to Him belong…" He saw himself raise his hand in the air, ready to strike.

"Oh, Daddy, no-o-o!"

"…they are…" He squeezed his eyes shut, tears streaming. "…weak…but He is strong."

His phone pinged, announcing a text.

Through his tears, he looked at the name flashing on his screen and sighed with relief.

Jordan.

His relief vanished as soon as he read the words:

"I'm in trouble, Mr. C…."

JORDAN

Trouble had been an understatement. Jordan sat in the airport lobby with Josh at his side. He'd managed to procure a wheelchair for his friend, after explaining to the attendant that Josh had been injured in a wreck. He'd also been granted the right to sit in the back of the plane with him to handle his care. Those details had seemed daunting feats, but they couldn't hold a candle to the war in his soul.

A glance at Josh's tight features both comforted and accused him. He knew the pain meds he'd given him earlier were wearing off and it was time for more—but that wasn't something he could give him. Not yet. Instead, he checked his watch. Thirty more minutes until they boarded. Reaching into his pocket, he pulled out the sleeping pills and dropped three into his hand. He'd researched the effects of an overdose and felt confident he'd landed on a number that would effectively knock Josh out for the duration of the flight without causing him harm.

"Hey," he quietly called, nudging Josh's arm.

"No."

Crap. He tried again. "Josh, time for your meds, man."

"Mmm."

Jordan leaned closer. "You're hurting, right?" His conscience accused him of his deception, but he was afraid of being found out if he gave Josh both meds. It had to be this way. Josh would take the sleeping pills, thinking they were his pain pills, and then it would be an easy flight out of Florida. "Take your pain meds. You'll feel better." He held them out, relieved when Josh grabbed the pills. He kept his eyes on him as he offered a bottled water, ensuring he'd taken all three.

Josh shifted in the wheelchair, growing agitated when he couldn't get comfortable. "Man, forget this," he said, moving to stand.

His pulse quickening, Jordan jumped up to intercept him. "You need to stay in the chair, Josh."

Josh yanked his arm free from his grasp but cried out as pain seared his ribs, making him fall back into the chair. Cursing, he glared up at Jordan through bleary eyes. "Where are we?"

"Right here." He nervously evaded, praying it would work.

It didn't.

Josh forced himself to focus on Jordan's face and read the fear in his eyes. Something was wrong, but he couldn't focus through the fog clinging to his mind. His gaze shifted to the airport lobby, taking in the people with baggage. Dread filled his bones and his body went cold. "J, where are you taking me?"

Jordan's face paled as he sat back down, but he would not relent. Josh's life was on the line, and he would see this through. "I told you," he said evenly. "We're going home."

Josh sat completely still—Jordan's words sinking into his mind. Closing his eyes, he began a mental checklist of his situation. Every part of his body registered pain. Dizziness continued to persist at random. Nausea was his constant companion. He had no money, no house, no car.

And Jordan was taking him to Highshore.

His eyes flew open, and he spat curses, rapid-fire, at his friend. "Take me back to the hotel, or I'll kill you with my bare hands."

A steady calm flooded Jordan as he stared him down.

"No. I meant what I said, Josh. We're going home."
Josh's breath quickened, and he felt the room closing in around him. He had to get out of here! He tried again to push himself out of the chair but failed. "You'll never get me on that plane, Jordan."

"Watch me," Jordan retorted.

"I'll fight you the whole way. I'll make a scene, and they'll kick us both off!"

"No, you won't." Jordan glanced at his watch.

Ten minutes to boarding.

Panic teased the recesses of Josh's mind, but before it could take root, he was hit with another wave of dizziness that derailed his thoughts. "Agh!"

Jordan leaned closer to him, ready with water once the spinning stopped. "Breathe," he reminded him.
Josh gripped the arms of the wheelchair tightly until his face finally relaxed.

Empathy for his friend filled Jordan's heart when Josh let out a whimper of desperation.
"Don't do this, Jordan. Don't do this to me, man!"
Forcing his heart to harden, Jordan held out the water. "Drink this," he urged.

Josh obeyed.

"You tired?" Jordan watched his features, then glanced at his watch.

Five minutes to boarding.

"I can't...I..." Josh's eyes met Jordan's right before he gave into the meds that pulled him under.

"Forgive me, God," Jordan whispered, standing, and pulling out one of his baseball caps. Placing it on top of Josh's head, he pulled it low over his face and wheeled him to the front of the boarding line, feeling as though he were kidnapping his best friend.

Once on the plane, he pulled out his phone to read the slew of concerned texts from Josh's dad.

Mr. C: What kind of trouble? Are you boys alright? Did something happen?

Mr. C: Jordan, talk to me. What's going on? How can I

help?

Mr. C: Come on, son, I can't help if I don't know what's wrong.

Jordan stared at the messages, unsure how to explain the craziness of the past two hours. Should he come clean and confess what he'd done? Garrett already knew he was with Josh. Would it hurt to let him know he was bringing him home?

Jordan: Some stuff happened…I made a rash decision that may or may not have been a smart idea. Josh is okay, but I'm pretty sure I just destroyed our friendship.

He was in desperate need of sleep and was hardly functioning as it was. Jordan swiped to the alarms on his phone and set an alarm for two hours. That would give him enough time to rest but would jolt him awake in enough time to figure out how to get Josh off the plane without tipping off their location. His eyes grew heavy as sleep pulled him in, and he laid his head back on his seat, giving in to exhaustion.

Garrett stared at the text on his screen, his hand rubbing the stubble on his jaw. He'd laid Nevaeh in her bed an hour before and had kissed Elysia goodnight, but there was no way he could lie down with his wife knowing his boys were in trouble. Jordan's message was cryptic, and he couldn't make sense of it. What could he have done to destroy his friendship with Josh? Were the two still together? Had he abandoned Josh somewhere? The thought of his son lying vulnerable and hurt pulled at his heart. He hit the reply button and began to type.

You gotta give me more details, kid. I can't help if I don't know what's going on. How did you destroy your friendship with Josh? I didn't think that was even possible…

Jordan's alarm pulled him from a deep sleep. When he pried his eyes open, he was disoriented, and it took him a minute to realize where he was and what he'd done. He turned the alarm off and noticed the text from Garrett. As he read, a sinking feeling hit his gut, and he glanced in Josh's direction. He was stirring. His features pinched as he moaned in his sleep. Assuming Josh would wake up in a world of pain after missing his last dose of meds, Jordan reached into his bag and withdrew the pain pills to have them ready. With a sigh, he answered Garrett.

Jordan: Well, we're on a plane heading to Highshore, and Josh knows nothing about it. So, yeah. Pretty sure I've destroyed us.

He only had to wait a moment for the response.

Mr. C: WHAT?!?!?! Jordan, what happened???

Beside him, Josh moaned and stirred. Jordan pocketed the phone and focused on his friend. "Here, drink this. It'll help."

Josh grabbed the water bottle from Jordan's hand and gulped until it was empty. His eyes focused blearily on Jordan's face. "I can't breathe," he whispered. "Hurts. So bad." He squeezed his eyes shut. "Feels like I've been in a fight all night."

Jordan winced at the guilt stabbing his heart. "Here, take these. You'll feel better." He slipped him the pain meds, along with another sleeping pill, watching to ensure Josh swallowed all of them. He knew it was wrong, and he prayed it wouldn't hurt him, but he only had one thing in mind: getting Josh off this plane and safely to his apartment without him losing his mind and trying to run off and get himself killed.

Chapter 12

"A wise son heeds his father's instructions, but a scoffer does not listen to rebuke."
~Proverbs 13:1~

RHEA

Hot water poured down on Rhea until her skin was red, but she didn't move to adjust the shower faucet. She stared blankly at the wall, fighting the bouts of panic bursting through her chest. She had a decision to make, but no courage to decide. Her body trembled and she felt her knees grow weak—a sign that she'd endured too much heat for too long. With mechanical movements, she twisted the knob and turned off the shower before reaching for the towel and wrapping it around herself.

Cold air whooshed around her as she opened the door. Stepping to the mirror, she stared at her reflection, tears springing at the panic wreaking havoc on her features. She checked the time and gasped. Sterling would be home soon. The last thing she wanted was for him to find her like this. She had to regain control of her emotions before she gave herself away.

Quickly, she set to work on her makeup. Applying enough concealer to hide the puffiness around her eyes, she threw on a muted shade of eyeshadow, contrasting it with a brighter color on her lips. With a sigh, she traded the towel for a simple sundress and blow-dried her hair until the curls bounced around her waist. Leaning closer to the mirror, she examined herself.

"Come on, Rhea. You can do this," she encouraged her reflection. "Sterling cannot know." Her eyes narrowed. "He will not know."

Moving to the bedroom, she went to her bedside table and pulled open the drawer. She eased herself onto the bed as her fingers worked the false bottom of the drawer and freed the latch. Sliding her hand into the compartment, she pulled out a picture and stared down at the carefree faces of the couple looking back at her. A smile teased her lips as she stared at the boy—then, only fifteen years old. He wore a goofy grin, and his eyes spoke of a confidence she'd always envied, though she knew the truth of the secrets plaguing his soul. Her finger traced the outline of his blond hair, following his bicep as his arm draped around the shoulders of the girl. Turning the photo over, she read the inscription she knew by heart.

Josh and Rhea–No one can break us!

Rae, you're my forever love–don't you ever forget!

A tear slid down her cheek. She hated herself for looking at this picture. Even more, for her desire to talk to this boy and pour out her heart about the terror pulsing through her–the terror only he could understand.

"Josh," she whispered.

He'd know what to do. Whenever trouble came their way, he'd always gotten them out of it. He had a way with words that put her to shame and could fast-talk his way through anything.

Where was he now? He'd promised to come back for her. She'd waited in Highshore for two years before giving up on him.

It hadn't been hard for Sterling to win her interest. Her heart was shattered by the boy who'd left her behind, and she no longer cared what happened in her life. But Sterling was different than what she'd expected, and it didn't take long for her to realize he truly cared about her. Three months after they'd started dating, she found herself in a whole new city and determined to put Highshore–and Josh–out of her mind. What she hadn't banked on, was how hard that would be, and now she found her heart loving two men at the same time.

A chime sounded from below, announcing Sterling's arrival. Quickly, Rhea shoved the picture back into its hiding place, but pulled out another, her gaze fixated on the baby girl. Tears filled her eyes as her heart reminded her of her empty arms.

"Rhea, I'm home," Sterling called.

Her heart ached at the joy in his voice. He was always so cheerful—he didn't deserve to be with a girl who kept secrets buried within her soul. Pressing a kiss to the picture, Rhea placed it back with the other and shut the drawer, grabbing the book off her nightstand and pretending to read.

"Rhea? Baby, you here?" he called again, and she knew she had to answer.

"Up here!" She forced normalcy into her tone, channeling their usual rhythm. His footsteps pounded on the stairs, and she jumped up and began smoothing the bedspread. "I was just finishing my latest thriller novel. It's about this guy whose car breaks down on a deserted road and he loses his—"

Sterling's arms wrapped around her, and he spun her to face him as he pressed his lips to hers.

Her panic dissolved into the strength of his embrace, and she relaxed into him. When he broke the kiss, her eyes went to his. "Good meeting, I assume?"

"Terrible." He rolled his eyes. "I had to get out of there and get home to you." He glanced at the novel she'd discarded on the bed and cocked his head. "I thought you said you were finishing your book."

Rhea's gaze flew to the book. "I was. I only have one chapter left."

Sterling grinned and picked it up. "You don't track your place with your bookmark?"

She stared at the bookmark placement and swallowed. It was near the beginning. "Normally, yes, but I was so excited about the chapter, I forgot to move it back after reading."

He tweaked her nose and placed the book on her nightstand. "Your head is going to explode with all the books you shove into it."

"I'd rather it explode from novels than boring law books," she retorted, giving him a playful shove.

"Yeah? You think my law books are boring?" Sterling grabbed her and fell to the bed, tickling her until she couldn't breathe.

When she moved close and nestled into him, he kissed her brow. "Baby, why were you afraid when I told you the name of my dad's new client?"

Rhea tensed and the panic pulsed again. "I'm not sure," she lied. "I must have thought you'd said another name."

She was off the bed before Sterling could stop her. Frustrated, he sat up and watched as she busied herself at the dresser. "Rhea, talk to me. What name did you think I'd said? Who are you afraid of?"

She closed her eyes and willed her body to stop trembling. Maybe she should just tell him… Panic erased the idea as soon as it had appeared. "No one, baby," she lied again. Would he believe her? "At least, not anymore." She spun to face him, a new lie forming. "There was this bully from high school. She had the same last name as the client. But she doesn't live here anymore. I guess hearing the name just triggered me."

Sterling watched the smile flash across her face but focused more on the fear in her eyes that told him she was lying. Up to this point, he'd been convinced their year-long relationship was built on trust, but it was clear he was wrong. He studied her a moment longer, reading the tension in her body and the way her eyes pleaded with him not to push her for the truth. Forcing a smile, he stood and loosened his tie.

"I'm going to shower. Let me know how the novel ends." He walked to their bathroom and shut the door. As he turned on the water, something the client had said rushed to his mind and he froze.

"She has a beautiful name…"

How had Nichole Sherard known Rhea's name if she'd never met her?

GARRETT

"Penny for your thoughts."

Garrett's distant gaze met the concerned eyes of his wife, and he offered her a smile meant to put her mind at ease. "I'm going to pour myself some coffee. Want some, love?"

Elysia nodded and sat down at the kitchen table. Propping an elbow, she rested her chin in her hand and watched him as he poured the steaming brew into two cups, adding cream and sugar before joining her. She smiled as she took the cup from his hands and sipped, the heat warming her throat. "You've been very distracted lately. I've noticed you've been coming to bed later than usual the past few days. Do you want to talk?"

He sipped his coffee, buying time. How could he explain what had happened without telling her about their son? The betrayal of his silence on the matter stabbed him through his heart. At last, his blue eyes met her brown, and he sighed. "Do you trust me, Lyse?"

She studied his face, unnerved by the haunting in his eyes. She was worried. It wasn't like Garrett to keep things from her—he knew the importance of disclosure in their marriage. Whatever had his silence must be serious. Her finger traced the lip of her cup as she wondered at the wisdom in pushing the matter. "I trust you, Garrett, but I won't lie and say I'm comfortable with this. I can tell that something is wrong. I don't understand why you won't talk to me, but I will trust you to tell me if it is important for me to know." Her eyes seared through his, and she watched as he shifted beneath her stare. Elysia cocked her head to the side. "Is it important for me to know?"

She had him with that question. Yes, it was important for her to know. Josh was her son—she had every right to know all that had transpired. But to tell his secret meant a betrayal of both Jordan and Josh. A burning need to protect Elysia from heartache also kept him quiet. What if Josh was on his way back to Highshore? Jordan had indicated he was coming, not only against his will but against his knowledge. Garrett could only assume Josh would leave the first chance he got—most likely without bothering to see his mother. He couldn't risk Elysia getting her hopes up only to have them dashed against their son's strong will and defiance.

"Cameron."

He glanced up, startled. She only called him by his last name when things got serious. He swallowed hard. "It's very important that you know, babes. But it's not time. Can you trust me? Please?" His eyes implored her for understanding and grace.

After a moment, she nodded, but the set line of her jaw sent a clear message to the man across the table: Do not mess with the stability in my life, Garrett Cameron. God knew he'd done enough damage to her in the past. As he read the lines in her face, Garrett pleaded with God for wisdom. He cleared his throat and stood. "I've got to go see Levi. I'll be back soon."

When she didn't move or acknowledge him, he awkwardly bent to kiss her, the chill from her veins giving him pause an inch from her mouth. He stood and gently touched her hair. "I love you, Lyse."

Garrett walked the short distance through the woods to Levi's door. On his way, his mind whirled, and his heart pleaded for a respite from the chaos fighting within. Something was wrong, and he needed Levi to help him find out the truth. His knock was answered swiftly, the upbeat attitude of Levi's wife warming his soul. "Laura," he nodded at the woman who could be Jordan's twin. "Levi home?"

"In the study. Come on in, Garrett. Want a drink?" She swung the door wide and let him pass, shutting it behind him.

"No, that's okay. Thanks anyway. I just need to speak with Levi." He followed her down the hall to the study, grateful when she left the two alone, and closed the door.

"Garrett! Didn't expect you today. How's it going, my friend?" Levi had papers covering his desk, but a jigsaw puzzle held his attention.

Garrett sat across from the desk but didn't relax in the chair. His back was stiff, hands locked together as he leaned forward. "I have a problem, and I need your help to solve it."

Levi's face erupted in a smile. "You know me and problems needing solutions. I'm your main man."

Garrett smiled. Jordan may have his mother's looks, but his personality was all his father's. "Remember that client you referred to me last week? The one Jordan said was a friend, but wouldn't name?"

Levi nodded. "I remember. Why–did he not pay?"

"It's Josh," Garrett blurted.

"What?" Levi leaned forward on his desk. "How did I..." He shook his head in disbelief. "Why didn't Jordan tell me? Why didn't you tell me?"

"Josh doesn't know I'm involved." Garrett waited for that to sink in.

Levi thought about this, then nodded. "Oh...I see." He sat back in his chair. "So, all this time Jordan..." His voice trailed off as he connected the dots.

"...has been with my missing son." Garrett filled him in on Josh's arrest and need for legal help. He told him about the wreck and how Josh had been rendered helpless, with nowhere to turn. "I think Jordan did something that could put both boys at serious risk. I need your help to see if my suspicions are right."

"What did he do? He hasn't answered my texts since yesterday."

"Mine, either. I think he brought Josh home last night."

Levi's jaw dropped. "What!"

"I think he did, but I can't go over there to see, and he's not answering my calls or texts." His eyes fell to his hands. "I have to know, Levi. Can you please go check?"

Levi nodded and stood.

"Absolutely. I'm headed there now. Stay by your phone, old buddy, I'll have the answer shortly."

Garrett watched his friend rush from the room, knowing he'd be right back. He counted to five before the door flew open, and Levi shot to his desk in a flurry of movement. "Forgot my phone," he muttered as he rushed back out, leaving Garrett shaking his head at his constant state of distraction.

JORDAN

Heavy pounding startled Jordan from a deep sleep. He forced his eyes open and surveyed his surroundings, trying to make sense of where he was at. His mother's mirth-filled eyes stared down at him from the picture frame on the wall. His grandpa's antique cuckoo clock shrieked from its perch on the mantle, and the pounding on his door intensified. The fog of sleep was slow to evaporate as he rolled from the couch and stumbled to the door. Peering out the window, he groaned when he saw his father standing on the step. "Aww, man…" Knowing he'd have to come clean with what he'd done, he braced himself for the lecture that was sure to come. Not even trying to put on pretense, he unlocked the door and opened it a mere crack, knowing his father wouldn't take the hint. "Dad," he croaked through sleep-laden vocal cords. "It's so early," he complained, keeping his body in the doorway.

Levi raised an eyebrow at his son, taking in the mess of brown hair and sleep-clogged eyes looking back at him. He knew by Jordan's demeanor that Garrett's suspicions were correct—Jordan had done something he didn't want his father to know about. "It's ten o'clock, boy," he stated, amused when Jordan winced and leaned his head against the door.

"Dad, it's been a really…really long night. If you could just…come back, say…in three days?" His eyes were closed, and he felt his mind trying to slip back to sleep.

"You hidin' a girl in there?" Knowing this wasn't the case, Levi laughed when Jordan predictably grew defensive.

"Not funny." Jordan's eyes met his, his body still blocking the door. "You know me better than that. Just gimme a few hours, and I'll meet you for lunch or something, okay?"

"Jordan," Levi crossed his arms. "Move."

"D-a-a-a-a-d," Jordan groaned, but obeyed, opening the door for his father to enter the small living room.

Once inside, Levi surveyed the mess of bags and the disheveled couch tossed with pillows and a blanket. He raised an eyebrow as he turned to his son. "You sure about that girl?" The corner of his mouth slid into a smile. Jordan would never bring a girl home to spend the night. His son was far too committed to a life of following Jesus to pull such a stunt. He'd always boasted that he never worried about Jordan sneaking around with girls as a teen. Sneaking into secret databases—yes. But sneaking girls? Nah, not his boy.

Rolling his eyes, Jordan dropped onto the couch and grabbed a pillow to his chest. His gaze followed his father as he sat, unnerved at the way Levi's eyes roamed the apartment as though looking for something. A twinge of fear sparked in his gut.

"Dad," his voice cracked from sleep.

Levi met his eyes, relaxing into the easy chair across from him. No father had ever been prouder of their son than he. Jordan had been an easy kid—rarely got into trouble without the aid of his best bud. He'd always been sensible, with a good head on his shoulders, but a father knows when his kid is hiding something and, as he stared at his boy, he knew Jordan was hiding a secret today. "Wanna talk about it?"

Jordan shifted and looked at the window before glancing back at his dad. He dropped his gaze. "If I say no, do I get to go back to sleep?" His eyes met his father's, read his answer, and sighed. Most twenty-one-year-olds defied their dads. Most would never allow their father to force his way into their apartment and demand information from them. But he was not like most twenty-one-year-olds. He had mad respect for his dad. He trusted him and valued his input. Plus…his dad still paid his bills, so there was that.

Here goes nothing…

"It's a really long story," he stalled.

Levi leaned back in the chair and crossed his foot over his left knee, the picture of relaxation. "I've got nothing but time for you, my boy." His eyes twinkled, and he knew full well that Jordan had hoped to detour his interest. Compassion replaced the mischievous glint in his eyes as he watched Jordan's features shift. A cloud of remorse had replaced the guarded look on his face, and Levi wondered just how deep a hole his son had dug for himself.

Jordan squeezed his eyes shut. "I found Josh."

Levi sat very still. The news was no surprise, not just because Garrett had already told him the boys were together, but because he knew that Jordan had relentlessly searched every avenue for his friend since Josh had disappeared.

Jordan focused on his dad. "I texted and asked him to call me if it was really him. So, he did." His voice grew quiet. "Dad. It was awful. He was living in Panama City, and he'd just been fired from his job. He had no house, no place to go, no car, and no money. Wanna know where he called me from?"

Levi gave a small nod, pained at the sorrow in Jordan's eyes.

"The park. It was night, and Josh was sleeping on a bridge in the playground." Tears pooled as the conversation played back in his memory. "He sounded so miserable and lonely out there. That's the whole reason he called me. He just…needed somebody. And he trusted me," he whispered, his eyes falling. "I asked him to let me go get him. Told him he could stay with me and get a job here and build a life. He wouldn't even consider it. Before we hung up, he made me swear not to tell a soul he'd called. So, I didn't."

"You shouldn't swear," Levi interjected, but the serious tone that usually came with that phrase was replaced with empathy for his boy.

Jordan met his gaze and breathed a shuddering breath. "You have no idea how badly I wish I hadn't this time, Dad. The next day I got another call. This time it was from an old contact I had at the paper. She lives in Panama City and called to tell me Josh was trending in the papers. She said he'd been in a bad car wreck and was in the hospital." He looked at his father, his features speaking volumes about the conflict in his soul. "I was in his father's backyard. Garrett was right there, and I never said a word to him about what I'd just learned. Instead, I had Serenity dig for more info. When she called back, she told me he was in police custody and a world of trouble. I called the hospital, but no one would give me any information on Josh, so I did the only thing I could think of–I went to him."

Levi glanced at his hands, struggling to comprehend his son's logic. It would have been so simple for Jordan to have passed the information on to Josh's father, yet his son had chosen loyalty to his best friend. "I admire your loyalty, son, but I think you now know that you should've involved Garrett from the beginning."

Regret burned in Jordan's chest, mixing with the desperate need for his father to understand. "Are you not listening to me? I swore to him, Dad. I swore. I couldn't break my word! He would never trust me again! And the whole time I was on the phone, Mr. C watched me like he knew. Dad, I felt so awful keeping it from them." Tears pooled. "But what choice did I have? If I had told them about the call, they would've been on the first flight to the hospital and Josh never would have forgiven me. So, I went to him myself." His voice was a whisper. A flash of anger sparked in his eyes. "But you already knew that, didn't you?"

Levi smiled and gave a small nod. "Yeah, son. I did. What happened after you went to him?"

"Remember when I called and asked you for that lawyer?" He waited for his father's nod. "When I got to the hospital, the cops wouldn't let me go see him. Serenity had an inside guy on the police force, so I at least had an idea of what Josh was facing. They said they caught him with coke. Coke, Dad. Josh." He stared hard at his father, ensuring he understood the ludicrous notion of Josh and coke being in the same sentence.

Levi's brows rose. "That can't be right."

"It wasn't. Mr. C got to work on his case, partnering with a lawyer in Panama City. They found out that the coke had been planted on him while he was unconscious. If I ever find out who framed him, I'll bug every device that prick owns," Jordan grumbled.

Levi hid a smile. This was the part where most young adults would have said "I'll punch him in the face!" but not Jordan. His boy was a whole different breed. "I assume Garrett got the charge dropped?"

Jordan winced. "Charges. Dad, it was so bad. Josh was charged with assault with a deadly weapon, evading arrest, grand theft auto, speeding, reckless driving, possession of coke, and the list goes on." He rolled his eyes.

"Say what?" Levi stared in disbelief. "You're joking, right?"

"Nope. They really wanted to lock him up, but Mr. C is too good at what he does. He had him freed in no time. When Josh was released from the hospital, I took him to a hotel Garrett paid for. He told me to keep Josh there with me for as long as he would stay and to make sure he didn't run off without a large sum of money that Garrett would provide. It never came down to that, though. I did have to argue with him when he first got out. He tried to walk off instead of getting in the cab with me." He rolled his eyes. "He's still just as stupid and stubborn as he ever was."

When Jordan told him about their conversation in the hotel room—and about the boss who'd gotten through Josh's rock-hard exterior—Levi smiled, pleased to know Josh had found someone who could reach him.

"Throughout the night, Josh was super out of it. He kept getting bad dizzy spells that made him violently throw up. I started getting nervous and thinking about how, eventually, I was going to have to leave him. I didn't like the thought of him getting back on his feet by himself, so I—"

Levi studied the shift in Jordan's eyes, noting the nervousness that had overtaken him. "What, son? What did you do?"

"I told him I was taking him home, and he agreed." Jordan held up a hand to stop his father's argument. "It was an intense situation, okay? My best friend was lying helpless in that hotel room with no hope in sight. There was no way I was leaving him there alone. So, I...traded in the hotel fair for two tickets home." He glanced up, trying to weigh the impact of this news on his father.

Levi brought a hand to his chin and mulled over that last sentence. "So...Josh is here," he clarified. At Jordan's solemn nod, he continued. "In this apartment?"

Jordan's gaze fell on his bedroom door. "Right there."

Levi thought some more. "So, you're telling me that he agreed to get on the plane with you and agreed to come back home. Is that right?"

Silence.

Jordan took a deep breath and blew it out hard. "Uh, not exactly." His hand went to the back of his neck, his eyes fixed on his father.

"Son..." Levi didn't like where this was going.

"I told him I was taking him back with me, but he was in too much pain to care. Then, once we were at the airport, I...um...I slipped him three of his sleeping pills and knocked him out for the flight. He woke up when we were about an hour outside of Highshore. He was super groggy and in a lot of pain. He was exhausted and focused on lying down. I knew we'd be landing soon and would have to take a cab to my place. I also knew that Josh would be coming out of his fog before we got off the plane, so, I..."

Levi locked eyes with his son, curious at the guilt that had surged into his gaze. "Jordan?"

"I gave him more sleeping pills," he whispered. "By the time I got him into bed this morning, he was too drugged to care where he was."

Levi shot to his feet. "Jordan! You mean to tell me that

kid has no idea he's here?!"

Panic surged through Jordan's veins. "Shhh! He'll hear you! Just, please." He placed a hand over his face, his fingers trembling. "Please, just sit, Dad. Calm down before you wake him up. I'm not ready to handle this, okay? Battling a drugged-up Josh is one thing, but battling a sober Josh is something I am not able to face right now."

Levi heard the plea in his son's voice, but there was no way he was able to sit down with fear pulsing through his veins. How could Jordan have been so stupid? How could he have made such a foolish decision? He paced the floor in front of his son. "Do you have any idea what that kid's gonna do to you when he finds out what you've done? Has it slipped your mind that he decked you five years ago over a game of cards?" Concern for his son's well-being rippled across his face. He'd seen Josh do heinous things with his fists over the years. A soul burdened with hatred and anger was capable of massive damage when that energy burned through its veins. A paralyzing thought hit him, and he came to a halt, pinning Jordan with a hard stare. "What about his parents? Are you just gonna, oh, I dunno, let them bump into him by chance?! Jordan, what were you thinking?"

Righteous indignation burned his reasoning to ashes. "What was I thinking? I was thinking that my idiot friend was gonna get himself killed. Wind up dead somewhere in the streets. That's what I was thinking. Where's the 'good job, son, you followed your heart and rescued your friend from a life of misery and heartache,'?" He stood, going toe-to-toe with his father and forgetting to keep his voice down. "And I'll have you know that there has never been a time when Josh has hit me that I didn't let him."

Levi's eyes grew, his head bobbing in sarcastic agreement. "Oh, sure, sure! So that time you angered him because you foiled his plans to jack that car in ninth grade and he beat you so bad I had to take you to the hospital—that all took place because you were generous enough to let the tough guy kick your butt? Or how about when he busted your lip because you were about to rat him out to the teacher for placing that snake in her desk drawer—you let that happen, too?"

Jordan bristled. "Just stop, okay? You've made your point—I get it. I messed up big time. Made a stupid decision. But there's no going back now, so just take your sarcasm and leave so I can figure my way out of this mess I'm in."

When his father didn't budge, Jordan went to the door and yanked it open, waiting.

Levi stood in silence, shocked by his son's response. The two so rarely fought, but when they did it was bad. His wife's words, spoken many times before, flooded his mind as he looked at the man across from him: *He is your behavioral twin, Levi. If you spark a fire in his soul, you won't be able to extinguish the fight. Let him be and he'll come around.* Heeding Laura's wisdom, he walked to the door, pausing in indecision. If he left, Jordan would be alone to deal with Josh's wrath. If he stayed, he risked further angering the boy he loved. Sighing, he stepped out onto the porch and turned to Jordan. "I'm just a phone call away. If you need me."

"I won't." Jordan's eyes were steel as he raised his chin at his father.

Levi nodded and turned for his truck. As he climbed in, he paused. "Jordan?"

"What?" he bit through tight lips.

"Watch your back."

Jordan seethed as he watched his father back out into the road. He slammed his front door shut, knowing he was wrong, but too angry to care. Far too angry to resume his rest, he snatched a book from his bookshelf, plopping onto the couch to read and await the fate he knew would be coming once Josh realized where he was.

Chapter 13

"Even my closest friend whom I trusted, the one who ate my bread, has lifted his heel against me."
~Psalm 41:9~

JOSH

Josh stirred beneath the blankets. His head pounded in rhythm with the throbbing in his aching ribs. He'd slept hard; his mind filled with dreams of his past that had seemed all too real. He rolled onto his back and opened his eyes, taking in the unfamiliar sights surrounding him. His thoughts were jumbled, tripping over one another as he tried to piece together the past few days. He remembered leaving the hospital with Jordan and going to a hotel, but his memory offered very little of the events post-arrival. His gaze wandered and confusion swirled in his mind, threatening to overtake him. Nothing in this room held a sense of familiarity. Had they switched hotels without him realizing it? Or maybe his memory had taken a hit in the wreck and was now showing face. Jordan was nowhere in sight, but he knew he'd find the answers needed to fill in the gaps if he found him. Grunting his way to the edge of the bed, Josh dropped his bare feet to the carpeted floor and stood, heading for the door. He stepped out into another unfamiliar room but welcomed the sense of relief in his soul at the sight of Jordan stretched out on the couch, a book hiding his face. The creak of the door alerted him to Josh's presence, and Jordan lowered the book, leaving Josh to wonder at the brief look of panic that flashed in his eyes.

"Hey, man." Jordan's voice sounded strained to his ears, and he told himself to play it cool. Even as the thought entered his mind, his nerves squeezed the breath from his lungs as Josh paused in the doorway. He sat up and put the book aside. "Sleep okay?"

Josh surveyed the room, confusion wrinkling his brow. This was not a hotel… "Jordan, where are we?" His voice was thick from pain and sleep.

"You didn't eat last night—you hungry?" Jordan stood and turned for the kitchen to buy himself time. Please, God, please—he begged. But for what? For Josh to be calm in the face of his deceit? For him to accept the betrayal from his best friend? He lowered his head in shame and grabbed a bowl from the cupboard.

Josh's pulse quickened as he watched Jordan, noting how he worked to avoid looking in his direction. His eyes darted from one thing to another as he began to put the pieces together. Familiar faces stared at him from picture frames on the wall. He studied one, his heart squeezing from mixed fear and regret as he recognized the laughing eyes of Jordan's mother. He forced himself to look out the window, dread creeping into his bones. The beach that spread below, with its sun-kissed sand and deep blue waters, held no beauty in the eyes of its beholder. The sands where he'd spent countless days awakened a terror he thought he'd buried long ago and suddenly he knew. He scrambled away from the window as though it had erupted in flames. "Tell me you didn't, J. Please!" His hand went to his head, his pupils the size of hockey pucks.

Jordan stood behind the counter and watched as panic took Josh captive. He felt lower than scum at the fact that he was the reason for it all. Who did he think he was, making this life-changing decision for his friend? His father was right. He had been foolish and now Josh was paying the price for his selfishness. "Josh, let me explain." He moved around the counter but froze when Josh frantically backed away. The gesture was a punch to the gut—a declaration of the broken trust.

"NO! You have no idea what you've done!" Hot tears seared his cheeks. It was all coming together now. Jordan showing up at the hospital, getting him a lawyer to keep him out of prison, taking him to the hotel to give him time to heal. It had all been charged with one underlying motive to trick him into returning home. His senses were overloaded as he worked to comprehend the level of betrayal he'd just been dished. His mind whirled as he tried to breathe. The one thing he couldn't figure out was how Jordan had convinced him to get on that plane. He couldn't remember anything after the hotel, and it made him sick. Had he drugged him? His eyes flashed at the thought. Surely not...he would never...

Jordan swallowed hard, reading each emotion as it sparked across Josh's features. The trust that had always enabled their friendship to withstand fire was burned up in the flames of his betrayal. As he watched Josh's eyes flit across the room, panic surging in his pupils, he knew there was nothing he could say to undo the damage he had done.

"Josh, sit. Please," he pleaded.

As though he hadn't heard him, Josh paced the room like a caged lion. "I've gotta get outta here." Sweat began to stain his shirt as his eyes darted around the room. "Hold on, man. Let me explain." Jordan held a hand toward his friend, dropping it back to his side when Josh leaped away, facing off like the two were matched in a boxing ring.

Highshore. He was in Highshore. The city of torment where his father roamed the streets with his head held high and the townsfolk bowed to him as though he were king. "How could you?" The words evaporated from his lips as his eyes landed on Jordan's guilt-ridden face. He squeezed his eyes shut, panic pushing the tears through his eyelids. The vise grabbing his chest tightened and his eyes flew open. "You blindsided me, J." Cursing, he swiped at his tears. "You betrayed me. My best fr—" He choked on the tension in his throat. "My best friend," he whimpered.

Something inside Jordan broke, allowing his hatred for himself to saturate his soul. "I couldn't just leave you there like that," he whispered. "You agreed to come with me..." His conscience accused him of the lie, adding venom to the hatred in his veins.

Josh gasped, fighting for air, as his memory fought to make sense of what Jordan had just said. Was it true? No...he would never have agreed to come back to this place. "Why you lying to me, man?" His vision clouded through his tears. "Tell me the truth, J. Just tell me the truth—please! You've always been the straight shooter. You used to hide in the shadows if I told a lie, even if you had nothing to do with it. So why, Jordan? Why you lying to me?" His voice shook from the fear in his veins. "How did I get here, Jordan? How?!"

Tears of desperation splashed Jordan's eyes and he furiously blinked them back. "I'm not lying, I swear. You were in a lot of pain, Josh, and the dizzy spells weren't letting up. I told you I was taking you home with me so I could take care of you, and you said 'okay.' I would never have forced you to come back, Josh. You know that!"

Liar!

The hatred in his conscience sounded loud and clear. Anger battled the voice inside of him. He was tired of his heart betraying him and fought to overcome the accusations. Josh had agreed to let Jordan bring him home.

"I don't believe you," Josh growled through clenched teeth. "I would never have agreed to come back here if I was in my sound mind, Jordan. What did you do to make me agree to this?"

Silence.

"What did you do, Jordan?!"

Jordan swallowed hard. There was no way around it. He had to come clean. "You had a prescription for sleeping pills..."

Shock rippled through Josh's muscles, twisting them into knots. His nerves surged, shooting a tingling pain throughout his body. "You drugged me?"

Jordan watched as panic transformed into rage, and he began to worry. When Josh took an abrupt step toward him, he longed for his father's presence. But, no...he deserved whatever he had coming. "Josh..."

"Shut up! Don't you dare talk to me! Don't you ever talk to me again, you self-centered prick!" The anger evaporated into sorrow, and his face crumpled. "I thought you were my friend, Jordan. I thought I could trust you.

You were the only one in my corner, man, and you stabbed me in the back!"

Anger surged past the guilt knifing its way deeper into Jordan's heart. "For once in your life would you just listen to someone who cares about you?! I am your friend, Josh. That's why I brought you here—you need help, man! You have nobody! You have nothing! If I had left, you there alone you would have died—you're just too stubborn to admit it!"

"No! Friends don't drug their friends! You are not my friend, Blayze."

Jordan lunged, shoving Josh hard. "When are you going to wise up and recognize the people going to bat for you, Josh?"

His impulse was his worst enemy. Josh's fist slammed into his eye, knocking him into the counter behind him. A yell escaped his lips as Jordan gripped his back, pain shooting through his spine. The sucker punch to the gut dropped him to the floor and he watched Josh back away, his fist still cocked, lips pursed as he turned and disappeared into Jordan's room. When the bedroom door slammed shut, Jordan groaned and pressed a hand to his rapidly bruising eye. "Jordan, you're an idiot," he muttered. His gut told him to call his dad, but his stubborn pride refused the request. Instead, he dragged himself to his feet and limped to the freezer to fish out some ice for his eye. Every fiber of his being longed to barge into the bedroom and plead with Josh to stay, but he knew better. Self-control had to take precedence over his desire this time. Forcing his back to comply, he lowered himself onto the couch to wait, his eyes never leaving the bedroom door.

JOSH

Josh collapsed on the bed, moaning as waves of pain radiated throughout his body. Slugging Jordan had rendered him immobile. His vision clouded from the pain slamming his ribs. Panic threatened anew at the possibility of his father finding him in town. He couldn't let the pain get the best of him. He had to get out of this place. Ordering himself to stand, he swallowed two of his pills. Digging through his duffel bag, he withdrew a change of clothes, pulling them on as he bit back the pain. Reaching into the bag, he fished out his phone, cigarettes, and lighter and shoved them into his pockets. With stiff movements that took his breath away, he pulled on his socks and sneakers and stood, dreading having to toss his bags over his shoulder. He squeezed his eyes tight, psyching himself up for the intense pain he was sure to endure, grabbed the straps, and carefully lowered the bags across his chest. He winced, but determination and fear propelled him forward. Pulling the door open, he stepped into the living room, glaring when his eyes fell on Jordan.

Jordan helplessly looked on as Josh limped to the door. His friend needed rest to heal, but he knew better than to try and convince him. "Josh, where you going?" He followed him to the door. "You can't leave. You've got no money and no place to go. Please, Josh, be smart. This isn't smart!"

Josh gripped the doorknob and turned seething eyes on Jordan. "I am not gonna just sit here and let him find me. I'd rather die on the streets than give him the satisfaction of ever seeing me again. I've had enough hell to last a lifetime from that man, and I refuse to be anywhere near him. I'm going back to Florida, and you are gonna stay out of my life. I never want to see you again, Jordan. Not for as long as I live."

"Josh, please. I'm sorry! I am so sorry, man. Let me make this right!" His plea fell on deaf ears as Josh stormed out the door and down the sidewalk.

"Forget you, Jordan," he called over his shoulder.

Jordan let out a frustrated yell into the air and shut the door.

"He'll be back," he said to the empty room. "He has to come back. Where else can he go?"

Chapter 14

"And he said to his disciples, 'Temptations to sin are sure to come, but woe to the one through whom they come!'"
~Luke 17:1~

ASHER

"...and all the bases were loaded, Dad! Then the pitcher pitched that pitch, and it was on! I swung and hit that sucker right into the outfield, Pops. Everyone went wild!" The chatter stopped, the bright, brown eyes dimming as the mop-haired little boy realized his story had fallen on deaf ears. His shoulders slumped as he watched his father stare at the computer screen as though he'd been hypnotized. "Dad?" His voice was small.

Asher cried out when something hit him on the back of the head. Throwing his hands up to shield himself from the blows that kept coming, he looked up in surprise at his bride of six years.

"Your son is trying to talk to you!" Bridget smacked him three more times with the rolled-up newspaper before throwing it at his face, her amber eyes flaming. "You missed his game and now you can't even listen to him tell you how he hit the winning ball! Father of the year, Asher," she growled. Bending at the waist, her dirty blond curls fell over her shoulder as she put herself inches from his face. "I don't know what has gotten into you these past couple of weeks, but you had better remember that you have a family or else." The threat hung in the air as she spun on her heel and wrapped her arm around their son's shoulders. "Come on, Ty, I'll fix you a sandwich. Let's leave Daddy alone with his stupid computer—it's more important than us right now."

Asher watched his son glance back over his shoulder—sadness and disappointment registering in his eyes. He sighed and hung his head as his family disappeared into the kitchen. He could hear Bridget's anger in the dishes she pulled from the cabinet—each plate banging on the countertop. She was right. He'd become detached and unavailable since she had come back into his life. If Bridget only knew the amount of danger he was killing himself to keep them out of, then she'd understand. Maybe. A bell sounded from the computer, alerting him to a new message. His heart clenched from dread. Opening the message, he read and bit his lip hard.

"I don't think he heard a word I said, Mom." Ty's voice sounded from the next room.

"It's okay, baby. Daddy's just being a jerk. You know work makes him crazy sometimes."

Asher gritted his teeth at the truth in her words.

"I just want my dad back..."

Forcing himself to block out the pain in his son's voice, he focused on the screen.

"Joshua Cameron, Jordan Hendricks. Flight 107—westbound flight to Highshore, California."

Asher studied the departure and arrival dates and times, then lowered his face into his hands. This couldn't be happening. Cameron wasn't just out of jail; he was also back in Highshore. He screamed a slew of curses into the air and tossed the keyboard across the room.

"Oh, that's real mature, Asher." Bridget's voice sounded behind him.

He squeezed his eyes shut and reminded himself that he loved this fiery-tempered woman. "Not now, Bridge," he breathed hoarsely, adrenaline spiking. She laughed, and he knew he'd just incited an argument.

"That's rich...you think you can just dismiss me like you did Ty? I don't think so, bud." She yanked the keyboard off the floor and slapped it down in front of him. "I want to know what's going on, and I want to know now."

Asher stared at her as she crossed her arms and raised her chin. "I can't...I can't tell you, Bridget." His voice was thick with regret.

The hardness in her eyes dimmed as she studied the torment on his face. She crossed her arms over her chest and hugged herself tight. "Can't," she said dully. "Can't, Asher? Or won't? I swear if this is about Addison, I'll kill you. Do you hear me? If you're messin' around with that girl again, we are done, Asher. Done! I'll have Ty and me packed up so fast your head will spin."

Asher's veins turned to ice as hot tears exploded from his tear ducts. He had to get from under this blackmail—and fast before it destroyed his marriage. He stood and reached for her, dropping his arms at his sides when she stepped back and raised her chin. Her lower lip quivered, and he wondered if he could hate his blackmailer any more than he already did. "Baby, please listen to me. I haven't seen or heard from Addison in three years. When I told you I was done with her, I meant it. I am so sorry she ever happened, okay? You're my girl—just you. You and Ty are my whole world, Bridge. But this…" He sighed, a tear escaping his eyelid and sliding down his rough cheek. "This is bigger than both of us and if I don't deal with it now, it could end badly for our family. If something were to happen to you and Ty…" His voice trailed off, his eyes looking to the ceiling.

Bridget studied him a moment longer, her mind working to make sense of the hidden messages between the things he'd said. "It's not about Addison." Her eyes implored.

Asher shook his head. "No. I swear, babe."

She sighed and dropped her arms. "Whatever you're messing with, make sure it doesn't come through that door." She took a step toward him and brushed his arm with her fingertips.

"I promise I'm doing my best to ensure that doesn't happen. I just need you to trust me, okay? And keep Ty with you as much as possible."

She nodded, accustomed to cases he worked on getting too close for comfort. She knew the drill. This was nothing new. But for some reason, there was fear in his eyes. Her heart skipped a beat. Asher wasn't one to show fear—ever. The case he was working on had to be serious. "Okay. I'll keep Ty with me for a few days. Maybe leave town for a while…?"

Asher breathed a sigh of relief; grateful she was catching on to the underlying tone of imminent danger. He weighed her suggestion of skipping town. No, that wouldn't do anything but alert his blackmailer and create suspicion that he was up to something. His family was safer at home with him. "No, don't leave yet. But keep your bags packed so you can run the second you get word from me to do so. Understand?"

Bridget nodded and let him kiss her. "Stay smart, Ash," she whispered against his lips. "Whatever you do, get out of this mess quickly so you can get back to us."
"I promise," he breathed. Pulling her into him, he held her tight, praying to the God he didn't believe was interested in him. *God, get my family out of this mess I've made…*

JOSH

Josh fought to keep his focus through the mixture of pain, fear, and panic. Each step was made heavier by the weight of his bags, yet he pressed on. The neighborhood and streets were familiar, yet his destination remained unknown. He passed by the locally owned grocery, the weight of the townsfolk's stares penetrating his weathered soul.
"Is that Garrett's boy?" Mrs. Jemson asked, her sack of groceries forgotten on the porch beside her.

"Well, if it isn't the heathen, himself, crawling back home." Luke Wallace's eyes followed Josh's slow gait down the sidewalk. "Your mama's stopped crying for you now. What's the use coming back here after all these years? Looking to stir up more trouble?" He laughed uproariously, as though he'd made a great joke.

Josh gritted his teeth around the cigarette smoldering in his mouth and kept his eyes low as he passed.

"He doesn't even bother to say hi." Miss Helen's voice resonated with offense. "Always was a rude one, that boy. Just look at all that ink on his arms—and would you look at that! He's smoking! Such a disgrace! What, with his daddy an upstanding lawyer and his mama a saint, nonetheless."

Their snide comments continued to jab at his wounded heart. Deciding he'd had enough, Josh turned down Seacrest Lane to escape further jeers from the ones he knew would occupy a pew on Sunday. Passing by the town's most frequented hangout, the smell of Hal's famous pizza lassoed the wind and teased his nose, making him wish he had five dollars on hand.

Little had changed in the four years he'd been gone; Highshore had a reputation for being the town that stayed frozen in time. A new business had popped up here and there–a few unfamiliar faces. Most people he saw on the streets, he knew; the shocked stares, followed by wagging tongues as he walked, confirmed they remembered him, too. In the distance, Josh could make out Highshore Elementary's bright, green sign that had weathered years of storms and graffiti, announcing the school football team remained undefeated. He swallowed hard as he approached the school. Nearing the playground, his memory was assailed by recollections of his past.
His feet stopped at the large, foreboding entrance to the schoolyard and his eyes fixed on some distant memory invisible to the people passing by. In the far corner of the playground, he could see himself as a frightened ten-year-old boy, surrounded by a gang of angry teachers. "Frightened" was not how they described the child caught stealing from the principal's office.

"Belligerent," they'd said.

"Defiant and mean-spirited," said another.

He'd never told them why he'd stolen back his math test—to evade his father's wrath at the bold 65 marked in red across his paper.

The principal had been enraged and was intent on making an example of him. He'd called his father and had forced Josh to tell him what he'd done. His father had been humiliated. That night was the worst beating he could remember. That beating was the reason his back was covered in ink today. The scars left by his father's drunken rage were deep and alarming. The next day, he was back at school, and none of the teachers knew the effect their outrage had on a small, defenseless, little boy whose daddy saw him as a challenge.

A child's ear-splitting scream jolted Josh back to reality and his heart thumped wildly. His gut clenched as a man shouted angrily. He sought the source of the scream, fixating on a small boy refusing to comply with his father's decision to leave the playground. Panic turned his blood to ice. He swiped a hand down his face and tried to focus, his senses on overdrive. Move! He forced himself down the sidewalk, fear nipping at his heels.

Passing a row of townhouses, he was vaguely aware of the occupants puttering in their yards. An older woman stood on her porch; a row of dust-laden rugs draped across the railing. She raised her broom high and proceeded with their beatings, dirt billowing around her in a suffocating cloud. With each thwack of her broom, terror seized Josh's mind, holding it captive and forcing him to relive his childhood. His shoulders tensed, and his back grew tight. Tears of desperation fell from his eyes, his subconscious anticipating the beating due to him.

Not again. Please, no! He pleaded for an escape from the memories playing their reel for him to see, yet they taunted him further, mocking his pain. He could hear his father's voice and smell the alcohol on his breath. The broom cracked against the rug, a sharp, unforgiving thwack that carried out its task until the rug slipped to the ground in surrender to the harsh beating. His father lunged for him, and he ran. The pain in his ribs intensified. With each smack of his shoes against the pavement, he felt like a sledgehammer was beating his bones. At last, his body demanded rest, and he stopped running, easing himself into a slow walk.

"No matter what you're going through, Jesus loves you, Josh. He will protect you." The words of Jordan's mother pushed through the panic and brought reason to his soul. Laura had spoken those words to him countless times as a boy, but he'd never understood. If Jesus loved him, why was terror his constant companion? You'll protect me? he challenged. Where were you when he was beating me senseless all those years? Laura was wrong. Jesus didn't love him. Nobody loved him. Even his best friend had betrayed him.

Thoughts of Laura and Jesus brought Titus to his mind, and he pulled his phone from his pocket. Not giving time to talk himself out of it, he dialed his boss, desperate for the familiar voice of someone he could count on.

"Josh?"

Relief flooded his aching bones at the sound of Titus' confident baritone. "Titus," he breathed through a cloud of tears in his throat. He coughed hard, wincing at the stabbing in his ribs. "Titus," he repeated.

"Josh, what is it? What's wrong?" Concern and regret laced his tone.

He took a shuddering breath and stopped walking, easing himself to the curb, every ounce of strength spent.

"That Book you gave me…"

Titus sucked in a breath, letting it out in one harsh huff. "Yeah…?"

"Does it have any advice for a guy who's hit rock bottom?"

He squeezed his eyes shut, ashamed of how weak his words were. He couldn't remember the last time he'd felt so lost and helpless, and he hated himself for it.

"It sure does." Titus' voice was calm and quiet, his empathy coming across the lines. "It's full of advice for guys who've reached rock bottom. The answer always comes back to Jesus."

Josh sniffed and laughed. "Yeah, okay. So, some dead guy is gonna get me out of this hole I'm in."

"Jesus isn't dead, son. If you read that Book I gave you, then you'll see. His Words are alive, and they spark life in the reader. Have you checked it out yet?"

Josh's mind took him back to the cafe where Titus' secret had leaped off the page and slapped him in the face. "Yeah. Yeah, I did." He grew quiet, thinking. Then dove right in. "Who'd you kill, Titus?"

Titus gasped, then coughed as though trying to cover his shock. "Um, well I…It's not, um…" He sighed. "Read the book of Romans—chapter seven. Everything you need to know is in there." He waited a moment for Josh's response. When there was none, he asked the question on his mind. "Are you safe?"

Josh squeezed his eyes shut. "I'm in Highshore."

"But isn't that where you're fr—"

"I have to go." Josh cut him off, afraid of where the conversation was heading. "For what it's worth, I'm glad we met. Good luck in life, Titus."

"Josh, wait, you're talking like I'll never see you again."

"Maybe you won't." Josh hung up the phone and slipped it back into his pocket. Grabbing one of his bags, he shifted through its contents until he found the Bible Titus had given him and pulled it out. He thumbed through the worn pages, searching. For what, he wasn't sure. But Titus swore by the contents of this Book, which compelled him even more to search for the answers to all his problems. He'd never had a Bible before. His parents had always flirted with the idea of church, attending only on special occasions, or when his father needed to look good in front of somebody. He'd gone a few times with Jordan over the years, but never consistently. Everything about the Book he held in his hands was foreign to him. What was it Titus had told him to look for? The book of Romans? What kind of sense did that make anyway? Titus had only given him one Book…not two. He switched from thumbing through to carefully turning each page trying to make sense of it. Titus' writing was scrawled everywhere, sometimes commenting about certain aspects of the Book, but mostly it seemed to Josh that his boss had written his life's story on the pages.

"Ephesians," he read aloud, noting how the book seemed to be divided into titled chapters or something. He stared a while longer at the page and noted the small print: The Book of Ephesians. "Okay..." Josh wrinkled his brow and flipped to the front of the Bible, relieved to find a contents page. "Genesis, Exodus..." He read through each title until he found Romans.

Feeling like he was getting the hang of how the Bible worked, he glanced at the page number and flipped the pages, stopping when "Romans" seemed to shout at him in its emboldened font. He spotted chapter one and turned the pages until he found chapter seven. *Okay, now I'm gettin' somewhere...*

Titus' writing covered every space on the page. Josh paused, unsure whether he should start with the chapter or with Titus' words. Deciding to read the chapter, he began, feeling like he was reading a foreign language. Toward the middle of the chapter, Titus highlighted the words in bright fluorescent yellow. Confusion clouded Josh's mind as he read, and he decided to read it out loud in hopes of comprehending.

"For we know that the law is spiritual, but I am of the flesh sold under sin. For I do not understand my own actions." Josh paused, his finger following Titus' scrawl beside the words: *God, why did I take Grandpa's car that night? Why?!* He sucked in a breath, his gaze shifting to a family across the street. *Titus stole a car? It couldn't be...* He read on. "For I do not do what I want, but I do the very thing I hate." Titus' handwriting arrested his attention: *I didn't want to take it—I knew better! God, I hate this part of me!* "Now if I do what I do not want, I agree with the law, that it is good. So now it is no longer I who do it, but sin that dwells within me. For I know that nothing good dwells in me, that is, in my flesh. For I have the desire to do what is right, but not the ability to carry it out." Josh stopped and closed the Book, his mind a mess of confusion. *What kind of nonsense was this? Every idiot knows he's responsible for his own choices. What a pansy* move to blame some idea for your actions. "Sin made me do it" was just a cop-out. The question was, what was Titus claiming that sin had made him do?

"There's a boy in the street."

Josh's head snapped up to see a little girl staring at him across the street, her blond curls gleaming in the sunlight. Her bright green eyes held a haunting familiarity that he couldn't place.

"Nevaeh, don't point. It's rude." Her mother shushed her and glanced at Josh before grasping her hand in hers and leading her away.

"But, Mommy, he looks so sad," the little voice whined as her mother dragged her away. "Maybe he needs Jesus. I can go tell him about Jesus, Mommy." Her mother continued to pull her along, reassuring her the boy would find his way.

Josh stared after them, all breath gone from his body. His ribs screamed at him, but he ignored the pain because that wasn't the little girl's mom. It was his mom. His mother had been within feet of him. She'd looked right at him and hadn't recognized him. His heart clenched as he watched them fade into the horizon. What was she doing with a little girl, and why was the little girl calling her "mommy?" He was desperate to run after them. Fall into his mother's arms and beg her never to let him go. But he didn't dare. That was one dangerous step toward a deadly slope he was unwilling to tease. His hands gripped the Bible as he hung his head and forced back the tears. He placed the Bible back into his bag and zipped it closed.

The little girl's observation of him reminded him of his current circumstance and he realized that he had to do something, fast. Josh clung to the bags he held in his lap, the pain in his body causing him to long for the sweet release of death. He had to focus. He needed to figure out a plan. The tears he'd blocked now stung the back of his eyes. Who was he kidding? There was no plan to figure out. He was stranded in hell with no money, no place to go, and no friend worthy of his trust. He groaned into the fabric of his duffel at the sound of rumbling overhead. Large drops of rain slapped at his back. Defeat rode in on the coolness of the clouds' tears, soaking both body and soul. Within seconds, the gentle rain turned torrential, and he pulled himself tighter into a ball.

"Hey, son, let me get you someplace dry."

Josh raised his eyes, blinking the water from his lashes. "Levi." The name brought an immediate sense of relief and peace. "How did you know—"

"Come on, Josh." Levi cut him off, extending a hand to the younger man. "You're soaked to the bone. My truck's right over here." He helped him to his feet and hoisted his bags to his shoulder. Josh wordlessly followed him to the simple pickup and pulled himself inside, relaxing his battered body into the seat.

"Hungry?" Levi asked, glancing at his wearied passenger.

"Yes."

"I'm sure Laura's got a feast cooking at home. Interested?"

Josh squeezed his eyes shut. "Yes." *What am I doing?*

"Where you headed?" Levi kept his tone calm, though the sight of Josh made him worry for the safety of his son, and it took all his strength to keep from asking if he'd left Jordan in one piece. Taking in the way Josh winced with each breath, it became clearer why Jordan had been so desperate to help his friend, no matter the cost. His heart constricted at the thought of the terror he knew must be consuming his companion.

Josh's jaw set with renewed determination. "Home."

Levi drove in silence as he considered the statement. "Where's home?" he asked quietly.

"Not here," Josh quipped.

Levi nodded. *Fair enough.* "Quite a storm…you're welcome to stay with us until it passes." As though reiterating the statement, a flash of lightning fell from the heavens, a resounding boom offering its good riddance.

Josh sighed. Even when the storm cleared, he'd be on

foot; at the mercy of any passers-by who took pity. It was a thought he didn't relish, with the amount of pain he was in.

Studying his face, Levi prayed for wisdom regarding what he was about to do. He drove to a nearby ATM and stopped. He felt Josh's eyes on him as he withdrew six hundred dollars from his account. Turning to face Josh, he pressed the money into his hands. "Son, you're on one heck of a journey, and I know it's getting the best of you right now, but don't give up."

Josh stared, speechless at his generosity, the weight of the money leaving an impression on his tattered heart.

"I want you to take this. Come home with me, eat a hot meal, take a hot shower, and get a full night's sleep. In the morning, if you still wanna head home, I'll take you to the airport myself. But if you change your mind and decide to give this place another shot, you keep that money and stay with us until you decide what to do."

Josh blinked back the sudden tears in his eyes. "Why would you do that for me?"

"Because you're worth it."

Leaning his head against the rain-soaked windowpane, Josh quietly wept as panic and fear were replaced by something he'd only dreamed of—unconditional love. The heathen was home.

Chapter 15

"By this we know love, that he laid down his life for us, we ought to lay down our lives for the brothers."
~1 John 3:16~

LEVI

"Well, here we are." Levi kept his voice steady as he parked his truck outside his home and turned off the ignition. He waited in the silence of the cab; his gaze focused on Josh's features.

Josh's right hand gripped the door handle, but he remained frozen in his seat as he stared at the large house in front of him. So familiar and welcoming—yet intimidating and frightening. His eyes scanned the yard and the edge of the woods, searching for his predator.

Levi read the fear. "He's not here. You have my word."

Josh met his eyes, staring hard, then nodded.

"Ready? I know Laura's gonna freak." Levi grinned, hoping to lighten the mood, but Josh only nodded and pushed the door open. Levi followed, grabbing Josh's bags from the backseat. As he neared the front door, he could feel the tension winding Josh tighter with each step. "That hot shower will do you good," he commented, shoving the key in the lock and twisting the door open. "You can have Jordan's old room—it's still pretty much the same."

"Decked out in nerd?" A smile flashed across Josh's face as he glanced at Levi.

"You know it." Levi laughed as he shut the door behind them. "Why don't you stay here a sec, and let me go get Laura? I'll be right back."

Josh watched him go, the tension in his muscles beginning to ease. Just standing in the foyer of this home that held so many of his happy memories was like walking into a warm embrace. He closed his eyes and allowed the warmth of his memories to squeeze his soul tight as though welcoming him home.

Levi crept up behind his wife as she washed the dishes.

From a radio on the counter, Casting Crowns sang about God's grace, and Laura joined in with her soft alto. He loved to hear her sing. In his opinion, she was better than all those famous singers. He grinned as he watched her throw her head back and belt out a line, biting back a laugh as he wrapped his arms around her and she screamed. "Hey, baby," he whispered against her ear.

"Levi Hendricks! What have I told you about sneaking up on me like that?" She rewarded him with a wet slap to his chest but melted into him when his lips melded with hers. Pushing against him, she searched behind him. "Where are the groceries I sent you after?" She pulled from his embrace and headed for the living room, surprised when he grabbed her wrist and pulled her back to him.

"Well, love, I left them in town…" He squinted his eyes. "…at the store…on the shelves where they sell them." He looked down at her features, unable to squelch the laughter bubbling in his throat. He kissed the frown from her lips and breathed in her lilac-scented hair. "If it helps, I have a really good reason for bailing on grocery duty."

"This better be good, because your chicken dinner is at the store, sir," she grumbled into his chest.

"I brought home a stray," he whispered against her hair.

Laura pushed him and stepped back–her mouth agape. "No, Levi. No dogs!"

Levi shook his head, scrunching his nose in innocence. "I'm sure no one calls him a dog… If they do, then they ought to be ashamed of themselves, because that's just rude."

She studied him, trying to figure him out. "What are you up to, Hendricks?"

He took her hand and pulled it. "Come see." His heart leaped with excitement as he walked her into the living room where he'd left Josh in the foyer. He came to a halt and glanced at his bride, surprised when her eyes fell on Josh, and she jumped back, almost hiding behind him.

"Levi!" she hissed in his ear. "Who is that man standing in my foyer, and why does he look like he belongs in a gang?"

Levi's eyes lit from the grin spreading across his face. He bent his head over his shoulder and focused on Josh's amused features. "He can hear you, you know. You better play nice, or he might get mad."

At that, Josh burst into laughter and shook his head. "You're wrong, Mr. H."

Mr. H…

Laura froze, her hands gripping Levi's arm tight as she stared at the stranger in her foyer. "Wait…only Josh calls you Mr.…" A gasp escaped her lips, and tears exploded behind her eyes as she shoved Levi out of her way and strode up to Josh, staring at his features. "Josh, baby?" Her voice was thin as she looked him over, taking in his tattoos and the hardened lines of his face.

Josh glanced over her head at Levi, who offered him an encouraging smile. His eyes fell back to hers, and he nodded. "It's me."

Laura screamed and lunged, grabbing him in a tight embrace.

"Aghh!" He yelled in desperation, his eyes closed tight as he gently pushed her off him and fell into the wall with a gasp. He felt as though he'd been knifed but was more concerned with erasing the look of shock on her face than with his well-being. "It's nothing." He forced the words through gritted teeth.

Laura's face was a mask of horror as she watched him grip his ribs. "What's wrong?"

Levi wrapped an arm around Josh's waist, helping him to a nearby chair. "Easy does it," he breathed beneath the added weight as he lowered and helped him get comfortable. "You good?" he asked, studying Josh's pale features.

Josh gave a slight nod, his mind consumed by the burning in his ribs. He forced his attention to Laura, wanting to erase the worry coloring her face. "You don't look…any older…then I remember," he breathed through the pain, his mind begging his body to give him a break. "What are you…twenty-nine?"

A smile bloomed across her features, laugh lines exploding around her grayish-brown eyes. "Oh, stop." She laughed. Her laughter faded as she sat down on the ottoman in front of Josh's chair and placed a gentle hand on his arm. "Baby, what happened? Why are you hurt?"

Josh glanced at Levi, then smiled at Laura. "Would you believe me if I told you I was completely blameless and was injured due to absolutely no fault of my own?"
She stared at him, a frown tugging at the corners of her mouth. "Not for a second. The Josh I know has always been responsible anytime he's been injured. So, what did you do?" She raised a brow at him, her heartwarming at the sight of this boy she loved.

"I totaled a car and nearly totaled myself along with it," he admitted, a sheepish grin on his face.

Laura's eyes dimmed. "Were you racing again?"

He started to shake his head no, then paused, thinking. "Well, not exactly…I just, um, lost control."
She stared at him, studying the healing wounds around his head and arms. "I'm glad you're safe, Josh—and that you're home. I can't believe you're back. baby, we've missed you so much!"

"Josh will be staying the night with us. Possibly longer." Levi chanced a glance in his direction.
Laura smiled and jumped to her feet. "I'm going to bring you some of my iced tea. Don't move," she warned over her shoulder.

Levi laughed at her excited demeanor, though he couldn't blame her. His heart was bursting at the seams over having Josh in his home. After four years of silence, seeing him safe—and mostly whole—was a long-awaited relief. He studied his tired features and searched his mind for a topic that wouldn't force him to throw up his guard. "You know, they're training hard for the state surfing competition right now. They've got a few surfers this year

I think just might make the qualifying series."

Josh's eyes lit with interest, assuring Levi he'd chosen the right topic. "Man, I miss competing. What's the forecast?"

Levi grinned. "They say they're expecting near double overhead. That'll be a sight to watch the groms try and take that on."

"Who's looking the most informed this year? Anybody I know?"

"Rad the Fab Dad is in on it this year. You remember, Ryan's father?"

Josh raised an eyebrow. "You've gotta be kidding me. Last I saw him, he was a total kook."

Levi laughed. "That was over four years ago; he's become quite the charger. His boy's not such a junkyard dog anymore, though he wants one more year of training before he competes." He smiled at how Josh became animated, relaxing his body as they talked shop.

"Does your mother know you're here?" Laura's cheerful voice sounded, just before she appeared with a glass of iced tea in each hand.

Levi groaned as he watched Josh's entire demeanor change before his eyes. Josh's shoulders tensed, and a guarded look sparked in his eyes as he took the glass from her hands.

Sipping the tea slowly, stalling his answer, Josh took in the way Levi caught his wife's attention, silencing further inquiries she might have made. "I could use a shower before dinner. I think I'll head upstairs."

Levi nodded, uneasiness settling in his bones as he prayed Laura's question hadn't ruined their attempt to reconnect. "Yes, of course. Make yourself at home." He watched as Josh gritted his teeth and bent for his bags. "Let me take them up." He leaped from his chair but froze when Josh held out his arm.

"No. I've got it." Josh gripped the bags and hoisted them to his back, ignoring the sting of tears. Heading for the stairs, he turned to Laura, his voice flat. "My 'visit' wasn't planned. Mom knows nothing about me being here, and I'd like to keep it that way. I'm going home tomorrow."

Laura watched him climb the stairs with laborious effort, his hand gripping the railing with each step. Her heart burned in her chest. Part of her wanted to shake him and scream at him for how wrong he was. Another part of her felt nothing but sorrow and empathy for this lost boy fighting for survival in his dark, cruel world. Her eyes shot to Levi as she brushed past him and headed for the kitchen. "Dinner will be ready in an hour," she called over her shoulder and disappeared.

Left alone in the foyer, Levi cleared his throat and sighed. Well, that could have gone better… Taking advantage of being undetected by Laura or Josh, he pulled his phone from his pocket and took the stairs two at a time. He passed by Jordan's room, satisfied to hear movement inside—a sure sign that Josh wouldn't overhear the phone call he was about to make. Checking over the rail for Laura, Levi pulled open the door to their bedroom and stepped inside, shutting the door behind him. Quickly, he dialed Jordan. He needed to know his son was okay. He also felt a strong obligation to let him know Josh was safe.

"What?"

Levi sighed at the sharpness in his son's voice. He missed his boy and wished Jordan would let his pride go. "Hey, son. I just wanted to let you know that I picked Josh up in town this evening. Found him on the curb. He's agreed to at least stay the night—eat a hot meal, get a shower. Hopefully, he'll have a good night's sleep."

"You telling me this so you can rub it in my face?"

Levi blinked, shocked. "Um…no? I'm telling you so you won't worry about your friend." He placed the call on speaker and laid the phone down on his dresser as he searched for a fresh shirt.

"Worry? Oh, there's no worry on my end. I'm done worrying about what happens to that jerk. I gave up almost two weeks of my life for that guy and where did it get me?

My best friend accuses me of betrayal and my father thinks I'm an irresponsible prick!" Jordan's voice rose with each accentuated word.

In the next room, Josh stood at the linen closet in Jordan's bathroom searching for a towel. He hadn't intended to eavesdrop on Levi's call, but Jordan's voice had captured his attention, and he stood frozen, listening to every word.

Levi thought about his answer before speaking. "I don't think you're an irresponsible prick, Jordan. I just—"

"Man, save it! I heard you loud and clear, okay? I know you think what I did was wrong. I know you don't support my choice to bring Josh back home. But you didn't see what I saw! You didn't see your best friend handcuffed to a bed while he was healing from a crash he created. You didn't watch this idiot fight for his stupid pride and independence even though it would cost him his life! You didn't see all that, so don't you dare judge me!"

Josh leaned against the wall, surprised at how Jordan spoke to his father. This was not the Jordan he knew. Four years ago, he'd been the picture of respect. Jordan's voice dropped a level, and Josh pressed his ear to the wall to hear, raising a brow when his friend began to curse at his dad.

Josh held his breath, waiting to see how Levi would respond. When no answer came, he realized Levi was just as shocked as he was by Jordan's unexpected behavior. After a few moments, he picked up the low baritone of Levi's voice.

"I can tell you're angry with me, Jordan. I'm sorry, son. I never meant to hurt you. It's just…when I realized what you'd done it really freaked me out. I knew Josh would feel betrayed, and I could only assume he'd attack you." Levi grew quiet, then asked the question that had haunted him since he'd found Josh. "So…did he attack you, Jordan?"

Josh listened, trying not to breathe for fear of missing Jordan's answer.

"Save yourself the trouble and don't worry about what's going on with me. In fact, why don't you just put all your energy into your new favorite? He sure could use that extra dose of love right about now. But just so you know, he won't be there in the morning, so don't set your hopes too high."

Josh set his jaw. Where did Jordan get off talking to Levi that way? He fought the urge to go back and smack some sense into his thick skull.

"What makes you think he won't be here in the morning?" Levi kept his voice level, though his tension was mounting.

"You're only eight acres away from his dad. Once that sinks into Josh's head, he'll be gone. Mark my words, Dad. He will not be there when you wake up. I know him. I've seen his disappearing act more than you know. Don't say I didn't warn you—and don't look for me to help you find him when he's gone. I'm done with this mess. If Josh wants to screw his life up, so be it. That doesn't mean I have to watch."

Josh clenched his right hand into a fist and closed his eyes. Jordan had a point. A point that drove fear into his soul. What had he been thinking coming here?

"I have to go. I have a lot to catch up on in journalism," Jordan told his dad, impatience biting at his tone.

"Uh, yeah, okay. So, I'll see you at church on Sunday?" Levi's voice held a hint of hope.

Jordan laughed. "Don't count on it. I told you; I have way too much to catch up on since I took two weeks off for nothing. I'll be busy. I'll see you when I see you."

Anger smoldered in Levi's chest. He hadn't done anything to deserve this treatment from his son, and Jordan's act was growing old fast. "Look boy, treating me this way is one thing, but I swear, Jordan Blayze, if you brush your mom off and start ignoring her then it'll be me and you, pal. You got that?"

"You gonna fight me, Pops?" Jordan challenged.
Levi picked up a glass, framed picture of his son and threw

it across the room, satisfied when it shattered to the floor.

"Remember what I said," he warned. "Now I'm hanging up before you really make me mad."

With mechanical movements, Josh pulled a towel from the shelf as he thought about what to do. He didn't think he'd make it far if he set off that night—he desperately needed a full night's sleep. Not realizing Levi was dialing his enemy on the other side of the wall, he turned the shower hot and climbed into the steam.

Levi let the phone ring twice before wising up and taking it off speaker. The last thing he needed was for Josh to find out he was confirming his whereabouts for his dad.

"Was I right?"

"Sure were. I knew the second I saw Jordan that he was hiding something from me. He didn't even want to let me in. I finally dragged it out of him, and he confessed that Josh was asleep in his room."

"How'd he get him to agree to come back?" Garrett's voice held his disbelief.

"Well...he drugged him. Josh had no idea what was happening when they boarded the plane. Woke up this morning and realized where he was. I think he gave Jordan what he had coming, but Jordan won't admit it. He's acting...off. Not himself at all, Garrett. I'm worried about him. I just got off the phone with him and he was cocky, disdainful, and just plain disrespectful. Even challenged me to fight him," Levi added, still unable to comprehend the conversation he'd just had with his son.

"You sure you're talking about your son and not mine?" Garrett asked incredulously.

"Right?! I don't know what's going on, but this whole thing with Josh has gotten to Jordan. He won't even commit to church Sunday." He let that sink in before continuing. "Jordan. My kid. The one who never goes anywhere without his Bible, and whose soul is eaten alive if he misses a service."

Garrett sighed. "I agree. Something's wrong. He'll come around, though. Jordan's got a good head on his shoulders." Unable to hold back any longer, he asked, the question plaguing him. "So...my boy's with Jordan?"

"No. He's with me."

Garrett swallowed hard. "With you? Like...at your house?"

"In Jordan's room as we speak." Levi smiled.

A moment passed before Garrett was able to speak.

"Man, he's so close, Levi. Eight acres. It may as well be eight hundred miles."

Levi nodded. "Yeah, I get what you mean. Keep your head up—you never know what's going to go down. I convinced him to eat a hot meal and get a full night's sleep. Jordan suspects he'll run off before daylight, but I'm hoping for a sensible decision from the boy. I'll keep you informed. What's your move?"

Garrett sighed. "I mean...what can I do? He hates me. I can't just show up. I can't invite him over for dinner. I can't do anything except hope he asks to see me, which, let's face it, will never happen. Has he asked for his mom?"

"No. But we haven't had a chance to talk yet. We came home and Laura saw him and freaked. It was so great. She was psyched and he seemed happy to see her too. But then she kinda spooked him, I think. She asked if Elysia knew he was here, and he shut down right away and said he didn't want her to know."

"...because if she knows, then he's afraid it will get back to me. Levi, all of this is on me. I've destroyed my family, and there's no way to mend them. Elysia can't see our son because of me. I haven't even told her he's here!"

Levi shook his head. "You can't live in the past, Garrett. That's what Josh is doing, and it's killing him. You have to keep moving forward—just like you've been doing. Above all, keep your eyes on Christ. As far as Elysia goes..." he sighed. "I can't tell you what to do there. I know she's going to be angry with you for keeping this from her. On the other hand, if she knew, there'd be no stopping her from coming over and seeing him. That has to be your decision, bro. Let me pray for you."

"I'd appreciate that."

"Lord, be with Garrett as he seeks Your will in this matter. We understand how important it is to be open and honest in our marriages, but this is such a tedious issue, Father. Please show him whether he should bring Elysia on board now or wait a while longer. Give him peace in his heart, and help him to trust You above all. Thank You, Jesus. Amen."

"Thank you." Garrett's heart warmed as the peace of the Savior washed through him. "I have to go—she's coming up the stairs. Thanks for keeping me informed. Please keep me updated, Levi."

"You got it." The dial tone buzzed, and he clicked off the phone.

Tousling his hair in the mirror, Levi left the room, satisfied to find Jordan's door still shut. The buttery aroma of garlic bread wafted up from the kitchen, and his mouth began salivating as he took the stairs two at a time. "What's cookin', good lookin'?"

Despite his cheerful tone and upbeat step, Laura rewarded him with a glare. "He's wrong," she stated as she pulled the bread from the oven and slapped the pan down on the stove.

"Okay..." Levi approached the table and sat down, his eyes never leaving his wife's tense features. "Who are we talking about, love? You tell me, and I'll side with you right away," he teased, earning himself another glare.

"That boy," she snapped. "Coming back home and refusing to see his mother!" She slapped down three napkins and forks onto the table, nearly tossing the glass plates into their respective places.

"Lar..." Levi began.

"Don't you 'Lar' me, Levi Hendricks!" She slammed a glass onto the table, her eyes flashing fire. "His mother has worried herself sick for four years over his safety. She has confided in me more than once that she just knew he had either killed himself or gotten himself killed! And he waltzes in here and says that she is not to find out that he's here?! Over my dead body! Who does he think he is?"

Panic burst across Levi's chest. "Laura don't interfere…" he warned, but he knew that look in her eye. Once she set her mind on something, there was no going back. Detecting movement from the entryway, he shot his wife a pleading look as Josh walked in and sat in a chair at the table.

Josh's eyes went from one to the other, noting how the room had grown quiet when he'd entered. "Um…did I interrupt something?" he asked, wondering at the way Laura's eyes narrowed in his direction.

Laura flashed a glance at Levi before turning back to the stove to dish up the spaghetti she'd prepared. With each serving she placed onto a plate, the large, metal, serving spoon smacked the glass, sending a clear message to the occupants in the room.

Levi cleared his throat and breathed a small laugh as Josh reached for his iced tea. "Hungry?"

Josh raised an eyebrow over his drink. "Starved." He placed the glass on the table and glanced questioningly at Laura's back.

Levi pretended not to notice, jumping up and grabbing plates from Laura as she completed each one. "Soup's on!" he announced in exaggerated excitement as he placed the steaming spaghetti in front of Josh and returned to his wife's side for the second plate.

"And why isn't Jordan here?" Laura spun around and demanded from Levi, then Josh, as though the two had been privy to her thoughts. "His best friend is eating spaghetti in my kitchen and my son is nowhere to be found." Her eyes flashed between the two and she ripped her apron from her waist and tossed it onto the counter. "Both of you are wrong," she seethed. "I know something fishy is going on here, and I don't like it. Not one bit. Now," she pulled out a chair and dropped into it, crossing her arms over her chest. "Which one of you is going to spill the beans about what happened?"

As though on cue, Levi and Josh shoveled a huge helping of spaghetti into their mouths, neither one wanting to fess up about Jordan. Levi, protecting his wife from their son's drastic change in behavior, and Josh, not wanting to let on that he'd slugged Jordan only a couple of hours before.

"Good spaghetti!"

"Man, this is so good!"

The two spoke simultaneously, each one nodding like idiots under Laura's harsh glare.

"Alright." She stood, and both of their forks froze mid-air, eyes locked on the woman in front of them. "I'll call him, then." She took a step toward the phone, watching. "And I'll invite him to dinner so he can see his best friend and be as happy as we are to have this rare privilege."

Both guys exchanged looks and shouted "NO!" as Laura picked up the phone to dial.

"I mean, um...he's probably sleeping," Levi offered weakly.

"Probably working..." Josh followed, averting his gaze to anything but her eyes.

Laura turned and stared. "You both have five seconds to talk before I call my son."

Levi and Josh exchanged another look before Levi sighed. "Babes, Jordan isn't gonna come to dinner."

"And why not? Spaghetti is his favorite...and Josh is here."

"He's mad at me," they answered together.

"Yeah, he's totally mad at Mr. H, I mean..." Josh twisted the spaghetti onto his fork and shoved it into his mouth, working hard to maintain a look of innocence under her mom-glare.

Laura's eyes narrowed. "You're both full of shit." Josh choked on his spaghetti and had to sip his iced tea to recover. He wished Jordan had been here to witness this moment in history: Laura Hendricks, Bible thumpin' churchgoer, says "shit."

"I'm calling my son." She turned to the phone and

dialed.

Josh hung his head and sank lower into his seat, glancing up as she placed the phone to her ear, her eyes boring right into his. "I hit him," he blurted, surprised by his own candidness. Laura's brows knit together. "Twice." He squeezed his eyes shut, then squinted up at her.

Four years. Four long years without her influence, yet one night in her kitchen drew every ounce of respect front and center, exposing him to the elements. With a sigh, he noted Levi's eyes on him as well.

Laura hung up the phone and placed it on the counter, returning to the table and sitting down. "So, he knows you're here," she stated.

Josh nodded, pushing the spaghetti around on his plate. "He ought to, since he's the one who drugged me and dragged me here," he grumbled, his respect for Laura taking a backseat to the fresh wave of anger toward Jordan.

Laura's jaw dropped. "What?!" She glanced at Levi to see if this was news to him, glowering when she realized it wasn't. "You knew about this?"

"Uh…yeah." Levi's brow creased. "I found out today. Seems Jordan has been on quite the journey these past two weeks."

Laura sat still, processing all she'd just learned. Compartmentalizing it in a matter of seconds, she sipped her iced tea and took a dignified bite of her spaghetti before offering her response. "Well, you're here now," she addressed Josh. "And your mother deserves to know that. The question is, are you going to be the one to tell her, or am I?"

Levi groaned and hid his face in his hands. She never listened to him…

Josh sat motionless; his eyes fixated on the flower pattern spread on his plate. Anger brewed in his chest at having his hand forced, but his love and respect for Laura kept him from lashing out. "Mrs. H, I cannot tell Mom I'm here, because I am not staying here." He raised his eyes to hers, the storm gaining strength in their clear blue hue. "I will not hurt her again."

Laura stared, noting the controlled emotions on his features. "Give me one good reason why you're insisting on leaving tomorrow." She raised her chin stubbornly, gesturing toward him. "Look at yourself, Joshua. You need rest. You don't need to be running to who knows where to get away from the demons of your past, son. You belong here with people who love you."

Levi pleated the tablecloth between his fingers over and over, his eyes bouncing between Josh and Laura, curious as to who could out stubborn whom.

"My father is right across the woods." Josh leaned his elbows on the table, the fight rising. "Maybe he's bewitched all of you while I've been gone—convinced you that he's some stand-up, righteous guy—but the truth is, he's a no-good prick who doesn't deserve to breathe. He always has been, and he always will be. I want nothing to do with him. I'm leaving in the morning, and my mom will not know that I am here, because I refuse to break her heart." Josh pushed his plate away and forced his body to stand, his face masking the pain the movement caused.

"Sit down," Laura ordered, her eyes locked on his. Levi saw the moment the anger surged over the barrier Josh had placed. He was instantly on alert, ready to pull Laura away from him if needed. "Lar." He tried to warn her, but she brushed him off.

"No. Sit down, Joshua. Eat your dinner and knock off this nonsense."

"I'm not your kid, Laura." The words were out of his mouth before he could stop them, and it was too late to take them back as he watched them lash her heart, her face falling. All the years she'd poured into his childhood… He took a deep breath, his resolve strengthening. "I won't sit down, and I won't finish my dinner. Thank you, but I've lost my appetite."

She watched him storm out the front door, slamming it behind him. Heard her husband's relieved sigh at having the conflict dissipate. But she wasn't done. Laura stood to her feet, the picture of grace, and calmly walked to the front door, pulled it open, and stepped outside. She found Josh sitting on the steps, his back leaning against a brick pillar, cigarette in his mouth. "What is this?" she asked, shocked. She sat on the step beside him and pulled the butt from his lips, tossing it to the ground.

Mouth agape, Josh extended his hands upward as he looked at her. "Mrs. H, come on!"

Her brow shot up, satisfied when he relented and rolled his eyes with a groan. "You're angry with Jordan." Her voice was calm. "You've been seriously injured. You're in the same town as your mother, yet you plan to leave without kissing her face." She paused, letting her words sink in. "The Josh I know isn't an idiot. He makes calculated, smart decisions. Look what you accomplished—you disappeared so far off the grid it took Jordan four years to find you."

His eyes met hers, and he glared. "I never asked him to find me, so this mess is all on him."

"You listen to me, and you listen good, young man." She swooped down the steps so she could face him at eye level. "I've watched that boy search the globe for countless hours over the years. I've listened to his excitement when he thought he had a lead. I held him in my arms when a lead was a dud, and he cried his eyes out over losing his best friend, so don't you dare disdain him for succeeding in his mission to be there for you!"

Josh dropped his eyes, focusing on his hands. "He did all that?"

"Yes, he did. It destroyed him when he found out you'd run away. He kept telling me you'd never come back, and he couldn't handle that." She watched his face carefully, reading the expression in his eyes. "Jordan never gave up on you. Not once. And he never will. He may be angry right now, but he will come around, that much I know. The question is...where will you be when he does?"

Josh looked at her, but she stood without another word

and turned for the door. "And your mother." She turned to look at him, one hand holding the door open. "She deserves to know you aren't dead, son. If you've no interest in your father, so be it. But don't punish her for his sins." She stepped inside and shut the door, leaving him alone with the darkness around him, his thoughts in his head, and the smoldering butt of the cigarette she'd thrown to the ground.

Chapter 16

"I cry aloud to the Lord; I lift up my voice to the Lord for mercy. I pour out before him my complaint; before him I tell my trouble"
~Psalm 142:1-2~

STERLING

"Back again, I see." Sterling's eyes tracked Nichole as she walked into his office, her red high heels clicking against the floor.

"Yes," she answered, her voice clipped. "And this time you will put this contract through."

Folding his arms over his chest, Sterling leaned back in his chair, brows raised at her boldness. "Sure. If it's legal."

Her red-stained lips curved into a smile as she slid a folder toward him. "You've been practicing law for...what, three years?"

He bristled as he opened the folder and perused the document. Honestly, she'd overestimated his years as a lawyer by one year, but he wasn't about to tell her that. "Mrs. Sherard, unfortunately for both of us, my father has chosen me to be the one to represent him in this deal. Let's make the best of it, shall we?"

Nichole's smile stretched further as she watched him. Her eyes roamed his office, and she noted with amusement that the picture of him and his girlfriend was absent from his desk today. How cute. He's protective over her... Deciding to toy with him and see where his mind was at, she crossed one leg over the other and fixed her skirt. "I thought I saw your girlfriend at the market this morning. You like melons, I see."

Sterling's eyes shot up, and he frowned, not only at this intrusion into his thoughts but also at the ludicrousness of her suggestion. "My girlfriend doesn't go to the market. Not that it's your business," he muttered, returning to his work.

Nichole had to press her lips tight to keep back the

laughter threatening. Noting the decor in his office, she made a mental note of the awards and certificates along the walls. His credentials were impressive–she'd give him that–but he was still a no-account lawyer in her book.

"This is an acceptable contract, Mrs. Sherard. I need you and my father to have your signatures notarized, and then you may finalize the deal. Now, if there's nothing else…"

She read the eagerness in his eyes and laughed. "You do have a lot to learn, don't you, boy?"

Sterling set his jaw. "I think we're done here."

"I think not."

His eyes narrowed, and he shoved the folder toward her. "What other business do you have with me?"

Nichole relaxed in her chair. "How's Rhea doing?"

Sterling's cheeks flushed. "Mrs. Sherard, I'm not sure how you know my girlfriend's name, but she has nothing to do with my father's sale. Please leave."

"Has she told you about Joshua?" She smiled and drummed her fingers on the arm of the chair.

His brow furrowed in confusion. "Who?"

Nichole feigned shock. "You don't know about the childhood sweetheart who stole your girlfriend's heart and never returned it?"

"What makes you think you know anything about my girlfriend?"

The smile back in place, Nichole picked up the folder and stood. "I know everything about your girlfriend, Sterling. Rhea is my daughter." She walked to the door and opened it, turning to enjoy the shock on his face. "You'd better do some digging into her past. Find out about Joshua—if he resurfaces…" Her laughter seemed to roll in on a sea of malice. "You're history."

GARRETT

"I have something to tell you." Garrett sat on the grass beside his wife; his eyes fixed on their daughter's grave. Though it had been over twenty years since they'd lost

Nilah, they still grieved for the baby they never got to raise. He picked at a blade of grass, his muscles wound so tight he could hardly breathe as his gut clenched with nerves.

Elysia glanced at him, a soft smile on her face. Leaning against his shoulder, she sighed. Her eyes were puffy and red from crying. She could never visit Nilah without shedding tears. Feeling Garrett's tension, she sat up and looked at him, surprised by the intensity of his gaze. Concerned, she reached for his hand, but he pulled back and ran his fingers through his hair—a sure sign that something was wrong. "Baby, what is it?"

Garrett swallowed hard and squeezed his eyes shut, his heart warning him that he was about to destroy his marriage with what he was about to say. "Lyse, I don't know how to tell you this." He choked back his tears, unable to meet her eyes.

"Garrett, what's happened?"

He squeezed his right hand into a fist on top of his thigh and focused his attention on the sky. "Something happened a couple of weeks ago. Something…that I couldn't tell you." He sniffed. "Before I say this, please know I never meant to hurt you. I did what I thought was right. I'm not sure if I'm doing the right thing by telling you right now. I don't know anything anymore!" Tears rolled down his face. "God, help me." He trembled.

Fear gripped her chest. What had he done? "Whatever it is, baby, you can tell me. You know we'll work through it, just like we always do."

His eyes locked on hers as his fingers played with the grass. "I know where Josh is."

Elysia sat motionless, staring at him as though he was a stranger. Her mind played his words again, unable to comprehend. "You wh-what?"

"I know where Josh is," he repeated. "But…he doesn't know that I know."

She blinked hard, her thoughts whirling. "Garrett, how…?"

He swiped a hand down his face, warring within himself over the details he needed to explain. "Lyse," he began but stopped and took a deep breath. "I'm so sorry, baby."

Her eyes flashed. "Just tell me!" she bit out harsher than she'd intended, her nerves tingling as icy dread pulsed through her veins.

"The other day, Eunice passed me a client's message. The client was Jordan. He told her about a friend who needed a lawyer." He paused to study her, his back rigid. "The friend was Josh."

Elysia's eyes closed, and she released her breath in a rush. "Tell me everything, and do not stop until you're done."

His voice shook as he dove into the account of Josh's arrest and the charges against him.

Her mouth dropped with each one. "But Josh doesn't…Josh has never…" She shook her head, looking up at him. "Josh wouldn't touch drugs," she whispered, tears pooling in her eyes.

Garrett nodded. "Yeah. I know. That's one way I knew some charges had been fabricated." Forcing himself to continue, he explained the wreck and Josh's injuries, not stopping until he'd informed her about Jordan bringing Josh home.

Elysia stared at him in disbelief. "Josh is…here?"

He nodded.

"H-have you seen him?"

"No," he whispered.

"Where is he?"

"With Levi. He and Jordan got into a fight. I assume it was over Jordan drugging him and putting him on the plane. Josh got mad and took off, and Levi found him wandering the streets."

Elysia remained quiet for some time, processing. "He's at Levi's."

"Yes."

"With Laura."

"Yes."

"Josh is alive." She gasped.

Garrett nodded. "Yes, he is."

"I just knew...I worried he had..."

"I know."

She sat up straighter, her eyes narrowing fiercely. "All of you knew," she seethed. "And you kept it from me. You kept my son from his mother!"

"We had to, baby. I wasn't supposed to know anything about his situation, yet I suddenly knew everything." His voice was quiet, uncertain—a plea for understanding projected with each word. He couldn't read her.

Elysia jumped to her feet, shaking off his attempts to grab her.

Unnerved by her sudden shift in energy, Garrett scrambled off the ground. "Lyse..."

She ignored him. "I have to go to him."

"Elysia," Garrett stepped forward and reached out, stopping inches from her arm. He couldn't let her show up unannounced—his son would run for sure. "Elysia!" He intercepted her as she tried to walk to their car, his arm blocking her. Placing his face inches from hers, his eyes intense, he fiercely whispered, "Where are you going?!"

"Get out of my way, Garrett," she hissed through gritted teeth, her eyes flashing fire as she tried to pull from his grasp.

"Elysia...baby," he pleaded. "He doesn't know that we know he's here! If he knows, he'll run—don't you understand?"

"No!" she screamed in his face, tears streaming. "He will not run from me! He doesn't hate me, Garrett! It's you he hates. Now get out of my way, and let me see my son!"

He never saw the hand that slapped his face and sent his glasses flying to the ground. Panic pulsing, he watched her run to their car and stop to look back at him, her words stabbing him in the heart.

"Do not follow me, Garrett Cameron!" she warned, ice in her glare. "I will not have you running my son off again!" Without another word, she pulled the car door open and climbed inside. In a moment, the engine roared to life, and she peeled out of the cemetery and down the road, leaving her husband alone with his aching heart.

STERLING

Sterling sat in his driveway, hands on the wheel as he stared at the home he shared with the girl he loved. A stranger, according to the woman claiming to be her mother. Though he'd run after Nichole to press her for more information, she'd decided she no longer cared to give him the time of day and had left in the hallway of his office building with more questions than answers. He'd left work right after, needing time to clear his head. He'd thought about what she'd told him as he'd driven out to the pastures owned by his family. It was an hour's drive from home, giving him plenty of time to think, but he wasn't any closer to answers than before Nichole walked in his door.

He closed his eyes and turned the radio up, trying to envision Rhea in the house. She was off today, so she'd probably be trying her hand at a new hobby in her art room. Was she thinking of him? Was she thinking about his meeting with her mother? Or the lover she'd managed to keep hidden from him? Was any of this true about her? He opened his eyes, his hands gripping the wheel tighter. He couldn't decide how he felt about the lies—assuming they were lies—and that scared him. He and Rhea rarely had disagreements. He loved everything about her and had understood she felt the same way.

So why hide an entire life from him?

When he saw her peek out the window and wave, Sterling forced a grin and waved back before turning off the ignition and walking inside.

Rhea's squeals could be heard before she appeared at the end of the hall. Dressed in overalls and a turquoise tank top, she barreled toward him, sliding in her socked feet and falling into his arms with a laugh.

The cutest liar he'd ever seen… Sterling pushed back the thought and wrapped her in his arms, pressing a kiss to her lips.

"Chloe came over today, and we had the best time painting fall leaves on our mural for the café," Rhea rambled excitedly.

"Oh, yeah? That's great, babe." As she pulled his suit coat off his shoulders, he wondered how he should approach asking her about her mother and old boyfriend.

"We took a trip to the bookstore after lunch, and I grabbed that new series I've been wanting so badly. You know—the one you told me to buy the other day?" Rhea walked his suit coat to the closet and hung it up.

"Uh huh. Good job. It's about time you bought yourself something new."

"Chloe bought a horror book, by Stephen King. I tried to warn her against it—you know how freaked out she gets—but she wouldn't listen."

He couldn't resist any longer. "Baby, come here for a minute."

She turned to face him, her smile fading at his pensive features. "What's wrong?"

He tensed. "Just…come here and sit with me." Sitting on their bed, he patted the space beside him.

Rhea kept her eyes on him as she walked to the bed and sat with her back against the headboard.

"How come I've never met your parents?"

Breathing a laugh, Rhea shook her head. "My…parents? Baby, you know I don't like to talk about them."

"Yes. You said your father ran out on you when you were young, but you've never mentioned much about your mother."

Her eyes dimmed. "Sterling, why—"

"I met someone this week who claims you're her daughter." He watched her face pale, telling himself to ignore the empathy in his heart. "Dad's client, to be exact."

Rhea stared at their bedspread, frozen with fear. This couldn't be happening.

"I wondered why you seemed so shaken the other day when I'd mentioned her name. I knew your reason was a lie—I just couldn't figure out why. Your mom told me something else, too."

Rhea began to tremble. No, no, no!

"Who's Joshua?"

Tears shimmered in her eyes as she stared wordlessly back at him.

He reached out and gently cupped her chin, forcing her to look at him. When she didn't answer, he released her and sat back, shock resonating on his features. "Rhea, we're a team, baby." His voice belied the betrayal pounding his heart. "We don't keep secrets. All I want to know is why you kept all this from me."

She pulled his hand from her face and sniffed, wiping the heels of her hands down her wet cheeks. "I can't believe she found me," she whispered.

Concern sliced through him. "Why are you scared of her, Nic?"

"Please," Rhea's lips quivered. "Don't call me that."

Confusion clouded before understanding dawned.

Sterling grimaced when he made the connection. "Baby, I had no idea..."

She slid from the bed and moved to the vanity, staring at her reflection in the mirror. Her bright green eyes stared back at her, dim from the bombshell Sterling had just dropped at her feet.

He knows!

Not just of her mother, but of Josh!

The realization snagged her soul, dragging it into a dark hole of helplessness. What was she going to do? Now that her mother knew where she was, she'd be relentless in pursuing her. She would destroy everything in her path to get to her—including Sterling. Her heart pounded when she caught movement in the mirror and saw Sterling walking toward her. Spinning to face him, she pressed her back against the vanity.

"Why are you afraid of her?" Sterling asked again. His voice was tender, laced with the compassion he felt for this girl he loved.

Rhea shook her head. "She's...done horrid things. I never talk about her, because I was trying to forget about her."

"And Joshua? Has he done horrid things?"

Run away with me!

Her mind was thrown back four years prior. She could still see the horror in his eyes when he realized she wasn't going with him.

"No," she whispered, staring at the face of the seventeen-year-old boy forever frozen in her memories. "He defended me."

Sterling's features clouded, but he forced himself to think of her before himself. "Well, then, where is he? Why isn't he here with you?"

Rhea's eyes met his. "Because he ran away from the monster that was his father and never came back." Swallowing hard, he forced himself to ask the question that struck fear in his soul. "And if he did...come back?" The tears clouding her vision were her only answer.

LAURA

Laura sat on the floor in her living room, the vacuum cleaner sprawled in pieces around her. The machine hadn't been functioning properly for days, but she'd ignored it right up to the point where it had started spitting the dirt back at her instead of storing it away. She held the base of the vacuum firmly in one hand, a poised screwdriver in the other, prepared to unscrew every piece if that was what it took to gain its compliance. She brought the screwdriver down to the first screw, stopping short at the incessant ringing of the doorbell. With a sigh, she shoved the vacuum to the floor and stood.

"Laura! Laura, please!"

Her brow creased as she dusted her hands across her

jeans and hurried for the door as the bell sounded with added persistence. Surprise registered in her eyes at the sight of her friend's tear-streaked face. "Elysia, what is it?" Ushering her inside the foyer, she gently placed a hand on the other woman's arm.

"Where is he?" Pulling free of Laura's grasp, Elysia's eyes searched the room for Josh. "Tell me where he is." She turned to her friend, her eyes pleading. "Please, Laura! Where is he?!"

Laura breathed a deep sigh and shoved her hands into her back pockets, mentally kicking her husband and Josh for putting her in this position. "He's not here, sweetie." Elysia's features crumbled as tears streamed down her face. "No," she cried, a hand going to her mouth. "I didn't get to see him. My baby was here, and no one told me! Why didn't you tell me, Laura?!"

"Oh, honey." Laura's voice cracked. "I didn't mean he'd left town. He's just out running around with Levi. I'm so sorry—I should have thought before I said he wasn't here."

Elysia wiped at her cheeks, hope blooming. "He's still here?"

Laura nodded, a small smile on her face. "Coffee while we wait? They shouldn't be too much longer—Levi is counting on a roast beef sandwich for lunch." With the gentleness of a mother leading her frightened child, she led Elysia to the kitchen table and set a steaming cup of coffee in front of her.

Elysia's hand trembled as she gripped the mug and drank of the warmth it offered. "Please," she whispered as Laura joined her with her own mug. "I need to know everything you know about Josh. Garrett told me—" She stopped, gasping as her tears surged. "He told me Josh had been in an accident and was injured."

Laura nodded, confirming. "Yes. He's getting around fairly well, though he scared the life out of me when I gave him a hug and he screamed." She winced. "Seems his ribs are pretty banged up. He has a lot of cuts and bruises that are still healing. Other than that, he seems alright. He hasn't told me anything about the wreck." She smiled, stroking the side of her cup. "He did try and tease me by telling me it wasn't his fault, but he knew I knew better."

Elysia listened intently, her coffee forgotten in her hands. Her brow creased as she thought over the details she'd learned that morning. "Garrett said Jordan drugged him?"

Laura sighed; her heart grieved over the son she hadn't heard from since the incident. "That's what I understood from Levi, yes. He filled me in on a lot more last night. He said the boys were in a hotel, and Jordan was caring for Josh. Apparently, Josh was suffering from nausea and dizzy spells. Jordan told his dad that Josh could hardly function, he was so miserable. Jordan told him that he was going to bring him home with him and that Josh had agreed."

Elysia's brows shot up. "Somehow I doubt that." Her phone vibrated on the table, arresting her attention. Glancing down, she read the text from Garrett:

Taking Nevaeh out for a while. Need to clear my head. No need to fix her lunch—we'll be gone for a few hours. …love you…

She closed her eyes against the rush of tears, her husband's pain coming loud and clear through his text. Quietly taking note of what she'd just seen, Laura decided not to comment or ask questions. "Jordan admitted to drugging him with the sleeping pills the doctor had prescribed. He told his father that his fear for Josh's safety overcame all reasoning, and he could only focus on getting Josh on the plane and back home."

"Garrett said Josh became angry with Jordan and took off for the streets," Elysia said quietly. "What happened?" Laura shifted and took a sip of coffee. "Levi told me that when Josh woke up and realized what had happened, he panicked. When Jordan tried to explain, Josh wouldn't have it. He packed his bags and set out on foot. That's when Levi found him on the curb." Her eyes focused on her friend, concerned when Elysia gasped and fresh tears pooled. "Elysia?"

"It was him," she whispered. "The boy Nevaeh saw on the street."

Laura wrinkled her brow in confusion. "Nevaeh saw him?"

Elysia nodded. "Yes. We went to town for a few groceries. We were walking to Buster's Ice Cream Parlor, and she stopped me and pointed to this guy—to Josh," she cried. "Laura, I saw my son yesterday! I saw him, and I didn't even recognize him. Nevaeh was telling me he needed Jesus, and he looked sad. I pulled her away from him. Laura, I thought he was a street bum—a threat to my baby girl. I should have recognized him! I should have run to him and squeezed his neck and kissed his cheeks!"

Laura went to her, pulling her into a tight hug as she cried. "Shh, honey. There is no way you could have known that it was Josh. When Levi first brought him home, I hid behind him because I thought Josh was a gang-banger! He looks nothing like what I remember. The only thing recognizable are his eyes. Even his hair is in a different style these days."

Elysia laughed, squeezing Laura's neck before letting her go. "There were tattoos all over him. He had such an empty expression in his eyes—I just knew he was some street bum strung out on crack or drunk as a skunk. Never in a million years would I have ever thought he was my son."

Laura nodded, returning to her seat and sipping her coffee. "He looks like his dad," she said quietly.

Her eyes dimmed. "I was awful to him this morning." She thought back over the things she had said to Garrett, her conscience pricking. "I even slapped him when he tried to keep me from coming here," she admitted, her face coloring with shame. "He didn't want me coming, because Josh doesn't know we're aware he's here. He told me if I came, I'd run him off." Her eyes met Laura's, a spark flashing. "Laura, that made me so angry. How dare he talk to me about running off my baby when all of this is his fault? I said hateful things to him. I told him not to follow me—that I won't let him run Josh off a second time." Her eyes fell to the tablecloth, her fingers white as they gripped her mug. "You should have seen his face. He was devastated."

Understanding settled in Laura's eyes as she reached out a hand and squeezed Elysia's. "You're being too hard on yourself. I'm sure it hurts Garrett to know he can't just pop over and see his son, but he understands why. He wants a relationship with the soul he destroyed—it's not going to happen overnight. These things take time. Josh may never come around, and he needs to be prepared for that. Don't beat yourself up over your anger toward him. I'm fighting my own anger with Levi and Josh right now because neither of them wanted to tell you he was here. I let Josh have it last night—told him how wrong he was for keeping this from you."

"What did he say?"

"He told me he wasn't going to tell you, because he refused to break your heart again when he left for home." Elysia's brow creased, and she sighed. "He ran all the way to the other side of the States, Laura. Can you imagine Josh hitch-hiking all the way to Florida with random strangers?"

Laura grinned. "Yes…yes, I can see him doing that. You raised quite the free spirit."

Elysia took a long sip of the bold coffee, hoping its effects would kick in soon. "What do you think he'll do?" Her question was filled with hope, her eyes earnestly searching Laura's.

"It's hard to say at this point. Last night he seemed anxious to leave. But this morning Levi got him all excited about the surfboard he's had stored with us all these years, filling his head with restoring it and taking it out on the waves. They're actually browsing Al's Surf Stop for supplies now."

Elysia squeezed her eyes shut. "Do you think he'll talk

to me?"

Laura's smile was gentle as she answered, confident she was speaking the truth. "Oh, yes. He misses you dearly and even talked with me about you over dinner last night. He had both Levi and me confirm that you are happy, well, and safe."

Silence fell between them as Elysia thought on this, her stomach churning at the thought of Josh worrying about his father hurting her while he was gone. A thought hit her, and she sighed. "How are we ever going to get him to see the changes in Garrett? He'll always see him as the monster he knew."

"You have to give Josh the freedom of choice, Elysia. We can't force him into a relationship he wants nothing to do with. If his relationship with his father is meant to be, then it will be." She stood. "Let me refill your cup."

Elysia vacantly stared across the room, her mind imagining the conversation she was about to hold with her son. She didn't want to give him freedom to make the best choice for himself. Left to his own choice, he'd choose to run. Hadn't he always? No, what she wanted was to force him to stay, but she knew Laura was right. It had to be his decision. Her stomach flipped from nervous excitement. She'd begged God for years for this day, eventually giving up on her pleas ever being heard. Now that it was finally here, she found herself praying for restoration of the connection once held so dear.

"Man, that was sick! Did you see him land that aerial on that wave? He's definitely gonna be ready to compete."

Laura glanced toward her friend. From where she stood, she had a clear view of Josh and Levi as they stepped through the front door, and she wondered at the sudden knot in her stomach. "You okay?" she quietly asked Elysia, who looked as though she would bolt for her son, yet remained frozen in her chair.

Elysia wasn't given the chance to answer before Levi rounded the corner, Josh right behind him.

"...the way his board flew up and then..." Josh's voice

trailed off as his eyes fell on the woman at the table. Her brown eyes locked with his blue, neither noticing that Laura and Levi had slipped quietly from the room, leaving the two alone. Tears streaked Elysia's face as she stared up at the man who'd replaced the boy she remembered.

Josh swallowed hard and slowly shook his head, one hand gripping the door frame tight. "You were—" He cleared his throat, his eyes falling to the floor where he closed them tight. "You weren't supposed to find out I was here. No one was supposed to…I didn't want to…"

Elysia slowly stood, terrified to embrace him, terrified to not. "I had to see you," she whispered. "I can't believe you're standing here. Look at you, so tall and handsome. And with so many tattoos." She laughed nervously.

Josh ran a hand across his face, helplessness gripping his heart as he watched his mother succumb to her tears. "I never meant to hurt you." He sniffed. "I just couldn't take another day with him, Mom. I just couldn't."

She stepped forward and pulled him into her arms, holding him tight as they both sobbed. "It's okay," she soothed, caressing his hair with her hand. "You're home now. I have so much to tell you—so much I never got to explain."

"I'm so sorry, Mom," he cried, holding her tighter despite the intensifying pain in his ribcage. "I never should have left you alone with him. The thought of him hitting you haunts me every day. If he's touched you, I'll kill him—I swear."

Sorrow gripped her heart at his words. "Shh. Not now. Come eat lunch with me."

He pulled from her embrace, uncertainty lining his brow. "Mom, I can't…"

"Come on, I'll take you to The Strand. It's always been your favorite. We can talk over burgers." She tried to keep the pleading tone from her voice, but knew she failed miserably. She reached out her hand and gripped him with more force than intended, terrified he would give into the fear in his eyes and run.

Against the warning bells in his head, Josh was powerless to resist the gentle tug of his mother's hand on his. Nodding his consent, he smiled as her eyes lit up, and he followed her out the door.

Elysia excitedly climbed behind the wheel of her car and started the engine, proudly looking over at her boy. "I just need to run home and grab my purse. I forgot it in the rush to come over here." Her smile faded at the sudden tension on Josh's face. It was then she realized her mistake, and her anger toward her husband rekindled.

Josh's hand gripped the handle on the door, his mind telling him to bolt, his heart urging him to stay. Home. The place he'd run from. The place his father still dominated. There was no way he could go back there…

"He's not there, baby…"

His mother's voice faded in and out as he willed himself to keep his word and go with her. I can't do this. His fingers tightened their grip, panic pulsing in his veins. All at once, a lightning bolt of pain slammed his ribs, and he squeezed his eyes shut tight as he fought the urge to throw up.

"…out running errands…"

The world around him was closing in fast. Josh forced himself to suck in a deep breath, suddenly aware of his mom's hand on his arm. He opened his eyes and looked into hers, tears brimming as the panic completed its dance. "I'm so sorry," he said in a hush. "I cannot do this," he whimpered, begging himself to overcome his fears and just go with her to avoid breaking her heart.

Elysia blinked hard as she gripped his arm. "He won't be back for hours, Josh. Please, baby. Josh…baby…please." Her words tumbled over each other as she pleaded with him to stay.

Breathe, he ordered his lungs. He let a moment pass between them, gathering his senses and commanding them back into place. At last, he gave a short nod and offered her what he hoped was a reassuring smile. "Okay, Mama, let's go eat. I'm starved."

Relief flooded her, and she relaxed as she drove the two blocks home, parking in front of the door. "I need to let the dog out. Come in with me?"

Josh watched as she stepped from the car. In her eyes danced a silent plea, and he found himself giving into her again. "Sure." Despite his attempt to take her word regarding his father's whereabouts, he remained watchful, guarded, as he followed her inside.

Assuring she'd only be a moment, Elysia headed for the kitchen, leaving Josh alone with his thoughts. He scanned the room, blocking the multitude of painful memories that threatened to send him running. His eyes rested on a photo hanging on the wall, and he felt his blood grow cold. Behind the glass, his mother's face beamed radiant and bright. Beside her, with his arm draped across her shoulders, sat the man responsible for the hatred boiling in his veins. He resisted the urge to rip the smiling face of his father away from his mother. Confusion knit his brow at the sight of a little girl nestled between his parents. She looked familiar. He leaned closer to study her face and set his jaw.

"There's a boy in the street…"

The little girl's voice floated to his mind from yesterday's memory, and he wondered who she was. Maybe a cousin? But why would she be in a family photo with his mom and dad? Maybe they'd adopted, he wondered, making a mental note to ask his mom over lunch. To his surprise, he found the walls filled with pictures of the girl, with his own image displayed here and there. He heard his mother step outside with the dog, and he walked to the staircase, his hand resting on the rail.

Josh looked up at the carpeted stairs that led to his old room, and his pulse quickened. Part of him wanted to go up to the room where he grew up, but he knew if he gave in to the urge, he'd have to face the demons that went along with that. He turned away only to turn right back. Taking a deep breath, he took the first step, then another, until he stood at the top of the stairs, his bedroom door a mere foot away from where he stood. Placing a hand on the knob, he steeled himself and opened the door.

He was not prepared for what he saw.

Walls that had once proudly shouted his rebellion with graffiti and punk rock posters were now plastered in My Little Pony pictures set against a backdrop of pink that reminded him of Pepto-Bismol. His senses tingled from the shock as his eyes took in bookshelves lined with endless stories that would spark the dullest of imaginations. Dolls, dress-up clothes, three toy boxes and a bed draped in all things pink were only part of the contents of the room. Nausea teased his stomach as he wondered about the child his parents deemed worthy of such an investment. As a boy, this room had held the simplest of items—the bare necessities. His toys had been scarce, not due to a lack of resources, but because his father refused to buy him anything unless the purchase made him look good to those around him.

Numbly, he closed the door and stood still in the hallway, thinking. *Maybe Mom is fostering her. Or maybe it's a kid from the neighborhood who needs help. Why didn't she mention her to me on the way over?* Deciding to confront his mother now rather than later, Josh headed for the stairs, finding himself paralyzed from fear as the front door opened below him.

"Come on, princess, let's get you inside before the sun melts you like a popsicle." Garrett was rewarded by his daughter's uproarious laughter as the two stepped into the house.

Reaching out a hand for the comfort of her father's touch, Nevaeh refused to budge as she pointed up the stairs. "Daddy, who's that man looking at you?"

Garrett's smile faded as he followed her gaze. His knees went weak. His body trembled. His heart thundered in his chest, threatening to explode the rib cage that contained it. The years of torturous shame and judgment couldn't hold a candle to how he felt in that moment as he took in the look of stark terror on his son's ashen face.

Chapter 17

"It is an honor for a man to keep aloof from strife, but every fool will be quarreling."
~Proverbs 20:3~

NICHOLE

Nichole Sherard was accustomed to having things her way. Her husband's high position in the town of Highshore had made it easy for her to obtain the respect of others, though few would admit she'd earned it. A woman of great luxury, she saw herself in a class far above most and had no problem making it known by throwing her weight around and intimidating even the strongest men. For this reason, she found herself highly agitated in the lobby of the Seascape Hotel—the newest, fanciest hotel Highshore had to offer. "So, you are telling me that the room I've requested is unavailable. To me?" She stared in disbelief at the young man behind the desk.

The manager's smile lay somewhere between sincerity and amusement. He shrugged his broad shoulders, his eyes dancing at the opportunity to set this entitled woman in her place. "It's like the receptionist explained to you, ma'am: that room was reserved before you arrived. You cannot reserve a room without an actual reservation. Your husband's position in this town holds no credit here. I highly doubt the occupants of our royal suite will vacate based merely on the fact that you're the city manager's wife. You're like…not even the city manager." He threw that one in just to incite a rise, his grin stating as much.

Nichole tapped her long, manicured nails on the concierge desk, their red tint perfectly matching her overly-painted lips. The nerve of this insolent fool. Was he even out of college? She scrutinized him and decided it was time to school this little boy. "Do you not understand that I could have your job for this?"

Zion Bristol's face exploded into a broad smile. "Well, seeing as my father owns this hotel, it's doubtful—

ma'am," he added, egging her on.

Nichole bristled. "Then tell me—what room is available for a woman such as myself?"

Zion's brow rose. "The dungeon?"

Her face told him he'd pushed too far, and he quickly backtracked. "Let me check our availability, Mrs. Sherard. I'll have a room key available shortly." He clicked through the reservations, aware of her searing glare as he worked. "I will not accept mediocrity, young man, though I suppose I can't expect much from a hotel that allows vermin like you to run things."

"Ah, but you don't consider that my father rather likes vermin. It's how people like you are able to land a room here," he stated with a wink, relishing in the bright flush of her cheeks. "We have a suite available near the pool. I'm sure our poolside bar and grill will suit your requirements. Good food and a tan—can't get much better than that!"

The haughty stare she offered him held enough chill to rival the Antarctic. "For a new hotel chain, you have very poor customer service. I will be leaving a scalding review of your service on Yep."

Zion's brows shot up, and he failed to contain his laughter. "Um…you mean Yelp?"

"Whatever! I will see that this hotel is avoided by the kind of people I consort with!"

"Yes, please! Keep the trolls away until we complete the bridge!" He grinned and held out a key card. "Suite 305, Mrs. City Manager's Wife, ma'am. Room service is available twenty-four hours a day. Enjoy your stay at the Seascape Hotel."

Nichole snatched the key with a huff and adjusted the wide-brimmed, black hat perched atop her shoulder-length, reddish-blond hair. Her thin fingers dusted at her pristine outfit as though his very presence had soiled her attire. "I expect my bags to be delivered to my room within thirty minutes. Is that understood?"

"Absolutely. I'll send them right up, along with your broom."

"Excuse me?" Her penciled brows rose as she entertained the thought of throttling him.

He flashed his most charming smile. "Thank you, Mrs. Sherard. It's a pleasure doing business with you."

"Of course, it is." Throwing her nose in the air, she briskly walked toward the elevator, her four-inch heels clicking loudly against the marble floor.

Zion whistled as he watched the elevator doors close. "Wouldn't wanna be married to that woman."

Once inside her suite, Nichole unpacked her laptop and kicked off her heels. She loathed the idea of staying in a hotel for any length of time but refused to stay in her home while renovations were underway, though her husband had refused to leave.

Lance wasn't the brightest of men, but he was useful to her current cause. Once he outlived his usefulness, she would discard him like a worn shoe and move on to a man who could prove to be more useful than he. Until then, she would continue to run Highshore from behind the veil of her husband's title.

She picked up her phone and dialed, tapping her nails as she waited.

"Yeah."

"I need all the dirt you can get on Sterling Oliver."

"Oliver? The real estate broker's son?" Asher's tone displayed his confusion.

"Did I stutter?"

"Uh, no, but wha—"

"Questions are luxuries only clean cops can afford," she snapped. "I found my daughter. The little tramp is playing house with this goodie-two-shoes lawyer, and I need everything you have on him. I want someone watching Rhea around the clock. If she so much as goes within two miles of Highshore, I want her detained until I get there. Am I understood?"

"Yes."

She drew a pattern on the armchair with one of her nails. "Anything…you need to…tell me, Asher?" She drew her words out, anticipating the pounding of his heart.

"Uh, no?"

Nichole smiled a tight smile. "Ty's a decent ball player, isn't he?"

The line fell silent, his fear sparking across the wires. His breath became heavy as he formed his answer. "My son is off limits, Nichole."

"Well, aren't we ballsy today?" she laughed. "Have you learned nothing since dealing with me? Nobody is off limits, Asher Holmes. You lied to me. You kept information from me that is of the utmost importance. Since it seems I've not made myself crystal clear in the past, I'll spell it out for you. No one lies to me and gets away with it, Captain."

"What're you–I didn't–I don't know what you're talking about!"

His panic made his voice staccato, and she envisioned him fighting to breathe from fear of what she might do. "Joshua Cameron is out of jail, you imbecile!" she screamed into the phone. "Did you honestly think I wouldn't find out?"

"I-I-I didn't know!"

"It's your job to know. And since you failed to do your job, Asher, you must pay the consequences."

"Nichole, I swear I didn't know! Last I heard he was still locked up, but I can make it up to you!"

She smiled and drew a slash through the face she'd drawn. She liked where his thoughts were going and was just curious enough to see how he would try and redeem himself. "I'm listening."

"I have an informant who works with his best friend. Let me sick her on him, and I'll get you everything you need to know. Please."

"You have twenty-four hours to give me something I can use. Otherwise, Ty will know more about me than you want him to. Do I make myself clear?"

"Crystal," he bit.

"I want an exact location on this hoodlum. If he so

much as gets within miles of this city, I will own you. And if I ever find out that you're keeping information from me again you can kiss your little career goodbye. Twenty-four hours, Asher. Clock's ticking." She hung up before he had a chance to respond.

JOSH

Josh felt as though he'd taken a blow to the stomach. His breathing was labored, his lungs managing only shallow breaths. His eyes were fixed on his father's face, and he noted with confusion the regret and agony lining his features. A small whimper drew his focus to the little girl clutching his father's leg. Her golden curls swooped into her face and provided a protective canopy over her eyes, keeping them hidden from the stranger above her.

Garrett stood frozen in the entryway, the breeze from the open front door the only sound to be heard, time had come to an abrupt halt. The world outside faded into a sense of nothingness. He longed to say something but had zero doubt that even one word from his lips would send his boy away forever. His hand gently gripped Nevaeh's shoulder, more for his comfort than hers. He stared at Josh, waiting for him to make the first move.

"Okay, baby, I'm ready to…" Elysia's cheerful voice faded at the sight of her husband and child, her eyes following their gazes up the stairs. "Oh, no," she whispered. The intensity in Josh's eyes confirmed her fears—reconnecting with her over lunch was the last thing on his mind. Josh looked at her, the expression on his face reminding her of a mouse trapped in a maze. But it was the way his jaw set in anger as he turned his icy stare on Nevaeh that caused his parents' blood to go cold.

"How long did you wait?" His words were only a mere hint of the dangerous thoughts within.
Elysia forced the answer from her tight throat. "What do you mean?"

"Don't play stupid, Mom!" he shouted, his voice resonating in the staircase and causing her to jump. "How long after I'd gone did you wait before replacing me with her? A week? Maybe a month to save face? Did you figure if you tried again, you'd get the kid you wanted the first time? The kid who could make you proud? Is that it, Dad?" He spat the title through gritted teeth, his eyes swinging to Garrett and bearing straight through his soul.

Garrett swallowed hard, lost on how to replace his son's assumptions with the truth. "It's not like that," he began, willing himself to stay calm under the accusation. "We didn't rep—"

"Was she just so perfect when you saw her? The little angel you wanted all these years?" Josh took a few quick steps down the stairs. The terror he'd felt was shoved aside as rejection gave birth to the anger rooted deep in his heart. Pain stabbed his ribs, and he slammed a fist through the wall, eliciting screams from his mother and sister.

"No, Josh, you don't understand," Elysia tried, her heart pounding from the panic surging through her veins.

His eyes flew to hers. No longer the beautiful crystal blue she loved, they burned with ferocious intensity that threatened to consume them all. "I understand perfectly, Mom. He's wanted a girl this whole time—a boy just wasn't good enough. A boy was a threat to him—something to keep under his foot. Think I'm making this up? No." He laughed and shook his head. "Not even. These are his words to a little boy who was just eight years old!" He shoved a finger in Garrett's direction, hot tears burning his eyes. "My leaving was the perfect opportunity for him to play on your emotions and coerce you into having another—a replacement for the boy he hated." He dropped his hand to his side, his eyes falling on his mother's face. "And you went right along with him. Gave him what he wanted, shoving me out of your life forever."

Garrett swallowed hard. "No, son, w—"

"Where do you get off calling me 'son?!'" Josh interrupted, his sneakers pounding the rest of the way down the staircase. "There's no one here to pat you on the back for being my father." He gestured around the room.

"No one's waiting in the shadows to give you their praise for raising me." He met his father's eyes, his jaw tense as he stared him down. "Drop the act. It's disgusting."

Garrett kept his eyes on Josh's fierce glare, unsure of his son's intentions. Beside him, Nevaeh clung tighter and hid her face behind his pant leg, trembling from head to toe.

"Is she your punching bag, too, or is she just such an angel that you could never raise a hand to her?" Josh stepped to the lower floor and knelt in front of the little girl who refused to look at him. "Does Daddy hit you, kid? It's okay—you don't have to hide it. He hit me, too. For years." He stood, his hand brushing Nevaeh's curls.

Warning bells went off in Garrett, blasting as loud as a firehouse alarm. He quickly scooped Nevaeh into his arms and took a step back from his son, but he could see in his face that Josh was far from through.

Undaunted by his father's decision to pick up the child, he addressed her further. "Does he call you worthless? Maybe tell you what a mistake you are? That he wishes you were dead, or never even born?"

"That's enough, Josh," Garrett warned. Nevaeh began to shriek from her sobs as she buried her face in his neck. "Elysia, take her." He passed her to his wife's outstretched arms, his eyes never leaving Josh's face.

"Check out Father of the Year over here!" Josh's face spread in a mocking smile. "So, you'll protect her, is that it? Suddenly you're a hero when it comes to parenting? Nobody touches baby girl but, hey world! Here's my son, go ahead and rip him to shreds!'" His jaw twitched as he raised his chin, fighting to resist the tears threatening to explode from his eyes.

Elysia held a hand to her mouth as she cried. *Say something, Garrett!* she mentally pleaded, but Garrett stood perfectly still. Not a word escaped his tight lips. He remained as firm as a boxer in the pique of the match, allowing his opponent to slam him with the blows.

"Well guess what, Dad?" Josh stood toe to toe with

Garrett, a near-perfect match in height. "I'm not a little kid anymore. Unfortunately for you, all those beatings really paid off. I can take three grown men and still be standing." A cold smile stretched across his face, death in his eyes. "And you're just one pathetic excuse of a man." He enunciated each word sharply, determined to make the weight of his point torment his father's mind as he toyed with its meaning.

Elysia gasped and held Nevaeh tighter. Surely Garrett would defend himself if hit... She took a step back as Josh's gaze fell on the frightened little girl in her arms. "Stay away from her, Josh," she warned, her voice trembling.

He laughed, low and mirthless, his eyes on the frightened child clinging to his mother. "You know, it's funny you're protecting her from me." He raised his gaze to meet his mother's eyes and cocked his head to the side. "Where was all that protection when your son was screaming in the barn? Or in his room? Or right there in the living room when his father hit him in the stomach with the fire poker?" He watched her face crumple before him, tears soaking her cheeks. Turning his focus on Garrett, he laughed. "And you...thinking you can be there for her. You don't have the slightest clue how to be a dad. What can you do for her? Huh? You'll do nothing but destroy her."

Garrett's and Elysia's eyes were frozen on their son as his gaze fell back on Nevaeh. "Well, I'm not gonna let that happen," he spoke quietly, as though to himself. "I'm gonna do for her what no one was brave enough to do for me. Not Laura, not Levi, not even my own mother." Josh's voice was deadly calm, his eyes almost manic.

Elysia's heart tightened. Ice cold chills shot through her veins, and she exchanged a wary look with Garrett. He motioned for her to leave the room, but her feet refused to budge.

"Once I'm done telling my story as an adult, you'll finally be behind bars and my little sister will be safe with me. Far, far away from you." He ignored the shocked look on his mother's face. "You will never see her again. I can promise you that."

"Josh, you don't unders—" Garrett's words were cut short as Josh completed his thought.

"Better yet…maybe I should just take her with me now and let the courts sort it out later. That way she'll have a chance at life. You know, with someone who doesn't beat the crap out of her every few days." He stepped toward his mother, his expression softening as he looked at Nevaeh.

"How'd you like to come live with your big brother?"

Nevaeh whimpered and dug her fingers into her mother's shoulder. Elysia looked at Garrett, panic dancing in her eyes as Josh stepped closer. Did he intend to take her from her arms?

"Leave her alone, Josh. You're scaring her. It's me you're angry at." Garrett blocked any further advancement, ushering Elysia to back away.

"I'm scaring her? Oh, that's rich." Josh laughed as he faced off with his dad, his body language warning of an impending fight. His pulse pounded throughout his head, his ribs screaming their protest; he welcomed the pain, allowing it to fuel his rage.

"Please, just listen to me. Your mother and I have been trying to te—"

Josh swung, his fist catching Garrett by surprise. Blood spewed from the older man's nose, and Nevaeh screamed, hysterically trying to escape Elysia's arms and run to her dad. Before he'd been given the chance to defend himself, Garrett's jaw caught a second punch, snapping his head back as a third landed in his stomach. The blows felt like he was being hit with a sledgehammer. Strong. Aimed with precision and force, as though his son had been trained by a professional fighter.

"Stop it! Stop!" Elysia screamed, but Josh's eyes had glazed over, and she knew he had only one goal in mind: twenty-one years of pent-up revenge.

I've gotta get 'im outside. Garrett's thoughts were

muddled as he tried to focus. A fourth hit landed in his eye, the screams from his family compelling him to go low and wrap his arms around Josh's waist, shoving him through the front door.

Josh let out a cry of pain and Elysia raced to the porch, her eyes wide with horror as Garrett and Josh fell like pillars of stone to the grass below. She held Nevaeh close to her chest, her heart beating wildly as Josh's fists delivered blow after blow, Garrett offering himself as a human punching bag.

"Fight back, you coward! Hit me!" Josh screamed into his father's face, adrenaline bursting through his veins as he pounded him. "I'm gonna kill you!" he shouted, fighting for the upper hand when Garrett managed to flip him and pin him to the ground.

Terrified her son would carry out the threat—and that Garrett would let him—Elysia could stand no more. Her body trembled as she delivered her own threat—the only one she knew would send him running. "Leave him alone, Josh. I'm calling the cops!" She watched him jerk free of Garrett's grasp, his T-shirt ripped to shreds, dirt and grass covering him from head to toe.

Garrett lay on his back, panting as the metallic taste of blood slid down his throat. He coughed and rolled to his side, spitting pools of blood from his mouth. Elysia's voice faded in and out as she repeated the threat, and he watched his son take off down the driveway. At last, he closed his eyes. He collapsed back to the earth and welcomed the pain in his body like a long-awaited friend.

ASHER

The Highshore Tribune wasn't much to speak of—just a rinky-dink, college-run paper that did more gossiping than actual reporting of the news. But today the Highshore Tribune was everything, at least to the lone occupant of the beat-up Buick Century parked in the parking lot. He'd been waiting for over an hour—his coffee long gone, right along with his patience. If Cali Bristol wasn't such a good informant, he'd have left long ago. She was never on time—always walking to the beat of her own drum.

He sighed and leaned back on the seat, focusing on Patsy Cline's voice as she belted her lyrics over the radio. Closing his eyes, he thought about his conversation with Nichole, panic teasing his soul. If Cali didn't come through for him, his family would be Nichole's new target. He could not allow her access to them. If Bridget and Ty knew about his past, they'd be gone forever. Swallowing hard, he glanced through the windshield and spotted a blue Mustang whip into the parking lot as though only the driver's life mattered.

Cali had finally shown up.

Asher watched her get out of the car, rolling his eyes when the college student swung her long, strawberry-blond waves over her shoulders in dramatic flair. He waved her over, tapping his watch as she strolled to his window. "You're late," he hissed.

She shrugged. "So, find a new informant." Tousling her hair, her eyes displayed her boredom. "It's not like I haven't already told you I don't have time to do your sleuthing for you, anyway. Go get another flunky." She turned to walk away but paused when he called her name. "Cali, wait. I know what you said, okay? But I wouldn't ask for your help if it wasn't an emergency. This case is big. Really big. And a lot of lives are at stake. I need your help, and I have the cash in hand. Please." Asher held his breath, a wad of cash gripped in his palm.

Cali rolled her eyes and turned back to him. "Make it fast, I have to get to work."

"You guys have an intern here by the name of Jordan Hendricks, right?"

Cali's brow shot up. "Jordan? You're interested in Straight Shooter? You've got to be kidding me. He's never shot a crooked arrow in his life. Why are you after him?" Asher shook his head. "He's not the target. A friend of his is, and this guy is definitely a crooked arrow."

"Okay, well what's the arrow's name?"

He sighed and gripped the cash tighter in his hand. "Listen, I'm gonna tell you, but I'm placing a tremendous amount of trust in you, Cali. You cannot mention this to anyone—especially to Jordan, understand? Not one word. If you can keep my target's name quiet, I'll make sure there are a lot more Franklin's coming your way."

She shrugged her shoulders carelessly, but Asher knew she was the best informant out there. "Whatever. Give me his name."

"Joshua Cameron. I need you to do whatever it takes to get Jordan spewing info about this guy, got it? I need to know where he's staying, who he's running with, if there's a girl with him, all of it. But do not tip off Hendricks! Whatever it takes, Cali." He stared into her eyes, leaving his implied meaning hanging in the space between them.

She laughed and crossed her arms over her chest. "Let me see the cash. There'd better be a whole lot of money there to back up this request, Asher."

"Believe me, it's right here." Asher handed her the wad and watched her count the money before pocketing it.

"Okay, get outta here so I can go find Straight Shooter. If he's even here." She shrugged. "Been a minute since I've seen him at work. Haven't seen him around town or in school either."

"He's here," Asher confirmed. "Remember, Cali. Not a word." He started the car and pulled away, smiling at the rear-view mirror when he spotted her getting into character by raising the midriff of her top a few inches. "That's my girl…" He had a good feeling about this.

Chapter 18

"For a prostitute is a deep pit; an adulteress is a narrow well. She lies in wait like a robber and increases the traitors among mankind."
~Proverbs 23:27-28~

LEVI

Levi wiped the sweat from his brow as he glared at the stubborn hedge he'd been trimming for the past hour. Grabbing the hedge clippers firmer in his gloved hands, he tensed his jaw, teeth grit and snapped the stubborn branch from its hedge. "Yes! That's what I'm talkin' about—take that, you stupid hedge!" He snatched the branch from the ground and shoved it at the hedge as though lording his victory over its defeat. Sudden movement from the trees surrounding his backyard caused his head to snap up as the branch slipped from his grasp and fell to the ground, his victory forgotten. "Laura!" he yelled for his wife as he took off for the woods, his work boots pounding the earth as he ran. "Laura, come quick! It's Josh!" The slamming of the screen door behind him assured him she was hot on his heels as he ran.

"Josh! Josh, can you hear me?" Levi knelt by Josh's still form and placed a gentle hand on his back. When no reply came, he bit his lip and prayed he was making the right decision as he carefully rolled him to his back, shocked to find his clothing ripped and bloodied, dirt and grass covering him. "Aww, kid." Levi groaned, wiping his hand down his face. "What happened?"

"Levi, what is it?" Laura rushed to his side and fell to her knees, gasping at the sight of Josh. "Is he breathing?" Panic edged her tone as she reached for him, pulling back when Levi placed a hand on her arm.

"Careful," he warned. "I don't know what's happened to him, but he looks rough. We don't want to move him just yet. You have your phone?"

"Yes." She nodded, pulling it from her pocket.

"Okay. Call Elysia. We need to make sure she's okay. It looks like he's been in a fight, and he was with her last. Let's hope, by the grace of God, she's okay." He felt his wife stand and walk a few feet away as she made the call, and he turned his attention to Josh. "Hey, kid. Nod your head if you can hear me," he called as he gently shook Josh's arm. Pulling his water bottle free of his belt loop, he drizzled the cool water over Josh's face, satisfied when Josh turned away. "Good, good." Levi smiled, giving him space.

"I've gotta...I've got to..." Josh fumbled with his words as he rolled to his side and cried out.

"Here, let's get you to your feet." Levi wrapped an arm around his shoulders, only to be shoved back, nearly losing his balance.

"Don't touch me...please," Josh pleaded, tears falling to the earth as he attempted to push himself up.

Levi backed up, his eyes displaying his grave concern. Toying with the idea of calling an ambulance, his wife's voice was suddenly in his ear, a sense of urgency in her tone.

"Elysia is on her way here. She told me to keep Josh here until she gets here. He and Garrett got into it," she added, her eyes flitting to Josh as he struggled to stand. "What do you think we should do?"

Levi contemplated the question, watching Josh fall back to the earth. "Let's get him to bed," he decided as he stood. He gently gripped Josh's arms, tightening his grasp when he tried to fight him.

"No," he breathed against the pain. "No! I have to go...can't...stay...here..." He tried to push against Levi's grasp, but the older man was done playing games.

"Listen to me." Levi pulled him closer, his voice in his ear. "You are going to kill yourself if you keep on with this nonsense. You have to rest, Josh. I'm taking you to bed, and you will not fight me—understood?"

Josh shook his head, tears streaming. Exhausted, he gave in to the defeat pulling him under and collapsed into

Levi's embrace. "Dad...he knows I'm here...I have to go..."

"Hey, it's alright, kid. I won't let him get to you; I promise. You're safe, okay?" He felt Josh nod against his shoulder. "You're safe, son." Levi's gaze found his wife's tear-streaked face and he gave her a wink. "Come on. One step at a—grab onto me as tight as you can, and we'll slowly make our way to the door." He gently repositioned his arm around Josh's waist and pulled him beside him. "Doing good," he encouraged. "Just keep going...you've got this." They made it to the porch before another spasm seized Josh's rib cage, and he doubled over, heaving from the pain.

"I'm sorry—I'm so sorry," he cried.

"Don't give it another thought. Just a little farther...one step...okay, now the second step. Okay, last step, ready? Here we go...okay, you made it! Alright!" Levi coached and cheered until they'd made it through the door and to the bottom of the staircase. "Okay, son, think you can handle these bad boys or are you crashing on the couch?" Desperate for a reprieve, Josh shook his head hard. "No. No, please...I can't do it..."

"Alright. Let's take a few steps to the right...that's it...just a few more...and here we go..." He winced when Josh screamed as he lowered him to the couch. "Easy does it. Okay, good. Let's pull your legs up there, too. There we go...alright. Now we're to the finish line—you did it, kid. Way to go." Watching him as Josh lay back on the cushions, Levi slowly pulled his sneakers from his feet and laid them on the floor before grabbing a blanket and covering him up. "Still have some of those meds the doctor gave you?" At Josh's slight nod, Levi felt Laura move for the stairs, intent on making her boy feel better. "Okay, stay with me. Laura's coming with them now—try and stay awake until we can get these pills into you."

Laura breezed past him and disappeared into the kitchen, returning a moment later with a glass of water. "Josh, baby. Sit up just a little, hon." She gently pulled his head up and slipped two pills into his mouth, offering the water to wash them down. Satisfied when he swallowed them both, she laid him back down and gently kissed his brow. "Sleep," she whispered.

From the entryway, Levi spotted Elysia's car pulling in and sighed. "Elysia's here," he informed his wife. "He has to sleep, Lar…" he warned.

She nodded. "Agreed."

Levi swung the front door open and smiled as he welcomed her in, a finger to his lips as he gestured toward Josh's sleeping form. "Come on in. We can talk in the kitchen."

"No," Elysia said firmly, her eyes filled with tears at the sight of her son. "I need to be with him."

The husband and his wife exchanged a look, but neither protested as they joined her on the sofa. For a while, no one spoke—each one lost in thought as they stared at the boy they loved. Laura broke the silence, unable to bear it any longer. "Elysia…what happened?"

Tears pooled as Elysia stared at her son. "He accused us of replacing him with Nevaeh and asked her if Garrett hits her and calls her names."

Levi ducked his head, his heart pained for this family. "How did Garrett handle the accusations?"

Elysia gasped against her tears. "He tried to get him to stop, but Josh was already gone. He kept coming down the stairs…and his eyes, Levi. His eyes were manic. Full of rage and hatred," she whispered.

The tick of the wall clock seemed to boom as it tapped out the rhythm of time.

"Josh came down the stairs and started talking about going to court and getting custody of Nevaeh. He told us he would tell his story as an adult, and then people would listen. He accused me of not protecting him from his father. Told me I've protected Nevaeh, but let his father have his way with him." Elysia took the glass of tea offered by Laura, nodding her thanks. "And the worst part?" Her gaze swung from Laura to Levi, her voice a tight whisper. "He was right."

Levi shook his head. "No. No, he wasn't. He doesn't know the whole story, Elysia. He doesn't know your side. Once he knows, he'll understand."

Elysia shook her head and sipped her tea. "Josh attacked him. Right there in front of Nevaeh and me. He told him he was a fighter because of the beatings. He hit him again and again," she whispered. "Nevaeh was screaming but he didn't seem to notice or care. He just kept beating him…and Garrett let him." Her eyes met Levi's, tears swimming. "He let him hit him."

Levi nodded. He understood Garrett's reasoning there. "That must have been hard to watch," he commented. "Garrett got him outside, and they both fell off the porch. Josh screamed, and I knew he'd further injured himself, but he just kept fighting. He told Garrett he was going to kill him, and I got scared. I threatened to call the police, and he ran. I never even got the chance to tell him…"

Laura sighed, glancing at Josh to find him still asleep. "It's alright, Elysia. You'll have your chance. Where are Garrett and Nevaeh now?"

"Garrett's in bed. I left Nevaeh with a neighbor. He's too out of it to care for her right now. I can't let Josh run away again. My heart can't take it," she cried.

"And he won't," Levi assured. Somehow, even though he couldn't ensure this would happen, he knew in his heart that he was speaking the truth. He glanced at Josh, then back to his mother. "Let him sleep. You stay here until he wakes up. When he wakes up, you talk your heart out. I promise you'll have the privacy you need. Don't worry—that boy isn't going anywhere."

CALI

One glance to the rear of the building confirmed Asher's prediction: Straight Shooter was back—his red Dodge Ram parked in its usual spot. A smile spread across Cali's cheeks, and she fluffed her hair as she threw open the door and made her usual dramatic entrance. "What up, my peeps?"

The Tribune buzzed with active reporters chasing the wind as they teamed up with partners to get the latest story. Joe and Gil nodded in appreciation as she passed, twirling a dance that made their mouths drool.

Rachel Limburg's soft brown eyes watched Cali's antics as she walked toward her. Having spent the last semester in the same class as Cali, her behavior was no surprise to the young editor-in-chief. During her two years at the paper, she'd watched her work the guys over, manipulating them into giving her whatever she asked for while breaking hearts and leaving the pieces in the dust.

Cali bounced to her side, one hand on her slender hip. Rolling her eyes in the opposite direction, Rachel pulled her red hair over her shoulder and wrapped it into a quick twist to keep it out of her face before assigning the day's tasks to her waiting reporters. "Kade, after the Jeremiah story, I need you to follow the trail of the missing windmills."

"Windmills." The reporter stared dumbly at her, his face a canvas of disinterest.

"Yes, windmills, Kade. Mrs. Lewis reported three more pieces stolen from her collection yesterday. We need to get on the trail and find out who's pulling these shenanigans. Now go," she softly ordered. Her eyes followed him as he walked away, grumbling over his shoulder about being her flunky.

"What's my assignment today, Miss Boss Lady?" Rachel closed her eyes but forced a smile when she turned to face her. "Cali, good morning. I need you to work on the church graffiti story. Chase down every lead, centering on the Haulbrook boys. You know they've been working their magic around town lately. I'd assume it was them who painted the building."

"Man, those Haulbrook boys are so intimidating, Rach. Can I partner up?" Cali's eyes showed her unease as she searched Rachel's face.

Rachel studied her, knowing she was up to something,

but unable to pin down her angle. "You aren't afraid of anyone, so what's your deal? I can't spare a partner for such a minor story."

"It's just that Paul Haulbrook came onto me the other day, and he's really big, you know? He could be holding a grudge. I mean, he may not even speak to me. If I had a partner, he'd probably open up some more..." Searching her face, Cali knew she wasn't convinced. Time for the ace up her sleeve. "I'd hate to let my daddy know I'm being subjected to harassment at work. He'd want some answers for sure. Are you ready to deal with that, Boss Lady?" She cocked her head, her teeth toying with her bottom lip as she tossed the challenge at the editor.

Rachel cocked an eyebrow at her, unamused by her game. But...whether she liked it or not, Cali's father owned the Tribune, and she couldn't risk losing her job over this princess. She breathed a resigned sigh. "Who do you want to partner with?"

"Oh, I don't know...just a guy who could take him, I guess." She studied her shoes as though lost in thought and then looked at Rachel. "How about Straight Shooter?" Rachel's eyes shot to where Jordan was hunched over his desk, feverishly perusing the contents of a book. Her heart sank as she watched her best friend. "Jordan? You want to partner with...Jordan?" A lump formed in her throat, and she coughed to regain her composure before forcing her attention back to Cali. "Why? I thought you couldn't stand him."

She shrugged. "He's too calm for me, but I need someone calm to get this story. So, partners?"

Rachel took a breath and needlessly shuffled the papers on her desk. Though she and Jordan did nearly everything together, their relationship hadn't gone past the friend zone, much to her displeasure. She'd seen many girls at the Tribune attempt to get close to him, but each one had failed. Jordan just wasn't that kind of guy. He was sweet and genuine—not one to chase after thrills and girls in tight skirts. He was practical and educated, desiring things of God and denying those of the world. That was exactly the kind of leadership she was seeking in a husband.

And now Cali Bristol was threatening any chance she might have with him. She didn't like it. Not one bit. But if she denied Cali's request, she could lose her job. No man could resist her charms, and as she watched Jordan sip his coffee, she wondered if he'd be the same.

Realizing Cali was still waiting for her answer, Rachel pulled her gaze from Jordan and glanced back at her. "Uh, yeah, okay…Straight Shooter. Call him over here. I mean, if he wants to and all…" She busied herself with a file, her head resting in her left hand as she worked. Out of the corner of her eye, she watched Cali dance her way to Jordan and bit her lip as she studied his response. She smiled when irritation teased his brow. "Uh-huh," she muttered under her breath. "Not every man is into you, Miss Thang."

"What was that?"

She turned, offering a half smile to her desk mate. "Nothing."

Jordan stared at the girl who'd dared interrupt his reading, his eyes narrowed. "You want me to be your bodyguard." His tone was dulled by disbelief. There were at least ten guys at the Tribune buffer than he, and she'd picked him? He rolled his eyes. "I don't have time for this, Cali. I have a huge load of work to catch up on from my time away. Go ask James—he's been dying for your attention."

Cali's gaze swung to the reporter, squeezing her arms tight across her chest as he waved and winked in her direction. "Ugh! As if." She scrunched her nose and turned back to Jordan, frustrated to see he'd returned to his reading. Her brow rose as a laugh escaped her lips. "Doesn't seem like you're doing much work now. What is that, a Bible? Could you be any more of a nerd?"

With a sigh of irritation, he cut his eyes to hers. "Not really helping your case much, are you? Do you mind? I'm kind of busy here." Doing what? His conscience challenged. Justifying myself before God? He winced at the thought and closed the Bible. "Fine," he muttered. "Let's go."

"I knew you'd understand," she gushed. "Paul is just way too much for me to handle. I'd probably slug him if he touched me again. Ready to get our marching orders from the boss lady?" Cali leaned her body forward, ensuring Jordan got an eyeful as she propped her hands on his desk and blinked long lashes at him.

Jordan rolled his eyes as he stood. He knew she was bad news. She was all guile—this temptress from hell. He had to give her one thing, though—her energy was magnetic and enticing. Telling himself he'd only entertain her for a minute before busying his mind elsewhere, he allowed his eyes to roam, snapping to attention when James let out a whoop beside him.

"Caught you lookin'! What would your God think of you now?" James teased as he pointed at Jordan. Jordan's gaze fell to the floor, shame burning his cheeks. "Get lost, James," he muttered before turning to Cali. "Let's go." His tone was clipped as he walked away.

"Don't mind him—he's an animal. Everybody knows you're not like that, Straight Shooter."

Jordan couldn't look at her. "Rachel's waiting."
"Well, then," Cali scoffed. "We'd better hurry before she gets mad! You know those redheads have a fiery temper." She winked at him and walked toward Rachel's desk.

"Here's my bodyguard. We're ready to roll!" Cali watched in amusement as Rachel glanced at Jordan and blushed. A thrill raced through her and a sly smile parted her lips. Pretending to examine her shoe, she gasped. "Oh, gross! There's dirt on my shoe!" She bent in front of Jordan, knowing her shorts did a poor job of covering her backside. She could feel his eyes on her and grinned. Perfect. Hook, line, and sinker. She smiled as she stood, hair flying.

Rachel cleared her throat and pretended to shuffle papers. "This isn't a difficult story. I expect it on my desk by the end of theday, if not sooner." She glanced at Jordan, swallowing her disappointment when he seemed reluctant to pull his eyes from Cali and focus on her.

"Anything else we need to know?" Jordan asked, eager to put the task behind him and distance himself from Cali.

"No," Rachel answered, her eyes meeting his. "End of the day, Jordan."

He studied her face, arching his brow at the intensity in her eyes. "You got it, boss," Jordan answered, pulling his keys from his pocket and turning to Cali. "Okay, then. I'll meet you there."

Rachel watched him walk away, sucking in a breath when Cali yanked the keys from his hands with a grin. "Are you kidding me? We're going to the same place! I don't bite, Straight Shooter." She laughed and pushed ahead, keys dangling from her finger as she teased him.

Rachel did not miss the storm that crossed Jordan's face as he followed her through the door. She wished she could run after them to see what he would do.

The sun blinded him as he stepped into the parking lot, one step behind the girl who'd just crashed into his life like a wrecking ball. "Cali, give me my keys." He glowered when she ignored him and unlocked his truck, slid behind the wheel, and shut the door in his face with a grin. "This isn't funny," he growled, pulling on the handle and finding it locked. Jordan ran his hands through his hair as he looked at her. "Open the door, Cali. I'm not comfortable with this."

"You want to get this story over with, right, Straight Shooter?" Cali called from behind the glass.

"More than you'll ever know," he grumbled.

A smile exploded across her features as she started the engine. "Well then, get in so we can get this over with." Rolling his eyes, Jordan resigned himself to her bidding and climbed into the passenger side. "We go there, talk to the brothers, and get back to the paper. Got it?" He cut his eyes to hers, his stomach flipping as she merely tossed her hair and peeled out of the parking lot.

ELYSIA

The sun was painting its purple hues along the horizon when Elysia noticed Josh's eyelids flicker. Gripping the edge of her seat, she leaned forward, her heart racing. "Baby?" she quietly called, willing him to look at her. "It's Mom." She gently brushed his hair away from his forehead, her fingers tangling in his locks.

"Mama," he breathed, focusing his gaze on her face. For a fleeting moment, he was spared from the memories. But that moment was short-lived as his harsh words flooded back to him, along with the look on his mother's face when he'd said them. He pulled the blanket off his body and forced himself into a sitting position. "About today…"

She shook her head. "Doesn't matter. All that matters is that you didn't run."

He raised his brow and breathed a laugh. "Yeah, well…" His voice trailed off as he met her eyes. "I'm really sorry, Mom. I never should have said those things to you—I didn't mean them. I was just so angry at him. How could he just replace me like that? Like I'm some trinket instead of his kid. And when I saw her room…my room…I just…lost it, Mom. I had nothing; you know?" Tears threatened his eyes as he looked at her. "He's given her everything, including his love. How could he just throw me away?"

She smiled softly, but the smile didn't meet her eyes. "Josh, about Nevaeh." Her heart skipped a beat, but she pressed on. It had to be said. She watched him avert his gaze and focus on the carpet, sorrow darkening its hue.

"Does she make you happy?"

Elysia almost missed the question. "What?"

"Nevaeh. Does she make you happy? Like Nilah would've?"

She closed her eyes. "She makes me very happy, baby. But she's not a replacement for Nilah."

He sighed. "You don't have to protect me from the truth, Mom. I'm all grown now. I can take it. I know how crushed you and Dad were when Nilah didn't make it." He grew quiet for a moment, studying his hands. "I hate her, you know. Nilah?" Josh glanced at her, shame coloring his cheeks. "I know it's not her fault, but I wish she'd never been born." He laughed. "God hates me, Mom. I've always known it. He cursed me by bringing me into this world on her birthday. Why did He allow her to be born, only to have her die the same day? Did He not see what would happen? Laura's always talked about Him being this all-knowing Being. Didn't he know my father would only be able to focus on his stillborn baby every time my birthday came around, instead of celebrating his son? Does God even care what I've gone through, living in her shadow like that? To have been beaten because of her all these years? I hate her so much." He sniffed. "And now I've been replaced by another sister. I hate her, too. I've known all these years how much you guys wished I had been a girl, Mom. I don't understand why you waited until I left before trying again. Was I in the way? Did ya'll want me out of your lives so you'd have more time to dote on Nevaeh?"

Elysia choked on the sobs in her throat. The pain of losing her daughter rippled through her veins and mixed with the torment her son had been forced to endure each day of his life. It was time. No more stalling. He had to know the truth.

"Josh, Nevaeh is not your sister." She swallowed hard. "She's yours."

Josh's blood ran cold, his pulse pounding in his ears. Sure he'd heard wrong, he shook his head. "What did you just say?" There had to be a mistake. He couldn't be a father. A daughter he never even knew of? Impossible…

"Nevaeh is your daughter, son." Elysia's jaw twitched as she fought back her tears. How many times she had dreamed of telling her boy this news! So, why did it feel like she was suffocating? Her chest seized, and she fought to breathe as he stared at her, disbelief etched onto his features. Say something…she mentally pleaded.

Josh cleared his throat and dropped his eyes to his hands as memory after memory of his past with Rhea flooded his mind. "There has to be a mistake." He raised his eyes to hers. "How do you know she's mine?" Tears rushed, and he roughly wiped them from his cheeks. Elysia's gaze was soft as she regarded him. "Have you seen her, Joshua?"

Josh's mind flashed back to the first time he'd seen her on the sidewalk. Those eyes…those had been Rhea's eyes staring back at him. No wonder they'd seemed so familiar. And that hair—it was the exact color of his, mixed with Rhea's curls. He shook his head. "I need to see her. I need to look at her to be sure. I can't… I don't have a daughter, Mom. This is crazy!" He quickly stood to his feet, immediately regretting the decision when a jab of pain stabbed his ribs. "I cannot have a kid! This is me we're talking about!" His eyes danced with panic as he paced the floor.

With greater calm than she felt, Elysia reached for her purse and withdrew a picture of Nevaeh. "She's a beautiful mix of you both."

Josh snatched the photo from her hands and dropped to the couch, wincing from pain. He perused the picture, searching the face of the little girl said to be his own. When it became painfully clear that his mother spoke the truth, he raised his eyes to hers. "She's mine," he acknowledged.

Elysia nodded, a smile tugging at her lips. "Through and through. She's the spitting image of your personality. Stubborn, proud, independent, and fierce. She has Rhea's musical talent—she never stops singing, and her voice is beautiful and clear. But she has none of her mother's timidity." She laughed as a memory came to mind. "You would have been so proud of her the other day. I was mortified, but you would have been cheering her on. A little boy tugged her hair and called her 'curly swirls' while we were at the playground, then he pushed her to the ground. Nevaeh got right back up, planted her feet, and decked him right in the nose."

Josh's brow shot up as he tried to envision the terrified little girl from earlier that day standing up to a bully. His heart panged when he realized he had been the bully today. "That little boy's mother was furious, but Nevaeh looked right at her and told her she needed to teach him some manners." Elysia shook her head and laughed. "Like I said, she's yours through and through." She grew quiet, noticing the pensive look in her son's eyes. "Ask me anything," she quietly said. "I don't know where to start."

Josh remained motionless, his mind whirling to connect the dots. Nevaeh. His daughter. Being raised by…his father?! His eyes hardened as the realization kicked in. "Where's Rhea?" he demanded; his tone cold.

Elysia shrugged and sighed. "I don't know, baby. It was a chilly night. I remember I had just started the fireplace when the doorbell rang." She paused, her eyes wandering to the ceiling as she looked at Rhea and Nevaeh so long ago. She shuddered at the tear-streaked face of the girl who'd placed her baby into her arms. "I was confused and excited, all at once. I thought maybe she had come with you. But she was standing there alone with this tiny bundle in her arms. When I asked about the baby, she told me she was yours. At first, I didn't understand. I thought she'd just visit and let us know we were grandparents. But then she told me why she'd come." Her voice caught. and she felt Josh's heavy stare. Grabbing her water from the side table, she drank deeply before setting the glass back down.

"Mom," Josh urged. He had to know the reason Rhea had chosen his father. Out of the millions of people in the world, why Garrett Cameron? His blood boiled in his veins as her betrayal began to take root.

"Nevaeh was just four days old when Rhea brought her to me. She told me she needed my help, but when I asked what had happened, she only told me that there were things she couldn't tell me—that she couldn't explain. She said Nevaeh wasn't safe with her, and that I was the only one she trusted with her."

Josh slammed a hand down on the table causing his mother to jump in her seat. "Safe? She wasn't safe with her? So, she chose my father?!" He gritted his teeth and moaned, rocking himself back and forth on the couch. The pain in his heart was ten times greater than the pain in his ribs. "So, you just let her abandon my kid with him? How could you do this to me, Mom?" He knew he wasn't being fair, but he didn't care. The mere thought of his daughter being raised by his tormentor was enough to drive him mad.

Elysia swallowed the sting of his accusation and forced herself to push back. "I'm not finished with the story, Joshua. I argued with her for a long while. She continued to insist I take the baby. I suggested I just watch her for a while, and she could come back to get her. I didn't know your father had come up behind me." She met his hard stare with the raising of her chin. "Rhea saw him and immediately called out. Told him he was the grandfather of a beautiful baby girl who needed him. She told him she couldn't keep her, and that Nevaeh wouldn't be safe in her care. She begged us to adopt her and raise her as our own, and then she…" She hesitated, which she immediately knew set him on edge. "She made us promise not to tell her anything about you or her. She gave me a picture of you two at the formal. On the back was a P.O. box where I could send the adoption forms for her to sign. And then she was gone."

"Just like that." Josh shook his head in disbelief.

She nodded. "Just like that."

"And you have no clue where she's at?"

"No. We never saw or heard from her again."

Josh's chest heaved, his vision clouding. "So, you adopted her? Without even giving me a chance?!" He raised his eyes, fire dancing in his pupils.

Elysia prayed for the grace to be calm in his fury and for God to make him listen and get past his rage. She breathed a deep breath before answering. "No. I refused to adopt her. Instead, I went down to the courthouse and established custody of her. She is legally in our care, meaning neither you nor Rhea can take her away from us without us signing her over or one of you taking us to court to fight for her."

Josh forced his mind to calm so he could comprehend. "I still have a chance at being her dad? At raising her on my own?"

She nodded slowly. "Yes. Assuming you're found fit to care for her."

Josh bristled. "You saying I can't take care of my own kid?"

She raised her brow at him and crossed her arms.

"Joshua, have you seen yourself lately? You can't take care of yourself right now. It requires a lot more than just wanting her, baby. You understand that, right? She needs a house. Stability. Steady income. A car to take her back and forth to school, church, and the doctor. She needs to get to know you, son." Elysia grew quiet and dropped her gaze, not wanting to say what was on her mind. But he needed to hear it. "She needs to trust you. And right now, you have anything but her trust after beating the only father she's ever known right in front of her." She stood to her feet, grabbed her purse, and stepped toward the door.

"Mom…" Josh stood, tears glistening in his eyes. She held up her hand. "I'll come back tomorrow. You need your rest." Stepping out onto the porch, she turned to face him with one hand on the doorknob. "Assuming you're still here when I wake up."

With the click of the door, his heart shattered, the picture of his baby girl still clutched in his hand.

Chapter 19

"Vanity of vanities, says the Preacher; all is vanity."
~Ecclesiastes 12:8~

JORDAN

It became evident after an hour with Cali that she had no intentions of following up on the Haulbrook boys. Jordan had given up trying to get her on task hours ago and as much as he knew he should call Rachel and fill her in, he had yet to pick up the phone. Instead, he'd allowed himself to be dragged all over town by the redheaded girl who made him forget about Josh and his father.

Their trek around town had been grueling, and he'd longed for her to shut up so he could think. But as time passed, he began to warm up to her, grateful for the distractions from the thoughts that plagued him. Currently waiting for her to return to their table where they'd just finished a meal, he spotted her coming back from the restroom. His cheeks flamed when she stooped to tie her shoelace, offering him a clear view of what should have been hidden beneath her shirt.

His phone's vibration drew his attention, pricking his conscience before he'd read the text he knew was from Rachel. A thumbs-up emoji signaled that she approved of his "progress" in the story and informed him that he was done for the day. He'd learned nothing of the Haulbrook boys, but he'd learned one key element about Cali's personality: she was a master deceiver. He'd watched her spin her web of lies and drape it over Rachel like a beautiful canopy. He watched her stand and walk back to the table, flipping that rich thick hair over her slender shoulder, and wondered at his quickening pulse. *God, get me away from this temptress...*

"Miss me?" Cali batted her eyelashes dramatically as she flounced into the booth across from him.

She was bold. This girl didn't care a thing about what anybody thought of her. She was the opposite of himself, and he was helplessly drawn to her charisma. She was also dangerous—this Jezebel. Ordering himself to pull it together, he took a deep breath. "Just heard from Rachel." Cali watched the doubt flicker in his eyes. "Don't worry about her." She leaned back in the booth, her chest pushing her tight t-shirt to the limits. "We'll get her dumb story done, okay? The Haulbrook boys were just so uncooperative today, weren't they?" A carefully placed wink, a display of tongue…yeah…his focus was right back on her. Good boy. "Enough about her and that lame paper. You've been hanging with me all day—let's hit your neck of the woods!"

His eyes shot up, heart pounding. "M-my neck of the woods? As in…?"

She rolled her eyes and leaned forward, elbows on the table. "You're so cute when you play dumb." She laughed. "Don't you have your own crib? Friends? Family?"

His chest constricted. "Y-you want to meet my family?"

"Don't be ridiculous! One look at me and they'd rip you away! Then all our fun would be a waste, wouldn't it?" She stroked his wrist with her forefinger.

Jordan yanked his hand away, rubbing his wrist beneath the table as though he could wipe away the tingling in his body from her touch. He thought about her words, knowing she spoke the truth. His father would never let him hear the end of his choice in company. Rolling his eyes, his heart grew hard at the thought. Screw his father. He'd already lost all faith in him, hadn't he? "Yeah." He forced a laugh. "They would. So then, um, what did you want to see in my part of town?"

She pretended to think, her finger going to the corner of her mouth where she chewed the nail. "I bet you have tons of friends. Who's the wild card? Let's start with him! We could go big—after all, we've worked so hard today; we deserve a little party time, don't you think?"

The corners of Jordan's mouth raised in a nervous grin. "I didn't exactly get the name 'Straight Shooter' by partying with friends," he commented, feeling like she already knew that.

She rolled her eyes, propping her chin on her hand and casting him a bored look. "Come o-n-n-n." She dragged the word out over a whine. "There has to be someone you know who knows how to have a good time."

"I mean, I have this friend, but he's in pretty bad shape, so he wouldn't be much fun. Besides," he added, "we're not talking right now." Jordan's chest tightened.

"Aww, you miss him," she stated, a mock frown pulling at the corners of her mouth. "What's his name?" Beneath the table, she slipped her feet out of her sandals and caressed his leg with her bare toes.

He jumped and worked to evade her. "Josh. His name is Josh. But like I said, he's laid up right now and can't hang."

"Well, then…let's bring the party to him!" She smiled big, her hot pink nails tapping the table as she thought. "What better way to mend a friendship than by bringing some fun back into his life? Why aren't you boys talking, anyway? Did you get into a fight over who's bigger?" She pouted at him, eyes working overtime.

Jordan shifted uncomfortably. "Ah, no." He breathed a nervous laugh. "He's just going through a hard time right now. I tried to help, but he didn't appreciate it. That's all."

She scrunched her nose as though she'd sniffed dog poop. "How rude. You don't seem the type to hang with someone as sorry as that guy. I mean, like…you have good character. Why are you letting him treat you like that?"

He had good character. She'd said it, herself.

"The lips of an immoral woman are as sweet as honey, and her mouth is smoother than oil. But in the end, she is as bitter poison, as dangerous as a double-edged sword."

He squeezed his eyes shut as the Proverb came to mind, but they flew open as he felt Josh's fist slam his gut all over again. Righteous indignation flared in his soul and pride burned the Proverb from his mind. She was right. Josh had no right to treat him that way. "I haven't spoken to him since he left my apartment."

"Oh. M. Gee. You kicked him out?" She burst into laughter. "There's some backbone, J!"

"J." Only Josh called him that. Jordan's gaze fell to the table. What was he doing with this girl? "I didn't kick him out," he said, eyes fixed on his empty plate. "I would never kick him out," he whispered. He reached for his phone and absentmindedly began to play with the screen, hoping she'd stop asking questions.

Cali watched him spin the phone, then grab it up and unlock it. He fiddled with the device, not bothering to lock it once he'd set it back onto the table. A grin exploded across her face, her freckles dancing along her cheekbones. Before he realized she had it in her hands, she'd snatched the phone and put it to her face. "Let's have some fun." She smiled coyly, ignoring the shock on Jordan's face.

"Um, Cali, I don't like people using my phone," he protested. As much fun as he'd had with her that day, his nerves were shot. "Please give it back." He shifted in his booth as he watched her thumbs fly over the keyboard. "Cali, what're you doing? I'm not kidding. Give me back my phone."

"Geez, lighten up, geezer. You act like you're hiding naughty pictures or something." Her thumbs froze, her eyes staring over the device, eyebrows raised. "Are you hiding naughty pictures? Tsk, tsk, Straight Shooter. What will the gossips say?"

His face reddened. "I'm not hiding anything, Cali. Just give me back my phone!" Realizing he was raising his voice, Jordan glanced around the room, ducking his head when he met the fierce gaze of Mrs. Howard, the town's librarian.

"I bet you get ulcers on the regular," Cali teased as her thumbs resumed typing. "There!" She proudly dropped the phone down in front of him, leaning back in her booth, arms crossed in front of her chest.

Hesitating, Jordan picked it up and glanced at the

screen. Josh's name stared back at him in bold type, and he groaned. "Aww, Cali, what did you do?"

"Read it and find out for yourself. And if you get mad at me for helping you out then you're no better than your lame friend, are you?"

What up, loser? Straight Shooter has a new gal on his arm. If you care to find out more, hmu with a text!!!! My phone number is 555-897-0896. C'mon…you know you're curious ;)

Jordan's face said it all. "Cali, to you this is a game. But to Josh and me? This is serious stuff. Our relationship is already strained because of me. I don't need a perfect stranger coming in and shaking stuff up any more than it already is." He ran a hand down his face and tried to calm his nerves.

"Relax, Jordan! You are so serious!" She suddenly stood and leaned across the table, her finger flicking a speck of food from his mouth.

Jordan found his eyes mere inches from her chest, and his pulse began to pound. He knew better than to entertain her. He leaped to his feet, side-stepping as she scrambled to get out of his way. "It's been a long day, Cali. We should go."

Shocked, Cali stared at him before gripping his forearm. "Was it something I said?"

He looked at her, swallowing hard before shaking his head. "We should go," he whispered, shame coloring his face at where his mind was taking him.

"Listen, what if I went with you to make things right with your friend? It's the least I could do after upsetting you." She grabbed her purse from the booth and rushed after Jordan as he made his way for the door, nearly running to keep up with him in the parking lot.

"Josh is staying with my parents, Cali." He glanced at her as he unlocked his truck and reached for the door. "I can't go there right now." Without another word, he climbed behind the wheel and started the engine, eyes facing front as she climbed beside him.

His silence was fine with her. They pulled out of the parking lot, and she smiled out the passenger window. Score one point—she now knew where Josh was staying. All she had to do was tell Asher, and he'd be able to find out the address and drag the crooked arrow wherever he needed him to go.

JOSH

It had taken Josh over thirty minutes to take a simple shower. The pain in his ribs continued to radiate throughout his body, but he didn't dare give in to his impulse to take more pain meds than prescribed. Been there, done that, and now he was in Highshore. Josh gritted his teeth and grabbed the duffel bag that held his cigarettes and the Bible Titus had given him. What a coincidence—the Lord's Book tossed in the same bag as the sinner's vice. Whatever. It was just a book, after all. The only words on those pages that had his interest were the ones explaining Titus' claim to murder. He withdrew the Bible and laid it on the bed, then snatched up his cigarettes and lighter, zipped the bag, and tossed it to the floor.

He was desperate for a cigarette. With Mrs. H. always hovering downstairs, he'd been unable to slip outside and steal a smoke—she'd just take it from his mouth if he did. But if he stayed near the open window in Jordan's room, he figured he'd have a chance to finish a cigarette in peace. Josh picked up the Bible and headed for the window, dragging Jordan's rolling desk chair. Grateful that the window quietly slid open, he raised it high and lit up before turning back to the page he'd marked the day before.

"So, I find this law at work: Although I want to do good, evil is right there with me. For in my inner being I delight in God's law; but I see another law at work in me, waging war against the law of my mind and making me a prisoner of the law of sin at work within me. What a wretched man I am! Who will rescue me from this body that is subject to death? Thanks be to God, who delivers me through Jesus Christ our Lord!"

Josh stared at the verses he'd just read, highlighted in bright, fluorescent yellow. He had no idea what they meant, but Titus had written in every free space on the page. Working to find a starting point in the handwriting, he began to read as he took another hit of his cigarette and blew the smoke out the window.

"Why would You choose me, God? Why do You want me after what I did? I never should have gotten behind the wheel of that car. I knew I'd had too many beers that night…"

He stopped reading and looked away, his heart thumping harder against his rib cage. Titus, a drinker? None of this made sense. This wasn't who he knew Titus to be. He'd never seen him with alcohol. Sighing, he took another hit, forgetting to aim the exhale at the window. Or maybe he didn't care. His eyes fell back to the page, though he wasn't sure he wanted to know more.

"If I hadn't been so selfish, Grandpa would still be here, and that little girl wouldn't have lost her mom. Why don't You just leave me alone, God? I'm not the guy for this job!"

What was he talking about? Josh ran a hand through his hair, frustrated when there didn't seem to be any more explanation on the page. His phone pinged, and he glanced at the screen to see Jordan's name. Rolling his eyes, he unlocked the device and read the text from Cali, his brows knitting in confusion. Was this for real? And if it wasn't a joke, why would he text this chick? Irritation swelled in his veins as he typed a quick reply to Jordan.
Yo, man. Who's this hooker on my line?

He clicked out of the text and flipped through his calls until Titus' name appeared. His thumb stabbed the send button, and he took another hit of his cigarette as it rang.

"I seem to be very popular with you lately."

Josh grinned at his teasing, his voice warming his soul. "Yeah, well, you've become quite the mystery."

Titus sighed and offered a small laugh. "Hey, whatever

keeps you calling this number. What's up, kid? You alright?"

Josh thought a moment before avoiding the question altogether. He didn't want Titus' sympathy. Not when it was his own doing that had gotten him into this mess. "I read the chapter, or whatever it's called."

"Oh." He paused, then, "So what do you want to know?"

"I've never seen you drink. Ever."

Titus laughed. "Yeah, well. Trauma will do that to a guy, won't it, Josh?"

"I guess." His voice was quiet, contemplative. He tapped the cigarette on the windowsill, smashed it out, and dropped it to the ground before realizing what he'd done. Cursing, he leaned out the window and peered at the evidence of his sin.

"Josh?"

He sat back and sighed. "You said everything I need to know would be here, but you only talk about drinking too much, stealing your grandpa's car, and him not being here anymore. And you mentioned a little girl losing her mom. None of this makes sense. How old were you?"

"Fifteen."

Josh whistled and breathed a curse. "Why'd you steal it?"

"I was angry at the world back then. I'd lost both of my parents when I was eight. See, my ship is the Tourista II. Theirs was the original. It went down in a bad storm that sprung up out of nowhere. Took them down with it."

Josh sucked in a breath, his mind flashing back to the jewelry he'd tried to steal from Titus' safe. He remembered the controlled anger when Titus had told him it was his mother's jewelry. "Titus, I didn't know. I'm so sorry."

"Hey, it happened. I'm a better man for it today."

Josh thought about this, confused. Titus must be delusional. Trauma doesn't make a better man. At least, that wasn't the case for himself. "So, you stole the car and got drunk. What happened next?"

Titus cleared his throat from the tears choking his voice. "I ran a red light while a young mother drove through the intersection with her baby girl. I hit the driver's side of the car, instantly killing the mom. I came out of that wreck without a scratch on me. I could hear the baby screaming from the backseat. I panicked. I was so scared; I couldn't think of what to do, so I called Grandpa and told him what happened. Not 911 so they could come and check the baby…I called Grandpa. I was only eight blocks from home, and it was one in the morning. Isolated streets—no one around to witness what had happened. Grandpa rolled up in Grandma's beat-up car and jumped out of the vehicle. He took one look at the mother and knew she was gone. He went for the baby, pulled her car seat out, and laid her on the ground. And then he…" Titus stopped, sucking in a sob.

Josh listened as Titus' breaths became heavier. He tried to picture his boss crying—something he'd never seen him do. Titus always had it together. Josh couldn't imagine him as a drunken, scared, teenager who'd just killed someone.

"…he called 911 and told them that he had been in an accident and a woman was dead. When he'd hung up, he quickly grabbed me by my shoulders and demanded I get into Grandma's clunker, drive straight home, and go to bed. And then I watched my grandpa climb into his wrecked car. He grabbed the edge of his shirt and wiped my prints off the steering wheel, the dash, the gear shifter, and the door. He looked at me one last time, that stern 'don't you dare defy me, boy' look he had, and mouthed 'go!' before shutting the door and planting himself as the murderer in my stead."

"What did you do? Did you leave him there?"

Titus' voice cracked. "I did. I obeyed Grandpa for the first time in my life. I climbed into Grandma's clunker and drove home, showered, and went to bed, only to hear Grandma's screams an hour later when the police called and told her that Grandpa had been in an accident, and someone was dead." He sniffed, his breaths coming in swift puffs. "Grandpa did fifteen years in prison. My fifteen years. All because he didn't want to see me throw my life away over a stupid decision made by a teen who was mad at the world. Grandma never admitted it, but she knew. I know she knew. I could tell it when she talked to me and looked at me. She never asked me for the truth, but our relationship was never the same after that."

"So, where's your grandpa today?"

"Back home with Grandma. He's never allowed me to say a word about what happened. We don't talk about it. It's like it never even happened. He was just as warm, accepting, and loving toward me as ever when he came home. It was Grandpa who pointed me to Christ repeatedly, but I'd always hated him for it. Right up until the day he gave himself to the system and let me go free. Like Jesus did."

"I don't know anything about that, but I have mad respect for your grandpa. I can't imagine being raised by a man who would do that for me."

"He's a rare gem, for sure. My life completely changed that day. I no longer did things just for the thrill of it. No longer chased that next high or had to be the toughest on the block. My perspective changed. Despite my past, I began to see who I could be in this world. Even though I no longer had a mom and dad, I knew I could make a difference. That's when I decided to continue my parents' legacy, buy the Tourista II, and share Jesus with others. I have to admit something to you, though. You're the first person I've ever told my story to."

"Why me? You've sat on this for fifteen years—why would you choose to tell me?"

"Because you're mad at the world, too. Your trauma eats you alive every day, and you can't see your potential to be someone in this world, because all you can focus on is running from your past."

Josh was quiet, Titus' words sinking deep into his soul.

He'd spoken with such assurance—like there was no doubt in his mind that this was true. And he was right. Looking at Titus now, he never would have guessed his history. Was it possible to overcome all the pain in one's past? It didn't make sense. Titus was rarely angry, never bitter. He was happy and carefree. But how? "I just don't understand how you got past all that and moved on. Something doesn't add up."

Titus laughed. "Keep reading that Book I gave you. If you really want to find the secret, you will. It's all in there."

"Titus?"

"Yeah?"

"I'm a dad."

"Wow, kid, I didn't know."

"Me, either."

Titus sucked in a breath. "How old?"

"Three. A girl. She's beautiful, man. But…" He hesitated, his gut twisting at vocalizing the truth. "…she thinks my dad is her dad."

"I see." Titus prayed over the torture he knew must be wreaking havoc in Josh's heart.

"I don't think my story will have a happy ending like yours."

"Well, son, your story will have whatever ending you choose. There's no such thing as fate—there's only choice."

Josh breathed a heavy laugh. "Yeah, okay. We'll see. I gotta go. Thanks for telling me your story, Titus."

"I'm trusting you'll make the best of it."

"Sure." Josh hung up the phone, wondering what Titus meant by those words.

CALI

"What did he say?" Cali was half in, half out of Jordan's truck, one hand hanging from the overhead bar. She cast Jordan a sly smile as he stared at the phone in his hand.

Jordan sighed and cut his eyes to her before dropping his

phone to the truck's seat and running a hand through his hair. He stared out the windshield, irritation seeping through his bones. "He called you a hooker." Her laughter jarred him, his gaze swinging to the girl he had quickly learned was addictingly insane.

"That's awesome—I've gotta meet this wild card friend of yours." She grinned as she stepped to the ground. Closing the door, she walked his open window and leaned in. "Thanks for a great day, Straight Shooter. I really had a nice time with you." She noted the reservation in his eyes, the way his muscles tensed as he gripped the steering wheel. Without warning, she leaned closer and kissed him soundly on his lips. She lingered, allowing him to get the full effect. She pulled back, hiding her laughter at the shock on his face. "Scoop me up tomorrow?"

"You can't just...you can't..." Jordan stammered as she bounced away from his truck and headed for her front door. "You can't just go around kissing random guys, Cali!" He raised a hand as she opened the door and turned around to grin at him. "Cali?" He called after her, wondering at the way the kiss left him wanting more.

Laughing, she turned and blew him a kiss before disappearing inside. "He's too easy."

"What are you doing hanging out with Jordan Hendricks?"

Cali rolled her eyes at her little brother, brushing past him. "Whatever I want; you need a new hobby."
Though she was two years older, Zion had always felt it his duty to protect his sister. Rushing up the stairs after her, he grabbed her arm before she could disappear into her room. "The guy's a quack, Cali–a total religious freak. Everyone in town knows that. What were you doing with him?"
She glared and pulled her arm from his grasp. "Get a life, Zion!"

"I'll tell Dad," he threatened, raising his chin. "I saw you kissing him."

Her eyes narrowed, and she grabbed a handful of his

shirt, pulling him down to her level. "You tell, and I'll tell him about your little street-racing incident last night. Yeah," she grinned as his eyes grew, "I know all about it, little brother. The whole town's talking about the '67 Mustang that couldn't be beat. It would be a shame for Dad to find out his priceless car was stolen by his idiot son so he could joyride with his buddies, don't you think?"

Zion cleared his throat and yanked his shirt free. His father had a collection of top-notch cars—cars he would kill for. The Mustang was one of the first ten off the factory line. It was irreplaceable. He kicked himself for being so stupid. "You need to stay away from that guy, Cali, before you get sucked into his crazy cult."

Cali shoved him into the hall and slammed the door in his face. One day soon, the threat of her father finding out about her wild ways wouldn't matter so much, but as it was, she needed his money and couldn't risk being cut off. She was already skating on thin ice with him and knew she had to mind her P's and Q's before he lost his temper. Pulling her phone from her pocket, she flung herself across her bed and punched in a number, waiting as the line connected and began to ring.

"Do you have good news for me, darlin'?"

Cali smiled. "Who's your favorite informant?"

"You, by far. How'd it go with Hendricks today? Work him over good?"

"You could say that. We have a second date tomorrow."

"Alright, that's what I'm talkin' about!" Asher laughed in relief. "What'd you get?"

"Well, you know…it was the first day, so…only a location." She waited for it, twirling her hair around her finger.

Asher whooped into her ear. "You kidding me right now, Cali? Where's he at?"

"Well, I don't have an address, but Straight Shooter says he's staying with his dad."

"No, no, no. You've missed something." The

excitement vanished. "Cameron won't go within a hundred yards of his father, let alone stay with him."

"Not his dad, you idiot. Jordan's dad. I have a name, but no address."

"Okay, now we're cookin' with grease. Hit me."

"Levi Hendricks. Saw it in his phone contacts."

"Perfect. It'll only take me a second to pull up that address. Anything else? Is he dating anyone? Visiting anybody?"

"Slow your roll. Like I said, one day. Jordan didn't want to talk about him. Apparently, the two little boys are in a pissing match right now and they're not on speaking terms."

Asher sighed, irritated. "Get them talking. And do it fast. I've got a huge time crunch on this case, Cali."

"Hey, I'm the best, remember?"

"Yeah. Just keep your head on straight and remember the goal."

The line went dead, and she dropped the phone to her bed and stared at the ceiling. The cover of night often gave her one of two things: a shield to hide her sins, or quiet black to smother her in the guilt of her wrongdoings. Tonight, it was the blackness that sat with her. Jordan was such a nice guy. Too trusting and kind-hearted. This world was gonna chew him up and spit him out and here she was aiding the process. She sighed and curled up with her pillow against her chest. She'd have to go easier on him tomorrow—the poor kid had just about died when she'd laid one on him. Fighting the guilt pricking her chest, she whispered into the night air, "No hard feelings, Straight Shooter. A girl's gotta make a livin'." Within minutes, she was fast asleep, the darkness pulling its blanket tightly over her mind and soul.

Chapter 20

"And behold, the woman meets him, dressed as a prostitute, wily of heart."
~Proverbs 7:10~

JOSH

"That cigarette isn't your friend, Josh, no matter how much you want it to be."

Josh's hand froze on the doorknob, his addiction situated between tight lips. Turning, he offered a sheepish smile to the woman wrapped in her bathrobe, sipping her coffee and staring at the book in her lap as though she'd never called him out on his sin. "Mrs. H., it's early. What're you doin' up?" Abandoning the front door, he slowly sat across from her, remembering to pull the cigarette from his mouth and clasp it in his palm before it was tossed into the trash with the others she'd claimed.

"I could ask you the same thing, though I'm pretty certain I already know the answer." She continued reading, her glasses slipping to the end of her nose.

Josh's gaze fell to the book, wondering at the sudden clenching of his chest as he realized she was studying a Bible. He wished he was brave enough to ask her the questions that plagued him, but admitting that he'd started reading the Bible would mean letting his guard down in ways that felt threatening to him.

Finally, Laura raised her head and pulled her glasses from her face, her attention set on Josh. "Have you heard from Jordan?"

Josh averted his gaze. "Ah, no." No need to mention the strange text.

"He's avoiding my calls. Won't answer my texts. I'm thinking of stopping by his place today. Want to come along?"

If only it were that easy… "Nah, Mrs. H., I'm straight. Jordan and I will patch. One day. Maybe. But before I can put any thought into him, I've got some stuff to deal with."

Laura smiled a knowing smile. "She looks like you, you know."

Josh focused on his hands. Were his thoughts that obvious? His mind had been consumed by thoughts of Nevaeh ever since he'd found out about her. "I'd say she looks more like Rhea, and from the stories Mom told me, she acts a lot like me." He grinned at her, pride lighting his eyes.

Laura laughed. "You know she won't be up this early."

He nodded. "Yeah. I know. But Mom always used to get up early. I really need to talk to her about some stuff. I was just gonna head over and see if she'd let me in."

"Of course, she'll let you in. Why would you say something like that?"

Josh's face clouded. "Because of the beat-down I gave my dad yesterday…? Mom's not too happy with me."

"Joshua, you forget your mother watched you go through hell as a child. Don't underestimate her ability to understand your need for revenge. Don't ask her to agree with it, but don't try and make it to where she doesn't understand."

Surprise registered in his eyes, and he sat quietly before standing and bending to kiss her cheek. "Thanks, Mrs. H." Her gaze followed as he limped to the door and pulled it open, cigarette peeking from his palm. "Do you want a ride, sweetie? You look like death."

He shook his head. "I need some air. Besides, maybe by the time I limp my way over there, Nevaeh will be awake." He threw a grin over his shoulder and was gone.

The walk through the woods was painful in more ways than physical. Josh grabbed a large stick to support him as he pushed through the trees and underbrush, each step flooding him with memories. To his left, he could still make out the tree house he and Jordan had built when they were eleven. He shook his head in disbelief that it had weathered all these years, and he found himself wishing Jordan was with him so he could reminisce. At the edge of his parents' property, he stopped by a large oak tree and ran his hand along its bark, searching. His face lit with a smile when his fingers slipped inside a small hole and touched something cold and round. Marbles. It had been his and Jordan's messaging system when either boy had been grounded. One marble meant "See you in a week, pal," two marbles meant "Two weeks a jailbird," and three marbles meant "Totally screwed, man. I'm in deep trouble." Josh's smile faded as he withdrew three marbles and held them in his hand. They were blue and green—his marbles. He'd placed three marbles so often that he'd stashed a fresh set in the bushes to keep on hand. Sighing, he pocketed the marbles, stepped into the backyard, and slowly walked toward the house.

Going over each room of the house in his memory, he remembered his father's bedroom door was closest to the front, and he walked to the back door to avoid waking him. He hadn't come to see him—and if he made an appearance while he was visiting his mom, he intended to block him out and carry on as though he wasn't even there. Josh shoved thoughts of his father out of his head and grunted as he climbed the four porch steps and crossed the deck to the back door. Taking one last, long hit of his cigarette, he willed the nicotine to flood his bloodstream and calm his nerves before smashing the cigarette out and tossing it to the ground. A faint line shone through the curtains, and he mentally begged his mom to talk to him. He softly rapped on the door and held his breath, the walking stick still gripped tightly in his fist.

The curtains were whipped to the side as his mother peered at him. The door swung open, and she stood there, that warm and welcoming smile that always put his mind at ease, set on her face. "Come in," she urged, moving to the side, and offering her hand for support as she led him to the kitchen table. "Coffee?" Elysia asked over her shoulder, already making her way to the coffee pot on the counter.

"Mom, it's me who came to see you—not Jordan." Josh grinned. "You know I don't drink that devil's brew."

She laughed and gripped her mug before joining him at the table. "I wasn't expecting you…here." She watched him, working to read the expression in his eyes.

"Uh, yeah." Josh's gaze held hers, uncertainty sparking in his eyes. "Is…that okay?"

"Of course! Baby, you're always welcome home." His face paled and he coughed to clear the lump in his throat. "I had some pretty intense dreams last night, Mom."

Nightmares were nothing unusual for her son. She couldn't remember a time when he'd had a peaceful dream. Her hand went to his, and she clasped it gently in her fingers. "Tell me."

"I dreamed this kid was screaming for help, only this time I wasn't the kid. This kid was a little girl with blond, curly hair, and she was screaming, 'Save me, Daddy, save me!' Tears rushed his eyes, and he roughly swiped them away. "Mom, it was her. It was my kid. She was screaming for me to rescue her from him. I woke up and tried to clear my head, but when I fell asleep, she was back, and I saw him…I saw him hit her. Just like he hit me."

"Shh, baby." Elysia rubbed the back of his hand, attempting to draw his focus. "He's never touched her, Josh. I promise." Her eyes were locked on his face, his features crumpling under the weight of the thought. "Look at me, son."

His gaze swung to hers.

"Your father has never touched your daughter. Do you hear me?"

He gave a small nod, but his eyes told her he wasn't convinced. "Have you ever found marks on her? Marks of any kind? Bruises he explained away? I remember so many times when he would hit me while you were gone and convince you I'd fallen off my bike or tripped over a log outside. Has there been anything, Mom?"

She sighed and rubbed her eyes. "Josh, when you were growing up, your dad used to drink a twelve-pack—if not more—every night. Not a day went by when I didn't worry myself sick over you. I knew your father would go into a drunken rage and take it out on you every time I had to work the night shift. I don't have those fears with Nevaeh."

"Because she's a girl," Josh said dully.

"No. Because your father hasn't touched a drop of alcohol since she showed up at our door. He threw himself into the Twelve Step Program and saw it through. Any time he was afraid of a relapse, he left the house and went to stay with our pastor until he knew he could control it."

"Because she is a girl, Mom." Josh leaned forward and placed his elbows on the table. "Why else would he suddenly stop drinking? He's sober now? Somebody give the man a medal. Where was all that effort when I was a kid? Why didn't I deserve a sober dad? It wasn't my fault Nilah died, Mom. I didn't take her from him, so why did he take my entire childhood from me?"

Elysia felt the sting of death all over again at the mention of her daughter's name, but there was no time to grieve the past.

Josh stood abruptly to his feet and pressed a hand to his ribs.

"Josh, baby, please don't leave. Please," she quietly pleaded, a hand reaching for his arm—quickly withdrawn when he yanked away from her.

"Why couldn't he love me? What was wrong with me, Mom?" His face twisted as he fought back tears. "You know what? None of that even matters. You know what I wanna know? Why didn't you leave my abuser? Why'd you let him do all that to me? Why'd you keep lying and telling me it would get better? That one day I'd be happy and wouldn't be afraid anymore? Look at me!" He took a quick step forward, hands gesturing to himself as the tears dropped from his cheeks. "I'm not happy. And I'm always afraid, Mama. Can't you see? He did that to me!" Josh trembled as he gestured to his father's closed door. "And you let it happen." He sniffed.

Elysia's heart snapped in two—years of pent-up fear and heartache pouring through her veins as she leaped to her feet and grabbed her boy to her, neither one mindful of his cracked ribs. "There's so much you don't know, Josh. So much I couldn't explain to you back then. I couldn't leave. As much as I wanted to, as many times as I tried. I couldn't."

"Why, Mom? Wasn't I more important than being with him? Aren't you supposed to love your kids more?"

"And that's exactly why I couldn't leave, baby." Elysia pulled free and gently sat him back in his chair before sitting across from him. "Your dad was a powerful man back then. I knew if I tried to leave, he'd fight me in court for you and win. And if he won, Josh, you would've been dead by now. The only way to keep you alive was to do what he said. Go to work, help pay the bills and stay out of his way. I went to work every day knowing I could come home, and you'd be gone—either dead or ditched somewhere I would never find you."

Josh swallowed hard, rocking in his seat. The fears of his childhood melded with his mother's fears and threatened to undo him. "I'll kill him," he promised, knowing in his heart he'd do it the first chance he got.

She shook her head firmly, her eyes glistening. "No, son. Your father is a good man now. He lives with the pain of his choices every day. He hates himself for who he was. For what he did to you—to us. But he's not that man anymore."

"No!" He stood, startling her. "Enough! First Titus, now you?" He looked at her in disgust. "That's not how life works, Mom. You don't get to be a monster your whole life and then decide one day that you're gonna be a better person. Guess what? I know I'm a monster, but I'm not duped into thinking I'll magically get better one day. No one can change me—not you, not me, not Titus, and not Jesus. I am who I am, and that sorry excuse of a man in there," his finger stabbed the air toward his father's bedroom, "is who he is, and he will never change. Get that? He'll never be a better man, because he's a monster. That's who he is. And you bet your life he's gonna get what's comin' to him. I'll make sure of that." Yanking his stick from where it was propped on the wall, Josh limped for the door and pulled it open. "I'll have to catch my daughter another time."

With a heavy sigh, Elysia watched him walk out and slam the door behind him.

HIGHSHORE BAPTIST CHURCH - PRAYER GROUP

"You'll never believe who's back in town." The elderly woman leaned forward in her seat; her Bible opened to the third chapter in James. The women of Highshore Baptist Church met every Wednesday morning for Bible study. During the two hours each week, gossip brewed thicker than the coffee settling in their mugs while Bibles lay neglected until the coffee grew cold.

"Is it Ollie Holton? I knew I saw him the other day at the bank." Claire Burke shook her head and tapped the Bible in her lap. "If the good LORD hadn't said to hold our tongues, I would have let him have it. The nerve of leaving his poor wife and kids to chase after that hot young thing on his arm!"

"No, no. I'll bet she's talkin' about Shana Kay. You all know why Shana Kay would be back in town." Sarah Flowers raised her brow, the wrinkles drooping in waves down her cheeks.

"Mmm-hmm…" The women nodded in unison, each one shaking her gray head.

"If you all will shush, I'll tell you who it is." Edith Jemson glowered behind her wide-framed glasses. It was her turn to host, and she took it personally when others tried to upstage her in her own home. "It's the Cameron boy, that's who." A collective gasp sounded around the room as the women gaped at her. She smiled behind her mug as she sipped her coffee, pleased that she'd dropped a solid bombshell on the gossip-starved group.

"Edith, you must be mistaken," clucked Hannah Lager. "You know he committed the awful sin. You know," she leaned forward, her wrinkled hand cupping her mouth, "suicide."

"Now that's just gossip, Hannah. Don't spread rumors, it isn't right," chided Sarah. "Edith, tell us what you know. Of course," she added, fidgeting in her chair as though feeling God's eyes on her, "so we can pray for the poor boy."

"Well, I was out buying my weekly groceries when he passed by the store. He looked right at me—and I know he remembers who I am because I used to catch him putting that devil's scrawl all over my fence when he was no more than thirteen years old. He knows good and well who I am." She nodded in earnest. "He looked right at me and didn't say not one word to me, or any of the others standing there. Not even a nod of his head for a hello."

"It's true! I saw him out running the town with Levi Hendricks yesterday!" Yvette Williams chimed in, her Bible slipping to the floor. "You know why he's come, Edith." Her brows curved upwards; her lips pinched into a tight frown.

"I do." Edith nodded, though she didn't; but she wasn't about to be upstaged in her own home.

"He's come for that baby, that's what."

"After all these years!" Polly Sanders gasped indignantly.

"It's a shame. No child should have to live with a heathen for a father. You do know why he left town, don't you?" Edith glanced around the room. "He was sneakin' around behind his poor parents' backs, runnin' around with every girl in Highshore. That's a fact."

"Nearly put his poor sweet mother in the grave. That boy never did know how to act. Always runnin' the streets, doin' exactly as he pleased." Sarah shook her head. "Saddest thing I've ever seen. His hard-working daddy did everything he could to give him a good life. Disgraceful."

"We need to be sure to lock our doors with him in

town," Polly worried her lower lip. "You do remember how the law was always catching him breaking in and stealing whatever he could get his hands on!"

"Oh, dear, you're right, Polly. I'd forgotten that. He can't be trusted to care for a child; someone ought to do something!" Claire gripped her coffee mug with white-knuckled hands.

"Surely Garrett won't allow this tragedy to occur. He's always been such a good, God-fearing man." Sara shook her head, sadly.

The clock above the mantle chimed the new hour, drawing Edith's attention. "Well, ladies, let's take a moment to pray over all we've learned and read over the taming of the tongue. Chapter three..."

NICHOLE

Nichole adjusted her Armani shades and looped her purse strap over her shoulder as she stepped onto the pavement. With a swift flick, she closed her car door, her bangle bracelets clinking. Her lips had been stained the color of cranberries; her high cheekbones accentuated by a blush too pink for her fair skin. The sun beat down its afternoon rays, causing the woman to despise the California summer. With severe strides, she marched to the Farmer's Market booth and browsed the local goods. Not one to subject her delicate body to trash from diners and fast-food joints, she perused the produce carefully, searching for the perfect fruits and vegetables for her lunch.

"Half off the cantaloupe if you buy a watermelon." The farmer offered her a friendly smile, his teeth darkened by years of enjoying too much chewing tobacco.

She smiled smugly at the round man, repulsed by his sweaty bald head and overalls that desperately needed to be washed. "Do I look like the type of woman who needs to purchase items at half price?"

His smile faltered, his beefy hands grabbing the straps of his overalls as he averted his eyes. "Uh, no ma'am. I only meant to—"

"Excuse me, I'll take a pound of grapes. Full price." Nichole's nose angled upward, and she crossed her arms impatiently as he gaped at her. "Well, get to it!"

"Yes, ma'am." The man quickly moved to gather the grapes, keeping his head down as he worked.

She perused the impressive produce he had to offer, thinking there wasn't a town within 500 miles that could outdo the crops of Highshore. She was busy admiring a shiny bushel of apples when she heard her name called. Glancing up, she groaned at the sight of Edith Jemson rushing toward her.

"Nichole, Nichole!" Edith breathlessly approached, her graying hair wildly escaping the bun tied on her head.

Great. Just what I need. The town's biggest gossip keeping me from my day. A tolerant smile flickered on her face like a light bulb giving up on its will to shine. "Edith. I was just leaving." She snatched the bag of grapes from the farmer's hand and pressed a crisp $20 bill at him.

Edith picked up her pace and followed Nichole to her car. "I saw you from across the street and just had to come tell you."

Nichole opened the car door and placed her bag inside.

"Edith, I haven't the time for idle gossip. I have a very busy schedule to keep and really must be going. Good day."

"Oh, but you simply must know!" Encouraged when the other woman paused to listen, she continued, eyes wide. "Garrett's boy is back in town, and word's out that he's come for that little granddaughter of yours. It's a cryin' shame, it is, what, with his reputation and all."

Nichole's body tensed, and she slammed the car door closed, stepping abruptly toward the older woman. "Excuse me?" Surely this old hag had no idea what she was talking about. Highshore had so much gossip, one could easily be led to believe it had rained lollipops and gumdrops. After all, hadn't Asher confirmed that Josh had been locked up?

Edith beamed at the shock written on Nichole's face. Her head bobbed, her plump cheeks jiggling like two bowls of Jell-O. "I saw the boy, myself. And Yvette heard his intentions with her own ears." She leaned closer, her hand providing a cover for her words. "If you ask me, I say he's aiming to rip her from Elysia's arms and run off with her like he tried to do with your Rhea."

Nichole bristled. "Edith, how long has that boy been back in my town?" *Of all the ignorant imbeciles I could've chosen to handle my business, I had to pick Asher!* Her perfect teeth clenched at the thought.

"Maybe a couple days or so. Got the whole town afraid." She nodded matter-of-factly.

Nichole's face twisted into a sinister scowl as she jerked her car door open and climbed behind the wheel, leaving the old gossip alone on the sidewalk. She didn't care one bit about the child—she'd wanted nothing to do with her since before she was born. But she refused to allow him access to the little girl. If her daughter refused to step up and be a parent, she would have to take matters into her own hands. Time to play the part of the doting grandmother. She slammed the car into reverse and peeled from the parking lot. "It will be a cold day in hell when I allow Joshua Cameron to get his hands on my flesh and blood."

Chapter 21

"If you are wise, you are wise for yourself; if you scoff, you alone will bear it."
~Proverbs 9:12~

JORDAN

"So, this is where the straight shooter reads his Bible and says his prayers." Cali's gaze roamed Jordan's living room, laughing when he flinched at her sarcasm. This guy really needed to lighten up… "Not a bad bachelor pad." She grinned. Stepping closer to the pictures displayed on the wall, she studied each one. "Who's the kid?" Her finger traced the outline of Nevaeh, frozen on the beach. "That's Josh's kid. Cute, isn't she?" Jordan smiled before disappearing into his room.

The two had stopped by his apartment so he could grab a clean shirt. An interview had gone south when the informant threw at him instead of answering questions. As he dug through his drawer for a fresh T-shirt, his stomach flipped with nerves as he recalled the lecture he'd endured from Rachel when she'd discovered the truth about the Haulbrook story. After reaming him out, she'd demanded the two wrap things up, and was not subtle in letting Jordan know he was in the doghouse. He anticipated at least a month of meaningless assignments with rookie reporters.

Grabbing a shirt, he shut the drawer with a sigh. "So, the wild card has a kid, huh? Bet he's a fun dad." Cali's voice dripped with sarcasm.

Jordan pulled his shirt off, unaware that Cali had wandered into his room behind him and was watching him from the door. "He doesn't know about her. And if he did," he pulled the shirt over his head, "he'd be a terrible father."

As soon as the words were out of his mouth, he recognized the bitterness charging them. Conviction slammed his heart. Who was he to badmouth his best friend? He turned to head back to the living room, stopping cold at the sight of Cali leaning against the door frame. "Cali, I uh didn't realize you'd come in. I was changing…"

Laughter exploded from her lips as she pushed off from the door and went to him, placing herself inches from his body. "You tryin' to tell me a girl's never seen your naked chest, Straight Shooter? You're more pathetic than I thought!"

Jordan blushed and snatched the soda-streaked shirt from the floor, tossing it into the laundry basket. "I don't usually have girls at my house. That's all." He walked to the door, aware she didn't follow. Pausing, he turned and stared hard. "Come on, Cali. We have work to do." He was not going down that road. Not with her. Not with anyone. His morals and commitment to Christ meant far more to him than some red-headed chick looking for a thrill.

"Come on, Jordan," she teased, "Aren't you just a little bit curious?" She toyed with the hem of her shirt, grinning when his eyes fixated on the skin of her flat abdomen. His heart thumped wildly, and his breathing quickened. "Rachel's waiting," he managed around the lump in his throat before turning for the living room.

A knock at the door sent his heart leaping from his chest. His eyes flew to his security camera. Dread filled his bones as he recognized the visitor. "Mom." Jordan's knees went weak. What would she say when she found Cali here? What would she think? She'd be so disappointed in him. "Um, Cali, could you stay here for a sec? I got to handle something." Assuming she would honor his request, Jordan opened the door and came face to face with the woman he respected more than any other. "Hey, Mama." He reached for her, grateful when she returned his embrace. It felt good to have some connection to the family he loved, even if he was still angry with his father.

"You've been ignoring me," Laura stated, stepping through the door and closing it behind her. She regarded her son with curious eyes, knowing in her heart something deep in his soul had shifted. "I haven't seen you since you left for Florida. Anything you wanna talk about, baby?" Jordan stared at her, his mind working to come up with an answer that would ease her mind and get her off his scent. "Ah, no. Nothing comes to mind." His hand went to the nape of his neck, a tell-tale sign he was lying.

Laura squinted her eyes at him, noting the gesture. She knew her son well. Making choices that bucked his conscience had never been easy, and he was a terrible liar. Deciding not to press—yet—she patted his arm and smiled. "Okay. But remember, just because you're mad at your father doesn't mean you're mad at me. I still want to talk to my son. I want to see you. Understood?"

"Yeah, Mama." He offered a small smile, knowing he wasn't fooling her. Movement from his bedroom door caught his eye, and he gasped when Cali emerged—shorts tight and cut above her pockets, crop top parading what the good Lord gave her. His eyes snapped to hers, desperation written all over his face, exasperated when she flashed him that smile and turned her full attention to his mom.

"Hi, I'm Cali, Jordan's girlfriend," she said, extending a hand to Laura. "What an honor to meet Straight Shooter's mom! I just adore your son!" She went up on tiptoe and planted a kiss on his jaw.

Shocked, Laura shook the hand offered, her eyes scanning the girl before swinging to her son. The misery painted across his features told her all she needed to know, and she fought the sinking feeling in her gut that he'd done something he would forever regret.

"She's not—Cali, you're not my—" Desperation seized him, and he dropped his eyes to the floor. Was she his girlfriend? Wasn't that what he wanted? "Say something, Mom," he urged, his tone quiet and pleading.

Laura stared at him, her heart and mind at war. Her mind reminded her of his age, while her heart pushed her to slap him into next week. "Can I talk to you outside?"

"Uh, we were just headed back to work. I'm—we're—

covering this really important story downtown, and Rachel is expecting us back any minute."

Laura crossed her arms, noting how he quickly stepped out of her reach. "I see. So, you're working today."

"Sure are!" Cali sidled up to Jordan and looped her arm through his, smiling and popping her gum.

"And you just, what, decided to make a quick stop to bang?"

Jordan's jaw dropped and Cali burst into laughter. "Mom!"

"Don't you 'Mom' me, young man!" Laura advanced on the two, backing them into the wall. "Does your boss know she's paying you to play around?"

Jordan shook his head in disbelief. How was this his life right now? "Mom, it's not like that!" Glancing at Cali, he yanked his arm from her grip and stepped to the right, putting distance between them.

"The appearance of evil, Jordan Blayze. Ring a bell? If it looks like a fish and smells like a fish, it's a fish!"

"Mom, you don't understand. I just needed to change my shirt!" He held out his hands, tears stinging his eyes.

"Yeah, all I did was watch," Cali added, her innocent tone sending Laura over the edge.

"Cali," Jordan hissed, his eyes on his mother.

"You may think you're slick, little miss thang, but I know your type. You're nothing but trouble. You don't care one bit about this boy. You're gonna use him, abuse him, and spit him out like chopped liver. You won't give two thoughts about what happens to him when you're through with him. And you!" She swung her eyes to her son, fire flashing. "You're stupid enough to let her do it! Don't expect me to stand by and watch it happen, Jordan. You know where to find me." She stormed to the door and yanked it open. "'Mom, I was just changing my shirt,'" she imitated her son as she stepped outside. "As though I was born yesterday!"

"Mom, come on, it's me! You know I don't play around like that!" Jordan followed her outside, vaguely aware of

Cali trailing behind.

"No, you used to not play around like that. I don't know what to expect from you lately. Cutting your father off, letting your best friend stay mad at you without even trying to fix it, ignoring your mother, and now her!" Laura pulled open her car door and climbed inside. "You'd better come to your senses, Jordan Blayze, and you'd better do it before you bring me a child to raise!"

Speechless, Jordan watched her drive off. He felt Cali wrap her fingers around his arm and he jerked free of her touch, taking a step backward. "Knock it off, Cali!" he snapped, his brows knit angrily. "This is all your fault! Why'd you come out of the bedroom? I told you not to come out of the bedroom! Now my mom thinks I'm sleeping with you!"

He was fun to play with. She enjoyed seeing him freaked out over his mother's opinions of him. But she knew it was time to stop jerking him around and start playing hardball before her chance to get to Josh got away. Cali placed a hand on her hip and frowned. "Maybe you can help me understand why you care so much about what your mom thinks of your decisions. I mean, you are twenty-one years old, aren't you?"

Jordan glared at her. "I care about what she thinks because she's my mother. It's called respect. You should try it sometime." He stared in the direction his mom had gone and found himself wishing for the courage to go after her.

"Jordan, your parents totally run your life. Don't you see that?" She cocked her head up at him, her eyes boring into his.

"No, they don't," he argued, but the seed had been planted and was spreading its roots looking for water.

"Yes. They do. Think about it. Your dad upset you so much that you haven't spoken to him since the argument. Your mom comes down here, lording it over your head like you owe him, then accuses you of wrong when you haven't even done anything! She wouldn't even listen to you explain. Like, she could really be telling people she caught you in bed with me just now. Your dad? Josh? I mean, are you just gonna let this stuff fly? When will you own your life and make them recognize you're not a kid anymore? You really need Mommy's permission to date me? If so, find yourself another chick to play, because I don't date little boys."

Jordan leaned against his truck and gave her a hard stare, considering all she'd just said. She had a point, even if it did sting. He'd allowed his parents to control his life. His father checking up on him? Making sure he'd be in a pew on Sunday? Even his best friend had cast judgments on Cali—calling her a hooker without even knowing her. Who did he think he was?

"Straight Shooter," Cali called, unnerved by the look in his brown eyes.

Jordan pushed off the truck and brushed past her as he went for the driver's door. He needed to think and couldn't do that with her around. "Get in, Cali," he ordered. "I'm taking you home."

ASHER

Asher sat in his office and stared at the address in his hand. "Got you, you little devil." A grin pulled at his mouth. He placed the paper on his desk as his gaze drifted to the windows overlooking the sea of desks in the department. His cops and detectives milled about, each busy with their assigned duties—oblivious of their captain's current investigation. He sighed and reached for a cigarette. He wasn't supposed to smoke in here, but who was going to stop him? He lit up and took a long draw, blowing the smoke at the ceiling before his fingers tapped the address into his computer.

"Levi Hendricks," he breathed. "Not even ten miles from the station. Easy bust." But how? Josh had already been busted for drugs—could he pull it off a second time? Highshore knew his rep. They might not buy it. Then, again…he wasn't a well-liked kid…who would care if a cop found drugs on him? He ran a hand down his face as he stared at the address.

From his desk drawer, his burner phone rang, interrupting his thoughts and causing his blood to run cold. Fishing it out, he took a deep breath before answering.

"Yeah." He gritted his teeth around the cigarette in his mouth, hating the fear in his voice.

"Either you are incredibly stupid, or you think I am incredibly stupid. Either way, it seems you are highly underestimating my ability to destroy you. Why am I just now finding out—from gossip, no less!— that Joshua Cameron is roaming free in my town?" Nichole's voice was stone.

Asher swallowed hard. How was it that she was always one step ahead of him? "I just found out," he lied. "I'm all over it—staring at the address he's crashing at right now. He's staying with his best friend's dad. I have an informant working the friend over as we speak."

Nichole laughed, a sure sign that his demise was pending. "I expect you to know his moves before he makes them. You should have seen this coming! My daughter is living mere miles from here, and now that gangbanger is back in my town. I'm sure you see my dilemma here.is back home. You still haven't given me a location for Rhea. She could run into him at any given moment, and I swear to you, Asher Holmes, if that happens, you will rue the day you were born."

"I have an idea where she is. I just haven't been able to confirm yet. I'll let you know as soon as I can—you have my word." Panic crept up the back of his neck.

"Listen to me, and you listen well. Go get my daughter. And when you have her, bring her directly to me. I don't care how it's done; just make it happen. If she isn't with me by the end of the week, I will end you. Your name will be in the papers so fast it'll make your head spin. Do we understand each other?" She breathed heavily into the phone. "Ty has a game tonight, doesn't he? I'll have to stop by and give him some…love."

The panic wrapped began to choke him. Asher's hand flew to his throat as he gasped for air, the cigarette slipping from his mouth. He stomped a boot on the butt, stifling the embers. "Stay away from my kid, Nichole." His heavy gasps squelched his attempt to sound threatening.

She laughed. "Don't worry—once the truth comes out, Ty will realize what a scumbag his father is. He'll eventually adjust to the gossip and hate speech they'll throw at him. He might choose the crime life—after all, it's what his father showed him. I'm merely the concerned citizen who wants a little boy to know the truth about his daddy. He deserves to know; don't you agree, Asher?"

"Nichole, don't," Asher croaked, tears stinging his eyes.

"Goodbye, Daddy Dearest."

The line went dead, and Asher fell to his knees.

JOSH

"Go back."

Josh cursed. "Did you hear what I just said?" Inhaling his cigarette, he flicked the ashes to the sidewalk.

"Yeah, I did." Titus kept his voice level. "You're wrong, kid."

Josh gritted his teeth. Titus didn't understand. If he'd heard the conversation firsthand, he'd be taking Josh's side. "How am I supposed to let this go, man? My mom thinks he's a saint, and the prick is raising my daughter!"

"Right. And you left the house without even laying eyes on your kid, so can we really point fingers here?"

"That's not fair."

"Isn't it, though? You expected your mom to make better choices for you as a kid. Now that you're grown, you feel she's defending the choices she made, and it's upsetting to you. I get that. But none of this is that little girl's fault. So, take your self-righteous butt back to your mom's front door, and go see your kid."

Josh breathed a sigh. "I don't know what to say to her,

Titus."

"And now we're getting to the root of the issue. You're scared, and that's okay. But don't take that out on your mom; she doesn't deserve that."

Josh remained quiet as he wrestled with his heart. He knew Titus was right. So now what was he supposed to do? "She's scared of me," he admitted.

"Your mom?" Titus asked, surprised.

"No. My kid."

"She doesn't know you. You're a stranger to her. Give it time, son."

"I, uh, kinda beat my father to a pulp in front of her."

"Ah…" Titus took this in, adjusting the advice up his sleeve. "God is a redeemer of all things, Josh. He brought you back home so you could meet your daughter. He's gotten you this far, now trust Him to take you all the way."

Josh rolled his eyes and cursed. "Enough with the riddles, man! What does that even mean—'He brought me back home?' Man, Jordan dragged me here—against my will!"

Titus sighed. "Been reading that Book?" When no answer came, he continued. "Read the Book, Josh. Things will start to make sense, I promise."

"Yeah, okay. I've got a kid to traumatize. I gotta go."

"Josh?"

"Yeah?"

"You can do this. You are not your father."

Josh stared vacantly at the trees; his cigarette poised between his lips. Titus' words hit him deep, knocking the wind from his lungs. "Uh, yeah. Thanks." He disconnected the call and pocketed his phone. Taking one last hit of the cigarette, he snuffed it out on the concrete and changed his direction.

The walk back to his parents' home was slow and painful. He knew he was pushing his body past its limits, but he didn't care. As he walked, he thought about how he might approach getting to know Nevaeh. Doubts came from all angles as he ran scenarios through his head, each ending in the little girl screaming in terror and begging his mother to keep her away from the scary man. He stepped into the yard and headed straight for the rose bushes his mother loved and tended each year. Carefully picking the best one he could find; he withdrew his pocket knife and cut it from its branch before heading to the porch. Standing to the side—just out of sight of the window—he gently rapped on the door and waited. The door opened just a crack as his mom peeked out and he extended the rose, placing it inches from her face. He smiled when she took it, laughing when she cried, "Who's there?"

"It's me, Mom." He came into view and offered a smile. "Told you I'm a jerk…"

Elysia stared at her son, twirling the rose in her fingers. "Yes. Yes, you are. Shame on you for running out on me like that," she scolded, but there was no lecture in her voice—only relief. "Come here, you." She reached for him, giving him a gentle hug as she pulled him through the door. "What brought you back?"

Josh thought about his answer as he sat down at the kitchen table. "Took the advice of a friend."

She raised an eyebrow, placing the rose in a cup of water before joining him. Josh didn't take anyone's advice. She welcomed this new sign of maturity in her boy. "Well, I'm glad you did. Nevaeh is in the living room watching Looney Tunes. Do you want to see her?"

Josh's features paled, but he nodded. "Yeah, I do."

He followed her into the living room, his eyes falling on the little girl captivated by the colorful bunnies on TV. Her tangled curls were everywhere—so much hair. Dressed in an oversized t-shirt, as though she'd just crawled out of bed, Nevaeh was the cutest little girl he'd ever seen. He stayed by the doorway, too afraid of spooking her to get any closer. He watched as his mother tapped her on the shoulder and made a face, causing his daughter to erupt in lilting giggles and exclaim "Mommy!" as she covered her small mouth with her hands.

Elysia scooped her up, keeping her back to Josh as she

spoke. "Someone's here to see you, baby girl."

Nevaeh squealed. "Who is it? Who? Who?"

"I want you to listen carefully to me, okay?" Elysia's eyes were serious as the little girl bobbed her head. "You remember the boy who hit Daddy, and Mommy told you that boy had a big owie in his heart?"

Josh winced and looked away.

"I don't like him," Nevaeh whimpered.

"You don't like what he did, but you don't know him, baby." Elysia's eyes found her son's, and her heart moved with compassion over the sorrow in his gaze. "He came to say sorry." She gave him a pointed look, satisfied when he offered a nod in return. "He'd like to speak with you now. Is that okay?"

Nevaeh stared at her before raising her chin, stubbornly. "No. I don't like him. He's a bully."

Elysia sighed and gave her a gentle squeeze. "I understand how you feel, baby. How about this—Mommy will hold you the whole time he's here. That way you can feel safe. Will that work?"

"No bullies. We don't play with bullies. 'Member?" Elysia inwardly groaned as her words came back to her. "Yes. I remember. We won't play with him unless you want to, okay? Now, he's come to say sorry, and it's the right thing to do to listen to his apology. We're going to sit down with him for a minute and let him apologize."

Josh watched his daughter cross her arms over her chest, surprised when she squeezed her eyes shut tight and refused to open them as his mother carried her to the couch and sat down, motioning for him to join them. He chose a chair opposite the two and slowly sat, looking to his mom for direction. When she merely nodded and smiled, he sighed, knowing he was on his own.

"Hi, Nevaeh." His voice cracked when he spoke, and he cleared his throat before continuing. "Uh, can I talk to you for a second?"

Her arms tightened across her chest, eyes squeezing tighter as her face scrunched from the effort.

"Okay…" Josh shifted in his seat and dropped his gaze to the floor.

"You hurt my daddy."

His eyes shot up, surprised to find her staring right at him, not an ounce of fear in her gaze. Instead, there was ferocity, and he recognized himself, wondering at the way his heart pained at that thought instead of swelling with pride. "Um, yeah. I did. I hurt your…daddy." He closed his eyes, nearly choking on the word. "I'm really sorry that I hit him." His voice rang with sincerity. It was true—he was immensely sorry for attacking his father in front of her. But that was the only thing he was sorry for. The attack was well-deserved. The prick had it comin', and he couldn't wait to give him some more.

"Daddy was bleeding," Nevaeh stated, her three-year-old voice pinning him to his chair. "And that was all your fault. You made a bad choice. You know choices have consinces." Her green eyes regarded him as though he was scum.

Josh raised an eyebrow at his mother. "'Consinces?'" he mouthed.

She smiled. "Consequences. Choices have consequences."

"Ah." He nodded and turned his attention back to his daughter. "Yes, they do. Like I said, I'm sorry I hit him. Do you forgive me?"

She smirked at him—his sweet little firecracker smirked at him. He shifted beneath her gaze.

"Sorry doesn't fix. It's just a band-aid for an owie." Josh looked at his mom and raised both hands, at a loss for how to mend things with his small negotiator. Hiding a smile, she raised an eyebrow at him, urging him to try a different approach. Scanning the room, his eyes fell on a bucket of Mega Blocks near the fireplace, and he lowered himself to the floor, ignoring the sudden stab of pain in his ribs. Though he felt Nevaeh's eyes on him, he didn't dare look at her for fear of losing her interest. Memories of castles and forts built by Jordan and himself in times past flooded his mind, and he quickly got to work, intent on constructing the best castle he could with the bulky blocks. It took him about five minutes to realize there was a huge difference between Legos and Mega Blocks. Try as he might, he could not manipulate the blocks like he wanted to, and frustration was mounting. This was getting ridiculous. Why was it so hard to make a decent castle with these large blocks?

"Oh, this is too, too much!"

Josh's head snapped up at the sound of her voice—far too bold and powerful for such a tiny body. He waited with rapt attention for whatever she might say next. Her eyes were focused on her grandmother's as she spoke, her little hands outstretched in exasperation.

"First, he hits my daddy, and now he's playing with my toys! And to make things worser and worser, he's doing it all wrong! Mommy, please! Make this boy leave my house!" She threw her head back and covered her eyes with the back of her hand in dramatic flair.

Shocked, Josh stared at her and then his mother, erupting in laughter. He quickly realized his mistake when she promptly exploded in a torrent of tears, her fair skin turning bright red as she wailed. "Great, I broke her," he muttered, his surprise growing as she grew louder with each breath.

Elysia's mouth twitched as she fought the smile threatening, regarding the little drama queen in her arms. "You didn't break her, that's your daugh—" She stopped herself, catching her breath as she quickly redirected. "That's just Nevaeh being Nevaeh. She's fine. It'll pass, just like always."

Josh cocked his head to one side, his stomach flipping from nerves. "She, um, she does this a lot?" What was he getting himself into?

The smile broke free, lighting her eyes as she laughed. "All the time, son. She's what most people would label as a 'threenager'."

"A three—a threenager." He repeated, connecting the

dots. "Ah, I get it." He laughed. Deciding to attempt another approach, he placed a block awkwardly on top of another, making the castle look even more defeated. Sighing dramatically, he played her pride. "I sure wish someone smart would come down here and show me how to do this. The king really needs a castle to live in—he's out here in the cold all alone." He shook his head in despair, deciding to kick it up a notch. He grabbed the king and matched his daughter's wailing. "I have no place to live! And this stupid villager doesn't know how to build me a castle!"

Nevaeh's torrents stopped, her focus now on her father. She watched as he made the king run around the carpet with his hands in the air, shouting at random plastic people to find him a builder who knew what she was doing. Her eyes flashed to her grandmother, then back to Josh. One fist wrapping around her grandmother's shirt, she slid off her lap and stood, staring, as Josh pretended to build. Rolling her eyes, she sighed. "No, not that block. It's too little. You need the one with the three bumps. No! That one! Ugh! Put it there, on the peerple one!"

Peerple. Josh held his laughter, thinking he'd never seen a cuter kid than her. He picked the king up and held it out toward Nevaeh. "Will you show this boy how to make me a castle, little girl?" He winked at his mother, noting how she was working to hide her laughter.

Nevaeh raised her chin, her eyes shifting from the king to her father, then back again. "Not until he 'poligizes to my daddy."

Josh froze, his heart pounding as though trying to beat free of its cage. He swallowed hard, feeling his mother's eyes on him, waiting. "Uh, yeah. Of course." His daughter's eyes were on him again, pinning him to the floor.

"It's your consinces. But 'member, sorry doesn't fix. You have to change your 'havior. Keep your hands to yourself."

Josh glanced at Elysia before dropping his eyes to the

floor. "Right. I think I've learned my lesson."

"You have to go do it now," she urged.

His eyes flew to his father's closed door. "Well, um, right now he's sleeping. We probably shouldn't wake him up. But I'll apologize as soon as I see him again, okay?"

"You better," she grumbled. She released Elysia's shirt and dropped to her knees. Grabbing a block with three bumps, she stacked it on top of another before grabbing three more and doing the same. "Look, like this."

He watched as she manipulated the blocks like a pro. He had to give her props—her castle outdid his attempts. Score one point for the baby, and zero points for the new dad.

Mental eye roll.

"Thank you, little girl! Now I have a home!" Josh grabbed the king and made him dance across the floor and into the castle, his heart warming when she laughed. Sitting back on her haunches, Nevaeh looked at him, hard. "What's your name, boy?"

Josh's eyes flew to his mother. Who was he? Josh? Brother? Daddy? Friend? He sighed.

"This is Jordan's best friend." Elysia came to his rescue, smiling when he relaxed.

Nevaeh's eyes lit up. "Jordan? I love Jordan! He's my best friend—he's not a bully." She scrunched her nose. "I need to talk to him about his choice of friends." There went those arms again, tossed across her chest as though she was queen.

Josh caught himself just staring at her, soaking her up. So much Rhea. So much himself. This little beauty who knew who she was yet had no idea. Would she want him? Would she accept him? Could he even pull off this whole dad bit? Watching her play with her new castle, he suddenly realized what he'd promised her. He had to apologize to his father for beating him to a pulp. Somehow, even though he still had zero regrets for what he'd done, being with her weakened his resolve for revenge. He was sure he'd agree to be best friends with his dad if it meant time with her. He could get used to this…

JORDAN

Jordan's conscience wouldn't ease up. No matter how loud he blasted the music in his truck, no matter what he focused his eyes on as he drove, all he knew was the burning conviction of the Holy Spirit in his chest. There was no doubt God was directing him away from Cali, but he wasn't ready to listen.

He was on a new assignment from Rachel—sans Cali. He could not have been more relieved to accept a story, especially one in Lambert, an hour's drive from wherever she might be.

Weary from his internal battle, Jordan turned down Selma Road and pulled into a gas station. Parking the truck at pump six, he pulled the keys from the ignition and went inside to pay for his gas and grab a cool drink.

His eyes scanned the choices of beverages, lingering on the beer aisle as he snatched a Big Red soda from the fridge. He'd never tasted alcohol. More out of respect for all Josh had gone through than for his conscience's sake. Shrugging off the sudden urge to buy a beer, he sighed and went to the counter to pay, uninterested in the small talk the cashier was attempting to exchange.

"Yeah, you have a good day too." He nodded to her and walked out the door.

Unlocking the truck, he tossed his soda inside and headed for the gas nozzle. He took in the beauty around him as he waited for his tank to fill. Lambert was known for its deep green grasses and towering trees—a perfect canopy of shade surrounding the city. The sight filled his heart with pain, shame washing over him again. God's majesty was all around him—evidence of His great love for all—yet he battled with the Spirit, testing the limits to see what he could get away with.

The gas pump clicked, startling him. Shaking the remaining drops into his tank, Jordan returned the nozzle and glanced at the pump beside him. His heart leaped in his chest, and he froze.

A woman stood pumping gas into her small car. Across from her, standing beside the passenger door, was Rhea. She looked different than he remembered, but he was sure it was her. His pulse quickened. Should he talk to her? Tell her that Josh had come home? Did he dare interfere in his friend's life—again? He saw her glance his way and quickly ducked out of sight, peeking through the columns. I have to talk to her. What if this is Josh's only chance to reconnect? Screw the fact the two weren't talking—this was his best friend's girl. This was major. His breathing grew heavy, and he clenched his fists, hating his indecisiveness. Just do it already, Jordan. He walked to the side of the pump and awkwardly smiled when the woman pumping her gas glared at him.

"Just what do you think you're doin', creep?" Chloe replaced the nozzle and snapped her gas cap shut, her hand reaching for the mace she kept on her keychain. "Back up, punk. I know how to use this," she warned.

Jordan held out his hands, eyes wide. "No need for the mace—I just wanna say hi to my friend, that's all." When Chloe's brow shot up and she turned to Rhea, he smiled awkwardly, shifting his focus to the girl regarding him as though she'd seen a ghost. "Hey, Rhea, how's it going?"

Rhea stood still—her eyes haunted. Even with his shades, she recognized him—and it terrified her. She cleared her throat and shifted nervously. "Do I know you?"

Jordan's heart sank and his smile faltered. He knew she recognized him. He could see it all over her face. Why was she pretending she didn't know him? "Yeah, you know me. I'm Josh's best friend, Jordan. Remember? We used to hang together all the time…"

She shook her head, turning slightly away as she tried to hide her tears. "You have the wrong girl. I'm sorry."

Chloe watched the exchange, her eyebrows knit with confusion. She'd seen the recognition on her friend's face and wondered at her denial. "Rhea," she urged, only to find herself on the receiving end of a fierce glare.

Jordan cast a sideways glance at Chloe and ventured further. "Rhea, Josh is home. He really misses you. If you'd like, I could maybe give you his number. Or you could give me yours so he could call."

She spun to face him, anger flashing in her eyes. "Look, I said you have the wrong girl. I don't know you, okay? And I certainly don't know anyone named Josh. Come on, Chloe, let's go." Rhea climbed inside the car and slammed the door.

Chloe hesitated before joining her, torn between staying out of it or slipping this stranger Rhea's number. Her eyes rested on his face, noting the conflict in his features. With a helpless shrug, she left it alone and got into her car. Dumbfounded, Jordan stared after them as they drove away. About to pray for guidance, he quickly changed his mind as his conscience reminded him of his sins. No, God didn't want to hear from him. And, if he was being honest, he didn't want to hear from God. His focus returned to Rhea. Maybe if she saw how much Josh longed for her, she'd come home. Climbing behind the wheel, he started the engine and let it idle while he thought about his next move. Josh was angry with him. Truth was, Jordan wasn't too fond of Josh right now, either. But that paled in comparison to Jordan running into Rhea. Josh would want to know. He deserved to know. Putting the truck in gear, he pulled onto the street and reached for his phone. Clicking on Rachel's name, he dialed and waited. She picked up on the first ring.

"Finished already?" she clipped.

"Ah, no. Actually, I'm gonna have to rain-check this story. I'm sorry, Rach. Something's come up. Maverick seemed interested—maybe pass it to him?"

"'Something came up.'" She sighed into the phone. "Is her name Cali?"

Jordan winced at the accusation, searching his mind for a response.

As though she'd never said it, Rachel moved on.

"Maverick will cover, but you'd better be here on time tomorrow, Hendricks. I'm getting sick and tired of finding coverage for you."

Taken aback by the chill in her tone, his defenses rose. "Yeah, okay. Later." He hung up and tossed the phone to the passenger's seat. What was that all about? Why was she asking about Cali? His conscience stabbed, and he gripped the steering wheel tight. "Would You just leave me alone already?" he shouted. "I didn't sleep with her! I've made it twenty-one years without even touching a girl, and I'm pretty danged proud of myself for it, so get lost!"

Prick, prick.

He slammed his hand against the wheel and ordered Siri to play Linkin Park at top level—a stark contrast to the normal worship music that usually kept him company. He blared Numb the entire way to his parents' house, pulling into their driveway faster than he'd intended. Shifting into park, Jordan grabbed his phone and shoved it into his pocket. As he pushed open the door, he noted his father's truck in the driveway and groaned. Great. Just what he needed. A dad lecture. His mind flashed back to his mother's shock when she'd discovered the scantily clad girl in his home, and shame colored his cheeks as he pulled out his key and headed for the door. What did she know? She'd never been a guy. She had no idea what it felt like to be under that kind of pressure. Jordan twisted the key in the lock and opened the door, his nose assailed by the aroma of his mother's homemade stew on the stove. For a split second, he wished he'd let his grudges go so he could enjoy dinner with his family, but he quickly changed his mind at the sight of his father walking toward him—a big smile set on his face.

"Your parents totally run your life…" Cali's words floated back to him, and he crossed his arms in front of his chest, hardening his gaze as his dad approached.

Undaunted by his cold appearance, Levi smiled big as he neared his son. "Jordan! Just in time for your mom's stew!" He reached for him, but Jordan stepped back, avoiding his eyes. Levi tried to fight the pain at his rejection, but the knot in his throat rebelled against his wishes. Jordan had never allowed such a great rift to come between them before; his heart grew heavier with each passing second.

"Josh here?" Jordan asked, keeping his eyes on the floor.

"Uh, yeah. Upstairs. Your room." Levi shoved his hands deep into his pockets. As Jordan bobbed his head at him in response, he wondered where his boy had gone.

"Did I hear Jordan?" Laura stepped up beside him, hope ringing in her voice.

Levi gestured to the stairs, and they watched Jordan head for his room and knock on the door. "Something's wrong," he commented.

Laura's eyes darkened. "I told you—it's that girl. You should've seen her parading from his bedroom in her skimpy outfit, hanging all over him! And he let her! And then dared lie to my face and say nothing happened." She crossed her arms in front of her, mama bear fury all over her face.

Glancing at his wife, Levi sighed—the serenity prayer coming to mind. Accept the things I cannot change… "Come on, let's check on dinner." Wrapping an arm around her waist, he led her into the kitchen, his gaze drifting to the banister just as his son disappeared inside his room. God, don't let it be true…

"What do you want?" Josh didn't even look up from where he was reading on the bed.

Jordan flinched, irritated at how comfortable his friend had made himself in his parents' home. How had his life become so flipped? Less than two weeks ago he was in his parents' good graces and Josh was still the one who'd run away—the rebellious one who'd wanted nothing to do with anyone. Grabbing his desk chair, he sat across from Josh, his gaze falling on the book. Realizing it was a Bible, he sucked in his breath. What kind of twilight was this?

"Dude, are you kidding me right now?"

Josh closed the Book and sat up, staring. "You got somethin' to say? Don't be a coward, spit it out." He watched Jordan flinch and noted the darkness in his eyes. His heart seized in his chest as he realized this was deeper than he was letting on. The fight behind his eyes was no longer about his and Josh's relationship—something had shifted in him, stirring a rebellion in his soul. His anger toward him evaporated, replaced with concern as he studied his tight features. "Why're you here, J?"

The ball of fury in his chest ignited, exploding throughout his body. "Where do you get off asking me why I'm at my parents' house? They're my parents. Not yours!" He knew he sounded like a five-year-old, but he didn't care. How dare Josh make himself comfortable in his old bedroom as though he was their son?

"Better check yourself, bro." Compassion for him dissipated. "You wanna fight, or what? Why you lookin' for me, anyway? Last I saw you, you stabbed me in the back—or have you forgotten?" Josh's eyes were wide—threatening. "Where's your hooker, J? Huh? She use you and toss you already?"

"Man, forget you," Jordan growled, rage boiling in his veins. "Look at you, all high and mighty. Reading the Bible like you didn't just waltz out of a cesspool of sin! Why, Josh? Why? Who you tryin' to impress—God? You're straight out of luck there, prick! He knows every dirty thing you've done, and He is not impressed."

"You're one to judge. You think you're so perfect, but you're no better than me, Jordan. Lying to everybody? Drugging me? Tricking me onto that airplane? Dissin' your parents for some crazy chick who doesn't give two craps about you?"

"You don't even know her! She cares more about me than you ever did!" Jordan shot to his feet. The only things keeping his fist off Josh's skull were the bruises still painting his body. "It's no wonder Rhea pretended not to know me today—she doesn't want anything to do with you. And who could blame her? She knows the truth—you don't care about her. You left her!" As soon as the words slapped Josh in the face Jordan regretted them, but it was too late to take them back and change course.

Josh's fingers gripped the edge of the mattress, his knuckles turning white. "What did you just say?" Jordan smirked at him. It felt good to be the tough guy for a change—the one on top. "Yeah, that's right. I saw your girl today—your hooker. That's all she was, right? Anything deeper than that, there's no way you would've left her behind. Betcha didn't know you left her with a kid to raise, did you?" His conscience leaped from his heart to his brain, screaming at him for his insensitivity.

Josh jumped off the bed and tackled Jordan to the floor, the two slamming into the desk chair as they fell. "Take it back," he screamed, his hand shoving Jordan's head into the floor. "Take it back!"

"Get off me!" Jordan yelled back, shoving against Josh's chest. He slammed a hand into his ribs, satisfied at the cry of pain that forced him to relax his grip on him. The bedroom door burst open, and Levi flew into the room. "Whoa, whoa, whoa!" Hooking Josh around the waist, he yanked him off his son, giving Jordan time to leap to his feet and square off with his friend. Pressing a hand against Jordan's chest, Levi pulled on all his strength to keep the two apart. "Stop it. Stop!" His eyes flashed fire as he looked at first one boy, then the other. Feeling their tension ease, he cautiously dropped his arms and stepped back. "Whatever has you two going at it, it isn't worth your friendship!" His eyes darted between them, resting on Josh's strained features. "You're already recovering from the last time you got into a fight; don't you think it's time for you to chill, Joshua?"

Josh glared at Jordan; his fists clenched tight at his sides. Raising his chin, he sent his message: This is far from over.

Jordan brushed a hand down his shirt, smoothing out the muss. His eyes burned as he regarded Josh, and then his father. "Man, forget y'all. You wanna be his daddy so bad, go right ahead. I want you off my back anyway, Pops. I'm outta here." He slammed his shoulder into his father's as he pushed out the door and pounded down the stairs.

Levi's eyes swung to Josh, one hand on the door frame as he danced with indecision. He wanted to race after his son, but Jordan's message was clear. Slamming a hand against the wall, he turned to Josh. "What the heck, kid?" Josh sat on the bed, wincing from the effort. His eyes met Levi's. "He saw Rhea today."

Levi's jaw dropped, and he stepped further into the room. "What?"

Josh dodged the question. "Look, I don't know, okay? I've never seen Jordan act like this before. Who knows if he's even telling the truth?" His voice cracked, and he quickly focused his attention on the rug.

Noting the tears glistening in his eyes, Levi sighed. "Hey. Whatever he said, he's just angry. He didn't mean it, okay? He'll get over it."

Josh nodded. "Yeah." He offered a half smile and watched Levi shut the door. The moment the latch clicked; Jordan's words washed over him again.

"That's all she was, right?... Left her with a kid to raise..."

He'd left her—abandoned her with their child. And now she was pretending they'd never met. He lay back on the bed, grabbed his earphones, and ordered Siri to play Numb.

Chapter 22

"And since they did not see fit to acknowledge God, God gave them up to a debased mind to do what ought not to be done."
~Romans 1:28~

RHEA

"You're going where?" Sterling gaped at Rhea's back as she withdrew a cardigan from their closet.

"Highshore. I need to check on a few things." Though her tone was calm, her pulse pounded in her ears.

"But…you never go to Highshore! You hate it there!"

Rhea sighed and pulled the cardigan on, her eyes fixed on him. "I have to check on something, Sterling. I'll be back before dinner. Don't worry!"

He shoved a hand through his hair, stepping back as she brushed past him and out of their room. "Rhea, baby. What is going on? Please. This isn't like you. Nothing's been the same since I told you about your mom. Talk to me. Let me in!"

She rushed down the stairs and grabbed her keys. Before she could reach the door, Sterling wrapped a hand around her wrist and stopped her. Startled, her eyes flew to his. "Let me go!"

He immediately released her but stepped in her way. "Baby, please. Tell me what you're doing. Let me come with you. I can help!"

"No one can help me!" she shouted, tears pooling. "No one. The faster you understand this, the better off you'll be." Her eyes searched his. "She's found me. Even worse, she knows about you. Your life is about to become much harder, Sterling." Rising on tiptoe, she kissed him. "I'm so sorry."

Without looking back, Rhea raced to her car. The panic was like a war within her as she drove to Highshore. Her mother would not win this time. She would get ahead of her evil schemes and thwart whatever plans she had to destroy all she loved.

Her mind raced with thoughts of Josh. Jordan had said he was back in town, but that was impossible. He would never come back to Highshore. Still, she had to be sure. If there was even a chance that Josh had come home, she had to get to him before Nichole Sherard. Her hands tightened on the wheel as she remembered Jordan had offered her Josh's number, and she'd refused to accept it. She would have to find him on her own and pray he would see her.

Sterling called three times during her drive, but she couldn't pick up. It wasn't fair for him to have to go through this. Maybe she should have been upfront with him about her past when they'd first gotten serious. Then he wouldn't have been blindsided when Nichole showed up to ruin their lives. Instead, she'd kept her past a secret, using vague answers whenever he questioned her about her family.

Crossing into the Highshore city limits sent her panic into overdrive. Her mother lived here, along with the goons who lapped at her heels for whatever crumbs she threw their way. Needing to gather her thoughts and a sense of safety, Rhea pulled into a Wal-Mart parking lot and shut off the engine, taking a moment to recenter herself.

"You can do this," she coached her panicking mind. Closing her eyes, she sat still and counted to twenty before opening them again.

It had been years since she'd crossed the city line and visited the town that held her captive to a past she'd fought to forget.

As she watched the crowd—some of whom she knew—she thought of where Josh might be. Jordan's house was first on the list. She assumed Jordan had his own place by now but had no way of finding him. She'd have to start with his parents. There was little to no chance the couple had sold their home in her absence. They loved their town. If she had no luck at their house, she'd search his old stomping grounds, starting with the caves she, Josh,

Jordan, and Rachel used to frequent. A wave of sadness washed over her as she thought of her old friends. She missed them. But this was no time to reminisce. She had to stay focused.

Deciding to walk into the store and get a snack before venturing further, Rhea stepped out of the car, locking it on her way through the parking lot. She absentmindedly browsed the produce section, but nothing teased her appetite. With a sigh, she settled on a cucumber and a container of hummus. She kept her head down low as she walked the aisles, not wanting to get trapped by any of the townsfolk and be pressed for information on her absence. She passed the cleaning aisle and nearly screamed when someone called her name.

"There you are."

Rhea spun around, her eyes widening in shock to see Asher within feet of her. Before she could scream, he locked her left wrist in his handcuffs and pulled her items from her right hand.

"Rhea Romans, you're under arrest for evading law enforcement. You have the right to remain silent…"

His voice faded as he locked her hands behind her back. A crowd formed, pressing in as the captain led his prisoner toward the front of the store.

"H-h-how did you find me?" she whispered, shock jolting her senses.

"You didn't think you could hide from her forever, did you, little one?" Asher spoke into her ear, his breath tickling her neck. "She's been looking for you. Mommy Dearest is done playing games. Time for your day of reckoning—I hope you've come to this city prepared."

His laughter sliced through her soul, emptying it of her last bit of hope as he loaded her into the back of his unit and drove them away.

NICHOLE

Nichole paced the floor of her suite as she waited for Asher's arrival. It had been two hours since he'd called.

Where was he? She had a busy day ahead of her and did not intend to waste time. At last, the doorbell buzzed, a sound long overdue. She hastily opened the door and ushered Asher inside. Rhea's elbow was grasped in his hand as he led her into the room, releasing her once the door clicked shut.

"Here she is. Now hand me the evidence and get out of my life." Asher looked dully at Nichole.

She brushed her fingers across Rhea's cheek, smiling when she flinched at her touch. "Go wait for me in the other room, Rhea, darling." She ensured the door had shut before turning back to the cop. "I distinctly remember telling you that you'd get your evidence after the job is done. It's not my fault you didn't comprehend." She checked her nails, her brows knitting when she found a chip in the polish.

The veins in Asher's arms bulged as his muscles tensed. Setting his jaw, he glared at the woman he loathed. He was desperate for freedom from this blackmail from hell. "The job is finished," he said through gritted teeth. "You wanted your daughter—now there she is!"

Her lips curled into a smug smile. "On the contrary, plans have changed. I'm taking a new direction on this—in court. I need you to play bodyguard around here for a while. Make sure she doesn't run off while I handle some business. The job is far from over, Asher, and I expect you to stay by my side and see it through to the end." She placed her mouth inches from his ear and annunciated each word, ensuring he understood the underlying threat. "You will do well to remember that your very existence in this town is at stake if you refuse me. I'll have you tossed in a prison cell so fast you'll be rotting before you've realized you're in there."

Asher clenched his fist and pictured what it might be like to throttle this woman. Ty and Bridgette would never understand his increased absences from home. Bridgette would have his head if he missed one more family outing—this would ruin his marriage. Defying Nichole, however, was suicide. He swallowed hard as she stepped away from him, her eyes cold. He had no choice but to do as she'd demanded—he'd figure out a way to smooth Bridgette over. He always had...

"We're done here. Go out to the hall and wait like the good boy you are." She winked at him, enjoying the way his eyes narrowed as his hand fumbled for the door and he stepped out. The moment he was gone, she turned and walked back to Rhea. "Pull yourself together, child, you look ridiculous." Nichole sat at the vanity and pulled out her blood-red nail polish, her mind set on fixing the chip.

Rhea watched her with hollow eyes. She swiped a hand across her face, noting with chagrin the streaks of mascara lining her fingers. "What do you want, Mother?"

Glancing at her in the mirror, Nichole's lips tightened as she painted her nail. "Rhea, darling, don't slouch. It's so unbecoming."

Rhea glared back and slouched even more. "Why am I here?"

Feigning surprise, Nichole's brows rose. "I've been worried sick over you, Rhea Nichole. How heartless is a child who can't even pick up the phone and call her own mother?"

Rhea rolled her eyes. "I guess you forgot about the part where you threw me out into the streets—pregnant."

Nichole stiffened. "Ungrateful little brat. After all I've done for you! This is how you talk to me?"

Rhea seethed. Her mother was the guilt trip queen, always finding a new reason for Rhea to "owe" her. She stared at her, disgusted by the narcissism that had robbed her of a good relationship with her mom years before.

"I've tried to reason with you in the past, Rhea." She said the name as though it repulsed her. "You are far too stubborn for your own good and only care about yourself. It's one thing for you to refuse to see me, but keeping my granddaughter from me is a whole new low." Nichole pulled at a tissue and wiped her eyes as she sniffed back her tears.

Rhea's lips quivered as she spoke. "How can you say these things to me? I gave my baby up because of you. Don't you dare talk to me about keeping her from you!" Hot tears burned her eyes as she released years of pent-up pain. "You told me not to come home as long as I still loved Josh. You refused to even call Nevaeh your granddaughter. You didn't want anything to do with his child. You did this. Not me!"

Nichole looked as though she'd been slapped. She watched her daughter crumple before her, burying her face in her hands as she sobbed. She felt her heart soften. She needed to take the focus off her actions. "Rhea, I've only done all this because I love you, honey. Why can't you see that?"

"Oh, please!" Rhea's head snapped up; her hair matted from tears. "Mothers who love their children don't force them to come see them under the guise of false arrests!"

Nichole tensed, her brow furrowing in a fierce frown. "Rhea, that's enough. Snap out of this pity party, and listen to me. I have some things to tell you. That gang-banger boy is back in town. What's worse is he's here for Nevaeh. You cannot let him get his hands on that girl."

Rhea pulled her knees up to her chest and hugged them. Josh was home, just as Jordan had said, and he knew about their daughter. Not only did he know, he wanted her. A smile played at the corners of her mouth as the realization sunk in.

"Rhea Nichole Romans, are you listening to me?" Nichole's whining cut through her thoughts, and she forced her eyes to her mother's.

"I have it all planned out," Nichole stated, as though the matter was hers to plan. "You will go to Elysia and tell her you want custody of Nevaeh. She'll sign her over to you, don't worry about that. Then you and the baby will move in with me. I'll take care of everything. Don't worry about a thing, darling. She'll have the best schools, the best tutors, the best of everything. We'll get her a nanny so she's not underfoot, and you'll go back to school so you can make something of yourself."

Rhea squeezed her knees tighter, building the confidence needed for this battle. "No," she said firmly. Nichole's eyes widened in shock. Had her daughter just defied her? This would never do...

"Let him have her. She needs her daddy, and he needs her." Maybe one day her mommy can be in the picture, too... "I refuse to take her from him, Mother."

Nichole leveled her gaze on her as her lips curved into a smile. "Does your new boy toy know you're still in love with Joshua?"

Rhea stifled a gasp as thoughts of Sterling rushed to her mind. She'd have to be careful of her next moves—she couldn't let her mother turn her sights on him. "I'm not in love with either of them," she lied. If she could convince her of this, both would have a better shot of escaping her mother's wrath.

Laughing, she leaned back in her chair. "You stupid little girl. You really want me to believe that don't you?" Rhea tensed, her mind racing as she searched for a way out.

"You are a terrible liar, and Sterling Oliver is an idiot to have ever believed you were in love with him. Now, you listen to me." Her red-stained lips pressed into a straight line. "I refuse to allow Joshua to go anywhere near you or Nevaeh. All he's good for is trouble, and you know it."

Rhea scoffed. "You don't even know him! You hate him because he's the only one in this pathetic town not scared of you. He's always refused to bow at your feet and kiss the ground you walk on, and you can't stand that. He's a good guy, Mom. I know he'll be an amazing father."

"I will not allow this," Nichole clipped, sitting up straight.

"It's not your choice." Rhea jumped up and headed for the door. "This conversation is over."

Fury burned through Nichole's veins as she followed her daughter out of the room. With a tight smile, she watched Rhea yank the door open and run right into Asher.

"Stop her," she calmly ordered.

Grabbing her by the arms, Asher pushed Rhea back through the door, shutting it behind him.

"You can't keep me here, Mother," Rhea seethed, shaking free of Asher's grip and facing off with Nichole.

"Sterling will look for me. He knows I'm here!"

Nichole smiled. Her eyes were slits of fury. "Quit being dramatic, child. You're not being held captive; you simply can't leave. Not until you obey me and go get that girl. If you don't, I will. I won't sit by and watch this monster ruin my grandchild."

Rhea raised her chin in defiance. "And if I don't?"

Nichole's eyes went to Asher. "I need a warrant for Joshua Cameron. He raped my daughter when she was just a teen and is now trying to gain custody of his daughter. I fear for her safety and request she be removed immediately from the home."

Shock jolted Rhea's senses, and a chill shot down her spine. "You wouldn't..." Her eyes searched Nichole's. "Mother, just leave her alone... please! She's so little. Josh's parents are all she knows. Don't make me take Nevaeh from them!"

Seeing she was getting nowhere; she pleaded with Asher. "Please, don't let her do this. All it takes is for you to refuse to do what she says. Please! Refuse her, and do what's right!"

Asher swallowed hard, forcing himself to ignore the desperation in her voice.

Nichole's lips curled into a sinister smile. "Enough of this nonsense, Rhea. No one will help you defy me, you foolish girl. Remember your place before you wind up in a world of regret. You have a lovely home in Lansford, darling. I believe Sterling would be making tea and heading to his study right about now, yes?"

Fear sparked in Rhea's eyes, making her mother laugh. "Okay," she whispered. "I'll go. But it's not as easy as you're thinking. I made sure Elysia couldn't just give her over to me. She has to go through court." She glanced at her mother, eyes narrowed. "Don't expect things to end the way you're hoping. Not everything goes your way."

"That's where you're wrong, darling. I always get my way." Nichole stroked her daughter's cheek. "Be a good girl, and go into the bedroom now. Mommy has work to do." Without waiting for her to obey, she turned and walked out the door.

JOSH

"No, not like that, like this. Color just a teensy-weensy bit—not too hard! Yes, perfect. Good job, boy!" Nevaeh's eyes lit up—she applauded her father's efforts on his coloring page. Her smile dropped into a fierce frown as she watched him pick up a purple crayon, aiming it for Minnie Mouse's dress. "What are you doing?! Not peerple! No! You'll ruin her whole year!"

Josh's hand froze, the crayon resting in mid-air. "What's wrong with purple?" Who knew coloring could be so complicated?

Nevaeh's hands rested on her hips as she regarded him. "She hates peerple. Don't you know anything?"

"Nevaeh." Elysia's warning tone sounded right before she poked her head around the corner. "Play nice." Little arms crossed over her chest as she stared at her grandmother. "Peerple, Mommy. Really?" When her grandmother's stern eyes stayed on her, she sighed and dropped her arms in defeat. "Sorry, boy. Here." She grabbed a pink and thrust it into his hands. "Do this one."

Josh obeyed and swapped out the crayons, coloring the dress to his daughter's liking. If this was what three looked like, what was he in for when she hit her teenage years? His eyes drifted to her, and he watched as she bent over the page, intently working at staying in the lines of Goofy's large black shoes. "I think you're better at this than I am," he commented with a smile.

Her crayon paused, her eyes shooting to his. "Uh-huh. My pictures always go on the fridge."

"That's because Mommy wants everyone to see how

good you color."

"I know." Her eyes dropped back to her paper, her broad strokes resuming. "I'm gonna be an artist police person when I get out of preschool." These words were spoken with certainty, leaving no doubt she knew where she was going.

Josh smiled at the back of her curly head. His hand reached to stroke her hair, but he stopped himself in-air. He had no right to touch her—she didn't even know who he was. The vise squeezed his heart.

"When I'm a police person, I'm gonna 'rest you if you hit my daddy. That's what police persons do—they 'rest people for hitting. Mommy says so." The crayon never stopped its dance as she announced her decision.

Josh shifted uncomfortably. "Well, how 'bout I try real hard not to give you a reason to arrest me when you become a police person. Will that do?"

Her eyes looked to his, eyebrows arched with perfection. She shrugged. "Don't hit my daddy, don't get 'rested. Simple." She stared at him, then leaped to her feet at the creak of a door in the background. Dancing across the living room, she shrieked at the sight of Garrett standing in the doorway. "Daddy, Daddy!" She bounced around his knees, holding tight and planting herself on his left foot, squealing when he laughed and stepped forward. "Higher!" she commanded.

Josh's eyes bounced from his father to Nevaeh as Garrett attempted to raise the little girl into the air, only to place her quickly back on the ground with a grunt of pain. Josh hid a smile as he watched him reach for a chair, dropping into it as though one more second on his feet would send him to the floor. Satisfaction swelled in his chest at the knowledge that he was the reason his father was suffering today. He deserved every bit of—

"Ahem."

His head snapped up to find his daughter standing in front of him, those arms crossed once again. Dread filled his bones as he remembered the promise he'd made her.

His father was awake, and now he had to apologize for beating the crap out of him, even though it was one of his proudest moments. Maybe she won't hold me to it...

"Daddy, boy has something to tell you."

Father and son locked eyes, neither one comfortable with the position in which they'd found themselves. Josh cleared his throat and glanced at his daughter to find her staring expectantly at him. Offering a half smile in return, he looked at Garrett, noting with added satisfaction the dark bruises painting their black, blue, and purple hues all over his face, his nose visibly altered from the blows. His eyes displayed his weariness, but they also showed him something that made uneasiness wash over him. Something he'd never before seen directed at him from his father.

Love.

Nevaeh tapped her pink Converse shoe on the floor, arms tightening across her chest. "Boy?"

His gaze fell on her, and he thought for the tenth time that day how challenging she would be when she hit her teens. "Um, right." He forced himself to look his father in the eyes, feeling like Nevaeh was taking notes. "I'm sorry." He nearly choked on the words.

"You have to tell him what you're sorry for," she informed. "It's Mommy's rule."

Garrett glanced at her, hiding a smile at the serious expression on her face. He didn't want an apology from his son; he certainly didn't feel he deserved one. But for her sake, he remained silent in his chair, wishing he could erase the tension on Josh's face.

"I'm sorry...for hitting you." He made sure his father read the message in his eyes: I will never be sorry. I hope you rot in hell.

"Next time I come, I'll ask Mommy if I can take you to the park." Josh knelt in front of his daughter, one knee on the porch. Deciding to test the waters, he ventured out. "Just you and me. Would you like that?" His eyes searched hers, noting when his mother's hand went to Nevaeh's shoulder and offered a slight squeeze.

Nevaeh glanced up at Elysia, receiving her nod of approval before giving her answer. "Okay, but 'member, no fighting, or the police will 'rest you."

"No fighting, I swear."

"Don't swear." She frowned at him.

Josh laughed as Levi's words came out of his daughter's mouth. "Sorry, kid." He stood and ruffled her hair, earning himself a look before she burst into a fit of giggles.

"I'll come by tomorrow, Mama," he promised, bending to kiss Elysia on the cheek. When she tensed at his touch, he stepped back to find her staring behind him, her mouth open in shock. "What is it?" He followed her gaze and froze, his hand slipping to his side.

"Who's that?" Nevaeh's small voice sounded far less bold as her finger pointed to the woman climbing from behind the wheel of her bright red car.

"Nevaeh, go inside," Elysia ordered under her breath. Instead of complying, Nevaeh's small arms wrapped around Josh's leg as she hid behind him. "She's scary." Her voice was muffled against his jeans.

Josh stood tall, shoving his hands into his pockets as he watched Nichole stride toward the porch with her nose in the air. "Look, Mom, it's Cruella De Vil." He smirked. No one detected the way his heart thumped wildly in his chest as she drew near.

"Josh!" Elysia hissed at her son, scared he would paint a brighter target on his back for this woman.

"Look at my baby! How big she has become!" Nichole gushed as she placed her hands on her knees and bent at the waist to smile wide at her granddaughter.

Josh felt Nevaeh's fingers dig into his leg as she peeked out at the stranger. Reaching down, he lifted her into his arms, wishing he could take in the way she immediately rested her head on his shoulder. No time to enjoy being a dad right now—not with this crazy lady setting her sights on his daughter. "Oh, you mean this baby right here? The one you've never laid eyes on?"

Nichole's gushing abruptly stopped, her eyes fixing Elysia with a cold stare as she stood. So, she'd been telling the street rat stories. She wasn't the only one who could tell stories. Her mascara-laden eyelashes flew open wide as she stared at Josh, as though noticing him for the first time. "Put her down! You've no rights to that girl! Elysia, how could you? How could you let her thug father touch her after what he did to my baby?"

Josh's and Elysia's jaws dropped at this, Josh's grip tightening on his girl.

"Don't play like you didn't know he raped her!" Nichole shrieked; fists clenched as she stared up at them.

"Nevaeh, go inside," Elysia ordered again.

"But—"

"Nevaeh, inside—now!" It was Josh who'd spoken, surprising himself at the authority in his tone as he placed her on the porch and pulled the door open in one swift movement.

She stared up at him, her eyes huge as tears pooled. "You're not my daddy!"

He watched her turn and run for the stairs, pushing the guilt aside as he shut the door behind him and stepped toward the porch steps.

"Josh, don't." His mother reached for him, but he evaded.

"Say it to my face." Stopping inches from Nichole, controlled anger pulsed for an outlet in his veins. Raising her chin, Nichole's smile was smug as she stared at the boy she loathed. "You raped my daughter and left her with that child to raise. You're nothing but a monster, and I've come to make you pay for what you did to her."

Josh cursed, his jaw twitching as the corners of his mouth danced. "You've got to be kidding me with this, Nichole. Of all the low life, messed up, rich schemes you've pulled over the years, this takes the cake." He shook his head, towering over her small frame. "You'll never pull this off. No one will ever believe that. Everyone knows how much I loved her!" His right fist squeezed and relaxed on repeat. "Besides, Rhea would never help you pin this on me. She knows the truth."

Nichole's smile was pencil thin. "Care to bet on that, sweetheart?"

Josh's blood ran cold, doubt flickering in his eyes. He followed her gaze as she looked back at her car, and his heart leaped into his throat at the sight of movement behind the darkened glass. "No." He shook his head. "She wouldn't…" He swallowed hard, his eyes flitting to hers, noting the contempt in her cold stare. Forcing himself to breathe, he clenched his. "Lemme talk to her," he demanded. "I won't believe it unless I hear it for myself."

"Suit yourself." Nichole scoffed as she went to the passenger side door and opened it. Leaning in, she locked eyes with her daughter. "Remember what we talked about," she warned. "He raped you. You were a scared, naive little girl, and he took advantage of you."

Rhea's eyes pooled as her lips quivered. "He didn't—"

"He did!" Nichole hissed, her breath swishing back a stray strand of her daughter's hair. "You're just too scared to admit it. I'll be right there beside you—you have no reason to be afraid. Go tell him you want that baby. Now!" She stared her down until Rhea unlatched her seatbelt and climbed from the car.

Rhea kept her eyes low as she approached him, her heart leaping wildly in her chest as she drew near. The scent of his cologne wafted to her nose, and a fresh onslaught of tears hit her eyes at the familiarity. It took every fiber of her being to keep herself from running into his arms, thoughts of Sterling miles away. She shoved her hands into her pockets, her eyes focused on her shoes. Her long, wavy hair draped across her shoulders, hanging freely to her waist.

"Rhea." Josh's voice was tight. "Rhea, look at me," he pleaded. When she refused, he looked to the sky, his mind wrestling his heart on his next move. Looking back at her, he caught her eye as she chanced a glance at him. There was so much he wanted to say…so much he needed to say…not here. Not now. Not with her watching them. He cast a heated look at Nichole, not missing the way she smiled in triumph over his discomfort. Working to ignore her, he refocused his attention on Rhea, deciding his best bet was to cut right to the chase. "Rhea, she's tryin' to say I raped you." He studied her face, searching for signs of shock or surprise, hurt to be met by an emotionless shell. "Tell her I didn't do it, Rae…" His voice was weak, his vision clouding. Did he even know her anymore?

Her mother suddenly beside her, Rhea took a deep breath and met his eyes, her voice small. "I've come for my daughter, Josh."

Josh shifted on his feet, a hand swiping down his face.

"You mean our daughter? The one I just found out about two days ago?"

"That's not my fault." Her eyes met his. "You left me, remember? Don't you dare pin this on me." Her voice quivered.

Josh gritted his teeth. He didn't want to do this with an audience. He'd always pictured their reunion as private—personal. His eyes shot to Nichole again, fury burning in his chest. "I begged you to come with me. I didn't even know about Nevaeh! And how about your choice to leave her with my father, huh?! What about that? Was that my fault too? Answer me!"

Rhea shrank beneath his fierce gaze, terrified at having to answer him for abandoning Nevaeh with his parents. "I didn't have a choice," she whispered, her heart willing him to understand. She winced beneath the sudden vise on her arm and glanced down to find her mother's fingernails digging into her skin. Remembering her warning not to get sucked into a conversation with him, she focused on the reason she had come. "I will be getting custody of Nevaeh, Josh. Don't try and fight me in court—you won't win." Her eyes were dull and lifeless as she stared at him, tears glistening.

Defeat washed over him as he watched Nichole usher the girl he loved back into the car. Something was wrong. This wasn't what Rhea wanted. He could read it all over her face. Besides that, she knew he hadn't raped her. "I'm not just gonna hand her over, Rhea. I have a right to get to know my kid," he called as she got into the car, her mother shutting it behind her.

"Do as you wish, boy, but the courts love sweet little mothers—not street rats like you. Once they see what you've done to her, they'll lock you up and throw away the key. You don't stand a chance with your rap sheet—no judge would give you that kid, so you might as well give up while you still have an ounce of your foolish pride left." Halfway behind the wheel, she turned to Elysia and waved. "Lovely to see you, dear. Lovely. Good day!"

Josh's eyes followed them until the car faded off into the distance. Two days into being a father to a child he'd known nothing about, and his daughter still had no idea he was her dad. And now he was being threatened with court—possibly jail time—for a crime he didn't commit. Where was all that Jesus stuff Titus had been telling him about now? Wasn't it about time some grace fell his way? Or maybe it was as he'd claimed all along—there was no redemption for pricks like himself. He was undeserving of the perfect love spoken of in the Bible. Undeserving of Jesus.

Chapter 23

"...human anger does not produce the righteousness that God desires."
~James 1:20b~

JORDAN

Jordan flipped a burger on the grill, enjoying the way Cali's hands rubbed his bare chest as she wrapped her arms around him from behind. "Hungry?" he asked, taking a swig of his beer. He shouldn't have waited so long to try it—he loved the taste and enjoyed the buzz tingling in his busy mind. It had been so easy to take that first sip once Cali had offered him one from the twelve-pack she'd brought.

He hadn't invited her—she'd just shown up at his door and announced they would grill out. After warring with the Holy Spirit all day, he was eager for a change of pace and had let her in, despite his better judgment. He needed something to be easy for a while, and she was definitely easy.

"Starved. Smells delish," she said against his bare back as she kissed him.

"Ready in five—promise." He turned in her arms and kissed her lips, his hand wrapped in her red hair. His phone buzzed in his pocket, and he sighed. "I need to see if it's Rachel. She's been working on a story that she's about to hand off to me. Watch the food?"

At her nod, he stepped aside and pulled his phone from his pocket, surprised to find Josh's name instead of Rachel's. Glancing at Cali, he stepped into his apartment before opening the text. He sucked in a breath when he found a picture—three marbles. Eyes wide, he ran a hand through his hair. "Oh, man," he breathed, cursing into the air. Josh was in trouble, and he needed help. He squeezed his eyes shut as he thought out his next move. Should he ditch Cali and run to him? Tell him to come here? Deciding on the latter, his fingers flew across the keys.

Come over, I'm free.

The response came in a matter of seconds, announcing Josh's desperation.

On my way

And a second text…

Thx man

Jordan sighed. It didn't matter that the two were feuding— they always had each other's backs at the first sign of trouble. What could have happened? He tried not to worry over him as he returned to the grill, smiling when Cali leaped back with a shriek to avoid grease splashing on her white shorts. His smile faded when his eyes fell on his beer, panic pulsing through his veins. "Uh, I need a minute." He grabbed his beer and disappeared into the apartment. Racing for the sink, he dumped the alcohol down the drain and ran water to wash down the smell. His eyes scanned the kitchen for any other signs of beer, satisfied when he found none. That should work…Josh shouldn't be able to detect anything. His conscience pricked and he gritted his teeth. "I told you to leave me alone already!" he growled.

"Excuse me?"

He glanced up to find Cali carrying a plate of hot burgers to the counter. Heat flooded his face, and he cleared his throat. "Ah, nothing. Wasn't talking to you. Sorry."

She eyed him, then shook her head as she covered the meat with foil. "Whatever. I'm gonna shower before we eat. I'm covered in smoke and grease."

"Uh, okay." Jordan worked to hide his discomfort at that thought. "I'll get dinner on the table." He busied himself setting out plates, adding a third in case Josh wanted to stay.

"Three?" Cali cocked her head to the side. "Who are you expecting?"

"My friend." He glanced at her as he set out three forks beside the plates. He sighed at her look of confusion. "The wild card." He threw out the hint, surprised when her face lit with a smile. "He needs to talk to me, so be cool."

"Aren't I always?" She winked at him before disappearing into his room.

Jordan was pouring tea into the cups when he heard the knock on his door. His pulse quickened and he found himself praying for guidance, then immediately chided himself for his hypocrisy. Either he wanted God, or he didn't. He couldn't have it both ways. He went for the door and pulled it open, his heart squeezing at the sight of Josh. "Hey," he greeted him.

Josh stepped into the room, his eyes falling on Jordan's bare chest. "Did I interrupt something?"

"Ah, no, it's all good." Suddenly aware of his exposure, Jordan reached for his black t-shirt and pulled it over his head. "What's up?"

Josh glanced at the table, then back at Jordan. "I can come another time…"

"No, now's good. I set a place for you. Hungry?"

"No."

"Okay, cool. What's wrong? Your text…"

"I know." Josh took a deep breath. "Nichole came to Mom's house today while I was visiting Nevaeh."

Jordan's jaw dropped. "What? Wait…you know about Nevaeh?"

Josh cast him a look. "You're the one feuding, so don't play hurt that you're not in the loop, J."

He had him with that one. "What did Nichole want?"

"She had Rhea with her."

Jordan's breath evaporated. "But Rhea hates—"

"I know. But she was with her, man, and they're tryin' to take Nevaeh. I just met her, J, and they wanna take her away from me."

"Josh, I'm so sorry…"

"That's not all. They're tryin' to say I raped Rhea. Tryin' to make it to where I can't ever have my kid with me. I'm screwed, J. I'm so done. Nichole's a monster—you know she gets whatever she's after in this town, and right now she's after me!"

As though suddenly remembering Josh's injuries, Jordan gestured to the couch. "Come sit, Josh. You're gonna injure yourself more if you don't start resting." Josh waved him off. He only had one thing on his mind: protecting Nevaeh. He looked at Jordan, desperation in his eyes. "What am I gonna do, J? I can't fight her and win. I have no money for a lawyer to take her to court. She's ruthless. She didn't even get papers first. She knows she's gonna win, so I'm no threat to her agenda. How am I gonna get Nevaeh now?"

Jordan shoved his hands in his pockets and thought. "Well, right now your parents have custody. So, Nichole is gonna have to go through courts to take her away from them, which won't be easy because they're both fit."

"We're talking about Nichole. She owns every city official in this twisted town. Everyone does what she says!"

Jordan smiled. "Not Judge Kramer. He hates her guts."

Josh cocked his head to the side. "He's still alive?"

Jordan laughed. "Yep. He's had a few cases in his courts Nichole tried to sway. None of 'em went her way."

"How do you know that?"

Jordan stared, hesitant. "I talk to your dad a lot. He shares some things about his court experiences with me. You know," his eyes lit up as an idea hit him, "you don't need money for an attorney." He looked pointedly at Josh.

"No." Josh's eyes hardened. "Forget it. I'll find my own way. I don't need that prick's help, and I don't want him anywhere near my kid."

"Well, too late for that. He's her acting father. He's doing a pretty good job with her, too." He realized a moment too late what he'd just done.

"Man, forget you," Josh bit. "Nevaeh's happy because of my mom—not because of him." As he spoke the words, he heard Nevaeh defending his father, and he knew it was a lie. She loved his dad, whether he liked it or not. The truth cut him like a two-edged sword.

"Well, hey there," Cali called as she entered the living

room.

Josh stared at the stranger dressed in nothing but a T-shirt and underwear. His eyes flew to Jordan, who looked as though he might be sick. He raised an eyebrow at his friend, waiting for him to explain the half-naked girl in his living room.

"Don't just stand there, J, introduce us!" Her voice was bubbly as she waltzed over and tangled her arms through the crook of Jordan's right elbow.

"You forget where you dropped your clothes after sleeping with my friend?" Josh's tone was cold.

Jordan's eyes seared through him before addressing Cali. "Cali, this is Josh. Josh, Cali." Every fiber in his being wanted to beg the girl to put some clothes on, but Josh wasn't about to push him around in his own house.

"So, this is the wild card." She licked her lips as she sized up her target. Asher would pay big bucks if he knew she was face-to-face with him.

Josh bristled and Jordan grimaced. Cali had zero tact. None.

"Anyone hungry?" Jordan pulled away from her and moved to the kitchen, watching Josh out of the corner of his eye.

Cali flashed Josh a smile, her next move clear. What was the fun of fake dating if she couldn't stir things up between friends? She walked toward the kitchen, hips swaying as she moved too close to Josh. Her right hip bumped into him as she passed, and she giggled flirtatiously, pausing right in front of him.

"I don't play that," Josh clipped, pushing her away, not giving it any thought when she cried out in surprise. "You're either his girl or you aren't. Do not play with me." His tone spoke of trouble if she persisted.

Fury colored her neck as she watched him join Jordan in the kitchen, not missing the way Jordan's eyes dimmed when his gaze met hers. She'd hurt him. How cute. She moved to the table and snatched a glass, sipping the beverage. "Tea? Really, J?"

Jordan froze. She wouldn't… His body went cold as he watched her move for the fridge. "Cali, I just poured those glasses. I thought they'd go better with the burgers; you know?"

Oh, please, God no…

"Better than beer? You crazy?" She had their attention as she yanked open the fridge and pulled out a case of beer, setting it on the counter.

Jordan's eyes flew to Josh as panic surged through him. He watched his jaw tense, his fists clenching and relaxing at his sides. When his gaze turned on him, an audible gulp sounded in his throat, and he cursed himself for his cowardice. This was his house! He could drink whatever he wan—

"Beer, Jordan?" Josh's voice was a tight whisper.

"Yeah, it's ice cold! Want one?" Cali dangled a bottle between her fingertips and held it in front of Josh's face. Hot tears burned his eyes as the betrayal hit him full force. Grabbing the bottle from her hands, he threw it, and it exploded against the wall, sending beer all over Jordan's kitchen. His chest heaved, and his jaw remained tight as he stared through Jordan.

Cali gaped at him; shock evident on her face as she scooted closer to Jordan.

Jordan's eyes remained fixed on his friend, shame coloring his cheeks. "Josh," he whispered through his tight throat.

Josh threw up his hands, warding off any excuse he might offer. Turning abruptly for the door, he pushed it open, turning one last time to look at the man he'd thought was his friend. He saw Jordan swallow hard. Saw Cali's hand slip into his. Then turned around and headed for Levi's truck, unaware that Jordan and Cali followed him outside.

Jerking the driver's door open, he climbed inside and slammed it shut behind him, shoving the keys in the ignition. Instead of putting the truck in gear, he gripped the wheel with both hands and rested his face on the steering wheel as he forced himself to breathe. Raising his head, he swiped at his eyes as he shoved the gear shifter into reverse and peeled out of the driveway. He fought for breath as he made the five-minute drive back to the Hendricks' home, relief washing over him when he spotted Levi on the porch swing, smoking his nightly cigar. Throwing the truck into park, Josh shoved the door open and stumbled to the ground, grabbing onto the door as his sobs overtook him.

Levi was beside him in an instant, concern etched across his features as he hooked Josh's arm around his neck and helped him to the porch, lowering him to the swing. Worry filled his bones as he watched Josh's shoulders rise and fall, but he wisely puffed on his cigar and waited for the moment to pass before asking the question on his mind. When Josh finally relaxed and breathed deeply, Levi pulled the cigar from his lips. "Wanna talk about it, son?"

Josh sniffed and focused his gaze across the yard. "We had a pact," he began. "Neither of us was gonna mess with alcohol. We swore to each other we'd never turn into my father. I thought Jordan had my back, man. I thought—" He stopped, his eyes welling. "I never thought he'd do it, Levi."

Levi's heart thumped wildly, and he told himself not to jump to conclusions. "What did he do, Josh?"

Josh ran a hand down his face, his chest squeezing the breath from his lungs. "He had a twenty-four pack in his fridge. It was half gone. And then she offered me one."

"Who?" Levi's mind was reeling.

"That chick he's sleeping with."

Levi hung his head, sorrow filling his bones over his son's actions. Forcing his mind back to the issue, he placed a hand on Josh's shoulder and squeezed it. "I'm sorry, son. I can only imagine what you're going through right now. I'm not gonna try and make excuses for Jordan—only God knows what he's dealing with right now—but I will say this: Jordan is your best friend. He loves you like a brother. He'd do anything for you. The Jordan we know would rather die than betray you, so, that tells you something is off with him right now. Just be patient, kid. He'll come around. He has to. His conscience won't leave him alone until he does. We both know that." He grinned.

Josh offered a half smile. It was true—Jordan didn't know how to make a habit of bad choices. It was one of the things Josh admired most about his friend. He couldn't shove everything down like Josh always did and forget how his actions affected others. He cared about people. Glancing at Levi, he took a shuddering breath. "Thanks, Mr. H."

Levi smiled, but his eyes remained dim. "Just give him some time." As he spoke the words, he knew they were as much for his heart as for Josh's.

GARRETT

"She really accused him of raping Rhea?" Garrett sat at his kitchen table, a finger tracing the circle of his coffee mug as he watched his wife. Every muscle in his body still ached from Josh's revenge, but he welcomed the reminder of God's judgment for his sins.

Elysia nodded. "She did. It was awful, Garrett. I wish you had been there to hear what I'd heard—that way you could help me determine if the threat is loaded or empty." Garrett's eyes darkened. "This is Nichole we're talking about. She doesn't make empty threats. Next time, come get me, Lys. I don't like the thought of you facing her alone."

"I just knew Josh was going to attack her out there. You should have seen his face. I was so scared. If he had hit her, she would have had him tossed in a dungeon somewhere." Her heart still skipped a beat at the thought, even after a full night's sleep since the incident.

"Josh isn't stupid, babe. He knows what she's capable of."

"He may know, but he's stubborn as a mule—just like

you. He doesn't let anyone push him around. Kid's got a mouth out of this world. He called Nichole 'Cruella De Ville'—out loud!" Elysia's eyes narrowed as she recounted.

Garrett laughed, picturing the scene. "Did she hear him?"

"She didn't let on if she did. You should have seen how Nevaeh clung to him when he picked her up. She's starting to warm up, and here comes Nichole to ruin everything! Josh is acting like a father. He's doting over her, playing with her, protecting her. All of that is about to go to crap because this jealous little Barbie hates our son."

Garrett smiled at her outburst before his eyes grew serious. "Let's transfer custody to Josh." His statement was as left field for him as it was for her, and his gaze quickly fell to his mug.

"What?" Elysia's jaw dropped, sure she'd misheard.

Garrett met her eyes. "If we transfer custody now, the courts will see he's established his parenting relationship with Nevaeh. It would make Nichole's case more challenging for her to navigate. It won't stop her, but it could help."

"Garrett Cameron, have you lost your mind? Our son attacked you yesterday. Or have you forgotten? What kind of a role model is he right now?"

"He attacked me, because I had it coming. It has nothing to do with Nevaeh. You've seen him with her—he wants to be her dad. He's not shirking his responsibility—he wants her."

Elysia leaned forward and rested her elbows on the table. "Sweetheart, you want to be Josh's dad too, but it's just not that easy, is it?"

Garrett dropped his eyes. "He deserves custody of his kid."

"And, I'm not against that—when the timing is right. Let him learn some more. Let him get a job for himself. We don't even know if he's decided to stay. Who knows what goes through that boy's head? He has a history of running. What makes you think he wouldn't repeat his past mistakes at the first sign of trouble when raising his daughter? Nevaeh needs consistency. She needs her dad to be stable before she lives with him."

He knew she was right, but it didn't stop the longing in his heart for Josh to have his baby girl. A fresh idea sparked, and he raised his eyes to hers. "Okay, so custody stays here for a while. That doesn't mean he can't take her places. Bond more. Maybe even take her overnight at times."

"To what home?" Her voice displayed her exasperation. "Levi and Laura's?"

"Well, yeah. They both love Veah. I'm sure they wouldn't mind her staying with Josh for a while."

Elysia's gaze softened as she reached for him. "Baby, I hear your heart. I just think you're rushing things a bit. Nevaeh still thinks we're her parents. This could destroy her if not done correctly. Right now, you are her daddy, and I am her mommy. In time, everything will come to light for her."

Garrett shifted, agitated. "But I'm not her dad—Josh is! She deserves to know that."

"No!"

They flew to the doorway, both going cold at the sight of Nevaeh standing there. Her small fists were scrunched up into tiny balls at her sides, her green eyes flashing.

"Baby..." Garrett's heart clenched as he wondered how much of what she'd heard had been.

"You're lying!" she screamed, her small face red. "You're my daddy—you! I hate Boy, and I never want to see him again—not ever, ever, ever!" She tossed her head back and screamed at the top of her lungs before bursting into tears and running from the room.

Elysia's eyes settled on her husband as she stifled her resentment.

Two children.

Both of whom she loved more than anything else in this world, shattered because of this man. She took a deep breath and reminded herself of his intentions. "Now we have to talk to her."

Garrett's misty eyes followed his wife as she rose from the table, his conscience accusing him. "Lys, I didn't mean to—"

She held up her hand and headed for the door. "We can talk later. Right now, I need to go find my daughter." Garrett sat frozen at the table, listening to Nevaeh's high-pitched screams over his wife's soothing tones.

Five minutes later, he heard the creak of the stairs, mixed with Nevaeh's whimpers, announcing their return. He glanced up, surprised to see Nevaeh twisting from Elysia's arms to get to him. He took her, his heart squeezing when she buried her face in his shoulder and cried.

"Shh. I'm sorry, baby. I'm so sorry," he soothed.

Elysia sat across from them and sipped her coffee as she watched her husband's face. Raising an eyebrow when he sent her a pleading look, she placed her mug back onto the table and crossed her arms in front of her chest.

Garrett knew what she was telling him: he'd made this mess, and he would clean it up himself. He sighed, his hand caressing Nevaeh's hair as she cried. "Um, baby girl… Mommy and I need to tell you something."

Nevaeh shook her head and grabbed a fistful of his shirt in her hands, her face still buried. "No! You're my daddy!"

Garrett sighed. How was she so perceptive all the time? He kissed her head and looked to his wife for support. Her gaze softened, and he smiled his thanks. "You remember Josh?"

Elysia cleared her throat and mouthed the word "boy."

"Um, you call him 'boy.'"

"I hate him," she mumbled against his chest.

"Yeah. Well, baby...he's Mommy's and my son. And you…" he glanced at Elysia, receiving a nod, "…you're his baby girl."

"No! You're my daddy. You!"

"I'm your grandpa, Nevaeh. And Mommy is your grandma. See, you have another mommy. Her name is Rhea, and she loves you very much. She brought you here to live with us, because she knew we could care for you when she couldn't."

Nevaeh shoved her hands against her ears and burrowed deeper into his chest. "You're lying!" she screamed.

Garrett sighed and hugged her tighter, his eyes clouding as he looked at Elysia. Standing, she approached them and placed a hand on Nevaeh's shoulder.

"Baby, come here," she urged, reaching for her.

"No!" Nevaeh's head shot up, her hand slapping Elysia away as she screamed. "I want Daddy. I want Da-a-a-a-d-dy!"

Tears sprung to Elysia's eyes, and she pulled back as though she'd been stung. "I'll be upstairs." Her lips quivered as her eyes flit to Garrett.

He watched her go while clinging to the little girl in his arms, and his heart broke in two at the realization that he was the cause of his wife's heartache all over again.

JORDAN

"What is wrong with you?"

Jordan crossed his arms over his chest and stared at his friend. "I don't know what you're talking about."

"Really, Jordan? Really?" Rachel's eyes flashed as she faced him, pain stabbing her chest. "I don't even know who you are anymore. The guy I've known since childhood has been replaced with some jerk whose morals have flown out the window!"

He bristled. "My morals? Let me get this straight. I finally choose to date someone and suddenly my morals are in question? You playing God, or just jealous?"

Her face blanched white and she shoved him. "Jealous?! Of her? She's a no-good floozy who thinks she can control any man with a pulse. She's done a fine job of controlling you, hasn't she, Jordan?!"

"She does not control me, Red!" he shot back, stepping

back when she came for him again.

He was used to her fiery temper. It was why he'd called her "Red" since grade school. The girl could fly from zero to one hundred in seconds.

Rachel breathed a mirthless laugh and shook her head. "You are so blind, Straight Shooter."

"Do not call me that!" He gritted his teeth and balled his fist. "I'm sick to death of you people always expecting me to do what you think is right. What about what I want, huh? Anybody ever think of that?!"

Shock slammed her, transforming her face into a look of horror. "What you want? What about what God says, Jordan? Do you not even care that you're sleeping with someone you're not married to?"

He cursed. "Unbelievable. Just like Josh and my parents, you've jumped on the bandwagon of assumptions. I have never slept with this girl!"

Rachel hid her surprise—and the hope rising within her. He hadn't slept with Cali? Maybe there was still a chance… "You could've fooled me! Every time someone goes to your apartment they're met with Cali in her underwear."

"Oh, okay." He scoffed, strutting around the picnic table where they argued. "So, you and Josh have been comparing notes about me behind my back. Well, note this, Red. I'm the one who's stuck around here for the last four years, while he ran away like a scared little girl, so maybe check and see where your loyalties lie before you go accusing your best friend of something he didn't do! I'm outta here." Casting a scathing look in her direction, Jordan stormed off toward his truck, leaving her to stare after him.

As he drove, he nursed his anger. What was the point of trying to stay within God's boundaries if everyone assumed he'd already crossed them? If he was honest with himself, his heart had crossed that boundary with Cali a while ago—what was stopping him from going all the way? What was the worst that could happen? It wasn't like this wasn't society's norm. No one would look down on him if he gave in...that is, no one except those who cared about him...

With determination, he picked up his phone and dialed Cali before he could change his mind.

"Hey, hot stuff," she greeted him.

Her acceptance of him warmed his soul. "Where are you?"

"Headed to you, of course. You home?"

"About to be. You have plans today?"

"Nope. I'm wide open..."

"Good. I'll be there in ten minutes."

He hung up, his heart firm in his decision.

It was time. He was twenty-one years old, after all. He would join the path of all the other guys in this world. Who could it hurt...?

Jordan had thought it would be easier to defy his convictions, but as he took Cali into his arms and led her into his bedroom, his conscience screamed in protest. The Holy Spirit's conviction weighed hard on his chest, but he refused to give in. This time, he would do things his way. Closing the bedroom door, he spun her into his chest.

"Jordan, what are you do—" Cali's words were cut off when he kissed her hard, wrapping his fingers through her hair. When he released her, she stared at him, wondering at this newfound boldness. "I didn't think you had it in you." She laughed.

"There's a lot about me you don't know." He smiled as he took her hand and led her to the bed. The line was crossed. The boundary disdained. His Bible lay open on his bedside table as his sins consumed him. The arrow who had aimed straight his entire life took a sharp left turn down an alley that would lead to nothing but regrets and heartache as he chased his Jezebel.

LEVI

Levi sat at the piano and mindlessly ran the scales of

D#, his fingers flying across the keys. He'd already taught three classes this morning and was due to teach his fourth in half an hour but no matter how hard he tried, he couldn't get his head into it today. Thoughts of Jordan barraged his mind, dragging his spirits further into darkness. Behind him, he heard the door open and click shut but made no move to see who'd joined him in the university classroom.

"Levi."

His lips tightened into a thin line as his fingers drummed the scales. Up and down. Up and down. Up and down. He heard Cypress clear his throat but still, he refused to come out of his thoughts.

"Levi," he called again, this time right beside him. Their friendship at the university was fifteen years deep—each driven by their love for music and their passion for bestowing that love into others—but Cypress couldn't mend his relationship with his son. He couldn't make Jordan snap out of this trance he was in and bring him back to reality—to God. And so, Levi played.

"Levi!" Cypress bent to see his face, noting with concern the intensity in his eyes.

His fingers abruptly stopped, chest heaving from the tension in his veins. Pulling his hands from the keys, Levi turned his eyes to his friend. "Jordan."

His son's name, along with the sorrow in his eyes, was all the other man needed.

Straightening, Cypress pushed his suit coat back and shoved his hands into his trouser pockets. "Go. I'll cover for you. Don't worry about a thing." He watched his friend leap from the bench and rush for the door. "I'll be praying!" he called as Levi disappeared into the hallway.

The drive from the university to Jordan's apartment was twenty minutes but Levi made it in fifteen. Stop signs became mere suggestions as he navigated the streets, his heart flooding with relief when his son's truck was the only visible vehicle in the driveway. Maybe that girl wasn't with him this time. Maybe he'd broken it off with her and was starting to realize the path he'd taken led to destruction.

Levi shoved the truck into Park and jumped from the cab, careful not to slam the door and alert Jordan of his presence. "Please God, just let him talk to me. Let my boy want to see his dad. Please." He squeezed his eyes shut, clearing the tears, and knocked on the door, his heart leaping into his throat when Jordan yanked it open.

"Hey, son," he managed around the lump he'd swallowed.

Jordan's eyes narrowed at the sight of his father, even as his heart burned with his sins. "What're you doing here? Come to tell me how to live my life again?"

Levi sighed. "I never used to need a reason to visit you." He studied his features, noting his tousled hair and wrinkled clothes. It was obvious Jordan had skipped class. What was behind all these decisions he was making?

Suddenly realizing his son was staring him down, he cleared his throat. "May I come in?"

"Aren't you supposed to be at work right now?"

"I just came from there."

Jordan paused at this, alarm shocking his senses. His father never left work early. "Is it Mom?" Please, God, no...

Levi stared, his hand stroking his stubbed chin. "Uh, no. It's you."

Jordan rolled his eyes. "Yeah, well, you're wasting your time. I have things to do." He started to shut the door, surprised when his father's hand shot out and stopped it from closing.

"Why are you shutting me out, son? I'm usually the first one you turn to when things get difficult. What's this all about?"

"I don't have time for this," Jordan evaded.

"No? Is that why you cut class today? Why you aren't at the paper half the time?"

Jordan's eyebrows shot up, the door opening wide as he stepped onto the porch. "You checking up on me?"

"Rachel called," Levi answered. "She's concerned."

"She has no business calling my father—I'm a grown man."

"You'll have to take that up with her," he replied smoothly. "But I deserve to know why I'm being shoved out of your life, Jordan. You owe me that much, don't you think?"

"I owe you? I don't owe you anything. You owe me! The decency of letting me live without you breathing down my neck all the time." Jordan's voice rose with each word, his face inches from his father's.

Levi's hand went to the back of his neck, tension mounting in his shoulders. *God, where is my boy? Give me some direction here...* "Son, where's all this coming from? You and I have always been tight. Can't you see why I'm concerned? Josh came home last night completely broken over some beer he'd caught you with. Beer isn't you, Jordan. That's not who you are."

"Josh needs to learn that the world doesn't revolve around what happened to him. What I do in my own home is no one's business but mine." Even as he said the words, his conscience screamed. He knew he was wrong. He knew every decision he'd made lately had been in direct rebellion against God, but he had no idea how to turn this around.

Aside from that, he knew there was no coming back from the betrayal he'd dished his best friend the night before. Without God's intervention, Josh would never forgive him for breaking their pact.

Tears clouded Levi's vision as he stared at his son. Jordan reeked of his sins, and Levi was broken for his boy. "Jordan, this isn't you," he repeated. "Whatever's got a hold on you, it's not too late, son. Please. Talk to me. I'm begging you, boy."

"There's nothing left to say. I'm done." He started closing the door, but his father's hand caught it once more.

"Dad, stop," he growled.

"Come to dinner," Levi pleaded, his mind whirling as

he concocted a plan. "Bring the girl. You're both welcome. We'd love to get to know her." He wanted nothing to do with the girl, but if welcoming her into his home was the only way to see his son, so be it.

Jordan rolled his eyes. "Mom hates her, and she doesn't even know her."

"Then bring her. Let Mom get to know her. Please, Jordan. Please. No judgment. No lectures. Just dinner."

Jordan stared for a moment before cutting his gaze to the side. He missed his parents. He knew Cali would be thrilled at the chance to officially meet them, though he wasn't sure dinner was a great idea with her in the mix. Did he really want to chance it? He looked back at his father's earnest face and sighed. Man, he missed his dad. "When?"

"Tonight," Levi said without hesitation. He knew he was chancing a huge fight with his bride over this, but he'd deal with that later. Right now, all that mattered was his son. "I'll even grill your favorites, just come."

Jordan gave a slight nod. "Okay. We'll be there."

Levi's face erupted in a smile, relief washing away the tension. "Good. Good." He stepped back, wishing he could pull his son into an embrace. "See you then."

"Yeah." Jordan watched him go, leaning against the door frame. Plucking a blade of grass from the side of the porch, he spun it in his fingers as his dad pulled out of the driveway. Though his father hadn't said anything, Jordan felt he knew what he'd done today. Sighing, he spun the blade to the ground and turned for his apartment, knowing in his heart that everything his dad had told him was the truth.

STERLING

Sterling was waiting for her when Rhea pulled up to their home. She'd been gone for hours. After leaving Josh, her mother dropped her off at her car and ordered her to return home. She'd not indicated plans involving Rhea, and that shook her to her core. The hour-long drive back to

Lansford was filled with thoughts of what Nichole might do. Would she really take Nevaeh from Josh and press charges against him for a crime he didn't commit?

She parked her car in the garage, her hands trembling. She knew the answer to this. There was no doubt in her mind that her mother would do this. So why had she allowed her to return to Sterling? What game was she playing?

Rhea didn't have time to think further about this before the garage door burst open and Sterling rushed toward the car. His pained expression told her of the worry he'd spent on her since she'd left him that morning. With a sigh, she opened her door and let him pull her into his embrace.

"I was worried sick," he breathed into her hair. "I'm so glad you're home. Come on." He wrapped an arm around her shoulders, flicking the door closed before leading her into the house. "I fixed your favorite dinner. I'm sure you're starved."

Rhea's mind played back the look on Josh's face when she'd refused to confirm he hadn't raped her. Her stomach lurched, and she broke free of Sterling's embrace as she raced for the toilet.

"Rhea? Baby?" he called after her, following her to the guest bathroom.

She could feel him hovering as she retched and wished he'd go away. Accepting the cold washcloth he'd brought for her, she wrapped her hair into a twist and leaned back against the wall, eyes closed.

"Baby, what's wrong?" Sterling sat on the floor with her, concern etched across his features.
She forced a smile and looked at him. "Nothing. Just not feeling so well."

"Come on." He stood and reached for her. "Let's get you upstairs."

When he scooped her up and carried her to their room, she laid her head on his shoulder, wishing she could protect him from what was coming. "I love you," she whispered, meaning every word.

Sterling's chest burned, and he squeezed her tight as he placed her onto their bed and sat beside her. Caressing her hair, he took in her pale features. "Did you find what you were looking for today?"

Tears rushed to her eyes. "My mother is the devil." She turned away from him and curled into a ball. "Please let me sleep."

He was quiet for a while, trying to understand. At last, he kissed her temple and stood. "Okay. I'll be downstairs if you need me."

Rhea waited ten minutes after he'd gone before withdrawing her phone. Pulling up the picture she'd taken of Josh and Nevaeh, she stared longingly. Nevaeh was perfect, with beautiful blond curls and bright green eyes that looked just like hers. She was everything she'd ever dreamed of and then some.

She sat up and rested against the headboard, her bare feet poking out beneath the too-long hem of her jeans. Her baby girl was wrapped in her father's arm, and the look of peace on Josh's face as he held her was like none she'd ever seen.

And here she was, conspiring to destroy them.

A tear streaked down her face, and she swiped it away. How dare she cry? What right did she have to these tears? Had she not just stood in his face and told him she was taking their baby away from him after he'd just found out about her? Had she not allowed her mother to accuse him of raping her when she knew he hadn't?

With a sigh, she looked back at the picture in her hands. What if... She sat up, staring. What if she could sneak off to where Josh was staying? If she could explain her side, and the reason behind what she had done, she could warn him to take Nevaeh and run away from the dangerous snares her mother was setting for him.

Checking her watch, she shoved her phone back into her pocket and leaped off the bed. It would take her about an hour to get to Levi's. She didn't know if Josh would be there, but she had to try. She owed him that much. Going to the dresser to brush her hair, she reminded herself to be quiet. She couldn't let Sterling find out she was leaving—he'd never let her go.

Quietly, she slipped down the stairs, listening for Sterling. About halfway down, she heard him in the kitchen, and her conscience pricked as she realized he was putting away the dinner he'd made for her. He would never understand. How could she tell him she was running off to protect the man she'd loved before Sterling Oliver was in the picture?

She made it to the side door and held her breath as she pulled it open and stepped into the garage. Exhaling, she climbed behind the wheel of her car and started the engine. The garage door whirred open, and she backed into the driveway at the same moment that Sterling rushed out, confusion furrowing his brow as he called to her.

Rhea watched him as she backed into the street, pausing before pressing the gas.

Sterling didn't know where she was going, but she knew that, once he found out, it would all be over. There was no coming back from this.

Determination sealed her fate as she drove away from their home, leaving him behind.

Chapter 24

"For I know my transgressions, and my sin is ever before me. Against you, you only, have I sinned and done what is evil in your sight, so that you may be justified in your words and blameless in your judgment."
~Psalm 51:3-4~

LEVI

The doorbell rang, and Levi's eyes shot to where Laura slapped forks onto napkins around the table. He cleared his throat and went to her, attempting to wrap his arms around her.

No dice.

She brushed him off and seared him with a glare. "Answer the door," she clipped. "And if that girl isn't wearing clothes, don't let her set foot in my house, Levi Jaidon!"

He backed away from her and sent up a prayer for God to bestow grace and mercy into his wife's heart for their son. A drawn-out whistle from above drew his eyes to the banister where Josh was grinning like a fool at Laura's temper. Levi sighed and dropped his head. All he'd wanted was time with his boy. Neither Laura nor Josh was making this easy for him. Laura's anger forced a lockdown in their communication, while Josh refused to come down if Jordan was in the house. Why bother trying? Jordan would most likely walk right back out that door once he felt the tension in the room. Forcing a smile, Levi pulled open the door, throwing up a prayer of thanks to find Cali fully clothed in jeans and a plain tee.

"My boy." His smile broadened as he reached for Jordan, grateful to feel his son's arms go around him, even if they were stiff.

"Cali, Dad. Dad, Cali," Jordan muttered as he stepped into the house.

"Pleasure," Cali smiled at Levi as she followed Jordan in.

Shutting the door behind them, Levi told himself not to stare as he tried to size up the girl working overtime to ruin his son's life. He wondered at her angle. What could she want from him? There had to be something… Reminding himself to play it cool so Jordan wouldn't leave, he gestured to the kitchen.

"Mom's in the kitchen finishing up the table. Ready to eat?"

"You got grilled veggies, Pops?" Jordan asked. "You promised my faves," he reminded, a hint of teasing in his tone.

Behind his back, Levi's eyes shut, hiding his tears of thanks at just a tad bit of normalcy from his son. "Sure do! Hot 'n ready to devour." He laughed as he led the way into the kitchen, noting that Laura was nowhere to be found.

"Have a seat." He waved to the table and smiled. "Mom's around here somewhere—probably out by the grill."

Jordan sat, pulling Cali down beside him and draping his arm across her shoulders. "Josh here?" Though he tried to hide his nerves, his voice squeaked from the tension in his chest.

Levi's eyes shot to the banister, then back to his son. "Sorry, son."

"He has got to learn to get over himself. The guy can't even take a joke." Cali rolled her eyes and laughed.

Levi froze, his gaze falling on this bold little girl who thought she could waltz into his home and say whatever she wanted. Taking a breath, he turned for the patio door and walked out to find his wife before he said something he'd regret.

"I told you, Cali," Jordan quietly spoke near her ear. "Be cool. This is my parents' house. Don't disrespect them."

She rolled her eyes and pulled free of his arm. "Oh, like you were so respectful to your father today?" Her brow shot up as she challenged him.

Jordan sighed, kicking himself for relaying their

conversation to her—and with pride, at that. Love was strange. He was so drawn to her, yet everything she touched burned up in his face. "Just be respectful, Cali. My mom doesn't play that."

"I wish she would try me," Cali clipped. The words had been carefully aimed at unnerving him. She enjoyed how his mind worked overtime to try and figure out her next move. He was so easy.

Watching him stiffen out of the corner of her eye, she knew her words had met their mark. Divide and conquer. Hadn't that been Asher's advice to her that morning? Dividing Jordan from his family was child's play, but she had to remember he wasn't the target. Josh was. Her eyes quickly scanned the top floor for any sign of him, grinning when she heard beats ramp up behind one of the closed doors. He was here. Now to draw him out.

Levi wandered back into the kitchen, a plate of steaming burgers in his hands. "Hope you two brought your appetites, we've got enough to feed an army!"

"Let me help you with that, Dad." Jordan grabbed the plate from his father, lowered it to the table, and nearly dropped it when his mother walked through the door. He swallowed hard as her accusations flooded his mind. He sat back in his chair, Cali snuggling up to his shoulder.

Glancing at the couple, Laura rolled her eyes when Cali gave her a pointed look and tossed a leg over Jordan's. Dropping her metal spatula onto the counter with a clang,

Laura picked up the salad bowl and vigorously washed the lettuce she'd already cleaned. "Did that girl seriously just throw her leg over my son right in front of my face?" she hissed at the sink, not caring one bit that her words could be heard by the occupants in the room. When she turned, all eyes were fixed on her, yet no one dared make a sound. "What are you all looking at? As though I'm the slut in this room," she grumbled as she tossed the salad bowl onto the table.

"Baby," Levi breathed into her ear, his hand on her back. "Take it easy. Please."

"I suggest you eat, Levi Hendricks." Her eyes bore into his before she sat at the table, Levi claiming the seat beside her.

Cali felt Jordan nudge her leg to the floor and she smiled. "Oh, silly me. I am so embarrassed! I'm just so used to it just being Jordan and me at home, I didn't even think twice." Her tone oozed saccharine, and she felt Jordan's surprise next to her.

"Um...here, baby, let me help with the iced tea." Levi rushed to grab the pitcher, eagerly filling glasses as his wife's glare pinned their son to his chair.

"You two are living together now?"

Jordan raised his chin, refusing to prove Cali right by allowing his mother to push him around. "She's stayed over."

"Yes."

They answered together, and Laura narrowed her glare. "Well." Her tone was level and cold. "I assume you've made other accommodations for rent, then?"

Jordan swallowed hard and looked at his dad, whose gaze was fixated on the tablecloth.

Coward.

He felt Cali's hand run up his thigh, and he shoved her off him. This was all her fault.

"Jordan?" His mother prompted; brow raised.

"There she goes... controlling your life again." Cali's sing-song voice was just loud enough to be heard as she sipped her glass of tea.

Laura leaped to her feet and Levi's hand shot out, gripping her wrist as he lowered her back down, his thumb caressing her skin.

"Don't worry about it, Mom," Jordan bit. "I'll figure out rent. You won't have to pay a dime next month."

"Oh, that's cute." Laura laughed, her eyes going to Levi. "Did you hear your son, babe? He thinks he can cough up fifteen hundred dollars for rent in two weeks. Isn't he funny?"

Levi cleared his throat, a nervous smile flashing across

his face. "Let's say grace, Laura," he urged from her side, his eyes begging her to let it go.

"How about you let her pray," Laura snapped. "Or does she know how, Jordan Blayze? Does she know the God of the Bible? Or did you just snatch her from a street corner and invite her into your bed?"

Jordan's cheeks flamed as his eyes met his father's. "We came here because Dad asked us to, Mom. We didn't come so you could attack my girlfriend."

The floorboards creaked from the entryway, and all eyes swung to Josh as he swiped a bottle of water from the fridge, a cigarette dangling between his fingers. His eyes locked with Jordan's as he swung the fridge closed and moved for the door without a word.

"This beer sure is good." Cali took a long sip from her glass, her gaze fixed on Josh as he stopped dead in his tracks and turned. "Tastes like a good beating."

A hush fell across the room as all eyes turned to Josh. His gaze flew between Cali and Jordan, the betrayal washing over him. Had his friend disclosed his most personal experiences with this girl?

"Time to go." Jordan grabbed her elbow and abruptly stood, his eyes never leaving Josh. When Cali didn't budge, he pulled her to her feet and pushed her past Josh. "Go, Cali. Now." His heart pounded in his ears when Josh's hand shot out and grabbed Cali's arm, yanking her back—his face inches from hers.

Cali's eyes were as big as saucers as she stared up at him, her arm screaming from the vise. Summoning all her courage, she reminded herself that she was on top—not him. Regaining her composure, she leveled her gaze at him and smiled. "I imagine it's going to be very hard to be daddy to that little girl, knowing your abuser had her first."

Josh shoved her hard. She slammed into Jordan, who caught her and pulled her through the front door. Jordan's eyes shot to Josh, who followed them with a glazed look. "Move, move, move!" he shouted to Cali, pushing her toward his truck. Please, God, don't let him hit her… please God…

Levi and Laura rushed after them, each worried over Josh's next move as he pursued Cali to the truck.

"Josh, she's not worth it," Levi called as he neared.

"You got a beef with me?" Josh demanded; fists clenched as he cut off Cali's path to the passenger side door.

Shoving a hand out, Jordan stopped him, his eyes holding Josh's. "We're leaving, man, just let her go." He kept his voice calm and steady, not wanting to give Josh any reason to start swinging.

Josh sneered at his friend. "So that's how it is? You tell her all my secrets, then you protect her?"

Josh's assumption slapped him in the face, and Jordan's hand fell to his side. "You think I told Cali about everything?"

"It's not what I think, it's the truth, Jordan! But it seems like the truth has become a foreign concept to you. You're nothing but a liar." Josh stepped toward him, laughing when Jordan stepped toward him too.

"Takes one to know one," Jordan threw back, mindless of his parents standing nearby.

"Yeah? Well, at least I admit to bein' a liar! I know who I am, but this stupid chick has you so turned around you don't know your face from your butt!"

Jordan shoved him and Josh swung, connecting with his left jaw and snapping his head back.

"Hey, hey, hey! Break it up, you two!" Levi grabbed Jordan, only to be shoved back as his son went after Josh. Hiding her smile, Cali decided to ramp up the heat. "Stop! Stop it!" she cried beside the boys as they exchanged blows. "He didn't tell me everything! Just some, okay? Like how you knocked up some chick and ran out on her and the baby."

Josh's fist froze midair, his eyes wide as he stared at his friend. Releasing Jordan's t-shirt, he dropped his fist. "'Some chick?'" His voice was small as he stared at Jordan. "You told this girl that I ran out on my kid?"

Jordan's eyes dimmed as he looked at Cali, his heart squeezing. "Why would you tell him that, Cali?" His voice quivered as he spoke. "Why would you lie and try to hurt me?"

Cali's eyes were huge as she worked her innocence. "B-but you did tell me those things…" She looked at Josh. "How else could I know he has a mile-long rap sheet? Or that his girl wants nothing to do with him anymore?"

Everyone began shouting at once. All hands grabbed Josh to try to pull him back. But no one could keep the fury from exploding through his veins as he slammed his fist into Jordan's truck, shattering the passenger's side window a mere inch from Cali's head.

Cali screamed and ducked, her hands flying to her head. "Take me home, Jordan! Take me home!" she wailed.

When Levi wrapped an arm around Josh's waist and hauled him back, Jordan ushered Cali into the truck and started the engine. Glancing up at Josh, he saw him point a finger at him.

"You keep that slut away from me, Blayze, or so help me, I will walk myself to that jail cell!" His right hand was bleeding—his old wounds having been ripped open—but Josh didn't seem to notice.

Jordan swallowed hard as Josh shook Levi off him, turned, and lit his cigarette before walking toward the road. Glancing at his parents, he let out a defeated sigh and looked down as they stared at him, shock and disappointment settling in their eyes. Casting one last look at his father, he mouthed: "Sorry, Dad." Revving the motor, he popped the truck into reverse and circled back down the winding driveway, Cali hugging her knees as she cried. This girl had just betrayed him to the fullest, ruining any chance he had left at mending things with Josh.

Decisions had to be made.

"I don't wanna see you anymore."

Jordan stopped the truck in the middle of the driveway and stared. Was she serious right now? She was dumping him? No, no, no… she didn't get to get off that easy. She'd done nothing but destroy him ever since they'd gotten together.

"Unbelievable," he voiced his surprise. "You're dumping me? I'm the one who should be kicking you to the curb!"

Cali cowered beside him as tears slipped down her cheeks. "Just take me home, Jordan. Take me home." Rolling his eyes and slamming his hand on the steering wheel, he threw the truck in drive and started to pull away, but froze when his gaze fell on something in the distance.

"Jordan, what's wr—"

"Shh!" He waved a hand at Cali, his eyes fixated to his left. There, illuminated by the moonlight, stood Josh. Only he wasn't alone. Rhea was standing there too.

JOSH

"Rhea," Josh whispered her name into the night air. Tossing his cigarette to the ground, he stamped it out—his eyes never leaving her face.

"I had to see you." Her eyes searched his for any sign of disapproval. When she found none, she breathed a sigh of relief and willed her trembling limbs to calm. Her eyes fell to his bloodied hand, and she gasped. "You're hurt!"

Josh glanced down and winced. "Uh, yeah."

Removing her scarf, she wrapped it around his wound. When she felt the blood had been temporarily stopped, she forced herself to explain why she'd come. "I didn't want it this way—I begged her not to do this, Josh. I begged her! Please believe me," she whispered.

His heart broke as he took in her tear-streaked face. He reached for her, grateful when she allowed him to hold her. Rhea's arms wrapped around his waist, and he welcomed the pain tearing into his ribs, knowing he'd accept more if it meant she was with him. Josh breathed in the rose-petal scent of her hair, pulling it back from her face and pressing a light kiss to her temple. "Don't cry, baby. Please don't cry. We're gonna be okay."

She pulled away and took a step back. "Josh!" Her

voice was urgent, rushed.

"Rhea, what is it?" Concern was etched across his features.

He wanted nothing more than to disappear into the night with her.

"I didn't come for this."

His eyes fell to the ring on her left hand, and his chest compressed against his lungs. "I see. What's his name?" He forced the words through tight lips.

Rhea wrapped her right hand over the ring and shook her head. "I need you to focus," she urged.

There was no explaining her desperate need to rush the delivery of her warning. As far as she knew, she hadn't been followed, but everyone knew her mother had ways of appearing out of nowhere, and she wouldn't risk letting Josh get distracted.

"I don't have much time. My mother has her sights set on Nevaeh." Her eyes searched his, ensuring she had his full attention. "She's coming for her, Josh, and there's nothing we can do about it. She will press charges against you for rape."

Nerves pushed a smile across his face, the ring temporarily forgotten as he stared at her. "Baby, she can't press charges—only you can do that. But since I didn't rape you, we have nothing to worry about. She can't touch us." Taking in the way her eyes dimmed, and her mouth twitched from unshed tears, he wondered what he'd missed. He'd thought of nothing else since Nichole's visit. Since then, he'd been sure he'd be free of any accusation if Rhea refused to press charges against him.

Rhea closed her eyes, fighting the urge to shake him. Had he forgotten who her mother was? What she was capable of? She had to put it to him straight—no room for pretense. Opening her eyes, she fixed her gaze on him. "Josh, my mom will press charges, and she'll have a recorded testimony from me to prove her allegations. She'll work the system, override the judge, and browbeat any lawyer you might retain. Then she'll take our baby from us, and you'll never see her again. Listen to me." She placed her hands on his forearms, her green eyes flashing with intensity. "You have to take Nevaeh and run."

"Rhea, I can't—"

"You're her only hope! Take her and go. Don't wait—please!"

Josh swiped a hand through his hair, uncertainty tormenting his mind. "My mom won't give her to me. She's already said so. She wants me stable before signing her over. I can't just take her!"

"No." She shook her head, lips trembling. "No, Josh. She's yours. Take her and go!"

"She's not mine," he argued. "You gave her to my father, remember?" Agony squeezed his chest as they bartered their daughter's fate.

"You can convince them to let you do this. You can tell them everything my mother has threatened. They'll give her to you. They have to!"

"Baby..." Josh touched her back, pulling away when she flinched. "I left you once." He sniffed. "I could never do that again. If Nevaeh and I go, you're coming with us."

Rhea laughed and looked at him. "You used to be so much smarter than this. You always used to be ahead of the game."

Confused, Josh raised his hands in the air, palms up. "I still am," he argued. "I'm not gonna let her do this to us."

Rhea glanced at her watch; the time illuminated by a soft purple glow. She had to go. Now. Her heart pounded as she thought of explaining her absence to Sterling. "I have to go," she cried. "Listen to me. Listen!" Her hands were on his arms again. "My mother is prosecuting you for rape. This is happening. She will force me onto that stand and force a false confession out of my mouth. Once that happens, it's over for you. You're going to jail. But don't think it stops there, because it doesn't. Once you're in there, she'll use everything she's ever known about you to destroy your character on the outside. She will work every angle until everyone in this pathetic town sees you as a full-blown rapist with every intent to rape your child. I know her, Josh. So, when I stand up in court and speak this lie against you, I want you to remember this one thing: I begged you to run."

Josh opened his mouth, but no words came out. He'd been struck numb at the truth in her tone. He watched her turn and walk down the street. She was leaving.

No.

No!

His hand shot out and gently gripped her arm, spinning her around. Pulling her body into his, he tangled his fingers in her hair and kissed her. His heart shattered all over again when she pulled away, tears streaming down her face. She stared long and hard, as though this was her last goodbye.

"I love you," he whispered, watching her back away. When she didn't respond, he called louder. "I love you, Rhea Nichole."

Please tell me you still love me too! his heart begged.

Taking one last look at him, Rhea turned for the street and disappeared into the night.

CALI

The moment Jordan's truck stopped in front of her house; Cali bolted for the door. He hadn't spoken to her on the drive home, but she was no longer worried about maintaining their relationship. Her hands trembled as she fumbled to unlock the front door. Once inside, she raced to her room and pulled out her phone as she climbed onto her bed.

Her tears flowed as the line rang, her heart still pumping wildly.

"Make it quick." Asher's tone was clipped.

"I don't wanna do this anymore." She sniffed and swiped a hand across her face.

"What happened? Are you hurt?" Concern replaced his irritation. It wasn't that he cared about his informant—he didn't—he just couldn't stand anything more weighing on his already burdened conscience.

"He broke a window—right by my head!"

Asher's mind whirled. "Who?"

"Josh! I took your advice and threw out details of his life I wasn't supposed to know. He took the bait and accused Jordan of ratting him out but came after me!"

"I told you not to provoke him!"

"Yeah, well you failed to mention he's a homicidal maniac!" Cali snapped.

Asher sighed as he thought, an idea brewing in his mind. He could use this…this could be good… "You say he attacked you?"

"Yes! With everyone there watching! If Jordan's dad hadn't grabbed him, he probably would've hit me! I'm not doing it anymore, Asher. I broke it off with Jordan, and I'm never going around him again."

Asher rolled his eyes. Drama queen. "Okay, baby girl. Don't give it a second thought. I'll take care of it. You did great, kid. Just great."

"I still expect my money," she reminded him.

"Yeah, yeah. You'll get it."

The line went dead, and Cali hugged her knees to her chest as she willed herself to calm. Her head flew up when her door opened. She glared as her brother walked in.

"Zion, you perv, get out! You never knock."

"What'd he do to you?" her brother demanded, straddling her desk chair as though she hadn't just ordered him out.

Cali rolled her eyes. "Nothing. Get lost."

He leaned forward, studying her tear-streaked face. "I'll kill him, if he hurt you."

She glared at him. "He didn't."

"Then why are you crying? Did Hendricks drag you to a church meeting?"

She gave him a pointed look.

"Did he force you to read a Bible?" Zion pressed.

"Zion, stop it. Go away. I don't wanna talk about it, okay?"

He was quiet for a moment, then ventured further. "You slept with him, didn't you?"

Her eyes shot to her open door. "That's none of your business! If you must know, I'm crying because of his friend–not because of Jordan."

His gaze narrowed, and she realized her mistake.

"What friend? What'd he do to you? Did he hurt you?"

"Why can't you be like normal little brothers and not care about what happens to me?"

His face fell. "You're my sister. Dad and Mom don't know about half the stuff you do out there. Someone's gotta keep you out of trouble, Cali."

"I can take care of myself. Now get out of my room."

Frustrated, Zion stood and walked to the door. "Watch yourself, sis. The town's starting to talk."

She glared at him. "Out!"

She shut the door, and she pulled her knees back into her chest and squeezed them tight, her near-miss with Josh's fist still heavy on her mind.

RHEA

It was almost ten o'clock by the time Rhea pulled into her driveway. Though she wished she could pretend she hadn't seen the car that tailed her all the way home, the truth was that Asher hadn't tried to hide that she was being watched. She wouldn't think about what this meant right now—she couldn't handle the pressure. Inside the garage, she turned the car off and waited. With each deep breath, she willed herself to calm, but instead of peace, she envisioned Sterling. Tears clogged her throat as she imagined him pacing the floor and wondering what had driven her from their home without an explanation.

He didn't deserve this. Sterling was a good man. And she was a liar.

She knew what to do, but the thought ripped her soul apart. Maybe she could pretend none of this had happened. She could tell him what a rotten day she'd had, fall asleep, wake up, and start all over again. She could pretend her mother's threats were just that—idle words spoken by a lunatic. After all, her mother hadn't given her any instructions after dumping her back at her car. Maybe she'd only wanted to shake her up—remind her who was in charge.

Who was she kidding? Her mother was a viper in a dress. Her threats were packed with venom and death. And Asher had followed her to Highshore.

There was only one way to protect Sterling, and she intended to follow through, even if it killed her. Parking in the garage, she'd barely shut the engine off when Sterling rushed for her car. She forced a smile but burst into tears when he opened her door. He pulled her into his arms and hugged her tight as she cried.

"Shh, baby," he soothed, kissing her temple. "It's okay. Whatever's going on, we'll get through it together."

"I'm so sorry," Rhea cried into his shirt.

"Stop. Let's go inside. We can talk once we get you calm, okay? Come on." He led her into the house, and they sat on the couch together, Rhea curling up against his side. "I painted the bathroom while you were gone. I hope you like it–I used the color you picked, even though I requested white…" He relaxed when she giggled through her tears, relieved to have her responding. His mind was filled with questions, but he refused to force her to talk. He would wait for her, even if it killed him.

"I'm so sorry, Sterling," Rhea sniffed, wrapping her arms around his waist and squeezing him tight.

He smiled and rubbed her back. "You scared me to death. But you're here now. Let's focus on that." He held his breath, waiting for her to volunteer something–anything–but she didn't.

"I was so stupid to leave like that. I should've told you." Her heart ached with the plans she was forming, but there was no other way to save him from her past. "Sterling?"

"Yes?" His answer displayed his eagerness, and his chest swelled with hope. Was she about to volunteer where she'd been all evening?

"I'm really tired. Can we just…forget today ever happened? I'd like to go to bed."

He closed his eyes. Why wouldn't she trust him with whatever she was dealing with? "Baby," he whispered.

Her chest tightened. "Please, Sterling." She pulled her legs tighter into her stomach and pressed her face against his chest. "My mother is a nightmare. Don't make me relive this night. Please."

Forcing himself to put her needs first, Sterling nodded. "Okay. Let's get you to bed."

Rhea clung to his neck as he scooped her into his arms and carried her to their bedroom. He helped her undress and climb beneath the covers, then climbed beside her and held her close.

"I love you," she whispered.

He smiled as he caressed her skin. "I love you, Rhea. We'll get through this. Together."

She lay awake in his arms long after his breathing evened out and she knew he was in a deep sleep. When their bedside clock read midnight, she slowly untangled herself from his arms and kissed him. Pulling on jeans and a T-shirt, Rhea reached for her bag and quietly packed.

Standing in the doorway with the bag draped across her shoulders, she gave the room one last look, her eyes lingering on the man who'd loved her for the past three years. Swallowing back a sob, Rhea slipped into the hall and shut the door behind her.

"Goodbye, Sterling," she whispered.

Life would never be the same.

Chapter 25

"I will arise and go to my father, and I will say to him, "Father, I have sinned against heaven and before you. I am no longer worthy to be called your son. Treat me as one of your hired servants."
~Luke 15:18-19~

ASHER

"You were right." Asher stared across the table at his blackmailer. "Rhea caught up with Cameron last night. I couldn't get close enough to hear, since she met him in Hendricks' driveway, but it doesn't take an idiot to guess she warned him."

The café wasn't busy—it was too early for the morning crowd. The two had each ordered a cup of coffee for their meeting, though Asher didn't plan on staying long.

Nichole smiled behind the steaming mug. Taking a long sip, she placed the mug down. "And what did our predictable little heathen do with this information?"

Asher shifted, praying his answer didn't set her off. "Well, I couldn't tail them both, so I left him there and followed her. She went back home. Stayed until around midnight, then slipped out with a duffel. Oliver wasn't with her."

Nichole raised a brow. "Where did she go?"

Asher pulled a piece of paper from his pocket and slid it to her. "To this address. Local girl. Works at the diner with Rhea."

"She left him." She smiled, tracing the numbers of the address with her nail. "Excellent. I expect it won't be long before he shows up demanding answers about his precious girlfriend who can do no wrong. You'll need to be available for when that happens."

He cleared his throat and leaned his elbows on the table. "Uh, actually, I wanted to propose something to you."

"I'm listening."

His heart pounded. "I know someone can help you convict Cameron in court." He swallowed hard. "But you have to release me from this blackmail before I'll tell you who." He studied her face, hope blossoming as she seemed to consider this.

Cold laughter slapped him in the face, and he knew he'd been played.

Nichole raised her chin, eyes narrowing. "I'll tell you what—you tell me who…or I'll set your demise into motion. How about that, puppet?"

A cold sweat broke across Asher's forehead. He cleared his throat, nerves constricting his airway. He saw no choice in the matter—he had to give in to her demands. "I heard from my informant last night. She says Cameron attacked her."

Nichole's eyes shifted; her interest piqued. "Attacked her—sexually?"

"No, violently. Says he would have beaten her to death if her boyfriend's dad hadn't pulled him off her."

She thought about this, letting the seed take root. This news could not have been more perfect. "How reliable is her information?"

"Never failed me yet."

"Would she lie on the stand?"

"No doubt."

"Easily intimidated?"

"Nope." Until today… He kept the thought to himself.

She smiled. "I want to talk to this girl. Set it up for later today. If this goes my way, I'll loosen your noose a bit. Now get out of my sight. Report back with the girl by five o'clock."

Without another word, she waved a hand at him, shooing him from the table.

As he walked to his car, Asher sucked in a breath. His plan had blown up in his face. His blackmailer still owned him, and he was helpless to change that. His only hope lay in the lap of a psychotic college student. "Please come through, Cali. Please."

GARRETT

"He asked us to meet him on neutral ground." Garrett stared at his wife as she leaned against their dresser. Any other day, with any other topic on her tongue, he'd be acting on his impulse to take her in his arms and kiss her. Her hands rested on the dresser, arms crooked at the elbows as she stared at him, chestnut hair falling over her shoulders. Those eyes...

"Did you hear what I said?" Elysia's tone was urgent, snapping his mind back.

"Uh, yeah. So 'neutral ground?' What's that about? He's been coming to the house just fine."

A sigh slipped from her lips as she pushed off the dresser and came to sit beside him on their king-sized bed. If only he could grab her in his arms and lay her back...

"He said he has to talk to us about something important. Something that can't wait." She looked at him, worry weighing in her eyes. "Garrett, something's wrong. I have a bad feeling."

He forced himself to focus on what his wife was saying. He reached for her hand and caressed her skin with his thumb. "Whatever it is, we'll get through it together, okay? Are we bringing Nevaeh?"

She sighed, tears filling her eyes. "I-I'm not sure we should."

Garrett felt sudden alarm in his spirit as her words sank in. What could Josh possibly want to discuss that had his wife so tense? And to want to speak with him? Telling himself not to borrow trouble, he met Elysia's tear-filled eyes. "And he asked for both of us?"

"Yes," she whispered, her eyes searching his. "Do you see why I'm so nervous now? Josh doesn't ask to speak to you. Ever. Something's wrong."

He had to agree with her. "We'll leave Nevaeh with Kenzie—you know she'd love to watch her for a couple of hours."

Elysia gave a slight nod, then rose from the bed. "We have to hurry. Josh said he'd be at the park at nine, and it's already 8:15. I'll run Nevaeh next door and meet you in the car." She left the room, her heart telling her that whatever her son had to say would change their lives forever.

JOSH

He was nervous. No, scratch that. He was downright terrified of what he was about to do. As he waited on the park bench for his parents to show, Josh pulled out Titus' Bible and opened it to the section Titus had told him about the night before. He read about a small boy fighting a giant—a giant even an army was terrified to face. Every time he opened this book, it read more like a fairy tale. How could Titus believe this stuff happened? A small boy killing this huge, scary guy with just a slingshot and a stone? Great story…if you're gullible and ten years old. But how was he, a twenty-one-year-old man, supposed to take this as a historical event and use it to push himself to face the giants in his life?

The sound of a car door brought his gaze to the parking lot. He swallowed hard at the sight of his parents headed his way. He quickly shoved the Book into his backpack—he couldn't let them catch him reading the Bible.

Couldn't show them this newfound weakness that often crippled his mind and soul. No, he had to display strength and control, or father would strong-arm him into caving.

"Hi, baby." Elysia reached for him, pulling him into an embrace. Her eyes went to his bandaged hand, but she said nothing as she kissed the top of his head and sat on the park bench beside him.

"Hey, Mama," he mumbled his reply, his eyes never leaving his father, who seemed careful to keep his distance.

"Josh." Garrett nodded at his son, wishing for the freedom to grab him into a hug, but knowing better.

Bobbing his chin, Josh got right to it before fear could make him change his mind. "Rhea came to me last night."

"What?" It was Garrett who'd spoken, shock evidenced

in his tone. He crossed his arms over his chest, his feet planted squarely on the ground, eyes flitting to his wife's face.

"Nichole is planning on taking Nevaeh."

"Oh, God, no." Elysia covered her mouth with her hand, tears spilling down her cheeks.

Josh's eyes shot to hers, angered that Nichole had the power to make his mother cry. "We're not gonna let that happen," he assured her. He forced his eyes to his father's, telling himself to eliminate all fear from his mind for his daughter's sake. "Rhea asked me to take Nevaeh and run. Told me her mom is going to take me to court. File charges against me for rape."

A sudden burst of excitement shot through Garrett. This was his chance to be there for his son! He dropped his arms, eyes bright. "I can defend you. I can get the charges dropped—we all know they're bogus anyway, I can—"

"No." Josh cut him off, staring him down. He shifted on the bench, not wanting to admit the pain in his ribs still weakened his body.

"What other choice do you have, son? You've got to fight her in court." Elysia kept her tone gentle, though she wanted to scream it in his face. Did he not realize how serious this all was? That he could lose his daughter forever? Nichole was ruthless. He didn't stand a chance in the courtroom without his father to back him up. Would he let his pride stand in the way of good legal defense? Even as she thought it, she knew he would.

Josh glanced at his sneakers. Here goes nothing...the reason why he'd asked for their time. "I told Rhea that I can't take Nevaeh because you guys have legal custody."

"True."

Garrett's and Josh's eyes shot to Elysia, each reading the stubborn set of her jaw.

Josh looked at his father, feeling in his gut he'd be the easiest to sway. "I'm asking you to transfer custody to me so I can leave with my daughter."

Elysia gasped and her gaze swung to Garrett, but he

remained focused on their son. "Garrett, no," she said firmly.

He stood, frozen in indecision. Everything in him wanted to give his son what he wanted, but what was best for Nevaeh?

"You can't do this without my approval." Elysia was on her feet now, positioning herself between her husband and son.

What was this? Was his mother fighting against him?

Unbelievable. Josh stood and faced them both. "This is Nichole we're talking about, Mom. She doesn't give two craps about my kid. All she wants is to destroy any chance I have with her and ruin my daughter in the process. I can take her and be gone. Disappear without a trace. You know I can—didn't I just come back from four years of being nothing? Nobody? None of you would have ever found me if it hadn't been for Jordan being a tech geek. I can do it again, Mom. Let me have my kid. Please."

She spun to face him, fire in her eyes. "She doesn't know you, Joshua. Right now, she's terrified of you. And you want me to just hand her off to you and trust she'll be okay? She may be yours by blood, but I have raised that girl since birth. She is my daughter. I cannot destroy her like this!"

Josh tried to push the hurt aside, knowing there was truth in her words. "We can tell her who I am, Mom. She'll adjust and then she—"

"She knows."

Elysia shot Garrett a withering glare. How dare he.

"What?" Josh looked at his father, confused.

"She knows who you are. She overheard Mom and me talking. She's angry and in denial, but she knows." Garrett met his eyes, tormented in his soul at the thought of handing his baby girl off and never seeing her again.

Josh took a second to comprehend. "Okay, so she knows I'm her dad. This is good. This could work." He turned his eyes to his mother, urgency burning in his gaze. "Mom, I'm begging you. Let me do this. I swear I'll keep her safe. I'll make sure she's alright—I would never hurt her. I love my kid. Please, Mom, please do this. For me."

Elysia shook her head. "Absolutely not." She folded her arms across her chest and raised her chin. She didn't care if she had to fight them both with her bare hands, they were not ruining this child's life. "The solution to your problem is standing right in front of you, Joshua. Take it, and leave your daughter out of it."

Josh gritted his teeth, his fists clenching at his sides. She didn't get it. "We don't have time for a court battle. Don't you see? Nichole never has just one plan, Mom. Never. She's always got some other scheme cooking in case her first doesn't pan out. Just let me have my kid. Let me have her! I can be gone within the next hour and you and Dad can sign her over and send me the papers to sign. Then she'll be mine, and Nichole can't touch her."

Elysia laughed in disbelief. "Do you really think she'll leave you alone once you have custody? She'll still throw rape at you, son. And you'll still have to go to court and risk losing Nevaeh to this woman. The safest place for Nevaeh is in our custody. The courts have nothing on us. They cannot rip her away."

Josh groaned and threw up his hands. "She can't prosecute me if she can't find me. Mom, come on! This is my daughter we're talking about! I didn't even know about her for the first three years of her life—let me be her dad!"

"That's not her fault!" Elysia shouted back. "You left! You did that. Not Nevaeh! So don't you dare punish her for your decision!"

Stunned into silence, Josh's jaw clenched as she spun on her heel and headed back to the car. "Dad..." His gaze pleaded with his father. "Talk to her," he begged. When hesitation flashed across Garrett's face, anger surged through Josh's veins, his jaw tensing. "You owe me that much!"

Garrett swallowed through his tears, feeling as though he'd been trapped between a rock and a hard place. "I'm so sorry, son." He turned and followed his wife, leaving

Josh alone to stare after them.

NICHOLE

"So, you've been acting as an informant for Asher and getting close to Joshua Cameron." Nichole stirred her tea with a delicate swirl as she stared at the girl across the table.

"No. Getting close to his best friend, Jordan. We, um, we've been dating." Cali fidgeted in her seat, unnerved by the intensity of this woman's gaze. Her eyes went to Asher. He gave her a reassuring nod, and she remembered to breathe.

"And what did you learn about Joshua during this time?"

Cali rolled her eyes, relaxing into her natural behavior. "He's a major prick who doesn't care about anybody but himself."

Nichole's stained lips crept into a tight smile. She liked this girl. She could use her. "I hear he attacked you?"

"He did. I threw out some info Asher had leaked about him earlier that day. I said it in front of his best friend, which made it seem like his friend had been spreading his business to me. Asher had advised me to do everything I could to break up their friendship so Josh would feel more isolated. Instead of retreating, the jerk attacked me! He chased me out of the house and pinned me up against Jordan's truck. He started yelling at me and slammed his fist into the window and broke it—an inch or two to his left and that would have been my head."

The smile grew. "And how did you respond?"

"I freaked out. I jumped in the truck, terrified he would hit me. If Jordan's dad hadn't grabbed Josh, he would've continued coming for me. I was so scared; I broke it off with Jordan and told him I never wanted to see him again." Cali shoved her strawberry-blond hair off her shoulder and crossed her arms over her chest.

"I see. Did Joshua ever make any sexual advances toward you? Even verbally?" Nichole's mind weaved her black widow's web—beautiful strands of silk intended to trap and kill.

Cali scrunched up her nose. "Eww. No."

"Have you ever been to court, Cali?"

"No."

"Are you afraid of the idea?"

"I'm not generally afraid of anything. My father is pretty high up—I've enjoyed a rather entitled life." Her mouth twisted into a half smile, and she winked in Asher's direction.

"Yes. Your father owns the new hotel in Highshore, correct?"

"The hotel, the paper, and some little run-down store he keeps for who-knows-what reasoning of his."

"Cristof Bristol—yes?"

"That's him."

"You seem rather angered about what happened between you and Joshua." Nichole steered the conversation back to the topic she needed.

"Of course I'm angry. Would've ratted him out to my daddy, except Asher paid me to keep it cool."

Nichole cut her eyes to that man; eyebrows raised.

He shrugged. "You want this in the papers?"

Right. Turning back to Cali, she smiled. "How would you like to get revenge against this boy?"

"You got a plan?"

She laughed. "I am never without a plan. I have deeply personal ties with Joshua Cameron. I will be taking him to court very soon for matters I won't discuss here. I want to pull you in as a witness. Once you're on that stand, I want you to tell the court what happened that night. I want you to sell it like you're on Broadway, understand?"

Cali's face exploded. "I'm the queen of selling it, lady. I can be whoever you want me to be."

"Perfect. Get on that stand, and knock his feet out from under him. Twist that story with enough embellishment to convince the court that you feared for your life—that he is a threat that cannot be trusted with a child."

She scoffed. "No embellishment needed. I wouldn't trust him with my dog."

Asher snorted.

"Not a word of this to anyone, got it? Not your father, big brother, Mommy, or your best friend. If this gets out, I will have my revenge—there's no daddy powerful enough to keep you safe from me. Are we clear?" Nichole sipped her tea, watching the girl over her mug.

"Crystal," Cali smiled. "How much you paying?"

"I'll send some cash your way through Asher—once I know I can trust you. Now go. The both of you. And don't be caught together after today."

ASHER

Asher sat in his office and stared at the three boxes he'd placed on his desk. Boxes that had been stored in his safe for years—untouched, yet never forgotten.

It's hard to forget helping an abuser slip through the system.

His conscience had plagued him—ramping up with Nichole's latest schemes to destroy Cameron. Unable to bear its weight any longer, Asher resigned himself to his locked office, hoping that facing his past sins head-on would enable him to push through this last leg with Nichole. He planned to remember. Then to shred. If he shredded the evidence that accused him every day, maybe he'd find peace while working within these walls. He sighed and picked up the next file to be shredded, forcing himself to open it and remember all that had happened.

All that he'd done—and not done.

All that Nichole had on him to destroy his life forever.

His breath quickened as he stared at the bruised face of a little boy on the paper in his hands. The boy's eyes were full of accusation.

Why did you let him do this to me?

Charged by a sudden burst of rage, Asher ripped the boy's face in two and placed it in the shredder. "I'm sorry," he cried. "I'm so sorry…"

When the face had been successfully shredded into the wastebasket, he turned to the next page, his heart slamming against his ribcage. He didn't want to see more. Didn't want to face the evidence against him—the proof of his crimes. But he didn't get the luxury of choice.

Nichole had made sure of that.

He shredded picture after picture. Bruises. Scrapes. Blood-stained clothing. When he came to a picture of the boy's back, mutilated by the man who was supposed to have loved him, Asher dropped into his chair and sobbed.

Thoughts of Ty flooded his mind. His own sweet boy, beaten. He would kill anyone who touched him, yet he had helped this little boy's father hide his sins. It didn't matter that he was a different person now. Didn't matter that his wife and child had no clue about his past. All that mattered was that his sins from years before were finally coming to bury him in his grave. Filled with loathing for his past self, Asher yelled murderously and threw one of the boxes across the room. He watched the files fly in the air and settle peacefully to the floor.

Peaceful. What a joke. There was nothing peaceful about those files.

Swiping a rough hand across his eyes, he snatched up the next paper from the box. A police report that never got filed. Never went before the judge. Instead, it had been confiscated by good ol' Asher Holmes, the crooked police captain who'd valued money and power more than a little boy's life. He forced himself to read.

Arresting officer: Silas Parlor

Parlor had been adamant about the arrest. He'd told Asher he'd never seen a child beaten as badly as twelve-year-old Joshua Cameron had been that day. To appease him and buy his silence, Asher had arrested Garrett, himself, and placed him in his squad car. It was easy to get him off—one altered police report here, another altered there…Parlor bought the lie that he'd screwed up his report, therefore putting Cameron back out on the streets. Two days after Garrett's release, Parlor quit the force and moved out of town, his guilty conscience eating him alive over an error he hadn't made.

Problem solved.

Only...the problem wasn't solved, because a little boy was still being beaten by his dad, and the crooked police captain was still okay with that. His hands trembled as he read further, wishing he could give into the impulse to shred without remembering. But no. He owed that little boy at least the courtesy of suffering through his past choices.

At approximately 7 PM, units were dispatched to 765 Pine Trail LN in response to a 911 call placed by a neighbor who'd heard screaming from the barn. Upon arrival at the scene, I found Garrett Cameron passed out drunk in the living room. No one else was found inside the home. Officer Herman and I walked to the barn where we found twelve-year-old Joshua Cameron severely beaten and unconscious against the interior wall. His injuries included that of...

Asher took a deep breath and covered his eyes, tears shoving through his tear ducts. He couldn't relive the injuries on that boy. Opening his eyes, he skimmed past the description and continued reading.

I arrested Garrett Cameron at 7:23 PM. When questioned at the scene about the state of his son, Cameron claimed to know nothing about what had happened, appearing to be distraught and demanding to know who had attacked the child. Blood stains on his clothing, along with his belt found in the barn, gave enough cause for arrest, and he was taken into custody and transported to the jail by Captain Asher Holmes.

Only he'd done no such thing. He'd driven his "prisoner" to the house of Lance Sherard—city manager—who was the third party in their circle of crime. Asher had left Garrett with Lance to sober him up and take his statement, then had rushed off to call Claire Burkman—the fourth party in their circle. Burkman was a seasoned CPS worker who thrived off making the next dollar. Between the four of them, they'd had it made.

Or so it had seemed.

Sherard had kept Cameron from getting burned, in order to carry out his agenda in the streets. A crooked defense attorney equals crooked politicians roaming free. Cameron was the best. Sherard would never let him go down for his crimes. Asher had kept Burkman doctoring her reports by keeping a steady cash flow in her pocket. And Asher? What had he gotten from this deal? Power and money. As captain, he was on top. No one could touch him, or so he'd assumed. He sighed, his hand feeding the file to the shredder. None of it had been worth it. He'd give up all his power and money for just one day of peace. Just one hour...

JORDAN

The only light in the room came from the glow of the flat-screen TV he'd mounted on the wall when he'd moved into his apartment. He and his dad had worked for over an hour trying to get that stupid thing on the wall so he could stare at it mindlessly for hours. Lots of laughs that day. Back when they were cool.

Now his only company was the newscaster droning on about the latest crimes in the city. No dad, no mom, no best friend. Not even the chick he thought he'd loved. The newscaster told him about a homeless man they'd found on the streets. Homeless because of a betrayal that ran deep—a betrayal from a friend. As he sipped his beer, Jordan shifted beneath the newscaster's gaze, feeling as though he was the center of the broadcast. He was no better than this homeless man's friend, sitting on his couch drinking a beer.

Beer. The very thing that had gotten his best friend beaten as a child.

Jordan closed his eyes and saw Josh as a twelve-year-old kid standing in front of him at school, lying through his teeth about why he couldn't play ball on the playground that day. Jordan's breaths quickened, his brow beginning to glisten. During Josh's hospital stay, he'd noticed the tattoo that now covered his back, hiding the scars he'd gotten from the beating that had kept him off the playing field that day. Anger and remorse gripped his stomach in an unforgiving vise, twisting the beer in his gut until he was forced off the couch and into the bathroom. When he'd finished retching the betrayal out of his system and had washed his mouth out, he returned to the living room and picked up his beer can. Walking into the kitchen, he poured it down the drain, running water to wash out the stench of it all. A sudden burst of energy drove him to the fridge, where he yanked the twelve pack from the shelf and slammed it down on the counter. With a yell, he popped the caps on all the cans and began pouring the alcohol into the sink, praying his betrayal would be washed down with it.

When the deed was done, Jordan bagged up the empty cans and box and walked them out to the dumpster. Satisfaction poured through him when he heard the tin cans clink against metal as the bag was tossed in. He didn't hurry on his way back to his apartment. Instead, he stared at the stars against the night sky as though looking into the face of God. Conviction gripped him, dropping him to his knees in the grass. Chest tight, breaths barely slipping through his lungs, Jordan cried out to his Creator, knowing the real betrayal had been of God, not of man.

"Oh, God…" His face twisted with his sobs. How could he have allowed himself to walk away from his Savior? "I don't deserve it, but I'm begging You. Forgive me." Jordan gripped his stomach, his face bent low to the earth. "I'm so sorry, Lord. I'm so sorry! I never should've fallen for that girl. Look where it got me, God. Look at me now! Look what I've done to my parents—to my friend! I'm broken, Jesus—desperate for Your hand of mercy. I can't fix this, Lord. I need you! I need You, God. Please be merciful to me. I don't deserve it—I disdained Your work on the cross. The death of Your Son on Calvary became nothing to me!"

Jordan's fingers gripped the grass beneath him as he cried aloud. "How do I move on from this? What can I do? Oh, God…"

"…as far as the east is from the west, so far does he remove our transgressions from us."

The verse hit him like a ton of bricks, and he cried harder. "Jesus, forgive me!"

"For I will be merciful toward their iniquities, and I will remember their sins no more."

Placing his hands over his face, his shoulders shook. "If You give me another chance with those I've hurt, Lord, I swear I'll do better. Just…let me have one more chance. Please, God."

"Yo, man…you a'ight?"

He raised his eyes and blinked through his tears to find a neighbor staring at him. As though realizing for the first time that he was slumped in the grass bawling his eyes out, Jordan leaped to his feet and dusted off his jeans. Sniffing and wiping his eyes, he nodded. "Yeah, man. I'm straight." He nodded his head at the guy. "Thanks."

"Whatever you done, God's big enough. 'Member that." The stranger bobbed his head at Jordan before walking to the dumpster.

His eyes watching the man, Jordan shoved his hands into his pockets. "Yeah," he whispered, dropping his gaze to the ground. "Yeah, He's big enough."

Suddenly, he knew what he had to do. No more of this nonsense. No more of his pride. His friend needed him. And his parents deserved an apology and an explanation of why he'd gone so crazy on them. First morning's light he'd go straight to the ones he'd hurt and make it right. All pride aside. Returning to the apartment, Jordan clicked off the TV just as the newscaster announced there was still some good in the world when someone found a lost dog and returned it to its owner. Grabbing his Bible, he sat down at his kitchen table and read the account of David and Bathsheba, weeping his way through the whole thing.

At two in the morning, when he could barely keep his

eyes open anymore, he headed to bed with a prayer for peace and courage, asking God to show him favor as he worked to mend his relationships with the ones he loved.

Chapter 26

"Finally, brothers, rejoice. Aim for restoration, comfort one another, agree with one another, live in peace; and the God of love and peace will be with you."
~2 Corinthians 13:11~

JORDAN

Jordan's plans to head straight to his parents' house to apologize were thwarted by a call from Rachel at six in the morning.

"Yeah," he croaked into the phone, his eyes mere slits in the darkness of his room.

"Can you be at the paper in thirty minutes?" Her voice was laced with excitement—a tell-tale sign she had a massive story brewing and wanted him to take the lead.

"Uh, okay…sure." He glanced at the glowing numbers on his clock and groaned. "Let me grab a shower and head out."

"Make it quick, Straight Shooter. This story's moving fast." The line went dead, and he threw the covers to the floor, forcing himself into action.

He made it to the paper in record time and found Rachel waiting for him—two large steaming cups of coffee in her hands. She thrust one at him and he took it, grateful that her attitude toward him no longer seemed armed with revenge. Taking a long sip, he sighed. Just what he'd needed.

"You look like crap," Rachel commented, glancing in his direction as she led the way to her desk.

"Gee, thanks, Red. Good morning to you too." It was true, and he knew it. Rebellion didn't look good on him, and God knew he was in desperate need of some deep conversation with his dad. "So, what's this story that dragged me out of bed before the sun said hello?"

She smirked as she sat in her chair and reached for a file. "Trust me—you will not bemoan your early rising when you see this story. But before we dive in…"

Her eyes dimmed and he shifted uncomfortably. "...are we good?"

He took another long sip of coffee, needing to buy some time before he answered. He owed her an apology for the way he'd treated her and disdained her advice. This was not going to be easy...

"I was wrong," he stated quietly. "You were right—about everything. Can you forgive me for being such a jerk?"

Rachel's face lit up as she smiled. "Of course I can—you're my best friend. I could never stay mad at you, Jordan."

When his only response was a quick nod, she forced herself to move beyond the apology, though she wanted to explore the reasons behind it. "So, this story—Pastor Zeke found four kids in the basement of the church last night—by themselves, with no guardian present and none to speak of. He's still with them this morning. Asked social services to give him some time before they take the kids. He thinks he recognizes them from a church service he held a few months back."

Jordan's brow rose at the mention of their pastor. "So, he knows who the guardian is?"

"He's not sure, but he thinks so. He didn't want to wake them, so he's waiting until daylight to begin asking questions."

"Ages?"

"His guess was between four and ten years old. I don't want you there alone—they need a female presence with them in case they're scared of men. I'm tied up with the grocery store arson from yesterday, so I can't be there. Cali is due any minute now—once she shows up, head out with her. Find out every detail you can about these kids."

Jordan froze, his heart skipping a beat. "Uh, how about you have Cali cover the arson, and you ride with me this time? We could use some catching up."

Rachel's eyes drifted to his, a curious expression on her face. Hadn't he and Cali been best buds like...a second ago? "Is there a reason you don't want her with you?"

He looked at his shoes and grabbed the back of his neck. Crap. There was no way out of this. Apologizing to her was one thing—coming clean about the extent of his sins was a different ball game. "Kids need nurturing, Rachel. You're better suited for that position, don't you think?"

Curious, she sat back in her chair, her pen resting between her fingers. "I have to lead the arson, Jordan. Cali can handle this. You've never questioned her abilities before…why now?"

I'd never slept with her before. Never been duped by her before. Never been dumped by her before… Forcing a smile, he met her eyes. "It's cool. I'm sure she'll do great."

A bell chimed, and the front door opened. Cali weaved her way through the sea of desks, dressed in a flowery sun dress that showed far too much of her chest. Her eyes flitted to Jordan; discomfort flashing across her face only to vanish as quickly as it had appeared. "You didn't tell me I'd be partnered on this." Her words were directed at Rachel, but her eyes stayed on Jordan, who refused to look at her.

Rachel stared at them, her senses on high alert. What was up with these two today? "Somebody wanna tell me what's going on here? Just yesterday you two were eager to work together. What's up?"

Jordan glanced at Cali, his stomach flipping when her eyes narrowed, and she raised her chin, a smile spreading across her face. She was up to something…he could see it all over her. He needed to beat her to the punch. Squash anything she might sta—

"What's up? Nothing. Nothing whatsoever." Cali swung her eyes to Rachel and winked. "I'd be happy to do the story with Straight Shooter. We're very familiar with each other. We make a great team, right Jordan? Especially beneath the sheets." Her face beamed as he withered in front of her.

Rachel swallowed hard, angry at the sudden sting of

tears in her eyes. So that's what this was. His apology was due to his guilty conscience. He wasn't seeking reconciliation with his life-long friend. They'd slept together. She looked at Jordan and almost felt sorry for the idiot as he dug his hands deep into the back pockets of his jeans and backed away from Cali. Quickly grabbing the file, she stood and walked around her desk toward him. Thrusting it at his chest, she hardly waited a second for him to take it before letting it go and shoving past him. "Get on this story before we're no longer the first paper to know about it. I want every detail you can find on these kids." She spun on her heel, eyes flashing through her tears. "And try to keep it professional out there, will you, Jordan?"

His fingers tightened on the file as the vise gripped his heart. He stared back at her, confused by the tears in her eyes and the tensing of her jaw. "Rachel, I—"

She held up her hand and closed her eyes. "Stop. I don't need to know the details of your personal life. It's not like we're friends. Just go." Her fierce gaze seared through Cali. "I swear, if your father didn't own this paper..."

Cali laughed. "Are you threatening me?"

"Cali, let's go," Jordan urged, his eyes flitting between the two.

Rachel smirked at her. "Let's just say there's no way in hell any other professional paper would hire you dressed like the slut you are. Now, go get my story."

Jordan watched her turn and walk away before glancing in Cali's direction. "Why did you do that?" he hissed out the side of his mouth before heading for the door.

"Don't act like you didn't enjoy every minute we were together, Jordan." She rolled her eyes as she followed him outside.

Stopping at his truck, he spun to face her, keys in hand. "Take your car. You're not riding with me on this."

Her lips curled into a smile, arms folding across her chest. "So, it's like that now, baby?"

Exasperated, Jordan threw up his arms. "What's your

game, Cali? Why you messing with me? You come around and spin my whole world out of order, get my head out of the game, ruin my relationships with those I love, then you wanna call me 'baby?' Heck no! We're gonna do this story together, because Rachel wants it that way—but you're gonna stay away from me and stay out of my life for good. Got that?"

"Blame doesn't look good on you, Straight Shooter—or should I call you Crooked Arrow now? I didn't ruin your life. That was all you. You're the one who let everything you love burn to ashes around you, so, don't put that on me. I'm flattered, though." She took a step closer to him, her chest inches from his. "And if you think I'm out of your life, you have another thing coming." She smiled. "I have a feeling I'll see a lot more of you in the coming months." Before he could think about her meaning, she turned and walked away.

"Been a while since I seen you around here." Pastor Zeke's voice was calm and quiet.

Jordan glanced at him before refocusing his attention on Cali. To his surprise, she'd taken to the four children and had sat down on the basement floor with them, a book in her hands and the youngest child snuggled in her lap. "Yeah. I've been...busy...these past few weeks."

"'Busy.'" The pastor nodded, his wire-rimmed glasses sliding down his nose. Sweat beaded atop his balding head, causing his brown skin to glisten beneath the basement light.

Jordan shoved his hands in his pockets. He had a feeling the pastor knew exactly what "busy" meant. "Actually..." He stared at the floor, following the swirls of paint with his eyes. "I've been a lot more than just busy, Pastor."

"I know." He softly replied, his eyes never leaving Cali.

The social worker hovered nearby, chatting on the phone, and writing furiously on a stack of paper as she worked. With no known next of kin, she'd agreed to grant

Zeke's request to act as a temporary guardian, giving him time to locate their mother.

Jordan sighed, his gaze shifting to study the pastor he'd known since birth. This was the man who'd baptized him after he'd come to Christ. He'd been there for him throughout his entire life and knew him almost as well as his father. "How much did they tell you?"

Zeke smiled but it didn't meet his eyes. "Enough. Always good to have folks in your corner who love you, boy. Don't blame them for confiding in an old man who takes you to the feet of Jesus."

Jordan's heart pricked. "Pastor, I've done some really bad things this month. Made some choices I deeply regret. Dug a hole for myself that I can't get out of." He stared at the older man, his lower lip trembling when he stared back at him—peace in his eyes.

"I know."

Frustration began to mount. He knew. Okay, what now? He didn't seem to be in the mood to offer up solutions. Jordan shifted as the youngest child began to cry in Cali's arms. He watched in awe as she soothed the boy by rocking and humming. This was not the Cali he knew. She didn't have a gentle bone in her body. "I can hardly pray anymore. Every time I try, I feel this weight in my gut. How dare I try to talk to God after all I've done? Who do I think I am? What right do I have to His mercy and grace now? I've ruined everything." He sniffed. "I followed my flesh instead of walking in Christ. How could I do this to Him?"

The kind eyes remained warm as the pastor smiled. "Jordan, you lost your way. In doing such, you forgot Who God is, boy."

Jordan's brow wrinkled. "I don't understand."

"What is grace?"

"Unmerited favor."

"Mercy?"

"Not getting what we deserve."

"So, when you talk to your daddy and ask him to

forgive you for shuttin' him out like you've done, what's going to be the result of that conversation?" Pastor Zeke's eyes held wisdom and confidence.

"He'll forgive me and move past it," Jordan answered without hesitation.

"No doubt?"

"No doubt."

"Why?"

"Because a relationship with me is more valuable to him than revenge."

Pastor Zeke smiled and gave him a pointed stare. Waiting for Jordan to nod in understanding, he continued. "Pray to God, son. Don't let Satan tell you He ain't listenin', 'cuz that's a lie. Pray to Him. Ask for forgiveness. Accept the consequences of your actions, and face the coming days knowing that Jesus done paid your price. You're a free man. Now walk in that freedom—go, and sin no more."

Jordan's heart pained at the Scripture. No need to worry about that—he was done messing with Cali. He nodded, tears staining his cheeks. "Thanks, Pastor. Thank you." He sniffed and swiped at his face.

"See you in a pew on Sunday?"

Jordan laughed. "Yes. Absolutely. I'll be here. And you—looks like you'll have four extras in your pew this week."

Zeke gave a slow nod. "For the time being, yes. It wouldn't be Highshore Baptist Church if something crazy wasn't in the mix." He grinned, but the grin quickly faded. "I know their mama. She'll be back when she gets to the end of that pipe dream she chasin'. That is, if the good Lord sees fit to save her from herself."

LEVI

"They wouldn't consider it. Mom wouldn't even hear me out, Levi! My father was more intent on listening to me than she was." Josh sat on the back stoop of the Hendricks's porch, cigarette in hand.

Levi gave himself a second to think before responding. He could see both sides to this story. He had equal empathy for both Josh and his parents.

"It's quite the request," he finally replied. "Those two are the only parents Nevaeh has ever known. I can see why your mother fears handing her off to a guy she's afraid of." Josh took a long draw on his cigarette. "Yeah. I get that. But Levi, you have no idea what Nichole is capable of. I'll never see my daughter again if she gets ahold of her. She'll take her, then lock me up and throw away the key. I have a chance to protect Nevaeh, but my parents won't let me." He glanced up at the older man, who'd leaned his back against the brick column of the porch. "I can be a good dad. I can keep her safe and show her love."

Levi sighed. "There's more to parenting than that, son. Especially in your situation. She doesn't know you. Right now, you're a threat to her world, and she's gonna fight that with everything in her power."

Josh stood and picked up a rock, chucking it across the yard. It pinged loudly off the side of the shed. "She's three, man. She doesn't have a choice about me being her dad. I didn't know about her before, or I'd have been here the whole time. I know now. I'm here now. And I want my daughter. Don't I have a say in this?"

"Sure. If you want to take your parents to court. Rhea gave them custody, Josh. She's theirs. Not adopted, no. But legally, they either willingly sign her over to you, or you fight them for her. Before you make that decision, think of your baby girl. Think of all the nights your mother—her mommy—has rocked her to sleep. All the days your father—her daddy—has played with her and held her in his arms. Are you willing to risk ruining whatever chance at a relationship you have with your daughter so she can be with you?"

"Are you even listening to me?" Josh threw his arms up. "If I don't take off with Nevaeh, then Nichole will take her. She won't care if my parents have custody or not. She'll find some reason to take them to court, prove them unfit, and ruin my kid's life. I'm not tryin' to be the prick that destroys Nevaeh for selfish reasons, Mr. H. I want my baby girl safe, and this is the only way I know how to do that." He pulled himself to his feet, his hand slipping to his side to dull the ache. "If that means I have to take my kid and run, then so be it. I've done it before, and I can do it again."

Levi shook his head, unnerved by the sudden shift in Josh's tone. "Don't do it, son. There's a world of trouble at the end of that dead-end street. You're no good to Nevaeh if you're in jail."

"Dad?"

Both heads snapped up at the sound of Jordan's voice. He stood just on the other side of the screen door, watching the two as though he didn't belong.

Levi's face exploded into a smile at the sight of his son. "Jordan," he whispered, tears stinging his eyes.
The screen door creaked open as Jordan stepped outside, his eyes barely touching Josh before bouncing back to his father. "I can come back...looks like you two were in a counseling session."

Josh didn't miss the hint of jealousy in his tone. "I'll catch you later, Levi." He popped his chin up at the older man and stepped toward Jordan. "Don't worry," he paused, his tone loud enough for his ears, alone. "There's still plenty of Daddy left over for you." He brushed his shoulder against Jordan's on his way through the door. The sting of Josh's words reduced him to a child as he found himself alone on the steps with his father. "I didn't mean to interrupt."

Levi's face twisted. "Son, you haven't sought me out in over a month. I don't care who I'm with. You interrupt me."

Jordan's gaze hit the concrete below. "Dad?"

"Yeah, son?" His heart pinched in his chest as he looked at him. His boy. His little slugger growing up, his best friend on the other side of childhood. *Thank You, Jesus, for bringing him here.*

"I messed up."

"Yeah."

Jordan's vision clouded. "I lost my virginity this week. Gave it to that girl. After working so hard to stay pure in Christ, Dad, I just...let her take it like it meant nothing to me."

Sensing the impending eruption, Levi reached for him. Jordan's frame shook with sobs as he wept onto his father's shoulder. "I held out so long. I was waiting for her. For my wife. And I gave it away! And she spit it right back in my face. And the beer…Da-a-a-d…"

Levi held him tighter as he sobbed, his heart tearing into pieces. "It's gonna be okay," he attempted to soothe him, though he felt completely inept.

"No. It's not okay! How could I do that to him? We swore, Dad. We've always sworn it! No alcohol. We were determined not to ever turn into Garrett, and look at me! Look at what I did!"

"You're not Garrett, son!" Levi's hand gripped the back of his neck. "You made a mistake, Jordan. You're human. You followed your heart down a bad path and messed up but look at you now! You're acknowledging your failures and you wanna make it right. You didn't destroy your life, and you didn't destroy Josh's. Josh is gonna be alright, Jordan. He'll eventually forgive you and move past your betrayal. But no matter how long that takes, you have got to forgive yourself."

"I can't. I hurt him bad. You should've seen him when Cali pulled that beer from my fridge. Josh was never supposed to know. I had tea on the table. The beer was out of sight. She just waltzed right over there and offered him one!"

Levi released him and stepped back, puzzled. "Does she know his background?"

"I told her the first night we drank together. I was hesitant to drink, but she was insistent, and I gave in. But not before I told her my reasons for not wanting to. She told me not to live in his shadow—encouraged me to 'be my own man.' I'm such an idiot, Dad."

"No. You're not an idiot, son. You just followed your lust, and it bit you in the butt. You won't repeat that mistake. But something's fishy about that girl, Jordan. She seems to have a pattern of sabotage for some reason. You still work with her?"

Jordan thought back on his morning and sighed. "Had a story to cover with her today. She outed me to Rachel. Blurted right in front of her that we'd slept together." Levi's heart broke, imagining the pain and embarrassment Rachel must have felt when she'd heard this news. It was no secret how she felt about his son. Everyone but Jordan could see it. His brow knit. "Why would she do that? What's her deal? Why is she coming after you like that?" Jordan shrugged. "Who knows? It's not like I'm the one who broke it off with her. I was going to that night, but she beat me to it. Maybe she sensed it and was trying to get revenge? I don't know."

Levi shook his head. "I'd ask Rachel for a reassignment. I wouldn't work with that girl if I were you."

"I did." Jordan sighed. "She said I had to go with Cali. Then she challenged me on why I wanted to be away from her, reminding me that I'd been eager to work with her before. I did this to myself, Dad."

"Well, son, maybe it's time to come clean to Rachel and tell her your reasons. Maybe she'll understand and let you off the hook."

Jordan thought about this, wondering why his heart sank to his feet at the thought of confessing his sins to Rachel. He didn't want her to know all he'd done with Cali. "Yeah. Maybe." Glancing back at his father, he flashed a smile. "I've missed you, Dad. I can't tell you how sorry I am for shoving you out of my life."
Levi's eyes watered. "I know, son. You have no idea how much we've missed you around here. Your mama is gonna be one happy lady when she comes home today. Even happier when you walk in that door on Sunday."

Jordan smiled. "I'll be there, Dad. I sw—"

"Jordan, don't swear."

He nodded. "Right. I promise you–I'll be there Sunday."

JORDAN

"Can I talk to you?" Jordan had driven back to the paper to talk to Rachel, prompted by his father's wisdom. Nervous energy zinged through his spine; his voice hushed from fear of being overheard.

Her gaze was cold as she regarded him. "About what?"

He sighed and glanced around. "Not here…outside."

Her brows knit in a fierce frown. "So, now you're concerned with keeping your business private?"

Jordan hung his head, shame washing over his features. "Rachel, please," he whispered, his hands on her desk. "I need my friend right now. Will you please come outside and talk with me?"

Studying the intensity on his face, empathy battled her pride. Reminding herself that her anger toward him wasn't justified, she sighed. "Fine. But I'm very busy, so you'd better make it quick." She stood and walked around the desk, her gray pencil skirt tastefully accentuating her body. Allowing him to lead her outside, she leaned against the brick wall and leveled him with an impatient stare. Unable to dance around the frustration in her brain, she blurted the question on her mind. "What's gotten into you lately? You're not yourself. All this?" She waved a hand over him. "These choices you've been making? That's not you. You don't do these kinds of things. I've known you for years, Jordan. Years. You have never allowed a girl to work you over."

He grimaced, guilt slamming his gut. "You think I don't know that? That's why we're out here." Jordan ran a hand through his hair and told himself to breathe. "I cannot work with Cali, Rachel."

Rachel glared. This again? "What is going on between you two? You've gotten along with her very well up to this point. Why the sudden change?"

"She broke it off with me."

Surprise flashed in her eyes. What kind of a girl gives up a great guy like Jordan? Cali was dumber than she'd thought. Crossing her arms, she raised her chin. "You're going to have to come up with a better reason than that if you want me to find you a new story to cover. You two work well together—I can't just break up a good journalistic team for pettiness." It was a lie. They made a horrible team, but she wasn't letting him off the hook that easily. It wasn't her fault he was uncomfortable in the bed he'd made.

Jordan's face belied his shock. "Rachel, please. I'll take any story you have—anything—just please don't put us together again." He swallowed hard, wishing he could interpret the flash of emotion across her face. He'd known her since grade school. Next to Josh, she'd been his closest friend and confidant. He'd always thought he'd had her pegged—knew everything about her. But as they'd entered adulthood, she'd grown more complicated, leaving him scratching his head more often. "Since Cali broke it off, she's been acting spiteful. Saying things to people, messing with people I care about. I don't feel comfortable around her anymore. Please. I'm begging you. Reassign me to another story. She can have the siblings' story—they took to her anyways."

Rachel studied him, her arms dropping to her sides. Her long lashes dusted her cheeks as she blinked, her red hair falling in waves around her shoulders. "The only other story I have right now is the fight over the sewers. City versus townsfolk." Another lie, but he didn't have to know that. He didn't deserve a good story after what he'd done. She caught herself, heat flaming up her ivory neck. What right did she have to be mad at him? As though she had some kind of claim on him? She raised her chin, waiting for him to turn his nose up at her offer.

Relief flooded his soul. "I'll take it." A smile pulled at the corners of his mouth, causing him to look even more boyish than he already had.

"Seriously?" She gaped at him. "I mean, yeah, okay. You can start on it right away. I'll need your interview on my desk no later than tomorrow afternoon."

"Thanks, Red. I really owe you one. So, just to be clear...no more Cali?" He held out his hand, palm down, as he asked the question.

Coward. She squared her shoulders and hardened her gaze. "Sure, whatever."

"You rock, Rachel." Jordan clapped her on the shoulder, all smiles, as he headed back inside to start his research.

Her gaze followed as he disappeared, and she was angry at herself when the warmth of tears stung her eyes. "Let him go, Rachel. He'll never see you as more than a friend." She sniffed and wiped at her tears before following him through the door.

Chapter 27

"Faithful are the wounds of a friend; profuse are the kisses of an enemy."
~Proverbs 27:6~

GARRETT

"Where did you say you were headed again?" Elysia pulled her hair back into a ponytail and grabbed the vacuum cleaner. She had a ton of stuff on her to-do list that morning, but there was something suspicious about her husband's behavior.

"I just needed to go to the place to get that thing I was telling you about yesterday." Garrett twisted the front doorknob in his hand and quickly stepped outside.

"The 'thing', Garrett? Honestly?" Elysia's hands went to her hips as she stared at her husband, her eyes narrowing.

"Yeah, you remember. We talked about it already. I'll be home soon." He closed the door behind him and breathed a sigh of relief. Quickly, he walked to his truck and yanked the door open, grabbing the paper he'd hidden in his glove compartment the night before. The "Help Wanted" ads burned in his hands as his eyes scanned the listings for one he thought might be suitable for Josh. If he could get him a job, Elysia would see how responsible he could be. Maybe then she'd sign Nevaeh over to him. Pulling out of the driveway, he prayed he was doing the right thing. He'd cleared his morning for this—even pushed back a high-dollar client so he could get an early start on the wanted ads.

At the end of eighth street, Garrett stopped behind a school bus and watched as it loaded a group of children. He tapped the wheel in time to the beat of a Casting Crowns song playing softly on the radio. When he was free of the bus, he took a right on Main Street, his sights set on the general store. They needed a bagger—it wasn't the most glamorous of positions—he knew his son was well over-qualified—but it was a paycheck, and that was all that mattered. As he neared the church, he glanced over to find Zeke outside. The pastor was pushing a lawn mower and sweating profusely in the morning sun, an activity that had been strictly forbidden by his doctor earlier in the year. With a sigh, he spun the wheel and drove into the church parking lot, parking near the door. Having seen him pull in, Zeke cut the mower off and wiped at his brow, relieved to have a reason to take a break from his task. "Hello there, boy. What brings you to church today? Ain't Sunday, ya know." He smiled and grabbed his water bottle, chugging heartily as Garrett approached.

Garrett smiled. A man twice Zeke's age could approach him, and he'd still call him "boy." It was Zeke's way of welcoming you in and dropping your guard around him. "What happened to the handyman we hired three months ago?"

The pastor looked at the bushes and shook his head. "Never cuts those bushes right. I got tired of listening to Edith's whining—figured if I do it myself, the gossip might stop." He rumbled a chuckle and swigged his water a second time.

Garrett frowned. "There's gonna be a whole lot more gossip if your heart does you in, Zeke. You can't be doing this stuff. You're not as young as you used to be."

Zeke's smile met his eyes. "Shouldn't you be at the office today?"

"Uh, yeah. I had some business that needed tending to. What if I told you I knew someone who could use a job?" The pastor studied him for a while, reading the earnestness behind his eyes. "Would this 'someone' happen to be a blond boy, related to you, and trying to get in good standing with his baby girl?"

Zeke was the most perceptive person Garrett had ever met. The man always knew what he was thinking before he opened his mouth. "That would be him, yes. He could really use the work, Zeke. And you're not supposed to be doing this stuff anymore—doctor's orders."

Zeke considered his request, his eyes looking off in the distance. "Is the boy running from the law these days?" Caught off guard, Garrett paused before answering. "Not that I'm aware…"

"Does he know how to cut a yard?"

Garrett thought back on Josh's childhood. All the years following behind him as he mowed, a beer in one hand and the belt in the other just in case his son happened to mess up. His heart twisted, and he forced his focus back to the present. "I'd say he's perfected it." He cleared his throat, fighting the tears that threatened.

"Tell you what," Zeke finished the bottle of water, sweat still pouring over his balding head. "Bring him by, and I'll have a talk with him. If I like what I see, the job is his. Know anyone who knows how to fix stuff? Got a busted pipe in the men's restroom that needs attention." He stroked his chin as though deep in thought. Garrett's face lit up. "Josh worked on the ship's maintenance crew before coming back home—I bet he'd know what to do with that pipe."

Zeke nodded. "Go get the boy. I'll be waiting in the office—where this sun can't find me."

"Yes, sir," Garrett beamed. "I'll go see if I can find him right now, sir."

"You do that." Zeke left the mower and headed for the church as Garrett rushed to his truck.

Excitement surged through Garrett's veins as he started the engine and pulled back onto the street. God was so good. Always coming through when he couldn't find a way. Now to see if Josh would talk to him without his mother present…

He pulled into Levi's driveway ten minutes after leaving the church. Spotting Laura's car near the garage, he noted that Levi's truck was absent. Assuming he'd already left for work that day, he prayed he'd find his boy home as he headed for the door. Nerves tingling, Garrett pressed the bell and waited. He heard footsteps approaching on the other side of the door just before it swung open.

"Laura." He smiled.

"Garrett, hi." She smiled back. "Levi's already at the college—left a little early today. Want me to have him call?"

"Um, no." He shifted nervously, his hand going to the back of his neck. "Is Josh here?"

Her smile faltered, eyes dimming. "He is…"

Unnerved by her reaction, Garrett second-guessed his choice to come. "Do you think you could ask him to come down?"

She sighed, hesitant. "What if he says no?"

"Tell him I have a job opportunity for him." He held out his hand, eyes growing large. "Not with me! Just…a job."

"Okay," she whispered, hoping Garrett wouldn't be crushed if his son turned his nose up at his request. "Do you want to come inside, or wait here?"

Garrett thought for a moment. "No. I'll stay here. Yeah," he confirmed his decision. "I'll wait right here." He sat down on the porch swing and clasped his hands together, elbows on his knees. She closed the door, and his eyes slid shut. "God, please just let him talk to me. Please."

The five minutes that ticked slowly by felt more like five hours. The door opened at last, and his gaze flew up to see his son emerging, cigarette in hand.
Josh stepped out onto the porch and shut the door behind him. His eyes locked with his father's as he placed his cigarette between his lips and lit up, taking a long draw as he leaned his back against the porch railing. "Laura says you want to talk to me?"

Relief flooded him. He was making progress. Not only had his son agreed to talk, but he was meeting his eyes. Thank You, Jesus… "Um, I know how hard you're working to get custody of Nevaeh. If you had a job, the courts would be more inclined to give her to you."

"I'm listening," he commented. He didn't let on about the tension in his body at being alone with his father.

"I know someone who's looking for a landscaper and maintenance guy. It's not much, but I know you could do the work. He, um, he wants to talk to you as soon as possible—assuming you want to, that is." He grimaced, feeling as though he'd butchered the offer.

Josh was quiet, his eyes on his sneakers as he took another drag off his cigarette. "Who is it?"

Garrett hesitated, knowing this would be a negative for his son. "Pastor Zeke."

Josh smirked. "Right. You want me to work at the church. This must be really funny to you, huh? Get your heathen son mowing the church yard out where all those gossiping bitties can see him doing 'the Lord's work,' and talk about how 'God's turned him around?'"

Garrett's face fell. "No, Josh. I'm just trying to help you get Nevaeh."

Josh pushed off the rail, standing over his father. "Then sign her over to me."

"I can't do that. Not by myself. The documents have to have your mother's signature. She won't sign them if she doesn't feel it's in Nevaeh's best interest. But if you got a job and proved to her that you're taking responsible steps to care for her, maybe Mom will sign."

Josh stepped back and took another long draw, blowing the smoke toward the porch ceiling. "Does Zeke know it's me needing the job?"

"He does."

"And he didn't flip his crap or demand I fill a pew on Sunday?"

"He did not."

"Okay. I'll talk to him. When?"

"Now."

Josh sighed, dreading the walk to the church. "Alright. Just…give me a minute to grab some pain meds. That walk is gonna be killer."

Garrett's chest tightened. "Um…I could take

you…son." He winced as the last word fell out of his mouth. He hadn't meant to say it. He prayed Josh wouldn't come unglued.

Josh's blue eyes met his father's identical ones as he considered this. "Alright. But only because of Nevaeh. Got that? You and me? We're not cool. I hate you just as much today as I did a year ago." He stepped closer, his hand reaching for the front door. "And I swear, if I ever find out you've put your hands on my kid—or my mother—I'll kill you, myself."

Garrett swallowed hard as he disappeared inside, his conscience burning. He'd agreed to go to the church with him. This was good. A very good thing. So why did it shake him to his core?

JOSH

Neither Cameron spoke a word on the way to the church, though Garrett was bursting at the seams to converse with his son. In so many ways, it was like sitting beside a stranger. He'd never really gotten to know his boy—had never cared to in the past. But now Josh was all he could think about. Who was he? What were his likes? Dislikes? Was he a hard worker? Dependable? Or had he been a thorn in his previous bosses' sides? He'd learned bits and pieces about his son through Jordan and Levi but wanted firsthand knowledge. A glance at the sullen figure beside him told him that wouldn't happen any time soon. There was so much to say. So much to apologize for… Garrett opened his mouth, but shut it just as fast, unable to start a conversation he knew Josh would reject.
When they pulled into the church parking lot, they found Zeke outside, tossing a ball with a young boy who looked to be around the age of seven. "Want me to go up with you?" Garrett asked his son as he parked the truck.
Josh glanced at him, his hand on the door handle. "So, now you wanna hold my hand? A little late for that, don't you think?"

Garrett watched him shove the door open and step out

onto the pavement. Leaning on the wheel, he chewed his bottom lip as Josh walked over to Zeke and the boy, the pastor's face lighting with a smile as he approached.

"I ain't seen you in a tall minute, boy," Zeke greeted him as he tossed the ball to the child.

Josh flashed a half smile before his mouth melted back into its solemn line. "My father says you have a position available?"

Zeke looked around Josh, his eyes directed at the lone man in the truck behind them. "What's wrong wi' him?" Josh fought an eye roll and shrugged. "Nothing, I guess. He's just waiting for me."

"We don't leave family in the car, son." Zeke waved Garrett over, growing adamant when that man hesitated before climbing from the truck and slowly walking their way, hands shoved into his pockets. "Who you hidin' from, Garrett?" Zeke teased, not missing the tension between the father and son—nor bothering to care. "Who's the kid?" Garrett needed to get Zeke's focus off himself.

The pastor's face exploded into a smile as he grabbed the boy under one arm and proudly squeezed him. "This is Isaiah. He's gonna be hangin' around here for a little while, making sure an old man don't get any older. Ain't that right, 'Saiah?"

"Tha's right." The little boy nodded his nappy head at the older two men, throwing his chin up at Josh as though challenging him to a street fight. "What you lookin' at, punk?"

Josh's eyes shot up as Zeke patted the boy's head. "'Saiah, this is a friend, not an enemy. Go put that ball away and run to the cafeteria to eat that sandwich we made earlier." When Isaiah hesitated, eyes sizing Josh up, Zeke nudged him with a hand on his back. "Go on now, boy. Get gone."

"He seems fun," Josh commented as the boy ran off. "No less fun than you were at that age," Zeke quipped with a wink. "So, you need a job, boy?" He turned to scoop up his baseball cap from the pavement and snugged it over his sweating head.

"I do."

"When can you start?"

"Now."

"How much you askin'?"

"Whatever you'll give me."

Zeke looked at Garrett and smiled. "Now that's a father right there. A man willing to work for whatever he can get, to make a life for his baby girl."

Garrett beamed beside Josh, careful not to make any comments.

"Your dad says you know how to fix stuff?" He turned the statement into a question.

"Yes, sir."

Zeke raised a brow. "You call ever'body 'sir?'"

Josh shifted, caught off guard. "Uh, no, sir. I mean, I um…"

With a laugh, Zeke clapped him on the shoulder. "Who was the last man you called 'sir?' Don't seem like that's a word that would be in your everyday vocabulary, boy." Josh thought a minute, then glanced nervously at his father before answering. "My arresting officer, couple years back."

"Listen here, boy. You be yo'self around me. None of this 'cleaning up the act' stuff. Understand?"

Josh stared. "Y-e-e-s…?"

"Good. Now, down to business. I understand you're tryin' to get some cash flowing so you can be a daddy to that little girl."

"Yes."

"This ain't the job for you," Zeke stated, staring him in the eye.

Josh crossed his arms over his chest, annoyed. "Then why are we both wasting our time?" Catching the attitude in his voice, he dropped his arms and muttered "sir…" before catching himself a second time and correcting with "I mean, um, Zeke?"

Hiding a smile, Zeke took a swig of water before answering. "Ain't nobody wasting time here, son. I understand you can maintain a yard, as well as fix stuff. Can you build?"

Josh thought about the question. "It's not that hard to figure out. I've built some things here and there."

Zeke looked at Garrett. "Can he build?" Garrett nodded, still refraining from speaking, afraid of overstepping his bounds.

"I'll have four guests in my house for the next few months. My house is small, boy. I need some space to put these little people. If you can build, you got a job at the church and with me. I'll keep you busy and pay you per job. How does that sit with you?"

Pausing only a moment before giving his answer, Josh nodded. "Yeah. Okay. Thanks, Zeke."

"Don't thank me. I should be thanking you that I don't have to push this thing in the hot sun no more. Alright, then. This lawn ain't gonna mow itself. You let me know if you need anything—I'll be in the office. And if 'Saiah comes 'round messin' with you, just send him right back inside."

"Sure." Josh grabbed the mower and was about to start it up when Zeke stopped him.

"We don't leave family hangin', boy."

Confused, Josh followed his gaze to his father, who stood uncomfortably like a third wheel in this party of two. With a sigh, he glanced back at Zeke to find his eyes fixed on him, pushing him to follow his lead. "Thanks for the ride. I'll find my way back."

"Yeah. Well, if you need a ride home, just call." Garrett pulled his keys from his pocket and turned to go. The lawnmower revved to life behind him, and he breathed a sigh of relief, mixed with a prayer of thanks to God for giving his son a second chance at life.

RHEA

The diner was packed. The local high school's football

team had a home game that evening, and the entire town of Highshore had suddenly decided they wanted diner food. Rhea tossed a tray of trash into the garbage and bussed another three tables before heading back behind the counter. She'd been working since eight that morning and was exhausted. Despite this, she'd asked Izaak to allow her to work a double. She needed to keep her mind busy—more than that, she needed the money now that she was on her own.

"Rhea, break," Izaak called above the noise.

Grateful, she clocked out and grabbed her phone before heading outside to get some air. Sinking to the sidewalk, she leaned against the brick wall and closed her eyes. She needed to check her messages, but her heart ached at the thought. Sterling had called her no less than a dozen times since six that morning. Leaving him was killing her, but she saw no other way. He'd already come to the diner to look for her, but she'd hidden in the back and begged Izaak to tell him she wasn't there. Sighing, she lit up her phone's screen and saw another dozen missed calls. "Sterling," she whispered, wiping her wet eyes. Why did he have to make this so much harder?

"Well, isn't that pathetic?"

Rhea's head snapped up, her heart filling with dread at the sight of her mother.

"You left him, and now pine for him. You stupid little girl." Nichole walked around her car and stood over her daughter. "Walk with me."

It wasn't a request, and Rhea knew resistance would be met with a scene. She couldn't have that. Quickly, she got to her feet and obeyed. Her mother led her to the back of the diner, where a sidewalk encircled a pond.

"'Oh, what a tangled web we weave,' darling." Nichole's dark shades kept her eyes hidden, but there was no mistaking the mocking in her tone. "Sterling reached out to me, you know."

Rhea tensed. He wouldn't...

"I'm meeting with him right after I leave you. I just

can't imagine how he'll take the news."

She forced herself not to ask what she meant by that. If she pretended not to care, maybe her mother would tire of the game and leave her alone.

"That poor man. What did he do to deserve the girl he loves running off to be with another?"

Dread filled her bones. She held her breath, afraid of the implication.

"It's terrible. Simply terrible, Sterling," Nichole's face twisted with mock concern as she foreshadowed her conversation. "I have nothing to say for my daughter's disgraceful behavior. If I hadn't seen it myself, I'd argue it wasn't true, but I did see it. She ran straight to Joshua Cameron and declared she will never return to your arms."

"Mother, don't." Rhea stopped walking and turned to face her. "He won't believe you, anyway."

Nichole's smile was tight as she pulled her sunglasses off. "I know you warned him," she hissed, stepping closer. "You ran straight to that street rat after leaving me that day. Don't think I know? Look, Rhea. Look at yourself in the arms of another man." She shoved a picture in front of her.

Rhea swallowed hard. Her suspicions had been correct. Asher followed her to Josh and took a picture of her embracing him. And now her mother was going to blackmail her.

"Did you honestly think I wouldn't find out? What did you tell him, Rhea?"

"Nothing," Rhea lied, knowing she wouldn't buy it for a second.

"I swear, Rhea Nichole, if you told that boy to take that little girl and run, I will find him. And when I do, I'll nail him for every piece of dirt I have on him, and he'll land in a prison cell so fast your ditsy little head will spin." Cold eyes stared through her daughter. Her long nails gripped Rhea's chin, forcing her eyes to hers. "Tell me, daughter, has running from me ever gone in your favor?" She squeezed the flesh in her hand.

Tears clouded her vision. Hardening her expression and setting her jaw, Rhea refused to cower. "Josh is smart, Mother. And he isn't afraid of you."

Nichole's face twisted into a menacing glare. "Smarter than me, darling? Let me let you in on a little secret. I've had men with Harvard degrees think they could outsmart me. One is dead. Another is in prison. Another is flipping burgers at a tiny little burger joint in a no-name town, thinking I know nothing of his whereabouts." Nichole smiled coldly. "No one can hide from me. Do you understand that?"

Rhea squeezed her eyes shut, knowing it was true. "Let him have Nevaeh, Mother. Please. What do you want with her? Leave her alone!"

Nicole's eyes narrowed. "It will be a cold day in hell when I allow that thug of yours to raise my flesh and blood. The lawsuit will be in motion shortly. There's nothing more you can do. I suggest you be a good little girl and get in the car. You're coming with me, so I can ensure you don't try anything stupid. If you so much as think about going back to Joshua, I'll see that he's never seen again. Do you understand?"

Rhea's chest tightened at the threat, knowing her mother had enough connections to follow through. This was all her fault. Josh and Nevaeh were in danger because of her. Knowing there was no use in fighting, she followed her mother to the car. She could only pray that Josh would take her advice and run with Nevaeh. Running was their last chance of hope…and hope was not a promise.

Chapter 28

"The Lord is not slow to fulfill his promise as some count slowness, but is patient toward you, not wishing that any should perish, but that all should reach repentance."
~2 Peter 3:9~

Three months later...
JOSH

The hedge clippers were growing heavy. He'd been trimming hedges since seven that morning, and his muscles were screaming for a break. Josh lowered them to the ground and wiped at the sweat dripping in his eyes. A smile spread across his face at the sight of Nevaeh chasing Zeke's newest addition to the house—a golden cocker spaniel puppy she had fallen head over heels for.

"Daddy, Daddy, look at him run!" she squealed, her blond curls bouncing as she raced across the yard. His heart warmed at the sound of his name on her lips. It didn't happen consistently—not yet. But she called him "Daddy" more often, interchanging the name for "boy" whenever she saw fit.

"Nevaeh, don't grab his tail. He might bite you," he warned as her hand shot for the dog who was just a hair faster than her three-year-old legs could run.

Josh sat down on the grass, his back muscles thanking him for the short reprieve. In an instant, his lap was filled with puppy and little girl, eliciting a laugh as he grabbed Nevaeh into a bear hug and kissed her head. "Zeke says he has ice cream. Hungry?"

She considered this, her dimples digging into her cheeks when she smiled. "Manilla or stawbee?"

He hid a smile. "Definitely manilla."

"Hmm..." She tapped her cheek with her finger.

"Okay! Can Leonard have some too?"

"Uh, no." Josh squeezed her tighter, breathing in the scent of strawberry shampoo and baby sweat. "Who loves you?"

Nevaeh's eyes shot to his, mischief dancing. "Leonard." She squealed past the laughter bubbling in her throat.

"Leonard?!" He feigned shock. "Is Leonard the one out here busting butt in the hot sun for you? No? Okay, then!" Josh smoothed her hair and stood her on her feet before pushing himself up.

He'd finally reached the point where his body no longer protested his every movement, though he'd had to cave and visit a doctor before finding full relief. The accident had left him with some battle scars, but that just added to the painting already covering his skin. Nevaeh pulled at his hand, compelling his feet to move. "Alright, alright. Let's go find Zeke."

"Grandpa says I can't call him that. He says if I call him 'Zeke', I'm in trouble." Nevaeh held his hand as they walked to the backyard of Zeke's home in search of the pastor.

"Yeah? Maybe you should stick with 'Pastor Zeke' instead, huh?" Josh's gut clenched at the thought of his father in the same sentence as the words "I'm in trouble." He knew his dad never hit her—wouldn't even consider a mild pop on the rear—but there was always that nagging "what if" in his mind that never let him drop his guard.

Zeke was ankle deep in mud as he picked through his tomato garden, humming "Amazing Grace" as he worked. This man had become like a second Titus to Josh. Always there to offer advice, encouragement, and a swift kick to the rear when he got off track. Josh had grown to respect him and was learning more each day about the value of following his advice. Though they talked of church often, Zeke never pushed him to attend, always leaving the ball in his court.

"Hey, old man," Josh called as they approached, a smile in his voice.

Zeke chuckled as Nevaeh charged for him, only to be snatched up by her father before she could lunge herself into the garden's mud. "Well, hey there, pretty thing." He smiled and grabbed his bucket of tomatoes before heading to the edge of the garden. His boots were thick with mud, creating a squish-squash sound when he walked.

Nevaeh threw her head back and laughed. "You need a bath!"

"I sure do," he agreed, placing the bucket on the grass. "Might even go jump in that pond over there to get this mud off my boots. What d'ya think of that?"

"No!" she squealed.

Zeke's eyes twinkled. "You wouldn't happen to want some of that 'nilla ice cream in my freezer, would you?"

"Yes!"

"You finish those front hedges, boy?" Zeke looked at Josh.

"Almost. Probably about ten more minutes and I'll be done. After that, you needed the gutters cleared?"

"I do." He looked to the sky and frowned. "Storm's coming in fast. Let's get that done before noon if you can."

"Will do. Let me get Nevaeh settled in the kitchen and I'll get back at it."

They began their walk to the house, Nevaeh bouncing around their heels. "You, uh, seen much of Jordan this week?"

It was a question he asked every Friday, although he already knew the answer.

Josh sighed, his eyes drifting to the older man. "Zeke," he whispered.

The pastor held up his hands in surrender. "Alright, alright, can't blame a man for askin'. Shame, that's all. Lettin' a good friendship like yours go to waste like that." Josh's heart pricked at his words. He missed his friend. It was weird being in the same town as Jordan, yet avoiding him like the plague. Jordan had tried countless times to make things right between them, but Josh would never get over the betrayal of Jordan flaunting beer in his face. He glanced down at Nevaeh, hoping she hadn't picked up on the dark shift in his mood. She was looking right at him as they stepped into the house, and he inwardly groaned. How did she always know? It was as though his daughter had found a window to his soul, able to peek in at any given moment without warning. He ruffled her hair and flashed a reassuring smile before ushering her to wash her hands.

"Anything new?" Zeke nodded in the direction Nevaeh had run, turning for the kitchen sink.

Josh shook his head. "Nah, I haven't seen Nichole around in months. She's probably hopped on her broom and headed to drive some other guy crazy."

Zeke smiled. Nichole was a tough one. He'd never liked her, though he felt wrong for it. There's just not much to like about a woman who treats her husband with contempt and acts as though everyone is beneath her. She frequented the church when she wanted to push her weight around with God's people. Always making a big show of her being there, as though filling a pew could make the townsfolk forget about all the evil she brewed. He'd lost count of how many times she'd pushed Lance to try and dictate what he preached from the pulpit. He'd had to remind her under no uncertain terms that he didn't get his marching orders from the city manager, but from God, alone.

"Well, I'm still askin' the good Lord to keep her away from you and let you be that girl's daddy. Gettin' anywhere with that mama o' yours?"

Josh hung his head. "Not really. She wants me to have a place of my own, a car, stability, all that mess before she'll sign her over. I found a story in the Bible the other day. It was about this dude who had to work for like...seven years just to get this girl he loved. Her dad was a real jerk and gave him the chick's sister instead. He made him work a whole other seven years for the girl he was after. I kinda feel like that guy right now. Why can't my mom just see that I love my kid and that I'll take care of her? Why is she making me jump through all these hoops? Even my dad wants Nevaeh to be with me, and he hates me. What's her deal?"

Deciding not to address that last statement, Zeke pulled

out the ice cream from the freezer and began scooping it into a bowl for Nevaeh, who had mysteriously been washing her hands for a solid five minutes. "Jacob."

"'Scuse me?" Josh looked at him, confused.

"His name was Jacob. And he loved Rachel very much. Never heard his story told with a ghetto twist before." Zeke chuckled, and Josh hung his head. "Kinda like it better your way. But yeah...he worked his butt off for that girl only to be given Leah instead. Boy was he angry. And rightfully so, I suppose. But his love for that gal, Rachel, that's what kept him goin'. And if you love that little monster in my bathroom who's probably flooded the place by now, then you'll keep goin' too." The old man's eyes twinkled as his words sank in, and Josh suddenly bolted to his feet.

Cursing, and immediately apologizing for it, he darted for the hallway in search of his daughter, crying out when he found her elbow deep in suds. "Aww, baby, come on...you know better than to play in the bubbles, Veah," Josh gently scolded as he grabbed a towel and dried the suds from her skin.

"Look, Daddy, the bubbles are floating to Pasor's sling!" Nevaeh's eyes grew large with wonder as she followed the bubbles upward.

"His 'sling?'" Josh asked in confusion as he wiped the countertop. His eyes followed hers and he nodded in understanding. "Oh, 'ceiling.' Right. You shouldn't have done that, Nevaeh. You made a big mess. Now go apologize and eat your ice cream."

"Alright." She bounced off for the kitchen, seemingly unphased by her father's rebuke. "Pasor Zeke, Pasor Zeke! I made bubbles fly to the sling! Oh, sorry!" she tossed in afterthought, clambering into a chair, and digging a spoon into the ice cream.

Josh followed behind her, his t-shirt sudsy and wet. "I'm sorry, Zeke. I didn't realize..."

Zeke waved him off and passed him a bowl of ice cream. "Wait 'til you realize she's been too quiet with a box of markers in her bedroom." He laughed, and his belly jiggled, causing Nevaeh to laugh too.

Josh took a bite, the cold cream sliding down his throat and cooling him off from the heat outside. He could get used to this. Peace and calm. Laughter. Good hearted family fun with his friend and little girl. His life was finally coming together.

JOSH

"Why are you so tall?"

The question caught him off guard as he lifted her from the tub and wrapped a towel around her body, her little face the only thing visible beneath the fluff. "Genes, I guess." Josh kissed her nose and began to dry her curls.

"What if you were wearing shorts?" Nevaeh's innocence sparkled in her eyes. Josh laughed, earning himself a serious frown from his daughter. "Not funny," she scolded. "Not nice to laugh."

"Sorry, kid." He smiled as he helped her dress.

"Why is your hair spiky, like pickles?"

"Pickles?" Josh questioned; brow raised.

"Yes. Pickles have spikes. Like your hair." She ran her fingers along his arm, tracing the art tatted years before. "Mommy says we can't draw on ourselves. Why did you draw on yourself? Mommy's gonna be mad."

It had been a long day in the hot sun, and Josh was ready for bed, but Nevaeh was wound up and full of questions. For a fleeting moment, he wondered how his parents had kept up with her all this time. "Grandma won't be mad," he replied, using her rightful title in hopes of encouraging Nevaeh to do the same.

Her brow creased as he tugged the nightgown over her head. "Well, I'm not allowed to do that, and that makes me mad. I want an angry man on my arm, too."

Josh tugged at his t-shirt in an attempt to hide the face on his arm. "Angry faces don't belong on nice girls' arms."

She stared at him, considering. "Are you not a nice

boy?"

He sat back on his haunches; weary from so many questions he didn't have the answers to. "I'm your daddy. That's all you need to know. Now, if we're done playing twenty questions, it's bedtime. Let's roll. Jump up, monkey."

She squealed and grabbed hold of his neck, laughing when he swung her around to his back. "I want a story," she demanded as he bounced to the toddler bed he'd set up for her in his room. His parents had finally agreed to allow her to spend every other weekend with him, as long as Levi and Laura were home. Anything more sent his mother into a panic, convinced he was plotting to take her and run.

Josh lowered her into the bed and tucked the princess blanket around her, careful to give her tiny toes plenty of room to peek out from beneath the covers, just the way she liked it. "How about a song instead?"

She bobbed her head, her face lighting with a smile. "Sing Jesus," she demanded.

Working with Zeke, Josh had picked up a lot of songs he'd been unfamiliar with just by listening to him sing throughout his day. Many of which had become part of his nightly routine when Nevaeh was with him. Her favorite, by far, was "Jesus Loves Me," a song he still saw as a mere fairy tale. He sat on the floor beside her bed and stroked her forehead as he began. "Jesus loves me, this I know, for the Bible tells me so…"

"Why don't you ever come to church with me, Daddy?" His hand froze on her head, the song forgotten. "Uh…"

"Why does my other daddy come get me every time and take me to church? Why doesn't this daddy take me?" I'm your only daddy. The thought burned in his mind, but he left it unspoken. He thought about her question, guilt burning in his heart as he realized he had no good reason to offer his child that she would understand. What could he say? He didn't believe in God? If that was true, why did he keep searching the Book Titus had given him? Why did he love being around Zeke so much, even when the old man had little to say that didn't include God or the Scriptures? Nevaeh's small hand gripped his arm, and he realized she was waiting for his response. He cleared his throat, fear pushing tears into his eyes. "I'll be there Sunday."

"Promise?"

"I swear."

"Don't swear, Daddy."

Josh smiled and smoothed down her hair. "Okay, baby. Okay."

Sunday hit like a ton of bricks. Nevaeh had made him call his parents first thing Saturday morning to inform them he would not need Garrett to pick her up for church Sunday—he would be taking her himself. He hadn't worked up enough courage to announce to Laura and Levi that he and Nevaeh would be attending service with them, but courage was a non-issue to the little girl who proudly bounded down the stairs in her Sunday best. The moment her feet hit the last step Nevaeh began to shout: "My daddy's coming with me today! Mrs. H, Mrs. H! My daddy's coming to church!"

A few steps behind her, Josh groaned—a gesture not missed by the woman in the kitchen as Nevaeh tugged at her skirt. "Veah, go eat your toast," Josh called. "Don't get crumbs on your dress, okay?"

"Okay!" Nevaeh released Laura's skirt and raced to the table, climbing into her chair, and grabbing her toast in both hands. About to take a bite, her eyes grew wide, and she froze. "Aww, man!" She squeezed her eyes shut tight. "Dear Jesus, thanks for this. It's a real treat to have bwead for bweakfast, even if it doesn't have sugar on it like my mommy's."

"Nevaeh!" Josh chided.

Her eyes flew to his, and she scrunched her nose. "I'm talking to Jesus. Can't get in trouble for talking to Jesus." She rolled her eyes and continued her prayer. "Jesus, help my daddy to get his butt to church today like he promised me." Josh's mouth fell open, and Laura laughed, a hand covering her mouth to avoid detection. "Okay, God, I'm real hungry now, so, I'm gonna go, okay? Man!" Her eyes flew open, and she munched on her toast, oblivious to her father's shocked stare.

"Nevaeh Lee!"

"What?" She gaped at him, mouth full. "Mommy says it all the time."

Josh crossed his arms over his chest. "Says what?"

Nevaeh pulled a face, her voice suddenly high-pitched as she mimicked her grandmother. "'Garrett, what really needs to happen is Josh needs to get his butt to church!'" Laura burst out laughing, earning herself a dark look from Josh. "Grandma isn't very nice sometimes," he grumbled. "Eat your food."

"Okay, Daddy." She shrugged her shoulders and rolled her eyes when she caught Laura watching. "He is so moody," she mouthed.

Glancing at Josh, Laura chuckled. "Honey, you have your work cut out for you with that one."

He sighed. "Yeah, no kidding."

"So, you're going to be joining us today?" Laura kept her voice gentle, knowing he was only going for Nevaeh's sake.

He focused on his sneakers. "That's what she says," he mumbled.

"You're a good daddy, Joshua." She patted his arm and smiled.

"Wevi!" Nevaeh shouted around the bread in her mouth as Levi came through the door.

"Hey, hey, Vea!" Levi mussed her hair, and Josh groaned. "What?" He turned to find him frowning. "What'd I do?" Holding his arms out at his sides, he stared at the young dad.

"Took me twenty minutes to brush her hair, Levi," he mumbled, feeling like the morning was stacked against him.

Husband and wife shared a knowing smile. Laura

moved to smooth Nevaeh's hair back into place and kissed the top of her head. She watched as the little girl reached for her milk a little too quickly, spilling some on the table and her dress. Before Josh could move, she'd grabbed it from her hands and helped her to the sink to wash up.

"I hear you'll be catching a ride with us this morning." Levi poured himself a cup of coffee, leaning against the kitchen counter as he drank.

"Nevaeh wants me to go with her," Josh replied.
He nodded. "Good. That's good, son. She needs her dad there."

"Uh-huh."

"Don't worry," Levi grinned over his mug. "Zeke's the same in the pulpit as he is in the yard. All around good guy, that one."

"Yeah." The statement did little to calm his nerves. When they finally loaded into Levi's truck to head to the church, Josh could hardly breathe from the dance taking place in the pit of his stomach.

The service had already begun by the time they arrived, but that didn't stop the congregation from turning to stare as Josh walked into the building, Nevaeh's hand clasped tightly in his. He stared them down until, one by one, they each resumed singing "Rock of Ages" with the choir. He kept his head down as he allowed Nevaeh to pull him into a pew, not paying attention to which pew she'd hauled him into until it was too late.

"Jordan, Jordan! My daddy's here! Look! It's my daddy!" Nevaeh's attempt at a whisper was equivalent to an elephant trumpeting into a foghorn. Josh's eyes shot to his right, his gaze locking with Jordan's before he pointedly turned away and focused on the choir.

Jordan's heart twisted in a mix of emotion as he watched his friend. He scooped Nevaeh into his arms and held her, his mind pondering the great feat she'd accomplished. Countless people had worked to get Josh in a pew over the years. All had failed. But this tiny little girl in his arms had defied all odds and dragged her daddy into a church building—into the very church he despised. He shook his head at the miracle beside him, sending up a prayer of thanks and asking God for wisdom on how to approach Josh after the service.

When the song had ended, Zeke walked to the pulpit, a smile stretching his plump cheeks as he gazed at the congregation he loved. "You may be seated, friends." There was a clatter of noise as the group sank back into the pews, an occasional eye drifting to the back, staring in awe at the town's heathen. The middle pew was alive with hushed whispers as the group of elderly gossips began to discuss the visitor. "Garrett's boy!"

"That's him!"

"That's her daddy!"

"Well, I say!"

Josh shifted in his seat, wishing he could get away with slipping outside for a smoke. His daughter would kill him if he tried, so he didn't dare move. Behind the pulpit, Zeke cleared his throat and leveled the gossip pew with a stare. The room went quiet, and he began to speak.

"We are honored—blessed—to have an old friend in the house this morning." He gestured to the back, eyes alive with happiness and hope. "Joshua Cameron is here with us! Visiting with his baby girl, Nevaeh. Welcome, son! You all have this fine young man to thank for the beautiful landscaping you see outside, as well as the fact that the men's restroom no longer leaks. Joshua has been hard at work for our church, and we are greatly indebted to him for his service."

Josh slid down in the pew to escape the eyes turning to stare at him. Why, Zeke? Why?

Scrambling from Jordan's arms, Nevaeh was suddenly at his side, her face scrunching with worry as she took in his features. "Daddy, say hello. What's the matter? Don't you like it here?"

Josh looked at her, his breaths shallow and quick, desperate for an escape. Refusing his impulse to run, he flashed her a smile and made a face at her, not caring when she burst out laughing during Zeke's prayer. He scooped her into his arms and held her tight, his heart relaxing just from her presence.

"Are you okay?"

He glanced at Jordan, his eyes looking him up and down before turning back to Zeke without a word. Jordan swallowed hard, unable to keep the disappointment from his face. Would Josh's rejection of him ever end?

"Turn in your Bibles to Luke chapter fifteen." Zeke flipped his Bible open and began turning pages. "Luke fifteen, verse eleven. And the Good Book says: 'To illustrate the point further, Jesus told them this story: 'A man had two sons. The younger son told his father, 'I want my share of your estate now before you die.' So, his father agreed to divide his wealth between his sons. A few days later this younger son packed all his belongings and moved to a distant land, and there he wasted all his money in wild living. About the time his money ran out, a great famine swept over the land, and he began to starve. He persuaded a local farmer to hire him, and the man sent him into his fields to feed the pigs. The young man became so hungry that even the pods he was feeding the pigs looked good to him. But no one gave him anything. When he finally came to his senses, he said to himself, 'At home even the hired servants have food enough to spare, and here I am dying of hunger! I will go home to my father and say, "Father, I have sinned against both heaven and you, and I am no longer worthy of being called your son. Please take me on as a hired servant. So, he returned home to his father. And while he was still a long way off, his father saw him coming. Filled with love and compassion, he ran to his son, embraced him, and kissed him. His son said to him, 'Father, I have sinned against both heaven and you, and I am no longer worthy of being called your son. But his father said to the servants, 'Quick! Bring the finest robe in the house and put it on him. Get a ring for his finger and sandals for his feet. And kill the calf we have been fattening. We must celebrate with a feast, for this son of mine was dead and has now returned to life. He was lost, but now he is found.' So the party began. Meanwhile, the older son was in the fields working. When he returned home, he heard music and dancing in the house, and he asked one of the servants what was going on. 'Your brother is back,' he was told, 'and your father has killed the fattened calf. We are celebrating because of his safe return.' The older brother was angry and wouldn't go in. His father came out and begged him, but he replied, 'All these years I've slaved for you and never once refused to do a single thing you told me to. And in all that time you never gave me even one young goat for a feast with my friends. Yet when this son of yours comes back after squandering your money on prostitutes, you celebrate by killing the fattened calf!' His father said to him, 'Look, dear son, you have always stayed by me, and everything I have is yours. We had to celebrate this happy day. For your brother was dead and has come back to life! He was lost, but now he is found!'"

    Josh listened with rapt attention to the parable, searching his mind for any memory of reading this story in the Bible Titus had given him. Was it possible these stories were more than fairy tales? Could a father have this much love for his wayward son? His gaze wandered to Garrett, seated across the aisle, and his heart twisted in his chest. Not his father. There was no love in him. Josh dismissed the progress he'd seen in his dad since he'd been home. It was all for show.

    His mind shifted to Nevaeh as he glanced at the little girl snuggled against his chest, eyes already drooping as she listened to the hum of the pastor's words. He knew he'd welcome her back if she ever ran wild, like the boy in the story. Maybe there was something to this Book after all...

    "We are the prodigal. You hear me? I say, 'We are the prodigal!' The prodigal is you! It's me! We wander away from the God Who loves us, and we go out there and sleep with the pigs, brothers. We sleep with those filthy creatures and eat the slop in their troughs, claiming we like it that way! But GOD, in His beautiful wealth of wisdom, longs for us to come home. He searches for us. Us! Despite the nasty, filthy creatures we've become. Hear me?" Zeke's face was red and sweat poured down his forehead as he jumped up and down behind the pulpit. His glasses slipped to the edge of his nose, unnoticed, as the man stared his congregation down.

"He don't care if you out there. He don't care that you smellin' like a pig, brotha! What God cares about is that you come home! Just come on home! Can't you hear Him callin' yo' name? Though He's surrounded by folks who stayed by His side, He out there worryin' after you! The one out there in the mud with them pigs! What you doin' out there? Huh? Why you eatin' with them pigs when God has feasts at His table, robes of purple, blessings all around waitin' on you? You'd rather be in the mud! You a fool, and so am I! Get home! You hear me? Git!

"Maybe you ain't never been home before. You ain't never experienced God the way some o' these other folks have. All you know is them pigs and you say 'Well, Pastor, how can I find my way to some place I ain't never been?' I got good news for ya, brotha! God has a place for you in His arms. Yes, He do! He been waitin' on you. For you to be done with them pigs and come to Jesus! Come! What you waitin' on? You wait too late and there ain't gonna be no more home to go to! His mercies are beautiful. His glories extravagant. But friend, don't be fooled! God don't wait forever! His mercies run out. While you playin' with them pigs, His mercies are dimming, ya hear? Don't wait! Don't be a fool!"

Josh sat frozen in the pew, sweat beading on his brow. Was he out there with "them pigs" as Pastor Zeke had said? Did God see him as nasty and filth-ridden? Did God want him that way? Surely not. Surely, he'd have to clean himself up before approaching such a holy God... He glanced at Jordan, marveling at the tears glistening in his eyes. What could have him crying about what they'd just heard? Jordan was with God already—everyone knew that. He walked it, talked it, and breathed it every day. What was his deal? So, he'd made some bad decisions. Big whoop-dee-doo. The guy was a saint, acting like a sinner. Josh rolled his eyes and refocused on the pastor's words.

"You comin'? Where you at? How long you stayin' in that mud, fool?" Pastor Zeke had come around the pulpit, down to where the congregation was seated. His eyes bore into each person.

"Come on! Come ask me about my Jesus. Come ask me where He be. Why does He want you? Why? Because His love extends to all, even filthy sinners like you. You're lookin' at a filthy sinner right in front of you! Yes, brotha, I'm talkin' about this ol' man right here." Zeke pointed a finger at his bald head, a smile stretching his face. Tears poured down his cheeks as he spoke. "God wanted me. He came and got me out of the trenches of hell. You don't believe me? Ask anyone who knew ol' Zeke back in the day. You tell any o'my college buddies where I'm at and they'll laugh you right in the face. The old Zeke liked that booze. That old fool liked them women. Yeah, buddy, that old Zeke, he was as nasty as them pigs. But God, He looked for me! And He lookin' for you, too! Where you at? Where are you? You comin'?"

Josh slid Nevaeh to the pew and laid her gently down, hoping she'd stay asleep. The room closed in around him. His breathing forced gasps for air. Keeping his eyes downcast, he slipped into the aisle and out the back door. The fresh air hit him in the face, and he gasped, sucking in a deep breath as tears stung his eyes. What had he been thinking to attend a church service? Sit through a sermon about a God he could never add up to?

He walked to the side of the church and lit a cigarette, inhaling the nicotine deep into his lungs as he leaned against the siding. "You don't want me, okay?" he spoke into the air. "I ain't worth it, man. I hate my father, I hate my best friend, I'm barely here for my kid, alright? So just keep Your distance, God. I'm not the guy for You. Trust me."

"He does want you, Josh."

Josh's eyes shot to Jordan. "Look who's playing 'savior' again," he mocked with an eye roll as he took another drag of his cigarette, blowing the smoke above his head.

Jordan sighed and chanced getting a step closer to his friend. "I can't save you, Josh, nor will I pretend to try." Josh laughed and shifted his weight. "Right. That's why you come to my rescue every time I fall. Gotta go grab the heathen—can't let anyone think you don't care…"

"That's not fair, Josh." Jordan's voice was quiet, his hands slipping into the pockets of his jeans.

"No?" Josh tossed his gaze in his direction, his face twisting in mock disbelief. "So, you didn't hunt down your wayward friend and fly across the United States of America, drug me, then drag me back home so you could save my soul? That was, what…all in my head?"

"You're my best friend, Josh. I have never turned my back on you. What was I supposed to do when they called and told me you'd been hurt? Leave you there, all alone, and wait for you to die?"

Josh's eyes belied his shock. "You've never turned your back on me, J? You didn't betray my trust and follow some skirt into the beer aisle? That was all my imagination too?"

Jordan's face was a mixture of guilt and remorse, his eyes dimming as his heart convicted him of his sins again. "You're right," he whispered through his tears. "I did betray you. I turned my back on you, and I can't even begin to tell you how sorry I am, Josh. I was wrong. So very wrong. If I could take it all back, I would, I swear. But I'm here now, Josh. I'm right here, and I swear to you, I'll never touch alcohol ever again. I'm done with Cali. She's out of my life for good. Just please, man. Please forgive me. Please."

"Forgive you? So that your conscience will stop

messin' with you? So you'll feel better about yourself?" Josh sneered in disgust. "No thanks, man. Imma leave you to that."

Jordan's eyes fell to the ground, and he forced himself to nod. "Okay," he whispered. "I guess I deserve that."

"Yeah. You do. Guess the saint's turned into a real sinner." Josh met his gaze, his eyes hard. "How's it feel to be just like me?"

"You left me."

Josh's eyes shot to Jordan's right, his heart sinking at the sight of his sleepy-eyed girl, her lower lip quivering as she stared at him. "No, baby," he whispered. Crouching down, he held out his arms for her, his heart squeezing when she shook her head.

"I wanna go home."

He nodded. "Okay, yeah. Come on, let's go."

"No! I wanna go home with my mommy. Not you." She turned her back to him, but stopped, her eyes narrowing in a glare as she looked at him. "That's a 'scusting habit. Mrs. H says so."

Josh looked down at the cigarette in his hand and sighed. Dropping it to the ground, he stamped it out and tried again. "Baby, come home with Daddy. Please?"

She shook her head. "No. You left me. I'm going with my mommy." Her chin up and Josh realized she looked more like him than he cared to admit. "'Bye, boy."

Boy. Her go-to name for him when she was mad.

"It's okay, baby," he whispered as she disappeared around the corner. "I'll always wait for you."

Chapter 29

"When I am afraid, I put my trust in you. In God, whose word I praise, in God I trust; I shall not be afraid. What can flesh do to me?"
~Psalm 56:3-4~

GARRETT

Garrett sat alone in his study. Peace was far from him as his mind tortured his soul. Clutched in his trembling fingers was a picture of his stillborn daughter–her silent image shouting memories he wished would have died along with her. A deep moan rose from his gut, and he clenched his fist as the pain began to take over. Closing his eyes against the tears, he wept from the desperation claiming him. He had to fight this. He could not give in to these memories.

In the past, he'd turned to alcohol during times like these—looking to booze to fill the hole in his heart that would never mend. As a Christian, and being three years sober, he'd learned to turn to God to ease the death in his soul, but God was far from his mind as he fought the hold Nilah still had on him, even 22 years after her death. He gripped the picture frame tighter, his tears dropping to the glass surface. "My baby." He sniffed. "My beautiful baby girl. You should still be here today…"

His mind played the reel from long ago. He saw Elysia, drenched in sweat and her face twisted with agony, as she delivered their first child. He'd felt nothing but pride as the doctor had coached her through each contraction.

"Just one more push ought to do it, Elysia. You got this. Come on, sweetie. Give it all you got."

"You're doing great, babe. I'm so proud of you," Garrett had whispered into her ear.

As much as he wished he could forget, the trauma from that day was seared into his mind. He gripped Nilah's picture tighter and remembered.

Garrett's eyes rested on the doctor's face, a hint of

panic at the expression he read. He sat up straighter, his fingers stroking Elysia's hair with greater force than he'd intended. "Doc, what is it? What's wrong?"

"Nurse, STAT," the doctor shouted as he worked to pull the baby free from her mother, tension lining his face. The room buzzed with nervous energy as the nurses ran from one end of the room to the other.

"She's blue…"

Garrett ran a hand down his face, his eyes darting from one nurse to the other.

"…not responding…"

Sorrowful eyes darted to the woman he loved.

"…the baby's not breathing…"

This couldn't be real…it wasn't happening…

"…the cord…"

Grief gripped his throat in a vice that refused to let go.

The room went still. Silent. A pin's drop to the floor would have felt like an explosion. Nurses wiped tears from their eyes, attempting to keep their emotions out of their jobs. The doctor cut the umbilical cord and sat back, defeat hunching his broad shoulders.

"Time of death: nine-fifteen PM." His words caught in his throat. "Stillborn, baby girl. Cameron."

A shrill scream shattered the silence around them, adding to the anchor of pain in each heart. Grief's icy blanket dropped over the room, suffocating all within. Garrett's tear-filled eyes shot to the woman he loved, and his chest exploded from the devastation shattering her features. His hand trembled as he tried to hold her, his strength crumbling with the weight of the cannonball wrecking his soul.

He was ready, the nurse was beside him. The still form of the baby he'd long-anticipated lay in her arms, cradled with delicate care and wrapped in a downy blanket the couple had chosen for her reception. Her face was blue. His stomach knotted at the sight. He took his daughter in his arms as tears poured down his cheeks, splashing the tender face he cradled to his chest.

"Nilah," he whispered. Her name alone broke him even more. He moved the baby closer to her mother, trying his best to hold it together as his wife wept beside him.

In his arms lay years of dreams. Prayers. Expectations. Promises he could never keep. He'd failed her. This beautiful baby girl. He'd failed to keep her safe. He was her father, and he'd been unable to keep her safe for even one day on this miserable planet. The realization hit him in the gut, twisting its cruel knife deep inside of him.

There was nothing left to do but lay his head down on his wife's pillow, their sweet girl between them on the bed, and join the mother as she wept.

A sudden noise sounded from the other side of his study door, jolting him from the memory. The door flew open, and Nevaeh sauntered to where he sat.

"Daddy, my tablet died, and now I'm bored." She worked to pry his arms free so she could claim his lap, irritated when he refused to let her.

"I'm busy right now, Nevaeh." Garrett turned his face away and furiously wiped the tears from his cheeks, begging God to draw her interest elsewhere.

"But I'm bo-o-o-r-e-d," she whined, nuzzling his elbow with her head.

Garrett bit back his irritation. "Baby, go find Grandma and play. Please, honey. I'm busy right now, okay?"

She pushed her bottom lip out and pouted up at him, only to be met with his stern eyes. "I can't." She sighed, pulling away from him. "Mommy's not here. She went next door to Mrs. Jenny's. I wanna go to the park. Will you take me? Please, please?"

Garrett sighed. "What if we call your daddy to come take you to the park?"

Nevaeh crossed her arms over her chest, chin shooting up. "No. I'm mad to him."

"Nevaeh, Daddy didn't leave you at church, hon. He just needed to go outside to get a little air, that's all."

The last thing he wanted to do was explain his son's actions to his granddaughter. He needed to get her out of here—he couldn't handle thinking of both of his children at the same time. This was Nilah's time.

"I need you to go play, babe. Go on. Shut the door, please." He stared her down until she backed out of the office and shut the door behind her.

With a sigh of relief, Garrett stared at the door a moment longer before pulling Nilah's picture away from his chest. He heard the doorbell but made no move to answer. He was in no mood for company. Vaguely aware of voices in the hall, he stood, intending to rehang Nilah's picture above his desk. His study door flew open, and Nevaeh raced in, shrieking with excitement. Before he could stop her, she barreled into him, knocking Nilah's picture to the floor and shattering the glass and frame at his feet.

Heartbroken, his temper soared. "How many times have I told you not to barge into my study, Nevaeh? Look what you've done!"

Reaching for a glass paperweight, he yanked it off the desk and threw it as hard as he could across the room, a yell escaping his lips as it slammed into the wall and shattered all over the floor. Nevaeh burst into tears, terrified by the anger demonstrated by the man who'd never shown her anything but love.

Garrett immediately regretted his impulsive decision and stepped toward her, tears pooling in his eyes. "Baby, I'm so sorry. Daddy didn't mean to, I'm so sor—"

The fist was in his eye before he ever saw his son. His head snapped back from the hard blow.

Josh pulled his daughter into his arms and held her tight as she clung to his neck and sobbed. Standing over his father, his nostrils flared with fury as his right hand clenched and unclenched at his side. "The only reason I don't beat you to death right now is because of this little girl. And let's get one thing straight, you sorry waste of oxygen, I am her daddy. Not you! Don't you ever let me hear you call yourself her father ever again. You understand me, prick?" Josh exited the room and stormed toward the front door.

Terror struck his heart, and Garrett jumped to his feet, tearing out the door after them. "Josh, wait! Wait!"

Nevaeh's eyes peeked over her father's shoulder as Josh stormed to Levi's truck and placed her in the backseat, slamming her door and turning to face his father.

"Wanna fight me for her? Come on. I dare you!" He stood, his clenched fists raised and ready to fly as he guarded his baby girl.

Tears filled Garrett's eyes from where he stood on the porch, unmoving. He knew he should try and stop him from taking her—it was what Elysia would expect from him. But he couldn't do it. She belonged to his son, and he deserved to have her. "Go, Josh," he whispered.

Shocked, Josh relaxed his stance, unsure. "What?"

Choking back a sob, he forced the word again. "Go. Take her and run. Hurry, before your mother comes home."

Distrust flashed in Josh's eyes, but he wasted no time in obeying. Racing to the driver's side of the door, he leaped behind the wheel and peeled from the driveway.

Dread seeped into Garrett's bones at the sight of Elysia walking back from the neighbors, eyes fixed on the truck speeding down the street. "Oh, God, help…"

"Was that Josh?" she called to him.

"Baby, I…"

"Garrett Cameron, do you have a black eye?" she demanded as she drew nearer. At his silence, panic seized her, and her gaze flew from him to the empty driveway. "Where's Nevaeh?" she demanded.

No answer.

Running across the yard, she screamed as she charged him, pounding his chest with her fists before he caught her in his arms. Shoving away from him, she dropped to her knees, burying her face in her hands as she sobbed. "I hate you, Garrett Cameron. Do you hear me? You have ruined everything all over again! I will never forgive you! Never!"

His heart shattered into a million jagged pieces, ripping his soul to shreds. The reality of what he'd just done slammed him full force. His breaths quickened into tight gasps, tears streaming down his face as he helplessly stood back and watched his wife leap to her feet and run.

Away from him.

And away from the chaos that always followed him.

"Where would he take her?" Laura was seated on her couch beside Elysia, her hand gently rubbing her back as she cried. Her question was directed at Garrett, who'd been pacing her rug for fifteen minutes. He and Elysia had arrived at the Hendricks's house minutes after Josh had fled with Nevaeh, only to learn they hadn't seen him since he'd left for their house that morning.

Garrett's eyes shot to his wife, his heart breaking all over again at her crumpled features. This was all his fault. Why hadn't he controlled himself? Bottled up his grief until Nevaeh was out of sight? "I don't…I don't know…" He gasped, disbelief washing over him. His son had taken Nevaeh. She was really gone. And he'd let it happen.

The front door burst open, and hope exploded across the room until Levi and Jordan walked in and disappointment settled like a wet blanket.

"What happened? Where are Josh and Nevaeh?" Jordan asked.

Laura grabbed her husband's forearm and squeezed it tight as he came to stand behind her. "We don't know. Josh went over to take Nevaeh to the park and he—" Her eyes cut to Garrett, whose gaze was fixated on the carpet. "He took off with her."

"What?" Jordan stepped toward his mom. "Why?" His mind raced with possibilities as he thought of where Josh could be.

"We have to call the police," Elysia whispered. "We have no choice. We have to turn him over to them—it's the only way to get her back."

Garrett's eyes flew to Levi's, tears stinging. "I need to

talk to you. Now."

Levi nodded, concern for his friend filling his chest. "Yeah, sure. Okay. Let's step outside." He released his wife's shoulder and followed Garrett to the front porch, closing the door behind them.

"This is all my fault." Garrett gasped. "Nevaeh came into my office when I was grieving Nilah. I was already upset, and she raced through there and knocked into me, breaking the only picture we had from the hospital after we'd lost her."

"Breathe," Levi urged.

"He will never bring her back on his own, but we can't call the cops, Levi!"

Levi scratched his chin. "Listen, Garrett, I know the last thing you want to do is turn Josh over to the authorities, but if you don't get them involved, he will leave the state with Nevaeh—you know he'll do it. You can't risk her like that."

As though he hadn't heard him, Garrett went on. "I lost my cool. I yelled at her, and I threw a paperweight against the wall. It shattered, and she screamed. I-I didn't see him there." His lower lip trembled. "I didn't see him until after he'd punched me in the eye. He told me the only reason he didn't kill me was because of her. And then he was gone."

Levi stared at his friend and told himself not to make the situation worse. "Garrett, I don't understand. We have got to call the cops. There's no telling how far he's gotten already! He has enough money for a plane ticket back to Florida—you hear me? I gave it to him myself when he first got here. If he leaves with her, he will never come back."

Garrett stared at him miserably. "We can't call the cops, man. If we call them, they'll bring him in for kidnapping. If they do that, he has zero chances of getting custody of Nevaeh, even if we deem him fit in the future."

Levi breathed a rushed breath. "Garrett, that may be a risk you're going to have to take. Right now, this has to be about Nevaeh—not Josh. Do you understand that?"

Garrett's face crumpled as he nodded. "I know. I know. I should have stopped him. I could have stopped him! I chose not to, though. Once she was in his arms, and I knew he was running, I saw it as a good thing, Levi. I...I told him to run."

"You what?" Levi couldn't hide his shock.

"I've been trying to convince Elysia to sign Nevaeh over for months now, but she wouldn't budge. I got wind last week that Nichole's stirring again. Been quiet for a while, but a fellow lawyer saw her at the courthouse last Tuesday. Said she was filing some papers. I knew it was only a matter of time before she swooped in and destroyed Josh. I couldn't let her get her hands on Nevaeh, and Elysia wouldn't listen to reason. So, when he took her, I let him. I never should have allowed it, Levi. How am I going to tell my wife I chose to do nothing?"

"Oh, man, Garrett. This is bad," Levi breathed. "This is really bad."

"Yeah," he sniffed. "We have to find him. That's our only hope. We have to spread out and search. Airports, bus stations, all over. We have to go now. I just...I don't know what to tell Elysia."

"The truth," Levi answered with confidence.

Garrett nodded. "I'll tell her...soon."

Levi's face displayed his disapproval. "You should tell her now, Garrett. It's only right."

He stared at him. "Would you tell Laura right now if it was you? If your son had just taken your granddaughter and run off to who knows where? Would you tell her now, or wait to see if you could find them first?"

Levi thought about this, then sighed. "You say the word, and I'll be right there to offer support." He clapped his friend on the back, giving his shoulder a reassuring squeeze. "Elysia loves you, Garrett. It may take her a while, but once this thing blows over, she'll be okay." As he followed his friend back inside, his heart told him he'd offered an assurance that was not his to give...

JORDAN

Jordan sat in his truck and stared across the parking lot of the airport, his heart in his throat. His father's truck was there—exactly where OnStar had said it would be. He scanned the parking lot for any sign of Josh or Nevaeh but saw none. Taking a deep breath, he pulled out his phone and dialed his father as he climbed from the truck and locked it.

"What'd you find?" Levi's voice was strained–barely audible over the shouting in the background.

"Your truck. He's at the airport. At least, he was. I'm headed inside now to ask if anyone's seen them. Who's shouting, Pops?" He peered into the window of his father's truck. Nevaeh's swirly-straw cup lay discarded in the seat, along with Josh's jacket.

"Elysia," Levi answered with a sigh. "Garrett's at the center of this mess, and she's not taking it too well. Listen, if you find any sign of them, call me. Understand?"

"I will," Jordan promised. "Good thing he didn't take off in your truck—add grand theft auto to this kidnapping charge. I can't believe he did this, Dad."

"I can. Josh will do anything to protect that girl. Can't really blame him for that, can we?"

"No. Guess not. I just don't understand. What spooked him?" Jordan pulled open the door of the airport and went inside. People rushed around him pulling suitcases, some with screaming children on their hips, each in a hurry to reach their respective terminals before their flights left without them. His eyes scanned the crowd, but Josh was nowhere to be found.

"Seems Garrett lost control of his temper around Nevaeh and threw something at the wall. Josh witnessed it and panicked."

"Aw, man, that's not good, Dad. No wonder he ran. I wish he'd talked to us. We could've helped!"

"That's not how Josh rolls. We both know that."

Jordan's eyes scanned the perimeter, his gaze settling on an enclosed garden to his left. Through a window, he spotted Josh seated on a bench watching as Nevaeh chased butterflies around the garden. He froze, his breath catching in his throat. "Got him," he whispered.

"You found Josh? Is Nevaeh with him?" Levi's voice was filled with hope.

"Yeah. I gotta go." Before he could hang up, his father began talking, rapid fire.

"Watch your back, Jordan. Remember, Josh will do anything in his power to protect that kid. He's already got a vendetta against you—do not give him a reason to attack. You hear me?"

Startled by his father's intensity, he slowly nodded. "Uh, yeah. Okay, Dad. Don't worry—I'll check in soon." "You do that, Jordan Blayze, or I'll be up there looking for you," Levi warned.

The line went dead, and Jordan took a step toward the garden door, his heart skipping in his chest. The bench was positioned away from the door, so Josh wouldn't be able to see him enter. Still, he was nervous. There wasn't another soul in the garden with them, and no one in the airport seemed to be paying them any attention. Taking a deep breath, he gripped the door handle and slowly pulled, thankful when it didn't make a sound. Gently pushing it closed behind him, his heart leaped to his throat as he noted the privacy of the garden. With only two windows facing the airport lobby, no one would notice if he fell into danger at the hands of his best friend. Swallowing his nerves, and praying for strength, he watched as Nevaeh tried her best to reach for a butterfly above her head. Her face was tear-streaked—eyes puffy and red. Jordan's heart twisted at the sight—had she been crying to go home? Had Josh forced her to accept this or were those tears from the anger she'd witnessed in her grandfather? She leaped into the air, squealing when the butterfly flitted just out of her grasp. The moment her feet hit the ground, her eyes shot to his, her face exploding in a smile. Panic pounded in his brain and, for a moment, he considered darting back the way he'd come. But no...this had to be done. He was

Nevaeh's only hope of getting home—and Josh's only hope of avoiding prison for years to come.

"Jordan! Daddy, Daddy, look!" She pointed. "Jordan's here! He's come to say goodbye!"

Alarmed, Josh turned to the door, his eyes flying to where Jordan had come to a stop a mere six feet away. Leaping to his feet, he grabbed Nevaeh and stared at his friend, danger flashing in his eyes. "What are you doing here, Jordan?" His voice was a deadly calm.

"I just want to talk, okay?" Jordan held his hands in front of him as he cautiously inched closer.

"There's nothing to say. You can stop right there, turn around, and go home." Josh's eyes never left his as his arms wrapped tighter around Nevaeh, as though he feared Jordan might snatch her from his arms.

"You don't want to do this, Josh. The police are coming," he lied. "They're going to arrest you for kidnapping, unless you turn yourself in."

Josh studied him, sizing up his words. His right brow creased, left raised in doubt. "You're bluffing," he challenged. Surely his mom hadn't called the cops on him... She would never end his life like that, knowing how hard he was working to be there for Nevaeh.

"I wish I was, man. Why don't you pass Nevaeh to me, and we can talk about this?" Jordan kept his eyes on his friend, mentally pleading with him to comply.

"No." Josh's eyes hardened. "I would rather go to prison for the rest of my life defending her than to ever give my father a chance to hurt my kid. I'll take my chances on the run, and you'd better stay right there."

His words made Jordan freeze and rethink his approach. Glancing at his watch, he wondered how much time he had before Josh's flight boarded. "Josh, please. I'm begging you, as your friend. Don't do this. They'll catch you right in front of her, man. You're risking being tazed in front of your daughter. They'll cuff you and haul you off to jail, and you'll never get another chance to be her dad. Please, man. Think about this."

"Daddy?" Nevaeh's timid voice sounded in his ear.

It took all his strength to keep his eyes on Jordan and not look at his child. "Not now, Nevaeh," he urged.

She twisted in his grasp. "Daddy, you're hurting me. Let go!" she cried, her small hands pushing hard against his chest as his grip tightened around her.

Jordan's features twitched as he watched Nevaeh become even more animated in Josh's arms. "Come on, man. You're hurting her. This isn't you. Let her go! Please!"

A flicker of doubt flashed in Josh's eyes as he glanced at his watch. Twenty-five minutes until boarding time. Their terminal was right across from the garden—he just had to get past Jordan to get there. He relaxed his grip on Nevaeh and shifted her in his arms until she rested her head on his shoulder and wrapped her arms around his neck. His eyes darted to the exit, but shot back in an instant. "Get out of the way, Jordan. Nothing you do will stop me from getting on that plane with my kid." He took a step forward, intending to go right through him if necessary.

"Don't do this, Josh. The cops will be here to arrest you any minute. Don't you get it? You're going to prison! Give me Nevaeh, and I'll tell them I was with you the whole time—I'll tell them you never intended to leave, only needed time to think. Please, Josh. Think about this!" Jordan's blood surged as he read the wild look in his friend's eyes.

Josh stepped forward, but Jordan wasn't going. "Move." His tone was hard. Cold.

Jordan shook his head. "I can't let you ruin your life like this. Nevaeh's?! I'm not goin' anywhere."

"Then I'll move you myself." He went for him, surprised when Jordan stepped out of his way, clearing his path. He rushed forward before Jordan could change his mind. Reaching for the door, he pulled it open and stepped over the threshold. In an instant, Nevaeh was ripped from his grasp, and Jordan burst past him, into the lobby.

Adrenaline surged through his veins as he grabbed a fistful of the back of Jordan's t-shirt and dragged him back into the garden, shutting the door behind them.

"Run to the other side of the garden! Go, go, go!" Jordan urged Nevaeh as he placed her on her feet just as her father yanked him backward and threw him to the ground. His shoulder hit hard, and he cried out as he looked up into Josh's rage-filled eyes.

Fury burned behind Josh's pupils, and his nostrils flared, fists clenched at his sides. "You're a dead man," he growled through his teeth.

Lying flat on his back, Jordan knew he had to distract Josh long enough to jump to his feet. Otherwise, he didn't stand a chance. "Think of your daughter, Josh. Nevaeh is watching!"

"This is for Nevaeh!" Josh shouted, even as she began to cry. "Don't cry, baby," he called, his eyes never leaving Jordan. "Give Daddy just a minute and we'll go, okay?" Grabbing a wad of Jordan's shirt, he yanked him to his feet.

"Josh…Josh, stop." Jordan's hands grabbed Josh's fist as he tried to free himself. "Stop it, man! You don't wanna do this!" He turned his face away, Josh's breath hot on his cheek as he pulled him closer.

"Yes, I do! You threatened my daughter's safety!" Josh drew back a fist and slammed it into Jordan's nose, throwing a second punch into his abdomen as he cried out and threw a hand up to shield his face from the blows.

"Stop! Daddy, stop it! You're mean!" Nevaeh screamed, tears pouring down her face.

As Josh drew back for another swing, Jordan took advantage of the arm in front of his face. Lunging forward, his teeth met flesh, and he bit down, hard. Josh hollered and shoved him backward in shock.

"You bit me!" Holding his arm in his hand for a moment, he observed his blood-streaked skin.

"And you busted my nose—we're even," Jordan mumbled behind the hand he'd pressed to his face.

A shrill ringing pierced the air. Jordan watched Josh's features as he cautiously reached into his pocket and withdrew his phone. Glancing down, he sighed. "Josh, it's Dad."

"Don't answer that!" Josh panicked, his eyes shooting to Nevaeh. "Jordan, do not answer that phone, man."

"If I don't answer, he'll come looking for me. You know he will. He already knows where I am." Jordan's thumb hovered over the green call button, his eyes never leaving Josh. His thumb inched closer as the ringing continued, but Josh was on him in an instant, snatching the phone from his grasp and throwing it as hard as he could, shattering the device against the enclosure. Shock exploded across Jordan's face as he watched the phone fall to the ground.

"Jordan, don't move!" Josh commanded, eyes ablaze as he held his right hand in front of him, placing distance between himself and his friend. "Nevaeh, come to Daddy, baby girl. Come on, kid, let's get out of here."

Nevaeh took a step forward, but Jordan stopped her.

"Nevaeh, stay right there!" Jordan's heart broke when she burst into tears. "Do not go to him, Veah!" He bit his lower lip, forcing the words from his mouth. "Daddy isn't safe!"

Josh's eyes swung to his, no sign of friendship left in his glare. "I'm going to kill you." The words were for Jordan's ears alone.

Jordan took a step back, blood dripping from his nose. He'd seen his friend angry more times than he could count, but nothing equaled the look on Josh's face in that moment. Fear struck his heart, sending shards of panic throughout his body.

He had to fight him—and fight hard. Before he could talk himself out of it, he lunged and took the first swing, his knuckles connecting to Josh's jaw with a sickening "thwack!" Before Josh could recover, Jordan landed a second blow to his chin, and a third to the ribs he knew hadn't yet healed from his accident.

Josh's head snapped back, his arms wrapping around his midsection as he yelled. Rage exploded inside of him, and his fists began to fly. Calculated blows slammed into Jordan's body. Right fist to his left cheek. Thwack! Left fist to the right cheek. Thwack! Right fist straight to the nose he'd already busted. Snap! Jordan's pain-filled screams confirmed what he already knew—he'd broken it.

Blinded by the pain, Jordan's eyes swam. He forced himself to keep fighting or die. Nevaeh's hysterical screams from the edge of the garden pushed him harder as he bent at the waist and charged Josh's midsection, tackling him to the ground and landing two blows to his face. Digging his knee into Josh's stomach, his left hand grabbed a fistful of hair as he slammed his knuckles into his right eye. With a guttural yell, Josh flipped him onto his back, and Jordan knew he was done for. His friend was stronger—a better fighter than he'd ever cared to be. It was over. The blows came fast and hard, waves of fury bursting free of their source and pounding his body without mercy.

"Daddy, stop! Stop hitting Jordan! Daddy! Da-a-a-a-d-y!" Nevaeh's wails floated through Jordan's mind as he drifted in and out of consciousness, Josh's rage-filled face dimming more with each blow.

As though realizing for the first time that his daughter was witnessing him beat the life out of his friend, Josh's right fist froze mid-air, his chest heaving as he climbed off Jordan and fell to his back, the taste of blood filling his mouth. He had to move. Levi knew Jordan was here. It was only a matter of time before he came looking for him.

Josh forced himself to his feet and looked down at his ripped and bloodied clothing. He'd have to move fast to get cleaned up before his flight. The challenging part would be to convince Nevaeh to go with him without a fight. He stepped toward her, and she screamed, pressing her back to the glass as she trembled.

"It's okay, baby. Come on, we have to go. We're gonna go to Florida, remember? You'll love it there." He reached for her but she shrank away. "Veah, come on. We have to go, baby." He scooped her up, his conscience pricking when she fought him and screamed. "Shh, baby. You're okay. It's okay. Come on, let's go." He walked past the limp body of his former best friend. He wouldn't allow himself to look at him—couldn't accept that he'd possibly ended his life.

"Jordan!" Nevaeh wailed as her father carried her. "Jo-o-o-r-d-a-n!" She stretched her arm out in his direction, tears streaking her face. "Jordan, wake up! Wake up!" she screamed, her small fists pounding against Josh's chest as he carried her farther away.

"Shh, Veah. He's okay. Jordan's just sleeping, alright? He's gonna be okay. We're okay, too, we just have to get out of here. Don't cry, baby. Don't cry." Using her body to shield the blood covering his own, he pulled the door open and stepped into the lobby, making a beeline for the gift shop across from them.

Jordan would be fine, his mind worked to reassure. A good Samaritan would find him. Someone would call for help. And that someone would call the police, and the police would find him.

And he would go to prison.

But until that happened, he would hold his precious girl in his arms and tell her his lie until they both believed it. "Shhh, baby. Daddy's got you. We're gonna be okay."

LEVI

Something was wrong. He could feel it deep in his soul. He'd tried Jordan's cell four times with no response. Checking the rear-view mirror for cops, Levi pressed the gas harder, shooting through an intersection without so much as a hint of a stop. The airport loomed in the distance as Levi's hands gripped the steering wheel until his knuckles turned white. "Please, God. Have mercy on my boy. Let my kid be okay, God. Please, God, please," he begged over and over as he whipped Laura's car into the parking lot. His chest constricted at the sight of Jordan's truck near his own—both vehicles void of life. Throwing the car into park, Levi jumped out and raced into the airport, his eyes searching for his son.

"Excuse me, have you seen this guy?" He grabbed a passerby's arm and thrust a picture of Jordan in his face.

"Man, get off me!" The man shook free and quickly stepped away.

Not to be deterred, Levi set his sights on another, only to be shot down faster than the first. He stood in the middle of the lobby and ran a shaky hand through his hair. "Where are you, son?" He asked the air. His eyes fell on the garden, and his heart dropped to his knees at the sight of his boy—bloodied and beaten, lying discarded in the grass. Breaking into a run, Levi shouted, "Call 911! Somebody call 911! Now!"

"I've got you!" a man shouted back from the lobby as he pulled out his phone.

Levi yanked the door open and raced to Jordan's side, falling to the grass beside him. "Jordan! Oh, Jordan," he cried as he gingerly touched his son's swollen face. Pressing an ear to his nose, he cried as his breath tickled his cheek. "Thank You, God. Thank You! Jordan, can you hear me, boy? Jordan, wake up, it's Dad. Wake up, son. Come on, boy. Show me your eyes," he pleaded. "Come on, son. Please wake up, please!"

With fumbling fingers, he grabbed his phone and dialed Garrett. "Come on, come on, come on…"

"Did you find him?"

"Meet me at the hospital. Bring Laura! Hurry!" Levi cried.

"Levi, what's happened? Who's hurt?"

"It's Jordan, man. Josh beat the crap outta my boy. Oh, Jordan," he whimpered. "Come quick, Garrett. Bring my wife!"

"We're on our way!"

The line went dead, and he sat back on his haunches. Helplessness filled his soul even as the paramedics rushed into the garden and fought to stabilize Jordan before loading him onto the stretcher.

"Please, God, please, God. Oh, God, please…"

Chapter 30

"Follow justice and justice alone, so that you may live..."
~Deuteronomy 16:20a~

LEVI

"...call the cops."

"...kidnapped Nevaeh!"

"...could've killed my son!"

"Everyone please just calm down!"

Jordan drifted in and out of consciousness, pain registering on all fronts as familiar voices floated in his mind. He attempted to turn his head, immediately regretting the decision. A low moan escaped his lips, and the voices around him drew closer.

"He's moving!"

"His eyes are flickering open—call the nurse!"

"D-a-a-d," Jordan moaned, his left eye slitting open, his right refusing to budge.

"I'm here, son." Levi pushed past the others and placed a hand on his arm. "I'm right here." He sniffed back his tears, a mixture of sorrow and fury colliding in his chest at the sight of his boy's pummeled face.

"Flor..." Jordan's eye slid shut, his face tense. "Florida..."

"Florida?" Levi's brows knit. "Josh and Nevaeh?"

Jordan gave a slight nod. "No... cops..."

Levi shifted on his feet. He didn't need the cops. He needed to find Josh and beat him senseless for what he'd done to his boy. "We have to find them, son."

"I'll...go..."

"Absolutely not." Laura was at his side, eyes blazing.

"Would everyone please clear the room? We need to run vitals again now that he's awake. Clear the room. If he checks out okay, he should be sent home to recover no later than tomorrow." The nurse stared expectantly at them as she held the door open.

In the hall, it was decision time. Levi hung his head and

placed a hand to the back of his neck. "How should we handle this?" The question was loaded—one that none of them wanted to answer.

"He kidnapped Nevaeh and beat my son unconscious." Laura's words were clipped and fierce. "We have to call the police. I love Josh just as much as I love Jordan, but the boy has seriously crossed a line this time."

"I agree." Elysia's eyes were dull from the day's battle. "I don't want my son locked up, but if something happens to Nevaeh, I'll never forgive myself if I didn't have him arrested."

Garrett crossed his arms over his chest and stared at the floor.

"Tell them."

He glanced up to find Levi staring right through him.

"I, um...we, uh...Elysia..."

She stared at him; chin raised. What could he have possibly done that was worse than causing the two people she loved most in this world to disappear from her life? "What did you do?" she accused.

Tears formed in his eyes as he glanced at his wife. "We can't call the police about Nevaeh."

"We have to, Garrett. He may not bring her back!"

"We can't." He sniffed. "Because if we do, they'll arrest him on kidnapping charges, then he'll never have another chance at getting custody of her."

Her face was set with determination. "This is about Nevaeh—not Josh! He's a grown man, Garrett, and he made a decision that put that child in danger. You seriously need to prioritize yourself right now, and quit living in the past!"

Her words stung, but she was right. He owed Josh everything, but at the risk of his three-year-old granddaughter?

"You have to tell her, Garrett," Levi pushed. "She deserves to know."

Garrett's lower lip trembled as his wife stared him down. "Baby...Nichole was coming...she was coming for him, and you wouldn't listen to me! I knew if she got her hands on Nevaeh, Josh wouldn't have a shot. When he took her and ran, he challenged me to fight him for her. I…"

He looked to Levi, who gave him a nod of encouragement.

"I could have engaged. Slowed him down. Stopped him, even. Instead, I told him to take her and run." He dropped his eyes, unable to bear the shock and hurt on her face.

Elysia shook her head, unable to comprehend what she'd just heard. "You let him take her?! You told him to run?!"

"Baby, I'm so sorry, I never should have—"

She held up a hand to stop him, the sting of Garrett's betrayal stabbing her soul. Her eyes shot to Levi and Laura before she turned and rushed for the parking lot.

"Elysia," Garrett called after her. "Lysie!" Tears pooled as he watched her leave, the hall an eerie calm as the doors whooshed open, and she disappeared outside. He started to go after her but stopped when Levi grabbed his arm. "Give her time, Garrett. She's not in a place to hear you right now."

Garrett looked in the direction his wife had gone, his face a mask of misery and regret. "I have to fix this, Levi." His eyes swam, guilt and remorse washing over him.

Laura gaped at him. All empathy for him had vanished once she'd heard his confession. "It's a little late for regrets, isn't it?" she snapped, her blood boiling. "Because of you, my son is lying in a hospital bed right now!"

"Laura." Levi cut his eyes to her, his expression holding a warning—a warning she did not heed.

"No! It's true! If Garrett hadn't lost his temper in front of Nevaeh, Josh would never have taken her and run. He would still be here, working hard to make a life for his daughter. But now we're in this mess, thanks to him." She stepped toward Garrett, eyes blazing. "Let me tell you something. I will be calling the police to bring that boy in for what he did to my son!" Laura's eyes flashed as she stared both men down before shoving past Garrett and rushing after Elysia.

Levi looked at his friend, wishing he could take back the words his wife had just said. "I'm sorry, Garrett. She shouldn't have—"

"No. She's right," he whispered, his eyes following her as she went through the doors. "We have to bring him in."

"How long would he get for assault?"

He shook his head, tears streaking his cheeks. "Not assault. Misdemeanor battery. He'll do two months, if he's lucky. More if the judge sees fit."

"How would they get him back to Cali?"

Garrett sighed. "We'd need a warrant, but I doubt the judge would grant one for a misdemeanor."

Levi raised a brow. "Garrett."

"Don't say it," he whispered.

"Garrett." Levi gave him a pointed stare.

Swiping a hand down his face, Garrett took a shuddering breath. "Give it time. Maybe he'll come back on his own."

"You really believe your son is gonna waltz his way back into this mess he left behind? That's not what Josh does, and you know it. He runs. And he keeps running until he's tossed flat on his back. You need to nail that boy for kidnapping that kid, and you need to make him come back to face the consequences of his actions!" His neck burned with the anger residing in his soul.

"Levi..." Garrett pleaded.

"He could've killed Jordan, Garrett. Don't you care about that? You're fighting for Josh in hopes of a relationship you never had. But my son has always been there for you. Always! You're gonna turn your back on him now?"

When Garrett didn't answer, Levi shook his head. "I'm going to go find Laura." He started to walk away from him, but turned back, pointing a finger. "Mark my words. I'm bringing that boy back here. And when I do, I'm gonna make him look at what he did to his 'best friend.' Then I'm gonna toss his gangster-wannabe butt in a jail cell."

TITUS

The first giveaway was a lamp burning in the den. Titus knew he'd left every light off before heading out to sea. He always had, and he wasn't a man to change his habits. He parked his truck and reached into his glove compartment for his gun before climbing from the vehicle and quietly closing the door. Keys in hand, he walked to his front door and tested the knob, surprised to find it still locked. His eyes scanned the windows near the door, frowning when none appeared to be broken. Unlocking the front door, he stepped inside, gun aimed in front of him. "Who's there?"

"You greet all your guests with a gun?"

Titus squinted in the dim light, surprise exploding on his face at the sight of Josh standing in the shadows. "Josh?! I could've shot you dead, boy!"

"But you didn't." Josh shrugged and walked past him, into the kitchen as though breaking into his former boss's home was completely normal. He grabbed an apple and bit into it, aware that Titus was standing behind him, mouth open wide.

"How long have you been here?" he asked, placing the gun on the counter. "And how did you get in?"

Josh shot him a look. "It's me you're talking to. You really should beef up the security in your home. Leaving it easily accessed by burglars while you're away for months isn't smart."

Titus flicked on the light, sucking in his breath at the cuts and bruises all over Josh's face. "You're in trouble," he spoke quietly.

"What was your first clue?" Tears filled his eyes as he dropped his gaze to the floor. His jaw clenched, and he swiped a rough hand at the moisture. "I made a bad move, man. A really bad move. Pretty sure I'm on my way to prison."

The older man's eyes softened. What was it about this troublemaker that always gripped his heart? "What'd you do, son? Am I harboring a fugitive right now?"

Josh shrugged. "Don't know. Probably."

"Josh," he sighed. "I'd take a bullet for you, kid, but I can't do jail time."

"Follow me," Josh urged, turning for the den. Titus's mind raced as he obeyed. At the sight of the sleeping little girl on his couch, he froze. "Is this—?"

"Yeah. That's Nevaeh. She's three." Josh leaned his shoulder against the door frame and took another bite of his apple.

"What happened? Who'd you get into a fight with, and why?"

Josh's eyes clouded as his mind drifted with the memory. "He lost it, man. Lost his temper with my kid and threw something into the wall. It broke all over the place with her right there, watching. She was terrified—like me as a kid. It was like watching my childhood all over again, Titus. My dad was yelling at her and then, out of nowhere, he calmed down and tried to smooth her over and called himself her father." Josh sniffed, the muscles in his face twitching. "I snapped. Couldn't think straight. Couldn't reason. All I could see was my father beating my kid. I took her and ran, but Jordan caught up with me at the airport."

Titus stared, waiting for him to continue. When he didn't, nerves twisted his gut. "And then...? What happened, Josh? Tell me."

He looked at him, misery swimming behind his eyes. "He tried to take Nevaeh from me. Told me the cops were coming, and I'd be arrested for kidnapping. He snatched her out of my arms, Titus. I saw red. I couldn't focus on anything except getting Nevaeh on a plane out of there, away from my father. I grabbed him, and I just started pounding."

"Where was Nevaeh during all this?" Titus interrupted,

fear gripping his chest.

"Jordan got her away from us. Man, what kinda father am I? I didn't even think of the fact that she was in his arms. He had to tell her to run away from us—like he knew it was going down like that. She watched the whole thing. There's no coming back from that, Titus. I ruined my kid."

"How did you ruin her, Josh?"

"I beat the crap outta him—right in front of her. He wasn't moving by the time I rolled off him. I may have even killed him—I don't know!" Josh trembled as Jordan's lifeless body flashed in his mind. "What if I killed him, Titus? He's my best friend. He's always been there for me. How could I do this to him? Titus," he sniffed, his fists clenched at his sides, "I'm done for. They're gonna find me, and they're gonna lock me away for good. I'll lose Nevaeh, man. I'll never get to be her dad. My mom's probably never gonna talk to me again. My father's a jerk. I may have killed my best friend. Levi and Laura will hate me forever. You don't want me anymore. What am I gonna do, Titus? I blew it! I had a job. I was workin' for a pastor. I really liked it." He swiped at his tears.

Titus's eyes shot up at this, but he wisely held his tongue.

"He'll never take me back. Nevaeh's grandma belongs in a psych ward. Been after me ever since Jordan dragged me back home. If she has her way about it, they'll throw me in a dungeon and forget I exist. I don't even have my girl anymore, Titus. She's got some other dude's ring on her finger now. Besides that, her mother brainwashed her into thinking horrible things about me that just aren't true. What am I gonna do?"

When he finally took a breath and collapsed into a chair across from Nevaeh, Titus offered his advice. "Go home, Josh. Turn yourself in."

Josh's head snapped up, his eyes alight with terror. "Did you listen to a thing I just said?! I can't go back! They'll arrest me and take my kid! Besides, even if I wanted to, I spent all my money coming here."

Titus sighed. "Why'd you come here, son?"

"Because I trust you."

Titus gave him a pointed stare. "Then go home."

Josh's lower lip quivered as he looked up at him. "I can't. They'll arrest me, man. Prison for life! And Jordan?" His face twisted. "He may be dead!"

"There's only one way to find out. That little girl deserves a father who's honest and brave. She deserves a daddy who isn't afraid to do what's right. To accept his mistakes, learn from them, and show her how to move past them. You can't do that for her if you run from this. Go home. Turn yourself in. Find out about Jordan. And start taking steps to make things right, even if it takes years."

Josh nervously tapped the side of the chair. "How?"

"Who do you trust back home?"

Josh thought for a moment, his face falling. "Jordan," he whispered.

"And?"

"Levi, I guess. But he probably wants to see me locked up just as bad as Nichole by now."

Titus perched himself on the arm of the couch, bracing his hands on his knees. "Okay, listen. Call Levi. Tell him you realize you made some big mistakes. Let him know how remorseful you are. Tell him you're coming back with your kid and that you'll hand her back to your parents. Tell him you'll be on the first flight back—I'll put you on the plane, myself, and pay the airfare. Tell him you'll do whatever it takes to make things right. And then let God take care of the rest."

Josh's vision clouded. "I can't do it, Titus. I can't!" His gaze drifted to his daughter's peaceful face; his mind tortured over what might become of her.

Titus leaned forward. "Yes. You can. Remember when you called me and asked me about David and Goliath? You challenged me on the accuracy of that story. This is your Goliath, kid. You fight this battle for her." He stabbed the air in Nevaeh's direction. "You hear me? You fight Goliath and end him, so she won't have to."

Josh stared at him, thinking. After a moment, he slowly nodded. "Okay." He gasped in surprise when Titus grabbed him in a bear hug. Tears burst from his eyes, and Titus held him as he cried. When his shoulders stopped shaking, Titus let him go.

"Ready?"

He glanced at Nevaeh and wiped at his face as he reached into his pocket and retrieved his phone. "No," he replied. "But I'll do it for her."

Titus nodded and smiled. "I'm right here with you, kid."

Josh picked up the phone and dialed.

LEVI

Levi's back was stiff from sitting in the hospital chair beside Jordan's bed. Despite his weary body and soul, sleep had evaded him. His anger toward Garrett had dimmed, though he'd hardly said two words to the man across from him since they'd gotten to Jordan's room. Garrett's foot tapped a nervous rhythm as he focused on Jordan's still form.

A shrill ringing caused both men to jump. Glancing at his phone, Levi bolted upright in his chair. "It's Josh!" "What?!" Garrett leaped from the couch and raced to Levi's side as he answered and placed it on speaker. "Josh?" Levi's voice sounded too high-pitched and strained for his own taste. When silence met his ears, he wondered if the call had been accidental.

"Yeah." Josh sniffed into the receiver; his voice low.

The fathers breathed deep sighs of relief at the sound of his voice. "Where are you, son?" Levi worked to keep his tone neutral and calm.

A moment's pause. "Panama City."

"Is Nevaeh with you—safe?"

"What kind of question is that?" Josh clipped. A voice in the background murmured, and he changed his tune. "I mean, yeah. She's right here, sleeping."

Garrett's eyes closed, and he pressed his fingers to his eyelids.

"Levi?"

"Yeah, son."

"I messed up."

Levi's eyes fell on Jordan, and he clenched his teeth. "Yeah. I know."

"Is Jordan...?"

"He's in the hospital. Should be out by tomorrow." He closed his eyes tight when Josh breathed a relieved sigh, knowing if he were in front of him, he'd fight him on the spot.

"Listen, I um..." He paused, and there was more murmuring in the background. He sniffed and whispered, "I'm gonna go back. I'll take the first flight there. I know it looks bad—it is bad. But man, I swear I only did it to protect Nevaeh. I thought my dad was gonna hurt her, and I just..."

Garrett's chest tightened as tears slipped down his cheeks. Levi reached out a reassuring hand and squeezed his shoulder.

"I'm gonna turn myself in, okay? Please don't send them after me. Not with Nevaeh watching. I'll get off the plane, and I'll...hand her over to my dad." His voice broke, and the murmuring was back. "And then I'll go to the station and give myself up. I'm so sorry about Jordan, man. I'm so sorry!" he sobbed. "I swear, I didn't wanna hurt him! He's my best friend! I swear..."

Levi sniffed and pressed his fingers to the bridge of his nose. "Don't swear," he managed through his tears.
Josh breathed a laugh. "Okay...okay...I'm gonna wake Nevaeh up, and then I'm leaving, okay? I promise I'll be there soon, just please. Please promise me you won't send them after me. Promise."

Levi looked at Garrett. "I promise. Don't let us down, Josh. We'll be waiting."

Josh's flight was due to arrive just after 10 PM. Levi

and Garrett left the hospital at 9:15, intending to meet their wives at the airport by 9:45. Neither one had enjoyed a pleasant conversation when phoning the girls about the latest turn of events. Laura was still intent on seeking blood from Josh as recompense for all he'd done to her son. Elysia didn't want to so much as see Garrett and had informed him that once "her baby" was back in her arms, she would be returning home without him.

The ride to the airport was quiet. Solemn. Each feeling as though they were headed to a funeral for someone they loved. Jordan had been adamantly against having Josh arrested for the assault, to the point that Levi and Garrett had to offer a false reassurance that nothing would be done so he'd calm down for the nurses. When the truck pulled into the parking lot, Garrett opened up about his conversation with his wife.

"Elysia wants me to find someplace else to stay tonight." His voice was quiet as Levi parked the truck and cut the engine.

Levi's brow furrowed, his mouth sliding into a frown. "For how long?"

Garrett stared out the window. "She didn't say. She really didn't say anything to me, except to ask for Josh's flight number. I'll be surprised if she ever forgives me for this, Levi. I've destroyed my family all over again."

With a sigh, Levi pulled the keys from the ignition and checked his watch—ten minutes until time to meet the girls. "One step at a time, Garrett. Let's take this one step together, okay?"

Garrett stared at him, his hand on the door handle. "For what it's worth, I'm sorry, Levi. I was selfish to protect him. You have every right to be angry with me."

Levi averted his gaze. "I'm not angry at you anymore, Garrett. Truth is, if things were reversed and it was Jordan running scared, I'd probably have done the same thing. I don't want Josh to be locked away, but I do want him to realize that what he did was wrong." He met Garrett's eyes, a spark of anger flashing. "And I want him never to lay a finger on my boy—ever—again."

Garrett's mouth twitched into a brief smile before settling into a nervous frown as the two climbed from the truck and headed inside. The women had beaten them to the lobby, sitting side by side as they waited for Josh and Nevaeh's arrival. By the looks on their faces, it was clear the guys were not welcome to sit with them, and neither one tried. Finding a bench near the exit, Garrett and Levi sat down to wait, both tense.

Levi glanced at his wife, wondering if her anger was directed at him too, or just Garrett. She wasn't meeting his eyes, which unnerved him. Was she fidgeting? What was her deal? She looked the same way she had on his birthday last year when she'd surprised him with a cruise, only this time she wasn't excited—just guarded. Her eyes were glued to the television, scanning the arriving flights as though her life depended on it. He didn't have time to draw Garrett's attention to his wife's behavior before she and Elysia leaped to their feet, faces tense and eyes peeled as people poured into the lobby from arriving flights.

Levi didn't have to scan the crowd to know the exact moment Josh stepped into view with Nevaeh in his arms. Elysia burst into tears, and Laura's mouth twitched as she watched him draw closer. There was a nervous tension in the pit of his gut that he couldn't shake. Something about the way his wife watched Josh walking toward them was very off. What was she up to?

And then he saw them.

From Josh's left, three armed police officers approached, one dangling a pair of cuffs in his hand. Levi's eyes shot to Laura, understanding hitting the pit of his stomach like a lead ball. "She called them," he whispered to Garrett, his tone panicked.

Exhausted and on edge, Josh never saw it coming. The cops rushed him, one grabbing his free wrist and cuffing it as another pulled his screaming daughter from his arms. His other wrist was cuffed as his eyes swung to Levi, shock and betrayal exploding across his face. "You promised!" he cried as the cop dragged him backward, offering Elysia room to rush in and grab Nevaeh. "I trusted you, Levi!" The cop pulled at him, but he jerked from his grasp, his eyes on Nevaeh. "I didn't get to say goodbye! I didn't get to kiss her; tell her I love her!"

The cop was on him again, his grip tightening on his arm. "You know, it's a good thing the kid you assaulted isn't present to press charges. If he was, you'd be looking at a felony charge."

Levi's jaw set in a hard line as tears rushed his eyes. He could feel Laura's gaze on him, but he refused to look at her. "Can I talk to him before you take him?" he called to the cop, who shook his head as he continued to drag him back. "Just for a second—please?"

"I said no, sir. We need to get him away from the kid right away."

Garrett's eyes clouded as Josh struggled against the cop's grip on his arm, a second cop rushing to grab hold of his other arm. "He's not a threat to his daughter," he called to the cops. "Just let us have a second!"

Laura's gaze lingered on Josh for a moment before she placed her hand on Elysia's back and led her away. "Daddy!" Nevaeh cried as she watched the cops pull him away. "Da-a-a-a-dy!"

"Nevaeh, Daddy loves you, okay? I love you, baby! I'm so sorry!" Josh cried as the cops hauled him toward the door.

"Garrett, what's our legal stance here?" Levi urgently whispered; his eyes glued to Josh's back.

"We have none," Garrett cried. "We have to respect the cops' answer—to buck that would be interfering with an arrest. Why didn't you tell him you didn't do this? He's going to hate you forever."

"Better for him to hate me than my wife," Levi replied. As the cops pulled Josh out the door, he had a sinking feeling that everything he loved in this world had just come to a devastating end. Nothing would ever be the same.

JOSH

"Don't I know you from somewhere?"

Josh stared at his booking officer, his eyes empty and cold.

"You look really familiar—could swear I've seen you before." The cop leaned closer to his computer screen. "Ah, that makes sense. You've got quite the record, kid. Seems you were a regular back in the day."

Josh turned away. He didn't have the headspace to ponder his past arrests. His mind was on his daughter. Was she okay? Would his mother offer her comfort about all she'd seen, or would she tell her that her daddy deserved to be hauled off to jail right in front of her? He squeezed his eyes shut to stop the fresh spark of tears.

"Yo, is that Garrett's boy?" A uniformed officer cursed, chuckling as he came closer. "I thought we were done lockin' you up. What're you here for this time, stealing an old woman's car?"

The booking officer laughed at the joke, but Josh's eyes grew hard.

"Can we just do this?" Josh snapped.

"Aww, the lawyer's son wants to hurry up and get a jail cell. Ain't that cute?" the cop teased. He glanced at the computer screen and whistled. "Disorderly conduct. Fighting, huh? Surprise, surprise."

"Either toss me in a cell or let me go, man."

"O-o-o-h! Tough guy, eh?" He laughed, ribbing the booking officer in the side. "Guess I should be scared—I mean, he was dragged in for beating the brakes off a guy. I should fear for my life, eh, Paul?"

The booking officer glanced at Josh and noted the storm billowing across his face. "Let him be, Slate. The guy's obviously had a long night."

"Aww, standing up for the criminal—that's so sweet," Slate teased before wandering off to spread his foolishness with another guy down on his luck.

"Come on, son." The officer gripped Josh's arm and pulled him to his feet. He led him toward a backdrop and stood him in front of a camera. "Stand still while the camera snaps your photo."

The camera clicked and flashed, and the officer directed Josh to turn to his left. As the camera clicked and flashed again, Josh's gaze fell on a uniformed man entering the station. The booking officer turned him again, and an uneasy feeling settled in the pit of his stomach as the man approached.

"Starks!" the man hollered across the room.

"Yo!" Josh's arresting officer called back as he rounded the corner.

"The prisoner you transported just now—I heard you run his name for a warrant check. I want to see your booking sheet."

"Sure thing, Captain." Starks handed the book to him and stepped back as he perused it.

After the captain had checked it over, he fixed his eyes on Josh. Terror gripped his heart, and he swallowed hard as he took in the hardened glare on Josh's face. "Do you, um...you know who I am?"

Josh rolled his eyes. "Should I?"

Asher didn't answer. He snapped a picture of the booking sheet before handing it back to the officer. Sweat beaded his brow. "Arrival time?"

The officer stared at the captain, a quizzical look on his brow. "You alright?"

Asher's lips pressed into a thin line. "What. Time. Did. He. Arrive?"

"Uh, like an hour ago, maybe?"

Without another word, he raised his camera and snapped Josh's picture, then turned and walked away, heading for his office.

The officer grabbed Josh by the arm and pulled him back to his desk. "Just a few more items to take care of..." He turned Josh's back to him and unlocked the cuffs before turning him back to his desk. "Press your left thumb in the ink pad and push your print here." Josh obeyed, allowing the officer to grab his right thumb next. "You, um, you know the captain?"

"What is with you morons? Don't you know how to just arrest a guy and toss him? Do we have to play twenty questions?" Josh's eyes flashed. His body ached. His mind wouldn't shut up. His heart had been ripped to shreds. He was exhausted and hungry and just wanted to be left alone.

"Sorry," the officer mumbled, placing the cuffs back on Josh's wrists. "I'll allow one phone call, but make it quick. You'll have to stay in the holding cell for the night, since we're packed upstairs. Do you choose to make a call?" His hand gripped Josh's arm as he waited for his response, his eyes searching his face.

Josh stared blankly at the wall, unmoving, as he thought.

"So, um…phone call?"

Josh glanced at him. "Yeah," he croaked, his mouth dry from the despair settling in the pit of his stomach.

The cop pulled on his arm, walking him down the hallway until they came to a phone booth. Releasing the cuffs, he took a step back, his hand on his gun. "Five minutes."

Josh stared at the phone before picking it up and dialing. He leaned his weight against the phone booth as the line rang, then mumbled his name into the receiver. As he waited for the recipient to accept the charges for the collect call, he rested his head on the upper ledge.

"Josh?"

"Goliath won."

"No, he didn't, son."

"Yes, he did. I'm going to jail. Levi betrayed me. I have no one left."

"What do you mean? I thought you guys had a deal that you'd turn yourself in. You're at the station, aren't you?"

"The cops ambushed me at the airport. They ripped my baby from my arms. She was freakin' out, man, and they didn't care. They didn't even let me say goodbye. I just wanted to call and tell you that. I'm going to jail. I don't know how long I'll be here. When I get out, I'm going back to Florida and leaving this place behind for good."

"No, kid. Don't talk like that. You're gonna get out, and you're gonna fight for your daughter. That's what you want. That's what you need. Do not give up in there, do you hear me? Don't give up!"

"Time," the officer called, stepping closer to Josh.

"I have to go. Just wanted to tell you that doing the right thing blew up in my face. Goodbye, Titus." He hung up and stood still while the officer cuffed his wrists.

He allowed himself to be pulled toward the holding cell without a fight, his heart sinking at the sight of how many prisoners were tossed in there together. The officer opened the door, removed the cuffs, and pushed Josh inside before closing the door with a loud "clang."

The prisoners in the cell eyed him as he stood in their midst, one advancing closer.

"What're you in for?" the guy asked, as though they'd known each other for years.

"Ending the last guy's life with my bare hands." Josh looked him dead in his eyes, unblinking. The inmate slowly backed away from him and left him alone. Finding an empty corner in the cell, Josh collapsed to the floor, leaning against the bars. His body screamed for rest, but sleep would not come easy. Especially since he'd lied during booking.

He knew exactly who Asher Holmes was.

He remembered every time Asher had come to his house after a beating and each report he'd falsified to cover up his father's crimes. And now, as he rested his head against the jail cell, instead of planning a future with his daughter, he was planning the demise of a criminal who played the part of a cop.

Chapter 31

"Many are the victims she has brought down; her slain are a mighty throng."
~Proverbs 7:26~

JORDAN

"Jordan, I have to tell you something." Levi stroked his chin as he watched his son prepare to leave the hospital.

"I'm listening." Jordan's movements were laborious as he worked to pull a fresh t-shirt over his head, careful to avoid his bandaged nose.

Levi studied his son, his jaw clenching at the obvious pain in his swollen eyes. Jordan was nearly unrecognizable after the beating Josh had given him the day before. "Need a hand?"

"No. Tell me what you need to say, Dad. I need to go find my friend."

"About that… your mom… um, your mom is really upset about what Josh did to you."

"I can take care of myself."

"Yeah. I know, son. But your mom...she's angry at him. And Elysia is furious that he took off with Nevaeh like he did."

Jordan's eyes shot to his father as he tugged his shirt over his bruised ribs. "He did what he thought he had to do. Mr. C scared the crap outta him, Dad. He thought he was gonna hit Nevaeh. Josh will do anything to protect her—remember?"

"Yeah. Well, while you were laid up last night, Josh called me."

Jordan's eyebrows shot up, and he winced. "What did he say? Are they alright?"

"Um...no. He ran to Florida, just like you said, but he called and told me he was coming back. He admitted to making some big mistakes. Said he regretted the fight and told me he would turn himself in to the cops, then hand Nevaeh off to Garrett without any trouble. He asked me not to send the cops after him, because he didn't want Nevaeh to see his arrest. I don't blame him for that and promised him I wouldn't. We met his plane last night, a little after ten." Levi paused, dreading telling his son the rest of the story.

"Dad," Jordan urged, impatience lacing his tone. He bit back a yell when he tried to reach for his shoes, immediately changing his mind with a frustrated sigh.

Levi grabbed the sneakers and passed them to his son. "Elysia and Mom met us at the airport. They had the cops take him in when he got off the plane. Josh is in jail, son. And he thinks I'm the one who put him there."

Jordan stared hard at his dad. "You're joking, right? I told you all—I don't want to press charges. How did this happen? I don't want my best friend doing time for fighting me. He was fighting for her! I knew what I was getting into when I went down there. I knew Josh would be incapable of rational thought and would be driven by fear. How could you let them do this?"

Levi sighed. "It was out of my hands, son. Mom and Elysia have grouped against Garrett and me. They won't talk to us. Elysia told Garrett not to come home. What would you have had me do?"

Tears squeezed through Jordan's eyelids. "How much is his bail?"

Levi gave him a blank stare. "Um…I'm not sure."

"You didn't call and ask? You just left him there?"

Levi's heart thundered in his chest. "Listen, boy. I don't want him in there any more than you do, but he almost killed you, and he kidnapped Nevaeh. He needed to be brought down."

Jordan scoffed. "'Brought down.' As though he's an animal, instead of the guy you consider as your second son? Should I expect the same thing if I screw up? You gonna toss me in a cell and throw away the key? Come on, Dad, this is Josh we're talking about! The same guy who used to sit at our table and bawl his eyes out just because you asked me about my day, and he didn't have a dad at home asking him the same question. The same guy who used to fall through the floor any time we invited him to church because he was too scared of what the gossips would tell his father. We know this guy. We have years of history, and you wanna let him rot in a jail cell because he did what he always does when he's cornered? He's so unpredictable that you didn't see this coming?"

"You're upset at Mom. Not me." Levi reminded him as he stood. "I was gonna let him turn himself in."

Jordan's eyes flashed. "But I didn't want the cops near him at all. I'm the one he attacked—don't I have a say?"

Levi stared at his boy, his arms crossing over his chest. "So, what do you want to do?"

"I'm gonna go get my friend out of jail! That's what!"

Jordan gripped the handle of his bag and pulled, sweat beading on his brow from the effort.

Levi shook his head in bewilderment. "He's never gonna learn if you keep catching him when he falls, Jordan! You could be dead right now! Do you understand that?!"

"He is dead!" Jordan shot back, putting himself in his dad's face. "Without Christ, Josh is a dead man walking, Dad. So, until Christ saves my friend from his own self, I won't expect him to act like he's alive. And you shouldn't either!"

"You can't bail him out, Jordan," Levi pleaded, grabbing the bag from his son.

"Wrong. I can't leave my best friend in jail. So, either come with me, or watch me as I walk out that door." Jordan stared him down, grateful when his father sighed and pulled the door open for him.

"Alright. Let's go. But if Mom asks who got him out, you leave me out of it. I want to sleep in my own bed tonight."

"Pansy," Jordan called over his shoulder.

JOSH

"Lawyer boy. Hey, lawyer boy!"

Josh's eyes slit open to find a guard yelling at the door to the holding cell, his gaze fixed on him. Straightening against the bars, he moaned as pain sliced through his back from having slept against the iron.

"Cameron!" the guard yelled a third time, his brows raised as though Josh was the stupidest inmate in the cell. With a sigh, he pushed himself to his feet, stepping over a sleeping inmate sprawled across the floor. As he approached the door, the guard sneered.

"Today's your lucky day, lawyer boy."

Josh stared at him; his eyes dull. "My father's the lawyer—not me."

The guard laughed, his eyes scanning his surroundings. "Yeah, okay." Reaching through the bars, he grabbed a wad of Josh's shirt and jerked him forward, smacking his face against the metal. "Don't think I've forgotten the summer of '19. Still have the scar you gave me when I went to cuff you and you pulled that shank on me. You're lucky I wasn't here when they booked you, or you'd be in solitary right now."

Josh swallowed hard, finding it hard to breathe with his collar wrapped in the guy's hand.

"Someone posted your bail." He grinned. "Waste of money if you ask me, seeing as we've been your permanent address since you were knee-high."

Working to keep the surprise from his face, Josh coughed when the guard released him and unlocked the door, grabbing his arm roughly and pulling him from the cell.

"Don't you wanna know who posted your bail?" The guard's breath was hot on his face as he leaned close.

"Does it matter? I'm free. Let me go." Josh stared at him, his gaze ice.

Walking him to his desk, the guard shoved him into a chair. "Can't go anywhere until you get all this crap signed. Gotta commit to follow through with your court dates—I expect you won't, but not my problem, lawyer boy."

Josh gritted his teeth. If this guy didn't knock it off... He reached for the papers tossed at him and began signing off on court dates and promises not to flee. When he'd finished, the guard tossed a bag at him.

"Take your crap, and get out of my face."

"You oughta thank me—your face looks better scarred," he grumbled under his breath and grabbed the bag.

"I can arrest you again." He glared.

"First you'd have to find your balls," Josh retorted before standing and walking out the door. The sunlight hit him in the face, and he squinted against the harsh beams. Before he could step off the front porch, a sleek red car screeched to a halt in front of him, its back-tinted windows sliding down to reveal the last person he would have expected to see. His pulse quickened, and his blood began to boil as long, red-painted nails dangled over the window's ledge. "Nichole," he bit through gritted teeth.

"Get in," she commanded, the thought that he might refuse never occurring in her mind.
He shoved a hand in his pocket and stared her down. "Why would I do that?"

"Because you love your daughter and don't want anything to happen to her." Nichole's eyes were unblinking as she made the threat.

Looking around as though expecting an ambush, Josh sighed and pulled the door handle, climbing in beside her. The door had no sooner closed than the driver took off, and the window automatically raised beside him. "What do you want, Cruella?"

She raised her penciled brow as she looked at him. "I'm sorry, did you want to stay in jail? Driver, turn back immediately," she ordered.

Shock flashed across his face, and he forced a quick recovery. "It was you? Why?" On guard, he straightened in his seat, one hand on the door handle even though the car had reached sixty miles per hour.

"Because, I want you out of my daughter's and

granddaughter's lives forever." Her red-stained lips spread into a thin smile.

"Look, Rhea's grown, okay? She's already made her choice clear. But Nevaeh? She's mine, and you will never take her from me."

The driver took a left, then a sharp right turn into a hotel parking lot. He parked the car and shut off the engine. "Ma'am?" he called to the backseat.

"Give us a second, Preston." She turned to face Josh, her eyes serious. "This is my offer. I will only say this once, so, try to keep that hoodlum head on straight for five seconds. Rhea is upstairs right now. You are to go up to her and discuss custody of Nevaeh. You are to sign your rights away, and then—"

"No way!" Josh interrupted, his hand working the handle to no avail. "Unlock the door—let me out of here, Nichole. Open the door, before I bust this window!" "You either sign away your rights or I'll strip them away—your choice."

"I'll take my chances in court, you crazy witch. Now open the door!" he shouted, his hand yanking on the handle. The door flew open, and he nearly fell out trying to get away from her. "You stay away from my kid, Nichole. Leave her alone, or I swear I'll come for you!"

"How cute." She laughed. "Thinking you can threaten me and beat me at my own game." Nichole stared at Josh from behind her shades. "Let's hope you don't miss that next court date, sweetheart." With a wave of her hand, the window rolled up and Preston pulled away, leaving Josh behind.

"Where to, ma'am?" Preston asked.

"Drive out to the street and circle back around. Park in the next lot over, facing the front door of the hotel. Make sure to stay hidden behind those bushes."

"Yes, ma'am." Preston obeyed. Finding the perfect spot in the lot next door, he killed the engine. "Ma'am?"

"Just sit tight. We won't be here for long." Nichole smiled and sipped her water, her eyes glued to Josh. She watched him shove his hands into his pockets and walk toward the street, heading away from the hotel. Her lips curled when his steps faltered and he froze, glancing over his shoulder. She could almost see the battle in his mind: run, or race to Rhea? Her hand gripped her bottle tighter as he spun on his heel and rushed back to the hotel. She watched him duck behind a car and check the street for signs of her. Then she watched him do exactly what she knew he would do—what she'd wanted him to do—listen to his heart instead of his mind. He waited until a couple walked through the door with a luggage cart and then ducked in beside the cart, slipping into the hotel and, no doubt, straight to the concierge desk to ask for a Ms. Rhea Romans. Hook, line, and sinker. A smile burst across her face, and she finished the last of her sparkling water. A low laugh bubbled up from her gut, exploding into a high-pitched, maniacal screech. She had him. She'd won the war. It was all over. Victory tasted oh-so-sweet…

JOSH

Josh rushed to the concierge desk, his gut pulling at him to abandon his mission. This was a stupid move. What was he even doing here? Playing right into Nichole's hands? But as the concierge approached, all he could think of was another chance to talk some sense into Rhea and convince her to go against her mother and fight for their family.

"I'm looking for Rhea Romans," he whispered as the guy leaned across the desk to hear.

"I'm sorry, who did you say?"

He cleared his throat, his heart dropping in his chest as Cali walked toward him. What was she doing here, and behind the desk? "Rhea Romans—what room?" he spoke a bit louder, his eyes on Cali as she stepped up behind the concierge.

"Don't answer that," she ordered.

The young man's fingers froze over the keyboard, and he backed away from the computer. "He's all yours, boss."

"'Boss?'" Josh questioned, his face hard.

"That's right." She smiled and raised her chin in the air. "My father owns this hotel."

"Golden spoon," Josh growled. "Come on, Cali, gimme her room number. Please."

She stared him down. "What if she doesn't want to see you?"

"Then, she can tell me herself. Give me the number, or I swear I'll knock on every door until I find her."

"You competing with the other guy who went up there last night?"

Josh tensed. "What guy?"

"You know…tall, handsome, sane…" Cali grinned. "Much more her type, if you ask me."

Gritting his teeth, Josh clenched his fist. "Give me the number, Cali," he demanded.

"This guy messin' with you?"

Josh glanced over Cali's shoulder at the guy walking toward them.

Rolling her eyes, Cali barely acknowledged him. "I'm fine, Zion. Get lost."

Ignoring her, Zion stepped to the desk and pinned Josh with a glare. "You're Josh Cameron."

"Well, aren't you smart," Josh quipped.

"You're Jordan Hendricks' friend."

Josh narrowed his eyes. "And?"

"You're the one who tried to hit my sister," Zion accused.

"Zi, let it go!" Cali hissed, but neither guy paid her any attention.

"You've got your facts wrong, prick. If I'd wanted to hit her, she'd have a dent in her ditzy little head. I don't try—I do."

Zion moved to go around the counter, but Cali grabbed him.

"Stop! Zion, I've got it!" She pushed hard against his chest, looking up into his glazed eyes.

"Better listen to that sister of yours. You don't look like you'd handle a beating too well, pretty boy," Josh taunted with a grin.

Zion sidestepped Cali, but she yanked him back.

"Stay here! Do not move!" Eyeing him as she backed her way to where Josh was standing, she pointed a finger at her brother. "Don't leave the lobby, Zion," she warned, ignoring him when he sulked.

"Sit, Ubu. Stay," Josh teased, and Zion's face flamed. Rolling her eyes, she cast Josh a look. "Follow me." She led him to the elevator and pushed the button. "What happened to you?" she asked, staring at the purple bruises on his face.

"Got into a fight. What's your excuse?"

"Jerk," she shot over her shoulder as the elevator doors swung wide and they stepped inside. Silence fell between them as they ascended, Cali's eyes bouncing from Josh to the floor. "Have you seen Jordan?"

Josh shot her a glare. "Why do you wanna know? You don't care about him."

"No?" She turned to face him, arms crossed over her chest. "How did he come out in that fight? Did you care about him when you were beating the crap out of him?" Josh stared, his eyes narrowing. "Who have you been discussing me with?"

Cali's cheeks flamed at the slip of her tongue, and she spun back to the front of the elevator. "Forget it. Just tell Jordan I hope he's doing okay."

The elevator dinged, and Josh stepped out before her, disregarding the "ladies first" part of his upbringing. He spun to face her, his arms keeping her from going farther. "That's far enough. Tell me her room number."

"Move, and I'll take you straight there."

"Why? So, you can report back to whomever you've been discussing my life with? No thanks. Room number. Now."

She swallowed hard but wasn't about to back off without a fight. "And, if I don't?"

Josh smiled, his eyes slits of fire. "I've already been in jail today. I've got no problem going right back in."

"Room 395—to the left," she whispered.

"Good girl." He patted her cheek and reached inside the elevator, pressing the ground floor button. He stood in the doorway until the doors closed and didn't move until he heard the whirring of the elevator as it shot her back to the lobby. Glancing at the time, he mentally kicked himself when he realized he'd already been in the hotel for ten minutes. Nichole wasn't going to give him much more time than that. He rushed down the hallway and stopped at her door, his fist rapping their old familiar code. Three raps. Pause. Five raps. Pause. One knock, then three quick taps. He drummed his fingers against the door jamb as he waited. "Please, Rhea. Please, please, please, please," he quietly begged.

The door flew open, shock and panic flashing across Rhea's face.

"What are you doing here?" She reached out and dragged him inside, closing the door behind him. "How did you even know I was here? You can't be here! My mother will be back any minute. Josh, are you insane?" Hot tears burned her eyes as she stared up at him.

"She already knows I'm here," he replied, his hands going to her forearms.

Rhea tensed and backed away, thoughts of Sterling's earlier visit flooding her mind. How was it that both the men in her life had chosen the same day to show up here? Sterling's visit had been shocking enough, but Josh's?

"Rae, it's me," Josh spoke quietly, his eyes pleading with her to remember.

She stared back at him, indecision dancing in her mind.

That was all he needed. Gently, and with grave caution, he reached for her. She didn't pull away, so he took her hands in his and leaned close, intent on kissing her lips, but froze at the sight of rope burns on her wrists. Anger pulsed through him as his mind filled with possible explanations for her injuries. "Who did this to you?" he demanded.

Her face paled, and she withdrew her hands.

"Rhea?" he pressed, feeling his heart might explode. "If Nichole touched you, I'll—"

"We were playing too rough." Her voice trembled. "He felt terrible, but it was my fault for not speaking up." The words rushed out as desperation gripped her.

Confused, Josh searched her face. "I don't under—" He stopped himself, reading in her eyes what she couldn't force herself to admit to him. His gaze was back on her wrists, and he gently held them. The marks were fresh. "What's his name?"

"Sterling," she whispered.

He stepped back, running a hand down his face. "Sterling? You replaced me with a guy named Sterling? What is he, some rich mama's boy parading you around like some sort of trophy?"

Rhea said nothing.

"Do you love him?" he asked, his chest tight.

Tears splashed to her eyes. "You left me. I didn't think I'd ever see you again."

Josh squeezed his eyes shut. "You didn't answer me, Rae." He looked at her. "Do you love him?"

Rhea's heart slammed against her ribcage. "I love you, Josh."

His breathing came in rapid bursts as he rushed forward and took her in his arms. When she didn't fight him, he kissed her harder, his body begging for control.

Snapping herself back to reality, Rhea shoved against him and backed away. "Josh!" she cried. "No! My mother talks of nothing but destroying you—do you understand that? She could kill you in a heartbeat and never bat an eye. She hates you with a passion and would shout with joy if you were hit by a train. Am I getting through to you?" Her eyes searched his. "You. Cannot. Be. Here."

"I'm not worried about that witch. I came to beg you to leave this place with me. Leave her. Leave Sterling. Leave it all. Come with me, and we can fight for our family together. Please, baby. Come with me." He grabbed her hands in his, eyes pleading.

She pulled her hands free and shoved them into the pockets of her jeans. "That 'witch' is my mom, and she's not a joke. She's dangerous. She's capable of bad things, and right now her sites are aimed at you and our daughter. Me running off with you will not get her off your trail—it will only make matters worse. Leave before she catches you here and goes straight for the jugular." Her gaze pulled to the bruises on his face, and she sighed. "Who were you fighting with?"

He dropped his eyes. "They wanted to take Nevaeh away from me." His voice was quiet. "My dad lost his temper with her the other day while I was there. I heard the whole thing from the next room. I went postal and took off to Florida with her."

Rhea's eyes grew large at this news. "You took her?"

Josh's jaw clenched. "Isn't that what you told me to do? Take her and run?"

"Well, yeah, but not if it meant fighting your family..."

Women. Would they ever make sense? "It was Jordan, and he deserved it. Snatched her from my arms and tried to run. I pounded his face in right before my flight."

Rhea's brows knit. So many questions, but there was no time. She had to get him out before her mother came back. "Why'd you come back? Where's Nevaeh?"

"With my mom. I came back, because I knew the cops would drag me back for kidnapping Nevaeh." He shook his head. "I was stupid. Should've ridden it out over there and settled Nevaeh somewhere safe." He reached for her, and she allowed it. "I can't do this alone, Rhea. Nevaeh needs both of us to fight for her—not just me. Come on, baby. Come with me." He drew her to him andher temple. Her neck. Her collarbone.

"Josh..." she murmured against his chest, her mind screaming in protest, her heart begging her to melt into him. "My mother..."

"Forget her. Haven't we waited long enough? Come here." He scooped her into his arms, wrapping her jean-clad legs around him as he carried her to the bed. He placed her down gently but stopped her before she lay back.

"Wait," he grinned, feeling like a schoolboy as he fished out his phone. He snapped her picture, then jumped onto the bed beside her and snapped another with her head against his shoulder.

Kissing her, he laid her back and laid down beside her, caressing her hair. Tears of relief trailed his cheeks as he held her—how many years he had longed for this moment! "Come with me, baby. This could be our normal—just you, me, Nevaeh… I can make it to where she'll never find us… Just please say yes…" He kissed her lips, his body taking control as his lust was gratified.

Rhea gripped him, her senses thrilled by his touch. Maybe she could give in to his request… make their dreams of being a family become a reality. Her subconscious screamed at her as she engaged. She knew her mother was near—she could sense her evil a mile away—but it didn't matter. Whenever she was with him, it was all okay. Everything was just right.

"Josh," she breathed against his chest. "I'll go with you," she whispered, tears streaming.

Her words mixed with the euphoric release of his body as he wrapped her in his arms and fell to his side, his eyes searching hers. "What did you say?"

Rhea trembled as she answered. "I'll go with you."
"Say it again," Josh whispered, his fingers tangled in her long hair.

"I'll go with you." She smiled through her tears.

A smile exploded across his face, disappearing as fast as it had formed when the bedroom door flew open and Nichole filled the room, draped in a cloak of evil.
But she was not alone.

"Joshua Cameron, you're under arrest for the rape of Rhea Nichole Romans." The cop reached for him and yanked him away from the woman he loved, dragging him backward. Wrestling his arms behind his back, he slapped the cuffs on his wrists and pulled him toward the door.

"No!" Josh screamed. His eyes shot to Rhea, who'd leaped from the bed as tears streamed down her face. She'd agreed to go with him. They were going to run away together. To finally be free of all this mess. His eyes registered his shock as they fell on Nichole's smug smile—evil Cruella De-Ville—the constant that always dangled Rhea just out of his reach. His mind whirled as he pieced it all together, calling himself every name in the book. Stupid. He was so stupid. He'd fallen right into her trap. Like the idiot he was, he'd done exactly what she'd wanted him to do. He mentally applauded her at her tactics as the cop read him his rights.

Wait a minute…that voice…he knew that voice…

As he was jerked toward the door, his eyes swung to the arresting officer. Asher Holmes glanced down at him, the Miranda rights flying off his lips as he dragged him past Nichole and into the hallway. Something snapped in his brain, and he let out a guttural scream as he wrenched out of Asher's grasp and raced back to Rhea, his wrists bound behind his back.

"Kiss me," he cried.

She hesitated, her eyes flying to her mother's icy stare.

"Kiss me!" Josh screamed, tears pouring down his cheeks. She pressed her lips to his, and his heart soared before Asher ripped him away and dragged him out the door.

Rhea burst into tears, wishing she couldn't hear his screams down the hall as he professed his undying love for her and begged her one last time to fight for Nevaeh. For him. For their right to be a family. And for all she claimed to love.

JORDAN

"He's not here."

"What do you mean 'he's not here?'" Jordan stared at the cop as though he had two heads. "My father watched you guys arrest him just yesterday!"

The lazy-eyed cop leaned forward on his desk, elbows

resting on the surface. "See, there's this little thing called 'bail'…ever heard of it?"

"Listen here, you prick—" A hand on his arm cut off the rest of his retort, and he threw an exasperated look in his dad's direction.

"Who posted his bail?" Levi asked, willing Jordan to stay calm before he got them both arrested.

"Santa Claus, for all I know. Why should I care? It's like I said—he's not here." The cop's eyes shot to the front entrance as a uniformed officer walked in hauling a prisoner beside him. "Well, at least he wasn't here." He stood, laughing, when Asher led Josh beside his desk. "This must be a record, Cameron. What was it…one whole hour of freedom?"

Laughter exploded across the department as the officers realized who'd been dragged through the door.

Jordan's heart flipped at the sight of Josh's downcast features. He studied him, noting how his eyes never came off the floor. Tears streaked down his face, and there didn't seem to be an ounce of fight left in his friend. "Josh," he called but received no sign of acknowledgment or indication he'd even heard him. "Josh, I'll get you out!" He turned back to the officer, urgency in his tone. "Can I speak to him?"

"Seems to me like he's not very interested in talking to you." The cop nodded in Josh's direction, pointing out how he allowed Asher to jerk him toward booking without a hint of resistance.

Jordan leaned forward, feeling his father's shock beside him at the sight of Josh. "But I want to talk to him."
The officer sneered. "Then get in line, 'cause booking has dibs. You'll have to wait around until visiting hours. That will be hours, just so you know." He laughed as though he'd made a joke.

"Is every cop in this station a jerk like you?" Jordan jumped to his feet, and the cop's hand shot to his gun. "Let's go," Levi stood and gripped Jordan's elbow. "Now, Jordan," he whispered near his ear.

"Man, get off me!" Jordan shook free of his father's grasp, his good eye focused on the cop. "I'll wait for visiting hours. Tell me where to go."

"Well, I'd say go to hell, but that would be unprofessional, so I'll just direct you to that nice cold bench over there." He pointed a fat finger to his right, and Jordan moved to sit down.

"Son, what are you doing?" Levi asked as he followed him to the bench. "You can't wait here all day. Josh didn't even look at us—something's wrong, Jordan."

"Exactly," Jordan snapped, crossing his arms. "And I'm not leaving until I find out what's going on with him. He posted bail, Dad. Now he's back not even two hours later?"

Levi studied the earnest expression on his son's face. He was right. Something bad had happened. "Want me to wait with you?"

"No. I'm fine. You have Mom to deal with, remember? I'll find my way home. Thanks."

He stared at his boy, pride swelling in his heart. Such a stubborn kid—a stickler for justice and an advocate for right versus wrong. At times he wanted to knock some sense into him, but at this moment, he applauded his son for sticking his neck out for his friend. "Okay. Call me if you need anything, you hear me?"

"Yeah." Jordan stared at Josh's back as the cops processed his second arrest in two days. "Dad?"

"Yeah, son?"

"She likes lilacs. Remember that."

Levi smiled, though his heart pinched at the thought of facing his wife's temper. "I'll go get some right now. You watch your back and keep your anger in check. I don't wanna bail you out of jail today."

JOSH

"He's been here all day, man. Have a heart and go talk to your friend."

The guard had come three times since Josh's booking,

informing him that a friend who "really seemed to care" had asked to see him any time visiting hours had opened.

Josh stared at the man from his bunk—his roommate's snores filling the small cell. Out of all the cops he'd encountered during his stay, Oscar had been the nicest one, treating the prisoners with respect. But none of that mattered to him. Nothing mattered anymore. He pulled his knees up and rested his elbows on top, clasping his hands.

"He's waited all day," Oscar urged.

"So, let him wait." Josh leaned his head back and wished the guard would go away, but he showed no sign of moving.

Oscar sighed, dreading going to Jordan and telling him—again—about Josh's refusal to see him. An idea came to mind, and he hid a smile at his own genius. "You know…if you're responsible for that kid's busted-up face, you owe him this visit." He focused his eyes on the floor, watching Josh out of the corner of his eye. His mouth twitched when Josh sighed. His plan was working.

Josh turned and dropped his feet to the floor. "Five minutes, that's it." He stood and walked to the bars, remaining still while Oscar unlocked the door and cuffed his wrists.

"You're doing the right thing, kid." Oscar was gentle as he pulled Josh beside him and led him to the visiting section. "Remember, no contact. You stay on your side of the table; he stays on his. Otherwise, you're right back in."

"Well, then, I found my out, didn't I?" Josh quipped.

Oscar shot him a look. "Just give him a chance, okay? He's desperate to talk to you." He opened the door to a tiny room with nothing but a table with two benches attached. "Due to the nature of your crimes, and the fact that you assaulted him once before, your wrists will remain cuffed to the table during this visit." He locked Josh's left wrist first, then his right, to the table.

"Whatever."

"Okay, he'll be brought in now. Play nice." Oscar left the room, locking the door behind him.

A door opened on the other side of the room and Jordan stepped in. He didn't miss the way Josh turned his gaze away from his swollen face.

"Hey." He sat across from him, his heart breaking at the lifelessness in his friend's eyes. "Josh, what happened?" He waited, but Josh only looked to his left and avoided the question. Frustrated, he sighed. "I want to help. Please talk to me, man. I'm your best friend—I'll always be your best friend. Just help me understand so I can get you out of here."

"Why?" Josh's gaze swung to him. "Why do you want me out of here? Why should you even care what happens to me anymore? Look at yourself, J. You need to stay away from me, man. I'm no good."

Jordan leaned forward, but a quick rap on the window reminded him of the rules to keep his distance and he sat back. "Josh, you attacked me because you felt threatened. You knew I intended to keep Nevaeh here in Highshore. You saw Highshore as a threat to her safety, and you weren't gonna let that happen. I'm not mad at you, man. I applaud your parenting. I would have done the same thing." He took a second to compose his thoughts, knowing Josh wouldn't give him much time. "Who posted bail?"

Josh's eyes slipped into a dark blue abyss of grief and remorse. "Nichole," he said with a bitter laugh.

Jordan's jaw dropped. "You can't be serious..."

"Dead serious. And I fell for it." His voice was a whisper as he focused on the table.

"Josh, talk to me. Tell me everything. I can get you help!" If Nichole was tangled up in his friend's mess, it was not a matter to be taken lightly.

"You can't help me. No one can." His right hand toyed with the cuff holding it hostage. "My own mother hates me now. She sees me as a threat to my baby girl. Your mom hates me, too, for what I did to you. My father's still the biggest prick ever...and your father betrayed me and tossed me into this jail after giving me his word he wouldn't. Rhea…" He sucked in a sharp breath, tears stinging his eyes. "…she was gonna run away with me, man. She told me…she said…" He sniffed and shook his head hard. "Doesn't matter. She's out of my life forever—her evil mother has made sure of that. I have no one." His eyes fell to the table, his heart squeezing tighter into stone.

"You have me! I'm not goin' anywhere; didn't I just say that?" Jordan looked at him earnestly, wishing he could convey how much their friendship mattered to him. "And, just to clear things up…my dad didn't do this."

Josh met his eyes, confused. "The cops were at the airport. They ripped Nevaeh from my arms and slapped the cuffs on my wrists in front of her. She was screaming. Your dad gave me his word that he would let me turn myself in. The cops were never supposed to have been there!"

Jordan took a deep breath, knowing his father hadn't wanted Josh to know, but it wasn't right for Josh to be angry with his dad when it was his mother who'd called the cops on him. "Mom called them. Not Dad."

Josh gaped at him, his mind working to put the pieces together. "Mrs. H turned me in? Laura?" He sniffed, wishing he could wipe the tears before they fell. His fists clenched against the table, his soul crumbling further inside of him. "Why would she do that to me? To Nevaeh? I was gonna turn myself in, J! I meant what I said!"

Jordan wiped his tears, hoping he'd done the right thing by telling the secret. "I think your mom had something to do with it, too. My dad said our moms shut both our dads out. Your mom even made your dad leave after he lost his temper, and you ran."

Tears streaked down Josh's face. "I'm going down for rape, Jordan."

Jordan's jaw dropped. "What…? How? Who?"

"No one," he cried. "I didn't do it, man. I didn't do it." He sniffed, attempting to wipe his face on his shoulder. "Nichole bailed me out and took me right to Rhea. I'm such an idiot. I fell right into her trap. I knew she was gonna pull something, but I didn't care. All I could think about was convincing Rhea to run off with me. Because of that, I'll never get to see my baby girl again. She's gonna take her away from me, and I'm gonna rot in jail for a crime I didn't commit."

Jordan's mind whirled. "She set you up," he stated the obvious.

Josh nodded. "Yeah. Had that crooked cop waiting in the shadows. She knew I couldn't resist Rhea, man. I'm such an idiot."

"Wait a minute. Rhea would have to collaborate her claims of rape for you to face conviction." Jordan leaned forward, earning himself another rap on the window. He waved a hand in apology and sat back. "There's no way she's gonna lie to that judge and say you did this."

Josh gave a mirthless laugh. "Yeah? Have you met Cruella DeVille? Seen her manipulate her like putty in her hands? The first time Rhea resists, she'll pull a custody card and threaten Nevaeh. Rhea will cave. Then she'll testify against me, and I'll go down for rape. They even have the 'evidence' to go along with her story. It was sheer genius, man. Nichole's a criminal mastermind. To make it worse, the whole town of Highshore sits inside her well-cushioned pocket. Get this—the cop who arrested me today? The same cop who used to come to my house when I was a kid. The same one who would look right at the evidence all over my battered body, then turn and tell his goons to alter the reports to make it look like a small squabble, usually labeling me as unruly and a flight risk."

"Asher," Jordan breathed, understanding dawning. "Josh, we need help. We can fight this, man, but we need help." He took a second before stating the thought in his mind. "We need your dad."

"Forget you," Josh spat. "I'd rather die in here than have him defend me. There are other lawyers, you know."

Jordan raised a brow. "Other lawyers who are gonna fight for free and get you out of a prison sentence?"

"We're done here. Guard!" Josh yelled over his

shoulder.

"I'm getting you out of here. Posting bail."

"No." Josh's eyes stared at the table. "Just let me be. At least behind bars I can't screw anything else up. Just go, Jordan."

"Josh, we can fight this, man! Don't give up! Don't let Nichole win!"

"Guard!" Josh shouted, his eyes on Jordan.

The door opened, and Oscar appeared. "You two boys play nice?"

"We're done here. Take me back." Josh watched as he unlocked the cuffs and helped him to his feet before cuffing him again. "Do not accept bail from this guy," he ordered. "I refuse it."

Oscar's brows rose as his eyes went from Jordan to Josh. "You, uh, you sure about that?"

Josh looked him dead in the eyes, his face devoid of expression. "Take me back."

Chapter 32

"You rule over the surging sea; when its waves mount up, you still them."
~Psalm 89:9~

GARRETT

Garrett sat alone in Jordan's old room—the room his son had occupied until his arrest. He stared at Josh's sparse belongings, his chest tightening at the thought of his boy behind bars. Since Elysia had refused to allow him to go home, Levi had extended his graces and offered him the room while he figured things out. He knew Laura wasn't thrilled with his presence but was grateful she hadn't refused him.

His gaze fell on an opened Bible peeking from beneath the pillow. Feeling as though he was violating his son's privacy, Garrett lifted the pillow with two fingers and peered at the Book. Covered in script and highlights, the Bible lay open to Christ's death on the cross. In awe, Garrett wondered if it belonged to Josh, or if it had been left over from when Jordan had lived here. Surely his son didn't own a Bible…that thought didn't add up to what he knew about his boy. Josh despised church. He hated anything to do with God, and resisted Christianity as though it were a plague. So, why was there an opened Bible in his room? He reached for it but froze at the sound of someone at the bedroom door. Quickly, he threw the pillow back into place and jerked his hand away, his heart pounding in his chest as though he'd been caught by Josh, himself.

A sharp rap on the door sounded just before Levi's urgent call. "Garrett. Garrett! You in there? I need to talk to you. It's important."

Alarmed, Garrett went to the door and pulled it open. Levi pushed past him with Jordan right behind him. They shut the door and grabbed seats around the room.

"What is it? Is it Josh?" Garrett's mind was filled with

worst-case scenarios of his son being beaten in jail...or worse.

"Something's happened," Levi began but Jordan took over, jumping to his feet and pacing the floor as though he hadn't been beaten within an inch of his life the day before.

"Nichole bailed Josh out of jail this morning," he started. His veins zinged from hot energy, and his swollen eye pulsed from the pressure.

"What?!" Garrett gaped at him, his heart dropping as cold waves washed through him.

"That witch bailed him out, then drove him straight to Rhea!" Jordan's fists clenched with the thought, wishing Nichole was in front of him now.

"No." Garrett sat back against the wall, shock vacuuming the breath from his lungs. "Please tell me he didn't..."

Jordan's eye shot to him, his jaw set. "He did. He fell right into her trap and went to Rhea's room. Nichole nailed him as soon as it was done. That's not all, Mr. C."

Garrett swallowed hard, his son's fate slamming his gut. It was over. Nichole had latched on to Josh's weakness and he was done for. "What else?" he asked weakly.

"Asher Holmes was the arresting officer." Jordan stared at him, watching as panic pounced behind his eyes.

"No..." Fear gripped him, squeezing him tight as memory after memory slammed through his thoughts. All the cover-ups. The false reports. Asher turning a blind eye to who Garrett had been.

"You can fight for him, Garrett. You can beat her," Levi urged, tears clouding his vision.

Garrett stared at him with vacant eyes. "He won't let me. He'll let her take him under. I know him—he won't let me touch this case with a ten-foot pole."

Jordan growled. "Then you do it anyway," he snapped.

Garrett's gaze swung to him. "I can't represent a client who doesn't want me to be his lawyer, even if he is my son."

"Then we convince Josh to hire you," Levi stated. "You're his only hope. The judges already know you. They'll listen to you and know he's your son—that will put him in their good graces."

Garrett let out a laugh. "The judges in this county hate my son. Because of me, they can't stand him. They see him as trouble—every one of them has locked him up in the past. He doesn't stand a chance in court." His eyes fell. "He's done for. It's over."

Jordan slapped the palm of his hand down on his desk, the "smack" resounding around the room. Fire blazed in his good eye as he stared at the older man. "You sound just like him right now, Garrett. You're both cowards!" Placing his face inches from his, he breathed heavily. "Fight. For. Your. Son. Fight for him! You're always so full of talk. 'Oh, if Josh were only here, things would be different. If only my boy would come home, I'd show him how much I care.'" Jordan straightened and shook his head in disgust. "He's here, Mr. C, and he's going to rot in a jail cell for a crime he didn't commit if you do not fight for him!"

Shocked, Levi stared at his son, wondering when he'd become so bold. Swinging his gaze to Garrett, he swallowed hard at the shame and sorrow coloring his face.

Garrett's eyes swam as he looked at Jordan, his words cutting deep. His admiration for this young man grew, and he thanked God that Josh had him as a friend. "Okay," he whispered. "I'll fight for him. But I'm gonna need you to convince him to let me do that."

"Done." Jordan crossed his arms over his chest. "You leave Josh to me. You just get to work on debunking whatever Nichole has against him. We can do this together—we're all he's got. Josh has given up, man. He's lost all hope. He feels like he doesn't have a friend in the world. He won't even let me bail him out—says he's done messing things up out here. If we don't help him, we'll lose him for good this time."

Garrett nodded, swiping the tears that streaked his face.

"Okay. I'll get right to work. Just, please…help him to see that my defense is his last hope."

"Nevaeh will see to it that it gets through his thick skull. I'm sure of it."

ELYSIA

Elysia sat on her couch as tears streamed down her face. Sniffing, she wiped a finger across her nose and tried for the millionth time to coax Nevaeh away from the front door. "Come on, baby, let's go get some ice cream. You love ice cream."

Nevaeh's face was splotchy red, her eyes bloodshot as she faced her. Exhaustion pulled at her features, but the little girl refused to give in to sleep. "I—want—my—daddy," she wailed, her lips quivering. "I—want—my—d-a-a-a-a-d-y!"

Elysia bit her lip, her mind and body beyond exhaustion. Coming home with neither Josh nor Garrett had been a nightmare. Nevaeh had screamed the entire car ride over and screamed through her bath and bedtime story. It had taken her hours to fall asleep, and then she was right back up as soon as the sun peaked above the horizon. As Elysia watched her, she wished she hadn't refused Garrett's attempt to come home. She desperately needed afrom the screaming but didn't dare leave Nevaeh alone. "How about we watch a cartoon? Huh?"

Nevaeh shook her head hard. "D-d-d-d-a-d-d-d-d-y!!"

Elysia felt something inside of her break. Enough was enough. She'd done the right thing by agreeing to have those cops come for Josh. He needed to realize the severity of messing with his daughter's life the way he had. She would not feel guilty for protecting Nevaeh, nor would she allow the child to cause her to feel trapped in her own home. Determination took hold in her mind, and she stood to her feet, her jaw tensing as she stepped sharply toward the screaming girl.

Nevaeh shrieked as she approached, throwing herself

on the floor when Elysia reached for her. "No, no, n-o-o-o! D-a-d-d-y-y-y!!"

"Nevaeh Lee." Elysia grunted as she scooped her into her arms, dodging a foot as it swung toward her head. "That's enough. That's enough!" she shouted, and they both burst into tears. "Shh, baby. It's okay. Let's go in here together, hmm?"

Nevaeh wailed against her shoulder as Elysia carried her to the rocking chair and sat down. Flicking on the TV, she put on an upbeat cartoon and attempted to rock her granddaughter. Refusing to sit still, Nevaeh fought her hold on her, causing Elysia's grip to tighten. "That's enough, baby. Enough. Be still and watch your show."

"I want my daddy," Nevaeh whimpered into her grandmother's chest. "I want my daddy. Let me have my daddy back. Please. Please!"

"Daddy's busy right now, Vaeh."

"Not busy," she cried. "D-a-a-a-d-d-y…"

"Shh, hush baby." Elysia kissed her head, startled when Nevaeh slapped her chest. "You may not hit Mommy!" Her eyes were stern as she pulled Nevaeh's hands away and held them, exasperated when Nevaeh threw her head back and screamed an ear-piercing screech, yanking against the hands that held her. Tears stung her tired eyes as Elysia gripped Nevaeh in one arm and pulled her tightly into her chest as she grabbed her cell phone from the side table and dialed Garrett.

"Elysia?" Garrett's tone was soft and full of hope.

"I need help," she whispered through her tears.

"What's wrong, baby? What's all that screaming about? Is that Nevaeh?"

Elysia stared at the child pressed against her chest, her muscles burning as she fought to keep from dropping her to the floor. "Please come," she cried.

"Come…home?"

"Just come. Please. Come now. I can't take any more, Garrett."

"I'm on my way. Hang tight, babe. Be there in a few."

He hung up the phone, and Elysia dropped hers back to the table and wrapped her other arm around Nevaeh, humming and rocking her back and forth as she continued screaming.

True to his word, the front door unlocked ten minutes after she'd called. Garrett rushed inside, the sight of his wife and baby girl filling his heart with warmth and fear.

"Here, let me have her." He reached for Nevaeh and the little girl instantly calmed down and laid her head on his shoulder, shoving a thumb into her mouth. Bouncing her in his arms, he focused his gaze on his wife's blotched face, reading the exhaustion that weighed on her features. "Elysia, go to bed, baby. I've got her, okay?"

"Do not leave with her, Garrett," she warned, allowing him to pull her to her feet. "She kept screaming for him." Her eyes studied Nevaeh's body as she hiccupped from hours of sobbing. "Or maybe she was screaming for you. I don't even know anymore, Garrett. This baby is so confused and heartbroken," she cried. "I just can't do it right now."

Garrett pulled her to him without thinking and pressed a kiss to her forehead as though she'd never told him she hated him. "I love you, Lys. Go to bed."

"Okay," she whispered, her fingers grazing Nevaeh's arm before she headed for the stairs. Turning, she called after him. "Garrett?"

"Yeah, love?"

"Will you sleep here tonight?"

He smiled as tears filled his eyes. "I would love to sleep here tonight, baby."

DETECTIVE DONAHUE

Detective Micah Donahue stared at the case file in his hands, a frown creasing his brow. A mixture of excitement and dread filled his bones as he read the title for the fifth time: Rape Victim—Rhea Romans.

He knew the name all too well. Her stepfather ran the town of Highshore by bribes, manipulation, and the sheer amount of terror his heinous wife was able to strike in the hearts of the townsfolk. Handling their daughter's case could go one of two ways for him, depending on how he proceeded. It could give him fame and fortune if he played his cards according to Nichole Sherard's demands, or…if he dared cross her, it could lead to his demise. She always had an agenda and if her daughter was sitting in his interrogation room, he was almost certain her mother was tangled up somehow.

Glancing down at the perp's name, he breathed a low whistle. Joshua Cameron—Highshore's very own tyrant, son of the best defense attorney Donahue had ever known. Josh was more than a known troublemaker—he was Rhea Romans' long-term boyfriend and, if he had his facts straight, the father of her child.

Cameron was a lot of things—Donahue had interrogated him countless times throughout the years—but he knew one thing for certain: that boy loved that girl. So, why was his name tossed in with hers on a rape charge? With a sigh, he braced himself and swung the door open, his eyes falling on the closed-off expression of his victim.

With a smile, he nodded, first to her, and then to the forensics nurse who sat beside her. "Hello, Rhea." Donahue sat at the table, ensuring the camera beside him was set to record.

Rhea sat as though carved from stone, her eyes fixed on the hands clasped in her lap.

"Can I get you anything? Coffee? Water?"

When she shook her head, he continued. "I know this is difficult to relive, but we want you to try and relax and get comfortable before we start."

Her eyes met his, and she frowned as though he'd said something stupid.

"Okay, let's begin." Donahue leaned back in his chair, stretching his long legs out in front of him as he observed her. "Just so you know, I'll be recording this interview, okay?"

No answer.

His eyes cut to the nurse, situated to Rhea's left.

Arching a brow, he asked a silent question that was answered with an ever-so-slight shake of the head. Frowning, he leaned forward and pressed "record" on the camera.

"For the record, my name is Detective Micah Donahue. Assisting me in this interview is Nurse Delilah Gill, with the Sexual Assault Treatment Center. We are interviewing Miss Rhea Romans."

Working to keep his face expressionless, he dove right in. "Rhea, can you tell me where you were when this incident occurred?"

"The Seascapes Hotel."

"You currently reside in Lambert, correct?"

She swallowed. "Not anymore. I'm, um, between addresses at the moment."

"Oh? You're relocating?"

"Soon," she evaded.

"What were you doing at the hotel?" Donahue cocked his head to the side, curious to see how she would answer.

"I was visiting my mother."

"So, the room where this occurred–it's your mother's?"

"Yes."

"Doesn't she own a home here in Highshore?" He furrowed his brow, confused.

"Yes."

"So…why was she staying in a hotel?"

"She's renovating her home." Rhea studied the wall behind him, her mind rehearsing her mother's coaching.

"I see. Was she there with you when the assault took place?"

"No."

"Do you know where she went?"

No answer.

"Do you know why she left the hotel?" he pressed.

"No. She only told me there was something she had to do."

"How long after your mother left did Josh show up at your hotel room?"

Rhea thought for a moment before answering. "Maybe an hour?"

Donahue wrote in his legal pad, thinking. "Tell me what happened after he showed up."

If you blow this interview, you will never see that baby again, Rhea Nichole. Her mother's words slammed her mind, and she squeezed her eyes shut. She had to sell this lie for all she was worth. She was Nevaeh's only hope. Though the well-rehearsed lie was on the tip of her tongue, she could not force the words from her lips.

The room was still, her silence deafening. Observing the fleeting emotions across her face, Donahue wondered at the way she kept her hands hidden beneath the table. Was she hiding them from him? "Rhea," he urged.

"Hmm?" she stalled, nerves rippling through her veins.

"What happened after Josh showed up at your door?" he repeated, keeping his voice steady.

"Come with me, baby!" Josh's eager eyes taunted her. With a shaky breath, she dove headfirst into the tangle of lies her mother and Asher had woven for her to lay before Donahue.

Five minutes. That's all the time it took for her to betray the only one who'd always been in her corner.

By the time she'd finished giving her statement, she was a stranger to herself. Her skin crawled, and she longed for a shower to wash herself from these lies.

Donahue scribbled on his legal pad; his eyes intense as he stared at the words he'd scrawled. His head snapped up, and he regarded the nurse with interest. "Delilah, did they do a complete examination of the victim at the Sexual Assault Treatment Center before this interview?"

"Yes, Detective, they did. The evidence has since been sent to the lab for analysis," the nurse replied.

Rhea sat straighter in her chair while they discussed her, attempting to get comfortable. The lights in the room were too bright. They were beginning to give her a headache. But nothing ached as badly as her heart.

"Rhea, do you know the offender?" Donahue asked, his eyes glued to her as he searched for anything that might tell him the direction they were headed.

"Yes," she whispered.

The offender.

Nevaeh's daddy...

He noted her tears. The tremble of her lower lip. The way she refused to look at him. "Can you pick him out of a lineup?"

She froze, her tongue refusing to betray him. She saw Nevaeh's smile. Pictured the look of contentment on Josh's face when he'd held her.

And then she thought of her daughter being raised by her narcissistic mother.

"I'm going to be sick," she whimpered, her face paling.

The nurse leaped to her feet and grabbed the trash bin, holding it for Rhea as she threw up. "I'll go for a towel," she offered once Rhea had sat back in her seat and closed her eyes.

Donahue's gaze followed her out the door before swinging back to Rhea. "Can you pick him out of a lineup?" he gently pressed, feeling antsy. What was going on here? Was she summoning an act for him, hoping to convince him that her story was true? If so, why? How had her well-known love for Joshua Cameron been reduced to this?

Maybe he was wrong, and the boy did assault her...

Rhea pressed a trembling hand to her eyes, her mouth tasting of bile. "Yes."

Terror seized her heart as his screams tore through her memory. The way he'd jerked free of Asher's grip just to kiss her lips one last time...

What was she doing?!

She squeezed her eyes shut against the tears. Her heart thudded as she recalled her mother frantically calling Sterling and begging him to rush over, spinning her web of lies and watching him become consumed by his hatred for

Josh. "Can I get some water?" Her voice squeaked with the request.

"Sure. I'll send Delilah as soon as she's back with a towel." He quickly displayed a mugshot lineup on the table, Josh's picture third in line. His eyes tracked hers as her gaze darted to his picture and bounced to the ceiling. "Rhea, are any of these the guy who assaulted you today?"

"I will raise her as my own…she will never call you 'Mommy…'"

"Yes." Her voice quivered.

He raised a brow. "Can you point him out for me?"

She stared at Josh's face. Noted the lifeless look in his eyes. He'd given up. There was no fight left in him. If only she could see him…

Her eyes went to Donahue's as she nervously shifted in her seat. Slowly, she pulled her right hand from beneath the table and touched Josh's picture. "This one," she whispered.

Donahue looked at the rope burns on her wrist and sighed. "What happened to your wrist?"

Rhea's hand shot back beneath the table, and she swallowed hard. "It's nothing."

He frowned and leaned forward. "May I see the other one, please?"

She froze. "…can I say no…?"

His brow rose. "Is there a reason I shouldn't see them?"

Her eyes stung as she withdrew her wrists and laid them on the table for his examination.

Donahue stared at the fresh burns, a frown creasing his brow. "I need to take some pictures of your wrists, Rhea." He reached for his camera. "This will only take a moment."

A piece of her heart died with each picture he snapped, but still, she said nothing. When he'd finished, she watched him study her wrists some more and knew he would press her.

"Did Josh tie you up or restrain you at any point? Is that how you got those rope burns?"

The door swung open, and Delilah handed Rhea a wet towel.

"Could you bring some water?" Donahue requested, hiding his irritation at the interruption.

"Of course." Delilah disappeared through the door once more.

"Rhea, can you answer the question, please?"

Her mother's warnings played back in her mind as she teased the idea of bailing on the agenda given to.

"Rhea," Donahue pressed. "I need you to answer."

Tears shimmered in her eyes. She had no choice but to comply. Her daughter's life was at stake. "He tied me to the headboard," she blurted the lie, forcing her heart not to feel.

Consulting his notes, he checked the time of Josh's release from jail that morning against the time the assault had been logged and frowned. Raising his eyes to hers, he furrowed his brow. "Where did he get the rope?"

Rhea stared blankly at him. "He brought it with him."

"He brought the rope with him?" he mused, cocking his head to the side as he watched her features. "Was Josh in the habit of carrying around lengths of rope when visiting you?"

"Uh...no." She fidgeted, unsure how to keep the lies going. Her mother had been positive that the detective wouldn't dare question her, knowing who her family was. She was unprepared to combat his doubt on her own.

"So, he gets out of jail, and the first thing he does is run and get some rope before rushing to see you?" Donahue raised a brow. He knew this couldn't be true. He'd investigated Josh enough in the past to know he was too impulsive to plan a crime. Josh was all about the next thrill—how far he could push the law while still getting away from it. Planning had never been part of his M.O. "I have to ask...were you two into any kind of bondage?"

Rhea's gaze flew to his, her eyes wide with shock. "What?! Eww! No!" she recoiled.

Donahue noted her reaction to the question on his legal

pad, glancing up when the door opened, and Delilah entered with a cup of water, setting it in front of Rhea before sitting beside her.

"You have a history with Josh, if I understand correctly." He looked at her, taking in the way she stiffened—read the guarded look in her eyes. The wall that shot up between them was almost tangible, but he didn't get the vibe that it was due to the rape. He'd crossed into some very personal territory for her—territory she held dear.

"Rhea, when did you meet Josh?" he asked.

"When I was in eighth grade."

"Were y'all friends?"

Her eyes slid shut as she thought about their history. She could see it so clearly—Josh standing up to boys who'd targeted her and becoming her bodyguard when danger was near. Opening her eyes, she forced herself to look straight at Donahue. "We were best friends."

Donahue worked to keep his expression neutral, but his mind raced to figure out her angle as he continued taking notes. "When did that change?"

Never, she thought, though she didn't dare say that out loud. Her heart squeezed in her chest at the thought of her mother. "Um, I guess four years ago."

"What happened to make it change? Why did y'all stop being friends?"

"He left me and disappeared," she whispered, feeling the stab of pain all over again.

"Come with me, Rhea!"

She shoved back the memory.

"I see." Donahue wrote this down, thinking. "What made him come back this way?"

"I don't know," she answered honestly.

Not wanting to lose momentum, he pushed forward. "Rhea, had Josh ever assaulted you before?"

Her face blanched white, and her features closed off.

"He's attacked you several times in the past. Make them believe it!"

She tensed as her mother's words rushed back to her memory. Her cheek burned anew from the slap she'd been given when she'd dared argue.

Donahue silently watched as the emotions played across her features, searching for any sign of fear—curious to find none.

"Yes."

His brow rose, and he scanned over Josh's priors. "Did you report the previous assault?"

"Assaults," she corrected, the word adding to the bile in her throat. "No. I never told anyone."

Donahue arched a brow, finding this difficult to believe. "Why not?"

Her eyes dropped to her hands. "He's older than I am. My mother never approved of me dating him and had warned me he was trouble. I didn't want to believe her, but when the assaults began, I started seeing what she was talking about. I was too scared to speak up, so I kept it to myself."

"Your mother is Nichole Sherard, correct?"

"Yes."

"She's a pretty important person in this town, wouldn't you say? Everyone knows her name."

"Yes." Rhea worked to keep calm despite the panic building in her chest.

"Does your mother have a lot of input about who you should or shouldn't hang out with? Maybe…whom you should date?"

No answer.

He nodded, tapping his pen on the table. "You said she didn't approve of Josh. How did she react when she found out you were pregnant by him? Was she angry? Hurt? Did she suggest you abort the baby or tell you to keep her?"

Tears pushed to her eyes, and she nervously wiped her palms along her jeans. He wouldn't stop staring at her, and his gaze felt as though he could see every dirty lie she'd handed him.

"Fear me, child. Not this joke of a town's police force."

"She was angry," she whispered, praying she wasn't about to ruin everything. "She threw me out when she found out."

He raised an eyebrow. "She threw you out…into the streets?"

Rhea stared at him, wishing she could trust him, but knowing she couldn't. "Yes."

Donahue sighed and shoved a hand through his hair. "I'm going to ask you point blank here, Rhea." He leaned forward, placing his elbows on the table. "Did Josh rape you, or did your mother influence you to make this allegation?"

Her face blanched white, but the thought of Nevaeh fending for herself against her mother sent her chin up in the air. "He raped me."

Frowning, he scribbled in his notes, buying time before he had to open his mouth again. The kid hadn't done it. He knew in his gut that Joshua Cameron was innocent of this crime. The question was—did he have what it took to stand against Nichole and her army of corrupt politicians and cops?

Raising his eyes to hers, Donahue made sure she could see that he knew she'd made a false accusation against the boy. "Is there anything else you'd like to add to, or correct in, your statement? Are there any questions you want to ask me before we conclude the interview?"

She shook her head, working to steady her trembling hands.

"Alright, then. This concludes the interview with Miss Rhea Romans. Time is now 12:34 PM."

Once he'd left the room, Rhea knew there was no going back. She had just betrayed the man she loved to protect the little girl she adored. Only God could help Josh now…

REAGAN

The late afternoon sun beamed down on the little outdoor coffee shop, blinding the lone occupant of table 13. The woman crossed her long legs, swinging her high-heeled foot with impatience as she checked her watch for the tenth time. She hated to be kept waiting. She had pressing business to tend to—children's lives hanging in the balance. There was no time to waste waiting on someone who thought the ground on which they walked was paved with gold. With a sigh, she grabbed her purse and stood.

"Hello, Reagan."

Reagan's lips formed a tight line as she watched Nichole approach. "I was beginning to think I'd been stood up." She sat back down, placing her purse in her lap.

Nichole laughed, dusting off a chair before sitting. She carried a large, stylish tote bag. Peeking out from the top was a manilla envelope with everything she needed to ruin the Camerons forever. "Nonsense, darling. Excuse me." She waved a hand at the barista clearing the next table. Snapping her fingers, she waved him over. "I'd like a caramel macchiato. Don't keep me waiting."

The barista rushed to complete her order, and Reagan gasped at this woman's entitlement. Clearing her throat, she shifted in her seat. "You mentioned on the phone that you had information on a case of mine—said it was urgent."

Nichole smiled and withdrew the envelope. "I do." She opened the seal and withdrew a stack of files and pictures. Placing one in front of the social worker, she tapped the face of the battered boy in the picture. "Remember this young man?"

Reagan's features went taut, and she paled as she stared at the photo. "This case is years old. I can't help him now."

"No, but you sure fought to help him then, didn't you, honey?" Nichole pulled another picture from the file and placed it on the table for Reagan's observation. "This little thing is his daughter."

"I'm glad the young man is doing well," Reagan whispered.

"Oh, he's not doing well. Not doing well at all. He was

arrested for rape this morning." She reached for the coffee rushed to her, sipping slowly as she watched the other woman.

Reagan's eyes dimmed, and her jaw tightened. "That's too bad. He had so much potential back then."

"Yes, well, you can't save them all. It's too late for him, but it's not too late for this little girl. She is currently in his parents' custody." Nichole waited for that little tidbit to sink into the woman's brain.

She pointed to the picture. "You're telling me this little girl lives in the same house as Garrett Cameron?" Nichole hid a smile. "Indeed, she does. She's my granddaughter. The girl her father raped today is my daughter."

Reagan's mouth parted. "I am so sorry… But… Why are you telling me all of this?"

"I need your help to get custody of this baby. She's better off in my care, far away from her abuser grandfather, and out of reach of her rapist father."

"Well, has there been a case of child abuse since Garrett has had the girl?"

Nichole sat back, feigning insult. "As though the many, many instances of child abuse in his past toward this little boy were not enough?"

Reagan frowned, thinking. "I can pull her on an emergency custody order. Keep her away from them long enough to present a case to the courts. I can't guarantee the judge will allow the order to stick, but it buys us some time. She'll be placed into your care, but you won't be allowed to leave the county with her unless the judge grants you custody."

A smile stretched her painted lips as Nichole sipped her coffee. "Perfect. All I want is for my granddaughter to have a chance at life. It terrifies me to think she might be enduring even a fraction of the abuse her father did."

"I was unsuccessful in getting Joshua out of that home," Reagan recollected with sorrow. "The powers connected to his father were too great for me to combat. Each time I thought I'd nailed him, another out would come his way and he would slip through my fingers again. But this time I will not fail. I will get this girl away from that man if it's the last thing I do. Do you have the address?"

"They never moved. Still in the big house in the woods."

"Perfect. Let's go visit them and bring this little girl some justice."

The black Lincoln Town car pulled into the Cameron's drive a little after 4 PM, a patrol car following behind. Reagan had obtained a court order straight from Judge McRory and was anxious to remove the girl from the home. Determination quickened her as she marched to the front door and rang the bell. The cop followed and positioned himself to her left. Straightening her pencil skirt and smoothing back her graying hair, she prepared to face the monster she'd come to despise. The door swung open, and her heart leaped into her throat at the sight of him. "Garrett Cameron?"

"Yes?" His eyes swung from her to the cop, then settled on the black car, a frown furrowing his brow when he spotted Nichole inside. "What is this?"

"Reagan Lopez, CPS. Remember me?" She offered a smug smile, thrilled when recognition dawned, causing his eyes to grow large.

"Uh, yeah. What can I do for you, Ms. Lopez?"

"Mrs. And you can hand over Nevaeh Lee Cameron without a fight."

Shocked, Garrett stepped outside and closed the door. "On what grounds?"

"Because you have a history of child abuse and have no rights to raise this child. I have the emergency order right here. There will be a hearing tomorrow, in which I will discuss your case with the judge. Until then, Nevaeh will be placed in the emergency custody of one Nichole Sherard."

"No." Garrett's jaw tensed. "No, this isn't right. You

don't understand! She's got it in for my son—she wants to hurt him! Please, Mrs. Lopez, I know you hate me, but Nevaeh's life is at stake here!"

"Really. The same way Josh's life was at stake for all those years?"

Garrett pushed his hand through his hair. "I'm not that guy anymore. I love my son, and I love my granddaughter. I would never hurt them!"

"But you did!" she shouted, stepping closer to him. "Now, I have an order from Judge McRory. You are ordered to give me that child, Mr. Cameron! To resist will be your arrest! Carlos," she shouted over her shoulder, and the cop stepped forward.

"Mr. Cameron, please bring the child out. We don't want any trouble—obey the judge's orders and let her go peacefully."

Garrett's breathing intensified as panic gripped his heart. "I'll go get her," he managed through the tears clogging his throat. Turning for the door, he disappeared inside and stood in the entryway, his mind racing. His heart dropped when Elysia appeared on the staircase, hair disheveled from her nap.

"Garrett, what is it?" Her face revealed her alarm as she rushed down the stairs. "Who's out there?"

"Reagan Lopez. And Nichole is in the car. They brought a cop—they've come for Nevaeh." He broke, tears pouring down his cheeks. "She's armed with an emergency order. Says I'm not fit to have her. Elysia, they're taking Nevaeh from us!" Garrett's voice went up an octave as his shoulders shook.

Shocked, Elysia rushed past him and burst through the front door, nearly running into the social worker. "You cannot take this girl from us! Please, you don't know what you're doing!" Elysia grabbed her arm, but Reagan shook her off. "We are the only parents she has ever known! Please!"

"If you won't bring her out to me, I'll get her myself. I suggest you move out of my way and do not fight me, or this officer will arrest you for resisting a court-ordered removal." Reagan stared her down and Elysia stepped aside, defeat washing over her in waves as the woman walked into her house in search of Nevaeh. Her eyes shot to the cop, who remained unmoving on the porch as though watching to ensure she didn't follow Reagan inside.

"She's eating a snack," Garrett informed the social worker as she shoved past him and made her way to the kitchen. He watched her approach his little girl and kneel in front of her.

"Hi, sweetheart, how are you today?" Reagan smiled, careful not to touch the wide-eyed child in front of her. Her heart broke at the sight of Nevaeh's red eyes and blotchy face—the leftover result from her meltdown that day. "Have you been crying, sweetheart?"

Nevaeh nodded; a sticky banana clutched in the palm of her hand. "I want my daddy," she whimpered.

"Yeah? Well, I have good news for you, baby girl. Your daddy called Mrs. Reagan this morning and wants you to spend time with your grandma. Would you like to go see her?"

Garrett gritted his teeth behind her. "She doesn't even know Nichole!"

Reagan swung her head around to face him, a glare set in her eyes. "If I want your help to do my job, I'll ask. But seeing as there's no chance of that ever happening, I suggest you back up."

Garrett shoved his hands in his pockets and clenched his fists.

"I have a grandma-mommy. She's mad at me right now."

"Oh." Reagan's eyes dimmed. "Why is she mad at you?"

"Because I want my daddy, and I screamed and screamed."

"Where is your daddy?"

"The pweece taked him away. He's been bad." Her

eyes grew large, the banana squishing in her tight grasp. "He hit Jordan. A lot a lot a lot. Like this." Nevaeh swung her free hand, fist clenched. "Jordan was asweep, and I said 'Wake up, Jordan! Wake up!' but Jordan didn't waked up. And then my daddy taked me on a plane to Fwoda. I didn't like that."

"No? Why not?"

"Because my grandma-mommy not in Fwoda. And no second daddy, either."

Reagan's brow rose. "Second daddy?"

Nevaeh pointed a finger at Garrett. "He's my grandpa-daddy." She scrunched her nose. "But I don't know why."

"Well. This is quite the mess, isn't it, sweetheart? How about we go outside and meet your other grandma—hmm?"

"Did grandma-mommy say it's ok?"

"Absolutely. Grandma-mommy will be completely fine with you going. Now, here," Reagan pulled a wet wipe from her purse and washed Nevaeh's face and hands. "Let's get you all cleaned up so you can meet her." When she had the girl looking presentable, she took her hand and helped her out of the chair, leading her beside her. Garrett looked on, helplessness taking him captive when Nevaeh's large green eyes looked back at him as she walked out the door.

"I'll need her car seat, please." Reagan addressed Elysia, who stood with silent rage dancing in her eyes. "Mrs. Cameron," she urged. "The child's car seat."

Elysia stared at the woman, her gaze falling to Nevaeh who innocently looked like she might be going on an adventure. Her heart thumped wildly in her chest as she moved to retrieve the seat from her car. She carried the seat to the black car, rage giving way to fury when Nichole stepped from the vehicle, her face smug with contempt and victory. Nichole yanked the seat from her hands and smiled. "Hello, Elysia. I did warn you I'd be coming for the girl."

"If you hurt this child, I swear I'll be coming for you!"

she hissed at Nichole as the other woman loaded the seat into the car. "This isn't over, Nichole. You cannot just destroy my family and have us back down. We will fight you in court, and we will win."

Nichole laughed, straightening to stare at her. "That's cute. Good luck with that, princess. Now move out of my way so I can get my granddaughter."

Elysia stood still as Nichole brushed her shoulder as she passed. Forcing herself to turn back and head to the porch, she bit back a sob when Nichole picked up Nevaeh, and the little girl's face scrunched as the first tears began to fall. "Mommy." She reached for her as she passed, panicking when Elysia did not take her from the stranger's arms.

"Mommy! Mommy!" Nevaeh's cries escalated as she was carried to the car and buckled into the car seat. "Shh, Grandma's got you now. You're okay. Hush, child. Stop all this nonsense," Nichole spoke sharply as she climbed beside her.

On the porch, Reagan instructed the cop to stand guard over the Camerons until they were safely out of the driveway.

"We're going to fight this," Garrett stated, pulling his wife to his side and slipping his arm around her waist.

"You're welcome to try, Garrett, but history is not on your side here." Reagan's nose went up as she stared at him. "You destroyed your son, and there wasn't a thing I could do to stop you, but the tables have turned. I will see you brought down if it's the last thing I do. Have a good day."

The cop remained on the porch as Reagan went to her car, his eyes never leaving the shattered couple. Once the car was out of sight, he gave his last warning before heading for his cruiser. "Sometimes you just have to know when you've lost the game. Don't try and follow her—that's a dumb move. Just accept that you've lost and move on with your lives."

RHEA

Rhea had seen this coming. But nothing could have prepared her for the torment in her heart as she held her daughter in her arms for the second time in her existence. Her mother had carried the screaming girl into the hotel room, tossed Rhea's bedroom door open, and shoved the child inside.

"Take care of your brat!" she bit before walking out the door and slamming it behind her.

It had taken Rhea three hours to calm Nevaeh. Hours of soothing, singing, flipping cartoon channels, and trying to read her a story. Nothing worked. Not until she reached out her arms and scooped her into a tight hug and softly sang "You are my Sunshine" against her ear. Rhea rubbed her back with gentle calm, awed by the fact that she was finally the one holding her daughter.

"My daddy sings me that song." Nevaeh sniffled against her chest.

Rhea's hand stilled for a moment before resuming her gentle massage. "He does?"

She nodded her curly head and shoved a thumb inside her mouth.

So many questions filled her mind, but she was terrified to ask, for fear of upsetting her again. Deciding to test the waters, she kissed the fair head before asking, "Does Daddy sing you a lot of songs?"

Nevaeh thought about this before answering. "Deedus."

"What was that?"

Nevaeh sat up and stared at her, her mouth opening around her thumb. "Jesus," she repeated. "And he tells me he loves me."

"Daddy tells you he loves you?"

Another nod. The thumb popped back into her mouth, and she lay against her mother's chest. The sniffles returned. "I want my daddy. I don't like my grandma—she's mean."

Rhea closed her eyes. "I don't like your grandma, either," she whispered. Allowing a silent moment to pass between them, she gathered the courage to ask the one question that plagued her. "Do you know who I am, Nevaeh?" She held her breath as she waited for her to answer.

"Yes." Nevaeh's eyes closed as she sucked her thumb.
"You're the pretty lady who keeps me safe."
Rhea smiled. "Nevaeh."
"Mmm?"
"Does Daddy ever talk about your mommy?"
"My grandma-mommy is daddy's mommy—we can't share. Daddy said so. My mommy-mommy is my real-life mommy."
"Do you know who that is?"
"Mmhmm." Her voice was growing sleepier.
"Who?" Rhea whispered, her heart skipping a beat.
"You."

Chapter 33

"Do not be deceived: God is not mocked, for whatever one sows, that will he also reap."
~Galatians 6:7~

JOSH

Josh's eyes were fixated on the door to the interrogation room, his nerves on edge over which detective might be assigned to his case. If it was Manson, he was screwed. The guy was so deep in Nichole's pockets that'd help her plant evidence on him if it helped lock him away. His luck wouldn't be any better if Plotter walked through the door. That guy hated him for all he was worth and would hand him to Nichole on a silver platter.

For the millionth time since his arrest, Josh bemoaned his stupidity at falling right into the trap she'd laid for him. If only he hadn't followed his impulse into Rhea's bed. If he'd just convinced her to run beforehand, they could have grabbed Nevaeh and been on the other side of the country by now. He cursed his foolish impulsivity. Why did he never think things through? Now it was too late.

The doorknob turned and he tensed, holding his breath. He hated the fear in his chest but there was only so much fight he could get away with in the middle of this piranha pool. The door creaked open, and the detective laughed at someone's joke before revealing his identity to his prisoner. When he finally stepped inside, Josh breathed a sigh of relief, followed by an inward groan.

Donahue. The detective who pretended to give a crap about his future. The guy was annoying as heck with all his lectures and admonishments, but at least he didn't get off on closing the blinds and giving him a beatdown. He'd been interrogated by him several times throughout the years. He knew how he worked—and how to get around him. But he wasn't stupid enough to think he'd be getting around Nichole's plans for him. His fate was sealed. He was done.

"Hello again, Josh." Donahue offered him a smile as he took a seat across from him.

Josh didn't miss the way his eyes dropped to the shackle around his left ankle.

Wanting to dive right in, Donahue started the camera. "You doing okay, kid?"

Josh gave him a look. "You serious right now?"

Another smile. Though he hated that he was in the system again, if Donahue were honest with himself, Josh was his favorite repeat offender. There was something about the kid that held his interest. He walked to the beat of his own drum and asked permission from no one. He leaped first and thought later. He was fearless—Donahue had to give him that—though severely lacking in wisdom. His street smarts rivaled hardened criminals—he was the best thief Donahue had ever locked up. And the kid never ceased to have a quick come-back for anyone who dared challenge him.

There was one thing, however, that Donahue was convinced he wasn't, and that was a rapist.

Setting his jaw, he determined not to leave any stone unturned during this interrogation. "My name is Detective Micah Donahue. Today's date is May 24th, 2019. The time is now 11 AM. Interviewing Joshua Cameron about an alleged sexual assault that occurred on May 23rd, 2023 in Highshore—Del Norte County."

Passing Josh a copy of the Advise of Rights form, Donahue instructed him to read along with him as he read. "Do you understand this form?"

"Yes."

"Do you agree with it?"

"Okay."

He bit back a smile. Josh never made anything easy for anyone. "Yes or no, Josh."

"Okay…yes."

"Alright. Go ahead and sign." He passed him a pen, and Josh scrawled his name on the paper and slid it back to him. "Do you know the victim, Rhea Romans?" Donahue noted the flash of pain that shot across Josh's features.

"She's not a victim!" he spat.

"Do you know her?"

Josh rolled his eyes and slouched in his chair. "You know I do."

"Yes or no, kid."

"Yeah, Donahue. I know that girl."

"How do you know her?"

"She's my…" Josh stopped himself and shoved a hand through his hair. "I love her," he admitted quietly.

"How long have you known her?" Donahue asked.

"Since my freshman year of high school."

"Have you had an intimate relationship with Rhea?"

"What do you think?" Josh snapped, his walls shooting higher.

"Yes or no, please."

"Yes."

"Tell me what happened yesterday. You were in jail for a disorderly conduct charge, correct?"

"Yes."

"Who brought that charge? Was Rhea involved in charging you?"

Josh smirked. "Nah, man. That was my mom and my best friend's mother."

Donahue jotted a note on his legal pad, then brought the pen to his chin as he asked the next question. "So, you got locked up for disorderly conduct—what happened then?"

He shrugged. "I got bonded out."

With a sigh, Donahue leaned forward. "Josh, I get that you're angry, kid. I would be too. But I cannot help you if you're not transparent with me."

Josh averted his gaze, frustrated by the tears clouding his vision. He'd give anything to shake free of the chain on his ankle. He needed to burn some of the energy being trapped by his nerves. He felt Donahue's eyes on him and set his jaw. As much as he hated to admit the truth, he knew the detective already knew. Might as well go ahead and tell him. With a sigh, he met his gaze.

"I didn't know who'd posted my bail until I stepped outside the jail. This car whipped up in front of me, and Nichole Sherard rolled her window down and told me to get in."

Donahue's brows rose at this. He couldn't imagine this kid ever obeying such an order. "Who is Nichole Sherard to you?"

"A villain from a Disney movie," Josh quipped, a smile teasing the corners of his mouth.

He grinned. "Care to explain?"

"She's the pits, Donahue. A real-life Cruella De'Ville. She's had it out for me ever since Rhea and I met. Hates my guts."

"So, it's safe to say you two don't get along…"

"Might wanna adjust those hearing aids, dude." Josh crossed his arms and raised a brow.

Ignoring the remark, Donahue pushed forward. "Help me out here. If she has such animosity toward you, why do you think she bonded you out?" He watched Josh's features tighten as he sat straight in his chair. *Now we're getting somewhere, kid…tell me everything…*

"She bonded me out because she concocted a plan with that crooked captain of yours—Asher Holmes."

Donahue's features clouded at the mention of his captain. *He knew his tactics all too well…*

"She convinced me to get in her car by threatening my kid. When I finally agreed to go with her, she started pushing me to sign over my rights to my daughter—told me she wanted me to go to Rhea's hotel room and tell her I was giving up. I refused and told her to let me out, but she'd engaged the child locks so I couldn't open the door. That witch drove me straight to the hotel where she and Rhea were staying and dumped me out in the parking lot."

"So, you got out at the hotel on your own?"

"Well, yeah," Josh snapped, his eyes flashing fire. "I wasn't about to ask her for a ride home."

"Did you guys make any stops between the jail and the?"

"No."

"Okay, so she dropped you at the hotel, and then what happened?" Donahue held his breath as he watched Josh withdraw. No, no, no! Come on, kid! Fight!

"I went to her room, like an idiot." He dropped his gaze to the floor. The metal shackle around his ankle taunted him with its hold on his soul. "Played right into her hands."

"So, you two had sex?"

Josh squeezed his eyes shut. "Yes."

"Was it consensual?" Donahue did not take his eyes from his face.

Josh's head snapped up, meeting his eyes dead on. "Yes, it was consensual. We were planning to run off together. Go get our baby girl and leave all this crazy mess behind."

Donahue raised a brow. "Really. So, did Rhea ever tell you to stop, get off her, or leave?"

Josh adamantly shook his head. "No, man. She was happy. We both were until her crazy mother and that crooked cop busted in on us and yanked me away from her!"

His brow creasing, Donahue scribbled on his legal pad, then held up a hand. "Okay, hold on. Back up. Rhea stated that you tied her up and forced yourself onto her. Where did you get the rope?"

Josh's jaw dropped. "I didn't have a rope. And I didn't force her to do anything."

Donahue withdrew the photos of Rhea's wrists and showed them to him. "Can you explain where she got these rope burns?"

Josh's eyes fell to the pictures, and fury seized his chest as he cursed. "Unbelievable." He shook his head, tears stinging his eyes. "I didn't do that to Rhea—her new boyfriend did, and they're pinning it on me!"

Donahue raised a brow and leaned forward. "New boyfriend?"

Josh rolled his eyes, forcing the name past his lips.

"Sterling Oliver. Rae told me he'd been too rough with her the other night. Left those marks on her wrists."

Intrigued, Donahue wrote the name on his legal pad, determined to talk to him. "Has Rhea told you anything else about him?"

"No." Josh squeezed his right hand into a fist. The thought of Rhea with another man had been prevalent in his mind since he'd found out.

"Okay." Donahue took a deep breath, his eyes on his notes. "You mentioned that Nichole and Asher busted in on y'all. Can you tell me what happened?"

Josh's jaw clenched as the memory played back in his mind. "They set me up, man. It was like they were watchin' us or something. He waited until we'd finished, then busted in and jerked me away from her. Think about it, Donahue. What was your captain doing making an arrest? Why was he even there? It's because of that crooked, no-good, lyin', manipulative piece of crap, that's why!"

Donahue watched him, a grin brewing. "Sounds like you've solved your own case, Cameron."

"Hey, I may hate my father, but that doesn't mean I don't know how to play this game of law. Doesn't take a genius to pay attention."

The grin faded as he refocused. "Okay, so let's go back over a few things. You said that you got out of the car at the hotel. At any time, did you find a piece of rope behind a dumpster or on the ground?"

Josh stared; blank-faced. "You know, for a smart detective, you're really stupid."

The smile tugged once more.

"Didn't we just establish that I did not show up at my girl's door carrying a rope?"

"Alright." Donahue held up a hand in surrender. "So, you state that you, at no time, restrained Rhea by tying her up. You also state that you had no rope when you went to the hotel room. The sex was consensual, and Rhea never told you to stop, or used any words to that effect?"

"That's my statement."

"Have you ever assaulted Rhea in the past?"

"Bro." Josh sat back hard.

"Yes or no."

"Nah, man."

"She's stated that you have—several times, in fact—and that she didn't report it."

Josh raised a brow. "And you believed her? So, you're telling me that, with a mother like Nichole Sherard, I could have gotten away with assaulting Rhea several times, and no one would've known about it? Man, you think that witch knows my every move now? When I was a teen, I couldn't skip class without her knowing! Get outta here with this mess, Donahue."

"Why would Rhea fabricate a false charge against you?"

Josh rolled his eyes. "'Cause her mother put her up to it! She's manipulating her so she can destroy me and get me out of Rae's life!"

The detective jotted down a few more notes. "Is there anything else you want to add? Anything you want to ask me?"

Josh's features dimmed as the reality of his situation sank in. Looking at the older man, he fidgeted. "I'm not gettin' out, am I? Her reach stretches too far."

Donahue's heart pained. "That's not for me to decide, son."

JOSH

"You have a visitor." Oscar stood on the other side of the bars, empathy for his prisoner squeezing the breath from his lungs. He'd watched Josh give up his dinner tray the night before to a guy pitching a fit about never having enough. The seasoned guard knew it wasn't from fear that Josh had given up the tray, but rather out of a state of giving up. He'd seen it countless times before. The same empty expression, lack of emotion. Dull. Lifeless. But this prisoner was different. It was as though the key still hovered near his broken heart, just waiting to be summoned to piece it back together again. Oscar was determined to see Josh summon that key. "Wanna go see who it is?" he asked, unlocking the door before Josh could answer.

Josh barely glanced his way as the guard entered, ready to escort him to the visiting room. "I'm straight," he mumbled, leaning against the wall and closing his eyes.

"You sure about that? It's the pastor from Highshore Baptist—says he wants to check in and see how you're doing in here." He carefully watched Josh's expression, searching for any sign of care or surprise. Disappointed to find neither, he decided on another approach. "Tell you what. You talk to this guy, and I'll add money to your books. Deal?"

Nothing.

"Come on, man. I've seen you scrounge for paper in here. Wouldn't you love your own stash? A pencil? Something to get those thoughts out of your head?"

Josh brought his eyes to Oscar, and he sighed. He would kill for paper and a pen right now. No one else out there would be adding to his books, that was for sure. Dropping his feet over the side of the bed, he stood. "Why do you care so much about what happens to me?" he asked as Oscar led him out of the cell.

"Because someone out there is waiting for you to come home." Oscar brought him into the visiting room and sat him at a table before buzzing the visitor inside. "Fifteen minutes," he warned before shutting the door behind him.

Zeke entered the room and took the seat across from Josh, his usual smile plastered across his face. "Hey, boy, that grass ain't gonna cut itself. Why you lettin' them keep you in here without a fight? E'rbody knows you didn't rape that girl. It's not in you like that."

Josh's eyes clouded as he looked at the pastor. "Doesn't matter if I did or didn't. Her mother will see to it that I stay here. It's over, Zeke. I'm done."

The older man's brow rose. "You told your daughter

yet that she ain't worth fightin' for? That her ol' man's just gonna let the system beat him down and keep him outta her life?"

Josh fidgeted in his chair, a brief spark of the old familiar fire lighting his eyes. Dimming as quickly as it had come, he stared down at the table. "You got it all wrong, man. Nevaeh is worth everything to me. That's why I'm stayin' right here. I'm no good, Zeke. I'll only destroy her."

Zeke scoffed and rolled his eyes. "So, it is as serious as Jordan told me." He stared Josh down, fury dancing in his pupils. "You really gon' just lie down and die then. Just give up and let e'rbody around you feel sorry for you." Josh met his eyes, irritation tensing his jaw. "I can't beat her, Zeke. You don't know Nichole. She's a monster. She doesn't care who she takes down, as long as she gets what she wants. She's after my kid, man! If I'm in here, she'll stay away from her!"

"Wrong!" Zeke slapped the table with a loud thwack and leaned forward as Josh jumped. No one came in and told him to back up—Oscar didn't dare interrupt the progress happening before his eyes. "I do know that woman! She's as evil as they come, son. I hate to be the one to break it to you, but she's already got your kid. So, git up off yo' butt and fight for that girl!"

Shock slammed into Josh's features, pulling his mouth open as he gaped at Zeke. "W-what're you talkin' about?" He leaned forward, tears pooling in his eyes. "Tell me you're lying. Please, Zeke. Tell me you're just trying to get me to fight for myself!"

Zeke sat back hard, tears glistening in his eyes. "It's not always about you, boy. That little girl was ripped away from your mother and father last night under the guise of your father bein' unfit to care for her. Nichole was armed with a CPS worker and a cop. They didn't stand a fighting chance. They were forced to hand over yo' baby girl or join you in a jail cell. That baby you love so much—the one you've decided you can't fight for no mo'? She is terrified right now. She's with a crazy woman who don't care one bit 'bout her. And you in here sayin' you ain't no good for that little girl. No sirree, son." He rested his elbows on the table, eyes fierce. His voice was low and urgent as he spoke. "You fight, Joshua. You git yo' daddy in on this case, and you nail that woman with ever'thing you've got. Then you sit back, and you watch the good Lord work things for yo' good, you hear? You watch Him! And then you trust Him, boy. You trust, 'cause He done taken you from ashes and brought you out smellin' like a rose, un'erstand?"

Josh stared, unmoving. His thoughts were consumed with images of Nevaeh screaming for him, terrified of people she neither knew nor trusted. He thought of his mother—how empty and helpless she must feel, knowing she was unable to stop Nichole from taking his daughter. And then he thought of his father. His lawyer dad. His jerk of a lawyer dad. And he made a decision.

"I have to go," he whispered, his eyes never leaving Zeke's. "The grass won't cut itself."

Zeke's face exploded. "Yo' right, son. That grass is gettin' higher and higher each day. Git yo' butt back to work, you hear me?"

"Guard," Josh called, swiping a hand down his face. "Guard!"

Oscar reappeared, offering the pastor a grateful smile and a wink behind Josh's back as he approached and led Josh out of the room.

Zeke watched him go, his heart burning in his chest. "I'm sorry, Lord," he whispered. "Maybe I shouldn't have been so hard on the boy, but You know I gotta speak that one's language to get through that thick skull You gave him. Git him outta here, Jesus. Give him another chance. I'm asking, okay? Protect my boy, Jesus."

He sniffed and stood, glancing in the direction Josh had gone, grateful for Jordan's phone call this morning begging him to persuade him to fight. "I got yo' back, boy," he said as he stepped through the door.

"There's $20 on your books," Oscar stated, leading Josh back to his cell.

Josh nodded his thanks but remained quiet, his eyes focused on the ground.

Oscar checked his surroundings, ensuring no one would eavesdrop on what he was about to say. Nodding to a fellow guard, he turned his nose up at another. Leaning close to Josh's ear, he whispered, "I know who put you in here."

Josh's steps slowed but Oscar pulled him along.

"Don't slow down. Just listen. The barn isn't safe. Most of these guys are on her payroll—including the captain. She's got dirt on most of them, so there will be no backing down. There's a handful of us who can't stand her highness and have resisted her attempts to control us. We've been teaming up behind the scenes to take her down but, up until this point, have been unsuccessful. We can't do it alone—we need your help." Noticing a set of eyes on them, he yanked Josh's arm and raised his voice. "Go ahead, wise guy, keep talkin'—see if I don't toss you in the hole!"

"Be cool, man, be cool." Josh fell into the game.

Drawing closer to his cell, Oscar lowered his voice. "Call your dad. Hire him. Once you've done that, tell him to contact Lance Sherard, and let him know that Oscar Hairgrove says hello."

"What?" Josh squinted at him as they stopped in front of his cell.

"Just do it," Oscar hissed, unlocking the cell and shoving him in. "Wait until shift change, then ask for a phone call." His eyes drifted to the inmate watching them from the top bunk. "You got somethin' to say, punk?"

"Naw, I'm straight, guard." The inmate averted his gaze.

Oscar locked the cell and glared at Josh. "You're lucky shift change is in an hour, 'cause I'm sick o' lookin' at you."

Josh took the hint and settled onto his bunk to prepare for the impending phone call that would forever alter his relationship with his father.

His hand trembled over the receiver, sweat beading on his brow. Josh had been staring at the phone for far too long—he knew he was eating into his call time, but working up the courage to dial that number was proving harder than he'd thought. Forcing himself to put Nevaeh before his past, he picked up the phone. His fingers drummed the booth as the line rang, his heart slamming harder with each beat. The line clicked, and he spoke his name into the receiver and waited, praying his father would accept the collect call.

"Josh?"

"Dad," he croaked.

"Josh, are you okay?" Garrett's voice belied his fear.

"Dad, listen to me. I don't have time to explain. I need to…I need…" He closed his eyes tight and forced the words past his lips. "I need you to represent me. Please."

"Yes! Yes, of course! I'll need to come down there and confer with you about the case—go over the, and get your statement... You'll have to sign consent forms and payment waivers and—"

"Dad," Josh interrupted. "Call Lance Sherard. Tell him Oscar Hairgrove says hello." He held his breath, hoping his father understood the code that was lost to him.

"Oh," Garrett breathed. "Oh…Get off the line. Right now. Don't talk to anyone in the barn about your case. Keep to yourself and wait for me. Just wait, son. Don't talk to anybody!"

The dial tone buzzed in his ear as Josh lowered the receiver to his lap. His chest squeezed, and he found it hard to breathe. He'd just invited his father into his life. Just asked his abuser for his help. Squeezing his eyes shut, his stomach roiled. For a moment, he thought he might need to find a trash can, but the feeling passed. He checked the time and noted he had ten minutes left. He had to act fast. He dialed the number, hoping his fried nerves hadn't warped his memory. Leaning his forehead on the phone booth, Josh listened as it rang. Once, twice, three times…The line clicked, and he spoke his name, his left hand opening and closing on repeat.

"Josh, is that you?"

He breathed a sigh of relief. "Titus."

"What's wrong, kid?" Worry danced in his tone.

"I've been arrested."

After a pause, Titus answered, "I'm aware…"

"No." Josh sighed, frustrated. "Arrested again." He explained everything as quickly as he could. "Titus," he said on a sob. "I had to ask my dad for help."

"Breathe," Titus urged. "Take it slow. Just breathe. Tell me the rest."

"I can't explain it over the phone. I can't do this, man. I can't do this! Nevaeh needs me, and I can't do it. It's like all my strength is just gone. I'm nothing anymore. How am I gonna sit in a courtroom and listen to him defend me when all he's ever done is destroy me? I can't trust him, Titus. I'm trying, but I can't do it!"

"Josh, listen to me," Titus spoke calmly. "You're gonna go into that courtroom and face that judge, and you're gonna let your father do what he does best. I've looked him up, kid. He really is the best defense attorney out there. He can get you out of this. Sometimes God requires blind trust. You have to trust. Don't trust your dad—trust God."

"You always say that." Josh sniffed, wiping at the snot dripping from his nose. "How can I trust someone I don't even know? All those stories in the Bible, they're interesting, but they're just stories to me, man. You tell me they're real, but I'm not some gullible little kid who believes in fairy tales, Titus. I'm not stupid."

Titus sighed. "Maybe you should try letting yourself think like Nevaeh for a bit."

Josh thought on his words, confused. "What do you mean?"

"Nevaeh trusts you?"

"Uh…probably not much…"

Titus breathed a laugh. "Well, before you pounded your best friend in front of her, did she trust you?"

"Yeah, I guess."

"Did she know you?"

"Not really."

"But she went willingly whenever you asked her to stay with you, right?"

"Eventually."

"That's blind faith, son. We walk by faith—not by sight. You can't see God. Right now, you can't feel Him, because you don't know Him. But you know He's there. Quit looking for Him with your eyes and start looking for Him with your heart."

"Titus?"

"Yeah, son."

"I'm scared." The admission hit him like a ton of bricks. The fearless hoodlum, scared? The truth was unreal to him.

"That's okay. Just breathe. Being scared doesn't show a lack of courage, Josh. Fear is a normal response to things we don't understand. Courage is looking fear in the eye and saying you'll do what it takes despite that fear. So, you go to court and fight for yourself—for Nevaeh—and sit back and watch the miracle unfold in your father. According to what you've told me, your father was an awful man. But now he is standing up to fight for his son. That's God, boy. That doesn't happen with a mere man."

"He's just doing it for show," Josh commented bitterly.

"Maybe. But what if he's doing it for you? Because God has brought him to a place of understanding and has restored his heart to a place of healing?"

Josh sniffed, his heart deflating more with each passing second. "I gotta go."

"Fear doesn't show alack of courage," Titus repeated. "Remember that."

Josh nodded. "Yeah." He hung up the phone, startled

when the guard grabbed his wrist before the receiver connected to its base. "Hold up, man, let me get to my feet—I'm not fighting you," he protested, gritting his teeth when his arm was yanked backward and pinned behind his back. "I'm not fighting you!" he shouted, hoping to draw the attention of the other guards, but no one came to his rescue.

"You tellin' me how to do my job, lawyer boy?" The guard jerked him backward off the stool and pulled him to his feet before slamming him into the wall. Putting his mouth close to Josh's ear, he sneered. "My name's not Oscar, punk. I work for the other team. Better mind your p's and q's with me, hear?" He pulled him off the wall and shoved him forward, his fingers digging tighter into his arm with each step. "Hear they got your trial date. Hope you're ready to be put away for a long, long time."

The guard's laughter stayed with Josh long after he'd been shoved back into his cell.

GARRETT

Garrett's pulse raced from the adrenaline pumping through his veins. Alone in his study, he heard Elysia working on the dishes in the kitchen. She'd hardly said two words to him since Nevaeh had been taken, but all that was about to change. He could feel it. First, the phone call to Lance. He picked up his phone and dialed the number he hadn't called in years. Lance picked up on the second ring.

"Lance Sherard speaking." His voice was strong and confident. Not the voice of a man easily manipulated, though his wife portrayed him as such.

"Lance, it's Garrett Cameron."

"Garrett! How are you, old friend?"

Not daring to reveal anything over the phone, Garrett blurred the truth. "Still alive and kickin'. Been a while—wanted to call and check in. Saw a friend of yours today."

"Oh, yeah?"

"Yeah. Ol' Oscar says 'hello.'"

Lance breathed a laugh. "Oscar, eh? Well, tell that old goat he owes me a game on the green, and there won't be any mulligans this time!"

"Will do, will do." Garrett chuckled, reaching for a pen and paper. Quickly, he scribbled the message onto the pad. "Listen, something's come up, and I've got to run, but let's do lunch. Say, tomorrow, at The Strand?"

"I'll be there," Lance concurred, and the line went dead.

Garrett placed the phone on his desktop and stared at the message, allowing the words to sink into his mind. No mulligans—no do-overs. Lance was on board with the plan. It was now or never. He had to nail this case, or Nichole would win the final round. Grabbing the note, he shoved it into his pocket and went for the door. As soon as he told Elysia that Josh had finally asked for help, he'd hit the ground running. Depending on who the judge was, the trial would start in a couple of weeks. As he stepped into the hall, he embraced the thought of sleepless nights and burning the candle at both ends. If it meant getting his boy out of jail, it was worth it. He hoped Elysia thought so too.

She was elbow-deep in suds when he approached her. Nevaeh's absence had snuffed out the usual song on her lips. He longed to take her in his arms and assure her that it would all be alright, but he didn't dare. He watched her shoulders tense when she detected his presence, a heavy sigh escaping her lips. "Baby," he began. "Josh called." Her hands stilled in the water. He had her attention. "He wants me to represent him." She closed her eyes, her lips trembling as she fought her tears.

"Thank You, Jesus," she whispered.

"His trial date should be set—I've gotta go to the court to retrieve his files. Um...it's gonna take a lot of time, Lys. I won't be home much."

Elysia pulled her hands from the water and dried them on a towel as she faced him. "Whatever it takes, Garrett. Just bring him home. And get Nevaeh away from that awful woman."

He nodded, his mouth terse. "Yeah. Can I...?"

She moved into his arms and allowed him to hold her, closing her eyes when he kissed her neck. "I love you," she whispered. "I'm still so angry with you. But I love you."

He squeezed her harder. "I'm gonna give him all I've got, babe. I love you." Garrett released her and pulled his keys from his pocket as he headed for the door. "I'll call later to let you know if I'll be home for dinner." The moment she nodded her reply, he was out the door to face the giants looming in the shadows.

TITUS

Titus stared at the wall in front of him. If he was honest with himself, he'd been staring at the same spot on the wall ever since he'd hung up with Josh. He couldn't shake the nagging feeling that he needed to go to him, but he couldn't justify the thought. What would he do when he got there? Sit in the gallery, smile, and wave to the boy while his whole life came undone right before his eyes? He sighed and tapped his pen on his desk. He had to do it. He had to go and support him through this.

"I must be crazy, Jesus," he muttered as he sat up in his chair and grabbed his keyboard and mouse.

The computer screen came to life, and he quickly typed Garrett's name and law firm into the search bar. The contact information stared back at him within a millisecond, and he knew what to do. He would go to Josh and sit with him through each conference with his father if that's what the kid wanted—but not without Garrett's blessing. He picked up the phone and dialed the number, his stomach flipping as though he'd suffered at this man's hand.

"Cameron Law, how may I help you?" The female voice on the other end of the line was curt.

"May I speak with Mr. Cameron, please? This is Titus Delancey—his son's former boss." He held his breath and prayed she'd put him through.

There was a pause before she grumbled, "Mr.

Cameron's a very busy man."

"Yes, I understand. I'll just be a moment. Please."

With a sigh, she placed the call on hold and classical music tickled his ear. He watched the secondhand circle the face of the clock on the wall twice before the music faded and he was greeted with a rushed "hello."

"Mr. Cameron, my name's Titus Delancey. I'm Josh's former boss out in Florida."

"I've heard a lot about you. May I ask the reason for your call?" Garrett's voice was guarded.

"Well...I'm not sure what Josh has told you, but he's kinda like a son to me." Titus paused when Garrett sucked in his breath, mentally kicking himself for stepping on the father's toes. "I, uh, I talked to him today, and he filled me in on what happened. I know about his upcoming trial and that he's having a hard time with it all. I called to ask your blessing to fly out and be with him during your consultations, as well as during the trial."

A long pause followed before Garrett spoke, tension winding with each word. "It's not protocol to have someone in on the consultation. I mean, Josh would have to give his approval. My son is in good hands with me. May I ask why you want to sit in?"

Titus swallowed hard. "I don't doubt your ability, sir. I've been spiritually coaching him for the last three years and, well...I hear you two haven't had the best history together. I know Josh could use a friend. I just want to be there for him—I'm not looking to encroach upon your relationship with the boy. I know you're working hard to establish a bond with him, and I respect that. If he doesn't want me there, I'll leave but I'm asking for your consent."

Garrett swallowed hard, fighting his heart with his answer. He had to put Josh before his desires. Finally, he answered, his throat tight."I think it's a great idea. My son could use all the support he can get. Our first consultation will be tomorrow morning at nine. Think you can make it by then?"

"Absolutely. I'm taking the first flight out. And

Garrett?"

"Yes?"

"Thank you. This means a lot to me, and I think it will mean a lot to Josh too."

"Yeah. I think you're right."

"If you could keep this between us? I'd like to surprise him."

"Of course."

After jotting down the location of the police station, Titus hung up the phone andto work on packing his bag. He prayed non-stop as he worked, and then prayed some more on his way to the airport, begging God to show up in the trial and show Josh Who He was.

RHEA

"I'm hungry."

Rhea cradled her daughter closer to her on the bed and gently shushed her. "I'll get you something to eat soon, I promise." She strained to hear the voices in the other room.

Her mother had answered a knock at the suite's door five minutes prior. Whoever was in the room with her, had her very upset.

"Josh says you guys made a stop between the jail and the hotel. Can you tell me about that?"

Rhea sucked in a breath. Detective Donahue.

"Do you see?! That lying little heathen! We did no such thing! We drove straight to the hotel. He promised he would say his goodbyes to my daughter and leave Highshore forever."

Nichole's voice escalated, and Rhea felt the tension in Nevaeh's shoulders as the little girl buried her face in her side.

"I don't like her." She sniffed. "She's scary. I want my daddy."

A sigh escaped Rhea's lips as she stared at the door. "How about we watch cartoons, hmm? Would you like that?"

"No. I want her to go away. Can you make her go away? And that man, too?"

If only... Rhea kissed her fair head. "Don't focus on them, baby. Look at me. Don't worry, you hear me? I won't let anyone hurt you." She pulled her into her lap and held her tight.

In the next room, Donahue fought the smile tugging at his lips. "So...you're telling me that you trusted the word of a guy whom you, yourself, have labeled as a lying little heathen?"

Tears pushed through mascara-laden lashes as Nichole latched onto his arm. "I was desperate," she squeaked. "This was my last chance at getting him to leave her alone! Can't you understand my need to protect my daughter?"

Donahue pried her off him and moved her aside, stepping further into the room. "It's not me you have to convince, lady. Can you tell me where Rhea was when you found her?"

Nichole's face blanched white. "She was in her bedroom, tied to the headboard."

"Tied with what?"

"A rope. It was awful! I had to untie her while Asher arrested that boy."

"I see. Where'd he get the rope?" Donahue observed her, noting how she seemed to weave the answer in her mind.

"I suppose he found it somewhere here; he didn't have any rope in the car."

He raised an eyebrow. "So, you think he found the rope lying around here someplace? Have you seen a rope here before?"

Flustered, she breathed an annoyed laugh. "I can't be certain. Are we done here? I have things I need to tend to."

Irritation teased his nerves as he looked her over. "May I look at the bedroom where the assault was said to have taken place?"

Nichole stiffened and her eyes went cold. "Just a moment."

He watched as she went to the bedroom door and cracked it open.

"Rhea, darling, Detective Donahue needs to see your bedroom. Why don't you and Nevaeh come into the sitting room for a moment?"

Rhea's eyes remained downcast as she led a small girl from the room and sat on the couch, pulling the girl onto her lap.

"Hello, Rhea." Donahue offered a smile, noting the tear-streaked face of the little girl. "I hope you're feeling better."

"What do you mean by that?" Nichole questioned, her eyes cutting to Rhea.

"Last time we spoke, her stomach was a bit upset. Probably just reacting to the stress of the situation." With interest, he studied the way Rhea avoided her mother's eyes as she pulled the little girl into her lap and sat on the couch. "Is this your little girl?" he asked, his eyes on Rhea's face.

"Yes," she whispered.

"Was she here when the assault took place?"

"No, thank God." Nichole swooped beside him and tugged at his arm as she stepped toward the bedroom.

Annoyed, Donahue extricated himself from her grasp and refocused on Rhea. "Do you know a Sterling Oliver?" Her face paled. "He's…" She glanced at her daughter and swallowed hard. "We were dating."

"Were?" His brow rose. He could feel Nichole's tension behind him. "Rhea," he stepped toward her, "did Sterling cause those burns on your wrists?"

"How absurd!" Nichole shouted, her eyes flashing. "As though my daughter hasn't been through enough!"

Donahue read the truth in Rhea's eyes before speaking. "You're right," he said, glancing at her mother. "My apologies." He stepped toward the bedroom, Nichole hot on his heels. Turning, he gave her a tolerant smile. "If you don't mind, I'd like to check the room alone. Thanks."

Fury burned her cheeks as Nichole watched him from

the doorway. She didn't like this detective–he was stubborn and determined. Her eyes narrowed. He had no idea what she was capable of. Making a mental note to look into him and find something she could use against him, she forced a tight smile and folded her arms across her chest as he scrutinized the headboard.

Donahue pulled out his camera and snapped several pictures of the headboard. There were several slots in the design, making Nichole's and Rhea's claims plausible. A rope could easily have been tied here…in fact…He leaned closer, frowning when he spotted small threads of rope clinging to one of the slots. Carefully, he collected the threads and placed them inside a paper bag, rolling it up and sticking it into his pocket. Staring at the headboard a moment longer, his brow furrowed at the sight of fresh scuff marks on the wall near the bed. Snapping pictures of them, he turned to the door, his mission burning in his chest. He needed to talk to Josh again–see his reaction to what he'd just learned. Someone was lying, but Donahue still wasn't convinced it was Josh.

"Isn't it tragic?" Nichole dabbed her eyes as he walked past her and headed for the door.

"A real travesty," Donahue quipped, rolling his eyes at the hallway as he stepped from the room. "I'll be in touch."

Back at the jail, he wasted no time requesting that Josh be brought to the interview room. The moment Josh walked inside, Donahue narrowed his eyes at him. "Sit down."

Josh obeyed, meeting his hard stare with a smirk and the raising of an eyebrow.

"You remember your rights?"

"Yeah."

"You wanna talk to me?"

"'Bout what?"

"Answer the question, Joshua."

"I think I just did."

Donahue shifted in his seat, fighting the urge to throttle

him. "Yes, or no?"

"Relax, man. Yes, I'll talk to you. What are we discussing today? The weather?"

"I think you lied to me."

"Well, that's an easy one–I didn't."

"I went to the bedroom, Josh. I saw the headboard, and there were scraps of rope on it." He watched as confusion clouded Josh's face.

"What're you talkin' about, Donahue? I already told you–I did not have a rope on me. Check the cameras!"

Donahue pulled out the photos and scraps of rope and laid them out in front of him. "Now, boy, don't you be playin' with me. I gave you the benefit of the doubt and want you to be straight with me."

"Wait a minute!" Josh leaned forward and pointed at a picture. "That's not the headboard! Are you sure you were in the right room?"

Donahue slapped a hand on the table. "Of course, I was in the right room! Nichole was there, Rhea was there, and your little girl was there too. I looked at the headboard, and I found this scrap of rope. You can't talk your way around the evidence, Josh."

"Listen to me, man," Josh argued. "That's not the headboard that was on that bed, and I can prove it!" Sitting back in his chair, Donahue raised a mocking brow and nodded. "Oh, this should be good. Give it your best shot, buddy."

"Pull my phone," Josh urged, his jaw setting. "I took pictures of my girl sittin' on the bed–you can see the headboard behind her. I also took a selfie with her on the bed, 'cause it's been years since we've had any pictures. Is that enough of a shot for you, buddy?" His eyes flashed as Donahue took in this news. "The headboard in our picture is not the headboard in your pictures. Prove me wrong!"

The detective stared at him a moment before answering. "All right, son. I hope you're not yanking my chain because I don't have time to sit here and play games with you. I'm willing to believe what you tell me is true, but don't you run any games on me–you hear me?"

"I'm tellin' you, Donahue. That headboard was not there. Pull the pictures. You'll see for yourself."

Chapter 34

"The Lord will fight for you, and you only have to be silent."
~Exodus 14:14~

JORDAN

Jordan stared at his computer—his untouched coffee long gone cold beside him. It was 8 AM. Josh would have his first conference with his father in an hour, and his fate would unravel. His stomach twisted with nerves, and sweat trickled on his brow. Across the newsroom, Cali sat, buried in some article she'd been working on non-stop for days. The two hadn't said two words to each other in months. It was better that way. He couldn't stand the sight of her after all she'd done. And what was with that cardigan she'd taken to wearing lately? Didn't she realize it was a zillion degrees outside? Rolling his eyes, he sighed and forced himself to focus on his screen.

"The Highshore parks are in danger of extinction—city manager, Lance Sherard, refuses to budge."

Jordan sat back in his chair, his fingers slipping from the keyboard.

"Hey, Straight Shooter."

His eyes flew up, and shame colored his cheeks as Rachel came into view. He sat up straighter, his nerves driving him to reach for his cold coffee and take a swig. Pulling a face, he spat out the bitter brew, his cheeks flaming again when Rachel laughed and pulled up a chair beside him. "Rachel, um, I'm kinda busy here..."

"Yeah, I can see that." Her brows knit as she stared at the blinking cursor on his screen. "I gave you this assignment two days ago—what's going on with you? Are you okay?" Her heart ached for him, but she didn't want him to know. Biting the inside of her lip, she forced herself to go into boss mode. "If I need to reassign this to a more competent reporter, I will."

Jordan glanced at her, a frown pulling at his mouth.

"How 'bout you give it to Cali? She's plenty competent." He tossed his pen across his desk and shoved a hand through his hair.

She loved it when he did that. Those thick brown locks of his.... Rachel! She scolded herself as her eyes found Cali hard at work. "Cali has enough on her plate as it is. Besides, it's not like you to shirk your work, Jordan." Rachel focused her gaze on his worried features. "What is it?" she asked softly.

He sighed. "Josh is in major trouble right now, and I can't be there for him."

She didn't answer right away. She hadn't seen much of Josh since he'd come home. They'd been a pack during high school—Josh and Rhea, an item...and Jordan and herself, always just...good friends. She and Rhea had always eye-rolled the boys when they'd gotten into trouble, but she'd been secretly afraid of Josh and his impulsive behavior. Swallowing hard, she forced herself to be there for Jordan. After all, this was his best friend. "Why not?"

He looked at her. "Because he's about to confer with his lawyer. Attorney/client privilege and all that jazz."

"Oh." She nodded.

Jordan sat quietly, his gaze pulling back to Cali. His eyes narrowed when he found her focused on him, a smug smile set on her face. He fought the urge to stick out his tongue like a fourth grader and pulled his attention back to Rachel. "I need some air. Wanna come?"

Surprise registered in her eyes as she watched him stand. He reached for her hand and pulled her up before she could protest, leading her toward the exit and onto the sidewalk. "Jordan, we have work—"

"We can't save the park from the city manager by writing about it. Forget the stupid paper for a minute. Let's talk about you. What's going on with Rachel?"

She stared at him, baffled by his sudden interest. "Jordan, are you sick? What is up with you?"

"Sick? Nah. Just needed to stretch my legs a bit, and

you've always been a great conversationalist." He strode on, not realizing her hand was still clasped in his.

Rachel watched his jaw clench and relax, feeling the tension in his fingers as they gripped hers. Any other day she might be thrilled to find herself in this scenario, but today something was definitely wrong with this boy. She knew him well enough to know when something was eating his soul. "Jordan, talk to me."

He didn't answer right away. His gaze was transfixed on the path. "This could be the end for him, Rach."

"Or it could be his new beginning," she offered.

"Josh is terrified of his dad. I can't imagine this consultation going over well. Mr. C is Josh's only hope but Josh doesn't trust him. You have to be able to trust your lawyer, Rachel." His voice grew distant. "I'm scared for him."

Rachel walked beside him, her strides half the length of his. "Jordan, did I tell you I'm covering this story?" His eyes shot to hers. "What? No, you didn't. As in— you'll be a courtroom reporter, or you'll be interviewing post-trial?"

"Both."

"Whose side are you on?"

She cut her eyes at him and stopped walking. "I'm an unbiased reporter, Jordan, you know that. But if you're asking my opinion..." She let her words fall.

Jordan dropped her hand as though it was a bomb and stepped back. "He didn't do it!"

"Jordan, you don't accuse a rape victim of lying..."

"She's not a rape victim! She's a victim of her mother! How can you stand there and accuse our friend of raping the girl he loves?"

"Rhea is our friend, too! And Josh has a horrible reputation, Jordan. We both know how he is..."

"Josh is a lot of things, but he is not a rapist, and I will not stand here and let you call him one."

"Jordan, I—" Rachel reached for him, but he jerked away.

"No! You're wrong," he snapped. "You'll find out just how wrong you are when you cover his trial. Maybe then you can look at the situation from a human's perspective and not a logical journalist's for once in your life. Maybe then you can remind yourself of what Nichole is capable of!" He turned his back on her and rushed down the sidewalk, leaving her to find her way back to the newsroom alone.

Shoulders slumped; Rachel stared after him in confusion. For one moment—one blissful moment—she'd had her best friend back. The friend she'd had before Cali Bristol had trampled his heart. If she hadn't opened her big mouth maybe she would have had the chance she'd longed for all this time. Maybe.

DONAHUE

"Perdòn." Donahue lightly touched the elbow of a passing maid at the Seascapes Hotel. Josh had told the truth about the headboard—now he needed to find someone who could explain why the picture showed something completely different than what was in the room. "Mi nombre es la detective Donahue. ¿Puedo hablar contigo un momento?"

"¿Qué necesitas usted?" The maid barely acknowledged him as she unlocked a room and pushed her cleaning cart inside.

"Un minuto de usted tiempo, por favor." He cast her a smile and hovered in the doorway.

When she saw he wasn't going anywhere, she rolled her eyes. "I'm very busy, Señor."

"I'll just be a moment," he assured her.

Sighing, she dropped a stack of sheets onto the bed. "Where we will talk?"

"Here's just fine." He smiled. "I need to ask you about room 350."

She tensed, and her chin shot into the air. "¡Mujer terrible y malvada!"

Hiding a smile, Donahue pulled a concerned face.

"Who's a terrible and evil woman?"

Mumbling to herself in Spanish, the maid yanked the dirty bedclothes from the bed and began dressing it with the new as though she'd forgotten Donahue's presence.

"Señora," he called but was ignored. Stepping closer, he tried again. "Señora, if you could just look at these pictures for me…"

With a huff, she abruptly turned and stared at the pictures in his hands.

"This picture was taken yesterday morning." Donahue held up the picture Josh had taken of Rhea on the bed. "This picture," he showed the one he'd taken during his examination of the room, "was taken today. Can you tell me why these headboards are different when the pictures were taken in the same room?"

She laughed and shoved a hand through her wispy brown hair, spouting rapid-fire Spanish. "¡Ella está loca! ¡Una loca! ¡La gente le teme!"

Donahue's brows rose. "People fear her?"

The maid met his gaze, her mouth twitching at the corners. "Cierre la puerta, señor."

Glancing behind him, he obliged her request, cautiously stepping forward when she waved him to her.

"The Señora…she no like the boy. Say he must pay for the love he have for la hija de la Señora. She tell the man…he must make scene for boy or lose todo lo que le gusta—all that he loves."

"What did she mean by 'make scene?'" Donahue asked.

"La loca y fea…she tell man to make like boy do something bad to la hija." Her eyes widened as she explained, her voice dropping like she feared being overheard. "El hombre asustado—he take old bed and say to la hija del gerente—'we must take to store room and hide.' I help—mi jefe, she tell me to help move bed. They pull new bed from another room, and then…"

Donahue leaned closer. "Then what happened? …Señora?"

"I see man tie rope to bed and move like this—" She

moved her hands side to side, indicating a back and forth motion.

"Are you certain of this? ¿Estás seguro de esto?"

"Si, Señor. I understand perfect Inglès. The lady…she hear only Español, pero I speak much English." She smiled. "I hear…everything."

Donahue straightened and stuck out a hand to shake hers. "Perfecto. Muy bueno. Thank you, Señora. Thank you."

GARRETT

Garrett stood outside the jail and watched the cab pull up in front of him. Before the man stepped to the curb, he knew it was him. He averted his gaze and turned away, working to keep it together for his son's sake. Josh would want this. Josh would be happy to see him. Josh was the focus, not himself. He felt the man approach and plastered a smile to his face before turning to greet him. "Titus?"

"That's me." His smile was easy, his handshake firm. "Are we ready to do this?"

Garrett's features tightened. We? He's my son… "I'll need to get set up first. Another lawyer should be here soon—his name's Khyron Thompson. I'm calling him in as my second chair on Josh's case. He'll join you in the lobby, and I'll call you both once I'm ready."

Taking the hint, Titus nodded. "Okay. Lead the way."

Garrett pulled open the station door and stepped inside, not bothering to hold it open for the man behind him. He walked to the front desk, where he and Titus received their visitor's badges and went through security. Once through, a deputy escorted Garrett to an interview room while Titus sat in the lobby.

From where he awkwardly sat in one of the hard plastic chairs, Titus observed his surroundings as he waited. The station was cold, not just from the a/c blowing snowballs from the vents. It was obvious that corruption reigned here. He focused on a man talking to a uniformed officer—his conversation loud enough for Titus to catch bits and pieces of what was being said.

"...Cameron...out of control...had to handle things."

"Blasted idiot! That kid is about to be interviewed by his lawyer! How bad did you rough him up?"

Titus' eyes narrowed as the two walked away, their voices angered and hushed. Glancing around, he wondered if there was something he could do to advocate for Josh. Whom should he speak to? Would they even listen? Maybe he could tell Josh's dad once he let him in the room...

Inside the interrogation room, Garrett ensured his laptop was running smoothly and ready to take rapid-fire notes from Josh's testimony. He could feel the time lapsing—he knew he should call Delancey in so they could call for Josh and start the interview. But that wasn't how he wanted this to go down. He wanted time alone with his boy, and he was going to get it. Josh didn't know Titus had come, so withholding that information wouldn't hurt him. There were things that Garrett longed to say to his son. Things he didn't want the wanna-be-father to be privy to. He opened the door and requested the guard to bring Josh in, then sat down in his chair and waited.

The door opened, and Josh was led in by a burly guard with a Pitt-bull face. Garrett did a double-take of his son at the sight of pain dancing across his features. Dressed in orange prison garb, his right hand was pressed into his ribs, while his left arm was locked in the tight grip of the guard's meaty fingers as he pulled Josh into the room and shoved him down into his chair. Without a word, the man slammed Josh forward onto the table, the left side of his face smacking the surface as he cried out.

"Hey!" Garrett yelled, leaping to his feet. "What's with all this unnecessary force you're using on my client? Why the cuffs?"

"Your client hasn't been in the best of moods today." The guard sneered and locked eyes with the lawyer. "He's gettin' cuffed, because he attacked one of the guards this morning—like an idiot." Yanking his left wrist in front of him, he snapped the table cuff on him and cinched it tight.

"Come on, man!" Josh winced, the metal biting into his bone.

"Take it off," Garrett demanded, his eyes blazing.

"'Scuse me?" The guard threw his chin up and yanked Josh's right wrist forward.

"I said, 'Take it off.' Take it off and cuff him humanely, or I'll go over your head so fast your head will spin."

The guard laughed as he looked from Garrett to Josh. "Well, would you look at that? The man who used you as a human punching bag telling me to be gentle with his baby boy. So, we ain't beatin' him no more, Dad?"

Josh gritted his teeth as the guard gave in to his father's demands and cuffed him again, this time giving his wrists some wiggle room. Once he'd shackled both ankles to the floor, he stood and stepped to the door.

"There you go, princess. Now you two play nice in here." The guard laughed and walked out the door.

Josh dropped his gaze to the table. The pain in his beaten ribs was enough to bring tears to his eyes, but he refused to give in.

Garrett cleared his throat and slowly sat back in his chair. "You okay?" he asked, his voice subdued.

Josh remained quiet, his jaw tensing. His left fist opened and shut. Opened and shut—again and again as he worked to quiet his nerves. "Can we just do this?" He detested the pity in his father's eyes—as if he needed this man to feel sorry for him.

Taking in his son's tight features, and the cuffs keeping him bound to the table, Garrett sighed. "Is what that guard said true?"

Josh met his gaze. "What do you think?" he wheezed, the pain taking his breath away.

Garrett's lips pressed into a thin line. "This is important, Josh. Did you instigate this, or did they jump you?"

He raised his chin. He could still feel the guard's boot

as it slammed his sides repeatedly after he'd been thrown to the floor.

Garrett decided to let it go for the moment, determined to find out the truth once he'd finished with his son. Typing a few lines onto his computer keyboard, he tried not to make it obvious that he couldn't keep his eyes off his boy. Was that fear in his gaze? Regret? He didn't know, but he wished he could ease his mind. "About what that guard said…"

Josh's eyes shot to his, and his features tightened. "Forget it."

"Um, yeah. Well, here's the thing. Ever since you came home, I've been wanting to talk to you alone but, uh, the opportunity never presented itself." He chanced a glance at him, his stomach lurching at the storm billowing behind his eyes. "Nothing I could ever say or do will ever be able to erase what I did to you all those years."

Josh shifted in his seat, his eyes darting to his left. "This isn't why we're here," he mumbled.

"No. No, you're right, but please hear me out. This needs to be said. I've needed to say it for years." Garrett cleared his throat, his eyes misting. "I was wrong, Josh. I was so very wrong. I was a drunk and a fool. When your mom found out she was pregnant with Nilah, I was ecstatic. I'd always wanted a daughter. My head was filled with dreams of taking her to father-daughter dances and her prom. We had her nursery all decked out in princess decor." He paused, suddenly aware of Josh's discomfort.

"I don't want your excuses, Dad." His jaw tensed. "I get it, okay? Nilah died, and I replaced her. I'm not a girl, and I ruined your life. Now can we please just talk about how to get me out of here?"

"No, no." Garrett's eyes dimmed as pain stabbed his heart. "I'm not coming across right. I'm not trying to make excuses for what I did to you. I was a monster—I know that. I allowed your sister's death to turn me into something I never imagined I could be. The pain from losing her transformed into hatred for you when you were born. And then you were born on her birthday/date of death as well...I just...I lost it, Josh. I lost who I was. I began drinking to hide the pain, and before I knew it, I'd turned into a functioning alcoholic who fought for strangers by day and terrorized his family by night."

"Stop. Please, stop!" The tears broke free, streaming down Josh's face. He yanked against the cuffs as though their hold would relent and grant him his freedom.

Garrett's lips quivered as he watched his son shrink away from him. "I just want you to know how sorry I am. I want you to know that I love you. I love you so much, Josh. And I'm so proud of who you've become."

"Proud of who I've become?" Josh yelled at his father, ignoring the stabbing in his ribs. "You mean proud of this monster you created? Proud that I ran away from you and didn't even know I had a daughter to raise? Proud that I'm in jail right now, because I've been accused of raping the girl I love? Save it, man! Just get me out of here so I can get back to my kid. Hopefully, I don't screw her up the same way you screwed me." Josh's fists clenched tight in their bonds, his eyes searing into his father's.

Garrett sat still, allowing the silence to fall like a wet blanket. He contemplated his next words carefully, weighing how Josh might receive them. Concluding that he had to say it no matter how it was received, he took a deep breath. "Josh, I remained a drunken monster long after you left—right up until the moment Rhea showed up on my doorstep and put your daughter into my arms. When I held that baby and looked into her eyes, I knew God had given me my second chance."

"Stop," Josh begged, the tears flowing again. "She's not Nilah! She's not your daughter! She's mine, you hear me? Nevaeh is mine! Stop talking about her like she changed you, 'cause she didn't! You're not different—you're not!"

Garrett forced himself to continue, despite the fear knotting his gut. "You're right, Josh. Nevaeh didn't change me. God did. I stopped drinking that day. I got into Al-anon. I went every time the doors were open. I started talking to Zeke—not going to church, just talking to him. Asking questions. I stopped hanging with crooked officials. When I wasn't at the office, I made sure I was home. I helped your mother around the house. Helped her with Nevaeh."

"Yeah? You did all that? Well, that's just great. That's all just so awesome." Josh sniffed, hating himself for the insecurities rising in his veins. "Were you satisfied then? Huh? You got the girl you'd always dreamed of; your wife didn't hate you anymore, and your son was out of your life forever. That what you wanted? Was that it? You didn't even come after me, Dad. Didn't even act like you cared I wasn't there anymore. Don't come to me with this bull, man, just don't."

Garrett shook his head, tears pooling. "You're wrong, Josh. The first week we had Nevaeh, I asked Jordan if he'd found out anything about you. I was scared, don't get me wrong. Most of me didn't want to find you—I knew I had hell to pay, and I was too cowardly to face you. I had no clue how to be a dad, but I knew I had done you wrong and wanted to start doing right by you. Seemed like every time Jordan found a clue, you'd vanish into thin air, and he'd have to start all over. I talked to different contacts across the states trying to find you, but I never came up with anything. I never gave up. I wanted to find you; to make things right and see you raise your daughter. I started going to church and studying the Bible. I even started sitting in on Zeke's Bible studies. God pricked me deep." He sniffed.

"The conviction weighing on my heart was relentless. One day, I just couldn't take it anymore, and I grabbed a picture of you in one hand and my gun in another. I locked myself in my study and told God that only He could save me from myself." The tears poured down his cheeks as he watched the torment on his son's face. "I put the gun to my head, and I pulled the trigger. Nothing happened. I was still there, holding your picture tight in my hand. At that moment, when I realized my life had been spared from my own hands, it was like God had reached in and yanked my heart out of my body and given me a completely new one that didn't have one stain."

"Enough!" Josh screamed and cursed at his dad, yanking hard against his cuffs. His chest burned with energy, his breaths were forced through tight lungs. "You wait until I'm captive to throw all this at me? That's messed up, man. That's messed up!" he cried. "I hate you. I hate you! Please, please just take my statement, and send me back to my cell. Please, I'm begging you." Tears soaked his cheeks as he closed his eyes tight and sobbed.

Garrett nodded; his face grim. His conscience accused him, but his heart was relieved. "I, uh, I have someone who wants to see you. Give me a minute." He stood and went for the door.

"Delancey. Thompson."

Titus' head snapped up, and he found Garrett's sorrowful gaze fixed on him as he stood in the doorway across from him. "Coming." He stood and shoved his phone into his pocket as he headed for the interview room, Thompson right behind him. His heart thumped wildly as he prepared himself to see Josh. Was the kid okay? Would he be happy to see him? Allow him to stay? The questions raced through his mind as he stepped into the room and froze at the sight of Josh's tear-soaked face. His gaze flew to Garrett, eyes narrowing fiercely as he sat beside Josh. "Hey, kid," he spoke softly, his elbows on his knees as he leaned toward him.

Josh's head snapped up at his voice, and his eyes flew open. His chest heaved as the air came in rapid puffs, relief overtaking his body and soul at the sight of this man who held his trust. "Titus," he breathed, "you came."

"Yeah, kid. Couldn't let you go through this alone." He offered a confident smile as he clapped him on the back.

"Thanks for coming." Garrett's voice was low as he leaned toward Thompson.

Khyron Thompson flashed his friend a smile and opened his briefcase. "I never turn down a plea for help from a friend—especially when that friend is you."

Thompson had interned for Garrett after graduating from California Western School of Law. After putting some clerk and court experience under his belt, he moved on to a larger law firm in nearby Sacramento. He'd cut his teeth on felony cases and had an impressive 98 percent win rate, which aggravated the local prosecutor. When Garrett had called and told him that he'd be defending his son in a sexual assault trial, he'd wasted no time in coming to his aid.

Clearing his throat, Garrett arranged the files and papers on the table before sitting down, his eyes focused on his computer. The tension in the room was thick enough to slice. "He doesn't have to be here if you don't want him to be—I can make him leave," he offered with a glance at Josh, knowing his son would never make this man leave the room.

"Make him leave?" Titus stared at Garrett; his brows knit. As though he had, what, strong-armed his way into this consult? Like he'd been the one to make the kid cry? Sheesh.

Focusing his attention on Josh, Garrett nodded to Titus. "He called and asked permission to sit in on the consultation. He felt like you could use a friend." He cleared his throat at the fresh splash of tears in his son's eyes. "...and I think he's right. So, if you're okay with him being here, we can begin."

"Yes," Josh choked. "He can stay."

"Alright, then." Garrett tried to hide his disappointment. Forced himself to push through as though he and Josh hadn't just shared the rawest moment of vulnerability in their relationship to date. "This is an associate of mine—Khyron Thompson. He'll be with us to the end. He's just as much your attorney as I am, and you should feel free to ask him anything. Okay, Josh, start at the beginning and don't stop until the end. Every detail is important. Nothing is too insignificant." He stared at the blank screen; fingers poised over the keys. When Josh said nothing, he looked up to find him fixated on the wall behind him. "Whenever you're ready," Garrett prompted.

"Um…so like…I guess I'll start with my bail being posted?" Josh glanced at his father, his gaze dropping to the table when Garrett met his eyes.

"Sounds good. You were arrested for disorderly conduct, and your bail was posted the next morning. Is that correct?"

"Yes."

"Okay. Who posted your bail?"

Josh looked at him, one brow raised.

"I have to hear all statements straight from you, not through heresay. Who posted your bail?"

"Nichole."

"Nichole who?"

"Dad."

"Humor me."

Josh sighed. "Nichole Sherard."

"Okay. So, she posted your bail, and then what happened?"

As Josh began recounting the conversation between him and Nichole on the drive to the hotel, anger pulsed through Garrett's veins. One look at Khyron and Titus told him their thoughts mirrored his—this woman was cutthroat and would stop at nothing to see Josh locked away for good.

"I went into the hotel and asked for Rhea. I made sure Nichole was gone first. I was positive she hadn't seen me, but I was wrong." Josh hung his head. "I knew better. It was a trap. I just…didn't care anymore. I to talk to her one last time…just us. Our entire relationship had been forbidden. Not one time did we have…" He glanced at his father, his pulse racing. Swallowing hard, his eyes bounced to Titus' confident gaze before continuing. "We never had support, you know? So, I went to her room and knocked on the door."

"Wait, wait, wait." Khyron held up a hand. "Nichole drove you to the hotel, told you to go up and see her daughter, then let you out of the car?" His brow furrowed as he stared at Josh. Leaning back in his chair, he pressed the end of his pen into his jawbone. "Why did you go into the hotel? You knew it was a trap, knew it was wrong, knew what her mother was capable of. Why did you play yourself right into her clutches?"

Titus' gaze swung from the lawyer to Josh, and he prayed the kid wouldn't lose his cool.

"I told you why," Josh clipped. His eyes shot to his father. "You call this helpful?"

Garrett opened his mouth, but Khyron cut him off.

"No, no, I'm serious." He raised a brow at Josh before looking at Garrett. "I don't play around with my clients. You know this." Fixing his gaze on Josh, he leaned forward and placed his elbows on the table. "I mean, you go in, planning to rape this girl, knowing her mom could walk in at any moment, yet you still did it?!"

"I did not rape her!" Josh screamed, jerking against the cuffs.

"Exactly." Khyron sat back, unphased by his outburst. "You knew she'd catch you in that room with her forbidden daughter, so, it makes no sense for you to rape that girl. And that is how we'll present it when you're on the stand. Now tell us the rest."

Josh's chest heaved as he stared him down, but Titus' calm voice kept him grounded.

"Come on, kid. You're almost there. You're doing great. Just tell them what happened after you knocked on Rhea's door."

Glancing his way, he breathed a shaky sigh before telling them what happened after Rhea had let him in. "...then she asked me who I'd been fighting with. I told her I'd taken her advice to take Nevaeh and run off with her, and she—"

"Wait a minute," Garrett held up his right hand and gaped at his son. "Taking Nevaeh was Rhea's idea?"

Titus watched the wall shoot up behind Josh's eyes. Saw the tensing of his jaw. Aww, Garrett...

Josh raised his chin. "Rhea was scared," he said, his tone daring his father to accuse her.

Realizing his mistake, Garrett dropped his hand and sighed. "I didn't mean to make that sound bad, Josh. I just didn't know she was behind your decision to run."

"No, you were behind my decision to run," he snapped. "She didn't make me do it. She didn't take her—I did." His eyes shot fire, the flames threatening to engulf his father at the hint of a wrong word.

Garrett worked his jaw, kicking himself for upsetting him. "I understand. What happened next?"

"I told her I couldn't do it alone—that Nevaeh needs both of us. I begged her again to run off with me. And then I…" Fear gripped his heart, and he froze as his mind played the reels of the night he'd run away from his father.

"Courage is looking fear in the eye and saying, 'I'm going to do this anyway.'" Titus stated, his voice calm and steady as he watched Josh's features dance. "Deep breaths, son."

Garrett bristled but held his tongue. He had to give it to him—the guy was good, and Josh responded well to him. But still…

Josh forced himself to tell his father what he'd done.

"Did she fight you?" Garrett asked.

"No," he whispered. Rhea's words flooded his mind, squeezing his chest. "Just the opposite. As soon as we'd finished, she told me she would run away with me. But they busted in the door right after that." Josh dropped his gaze, his right fist opening and closing with the memory.

Garrett paused; his heart pained at the realization that Josh had finally gotten the answer he'd sought for years from Rhea, only to be ripped away from her a mere moment later. "Josh, you said 'they' busted in the door right after—what did you mean by that?"

"As soon as we were finished, the door flew open, and a cop was dragging me off Rhea before I even knew what had happened. Nichole was right there with him, lookin' like she'd just won the lottery."

Titus' jaw clenched as he listened to Josh recount the events of that day. Why did this woman hate this boy so badly that she'd send him to jail and ruin his life like that?

Referencing the arrest report, Garrett's blood ran cold all over again at the sight of the arresting officer's name. "Since you've been in jail, has anything strange happened to you?"

Josh raised a brow. "Meaning?"

"How have the guards treated you?" Garrett asked.

"Why'd they jump you, Josh?"

Both Josh's and Garrett's eyes flew to Titus.

Titus looked at Garrett. "Heard them talking about it out there. Said he's been unruly."

"That's not true," Josh said, his voice tense. "I was minding my own business in my cell this morning when one of those idiots came to get me. He told me I had an interview with my lawyer soon, but they needed to talk to me first. They pulled me into a room and laid into me. Said they needed to remind me just how far Nichole's reach goes."

Garrett's jaw tensed. "They said that?"

"Yeah. They did." Josh met his eyes. "And when I looked at the cameras for help, one of the guards kicked me in the ribs and told me no one was watching. So, to answer your question—the guards have treated me like they know I'm your son."

Enough said. Garrett knew exactly what that meant, and it scared him to his core. The barn was dirty. It always had been. And he used to be part of that dirt. Now that he was on the clean side of the law, the dirty side would try to work their magic to reel him back into their mud. And when that didn't work, they would sling his dirty laundry at him for all of Highshore to see. His eyes hardened as he looked at his boy. Let them sling. He'd intercept anything they threw at him—and this time, he'd protect his son from their blows, even if it meant destroying himself in the process.

CHAPTER 35

"We are from God, and whoever knows God listens to us; but whoever is not from God does not listen to us. This is how we recognize the Spirit of truth and the spirit of falsehood."
~1 John 4:6~

DONAHUE

"How long were you and Rhea dating?" Donahue fixed his eyes on the man across from him. He was fidgety, and that made the detective suspicious.

"What do you mean 'how long were we dating?' Rhea and I are still together." Sterling's response was clipped. He was so over the assumption that he'd lost his girl through this mess. This was just temporary. As soon as he helped Nichole lock Josh away for good, she'd help him win Rhea's heart back.

Donahue raised a brow. "My apologies. I understood otherwise. Correct me if I'm wrong, Sterling, but you two shared a home at one point, right?"

"You will address me by my proper name–it's Mr. Oliver. We do share a home. She's just been staying with her mother off and on over the past few months."

"May I ask why?"

Sterling narrowed his eyes as his heart ached with Rhea's decision to leave him and pursue Josh. "No. You may not. Look, buddy–"

"Detective Donahue. You want respect? It goes both ways."

"Look, Detective, I'm an attorney, and I—"

"Civil," Donahue interrupted, earning himself a glare. "You're a civil attorney."

"Like I said, I'm an attorney, and I know my rights." Sterling rose from his seat and began gathering his things. "Are you charging me with a crime? You know, I didn't have to meet with you, and–"

"You're free to leave any time–you read your Advise of

Rights form. But I think you're as curious about me and this case as I am about you. So, why don't you sit right back down, and we can satisfy each other's curiosity?"

Sterling thought for a moment but then took his seat.

Donahue wasted no time. "What happened to Rhea's wrists, Sterling?" He failed to stop the grin before it appeared.

Sterling faltered for only a moment before he was back on point. "Joshua Cameron happened, that's what."

"How do you know Cameron did that? Did you witness it yourself?"

"No. I was told he did."

"Told by whom?"

"Rhea."

"Really? That's not what I was told. I was told that Nichole told you–not Rhea. Rhea was said to have been too embarrassed to even speak of it. So, who told you?" Donahue pressed, watching him squirm.

"Um, yeah. It was Nichole. But Rhea was there." Sterling dropped his eyes, unnerved.

"Tied to a bedpost?"

"Yes!" His head snapped up, relief flooding his face.

Donahue bit back a laugh. "What if I told you I had documented proof that there was no way Rhea was tied to the bedpost?"

Sterling regained his composure and stared him down. "I'd say prove it," he snapped.

"I plan on it. And, Mister Attorney, I know you don't practice criminal law, but are you aware of a little term called 'perjury?' If you get on that witness stand and knowingly lie, not only will you lose that valuable Civil Attorney's license, but you'll end up going to prison as well. So why don't you think long and hard and see if this is really the story you want to go with." Donahue's eyes flashed with his words.

Sterling swallowed hard and thought back over his conversation with Nichole. It wasn't that he trusted her—he didn't—it was that she'd made it clear that the only way for him to keep Rhea away from Josh was to follow through with her plans. She'd been generous to both Rhea and him. He'd seen Rhea's suite at the hotel—she lacked for nothing. Nichole had even arranged for him to visit her the other day. He'd been pleased when Rhea had seemed more at ease with him this time. So at ease, it had led to a romantic night together. Of course, he was in an interrogation room because of it, but still. The plan was moving forward. He felt confident in her ability to protect this lie.

He leaned forward, refusing to allow this detective to force his hand. "Josh Cameron tied my girl to a bed and raped her, and you're in here asking me what I know about her wrists? How about you do your job, Detective? Nail that guy for all he's worth!"

Donahue's smile was condescending, at best. "So, that's your story and you're sticking to it, eh?" Sterling sat back and crossed his arms over his chest, a grin teasing the corners of his mouth. "Indubitably." "Alright, then. Sure hope what Nichole is offering you is worth it."

She is, Sterling thought. Rhea is 100% worth it.

JUDGE FRANK

Judge Clayton Frank was an important man. Well-respected in his city. Of course, there was the usual backbiting and slander behind his back, but they talked about her, too, and it only added fuel to her fire. He had nothing but love and adoration for the red-headed queen of Highshore. She ruled her people with an iron fist—unforgiving and demanding the very air they breathed. He worshiped the ground she walked on and was anxiously awaiting the day she would summon him for their escape to the Bahamas, and he could leave this crazy city behind.

It hadn't surprised him when she'd approached him about a case on his docket. From the moment he'd seen Cameron's name, he knew Nichole would be hot on his heels, ready to pounce and destroy. He was eager to help her do that and knew exactly which ploys to play to nail the last nails into the boy's coffin. The only hang-up he could see was Garrett Cameron. He was a cut-throat lawyer and knew the law inside and out. Getting past him would be difficult, but Nichole's promises to him if they won this case gave him enough motivation to barrel right through him. He could have refused to allow the father to defend his son, but he told himself he had to make the case at least appear to be a challenge.

As he donned his black robe in his chambers, he glanced at his graying hair in the mirror. His salt-and-pepper locks drove her mad—she'd said this, herself, and he played her words over in his mind like the sweet morsels they were. He smiled at himself as he imagined the shocked expression that would play across Lance Sherard's face the day Nichole let him know she was running off with him—Judge Frank—the only man in Highshore who truly appreciated her for who she was. Soon, she would be Mrs. Clayton Frank. An electric current shot through his spine and he straightened the robe.

It was time. There wasn't a moment to lose—this was his moment! But first, he had to handle the pesky suppression hearing Cameron had pitched a fit to obtain. He intended to be as hard-nosed as he could get away with—he would not make this easy for the lawyer—but he was also aware of his need to toe the line. One wrong misstep and the whole thing would be tossed out of court. He would not allow that to happen.
Whether his father wanted to accept it or not, Joshua Cameron was finished.

"I hope you're ready, kid. I'm about to cancel your future."

GARRETT

"If you will just listen to me, you'll understand why I'm pressing so hard for Joshua Cameron's past crimes to be brought into the equation." Amelia Corazon, district attorney for over twenty years, breathed an exasperated breath as she cut her eyes to Garrett before turning back to the judge. "He raped the girl whom he's raped multiple times before—the jury has the right to know that!"

"She has no proof of these claims!" Garrett gestured toward her; his mouth open in disbelief as he appealed to Judge Frank. "Everything that comes out of her mouth is nothing less than an allegation. You can't try a case based on hearsay, and you know it."

Amelia squeezed her eyes shut as she forced herself to remain calm. They'd been going at it for the better part of an hour now, and she'd found Garrett to be nothing less than infuriating. Not only was he trying to be slick by slipping in witnesses who would merely muddy the waters of the case, but he also wanted to pretend like his tyrant son had a squeaky-clean past. Fixing her gaze on the judge, she focused only on him. "His reputation is renowned. The entire town knows the defendant and what he's done. They will not rest until he is locked behind bars for years to come, and the only way that will happen is if they're aware of his criminal history."

"You cannot seriously be considering this, Judge. She's talking foolishness! You can't prosecute a defendant based on past crimes!"

Judge Frank raised a brow of warning as he stared the lawyer down. "You'll do well to remember that this is my courtroom, and I will decide what will be admitted or suppressed."

Garrett gritted his teeth. "And you'll do well to remember that your courtroom is still a court of law, Clayton!"

"That's Judge Frank, Mister Cameron!" he yelled, his face burning. He couldn't wait to watch this lawyer's case fall apart.

Agitated, Garrett shifted in his seat. He'd been in Frank's courtroom many times before but had never encountered such an unreasonable roadblock as this. "Before you allow this ludicrousness to taint your reputation, Judge, I urge you to consider Johnson vs.

Mississippi 1988. Or how about Custis vs. United States 1994? Lackawanna County District Attorney vs. Coss? Shall I continue?"

Amelia pressed a hand to her temple as she watched the uncertainty flashing across the judge's face. Garrett was getting to him—she was losing the first round of this fight and was not happy. "This case is different!" she protested.

"No," Judge Frank said quietly, clasping his hands on the table. "No, it's not. He's right." His eyes settled on the prosecutor. He'd give anything to let Cameron's past crimes be on display in his courtroom, but he knew the law. If he allowed this, he was inviting the whole case to be thrown out, and that was something he could not do.

Garrett sat back in his chair and grinned. Victory tasted oh so sweet...

"Alright, Garrett," he spoke quietly, training his eyes on him. "Your suppression request is granted."

He nodded and winked at Amelia, whose cheeks flamed.

Her resolve strengthening, she decided to take a risk. "I insist on a compromise here, Judge. If you will not allow me to inform the jury of Joshua Cameron's history of violence, then I implore you to allow the suppression of certain evidence in this case that are inconclusive at best."

Garrett's jaw dropped, and his eyes flew to Frank. "What inconclusive evidence? Everything Detective Donahue brought to this investigation has been concrete!"

Judge Frank's gaze settled on the prosecutor as he waited for her to defend her appeal. He liked where this was headed—if certain evidence could be suppressed, Cameron would be convicted faster. "Madam Prosecutor?" he pressed.

Avoiding Garrett's stare, she honed in on the judge, ensuring she had his complete attention before speaking. "Detective Donahue insists that the defendant did not have access to a rope yet has failed to show evidence of this claim. On the contrary, the evidence displayed is proof that he did indeed bind the victim with rope!"

Garrett laughed and grabbed his briefcase, pulling out his evidence file. "You mean these pictures right here? The pictures that prove that the headboard in the hotel room had been switched for another one after my client had already been arrested?" He slapped the pictures on the table and shoved them toward the judge.

Judge Frank picked them up and studied them, a frown on his face. "Where's your proof the headboard was switched?"

"Right here." Garrett slid him another picture and shot a glare at Amelia.

"Your Honor, the only proof he has of this is the word of a maid who quit her job and disappeared. Her statement is null and void if she isn't here to testify!"

Frank raised a brow as he looked at Garrett. "Have you tried to find her?"

Garrett shook his head in disbelief. "She's gone. Vanished. To who knows where for who knows why. If you want my take on the matter, Nichole Sherard has something to do with one of my key witnesses disappearing into thin air, conveniently before my client's trial."

Anger brewed in his soul—not because of what the defense had said, but the contempt in which he'd said it. Telling himself to play the game of law the right way, he stared Garrett down. "No witness, no evidence. This is inadmissible in court." It brought him great pleasure to toss the pictures back at the lawyer in front of him.

"Thank you, Judge." Amelia smiled.

"This is ludicrous!" Garrett raised both hands in the air and gaped at Judge Frank. "The prosecution has failed to show why the evidence her own investigator brought her should be suppressed! As I stated, I have photographic proof, as well as witness statements that contradict the prosecutor's case against my client. To suppress these vital parts of the case is not only detrimental to my ability to defend my client but fundamentally unfair. I would go so far as to say that it borders on judicial malfeasance!"

"You are out of order, Cameron, and bordering on contempt! I agreed with your assertion that the defendant's past criminal history—including his previous assaults on this victim—cannot be introduced against him, so not prejudice the jury. However, in reference to this motion, I believe that the prosecutor has met her threshold for suppression of the provided defense evidence, and I grant her motion. None of the evidence provided by Detective Donahue shall be introduced as evidence in the trial of Joshua Cameron, except the interview of Ms. Romans."

"Unbelievable. What you're doing is illegal! You're boxing me in and making it difficult to offer my best defense for my client!"

"Tread lightly, Cameron." Judge Frank's tone was ice as he stared him down.

"I will not tread lightly, Frank—Sir—and, as a point of law, I will tread heavily right into the Judicial Boards chambers and demand that you be removed from this case on that very allegation! The prosecutor, though slip-shot as she is, is responsible for presenting a fair case for my client and maintaining a balance of justice for the victim. However, it is not the judge's job to put his finger on the scales and cause that balance to be shifted one way or the other! It is my assertion, sir, that with you presiding, that is exactly how this case will play out. As Defense, it is my sworn duty and responsibility to protect my client and ensure he gets a fair and just trial, as demanded by the Constitution. The only way I see that happening is for him to be judged by an impartial judge and jurisdiction!"

Heat shot through the judge's face as fear teased his senses. He could not allow this case to move to a new venue… "Who said anything about me being partial? You're in here throwing a fit because I won't give in to your demands. Why is that, Cameron? I'll tell you why! It's because that boy is your son. Damn me for allowing you to be his defender—you beat all, you know that? You're hot-headed, quick-tempered, ruthless, and biased. I should never have approved you as Defense."

Garrett slammed his palms down on the table and stood, reaching into his briefcase and yanking a stack of papers free. "Not partial? Not partial?" He threw a glare in the judge's direction before walking over to the court reporter. "I want this on the record—every word," he informed her before turning back to Frank and reading from the papers in his hand. "'Joshua Cameron is nothing more than a heathen. In fact, the entire town of Highshore has labeled him as such. He's the Highshore Heathen—that's who he is.'"

The judge gnawed his lip as Garrett read his own words back to him. Blast his foolishness in his chambers the other day! This was not good... If the lawyer could prove he was partial, the board was sure to listen. He had to back pedal, and fast. Leaning forward, he rolled his eyes. "You're making this a far bigger issue than it is, Cameron. The town has had its run-ins with your boy, but they're not prejudiced against him, they just don't enjoy having their cars stolen, or their neighborhood vandalized."

"Or their women raped," Amelia spat, eyes blazing.

Judge Frank threw her a glare. Was she trying to help this case move to a new venue? "Let's not be dramatic, Prosecutor. The defendant has only been accused of raping one of Highshore's women—not the whole lot of them."

"As if one is an insignificant number?" She gaped at him. As though he hadn't been interrupted, Garrett plowed right through their argument. "'Joshua Cameron is a nuisance...a menace to society. He should not be allowed to walk free in our town.'—Mayor Splendora. 'Our streets are not safe with the likes of this hoodlum roaming about. He should be locked away and the key tossed out of reach.' —Captain Holmes, Highshore P.D. 'He's a heathen. A tyrant. A thief and a rapist—no one is safe with this boy on the streets. He deserves nothing less than a beat-down and a harsh prison sentence.'—Nichole Sherard, wife of City Manager, Lance Sherard. Shall I continue?"

The judge shifted in his seat. "That's really not

necessary, Garrett. I'm sure we can come to some sort of…understanding…to keep the case at home court."

"No." Garrett laughed. "No, we really can't. We're done here, Judge. I have pressing business to tend to over at the Judicial Board."

Both the judge's and Amelia's eyes followed as Garrett packed his briefcase and stormed from the courtroom. Turning to Amelia, Frank frowned. "This is bad. This is very bad."

Chapter 36

"Shall not the Judge of all the earth do what is just?"
~Genesis 18:25b~

Two Weeks Later…
Day One of the Trial

Judge Alyjah Solomon was not a forgiving man. He upheld the law, regardless of who had broken it. Stature meant nothing to him. Age was irrelevant—the man had sent a twelve-year-old to juvie hall for petty theft when the kid had refused to show respect for his mother. Race was a non-issue. White, brown, black, yellow, or purple—if you broke the law in his town you were headed to jail. So, when Joshua Cameron's case had landed in his caseload, Judge Solomon had nothing but eye rolls for the repeat offender. His reputation was renowned across the counties sur-rounding the town of Highshore, and his rap sheet was a mile long. He remembered a fellow judge complaining about him years before, but more so, he remembered the boy's no-good defense attorney daddy. It was interesting to him that Garrett Cameron had sought to change venues from a Highshore court of law to one in Denton County, basing his appeal on the fact that his hometown was prejudiced against his client–he assumed the real reason behind this request was because the father was afraid his son would receive the sentence he deserved, instead of the one he wanted.

It was for this reason he had requested his bailiff to bring both the defense and prosecuting attorneys into his chambers before court began. He needed to ensure the two understood he wasn't the one to play with. Garrett had been in his courtroom before, but the prosecutor was new. He would not risk a trial like this without ensuring everyone was on the same page. He shifted his robe as the knock sounded at his door, calling for the bailiff to grant access to the lawyers waiting outside.

It was to Solomon's great satisfaction to watch the

tension play across Cameron's face when he stepped into his chambers and realized he was the presiding judge. Good. Let 'im sweat. Lawyers who saw themselves above the law deserved to have their feet knocked out from under them. "Come in," he called, waving them toward his desk. "Madam Prosecutor." He nodded to Amelia. "Defense." He forced back his smile when Garrett merely nodded at him.

The door opened once more, and a man rushed into the room. "My apologies, Your Honor. I was held up in traffic."

Solomon nodded at his prosecutor and waved him forward. "Madam Prosecutor, this is Prosecutor Adam Randall. He'll be sitting in for the sole purpose of aiding you should you need any assistance in our county. If you have any questions about procedure or how my courtroom works, please avail yourself to Mr. Randall–he is familiar with how I expect things to be done. Now, I won't waste your time. Let's get to the reason you're all in here. Mr. Cameron, you've defended clients in my courtroom in the past–you know how I run my court of law. You, however," he turned to Amelia, "have never prosecuted under my watch."

Garrett crossed his arms over his chest and waited for the speech he knew was coming.

"I expect you both to act like professionals in my courtroom. I won't tolerate any shouting or slick moves. I won't hesitate to throw you in contempt of court, so you play the game of law with fairness and respect. There will be no theatrics, and I will not accept any last-minute saves." His eyes locked with Garrett's. "You will address me as 'Your Honor' or 'Judge Solomon' at all times. Do you understand me, Defense? If I had been Judge Frank, I'd have tossed you in contempt the very moment you showed me a lack of respect."

Careful not to break eye contact, Garrett nodded. "Yes, Your Honor."

"Now, I have received a Freedom of Information Act

request from a local media station. I have decided to honor this request. There will be cameras in the courtroom that will be broadcasting the trial live. I expect you both to be on your best behavior. This is going out on national TV, and everyone will be privy to your actions in my courtroom. I expect you to remember that you are not in Hollywood–this is a court of law. Be professional."

"With all due respect, Your Honor, the media's presence will do nothing but add fuel to the fire already raging in my client's hometown." Garrett shifted on his feet, his arms falling to his sides. "You really want to make a show out of this?"

Solomon set his jaw. He shouldn't be surprised that Cameron was bucking him so soon in the game. He would have to put his foot down hard to remind him that he is not a judge to be played. "Do I need to remind you that this is my courtroom, and I am the one calling the shots here? The legislative board accepted your request for a change of venue. We cannot move this court anywhere the media cannot have access. You are going to have to work within the confines of my courtroom and the media. We will make sure that your client gets treated fairly and justly, but what we will not do is cater to your paranoia. Do I make myself clear?"

Biting back his response, Garrett dropped his gaze. "Yes, Your Honor."

His brow furrowed in a glare, Solomon glanced at the time and noted that it was ten minutes to ten. "Court starts promptly at ten. Do not be late–I won't tolerate tardiness. You're dismissed." He snatched up his reading glasses and placed them on the bridge of his nose before perusing a stack of papers on his desk.

"Tough judge," Amelia whispered to Garrett as they stepped into the hallway.

Not wanting to display his worry over the matter, Garrett grinned. "Buckle up–it's gonna be a bumpy ride."

Khyron checked his watch for the tenth time in five

minutes. If Garrett didn't hurry, he'd miss the opening statements of his own case. From the little he knew about Judge Solomon, he knew better than to arrive even a second late in his courtroom. With a sigh, he glanced down the hall and walked toward the lawyer.

"...getting closer to finding her then!.... Okay. ...No, it's great. Just great. I expect good results with this. Thanks!" Garrett hung up the phone and found Khyron's eyes on him.

"What was that about?"

"Nothing. Just some stuff I had to handle."

Raising a brow, Khyron threw his hands up. "Court's convening as we speak—you need to get in there before he tosses you in a cell."

"I'm right behind you," Garrett assured as he followed him down the hall.

Having Judge Solomon as the judge presented a big hurdle for Garrett's case. The judge had made no pretense in the past over his feelings toward him–in his eyes, Garrett was nothing more than a cutthroat lawyer who manipulated the law to get what he wanted. Despite that kink in his plans, selecting the jury could not have gone better. He'd cut loose anyone even remotely familiar with Josh, keeping only those who had never heard of him. Much to Amelia's chagrin, the judge had accepted the jury pool, and everyone was seated and ready to go directly after lunch, with the media set up on the sidelines.

"All rise. This court with the Honorable Judge Solomon presiding is now in session." The bailiff stood at attention, watching as the judge made his way to the bench and sat down.

Judge Solomon adjusted his glasses and took in the occupants of his courtroom. His silvery-white hair had begun its recession long ago, causing a more distinguished look that spoke of many years of wisdom. Just as he'd anticipated, the gallery was packed with citizens of Highshore—no one wanted to miss out on this high-profile case. To his right, the reporters waited to pounce as the case unfolded, each eager to soak up the drama and distribute the gossip to all who would lend an ear. He couldn't stand having reporters privy to his cases but had made the exception in light of the change of venue. Catching the defense attorney's gaze, he smiled a knowing smile when Garrett shifted in his seat. Defending his own son. Protocol? Not usually. Had the request been made directly to him, he probably wouldn't have signed off on it. But the request had been approved by Judge Frank, so he'd allowed it.

And then there was Nichole Sherard—the woman who, much like Garrett, saw herself above the law. Above justice. Above God, Himself. Her reputation preceded her wherever she went. He knew enough about her to know she was trouble, but not enough to know what to expect. This case should be interesting… "Everyone but the jury may be seated. Mr. Gilford, please swear in the jury."

"Please raise your right hand. Do you solemnly swear or affirm that you will truly listen to this case and render a true verdict and a fair sentence to this defendant?" Once he'd received the jury's "I do," the bailiff directed them to be seated.

"Mr. Gilford, proceed with the docket," Judge Solomon instructed.

"Your Honor, The State of California versus Joshua Taylor Cameron."

"Is the prosecution ready?"

The prosecutor briefly stood and sat back down. "Yes, Your Honor."

Judge Solomon nodded to Amelia. "Proceed."

Amelia stepped forward, her stride displaying her confidence; an air of justice surrounded her as she faced the jury. Eyes full of passion and fire, she began. "This case is about Joshua Cameron and how he meticulously planned the rape of Rhea Romans during the exact timing of her mother's absence. The evidence will show that Mr. Cameron manipulated the hotel staff into escorting him to

Ms. Romans' room so that there would be no mistaking which room he needed to enter."

She paused, her eyes drifting to Garrett. Clearing her throat, she raised her chin as he rested his own on his fingers. More than anything, she wished she could blast Josh's criminal history to this court, but she wouldn't dare cross that line. "You will see how he put his manipulative ways to work by listening to an overview of his history with the victim. A history filled with coercion, promises of undying love, failed attempts at taking this young woman away from the protection and care of her mother, and running off with her to keep her under his power and control. You will see how he was able to take a girl full of promise and potential and transform her into a high school dropout who lost all motivation for life. You will see how Mr. Cameron wooed her, claimed to treasure her, and then fathered her baby girl only to abandon her before the baby was even born."

"Aww, come on!" Josh exclaimed from beside his father, drawing all eyes to him. From the gallery, Elysia watched with bated breath as Garrett quickly placed a hand on his knee to silence him, but the judge leaned forward, eyes stern.

"Mr. Cameron, control your client or I will remove him from the courtroom." Judge Solomon stared Garrett down, his face hard.

"Yes, Your Honor. The defense apologizes—it won't happen again." Garrett turned to Josh and whispered, "Not a word, Josh. You have to trust me."

Josh sat back in his chair and fought the eye roll that threatened as he watched the prosecutor turn her nose up at him.

"Mr. Cameron used his power over the victim to convince her to let him into her hotel room while her mother was away. Disregarding the fact that Ms. Romans warned him of her mother's impending arrival, Mr. Cameron proceeded with his advancements upon her. He kissed her amidst her protests and forced her to stand in front of him as he touched her body. She continued to protest and ask Mr. Cameron to leave, but instead, he lifted her off her feet and carried her to the bed where he climbed on top of her and restrained her wrists with a rope."

Garrett's hand squeezed Josh's knee tight as he felt his son tense. To his left, he glimpsed Nichole's smug smile as she listened to the prosecutor's opening statement. On her right, Rhea appeared to shrink into her seat. His mind flitted to Nevaeh, and he wondered where the two had stowed his granddaughter during the trial. Was she safe? Scared? He couldn't dwell on that now. He needed his entire focus to save his son.

"Once he had her restrained, he proceeded to rape her. Ms. Romans was helplessly subjected to this man's control before her mother came home and found them. It is up to you, the jury, to remove a dangerous rapist from the streets of Highshore before he has a chance to strike again. Thank you."

From the prosecution's table, Adam Randall's eyes tracked Amelia back to her seat. She'd gone straight for the jugular and had already elicited a rise from the defendant. A smile teased the corners of his mouth as she sat beside him. This case was bound to be interesting.

"Defense? Your opening statement?" Judge Solomon's brow was raised as he watched Garrett.

"Yes, Your Honor." Garrett felt the energy pulsing through Josh's veins as he stood. Praying for strength and wisdom, he walked to the front and faced the jury.

"Good afternoon, ladies and gentlemen. Thank you for taking the time to do your civic duty by sitting in judgment on this trial." Glancing at the television cameras situated on the front row, he resolved to ignore the media altogether and focus only on getting Josh out of a prison sentence.

"The prosecution has laid out her case. She has informed you about how she will proceed, and what she hopes to achieve in this trial. As the defense, I must ensure she does her job correctly and remains fair and just when dealing with my client. As this is a sexual assault trial, you may hear some details that disturb you. This is not done to titillate or embarrass, but to uncover the truth. The only way to discover the truth is to expose every detail—no matter how painful or difficult.

"As she has stated, the prosecutor will attempt to convince you that my client planned and executed a sexual assault against the mother of his child. You will hear testimonies from various witnesses who will state that they were present at the time and will give their accounts of their involvements. You will hear the testimony of Rhea Romans, as well as the testimony of Detective Donahue, who interviewed the defendant."

Steepling his fingers beneath his chin, Garrett focused on each face in the jury. "I am speaking to a group of educated people. You all understand the concept of truth. You have all seen the law manipulated in the past and understand that just because a person testifies under oath in a court of law, this doesn't necessarily mean they are telling the truth. Every person is instilled with an ego—the imperative need to feel important, despite the cost. Sometimes, this reveals in others a specific drive to make themselves appear better than what they are."

He dropped his arms to his sides and hardened his gaze. "Joshua Cameron did not rape Rhea Romans, nor did he assault her. He loves both her and their child. The prosecution will try and convince you otherwise. They will paint him as a monster who seeks to destroy his family. However, much like egos, certain people thrive off agendas—evil agendas put in place to annihilate their objective. These people often make untrustworthy statements or claims, at best—while being downright perjury at worst."

"Objection, your Honor!" Amelia leaped to her feet. "The defense is attempting to taint the witness list before they have even had a chance to testify!"

"Mister Cameron, you are walking a fine line here."

Judge Solomon leveled a glare at Garrett.

"My apologies, Your Honor. Withdrawn." While maintaining an outward picture of humility, Garrett's heart leaped with excitement at his successful blow to Amelia's pending line of questioning.

"Objection sustained."

Josh shifted; uncomfortable the judge had been so quick to shut his father down. If this indicated how the trial would go, he was in trouble.

"Keep the faith, Josh." Khyron shuffled the stack of notes in front of him, determined to be ready at a moment's notice should his partner need him. "Garrett's drawn first blood. He's got the prosecution flustered."

Catching his wife's eye, Garrett was encouraged by the smile of approval set on her face. Having watched him in hundreds of court cases, she knew he knew exactly what he was doing.

"People with evil agendas are exactly what my client is up against today. They will do whatever is necessary to paint him in the worst light. They will refer to him as 'The Rapist' and 'The Heathen'—names created by these people with evil agendas, whose sole intent is to smear my client's reputation and try to taint him in your eyes. But I have faith that those who sit in the judgment of my client today will look past the evil and duplicity of these ego-driven people and see the truth. I believe that, by the end of this trial, we will prove, beyond any reasonable doubt, that Joshua Cameron is not guilty of the charges brought against him. Once you weigh the witness statements against the evidence, you will see that the only crime that was committed on the day in question is the fabrication of a scene and circumstances perpetrated, orchestrated, and executed by, not only the witnesses on the scene, but also by some of the law enforcement officers who were primary at the time of arrest.

"It is up to you to determine fact from fiction—to sift through these accounts and discover the truth from the lies. So, bear with us as we make this journey toward the truth.

Thank you."

"Prosecution, you may call your first witness." Judge Solomon clasped his hands as he waited.

"Yes, your Honor," Amelia stood. "I call Mr. Donny Chu to the stand."

Garrett studied the pimple-faced boy who seemed to tremble the entire way to the witness stand. "This ought to be interesting." He smirked as the kid was sworn in.

"State your full name for the record," Amelia instructed him.

"M-m-my name is Donny Lawrence Chu." He swiped a hand across his sweaty brow, casting a nervous glance at the judge before his gaze swung to Josh and bounced to his lap.

Unphased by the fact that her first witness was melting into a puddle of fear, Amelia pressed forward. "Please tell the jury where you currently work, Mr. Chu."

"Seascape Hotel...ma'am." He nodded to her.

"What position do you hold?"

"Concierge."

"Were you working on May 23rd, 2019?"

"Yes, ma'am."

"On the day in question, do you recall talking with the defendant, Joshua Cameron?"

"Yes, ma'am."

"Is that same man in the courtroom this morning and, if so, can you identify him to the court?"

Donny shifted in his seat, his eyes drifting to Josh.

"Yes, ma'am. He's sitting at that table." He pointed.

"Thank you. Let the record show that the witness identified the defendant as the person to whom he spoke on the morning of May 23rd, 2019." Amelia looked at the judge.

"Show reflected." Solomon nodded.

"Mr. Chu, at approximately what time did you have contact with Mr. Cameron?" Amelia carefully watched him, hiding her irritation when he hesitated. She'd thoroughly prepared him for this—had even told him he wasn't needed for much more than an opening voice—yet he sat in front of her and trembled like a leaf.

"Uh, about ten...maybe ten-fifteen that morning." Donny swiped a hand across his brow and adjusted the glasses sliding down his nose.

"Please tell the jury about your interaction with him."

"He, um, he was asking for a guest by the name of Rhea Romans."

"Did he ask for her room number?"

"Yes."

"Did you give it to him?" Amelia worked to keep her tone even.

"I didn't get the chance. My manager cut in and told me not to answer." Donny's gaze swung to Cali, who was the picture of calm.

"Oh? Why would she do that?"

"Uh, I don't...I don't really know. Ms. Bristol isn't in the habit of explaining herself to others. Ma'am."

"Thank you, Mr. Chu. That will be all." Amelia returned to her seat, keeping her eyes on her notes.

"Defense, care to cross?" Judge Solomon looked at Garrett.

"Yes, Your Honor." Garrett strode to the witness stand and smiled at the young man. "Mr. Chu, had you met Mr. Cameron before the incident?"

"No, sir," he squeaked.

"Please describe his behavior toward you that day."

"His, um, behavior?"

"Yes. Did he seem to be angry or anxious? Was he calm? Belligerent?"

"Uh...I mean...he seemed fine...he wasn't mad or mean or anything–at least, not to me."

Garrett raised a brow. "Was he mad or mean toward anyone else?"

Donny's eyes drifted to Cali, and he swallowed hard. "Well, no, but he did kinda get angry when Ms. Bristol stepped in."

"But not before Ms. Bristol stepped in," Garrett

clarified. "And never with you."

"No, sir. He was cool with me."

"Thank you, Mr. Chu. No further questions."

"Redirect?" Solomon asked Amelia.

"None at this time."

"Mr. Chu, you may step down. Prosecution, call your next witness."

"I call Ms. Cali Bristol to the stand." Amelia stood and walked toward the witness stand as Cali made her way forward.

"Raise your right hand," the bailiff instructed Cali. "Do you swear that the evidence you shall give to the court in this matter shall be the truth, the whole truth, and nothing but the truth, so help you God?"

"I do," Cali answered solemnly, pulling the long black cardigan she wore tighter around her body before taking the stand.

Josh's eyes narrowed as he watched her. Anger brewed in his veins when she made eye contact with him as she took her seat and flipped her hair for the cameras.

"State your name for the record."

"Cali Bristol."

"Ms. Bristol, your father owns the Seascape Hotel, correct?" Amelia asked.

"Yes."

"Were you working on May 23rd, 2019, the morning when one of your guests was assaulted in her room?"

"Objection!" Garrett slapped a hand down on the table. "Foundation, Your Honor."

"Sustained. Build your case, Prosecutor."

Clasping her hands behind her back, Amelia offered a tight smile. "Yes, Your Honor." She refocused on Cali, putting Garrett out of her mind. "Were you working the day that Joshua Cameron came into the hotel looking for Rhea Romans?"

"I was."

"Tell us about your encounter with the defendant."

"Sure. Josh demanded that I tell him Rhea's room

number, but I refused to give it to him."

"Why did you refuse?"

Her brows shot up. "Because I'm not a complete idiot, that's why. I knew why he was there."

"Objection—opinion," Garrett locked eyes with the judge.

"Sustained. Ms. Bristol, keep your statements to known facts."

Offering him an apologetic smile, she continued. "When I intercepted him, he was already getting angry with me. He even called me a 'golden spoon' when he found out who my father was. He was demanding her room number from me and, when I refused, he said, and I quote, 'Give me the number, or I swear I'll knock on every door until I find her.' You have to understand—my daddy's the owner of this hotel. I cannot allow anyone to disturb the guests, so I had no choice but to lead him to her."

"Oohhh, that girl!" Laura whispered furiously, but Levi paid her no attention. His gaze was focused on Cali. There was something strange about her mannerisms on the stand.

Sitting back in his chair, he took in the way she avoided looking at Amelia when answering questions. Who was she looking at? He angled his body forward, his eyes tracking hers. He frowned when he spotted Nichole's smug smile as she stared back at the witness. "What are you up to?" he whispered.

Amelia paced the floor in front of the witness stand. "Did you take Mr. Cameron directly to Ms. Romans' room?"

"No. I didn't have the chance. My brother heard him yelling at me and got involved."

"Did Mr. Cameron back off?"

"No." Cali's eyes drifted to Nichole before turning her attention to Josh as she spoke her next words. "My brother came tearing over to where we were, bowing up at Josh like he was going to fight him. I told him to let me handle it, and that's when Josh said 'Better listen to that sister of yours. You don't look like you'd handle a beating too well, pretty boy.'"

Garrett's eyes cut to his son, who shifted beneath his gaze, confirming Cali's statement.

"Did the two get into an altercation?" Amelia asked.

"No, but they would have if I hadn't stopped them. I told my brother to stay in the lobby and pulled Josh to the elevator."

"Did the two of you have a conversation in the elevator?"

"Yes."

"Please tell the jury about the conversation you had."

Cali's eyes never left Josh's face. "He was a black and blue mess when he came in that day—much like he is now." She gestured toward him. "When I asked him about it, he got really defensive. That made me super nervous because it was just us on the elevator, and I didn't want to be next, you know?"

"What do you mean by you 'didn't want to be next?'"

Cali dropped her eyes to her hands. "I had been dating his best friend before all this went down. The two had been at odds with one another—I knew Josh had been fighting with Jordan."

"Objection—lack of personal knowledge, Your Honor," Garrett protested.

"Sustained. Ms. Bristol, stick to the facts you've witnessed or have firsthand knowledge of." Judge Solomon settled his gaze on her, brows knit.

"Please tell the jury what happened next," Amelia urged.

"I told him to forget I'd asked—again, I didn't want to be next. The elevator stopped on Rhea's floor, and when the doors opened, I went to get off but he blocked me."

"He blocked you? From leaving the elevator?"

Levi's jaw tensed as he watched the hand signals fly from Nichole, wishing he could speak with Garrett and warn him about the exchange.

"That's right. He said, 'That's far enough. Tell me her

room number.' I told him to move and I'd take him straight there, but he refused and repeated himself. He said, 'Room number. Now.' I didn't appreciate his tone and was honestly scared for Rhea at this point, so I challenged him and asked, 'And if I don't?'" She stopped, her face paling.

"What was his answer?" Amelia asked, her eyes imploring.

"He said, 'I've already been in jail today. I've got no problem going right back in.'"

Garrett's jaw set, knowing Amelia would be all over this statement.

"Dad?" Josh quietly asked, his eyes studying his father.

"It's okay," he whispered back. "It's about to get ugly, but I've got you."

"Did you see this as a threat?" Amelia asked.

"Yes! That guy is dangerous! I wanted no part of his anger." Cali glanced at Josh before her gaze darted away.

"Ms. Bristol, has the defendant ever been violent with you?"

"Yes."

"Please tell the jury of any violence you've witnessed from the defendant."

"The first time I met him, he got all bent out of shape over me drinking a beer. Like, why should he even care what I drink? It's none of his business! But, whatever." She shrugged. "I didn't like him from the start. He had his best friend all tense any time he was near. Jordan had to walk on eggshells whenever he was around. I found him to be really controlling."

Josh squeezed his right hand into a tight fist beneath the table. He hated that girl. What did she know, anyway?

"Controlling how?"

"Well, like right before he came over, Jordan and I were grilling out and just having fun, drinking—something we had started doing together all the time." Her eyes went to Jordan and she pulled her cardigan tighter around her, her fingers playing with the fabric. "Jordan got a call from this guy, telling him he was coming over and he, like…freaked out and started hiding all the beer in the fridge. Who does that? Anyways, Josh got to the apartment and Jordan was all on edge. I went to shower, and when I got out, I wasn't wearing much—sorry, Judge—" She glanced at him before continuing. "I was headed to the kitchen, and this guy touched my butt as I passed—really freaked me out!"

Josh's jaw dropped. She was the one who'd bumped into him! He gritted his teeth as she continued.

"That's when I went and grabbed a beer from the fridge. I offered him one and he yanked it out of my hand and threw it across the room, shattering the bottle in a million pieces all over the floor, then the dude just stomped away and left!"

"Were you frightened?"

"Not nearly as frightened as I was the second time I saw him."

Garrett watched in amazement as her lower lip quivered. This girl had no shame…

"Describe the second incident."

"Jordan and I were invited to dinner at his parents' house—where he is staying." She pointed a finger at Josh. "Well," she laughed, "where he was staying before he ended up in a jumpsuit."

"Young lady, I'm going to remind you one time, and one time only, that you are in court." Judge Solomon stared her down.

Cali's eyes flew to Nichole's red face, and she ducked her head and submitted. "Yes, sir. We went to dinner, and Josh was there. He wouldn't even eat with us because Jordan wasn't doing what he wanted him to do, so he was mad. I said something he didn't like, and Josh came after me and shoved me really hard. It hurt pretty bad and I was super scared—it even scared Jordan. Jordan pulled me out of the house and down the driveway; we were trying to get to the truck before Josh could get to me because he kept chasing us. So, Jordan was trying to protect me, and he and Josh got into a fight and Jordan shoved him. Josh decked him on the jaw and then things really got crazy out there. Josh started punching and punching and punching—my head was literally inches from his fist. He was slamming Jordan's truck over and over and screaming his head off. I was so scared; all I could do was jump in the truck and scream for Jordan to get me out of there. I broke up with him right after that—I can't date someone who hangs out with crazy people, you know?"

"That sounds terrifying," Amelia agreed. "Have you had any further encounters with the accused?"

Cali stared at Josh, noting the way he shifted beneath her gaze. "No. I've stayed far away from him since then."

Amelia smiled. "No further questions, Your Honor."

"Defense, cross?" Judge Solomon looked at Garrett, his brow raised expectantly.

Eyes downcast, Garrett scribbled on his notepad. "No, Your Honor. Request to recall the witness at a later time."

"Alright, Ms. Bristol, you may step down. Prosecutor, call your next witness."

Josh watched as Cali stepped down, shock dancing across his features. Was his father seriously letting this go? Some defense he was. He shifted in his seat and leaned close to Garrett's ear. "What're you doin', man? She blasted me up there! That attorney is gonna put me away based on Cali's statements alone!"

Garrett finished writing the note he'd begun, not bothering to look up at his son. "I've gotten five people off murder charges in my career. Three of them were facing death row." His eyes met Josh's, and he raised a brow, his gaze steady. "I've got you, son. Trust me. Please."

Shaking his head, Josh sat back hard in his chair as Amelia called Zion to the stand.

After corroborating the details given by the concierge and Cali, Zion was dismissed without further questioning from either lawyer.

"Madam Prosecutor, call your next witness," Solomon instructed.

"Your Honor, I call Jordan Hendricks to the stand."

Amelia's eyes cut to Garrett, a smile teasing her lips at the frustration sparking across his features.

The color drained from his face as Josh watched his best friend get sworn in before taking the stand to testify against him. "Dad, why Jordan?"

"You beat the crap out of him, kid," Garrett whispered. "She's going to paint you as a violent offender."

Josh sat back in his chair, worry teasing his brow. The jury would eat this up–no one would believe he hadn't hurt Rhea after hearing Jordan's testimony.

"State your name for the record," Amelia directed. Her chin went up a notch, and her eyes narrowed as she prepared for battle.

"Jordan Hendricks." Jordan tossed his chin up in response, his gaze telling her to bring it on. Out of the corner of his eye, he caught sight of Rachel in the middle of the media—notepad in hand—and his brows furrowed into a glare.

"Mr. Hendricks, what is your relationship to the victim?"

Jordan shrugged. "We've been friends since the eighth grade."

"And your relationship to the accused?"

"You mean to Josh?" Jordan quipped; his stare unfaltering. "He's my best friend."

"How long have you known the accused?" Amelia annunciated the last word as she hardened her gaze.

"Man, like…fifteen, sixteen years? Long time."

"I see. To your knowledge, were the victim and the accused ever in a romantic relationship with one another?"

Jordan shifted in his seat, leaning back slightly. "He has a name, okay? His name is Josh—not 'the accused.'"

Josh smiled, grateful to have Jordan defending him on the stand.

"To answer your question, you already know they were together." Jordan looked to Rhea, then to Josh, before shrugging his shoulders. "For all I know, they're still together. Josh was smitten with Rhea from the first time he saw her."

Sterling reached for Rhea's hand, threatened by Jordan's statement. "I love you," he whispered near her ear, frowning when she pulled her hand away.

"Define 'smitten.' Would you say he was obsessed with her?" Amelia asked.

"No, lady." Jordan rolled his eyes. "Just normal teenage smitten. Let's not be dramatic here." He felt Rachel's eyes on him but refused to acknowledge her presence.

"Did the accused discuss their romance with you?"

"Josh and I are best friends. We've always told each other everything."

"How did he describe their first sexual encounter?"

Jordan's eyes narrowed. "Did you talk about your first sexual encounter with others?"

A murmur went up from the gallery and Judge Solomon smacked the gavel. "The witness will answer the question."

Jordan sighed and cast an apologetic look at Josh, grieved over having to put his business out in the open for examination. "He was excited. Said he'd never been with anyone like her. He told me he believed Rae was the one for him."

"'The one for him.' So, after having been with her only once, he declared her to be his own."

"That's not what I said," Jordan snapped. "You're twisting my words."

Amelia only smiled. "Their 'bond' didn't last quite as long as he'd hoped, did it?"

"You don't know what you're talking about." He worked his jaw, his eyes searing into hers.

"Do you recall, when Mr. Cameron was barely seventeen years old, he ran away from home?"

Jordan looked at Josh, his heart constricting. "I will never forget that day."

"But she forgot that day, didn't she?"

Sterling ran a hand down his face when Rhea tensed

beside him. Why was she insisting on clinging to this guy?

Amelia didn't wait for a reply. "Joshua was away for four years, is that correct?"

"Yes."

"Would you say it's normal to run away from someone you love?"

Jordan's gaze flew to Garrett, a cry for help dancing in his eyes.

Forcing a smile, Garrett gestured for him to stay calm.

"He didn't run away from Rhea. He ran away from…other things."

"Were you aware that Ms. Romans fell in love with another man during Joshua's absence?"

Jordan watched the color drain from Josh's face. Ducking his head, he kept his voice low. "No. Rae and I lost touch a long time ago."

"I see."

But the look in her eyes told him she didn't believe him.

"Did you have any contact with Joshua during his absence?"

"Not until his last week out there."

"Would you say he was different when he came back home?" Amelia glanced at her notes.

Jordan stared, his mind working to figure out her angle. "The guy was away from all his friends and family for four years. What do you think?"

Amelia locked eyes with him before turning to the judge. "Permission to treat the witness as hostile, Your Honor."

"Permission granted," the judge answered.
Determined to uncover the truth she was seeking, she refocused on Jordan. "Isn't it true that the accused has a reputation of having a volatile temper?"

Jordan shifted, not liking where this was going. "I guess."

"Yes or no, please."

"Yes." He sighed.

"Isn't it also true that Joshua Cameron often becomes violent when angry?"

Jordan glared. "Yes."

"What happened to your nose?" Amelia asked, feeling the smile threaten her lips.

Levi pressed a hand to his eyes. Beside him, Laura sat on the edge of her seat as she watched the exchange.

"I broke it," Jordan evaded.

"Please tell the jury how you broke your nose."

"Objection, relevance?" Garrett threw in, knowing the judge would allow it.

"Objection overruled. The witness will answer the question."

"I got into a fight with Josh, and he broke it."

"Are you afraid of him?"

Jordan scoffed. "Of course not. I deserved what I got."

Amelia stared at him a moment before turning to face the judge. "Your Honor, we submit People's exhibit #6 to be placed into evidence. A photo taken of Mr. Hendricks' injuries."

Solomon took the photo from her outstretched hand and looked it over. Nodding, he handed it back to her.

Passing the exhibit to Garrett, Amelia waited as he glanced at the photo and handed it back, but not before Josh caught a glimpse of the judgment heading his way.

Josh shifted in his seat, his knee bouncing in nervous rhythm as he waited to learn his fate.

"We object, on the grounds that this evidence is inflammatory and has no direct bearing on this case," Garrett contested.

"Your Honor, the prosecution aims to show a pattern of violence and abuse that the defendant had blatantly shown against someone whom he claims to be his best friend." Amelia's eyes held a flash of intolerance. Garrett Cameron would not show her up in this case. She would strike him down, regardless of cost.

"Objection overruled. Exhibit #6 is admitted." Judge Solomon ordered, holding a hand up to stop further protest from the defense. "Not a word. Proceed, Madam Prosecutor."

Placing the exhibit beneath the projector, Amelia turned to the jury and clicked the remote. A grotesque picture of Jordan in the hospital filled the screen, and the jury gasped at the sight. "Ladies and gentlemen, let the record show that this picture was taken the same day that the accused attacked this witness and left him half-dead in an airport."

Murmurs of shock exploded from the gallery as the jury stared at the picture and soaked up what they had just heard.

Josh ran a hand down his face as several shot him cold glares. "Dad?" he whispered.

Garrett didn't answer. His pen flew across his notepad, jaw tensed.

"No more questions, Your Honor." Amelia returned to her seat, feeling confident the jury was on her side.

"Cross?" Judge Solomon called.

"Yes, Your Honor." Garrett rose and went to the stand, his face a portrait of calm.

"You stated that you are the defendant's best friend, is this correct?"

"Yes, sir." Relief flooded Jordan as Garrett took over his questioning.

"Describe your relationship with the defendant."

"Josh and I used to do everything together. Told each other everything. We were in the same school, same class, and lived right across a field from each other for most of our childhoods."

"Have there been ups and downs between you two?" Garrett asked.

"Of course. We're both really stubborn and don't always see eye to eye."

"Did you see eye to eye the day Josh broke your nose?"

Jordan stared at him, doubt clouding his eyes. "No," he answered slowly, his gaze drifting to the cameras.

"What was the fight about?" Garrett kept his eyes on Jordan, though he knew the boy was growing uncomfortable.

A sigh escaped his lips as he looked at Josh. "I came between him and his kid. He saw me as a threat to her safety and he pummeled me to protect her."

"Do you feel that he was warranted to do so, as a father?"

"A father does what it takes to protect his kid. Josh thought I was going to rip Nevaeh away from him and walk her into danger. So, yeah. He was justified." Jordan's jaw tensed.

"Do you have any hard feelings toward him over the fight?"

"No. He did what he thought he had to do," he stated firmly.

"Do you trust Josh?"

"Absolutely."

"Even after the fight?"

"Yes."

"What makes you trust him?"

"Because I know he has my back, no matter what," Jordan said, his gaze unwavering.

"Has Josh ever stood up for you, physically or verbally?" Garrett crossed his arms in front of his chest.

Jordan breathed a laugh. "Man, he was always standing up for me in school. Defending me against all kinds of bullies."

"Would you say the same is true about him and the alleged victim?"

"No doubt. No one crossed Rhea without dealing with Josh first."

"Did you hang around with Ms. Romans and the defendant when they were dating?"

"All the time."

"Have you ever seen the defendant act possessively over her?" Garrett asked.

"Never."

"Was there ever a time in their relationship when you would have described Ms. Romans as being afraid of

Josh?" Garrett raised his brow, placing his pen beneath his chin.

"Never. Rhea loves him. All she's ever wanted was to be with him." Jordan's face displayed the conviction of his statement.

"She loves him, as in, presently?"

Jordan laughed. "Of course. I saw them not too long ago. She sneaked over and met him at the edge of my parents' property. There was no fear in her eyes. Only passion."

Sterling's eyes shot to Nichole, and he frowned. So, it was true. He hadn't wanted to believe it when she'd told him. He glanced at Rhea, pained to find her gaze on Josh.

"Interesting," Garrett commented. "Mr. Hendricks, do you see the defendant as a threat to you or anyone else?"

"He's only a threat to people who threaten those he loves."

"If you were to compare Josh's behavior four years ago with his behavior today, would you say his behavior has changed?"

"No doubt. He's calmer, happier, and more responsible. He's working hard at becoming the father his daughter needs him to be. He's building relationships with new people, and mending relationships with people from his past."

"Clarifying, you do not see Joshua Cameron as a threat to society? To Highshore?" Garrett asked.

"Absolutely not." Jordan looked at the media, wanting Josh's hometown to recognize the sincerity in his tone.

"No further questions, Your Honor." Garrett returned to his table, knowing the picture of Jordan would go much farther with the jury than the testimony they'd just heard.

"Prosecutor, care to redirect?" Solomon asked with his eyes on Amelia.

"Yes, Your Honor." Amelia walked to the stand and leveled Jordan with her gaze. "Mr. Hendricks, did you see the defendant on the day of the assault?"

Jordan shifted, nervous at what he might be walking

Josh into by his answer. "Uh…no. I didn't."

"So, you cannot say what his mindset was that day?" A smile stretched across her lips as she waited for his response. He was no match for her, this cocky little nobody.

"No, but based on my past experiences—"

"No further questions. The witness may be excused." Amelia turned on her heel, knowing full well she'd left him with his mouth hanging open.

"You may step down, Mr. Hendricks," Judge Solomon instructed. Looking at Amelia over his wire-rimmed glasses, he nodded. "Prosecution, you may call your next witness."

"Yes, Your Honor," Amelia stood. "I call Mrs. Nichole Sherard to the stand."

Garrett watched as she was sworn in, excitement dancing in his veins. He couldn't wait until it was his turn with her—he had every intention of serving her to the jury on a silver platter.

"State your full name for the record," Amelia instructed. The picture of a distraught mother eaten up by worry for her child, Nichole began her charade. "Nichole Claire Sherard."

"Mrs. Sherard, what is your relation to the victim?"

"I am her mother."

"You were the one who found the accused with your daughter on the day of the alleged rape, correct?"

Nichole stiffened, her eyes suddenly moist. "Yes."

"Tell the court about that day." Amelia strove to keep her voice even and calm, not wanting to upset the mother.

Dabbing at her eyes as she glanced at the cameras, Nichole answered. "I bailed Joshua out of jail that morning to discuss custody of my granddaughter with him. My driver and I picked him up, and I attempted to broach the subject, but he was belligerent. He refused to listen and was unreasonable when it came to my request."

Josh gritted his teeth, his right fist opening and closing at his side.

Garrett glanced at him and smiled. "It's fine. She's only hanging herself."

"You've done nothing to defend me so far—why should I trust what you say?" he spat under his breath. Swallowing his response, Garrett prayed for God to open his son's eyes to the truth.

"I simply wanted to reason with the boy and have him realize just how unfit he is to raise a child. When I saw that I was getting nowhere with him, I took him to my hotel to see if he would talk to my daughter. I was praying that she would talk some sense into his head. My driver parked at the hotel, and I told Josh to consider talking to her about signing custody over. He got angry with me, leaped out of the car, and tore through the parking lot like a madman."

"Oh, please." Josh rolled his eyes.

Nichole glanced at the cameras before swinging her gaze to Josh, her eyes boring into him. "I thought he'd decided to ignore me and go back to wherever hoodlums like him stay. I told my driver to take me to the farmer's market. While there, I ran into Captain Holmes. I asked him if he had time to come by the hotel and retrieve a file I needed to get to my husband—he often works directly with Lance. He agreed, so we headed to the hotel. I unlocked the door and heard noises inside—like muffled screams. The captain had heard them too and moved me aside to rush into the room before me in case something was wrong." She paused and sniffed, her eyes scrunching as the tears flowed.

"When he went into the room, I was right behind him, and I saw that boy on top of my baby in her bed. It was awful," she cried, pointing a finger at Josh. "Rhea was pinned beneath him, her wrists were tied to the bedposts. Her face…she was so scared…she looked at me and cried out 'Mama!' as the captain pulled that awful boy off my baby. I ran to her and pulled the ropes off her wrists. I could feel him watching me, and I knew he was wishing he could do to me what he'd just done to her."

"Objection, speculation!" Garrett could not hold back his eye roll as he looked at Nichole—as if his son would ever touch that woman.

"Sustained. Strike that comment from the record." Judge Solomon refocused on Amelia and nodded.

Satisfaction warmed Nichole's soul as she took in Garrett's agitated features. Score one for the master manipulator, and zero for the pathetic lawyer dad. So, they'd stricken her statement—no matter. Her words would forever be burned into the minds of the jury.

"Were you surprised to find the accused in the room with your daughter?"

"Yes!" Nichole placed a hand on her chest, eyes wide. "Rhea had been on a good path before this. She was dating a lawyer—a man of morals! Now she's so damaged and confused, she doesn't know what to think! When I left her in the hotel room, I assumed she was completely safe from harm—she was calm and watching a television program while sipping a cup of tea. Never in my wildest dreams did I suspect this boy would slip into her room while I was out."

From the gallery, Titus watched Josh's shoulders tense and prayed fervently for God to intervene.

"Mrs. Sherard, is it true that you have quite a history with the accused?" Amelia asked.

"Yes. It is true." Nichole dabbed at her mascara-laden eyes, her bright-red nail polish reflecting the light in the room. "It's been awful. Just awful."

"Oh, give me a break," Elysia muttered under her, her eyes searing into Nichole. "This woman, I swear!"

"Please tell the court about your history with the accused." Amelia began to pace in front of the stand.

"It all started when my husband decided to move us to Highshore. I fought it, but Lance was adamant, so I gave in. Rhea was already a fragile creature when we moved here—severely damaged by her father's abandonment."

Judge Solomon watched as Rhea crossed her arms and raised a stubborn chin. She was not happy with her mother for putting her on blast.

"When she started school here, she was placed in Highshore School—it's a combined middle and high school. At first, it was fine—no issues; but then she started coming home talking about this older boy she'd noticed and how he was 'just so dreamy.'"

Josh rolled his eyes and shifted in his seat. Rhea was not one to swoon, by any means.

"Before I realized what was happening, she was home less and less—always wanting to be with him. I started to worry because he showed signs of a bad reputation. I began to pay close attention to the others in town, noting how they all seemed to sense something was wrong with that boy. Lance would come home with stories of him being arrested for vandalism and auto theft, and this caused me to fear for my daughter's safety."

"Objection—priors are inadmissible." Garrett threw up his hand, his eyes fixed on the judge.

"Sustained. Strike that from the record." Solomon threw a warning look at Amelia, whose features were tight as she nodded.

"Did you take measures to keep Rhea away from the accused during her high school years?" Amelia asked.

"I tried my best," Nichole cried, her eyes on her daughter. "But Rhea was such a foolish girl and would never listen to anything I said! She told me I would never keep her away from him and that she didn't care if I died trying."

Rhea stared in disbelief as her mother succumbed to her tears. If she were a lawyer, she'd object to every word spoken by her insane parent. Glancing at Josh, she wished she could see his face and gauge how he was holding up. She rubbed her arms as she imagined his hatred toward her. If only he knew…

"Were you able to keep her away from him?"

Nichole scoffed, wiping her eyes. "No. I found out they were sneaking behind my back every chance they got!"

"How did you find that out?"

"It was all over the girl's face every time she came home from school," Nichole commented bitterly. "She made it clear that my thoughts on the matter were irrelevant, and she would be with him regardless of my opinion. I was so scared for her!"

"How old was she when they first had sex?"

Nichole stiffened, her eyes shooting daggers at Josh, who merely raised his chin and smiled coldly. "Fourteen or fifteen," she bit through grit teeth. "He took her virginity from her, like the monster he is."

"You strongly believe the accused raped your daughter back then as well, don't you?"

"Objection, leading the witness," Garrett countered.

"Sustained. Counselor, rephrase."

"Yes, Your Honor. Mrs. Sherard, did Rhea tell you she had consensual sex with the defendant?"

"No."

"What exactly did she say had happened?"

"She told me Joshua had pressured and coerced her into having sex with him, and that he'd told her if she ever told me what had happened, he would make her regret it." Nichole glanced at Josh, hiding her pleasure when his jaw tensed at her lies.

"Objection, hearsay!" Heat rushed the back of Garrett's neck as he leaned forward on his table.

"Your Honor, I intend to ask the same question to the victim, to confirm the statement," Amelia appealed to the judge.

"Objection overruled. The statement will stand."

"Mrs. Sherard, did you prosecute when you'd discovered what happened?"

Nichole scoffed and sat back, her red-stained lips parting. "You do realize that lawyer over there is his daddy, right? Garrett Cameron was all over it—conspiring with others to cover up what his awful son did to my daughter."

A low murmur rippled through the gallery.

"Conspiring with whom?"

"The police! There is a group of officers on the force in Highshore who are as crooked as they come! Horrid men who just laid down and did whatever that man told them to, simply because they knew he would get them off in court if they needed him! Disgraceful!"

"So, you never got justice for Rhea," Amelia commented. "Is it true that the accused ran away from home the same night he got caught with her?"

"Yes, it's true," Nichole seethed. "He knew if I found him, I'd have his head!"

Josh smirked. He'd never feared this woman's wrath a day in his life. She'd been small potatoes in his world—until now.

"Did you have a sense of relief when he ran away? Think your worries were over?"

"Absolutely. I couldn't have been happier when I found out he'd run. My daughter was still with me. She was safe. She was so depressed when he left—I had to put her in therapy to get the girl back to her normal self!"

Judge Solomon looked at Rhea, curious when her jaw dropped. He then watched Josh arch a brow in disbelief, and he knew in his gut this woman was lying. Turning his attention back to Nichole, he stared hard at her face, intent on understanding the motivation behind her lies.

"Your Honor, I'd like to present People's Evidence #20." Amelia pulled some papers from her briefcase and handed them to the judge. Once he and Garrett approved, she passed it to Nichole.

"Is this a copy of the therapist's report for Rhea?"

Nichole nodded. "It is. See where he declared her to be 'emotionally unstable?' That's what that boy did to my girl. He ruined her."

"If the jury will direct their attention to the large screen…" Amelia clicked the remote in her hand and the file filled the screen. She watched as the jury scrutinized the details on the document, including the doctor's name, the date, and the.

Tears sprang to Rhea's eyes. It was a fake. Her mother

had never taken her to therapy. The extent to which she would go to prove a lie was ridiculous.

"Rhea had a child as a result of her sexual encounter with the accused, correct?" Amelia's heart panged as the mother's eyes filled with fresh tears.

"She did. The child is three years old now. I don't even know her." She sniffed. "Rhea refused to even look at her when she was born. Gave her up on the spot! I never had a chance to get to know my granddaughter."

A hush fell like a wet blanket in the courtroom as the gallery processed the empathy tugging at their souls.

"That dirty heathen," Nichole suddenly shouted, pointing a finger at Josh, "has no business walking free in society! I will do whatever I can to make sure that my daughter is protected from this rapist!"

"Objection!"

"He's a degenerate! Nothing less than a troublemaker!" she continued, her face fiery red.

"Objection, Your Honor! These wild statements are prejudicial to my client and outside the parameters of the pretrial motion!" Garrett leaped to his feet, adrenaline pulsing through him.

"Sustained!" Judge Solomon slammed his gavel, but Nichole was not deterred.

Standing and facing off with Garrett, she raged. "He's nothing but a thug and a con—"

"Enough!" Judge Solomon slammed the gavel four times, fury burning in his eyes.

Nichole shut up, her eyes falling to the ground as the court stared at her in shock.

"You say one more word and I will jail you for contempt!" Solomon yelled.

Nichole sat down hard.

"Madam Prosecutor, do you have any more questions for this unruly witness?!" Solomon demanded.

Stunned, Amelia stared at Nichole. She'd had it in the bag. The conviction had been hers for the taking, and Nichole had ruined everything!

"Prosecutor!" Judge Solomon prompted.

"No, Your Honor."

"This court is adjourned for recess. Defense retains the right to cross-examine upon our return, but if your behavior hasn't improved, Mrs. Sherard, I will have you hauled out of my courtroom in a gag and chains. Do you understand?"

"Yes, Your Honor," Nichole quietly agreed.

Solomon slammed the gavel and abandoned his seat, leaving the court to find their own way out.

Chapter 37

"Though I walk in the midst of trouble, you preserve my life; you stretch out your hand against the wrath of my enemies, and your right hand delivers me."
~Psalm 138:7~

Judge Solomon's courtroom was far from calm once the court reconvened from lunch. The gallery was alive with furious whispering as the spectators discussed the case while waiting for the judge to appear, each one certain of their assumption regarding the verdict at the end of the trial. Some of their whisperings rose to a roar behind the council table where Garrett sat—their accusations and prejudices against Josh painting horrid pictures of his supposed sins. That was okay with him—let them speculate. They didn't know what he knew. No one in this court knew what he knew—and he intended to keep it that way, regardless of the fury burning his son alive right beside him.

"Did you eat?" he casually asked him.

Josh cut his eyes at him and glared. "Would you have eaten if two towns wanted to watch you hang for something you didn't do?"

Garrett smiled…and prayed for his boy. This was his fault—he knew that. But he intended to right his wrongs here in this room, with the whole world watching. His gaze drifted to the cameras, and he gave them a small wave and a nod. Might as well let the city of Highshore know he was aware of their judgments. He couldn't wait to waltz his freed son back into the town, head held high as they threw out humble apologies for judgments far too harsh.

His eyes trained on the door to the judge's chambers, he nodded at Khyron when it creaked open and the judge walked in. "You ready?" he asked.

"She doesn't stand a chance," Khyron grinned, obeying the bailiff when he commanded them to rise.

"Defense, do you care to cross-examine Mrs. Sherard?" Judge Solomon asked before he was even fully seated.

"No, Your Honor. Request to recall the witness." Garrett kept his eyes on the judge, though he was aware of the shock rippling through the courtroom like seismic waves.

"What are you playing at, Garrett?" Nichole hissed beneath her breath as she watched him. She'd prepared for his cross-examination during the recess, yet there he sat, as though he couldn't care less whether he examined her. He'd hardly done anything to defend his son, and they were well into the trial.

Her eyes narrowed as the judge ordered Amelia to call her next witness. She knew one thing: Garrett wasn't stupid—he was up to something. What bothered her the most was that she couldn't pinpoint what. However, he did have something stacked against him. She elbowed Rhea in the ribs and pointed at Josh, leaning into her daughter's ear. "He's furious. We've got this in the bag, Darling. That boy will snap on his father any moment—mark my words."

Overhearing her remark, Sterling hoped she was right. He frowned at the fear on Rhea's face and knew she was hoping the exact opposite was true.

"I call Captain Asher Holmes to the stand, Your Honor."

Nichole's gaze shot to the man as he stood, watching him like a hawk as he was sworn in. She had to be ready. She could not lose her focus.

"Please state your full name and position," Amelia instructed.

"Asher Holmes—captain of the Detective Bureau in Highshore," Asher answered, keeping his eyes fixed on the defense attorney.

"Captain Holmes, were you the arresting officer when the defendant was taken into custody on May 23rd, 2019?"

"I was."

"Please tell the courtroom about that day."

He shifted in his seat, his eyes locking with Garrett's for the briefest moment before bouncing to Nichole. "I had planned to meet with the city manager for lunch when I ran into his wife at the farmer's market. She told me she had some papers he needed to sign, but didn't have time to run them out there herself. She asked me if I'd mind swinging by her hotel and grabbing them on my way to lunch. I didn't see a reason to make her drive out when I was headed there anyway, so I agreed. When we approached her hotel room, we heard muffled screams coming from inside. I yanked Nichole away from the door and used her key card to enter. Once inside, I found Joshua Cameron on top of the victim. He had bound her wrists to the bed and was having his way with her—poor girl was terrified."

Levi watched the man's eyes, noting how he couldn't keep them off Nichole. Glancing at Garrett, he leaned forward and opened his phone's camera, angling it toward Nichole and sliding his thumb to "record." Careful not to be detected, he watched in amazement as she threw out signs for the captain to read. "You scrupulous little—"

"I rushed into the room and yanked the kid off the girl, then secured him in handcuffs and placed him under arrest. The girl was screaming and crying as her mom raced in all upset. She got the ropes off her arms and helped her dress while I hauled his little convict butt outta there."

"Objection, defamation of character based on information that has been banned from this case." Garrett pointed a pen at Solomon, his brow raised.

"Strike that from the record. Captain Holmes, you will respect the parameters of this case." Judge Solomon cast a disapproving look in Garrett's direction, clearly irritated by the manner in which he'd called out his objection.

"Did the defendant physically resist you?"

"He did. He actually got away from me and ran back to her—I can only assume he was trying to intimidate her further. I can't imagine what he'd thought he could have accomplished with his hands cuffed."

"Objection—speculation," Garrett argued.

"Sustained."

"No further questions, Your Honor." Amelia's smile was smug as she walked past Garrett's table.

"Defense, cross?" Solomon asked.

"Yes, Your Honor," Garrett rose to his feet.

Asher steeled himself as his former partner in crime approached. Garrett knew him well—knew how to read him and could always tell when he was lying. What he couldn't do, however, was prove he was lying. Of this, he was sure.

"Your Honor, if I may approach?" Garrett asked, a photograph in hand.

Judge Solomon waved him forward, taking the photo for his perusal.

"I'd like to present as evidence, Defense Exhibit #5. It's a photograph taken in the bedroom where the alleged offense occurred." Garrett's eyes held an amused light to them as Amelia stepped forward to view the picture.

"Any objections, Madam D.A.?" Solomon looked at Amelia, brows raised.

"None, Your Honor."

"Alright. Place into evidence." He handed the photo off to the court clerk, who logged and handed it back to Garrett.

"Captain Holmes," Garrett stepped to the stand, watching with amusement as Asher adjusted himself in the seat. "Is this the bed where you found the defendant and Ms. Romans?"

Asher stared at the picture, his eyes bouncing to Garrett's. Confidence strengthened his features as he answered. "It is."

His confidence wavered as a slow smile crept across Garrett's face.

"No further questions, Your Honor. I'd like to retain the right to bring this witness up for future questioning should the need arise." Garrett turned to walk back to his seat but spun on his heel, pen in the air. "One more thing…"

Silence blanketed the room.

"What is he doing?" Adam leaned into Amelia's ear, shocked by Garrett's unorthodox approach to defense. Amelia only shook her head, her frustrations mounting.

"You said he resisted you, correct?"

A grin teased the corners of his mouth. "Yes, he did."

"And was he charged with resisting arrest?"

"Uh, no, he wasn'—"

"Thank you, no further questions, Your Honor."

"You may step down, Captain Holmes," Solomon dismissed.

Khyron glanced at Asher, and in the same instant, the captain shot a confused look in Nichole's direction. "And the Black Widow's web begins to unravel…" he muttered as Garrett returned to his seat.

"Prosecution, your next witness?" Solomon called, glancing over the rim of his glasses as Amelia stood.

"I'd like to call Ms. Daphne Hoskins to the stand."

Garrett turned his attention to Josh as the forensics nurse was sworn in. His son's features were tight—his clenched jaw matching the fists at his sides. "Wait," he whispered, knowing his efforts to smooth the kid's anger would be in vain.

"Man, forget you," Josh spat. "Might as well have your sidekick represent me. You're doing nothing!"

Garrett's left hand opened and closed on repeat as he summoned his patience. "Please," he pleaded. "Trust me." Josh's cold eyes locked on him before he shook his head in disgust and looked away.

"Ms. Hoskins, please state your position and responsibilities for the court," Amelia addressed the nurse.

"You've got to cross-examine these witnesses, Garrett," Khyron leaned toward his partner.

"Not yet."

"In case you haven't noticed, your client is losing his patience with you."

Garrett's eyes narrowed. "My son—and you—are going to have to give me more time. I think my reputation has earned me that much, don't you?"

Glaring at him, Khyron set his jaw. "For his sake, I hope you're right."

"Ms. Hoskins, did you have the opportunity to examine Ms. Romans after the alleged assault?" Amelia asked.

"I did."

"Would you please advise the court of your findings?"

As the nurse confirmed for the jury that there had been evidence of the assault found during her investigation, Josh's features fell. He wished he could see Rhea's face. If he could just make eye contact with her, maybe she'd give up on this pursuit of lies.

"...along with the scrapings beneath the victim's nails," the nurse concluded.

"Thank you. No more questions, Your Honor," Amelia nodded to the judge.

"Defense, cross?" Solomon asked.

"No, Your Honor."

"Madam D.A., call your next witness."

"I call Detective Donahue to the stand." Amelia's red-stained lips pressed into a thin line as she prepared to question the detective. He would be more challenging than the others, but he was necessary. She offered him a tight smile as he was sworn in, telling herself to forget the heated conversation the two had found themselves in the day before. He'd tried to convince her of Josh's innocence—a laughable concept—and had told her he had the evidence to collaborate with his claims.

"Please state your name and position," she instructed.

"Micah Donahue—Detective with the Highshore P.D."

"You were the detective who interviewed the accused and the victim, correct?" Amelia asked, seeing Garrett's objection coming before it left his lips.

"Objection—alleged victim."

"Sustained. Prosecutor, the line," the judge reprimanded.

"Yes, Your Honor. Please answer the question." She smiled at Donahue.

"Yes. I interviewed both Rhea and Josh the day of the alleged assault."

"Permission to approach, Your Honor," Amelia asked, a jump drive in her hand. When Solomon waved her forward, she showed him the drive. "I'd like to present as evidence, prosecution exhibit #6–the video footage of Detective Donahue's interview with the defendant."

"Any objections?" Soloman asked Garrett.

"No, Your Honor."

"Place it into evidence," he instructed the clerk.

Once the drive was back in her hand, Amelia inserted it into her laptop and projected it onto the screen for the jury to see. Pressing play, she noted the way Donahue's brow furrowed in disapproval.

Garrett forced himself to breathe evenly as his son's hardened features filled the screen and Donahue's voice began to sound.

"Do you understand this form?"

"Yes."

"Do you agree with it?"

"Okay."

"Yes or no, Josh."

"Okay...yes."

Amelia paused the video, focusing her attention on the jury. "Note the defendant's belligerent responses to law enforcement–you will see a blatant disrespect of the very authority designed to keep the good citizens of Highshore safe."

Josh rolled his eyes, but one look at the jury's pinched features told him she had them all convinced. He was screwed. As the video continued, he longed for Jordan's reassuring presence at his side.

"Do you know the victim, Rhea Romans?"

"She's not a victim!"

"Do you know her?"

Josh rolled his eyes and slouched in his chair. "You know I do."

"Yes or no, kid."

"Yeah, Donahue. I know that girl."

The frame froze on Josh's anger-filled eyes, causing a murmur across the gallery.

"'She's not a victim,'" Amelia quoted, shaking her head. "This man shows absolutely no remorse for what he's done."

"Objection–innocent until proven guilty!" Garrett stood but sat back down at Solomon's glare.

"Sustained. Madam D.A., abide by the rules of this courtroom–don't make me remind you again," he warned.

"Yes, Your Honor." She pressed play once more.
"Have you had an intimate relationship with Rhea?"
"What do you think?" Josh snapped.
"Yes or no, please."
"Yes."
"Who is Nichole Sherard to you?"
"A villain from a Disney movie," Josh quipped, a smile teasing the corners of his mouth.
"Care to explain?"
"She's the pits, Donahue. A real-life Cruella de Ville. She's had it out for me ever since Rhea and I met. Hates my guts."
"So, it's safe to say you two don't get along..."
"Might wanna adjust those hearing aids, dude." Josh crossed his arms and raised a brow.

Amelia paused the video, focusing mainly on the women on the jury. "Imagine this type of animosity toward you as the mother of a young woman. By his own admission, Mr. Cameron was at odds with the victim's mother."
The video continued.
"Okay, so she dropped you at the hotel—then what happened?"
"I went to her room, like an idiot." He dropped his gaze to the floor.
"So, you two had sex?"
Josh squeezed his eyes shut. "Yes."
Just like Garrett knew she would, Amelia paused the

tape.

"Here, he's admitted to having willingly sought out the victim in her hotel room. Now, we have here a man fresh out of county, hunting down an innocent, unsuspecting woman." Amelia's chin rose as she made the statement, eyes flashing.

Josh stared at his dad, palms up at his sides. "Defend me!" He gritted his teeth, tears burning his eyes as his father sat motionless in the chair beside him.

"Trust me." The words were spoken with more calm than he felt. His heart ached at the pain on his son's face, but he couldn't make his move. Not yet.

After what seemed to be hours, Amelia cut off Josh's interview and faced Donahue.

"Detective, based on the evidence shown, Joshua Cameron is a volatile man. Would you agree with this statement?"

Donahue's gaze drifted to Josh, his heart empathizing at the kid's lost look. "You didn't play the whole ta—"

"Yes or no, Detective."

He raised his hand in protest. "But they only saw part of th—"

"I'm looking for a yes or no, please," Amelia restated.

Glancing at the judge, he found his hardened gaze on him.

"Detective, if you don't answer the D.A. as asked, you're going to find yourself tangled up in some dire consequences," Solomon informed him.

With a sigh, Donahue looked back at Josh. Their eyes locked, and he read the desperation there. His hand was being forced, but he wouldn't go down easy—he would go down like Josh.

"Detective Donahue, is the accused a volatile man, or is he not?" the D.A. pressed, exasperated.

Raising his chin in defiance, he folded his arms across his chest and shrugged. "Okay."

Her cheeks flushed, and she straightened her pencil skirt as her eyes shot to the judge.

"Detective, you are the prosecution's witness, and she wants you to answer in a certain manner. If you can't do that, then the court has no recourse but to treat you as a hostile witness, hold you in contempt until you decide to be a professional, and contact your command and see what repercussions can be placed on you. I guarantee that I will press for a suspension for subordination. This is what you're facing if you do not cooperate in my courtroom. Is that understood?"

"Yes, Your Honor," Donahue conceded, defeat tugging at his soul.

"Madam D.A., proceed," the judge instructed, adjusting the glasses that had slid down his nose.

Throwing her witness a warning look, she asked again. "Detective Donahue, is the defendant a volatile man?"

Looking her in the eyes, he set his jaw. "Yes. He is."

"Thank you. Please describe the victim's mannerisms during your interview with her."

He breathed a sigh before answering. "She was…agitated. Nervous."

"Did she seem scared?"

His gaze went to Nicole's smug smile, and he fought the urge to vomit. "Yeah, she did, but not of the def—"

"When did you first notice the rope burns on her wrists?" Amelia interrupted.

"About a third of the way into our interview."

"Did she attempt to hide them?"

"Yes."

"Did she explain what had happened to them?"

He frowned. "Yes."

"Please explain for the jury."

"But, see, her story doesn't match the ev—"

"Please explain to the jury what Ms. Romans said happened to her wrists." Amelia annunciated each word as though he hadn't heard.

"Let him speak!" Titus hissed beside Levi. "The guy is trying to tell us something! This is unreal." He cut his eyes to the man beside him, agitation burning his soul.

Tight-lipped, Levi nodded his agreement. It was obvious the detective had intel that the prosecution didn't want leaked to the jury.

Donahue's mouth set in a straight line. "She said the defendant had tied her to the bed. But that doesn—"

"No more questions, Your Honor."

Amelia's smile on the way back spoke of the triumph she felt in her soul.

"Defense, cross?" Judge Solomon asked.

Garrett nodded. "Yes, Your Honor." He watched the relief wash over his son's features as he stood and prayed for Josh's understanding.

"Detective Donahue, how long have you been on the force?"

"About twenty-eight years," he replied.

"Twenty-eight," Garrett repeated, clicking the pen in his hand. "Have you received any specialized training conducting interviews and interrogations?"

"Yes. I've attended several department-sponsored classes and training courses that taught me these techniques."

"So would you say, in your 28 years of experience conducting interviews and interrogations, you feel confident, based on your training, that you can determine if someone is lying or being honest?"

"Objection! He's inserting feelings and observations into a factual case!" Amelia cast a perplexed look at the judge.

"Your Honor, if I may…" Garrett extended a hand toward the judge, his features belying his impatience.

"I'll allow it." Solomon nodded at him.

"Detective, what sort of schools did you attend that enable you to determine whether or not someone is telling the truth?"

Fighting the smile that threatened, Donahue launched into his educational history, satisfaction filling his soul as Amelia shifted in her seat with each certification listed.

When he came to a stop, Garrett's eyes went to

Solomon, who focused his attention on Amelia. "Madam D.A.?"

"The prosecution recognizes Detective Donahue as an expert witness. I withdraw my objection." Amelia dropped her gaze the moment the words were out of her mouth.

Judge Solomon studied the victory behind Garrett's eyes as he faced Donahue. Well played, Cameron, he thought to himself as Garrett geared up for his next question.

"Detective, in your expert opinion, during which interview of these two young people did you believe the person was lying?"

"I believe the alleged victim lied in her interview."

Sterling gritted his teeth and wrapped an arm around Rhea's shoulders. How dare this man say she lied about the assault?

"Please explain," Garrett prodded the detective.

"During my interview with Ms. Romans, she was distracted. She evaded many of my questions, sometimes even refusing to answer. When I began to question her about who had allegedly assaulted her, she became sick and nearly threw up from nerves. I've seen a lot of victims grow ill over having to see their attacker—as though the picture could somehow come to life and attack them all over again. This wasn't that kind of illness. This seemed to stem from a place of fear for her attacker—not of him. She seemed really upset to be giving him up to me."

Sterling pulled his arm off Rhea and gaped at her. For a fleeting moment, she met his eyes, her expression telling him everything he needed to know.

"You foolish little twit!" Nichole hissed in her ear. "You sabotaged that interview on purpose!"

Terror struck Rhea's heart and jolted her senses. Her hand trembled as she swiped at a stray strand of hair. She could feel her mother's anger rising beside her, and her thoughts filled with Nevaeh's fate if Josh wasn't convicted.

"Did anything else stand out to you during the

interview?" Garrett clicked the pen in his hand as he stared at the other man.

"Yes. Ms. Romans kept her hands hidden for a large portion of the interview. She withdrew her right hand to point out Joshua's picture when asked—that's when I noticed the rope burns. I asked her about them, and she quickly hid her wrists again and told me 'It's nothing.' When I asked if I could see the other one, she asked me 'Can I say no?' When I asked if there was a reason I shouldn't see them, she reluctantly pulled them back out for examination."

"What else stood out, Detective?" Garrett asked, waiting for the one key he was searching for.

Donahue shifted and gnawed his lip. "The rope. I asked her where Josh had gotten the rope to tie her up. She looked like she'd seen a ghost. She was unprepared for my question and told me he'd brought it with him. When I challenged the logic of him being released from jail and picking up a rope before heading over there, she had nothing to say."

"And did you pull security footage to collaborate with this theory?"

"I did. Not one camera that captured him that day ever shows him with rope."

"Detective, did you ask the victim about her history with Joshua?" Garrett asked.

"I did. She explained their past together with fondness and longing, but when I asked her about any previous assaults she'd experienced at his hand, she claimed there had been many, but that she'd never reported them to the cops. When I asked her why not, she brought her mom into it. Said she was scared to tell anyone. I pressed for her reason, and she told me her mother had been furious with her when she'd gotten pregnant and had thrown her out into the streets."

A collective gasp echoed around the room.

Nichole gripped Rhea's leg and dug her fingernails into her skin, eliciting a gasp. "You can say goodbye to that brat of yours," she whispered, keeping a smile on her face for the media.

Garrett played both interviews again in their entirety—not pausing even once to explain what was already so plain for them to see. When the footage ended, the courtroom buzzed as the spectators discussed their opinions.

"No further questions, Your Honor."

"Madam D.A., any redirect for this witness?" Judge Solomon asked.

"None, Your Honor." Amelia rested her forehead in her hand. She could feel a headache coming on. She would have to fight even harder to persuade the jury against Josh after they'd seen Rhea's interview.

Solomon pulled his glasses from his nose and ran a hand down his face. He was tired and needed time to sort out the details of this mess—without noisy lawyers who only cared to bicker and fight. Grabbing his gavel, he raised it high. "This court is adjourned until tomorrow morning at nine o'clock sharp."

Slamming the gavel, he abandoned the courtroom and disappeared into his chambers.

Chapter 38

"They set a net for my steps, my soul was bowed down. They dug a pit in my way, but they have fallen into it themselves."
~Psalm 57:6~

GARRETT

"It would appear that Defense Attorney Garrett Cameron is out of his element defending his own son. The younger Cameron doesn't stand a chance with his father as his spokesman. The lawyer has only chosen to cross-examine a select few witnesses who've come to the stand thus far, leaving Joshua in an exasperated quandary. At one point, the cameras zoomed in on the boy and caught him telling his father "Defend me!" as tears filled his eyes. It is too early in the trial to determine his fate, but if Mr. Cameron is an indicator, then he doesn't stand a chance against District Attorney Amelia Corazon..."

Elysia watched the torment play across her husband's features as he stared at the television. There was so much she wanted to say, but she knew in her heart that nothing would ease the pain in his soul. "Eat something. Please."

He tore his eyes away to look at her. "Do you think he's watching?"

His question took her by surprise. "Baby..."

"Don't." He raised a hand to stop her. "Just answer me. Please."

She closed her eyes as she thought about how to respond. "I'm sure he isn't. Josh isn't social, and I can't imagine why he'd be in the common area instead of on his bunk."

"He thinks I'm letting them hang him."

She gnawed her lip, wishing he wouldn't torture himself. "He just doesn't understand."

"I'm not, you know."

Elysia placed her hand on his knee. "I know, baby."

Tears pooled in his eyes as his lower lip trembled. "I'm

fighting for him, Lyse. I swear I am. I will never allow anyone to hang our son ever again. I just need—" He sniffed and swiped a hand down his face. "I need him to trust me. For just one more day."

She reached for him, cradling his head as he sobbed.

JOSH

Josh tore his eyes from the television screen and stared at the food tray. He hadn't eaten anything during the past two days. Food held no appeal to him—his mind was far too consumed by the weight of his trial to give any thought to his body's need for nutrition.

"You owe me your tray! I won that last round, and you know it!"

He glanced up at the red-faced man two seats down from him. The guy had been on a rampage since the trays had been delivered—yelling at random inmates and bartering for their dinners. Breathing an impatient sigh, Josh grabbed his tray and stood, walking over to where the man had sat to try his luck with someone else. "Here." He dropped the tray in front of him. "Now, shut up."

All eyes were on him as he walked back to his cell, but he didn't care. His focus was on the newscaster's words.

"…if Mr. Cameron is an indicator, then he doesn't stand a chance against the ruthlessness of District Attorney Amelia Corazon…"

Truth was, he didn't stand a chance either way, and he knew it. Nichole's reach went too far. Each shift change, a new guard entered his cell to remind him of that fact. He was surrounded by his enemies, without a friend in sight.

Exhausted, he went to his bunk and sat up with his back against the wall to think. He desperately needed sleep, but his thoughts warred with one another, depriving him of the rest he needed. Rhea was a constant on his mind as he wondered where she was at with all this. He hadn't seen her even once during the trial but felt her presence in the courtroom, and it plagued him. She hadn't been questioned in court yet—would she stick by these lies to the very end?

Squeezing his eyes shut tight, he popped them open again to images of his father. His no-good defense attorney father—the best of the best, just not when defending him. He'd known better than to trust him. Had known he shouldn't have fallen for his games. Why had he let his guard down? He'd been so stupid to allow him to defend him! He imagined his father laughing it up with his buddies over a hundred-dollar steak, telling them how he'd fooled his dumb kid into thinking he had a chance. He pictured him reveling in the fact that he'd managed to convince him that he gave a crap about him.

The joke was on him—the loser in a cell with a rape charge draped around his neck.

He pulled his knees up into his chest and forced his eyes closed. He had to sleep. A train wreck was heading his way tomorrow, and he had to be ready.

But no.

Thoughts of Asher came next. Josh could still feel the impression of his hands on him as he'd pulled him away from Rhea. He heard him read him his rights. Heard the rushed and hidden whisper of "I'm sorry, kid" as he'd shoved him out of the room and led him to his doom.

Josh had already decided the captain's fate if they locked him away. It would earn him a life sentence—maybe even the death penalty—but what did he have to lose? They'd already taken his life. He had nothing more to live for, and he'd settled in his heart that he'd make sure Asher wouldn't either.

At last, sleep claimed him, as murder claimed his soul.

Day 2 of the Trial

Garrett arranged the papers on the table and told himself not to stare at his boy. Despite his effort, his eyes were drawn to the exhaustion painting his son's face, and he found himself reading every line on his tight features. "Did you sleep at all?"

Josh's eyes shot to his. "You're just showing them I was right about you. You know that, right?"

Pain stabbed his chest, but Garrett refused to look away. "Josh—"

"All of Highshore is watching. They all heard what that newscaster said about you. You're not fooling them, Garrett."

He'd seen it. The realization crushed his soul, but he couldn't let himself lose focus. Josh needed him to stay in this fight. At a loss to convince his son that he wasn't standing by and watching them tear him apart, Garrett closed his mouth and worked the end of his pen, clicking it on repeat as he studied his boy.

Josh's focus had shifted to someone entering the gallery, but his expression told him it wasn't Rhea. Garrett followed his darkened stare to Asher, and a sick feeling settled in the pit of his stomach as he worked to read the thoughts locked in his son's mind. He prayed that God would block Josh's plans and save him from further harm.

"All rise. This court with the Honorable Judge Solomon presiding is now in session."

From where she sat, Rhea had a clear view of Josh. Her stomach was in knots as she took in the closed-off look on his face. She knew she would be the first to testify this morning, and it scared her to her core. More than anything, she longed to proclaim his innocence to the world, but she didn't dare–not with their daughter's life at stake. At the start of the trial, Nichole had ripped Nevaeh from her arms and had secreted her off to an undisclosed location, intending to keep her there until Josh was locked behind bars for years to come. If she gave in to her heart's desires, their baby would be gone forever. Sterling's presence beside her unnerved her. She wished he'd lose interest in her and run far away from this mess, but he insisted on seeing this through with her.

As the court was seated, Josh turned in his chair, giving Rhea a clearer view of his face. Her gaze crossed his and her heart flipped when he stared back at her. Her pulse pounded at the familiar arch of his brow as he set his jaw when his eyes fell on Sterling.

I love you... she mouthed to him, devastated when he shook his head ever so slightly and looked away.

"Rhea!"

She jumped as her mother jabbed her ribs with her elbow, her brows knit in anger. "They called you to the stand!"

Nichole closed her fingers tight around her daughter's wrist and flashed her the picture she'd taken of Nevaeh that morning. "If you ever want to see this brat again, you will see to it that he's locked away," she hissed into her ear before shifting gears and wiping at her eyes, caressing Rhea's back as she stood and walked to the stand.

Rhea's mind was a fog as she was sworn in—her mouth speaking words her heart could never vouch for. She sat as stiff as a board as Amelia approached her, a sympathetic look in her eyes.

"Please state your full name for the jury."

"Rh—" She coughed. "Rhea Romans."

"Where do you live, Rhea?" Amelia asked.

She shifted in her seat, feeling her mother's eyes on her. "I currently live with my mother."

"And how long have you lived there?"

"Um, about three months, I guess." Rhea allowed her hair to fall across her face, shielding her from the eyes that watched her.

"Where did you live before moving in with your mother?"

Rhea's eyes went to Sterling, then bounced to Josh. "I was living with my boyfriend."

"And prior to this?"

She dropped her gaze. "With anyone who would take me in."

Amelia nodded. "Is it fair to say you're accustomed to moving around?"

"It's hard to find a place that feels like home."

"Would you say it's important to find a place that feels like home?"

Garrett watched the exchange, his eyes narrowing as he followed the prosecutor's thought process. She was trying to prove vulnerability. An insecure girl is an easy target for a rapist. The jury would buy into her argument—until his cross-examination ripped it apart.

"It is," Rhea answered, meeting Amelia's eyes.

"You and the accused were once an item, correct?"

Rhea's eyes fell on Josh and her features tightened. "Yes," she whispered.

"Did you see yourself making a life with him?"

She took a deep breath before answering. "I did."

"What would you say drew you to him?"

"He understood me and never judged me. He listened to me; not just pretended to listen. He stood up for me." Her eyes shimmered as she looked at Josh, memories of her life with him playing in her mind.

Amelia nodded and checked her notes. "Was Joshua what you would consider to be a 'bad boy?'"

"Objection, relevance?" Garrett argued.

"Overruled. Answer the question, Ms. Romans."

Rhea crossed her arms and held her elbows tight. "I guess so."

"Was that attractive to you?"

"Josh knew how I felt about his choices."

"Please tell the court how you felt." Amelia waited, aware of the rising tension in the courtroom.

Rhea sighed. "I didn't support his poor decisions, but I understood."

"Meaning?"

"Josh had a rough life. He did what he thought he had to do."

"Did the accused ever convince you to participate in his poor decisions?" Amelia asked.

"No. He respected how I felt. Josh normally didn't do that stuff if I was around. He was very protective of me."

"Did you ever feel like that protection was possessive?"

Rhea glanced at her mother, then Sterling. "Maybe once."

"Please explain."

"When he ran away from home, he tried to convince me to run away with him."

"And did you go?"

Rhea hesitated; her voice laced with self-doubt. "No."

"Why not?" The prosecutor asked quietly, her eyes studying her face.

"Because I felt pressured to go, and I was afraid."

"Of him?"

"Of everything."

"Please tell the court about the first time you had sex with the accused." Amelia's tone was gentle, her eyes urging Rhea to answer.

Rhea looked at her mother, read the expression on her face, and knew what she was expected to say. "Josh pressured me into it. Told me he'd make me regret it if I didn't give in."

Beneath the table, Josh's right hand worked itself into a fist, then opened and shut on repeat.

"Did you feel pressure the day Joshua showed up at your hotel room?" Amelia asked.

Rhea sat still, her eyes going from her mother to Josh. She swallowed hard.

"Unbelievable," Laura hissed at Levi in the gallery. "Watch Nichole's face."

Levi nodded, equally agitated by the obvious manipulation happening before his eyes. He kicked himself for not bringing it to Garrett's attention yesterday but was determined to do so the first chance he had today.

"Take your time." Amelia smiled at Rhea.

"I told him my mother was returning, and he shouldn't be there."

"Did he leave?"

"No."

Josh shifted in his seat, anger teasing his frazzled nerves. Beside him, his father scribbled furiously on a piece of paper, as though he hadn't a care in the world. For the millionth time since the trial had begun, he wished

Titus was by his side instead of in the gallery. At least that way he'd have a real father to support him.

"How many times do you remember asking the defendant to leave?"

Rhea thought of her answer. "Maybe three or four."

"Three or four times," Amelia repeated. "Were you afraid?"

Rhea looked at her mother, who raised her chin and gave her a hard stare.

Khyron's eyes narrowed as he followed Rhea's gaze to Nichole, noting how the girl constantly looked at this woman before answering questions.

"Ms. Romans, were you afraid of him?" Amelia gently prodded.

"Yes," she lied, unable to meet Josh's eyes.

Garrett felt Josh deflate next to him. "It's only just begun," he whispered. "I've got this."

Josh refused to acknowledge him.

"Tell us what happened after you repeatedly told Joshua to leave."

Tears filled her eyes, and she swallowed hard. Just stick to the script… she told herself, thoughts of Nevaeh flooding her mind. "He kissed me."

"Did you return the kiss?"

"Yes." She squeezed her eyes shut, her mother's coaching kicking in. "I was afraid to resist him. He kissed my neck, and I continued telling him my mother would be there any second and that he needed to go but he said, 'I'm not worried about that witch.' He asked me to leave with him—told me we could run away together and forget everyone and raise our daughter on our own."

Amelia's brows raised. "The defendant asked you to run off with him," she confirmed.

"Yes."

"And what did you say?"

"I reminded him of my mother. He said, 'Forget her,' and then grabbed me." Her gaze was pulled in his direction. She forced herself to look at the torment in his eyes as he watched her throw him to the wolves. Forced herself to realize that she was consciously destroying the man she loved—and then Nevaeh's face floated to her mind and her mother's control returned. "He picked me up and carried me to the bed. He threw me on my back and told me he would remind me why I don't say no to him."

A stabbing pain knifed Josh's heart as he watched Rhea feed the prosecutor her mother's lies. How could she do this to him? Betray him as though he meant nothing to her? Don't do it, Rhea, his eyes pleaded.

"He grabbed the rope and tied my wrists to the headboard."

Walking to the evidence table, Amelia picked up a bag and held it up for the judge. "Your Honor, I'd like to present People's Exhibit #15."

Solomon waved her over so he could examine it, then nodded. "Defense, any objection?"

Josh's eyes seared into him, but Garrett refused to back down from his goal. "None, Your Honor."

"Log this into evidence." Solomon handed it off to the court clerk.

"That evidence will end me," Josh's eyes swam with hot tears as he looked at his father, his anger boiling to the surface. "Why are you letting this happen? You know I didn't have a rope on me, Dad. You know!"

Garrett swallowed back his tears and prayed the judge's focus wouldn't be drawn to his son. "Donahue already proved your innocence in this—there's no footage to back up her claims," he whispered.

"Josh, you're going to have to trust him." Khyron leaned back in his chair so he could see around Garrett. "He's got you. I swear."

Shaking his head, Josh dropped his eyes to his lap. He couldn't watch Rhea confirm this lie to those who would condemn him.

"Are these the ropes the accused used to tie you to the bed?" Amelia asked, holding the bag out for Rhea's inspection.

Josh swallowed back a sob as he waited for her answer. He could feel the court's eyes and fought to maintain control. They wanted to see him undone and watch him crumble in front of the world. He refused to give them the satisfaction.

Rhea stared at the ropes, her face blanching white. There would be no coming back from this. Once she made this statement, telling the jury that he'd bound her, he would be finished. Her stomach lurched, and she resisted the urge to throw up. A sob caught in her throat, and she melted into a torrent of tears.

Every eye in the courtroom was fixed on her, except the eyes of the one she loved. Josh squeezed his eyes shut before popping them open, leaning back in his chair, and staring at the ceiling.

Studying her, Amelia's heart squeezed in her chest, and she cleared her throat. "Your Honor, I'd like to request a recess so my witness can have a moment to compose herself."

Solomon nodded. "This court will take a ten-minute recess." Slamming the gavel, he stood and retreated to his chambers.

Taking a deep breath, Levi saw the opportunity he'd been waiting for. "I'll be right back," he whispered to Laura and Elysia.

"Levi, what are you do—" Laura called after him, but he was gone.

Levi walked through the gallery, stopping a foot away from Garrett. Josh saw him first and furrowed his brow as Levi leaned in and whispered to his father.

"Garrett, I need to talk to you."

Surprised, Garrett nodded. "Okay, what's wrong?"

His eyes met Josh's, and he shifted on his feet. "Not here." He nodded to the door. "Step out with me?"

Glancing at his son, Garrett stood. "Sure."

In the hallway, Levi whipped out his phone and pulled up the pictures he'd snapped. "I've been watching Nichole during the trial. Certain witnesses who come up—she's signaling to them. It's like their eyes are glued to her, taking cues on how to answer when questioned."

"You're kidding." Garrett raised his brow. "Let me see." He leaned in to see the phone, his face redder with each picture. "This woman is unbelievable." Clapping his friend on the shoulder, his face broke into a triumphant smile. "You just got the pebble in my shoe tossed out of court, old buddy. Will you email those to me?"

"Of course." Levi ducked his head. "Laura's up there having a fit about all of this."

"Elysia holding up okay?" Garrett asked, features tight.

"She's stayed pretty quiet through it all. Her eyes rarely leave that boy in there. I think she's afraid this is the last chance she'll get to see him without bars keeping them apart."

Garrett's face fell. "I'm going to win, Levi."

Levi's eyes met his. "I really want to believe that," he answered quietly.

His jaw tensed. "Thanks for the heads up."

"You're welcome." Levi studied his face, praying for God to work in a way he didn't understand.

Garrett locked eyes with him. "I know you're all up there doubting my loyalties to my son, but I told you: I'm going to win this." Without another word, he turned and walked back into the courtroom, leaving Levi alone in the lobby.

Chapter 39

"With the merciful you show yourself merciful; with the blameless man you show
yourself blameless."
~2 Samuel 22:26~

Judge Solomon wasted no time in reconvening his court. He was anxious to hear the defense's side of the case but found his irritation toward Garrett rearing its head when the lawyer requested to approach the bench the moment thewas called to order.

"This better be good, Mr. Cameron." He frowned as he waved him forward.

"Oh, it is," Garrett assured.

Solomon listened intently as he explained Nichole signaling the witnesses, his eyes going to that woman. When Garrett had finished, the judge clasped his hands and frowned. "Thank you for bringing it to my attention. Now go sit down," he ordered.

Smiling, Garrett returned to his seat as the judge recalled Rhea to the stand.

Her eyes red from crying, Rhea told herself to focus on the prosecutor as she approached.

"Feel better?" Amelia asked, and Rhea forced a nod. Picking up the evidence bag once more, she held it out for Rhea's inspection. "Rhea, are these the ropes the accused used to tie you to the bed?"

She didn't allow herself to look at Josh as she answered this time. "Yes."

Josh swiped a hand down his face and shifted in his chair. Why? Why throw in the lie that he'd tied her down? Was it not enough she was accusing him of rape?

"Your Honor, I'd like to present the People's Exhibit #16."

Once more, Garrett withheld his objection, and the evidence was submitted.

"I'd like the jury to direct their attention to the screen.

The picture you are looking at is of Ms. Romans' wrists, taken onday of the incident. Note the lacerations and burns inflicted from the ropes Mr. Cameron used to restrain her to the bed."

Sterling ducked his head, cheeks flaming. He hadn't wanted to hurt Rhea, but Nichole had told him the only way he'd gain access to her is if he left marks on her wrists during their night together. He'd played it off as an accident and Rhea seemed to believe him, but he had doubts.

Garrett watched as the jury studied the picture, each member shaking their head in disbelief. A few cast nasty glares at his son, and he fought the urge to scream for them to wake up and see the lies. A glance at the witness stand confirmed his suspicions—Rhea's eyes had pooled with tears, and she refused to look at the screen. Not an ounce of satisfaction showed on her features as the jury oozed with sympathy for the girl. His eyes shot to Sterling and he frowned as he read the guilt on his face. Josh had claimed Sterling was responsible for Rhea's wounds. And he was determined the court would find out the truth. His thoughts drifted to Nichole, and he narrowed his eyes. He would have his turn. And when he did, she would regret ever messing with his boy.

Placing the evidence bag back on the table, Amelia directed her attention to Rhea. "Please tell the court what happened after the defendant restrained you."

Rhea closed her eyes, the weight of what she was about to do settling like an anchor in her soul. "After he tied me to the bed, he...he…"

Josh held his breath, his eyes transfixed on her. Was she backing out? Turning her back on her mother's plan to destroy him? Hope swelled in his chest.

"...he assaulted me."

The breath whooshed from his lungs, and tears sprung to his eyes. He felt as though he'd taken a barrel to his chest. She was going through with the plan. She was lying under oath to get him locked up forever.

Amelia crossed her arms behind her back. "If the jury would look at the screen." She waited for their attention before placing the images for all to see. "The lead detective on the case, and the victim's mother, took Ms. Romans down for a SANE examination immediately following the incident. You will note the results as follows: The DNA swabbed from the cervix and vagina of the victim were a perfect match to the DNA taken from the defendant, Mr. Cameron."

Josh squirmed beneath the cold stares of the jury. The prosecutor had succeeded in making him look like scum in their eyes. As it stood, he was a rapist—the jury was convinced. It was up to his father to turn the tables in his favor, yet his father seemed to have no interest in doing so. He glanced at Garrett's stoic features. Noted the set line of his jaw...and failed to interpret the look on his face. His knee bounced with nervous rhythm; his eyes glued to Amelia.

"No more questions, Your Honor."

"Defense, cross?" Judge Solomon looked over the rim of his glasses at Garrett.

"Yes, Your Honor." He stood, aware of Josh's eyes on him as he walked to the stand.

Garrett stared at Rhea a moment before he began, hardening his heart to the fact that she was the girl his son loved—the mother of his grandchild. Not today. Today she was just some girl trying to destroy his boy, and he would not let that happen.

"Ms. Romans, is it true that you met Josh in the Hendricks's secluded driveway during the night some months ago?"

"Yes." Rhea's eyes flitted to his, then bounced back to her hands, already feeling the intimidation. Josh's father was the best. He would see through her lies, and then what would become of Nevaeh? Her emotions were a pendulum between relief and terror.

"Is it also true that you were eager—pleased, even—to see him?"

Solomon looked on with interest. Though he didn't care for the defense attorney, he had to give it to him—the guy knew what he was doing.

"Yes."

"Was he expecting your visit?"

She swallowed hard. "No."

"Why did you meet him—alone, nonetheless—if you are afraid of him?" Garrett challenged.

"B-because I missed him—it had been years since we'd been together." Her eyes drifted to Josh, her heart breaking when he refused to look at her.

"So, you missed a man you claimed to fear. In fact, you missed him so much that you decided to meet him spontaneously."

Rhea held her breath, terrified of where he was taking his line of questioning.

"Why'd you do it, Rhea? What was the reason for this visit?" Garrett challenged.

Rhea searched her mind for an answer. Her eyes fell on Sterling's painful face, and she suddenly knew. "I had just broken up with my boyfriend. I had heard Josh was back in town and I couldn't stop thinking about him. During my time away from him, the only thing I could think about was what I liked about him. I forgot how awful he could be to me."

"Awful," Garrett repeated, a tight smile on his face.

"Ms. Romans, please tell the jury how old you were when you met the defendant."

"I was thirteen."

"Thirteen. And how would you describe your relationship with him during your teen years?"

Her gaze drifted back to Josh, longing settling in her eyes before she caught herself and refocused on the lies. "I met Josh during a vulnerable time in my life. He filled a hole left by my father's absence—made me feel special again."

"So, you haven't always been afraid of him?"

"No."

"What happened to cause this fear?"

Rhea paused, thinking. "He became controlling. He would get mad when I talked to other guys."

"Do you recall attending a high school dance in tenth grade?" Garrett asked.

"Yes."

"Do you remember an incident involving Billy Andrews?"

Her eyes went to his as she tried to figure him out. "Yes…"

"Can you tell us what occurred with Billy Andrews that night? Was there something specific that happened?" Her heart skipped a bit as the memories of that night flooded her mind. "Yes. He slipped some ketamine into my drink. Then he tried to take me to the locker room to 'show me a good time.'"

"I see. And did you find Joshua controlling that night?" Garrett asked.

Rhea's face blanched white. Josh had been a ball of rage after learning what Billy had done. It was the first time he'd physically defended her. The first time she'd felt he cared enough to sacrifice his own well-being for her. "No," she whispered. "He defended me."

"He defended you," Garrett restated, his eyes on her. "It was later, then, when he became controlling?" Garrett had to suppress a laugh as he watched her search for a fabricated time frame when Josh transformed from her knight in shining armor to the monster she was making him out to be.

Rhea squirmed, her thoughts racing. "As we got older, he wouldn't let me talk to other guys. He would get into fights with them if they came too close."

"I see." He looked into her eyes, ensuring she read the message behind his gaze: *I'm going to debunk every claim you make, little girl.* "Ms. Romans, has Josh ever hit you?" Doubt flashed across her face, her eyes drifting to her mother. "He tied my wrists to the bed…" she stated absently.

"Alright, we'll get back to that, but the question was, 'Has he ever hit you?' Yes, or no?"

Rhea's gaze fell on Josh, her breath rushing from her lungs when she realized he was staring right at her, his eyes begging her to tell the truth. "Never," she said quickly.

"Never," Garrett repeated, pausing so her confession could sink into the jury. "Before he came to your hotel room, had the two of you ever engaged in sexual intercourse?"

Her body went cold. "Yes."

"How many times prior?"

Her cheeks flushed red. "Many."

"Many times. So, during the eight years you've known him, you've been intimate many times together, but now he decides he has to rape you?"

"Objection, Your Honor. He's badgering the witness!" Amelia's tone belied her annoyance.

"Sustained. Watch your step, Defense." Judge Solomon gave him a hard stare.

"Withdrawn." Garrett held up a hand. "Ms. Romans, you claimed that my client tied your wrists to the headboard, correct?"

Rhea looked at her mother, who tapped her face twice. Solomon's eyes were glued to Nichole, fury rising in his chest as he watched Garrett's accusations against her come to life. "Wait a minute." He held up a hand, drawing every eye in the courtroom. "Bailiff, escort Mrs. Sherard out of my courtroom." He narrowed his gaze at the shocked expression of the mother. "You're in here signaling to this girl and manipulating her answers!"

The courtroom buzzed as each spectator processed this news.

"Bailiff, place her in a holding cell if necessary but do not allow her to leave!"

"I have never been treated with such a lack of respect!" Nichole shrieked as the bailiff reached for her arm.

Judge Solomon raised a brow in her direction. "One

more word and I'll hold you in contempt of court."

Garrett watched as she was led from the room, his heart leaping in his chest. Nichole escorted out during his cross-examination of Rhea's testimony? Couldn't get better than that. One look at the shocked expression on his son's face caused his hope to soar, and he prayed for God to help him hold on a little longer. When the courtroom doors closed on Nichole, he turned his gaze back to Rhea, curious at the lost look in her eyes.

"Counselor, ask that question again," Judge Solomon ordered, his eyes resting on Garrett.

"You claimed that my client tied your wrists to the headboard, correct?"

Swallowing hard, Rhea searched the room. Her gaze landed on Elysia's taut features and read the plea in her eyes. Shame washed over her body in cold waves. What was she doing? Destroying an entire family to appease her mother? No. She knew it went deeper than that. Nevaeh's future was at stake. She caught Josh's eye and willed him to understand, but how could he? "Yes," she confirmed.

"Where did he get the rope?"

"I don't know," she answered, chin raised. "He didn't tell me."

A low rumble of laughter rippled through the gallery, but Garrett's face grew more serious. "According to the evidence found during Detective Donahue's investigation, Josh was captured on several video feeds before reaching your room. Your Honor, if I may present Defense Exhibit #20."

Once he'd obtained Solomon's and Amelia's go-ahead, Garrett began the compilation of the footage that had tracked Josh once he'd left the jail, starting with the jail cameras and not stopping until they'd watched the videos from the hallways in the hotel.

The footage ended, frozen on a still frame of Josh disappearing into Rhea's room. "Not once did Nichole Sherard stop the car when driving my client to her daughter. Note his hands when he enters the room—

empty."

Josh's gaze went to his father, a spark of hope rising in his chest.

"Ms. Romans." Garrett faced her. "You say that my client tied your hands. My main confusion is this: according to everything we've seen so far with the video footage—as well as statements from your own mother—at no time was my client able to stop somewhere and purchase a rope. So, my question to you is, did he come into the room with a rope or was there a rope in the room that he may have used?"

Rhea's cheeks flamed. "Some of the details of the incident are fuzzy due to stress."

"'The incident,'" Garrett repeated. "Not 'the rape?'"

Rhea dropped her eyes to her hands and fought the tears threatening.

"Ms. Romans, you and Joshua were intimate before he moved away, correct?"

She stared hard at him, her heart locking down. One look at the judge, however, was enough to make her answer. "Yes," she whispered.

"How would you describe that last sexual encounter with Josh? Were you afraid of him?"

Her chin went up, her eyes sparking. Had he really asked her that question? "No. He was the least of my worries that day."

Garrett let the comment wash off his shoulders like water on an oiled duck. "So, there was no 'rape' committed that day?"

"No."

"Clarifying, you willingly had sex with the defendant without any fear of your wellbeing?"

"Yes."

Garrett submitted another piece of evidence for approval before turning to the jury. Holding a piece of paper in his hand, he explained. "Let the record show that during the alleged victim's statement, Detective Donahue asked if Josh had ever attacked her before, to which Ms.

Romans responded with 'yes.' Please refer to the screen to verify the statement I am referring to is factual and not fabricated."

He waited for the jury to peruse the screen, satisfaction resting in his soul at the furrowed brows sprinkling the crowd. Turning to look at Rhea, he folded his arms across his chest. "Rhea, do you understand what perjury is?"

She swallowed hard and tried to look at Josh, but Garrett moved to block her.

"Rhea?" he asked, his tone quiet and firm.

"Yes. I do."

"Are you telling the truth about what happened that day or are you being coerced into presenting this wildly inaccurate story?"

"Objection!" Amelia was on her feet, face taut with rage. "Badgering the witness!"

"No further questions, Your Honor." Garrett glanced back at Rhea before returning to his seat.

Amelia placed a hand on her brow as she searched her notes—worry written on her forehead.

"You do understand he just won that round, don't you?" Adam leaned in close, his eyes narrowing as he rebuked the prosecutor.

She shot him a fierce glare before turning back to her notes.

To her right, hope blossomed in the defendant's heart as his father sat down beside him—his presence strong and reassuring.

"Madam D.A., redirect?" Judge Solomon asked.

"Uh, no, Your Honor," Amelia answered, her eyes flitting to Garrett.

She'd underestimated him. He was proving to be cunning, and she didn't like that. "Defense, call your next witness," Solomon ordered.

"I call Sterling Oliver to the stand." Garrett glanced at Josh, surprised to see him watching him with interest in his eyes. Thank You, Jesus...

Sterling walked to the stand displaying more

confidence than he felt. As he was sworn in, he made himself meet the bailiff's eyes, but when Garrett approached, he dropped his gaze.

"Please state your name and occupation for the court."

"Sterling Oliver, civil attorney."

"Mr. Oliver, you were recently in a romantic relationship with Ms. Romans, correct?" Garrett asked.

"Correction." Sterling's eyes bore into Josh's steely gaze. "I am currently in a romantic relationship with Ms. Romans."

Garrett raised a brow. "This is news to the court. Ms. Romans just stated that she had broken off your relationship."

"We're taking a break," he clarified, his gaze drifting to Rhea.

Garrett's brows rose. "Is she aware of this 'break?'"

"Objection, relevance?" Amelia challenged.

"Overruled. Continue."

"She is aware, yes. It was her idea that we take some time off."

"I see. Mr. Oliver, had you been intimate with Ms. Romans the week of the alleged assault?"

Sterling had thought about this question throughout the trial. He'd weighed the costs and had been plagued with guilt over the fact that Rhea was clueless about how deeply he was involved in her mother's plot. Taking a breath, he read the expectant look on Rhea's face—and then he remembered Josh. He raised his chin. "No. Rhea and I haven't been together since she asked for a break."

Rhea's jaw dropped, but Sterling's determination only intensified.

Garrett's eyes bore into him. He didn't need his confession. He could win this case without it. "No further questions, Your Honor."

Sterling stared at the lawyer in confusion as he walked off the stand. He knew the man saw his lie, so why hadn't he pressed him? The thought unnerved him as he took his seat beside Rhea.

"Prosecutor, cross?" Judge Solomon asked.

"No, Your Honor."

"Defense, call your next witness."

"I call Nichole Sherard to the stand." Garrett shuffled his stack of papers as the judge ordered her back into the courtroom.

"I trust you intend to behave yourself on my stand, Mrs. Sherard?" Judge Solomon folded his fingers together, staring down his nose at the woman he'd lost all respect for.

"Yes, Your Honor." Nichole's tone was quiet and subdued, but Garrett wasn't fooled. She was merely toeing the line so she could stay in the game.

As Garrett approached the stand, he caught Nichole's eyes, noting the way her gaze hardened—her demeanor challenging him to bring it on.

"Mrs. Sherard, you made some bold statements against the Highshore Police Department, stating that some are 'as crooked as they come.' What, exactly, led you to say that?"

Her smile told him she was sure he had just opened Pandora's Box. "That department isn't known for its scrupulous ways now, is it? Their forte lies more along the lines of making sure old secrets stay buried."

"So, it's safe to say you don't trust them." Garrett locked his hands behind his back, preparing for battle.

"Not as far as I can throw them," she scoffed. "I wouldn't trust them with my dog."

"If what you say is true, then how can we trust anything that Captain Holmes has stated in this trial?"

Nichole's cheeks flamed and she gripped the chair arms tight, but Garrett cut her off before she could respond.

"He claims he found Ms. Romans bound with rope–even had a rope to place in evidence for us, and the alleged victim indeed had rope burns on her wrists. However, there's something very…off here, don't you think?" He cocked his head to the side, then forged ahead. "None of the footage has shown my client with a rope, and your own daughter can't decide how or when he supposedly produced said rope. Is it possible that Captain Holmes himself is part of the 'crooked as they come' crowd of which you are so adamantly against?"

"That boy tied her up!" she screamed, pointing her finger at Josh. "I saw the ropes myself!"

Garrett smiled. "Mrs. Sherard, do you consider it dangerous for someone to stalk another person?"

Taking a moment to recompose herself, Nichole smoothed her skirt. "Of course," she answered with confidence.

"Would you say that the defendant could have found you dangerous had he known that you'd been tracking him ever since he'd run away from home at seventeen?"

A sledgehammer slammed into Josh's gut, and he gasped for air. What was he talking about?

Judge Solomon leaned forward in his seat, aware that every eye in the courtroom was glued to the witness frozen on the stand. "Answer the question," he demanded, eager to hear what she had to say.

"You have no proof to back up that claim." Nichole's eyes were sheets of ice as she stared at the lawyer, angered that he'd thrown such a blow so early on in his questioning. What a brazen move.

He smiled. "Oh, but I do. Is it true that on the night Joshua ran away from home, you had him followed by a private investigator?"

Her cheeks flamed. "I needed to ensure my daughter's safety. Any mother in her right mind would've done the same."

Garrett's jaw tightened. "Mrs. Sherard, did you pay this investigator to pick my client up from where he was hitchhiking on the interstate that night?"

Nichole scoffed. "Of course not, that's ridiculous."

Garrett paused a moment, allowing the jurors time with her answer. "Are you familiar with a man who goes by the name of Drew Randall?"

Josh's brows rose as he watched his father. What did

Drew have to do with this mess? How had his dad even known about him?

Nichole mentally kicked herself for trusting Asher's choice of an informant. There was no telling why his name was being brought up in the trial—if he'd ratted her out, he would be dead. "It doesn't ring a bell," she lied.

"I see." Turning, he addressed the judge. "Your Honor, I'd like to present Defense Exhibit #22."

Once accepted into the evidence log, Garrett held a picture for Nichole.

"Do you recognize this man?"

She stared at the picture of a younger version of Drew, her back taut. Her eyes scanned the room for him. Was he here? "I haven't the slightest idea who this young man is." She stared at Garrett, daring him to prove her wrong.

Garrett locked eyes with her, neither one willing to back down. "No further questions at this time, Your Honor. Requesting the right to bring this witness back to the stand."

"Granted. You may step down, Mrs. Sherard." Judge Solomon nodded. "Madam D.A., redirect?"

"No, Your Honor," Amelia answered.

"This crap-show just keeps getting worse!" Adam hissed at her. "You should back off the case and let me handle it from here!"

"Shut up!" Amelia bit. She was over being criticized by this man.

Nichole's stomach flipped as the bailiff led her toward the doors. Garrett had something up his sleeve. She could feel it. One look at Asher told her he knew it too.

"Defense, your next witness?"

"I call Drew Randall to the stand."

Despite the hand gripping her arm, Nichole froze and whipped her head around to see the man walking toward Garrett. The extra guard hovering nearby told her he was still a prisoner–his stark white face told her he was terrified of the repercussions for testifying against her. So why was he here?

"Out in the hall," the bailiff ordered, tugging her arm.

Josh's eyes bounced from his father to Drew as the man was sworn in. He could not wrap his mind around the fact that Drew had been connected to Nichole. Was there anywhere he could go to escape this evil woman?

"Mr. Randall, do you know Captain Holmes?" Garrett asked.

Drew glanced at the murderous eyes of his brother and his insides turned to goo. "Yes."

"How do you know him?"

"He's my brother," he admitted.

"Half-brother," Asher growled from the gallery. He would kill him. The first chance he got–Drew would be dead.

"Your brother," Garrett restated. "Mr. Randall, is it true that you have been tailing the defendant ever since his ship landed several months ago?"

"Yes."

"Please tell the court your reason for this."

"I, um, I was hired to do so," he stammered, his gaze going to Josh. He winced as the storm darkened his eyes.

"Who hired you to tail him and why?" Garrett asked.

"My brother. He hired me to keep Josh from going back to Highshore."

Garrett raised a brow. "Did he give a reason for wanting to keep Josh away from Highshore?"

"No." Drew's gaze hardened at the memory. "He said I didn't need to know. But I found out later it was because Nichole Sherard had him working like a lap dog for her–she didn't want Josh to find her daughter."

"Objection, speculation!" Amelia protested.

"Sustained."

"So, to summarize, it is your belief that Nichole Sherard had Captain Holmes hire you specifically to keep my client away from Highshore? Is that your contention?"

"Yes, sir."

"But you failed in that mission, didn't you?" Garrett stared at the man, observing the way he was turning to jelly right before his eyes.

"It wasn't my fault," he nervously stated, his eyes drifting to his brother. "He got fired and crashed into a tree. I don't know how he got back here!"

Seeing he'd lost him, Garrett set his jaw. "No further questions, Your Honor."

"Madam Prosecutor, cross?"

Exasperated, Amelia shook her head. "No, Your Honor."

"Your next witness, Defense," Solomon instructed.

"I call Cali Bristol back to the stand," Garrett answered, studying his notes before walking to the stand.

Rolling her eyes, Cali walked to the stand and took her seat.

Her entire demeanor reeked of disrespect. He now understood why Levi and Laura held a sense of disdain for this girl.

"Ms. Bristol, when did you first meet Jordan Hendricks?"

Laura's foot swung from the tension in her veins. For the millionth time, she wished her son had never messed with that girl. Beside her, she knew Levi wished the same thing as his hand stroked his chin.

Cali stared at him, trying to get a read on him and failing. "He works at my dad's paper. I met him like…I dunno, two years ago, I guess? I came home from college and my dad made me take a job as an intern. Jordan had been there for a while already."

"When did you first take a romantic interest in him?"

"Objection, relevance?" Amelia contested.

"Your Honor, I'm going somewhere, if I may…" Garrett appealed.

Solomon eyed him, considering. He was growing tired of the prosecution dancing around the truth and was curious to see if Garrett could pin them in their lies. With a sigh, he nodded. "Sustained, but get there fast."

"Yes, Your Honor." Turning back to Cali, he focused solely on her face, needing to read every thought that flashed across her features. "Please answer the question."

"Maybe like...four or five months ago."

"To clarify, you worked with Jordan for approximately a year and a half but didn't show any interest in him until Josh was back in Highshore." Garrett stared her down, their eyes deadlocking as Cali tried to figure out what he knew.

Raising her chin and tossing her hair over her shoulder, Cali smiled. "Your point being? Josh being in town has nothing to do with Jordan's and my relationship. The heart knows no time." She sat back and tightened the cardigan around her body. "Besides, I don't even know when that guy came back to town—we don't know each other like that."

"No?" Garrett cocked his head in mock surprise. "But you knew enough about him to know what triggered him, correct?"

Cali stared, her mind furiously trying to stay ahead of his game. "Yeah, I know enough about him to know that any form of alcohol turns him into a violent maniac. I wonder why that is?" She smiled, confident she'd checkmated the lawyer with his own misstep. She was wrong.

Pulse pounding, Garrett's soul cried out to his Creator as he responded. "I'll tell you exactly why that is. It's because his father was a no-good sorry drunk his entire life and beat him within an inch of his life every chance he got. But you already knew that didn't you? In fact, you've been fed information about the defendant for months, isn't that right, Ms. Bristol?"

"Objection!" Amelia leaped to her feet, blindsided by the defense.

Judge Solomon's eyes rested on her. "Objection based on...?"

"Relevance, Your Honor. As was previously stated, this is a rape case."

"Yes, and you've dragged the defendant's background into the case. Don't dig up what you can't handle, Counselor. Sustained. Defense, proceed."

Elysia's eyes were glued to her husband, shock rippling through her at his slick admission to his past. What was he doing? She prayed he wasn't creating a noose around his neck.

"Ms. Bristol, do you know Captain Holmes?" Garrett asked, noting the surprise flashing in her eyes.

"My father knows everyone in this town. He is, after all, one of the richest guys in Highshore."

"Yes or no, please." Out of the corner of his eye, he caught sight of that man in the gallery, sweat beading on his brow as he watched her every move.

"I'm a reporter." She danced around the question. "I often work with law enforcement to either get the scoop on a case from them or for them."

"Yes or no, Ms. Bristol? Do you know the captain?"

"I've worked with him as an informant, yes." Cali resigned to the answer, her eyes meeting Asher's fear-stricken gaze. Whatever. She had no reason to protect him. Submitting evidence to the judge and gaining Amelia's approval, Garrett held up a picture for her perusal. "Ms. Bristol, is this you, standing outside the captain's truck in the Highshore Tribune's parking lot?"

Cali squinted at the picture. "Yeah, that's me. So? It's a free country. Can't a girl talk to whomever she chooses?"

Ignoring her, Garrett turned to the jury. "I'd like to direct the jury's attention to the aforementioned picture." He clicked his pointer, and the still frame of a security camera filled the screen. "Ms. Bristol, what was the reason for Captain Holme's visit on this day?"

"He needed my help on a case."

"On which case, specifically?"

"I believe there's such a thing as 'police/informant confidentiality,' sir." Cali smiled.

"Indeed." Garrett returned the smile. "If one truly is working with the cops on a case. On this day, Asher Holmes was off duty, working a separate operation from any other regarding the police force. He hired you—paid you in cash, even—to collect information on Josh. Isn't that right?"

"Objection, leading the witness?" Amelia's mouth was agape.

"Sustained." Judge Solomon shot her an annoyed look. "Answer the question, Ms. Bristol."

Cali raised her chin. "He told me it was for a case—I didn't go digging into his reasoning, okay? Said he needed me to get close to Jordan and learn as much as I could about Josh. He called him his target and said a lot of lives were at stake if he didn't get the info he needed."

Josh sat as still as stone as he took this all in. His heart ached for Jordan. Not only had this girl worked overtime to get at him, but she'd also played on Jordan's emotions.

"'A lot of lives,'" Garrett repeated. "Did the captain elaborate on why lives depended on your obtaining information about Josh?" Garrett asked.

"I don't ask questions—I just do my job and get paid. I never focus on the 'why.'"

"How insistent was the captain that you obtain this information?"

"Very. Wanted updates on the regular."

"Did he suggest you bribe Jordan to give up dirt on the defendant?"

Cali smiled, her gaze shifting to Jordan. "He told me to sleep with him to get his guard dropped so he'd start talking." She shrugged her shoulders. "So, I did."

"Confirming for the jury, you slept with Jordan to get close to him and learn more about Josh. Correct?" Even though he'd suspected, the truth still hit him in the gut, his heart squeezing with empathy for the boy who'd thought he'd found love.

"Sure did. Paid off too. I got lots of information to pass on to the captain. Zero regrets." Cali winked in Jordan's direction.

From the gallery, Laura's eyes shot daggers into the girl. "I want to find her mother and slap her in the face for raising such an awful creature as that!" she seethed.

"Shh," Levi rubbed her back, feeling the same way. He

was focused on his boy, however, and refused to give Cali the satisfaction of seeing his emotions.

Jordan closed his eyes, wishing he could fall through the floor as gasps emanated around the courtroom from people who'd known him since he was a baby. It was bad enough that she'd used him—horrible that she'd used him to get to Josh. But to have all of Highshore privy? He teased the idea of getting up and leaving mid-trial, but thought better of it, knowing he couldn't abandon Josh. His gaze swung to Rachel, wilting to find her eyes on him as she scribbled in her notebook. Would she really add his shame to her report to spread to the surrounding towns? His cheeks flamed and he forced his gaze away from hers.

"Ms. Bristol, did Captain Holmes ever mention Mrs. Sherard to you?" Out of the corner of his eye, he watched Amelia open her mouth to object, only to shut it again at the judge's harsh look.

Cali thought for a moment, glancing at Asher's pale face. "I don't remember him ever mentioning her, no."

"Are you aware of who she is?"

Cali rolled her eyes. "Who in this town doesn't know that crazy lady?"

"So, you are aware, then, that Mrs. Sherard is the alleged victim's mother and the city manager's wife?" Garrett waited for the judge to chastise him for the rabbit trail, but he did not.

"I know she's the city manager's wife. I didn't know she's the mom of the girl your son raped." Cali threw the barb, irritated when it didn't latch on.

"Allegedly raped," Garret corrected. "You were unaware, then, that Captain Holmes was working for Mrs. Sherard when he hired you to collect information on the defendant?"

Cali blinked. "And?"

"Yes, or no? Were you unaware?"

"Yes, I was unaware, but what does it matter? Why should I care who he was working for?"

"What if I told you that the information you were fed

about the defendant was not happenstance? It was carefully planned to manipulate Josh into acting, and reacting, in a certain manner to hang himself in court."

"Objection, speculation!" Amelia's tone demonstrated the level of exasperation in her veins.

"Defense, proof?" Judge Solomon asked Garrett.

"If I might beg the court's patience, Your Honor." He looked at the judge, a plea in his eyes.

"This court's patience is wearing thin, Mr. Cameron. Bring us to the point before I fine you for wasting our time, understand?"

"Yes, Your Honor. Thank you." His attention returned to Cali, and he continued. "For example, Ms. Bristol, you mentioned to the prosecution that Josh became irate at dinner after you said something he didn't like. What was it that you had said to him?"

Cali arched her brows and allowed her attitude to roam her features. "Just the truth—that he'd abandoned his little girl and how it must sting knowing his abusive daddy had first dibs on the kid. Oh," she smiled, "that, and I offered him a beer."

Josh bristled, his muscles twisting into tight knots.

"When you said these things to the defendant, did you know he would be triggered by them?"

Cali laughed. "Who wouldn't be?"

"Confirming for the jury: you knew Josh had a violent temper and you purposefully incited that rage by aiming carefully barbed remarks in his direction, hoping that he would take the bait and go after you. Have I spoken anything less than the truth just now, Ms. Bristol?"

Her eyes grew cold as she watched him. "Yes." She seethed. "You've failed to 'confirm for the jury' how it was you who abused the accused his entire life. It was you who beat on him for years. It's because of you he's terrified of alcohol, of love, and of any other human being who breathes." She sat back in her chair and folded her arms across her chest as she smiled smugly at him.

Amelia gaped at Cali, feeling like her entire case had

fallen through the floor. "Objection, Your Hon—"

"No!" Garrett snapped.

The courtroom was silent. Not a breath could be heard. The people of Highshore gaped at the lawyer, waiting for him to defend his honor as the loving father and upstanding citizen they knew him to be. Judge Solomon sat with bated breath as he stared, taking in the way Josh's face had blanched white.

"No." Garrett's voice dropped to a near whisper. Giving Amelia a weak smile, he nodded his head at her. "Thank you, Amelia."

Glancing from Cali to the judge, he ducked his head. "No further questions for this witness, Your Honor." Solomon's eyes were transfixed on Garrett before he turned to look at Amelia. "Cross?"

"No, Your Honor."

As Cali stepped down, Garrett started to walk to his seat but stopped halfway between the defense table and the bench and looked at Solomon. "Your Honor, may I request a moment to consult with my colleague?"

"Granted."

Leaning across the table, he focused on Khyron. "I need you to take over as lead."

"What?" Khyron's features belied his shock.

"I need you to take over the defense. When you do, I want you to call me to the stand to testify."

Khyron's mouth opened, but he was at a loss for words. "Khyron!" Garrett gritted his teeth, his tension mounting. He could feel Josh's eyes on him, but if he looked his way, he knew he'd take the coward's way out, and he could not risk that. "Do what I tell you to do. Call me to the stand as a witness."

"What do you want me to ask?"

"Just put me on the stand. I'll take it from there."

Considering his request, Khyron glanced at Josh, reading the fear and confusion in his eyes.

Desperate, Garrett reached out a hand and gripped Josh's forearm tight, causing him to jump. "Son...I know you have no reason to, but I need you to trust me right now." His eyes bore into his, tears shimmering. "Please."

Taking in the tight features of his father's face, Josh swallowed hard. "Okay."

A sob caught in his throat, and Garrett could only nod as he released Josh and looked back at Solomon. "Your Honor, I am relieving myself as the attorney of record for my client and having my associate continue with this case. I beg the court's indulgence—since I have been the support behind my client, whom we all know is my son, if I could indulge the court to allow a personal friend to join him at the defense table for the next portion of this testimony."

Judge Solomon looked over the rim of his glasses at him and raised his brows. "That is extremely unorthodox, Mr. Cameron. It's not something the court would—"

"Your Honor," Garrett interrupted, his soul pleading with God on Josh's behalf. "I'll not ask this court for anything else. I'm just asking for this one indulgence."

Josh held his breath as he watched the exchange, his heart pounding that his father went to bat for him.

Solomon stared down at his notes, thinking. At last, he raised his head and looked at Amelia. "Madam D.A., is there any objection to the defendant having an additional person at the defense table?"

"No objection, Your Honor," Amelia conceded.

"Defense, name the person you are requesting as a means of support for your client."

Garrett looked into the gallery, his eyes locking on Titus. "Mr. Titus Bristol."

Solomon nodded. "Mr. Bristol, please step up to the defense table and have a seat."

Titus couldn't get to Josh fast enough. He was thrilled that Garrett had chosen him to sit with his boy and was determined not to disappoint. "Hey, kid," he whispered to Josh once the bailiff had patted him down and he was seated.

Josh cast him a grin and swiped at the tears in his eyes.

"Titus," he whispered.

"My associate is ready to proceed, Your Honor," Garrett stated, his heart soaring with gratitude with the knowledge that Titus was at Josh's side.

Eyes narrowed as he worked to figure out this game, Solomon nodded. "Okay…Defense, call your next witness."

Khyron cleared his throat and looked at Garrett before standing. "Um, I'd like to call…Garrett Cameron to the stand."

Elysia gasped as tears filled her eyes. Her gaze locked on her husband; she was hardly aware of the low buzz in the courtroom as the spectators took in the abrupt change. "What is he doing?"

Jordan grabbed her hand and held it tight, his eyes glued to Garrett. "Trust him," he whispered.

Josh watched as the bailiff swore his father in, his mind working overtime to process what was happening. What was he doing up there? Why had he bailed on his case?

Once Garrett was on the stand, Khyron stared at him, uncertainty plaguing his mind. Locking eyes with his partner, he cleared his throat and took a leap of faith. "Please state your full name for the record."

"Garrett Cameron."

"Mr. Cameron, it's my understanding that you have information that is pertinent to this case."

"I do."

"Could you please tell the court what information you have to provide to the jury regarding this case?"

Garrett swallowed a sob as his gaze fell on his son. He read the mixture of emotions on Josh's face and took a deep breath. He owed this to him. It was time to let the facade go.

Slowly, he stood. His heart pounded through his ribcage and tears choked him as he opened his mouth to speak. "Highshore knows me as the lawyer who fights and wins. They know me as the man who gets things done. A family man, whose only desire was to raise his children right. A father who was—" He paused, images of Josh as a boy flooding his mind. "—who lived with severe disappointment in a son who refused to get it together. You all rallied around me when my boy left and offered your comfort and condolences. You told me I had done the best I could while assuring me Josh was nothing more than a rebellious, ungrateful teen who deserved to be held accountable for his actions."

The eyes in the courtroom watched his every move, not a soul making a sound as he spoke. The media kept their cameras trained on him, but he didn't glance their way.

"But it was me who deserved to be held accountable for my actions. While I fought in a courtroom for the ones you loved, I went home to a little boy who was terrified. He was terrified of me and the mere mention of my name."

Glancing at Josh's tight features, Titus placed a hand on his shoulder, sighing at the tension in his body. "You're okay, son. You're alright. Just breathe," he soothed.

"You all saw a man who fought for justice but that boy right there," Garrett pointed at his son, "saw me for who I was. A coward." His eyes went to his wife, their sorrow intertwining. "A coward too afraid to face his brokenness. Too afraid to fight to overcome the pain in his heart. Instead of fighting that battle, I turned to the bottle. I drank away my sorrows every day, sometimes coming to court and fighting your battles drunk, without any one of you ever realizing I'd had a drop."

Gasps emanated around the room as the townsfolk began to put the pieces together.

"I was full of lies. Full of excuses. I filled your heads with ideas that my son was a rebellious fool who just wouldn't listen. I magnified his every wrongdoing so that you all saw how awful he was. I gained your sympathy. Earned your trust. All the while vilifying my son in your eyes until you couldn't even stand the mention of his name. Eventually, Joshua gave up." He sniffed, his focus on his boy. Sorrow washed through him as Josh tried to hold back his tears but failed.

"He gave in to the stigma I'd created. He became 'the bad boy.' 'The Highshore Heathen,' as you all love to label him. He stopped caring because his father never showed him an ounce of love. To add insult to injury, he lived each day knowing that his mother only wanted the best for him." Garrett's eyes went to Elysia, whose tears streamed down her face. "Elysia fought with me daily to keep our boy safe, but I was stronger. I had connections. I had become the master manipulator in this town. She knew if she took him and ran, I'd be right behind her with an army to hunt them down and rip Josh away from her forever. She knew I had enough power to bury her in legal matters and fees and was heartless enough that I could do it all without so much as a grimace. She knew if she left, Josh would forever be vulnerable to his drunken father who didn't care, and so she stayed. She put up the farce with me, convincing you that all was well within our four walls."

Laura glanced at Elysia and reached for her hand when she noticed the tears streaming down her cheeks.

"It's my fault we're here today. It's all on me. All my boy ever wanted was to be free to love his high school sweetheart and all I ever did was sabotage them from the beginning. I did everything in my power to keep these two apart—to deprive him of all happiness, simply because I couldn't overcome my misery and pain. Between Nichole Sherard and I, they never had a chance. Both of us fought against them, each driven by selfish motives—me, driven by pain, Nichole, by her desire for total control. And so, we have the story of Josh and Rhea, folks. Just two kids who fell in love. Two kids, raised by selfish parents who couldn't see past their noses. I've destroyed my boy." Garrett sniffed. "Sucked the life right out of him. That's why I'm here today. Can I ever make up for the past? For what I've done to him? No. I'm not ignorant of the fact. But, today I stand in this courtroom—the very room I've betrayed him in countless times before—and fight with everything I've got to free him from the accusations that have placed him behind bars."

Garrett looked at Josh, thanking God to find his eyes on him. "Son, 'sorry' will never be enough. 'I love you' may never be received by you, and I have to accept that. But I'm standing here, in front of God and this court, and I'm letting the truth be known—you deserved a father, Joshua. You deserved to have your dad fight for you. Instead, you got me, and if you want to come after me for all the horrors I did to you throughout the years, there's a judge and a jury right there who, I have no doubt, will back you one hundred percent. If you ask the judge to lock me up and throw away the key, then I will eagerly hold out my wrists for the shackles long overdue. Whatever you decide, I just want you to know I don't regret you, son. I see now you're the best thing that ever happened to me. I love you, Josh." Garrett pulled out his handkerchief and wiped the tears streaming down his face.

Time stood still. No one spoke. No one moved. Judge Solomon sniffed back his tears, the pieces of the past falling together to create one large, clear picture for him to see. So much of his history with Garrett now made sense. He never would have pegged him to have been an abusive father. As the man had said, the judge had always seen Josh as the troublemaker Garrett had made him out to be. Realizing the lawyer had meant business when he'd asked his son to decide his fate, he turned to Josh. "Son? Do you wish to press charges on your father for crimes committed against you in the past?"

Josh couldn't breathe around the tears choking his throat. His father had just confessed his heinous sins against him in front of the entire nation. The gossips were in the gallery. The reporters were taking notes. Everyone would know about the events of today. Gone was the pretense of the perfect Cameron lawyer who could do no wrong. The gallery buzzed as they discussed their speculations over what he might do.

Titus' strong hand clasped his shoulder, his fingers squeezing him to remind him of his presence.

"Titus?" he cried, his voice small and strained.

"Right here."

"What should I do?"

Here was his opportunity. His one shot at legal justice—the vengeance he'd dreamed of all these years. He could put his father behind bars and forget about him for the rest of his life—it would all be over. But then…it would all be over. He would lose all the progress the two had made together over the past few months. His father had gone to battle for him against the one woman who longed to see him gutted. He'd placed himself between him and Nichole and had fought with all his might, eluding a sense of confidence Josh had never before seen in the man.

"What do you want to do?" Titus asked, his voice calm and quiet in his ear. "This is salvation, boy. God's eternal redemption playing out right before your eyes. That redeeming love I've been telling you about? It's alright here. What will you do with it? Christ's ultimate sacrifice—placing Himself on that cross for you. Taking the weight of all your sins upon His shoulders so you wouldn't have to pay the price for your wrongs. God's merciful forgiveness is at your fingertips right now. The choice is yours, Josh. Will you extend grace and forgiveness to this man and offer him the second chance Christ longs to offer you? Or will you make him pay for his wrongdoings? Justice won't erase the pain. It won't forgive him. It won't offer you a better life. It will take him from your mother–and from Nevaeh–and will be a constant reminder to you that your past is still there to haunt you at every turn. Your past will take on a new face and a new name. It will chase you down until you seek death and find it. However, there's freedom in forgiveness. God forgave you, boy, whether you see it or not. But His forgiveness of your wrongdoings doesn't erase them—you're still a liar, a thief, and an angry, bitter kid. His forgiveness takes away the debt you owe and makes your slate clean and clear. If you choose to forgive your father, it won't erase what he did to you, but it will free you from the burden of hatred. It's your choice, Josh. I support you all the way, no matter what you decide."

Josh twisted in his chair, his tear-filled eyes locking on his mom in the gallery. They both cried harder. He couldn't rip his dad away from her. Whether he liked it or not, his abuser had pulled himself together over the past few years and had become the husband she needed. He would never take that from her, even if that meant sacrificing revenge and justice and watching him walk away from the sentence he deserved. Turning to the judge, he wiped his face. "No, Your Honor. I don't choose to press charges against my father. Set him free."

He heard his mother's sobs in the distance and felt her tension release. He couldn't move. Couldn't breathe. He'd had the chance to make his father pay for all he'd done, and he'd chosen to set him free. Why? His eyes fixed on his hands; Josh mumbled three words.

The courtroom strained to hear.

"What was that, son?" Judge Solomon asked, staring intently.

Josh's gaze went up, his eyes fixed on his father. "I forgive you," he cried.

He watched his father crumple—this strong man who'd only ever displayed fury and power–and his heart broke.

Garrett fell to his knees inside the witness stand, burying his face in his hands as sobs wracked his body. Titus sniffed and wiped his eyes, overcome by the grace displayed.

"Order." Judge Solomon sniffed, his gavel weakly tapping. He coughed and cleared his throat, making a quick decision. "There's to be order in the court. Bailiff, clear the courtroom. Jurors, you're dismissed for the day. We will reconvene tomorrow at nine AM. Remember, you are not to discuss this case with anyone outside of the twelve of you. This court is now adjourned."

The judge rushed to his chambers, closing the door behind him before falling to his knees.

Unorthodox. Unconventional. Uncommon.

His courtroom had always had order. He was known for making things flow smoothly, processing cases, and getting defendants out the door in record time. This case was different. It had a hold on him that he couldn't shake. He covered his face with his hands and sobbed, his heart pained for the accused and for the defense lawyer he'd once despised. For the mother who'd been forced to relive her fears in front of the entire courtroom. As he cried, he prayed for grace and wisdom for the coming day, begging for the strength needed to see this to the end and bring Joshua Cameron the justice he'd longed for all his life.

Chapter 40

"But you, O Lord, are a God merciful and gracious, slow to anger and in steadfast love and faithfulness."
~Psalm 86:15~

JOSH

Josh stared at the cell bars, his stomach twisting into tight knots. He'd been unable to eat since the start of the trial, too focused on all that was transpiring. Exhaustion teased him but his mind refused him sleep. His thoughts were a jumbled mess from the constant reel playing his father's confession on repeat in his mind.

He'd forgiven him. For all that he'd done in his lifetime, Josh had just let him go free. He ran a hand down his face, working to process it all. Had he done the right thing? Would he regret not seeking revenge?

"You have a visitor."

Josh's head snapped up to find a gruff guard at the cell door. He didn't want a visitor. He wanted to be alone to gather his thoughts. "Who is it?" he asked, remaining on his bunk.

"What do I look like, an innkeeper? Either walk your butt out there and see or stay here. I don't give a crap what you do, but I'm walking away in three seconds. Three...two..."

Josh sighed. "Fine. Coming." He slid from the bunk and went to the bars. Considering the possibility that the guard only wanted to yank him from his cell to pass him another "message" from Nichole, he steeled himself.

The door clanged open, and the guard jerked his prisoner from the cell, his grip tight on his arm. Approaching the visiting room, he pulled the door open and shoved Josh in front of him, pushing him into the chair and cuffing his ankle to the table. "Fifteen minutes, tops. That's if I'm in a good mood," he growled as he opened the side door and motioned the visitors inside.

Josh stared as Titus and Levi walked in and sat across

from him. His two greatest mentors were in the same room, with one motive in mind: Making sure their boy was alright. Josh blinked back the sudden rush of tears and sniffed. "Hey," he mumbled.

"Hey, son," Titus smiled. "How you holdin' up?"

Josh's lower lip trembled, and he called himself a fool. "I let him go."

"Yeah. Yeah, you did. I'm proud of you." Titus kept his voice low. "How're you feeling about your choice?"

"I don't...I don't know. I can't feel anything. My head is pounding all the time. He deserves to be in prison, and I set him free."

Levi cleared his throat and glanced at Titus. Receiving a nod from the other man, he leaned forward.

"Off the table!" the guard barked over the loudspeaker.

Startled, Levi jumped back, his eyes searching the room. When his heart stilled, he focused his attention on Josh. "I need to tell you a couple of things."

Josh stared at him, nervous over what he might say.

"I didn't turn you in."

His eyes fell to the table, the memory of Nevaeh being ripped from his arms playing back in his mind. "I know," he whispered.

Relief flooded Levi's face. "You know?"

"Jordan told me. My mom and Mrs. H called the cops on me, right?" He raised his gaze to the older man, who nodded.

"They were just scared, son. They didn't know about our arrangement. All they could focus on was getting Nevaeh safely home."

"Yeah."

"Please don't be mad at them."

"I'm not."

Levi let out a breath, feeling Titus' eyes on him. Catching his glance, he thought back to their conversation only an hour before and pulled from its strength. "Josh, you did the right thing by letting your dad go free."

Josh's eyes dimmed. "I don't know. I mean, if I hadn't

set him free, I'd be fighting Nichole on my own, so I guess there's that."

"Josh, remember the lawyer who worked your case in Florida?"

Josh stared, blank-faced. "Yeah...? How did you kn-."

"Your dad sent him." Levi swallowed hard.

Josh's eyes shot to Titus, then back again. "What?"

"Your dad sent the lawyer who fought for your freedom in Florida," Levi repeated.

Josh cocked his head to the side. "No...it couldn't have been. Jordan promised me he didn't tell you he'd found me..."

"And he didn't. All I knew was that he had a friend who needed a lawyer. So, I gave him your father's phone number. He involved the other lawyer, and the rest is history..."

Josh's mind whirled, replaying that week in his mind. "So, that whole time...he knew where I was? He knew what had happened to me? That I was homeless? Everything?"

Levi glanced at Titus, who nodded for him to continue. "Yes."

"And he didn't come after me..."

"No."

"So, when I gave him that beating, he'd known I was in town the whole time, and he hadn't come for me?"

"That's right. He wanted you to come to him—on your terms, not his."

Josh looked at Titus to find him watching him. "He really has changed," he spoke through his tears.

"It's that salvation we spoke of, son. That same saving grace that came after me when my grandfather took on my murder charge that day."

Josh's face twisted. "Those stories in the Bible...they're not just fairy tales, are they?"

Titus and Levi smiled. "No," they answered together.

"It's as I told you," Titus said, "God's grace and redemption is demonstrated through blind faith. The faith that brought your dad to Christ is the same faith that compelled him to represent you when he knew you despised him. He believed God could overcome the demons holding you back. He believed God would bring you to a breaking point and turn your eyes to Jesus. Now, you may not see it—you may still deny it—but from what I witnessed today in that courtroom, that's exactly what's going on, Josh. God has taken your world and crumbled it at your feet. All the facades, all the fear...they're all in shatters around you. The question is, will you allow Him to finish His work and draw you to Him, or will you harden your heart and turn Him away?"

The door buzzed, cutting off any response Josh might have made. The guard stepped in and glanced between the men and Josh as he unshackled his prisoner and pulled him to his feet. "You're wasting your breath on this one," he informed them, yanking Josh toward the door. "Been locking him up for years." He grinned, placing his face inches from Josh. "He will never change."

Titus watched as the light that had sparked during their conversation was snuffed out and Josh's eyes went dim. Biting back his response, his gaze tracked them from the room before he turned back to Levi. "Now we pray."

"Relentlessly," Levi agreed.

JUDGE SOLOMON'S COURTROOM

Judge Solomon walked determinedly into court, intent on discovering the truth of State vs. Joshua Cameron. As he took the bench, his eyes observed the room's occupants. All jurors were accounted for. The gallery was full, as in the previous days. The defendant's mother was surrounded by her support group, as she should be, while the father was...absent. He scanned the crowd again, searching for Garrett, but he was nowhere to be found. Frowning, he looked at the defense table and watched Khyron prepare for the day. Solomon didn't know much about the younger lawyer but, as he watched him, he prayed he had what it would take to end this in Josh's favor.

"Where's my dad?" Josh whispered to Khyron. Even though his father had stepped down from the case, something was reassuring about knowing he was still present.

"He'll be here," Khyron whispered back. Looking him in the eyes, he offered a smile. "Trust him. That man loves you so much that he gave up everything. Remember what he's done for you."

"This court with the Honorary Judge Solomon is now in session," the bailiff called.

Josh didn't hear a word after that. The tension in his body kept his muscles rigid. He was so ready to be done with this trial from hell. So ready to move on with his life. But…would he be moving on with his life? Khyron stood beside him, startling him from his thoughts. He glanced at the stand and frowned, realizing they'd called the day's first witness.

Asher Holmes.

And he was staring right at him.

Josh's eyes darkened as the captain was sworn in. Murder filled his veins. It didn't matter if he moved on from this or not. Either way was a win-win in his book. Asher Holmes was going to meet his fate. It was all in the details…

"Captain Holmes, remember you are still under oath," Khyron began, his gaze pulled toward the court's double doors.

"Yes, sir." Asher nodded, his eyes still on Josh. The storm billowed across his features as Josh stared back at him, causing his stomach to flip.

"You stated that you found the victim bound to the bed, correct?" Khyron asked, clasping his hands behind his back.

"Yes, sir."

"And yet," his eyes went to his, "my partner disproved your statement with evidence that refuted your claim. Please explain to the jury your reasoning for standing by your assertion—remember, you are under oath, sir."

Asher swallowed hard. "Well, he only asked me where Josh got the rope, which I can't answer, as I don't know."

"So, you're saying that the video we showed the jury, which clearly shows the defendant having nothing in his hands, is not proof enough?"

"It's not my job to determine what the evidence shows," Asher quipped. "That's up to the jury."

"Right." Khyron's gaze went to the doors again, and his jaw tensed. "I'd like to present Defense Exhibit #30, Your Honor."

Solomon waved him up, and he and Amelia approved the evidence to be admitted.

Once back in his hands, Khyron showed the picture to Asher. "Can you identify this?"

"Looks like a headboard," Asher shrugged.

"Indeed. Does it look different than the one you saw earlier?"

"Um…yeah, it appears to be different."

"What appears to be different about it?" Khyron glanced at the doors again.

"Well, the design's different, and it looks like some marks are on it. This one is solid, whereas the other has slats." Asher shifted in his seat, willing himself to remain calm.

"Okay. So, what would you say if I had reason to believe this was the headboard that was in the bedroom where the victim stated she was assaulted? And that it was changed out with another? What would your reaction to that be?"

"Well, I'd say you got your facts mixed up," Asher stated, staring him down.

"Okay…why would you assume that?" Khyron's eyes pulled to the doors, and he nearly rocked on the balls of his feet as his nerves went into overdrive.

"Because, I was there the whole time and the headboard was never switched out, that's why."

"Okay, so your testimony is that this headboard has nothing to do with anything and the photo Detective

Donahue took of the headboard in the bedroom is the one that was there. Correct?"

"Yes. That's what I'm saying."

"And you're standing by that testimony, correct?" Khyron rapidly clicked the top of his pen, his eyes darting between the door and Asher.

"Yes, that's exactly what I'm saying."

"Okay. No further questions," Khyron stated, looking rather disappointed.

Josh shifted in his seat, his right hand opening and closing on repeat as he watched the liar on the stand return to the gallery. He'd have his turn. He just had to bide his time.

"Madam D.A., redirect?" Solomon asked.

"No, Your Honor."

"Defense, your next witness?"

Khyron stared at the door, his eyes slowly returning to the judge. "Uh, Your Honor, I…"

Josh watched him, his stomach twisting.

The double doors opened, and all eyes turned as Garrett walked in with a wide-eyed Hispanic woman. Khyron's face exploded in a smile, which he immediately worked to conceal. "Your Honor, I'd like to call Mrs. Rodriguez to the stand."

Solomon's gaze went to the woman, then to Garrett. One look at the lawyer's face and he knew victory was coming. "Mrs. Rodriguez, please take the stand."

Asher's face was stark white as she was sworn in. Hadn't they gotten rid of her?! How had Garrett found her?

"Please state your full name for the jury," Khyron instructed.

"I am Nancy Rodriguez," she answered, her accent heavy.

"Mrs. Rodriguez, do you need an interpreter?"

"No, Señor. I speak a leetle Inglès."

Nodding, he continued. "Please tell the court where you were working on May 23rd, 2019, when the alleged assault occurred."

She watched him for a moment, thinking, then nodded. "Seascapes Hotel."

"What was your position?"

"I am maid."

"Were you responsible for cleaning Nichole Sherard's room on the day in question?" Khyron asked.

"Si. I clean, yes."

"Do you recognize the alleged victim as an occupant of the room?"

"Si, si." She smiled and waved at Rhea. "Ella es muy amable—she very kind."

Khyron smiled. "Did you see anyone else in the room that day?"

Her expression darkened, and she pointed at Asher. "Ese hombre. Estaba con el diablo," she hissed.

"In English, please."

"That man. He was with the devil!"

"Your Honor, please have Mrs. Sherard brought in for just a moment," Khyron requested, and Solomon gave the order. "Mrs. Rodriguez, is this whom you are referring to?"

"¡Si, Señor, ella es terrible! She terrible!"

Nichole's eyes danced with fury as she regarded the maid.

"That's all I needed, Judge," Khyron informed him. Once Nichole had been led back into the hallway, he continued. "Mrs. Rodrgriguez, were you responsible for changing the sheets on the bed that day?"

"Yes, Señor."

"Please point out for the jury which of these headboards was on the bed in that room on the date in question." Projecting both pictures up on the screen, he waited for her answer.

The tension in the courtroom was palpable. Had the detective lied? Worse…had he been a part of fabricating a scene?

"This one." Nancy pointed to the solid headboard.

"This is bed in room."

"You're sure?" Khyron verified.

"Yes, Señor. I see man take board out and get new."

The gallery erupted into hushed whispers.

Josh glanced at his father, who'd joined him after bringing the maid into the court. Hope grew in his heart. He'd done it. He'd brought concrete evidence to prove that Josh had been set up. When his dad looked his way, he ducked his head, but pride swelled in his chest.

"So, in summary, you witnessed this headboard," Khyron pointed to the solid board, "switched with this headboard on the day in question?"

"I see," she stated firmly. "I see, and I make new bed."

"No further questions," Khyron smiled, returning to his seat.

"Madam D.A., cross?" Solomon asked.

"No, Your Honor." Amelia could feel Adam's disapproval, but what was she to do? This witness had been lost before now! Hot tears seared her lashes, and she called herself a fool. It wasn't like she hadn't lost cases in the past, but this one was hitting far too deep for her liking.

"Defense, your next witness?"

"I'd like to call Miss Rhea Romans back to the stand."

Khyron stood and walked forward, allowing Rhea to pass in front of him as she went to the stand.

"Miss Romans, please remember that you are under oath." Khyron's gaze settled on her and she shifted as she answered.

"Yes, sir."

"Miss Romans, earlier on in the trial, Mr. Cameron asked you if you understood the meaning of perjury. Please restate your understanding of this word for the court."

Rhea swallowed hard. Her eyes fell on Josh, and worry draped over her shoulders like a heavy cloak. He looked different today. Hopeful, yet guarded. But there was something else there that unnerved her. Vengeance. For her? Her mother? She forced herself to breathe and refocused on the question. "Perjury is a serious offense against the court," she stated as she trembled.

"That's right. I'm going to ask you a question, Miss Romans, and I need you to keep the consequences of perjury in your mind as you answer. Did Joshua Cameron rape you, or did he not?"

Tears streamed down her face as she stared at Josh. His eyes were locked on hers, and she read the plea there. And suddenly…she didn't care. About her mother, or her reach, or the countless minions she had to do her bidding. Suddenly, it was just her and Josh in that courtroom, and it was up to her to make the world understand his innocence.

"He did not," she cried. "My mother set him up." With a gasp, she continued. "She set us both up and is holding our daughter somewhere. She has refused to tell me where, unless I make sure Josh is convicted."

Sterling's jaw dropped. She'd caved. And now Joshua Cameron would go free.

Josh's entire body went cold, his eyes shooting to his father. "Dad?"

Though his nerves tensed, Garrett placed a hand on his boy's knee. "I'll find her. Trust me."

And this time, Josh knew that he would.

Once the final gavel had proclaimed his innocence to all and Josh was set free, the throng of well-wishers closed in around him. Josh shoved through them all and made a beeline for the girl on the witness stand.

"Rhea!" he called, his hands grasping hers and pulling her closer. His lips found hers as he tangled his fingers in her hair, thrilling when she wrapped her arms around him and clung tight. "Baby, I'm so proud of you. I'm so proud! You broke free, babe—she'll never mess with you again." He held her close as she cried against him.

"I'm sorry, Josh. I'm so sorry." Rhea cried into his chest, soaking his shirt with her tears.

"Shh, stop that. You did what you thought you had to

do to protect our daughter. Don't let it eat you up. I'm free, see?" He smiled and kissed her hair. "We're free to be together now—no interference." His eyes fell on Sterling, and he caught the jealous fire in his gaze. He watched the man turn on his heel and disappear into the crowd, then he dismissed him like the nobody he was. Feeling a presence behind him, Josh turned to find his father standing nearby, tears in his eyes. Clasping Rhea's hand in his, he stepped toward him.

"You did it, kid!" Garrett's hands were shoved into his pockets, energy pulsing in his veins. He watched his son, pride brimming in his eyes. "I'm so proud of you, Josh."
"Uh, yeah. Thanks." Josh nodded, unsure how to receive the declaration from this man. Beside him, Rhea squeezed his hand and caressed his thumb.

No longer able to hold himself back, Garrett reached out and grabbed his son into a tight bear hug, tears pouring down his cheeks. "I'm so proud, Josh. You handled all this like a rock. I love you, son." He squeezed tighter, his tears soaking Josh's hair. "I love you."

Josh stood frozen in his embrace, unable to breathe from the pressure in his chest. His father was hugging him. For the first time in his memory bank, his father was hugging him. Telling him he loved him. Crying over him. Josh sniffed and pushed free of Garrett's embrace. "Thanks, Dad," he whispered. "Thank you so much." Tears choked him as he verbalized the thought in his mind. "Thanks for fighting for me, man."

Garrett looked at his boy, pride swelling in his heart. "I will always fight for you, Josh. I swear."
Josh nodded, disbelief closing in. "Yeah," he agreed. "Okay."

"Josh!"
"You're free!"
"I knew you could do it!"

The crowd pressed around them, causing a desperate need for an escape to rise in Josh. Spotting Titus just outside the circle, he called out. "Titus!" His arm shot through the crowd until his wrist was grasped in Titus' strong grip.

"Alright, let's give him some room to breathe," Titus suggested as he pulled Josh and Rhea free of the crowd and out the door. Once in the lobby, he glanced at Josh's pale features. "Just breathe, son. Take it all in. Deep, slow breaths."

Josh gasped against the sobs, the weight of the past few days crashing in. "My dad..."

"Breathe..."

"Did you see? My father, he..."

"Deep breath." Titus rubbed his back as he hunched over.

"He hugged me, man. Told me he loves me!"

Titus glanced to his right and caught sight of Garrett watching him with his son. He didn't miss the jealousy in his eyes and felt great compassion for the man. He offered a smile and a nod. "Yeah," he spoke softly. "I saw, kid. I saw."

JOSH

The sun had long since surrendered to the night sky. Crickets chirped in the stillness of the air as fireflies blinked their hello to the lone occupant on the front steps smoking a cigarette. Behind him, the screen door creaked open, but he didn't bother to turn around. His mind refused to give him rest, insisting on playing the past few weeks over and over until he was sure he'd go mad.

"She wanted her daddy." Rhea's voice sounded behind him. "I hope that's okay." She smiled as she released Nevaeh's hand and sat beside Josh on the steps as their daughter clamored for his lap.

"Yeah." Josh quickly tossed the cigarette and waved the smoke away before wrapping his daughter in his embrace. "Of course that's okay." He smiled, kissing her hair as she settled against his chest.

True to his word, his father had wasted no time pressing Nichole for Nevaeh's whereabouts. He hadn't told Josh how he'd gotten it out of her, though Josh suspected he'd threatened her with a life sentence if she didn't tell him where she was. His father also hadn't told Josh where he'd found her, and Josh was grateful for that. He didn't need another prison term on his record, and that was the only reason he'd decided to push Asher Holmes forever from his memory, never to be thought of again.

Turning, his lips found Rhea's. He kissed her tenderly, still awed by his freedom to do so.

"Eww," Nevaeh commented, rolling her eyes.

Rhea laughed and blushed, pushing her hair behind her ear. Threading an arm through Josh's, she leaned against his shoulder and watched the stars twinkle down their approval. "You left your own party," she whispered. Josh shrugged, his heart squeezing. "Just can't do it right now. Surround myself with all of them? Answer all of their 'what now?' questions… I just can't, babe. I'm sorry."

"Shh. Stop it. You owe them nothing."

He nodded, squeezing Nevaeh tighter. Rhea was right. He owed them nothing. He was free to sit with his thoughts, alone on the porch with no one around but his family. His family. Josh squeezed his eyes shut at the thought. "Rhea?" His eyes flew open, heart racing.

"Mmm?"

"You are gonna marry me one day, right?" Josh's voice was laced with tension.

"Name the date, and I'll be there." She snuggled against his arm and closed her eyes as he relaxed beside her.

"So…no more Sterling?" he asked, watching her with worry.

Rhea tensed. She hadn't even seen him leave the trial. What would become of him? "No more Sterling."

He nodded and wrapped her hand in his.

Marry him. The boy she'd loved since eighth grade. With no Nichole Sherard to interfere. "Did you see her face when the cops cuffed Mom in the lobby?" Rhea laughed.

Josh grinned; Sterling forgotten. "Priceless. And Holmes, right along with her. They deserve to rot in there together."

"Daddy," Nevaeh's tone was sharp.

"Baby," he smiled.

"Be nice, or I'll tell Grandma-Mommy on you." Her face was stern before she popped her thumb into her mouth and stared into his eyes. "Dabby?" she spoke around the thumb.

"Yeah, baby."

"Don't wet them take me again."

Josh's eyes misted at the memory. "Never again, Vaeh. Never." He kissed her temple and held on tighter.

"So, will you pursue custody of her?" Rhea's voice was pensive, and that unnerved him.

"As soon as I'm stable, yes…but I was hoping that we could pursue custody."

"You were?" Tears shimmered in her eyes.
His brow rose in surprise. "Of course, Rae. You're her mother."

"I abandoned her…" she whispered, certain this would make him change his mind.

Anger sparked as he thought of all Nichole had put his girls through. "You didn't think you had a choice, babe. You were trying to protect her."

She grew quiet at that, her mind wandering. "I'm homeless right now, Josh. I don't know what I'll do, and I don't want Nevaeh dragged around."

Josh's heart pained in his chest. "I'm homeless, too. Just crashing with Levi and Laura 'til I figure some things out." He stared into the darkness as he mulled over an idea. Excitement charged through him, and he grinned. "Look at me," he gently prompted. When her eyes met his, he continued. "Leave it all to me, okay? Don't give it another thought. Just…stay here. Take Nevaeh." Josh transferred their daughter to her mother's arms and stood.

"Josh?" Rhea called, her nerves on edge. She wasn't comfortable being alone with all his family and friends milling around. In her eyes, they all hated her. How could they not?

"Don't worry, babe." He kissed her head and disappeared through his parents' front door.

The house was packed with the people he loved. He zig-zagged through the crowd until he found Jordan talking with Titus. Nodding to the older man, he looked at his friend. "Can we talk?"

Surprised, Jordan placed his drink on the table and stood. "Yeah, man, of course. Where at?"

"Upstairs—Nevaeh's room."

"Sure." Jordan followed his friend upstairs and sat on the Minnie Mouse rug covering the floor. "What's up?"

Josh shut the door behind him and lowered himself to his daughter's bed. "I just wanted to say how sorry I am for beating the crap out of you, J. I hope you know I only did it because I thought I had to."

Jordan smiled, his hand going to his still-bandaged nose. "Yeah. I know. I would have done the same thing had it been my kid. I'm sorry I put you in that position, Josh. All I could think about was you getting arrested for kidnapping, and I just couldn't let you go down like that."

Josh laughed and ran a hand down his face. "How are we friends, bro? I get us into the worst crap ever and you just keep coming behind me and cleaning up the mess. Why?"

Jordan's face grew serious. "Grace—unmerited favor. God cleans up my messes all the time, Josh, while keeping His love freely flowing toward me. How could I not do the same with my best friend?"

Grace. There was that word again. Josh shifted uncomfortably. "Yeah. Hey, listen, I have something to ask you."

Jordan smiled, knowing his friend was resisting the pull of God's grace. "Shoot."

"Still looking for a roommate?" Josh looked sheepish, hopeful.

Jordan's eyes lit up. "Heck yeah, bro! Just you, or Nevaeh, too?"

Josh grimaced. "Well, Nevaeh will be with me a lot, but I still have to work out custody with my parents. I'm also trying to convince Rhea to let herself share custody with me. Here's the thing, man, she doesn't have a place to go. So, I was thinking…if I move in with you, then Rhea could take my spot with your mom and dad until I can afford to get us a place of our own. What do you think? I'd ask her to move in with me, but you'd probably throw a Bible at me or something."

Jordan's face exploded in a smile. "You gonna marry her?"

Josh cursed. "How is that even a question, Jordan? I've only loved that chick for the past eight years…of course I'm putting a ring on her finger! But until I can do that…"

"Yeah, of course, man! I know my parents will go for it."

"I'll split the rent, J. No worries there. I'll get a second job to cover everything. I'll get us a car soon, so we won't be in the way." Hope swelled in Josh's heart as he verbalized his dreams. This was happening. This was really happening. He was making plans to provide for his family. "I'll even help Rhea pay your parents some rent. She's got that job in Lambert but I'm gonna see if she'll find one closer to home. Besides, I don't trust Sterling to keep his distance, and I don't want him coming within a thousand feet of my girl."

"He's a prick, for real," Jordan agreed. "So, when are you moving in? I've got that spare bedroom in the back that I use for storage—I'll clean it out and help you set it up for you and Nevaeh. Just say the word."

"Tomorrow?"

"That works," Jordan grinned, "as long as you promise me one thing while you're living with me."

Josh braced himself. "What's that?"

"You have to commit to church at least one Sunday a month."

Josh stared, weighing the seriousness behind that request before catching the laughter in his friend's eyes.

Shoving him, he stood. "You're a real prick, J," he grumbled.

Jordan leaped up and followed him out the door. "I swear, the roof would stay right where it's at, bro! And hey, you get a free meal out of each service! It's a win-win!"

"Not dragging me to church, Jordan, so save your breath." Josh grinned and shoved him.

"Nevaeh won't let you bail, Josh, she loves Jesus through and through…" Jordan's voice trailed off as the two went down the stairs and back to the waiting crowd.

As they mingled with the ones they loved, there was a reassurance building in the two friends' hearts. A hope that blossomed with the promise of new things to come, new adventures to trek, and, no doubt, new trouble to forge their way through. This time, together, with a team of supporters by their sides.

Chapter 41

"For by grace you have been saved through faith. And this is not your own doing; it is the gift of God, not a result of works, so that no one may boast."
~Ephesians 2:8-9~

JOSH

One month after the trial…

"You finished in the back, boy?"

Josh wiped the sweat from his brow and glanced up to find Zeke walking toward him, iced tea in hand. Grateful, he accepted the cool beverage and downed it in one gulp before answering the question. "Almost. Gotta grab the twelve-footer and climb up that tree to finish that last branch. Did you say you needed a rose bush transplanted at the church today?"

"If you can swing it, yes. What time is the auto shop expecting you today?"

"Three-thirty. I can make it, sir."

Zeke's brow rose. "So, we're back to 'sir?' The inside done changed my boy." He grinned.

Josh placed a hand on the back of his neck. "Sorry, Zeke. There's just somethin' about an added sense of respect when talkin' to you, you know? You scare me sometimes," he admitted with a laugh.

"Ain't me you oughta fear, boy, it's Him." Zeke pointed to the heavens.

"Oh, He scares me too," Josh muttered. More than he cared to admit…

"Gonna be in that pew on Sunday? Bring your girl and her mama with you? Gotta set that example, son." Zeke gave him a knowing look as Josh ducked his head.

"Uh, yeah. You know Nevaeh's not gonna let me skip church, Zeke. We'll be there."

"See to it you are—you won't regret it." Zeke smiled. "Now you better git gone, boy, and finish that tree. Don't wanna keep Mr. Nguyen waiting, now."

"No, don't wanna do that." Josh laughed at the thought of his second job and the owner who ran the auto shop. Even a minute late earned him a harsh reprimand, and he'd made it his goal to be five to ten minutes early for every shift to keep the man happy. Being on time had become easier since buying a used car from the shop two weeks before—reliable transportation that hadn't cost him more than he could afford. Checking his watch, Josh nodded at Zeke. "Gotta get done—we'll chat later."

"At the altar on Sunday, I presume," Zeke teased.

"Yeah, yeah. Sure." Josh grinned.

GARRETT

Garrett sat at the kitchen table, coffee long forgotten and cold. He gripped the letter in his hands, his fingers trembling as he read the words for the tenth time. The front door banged open, and he quickly shuffled the letter under his Bible, stretching his arms out for the little girl barreling towards him. "There's my girl! Hi, Nevaeh!"

"Grandpa!" She threw herself into his embrace and wrapped her arms around his neck, squeezing tight.

"Elysia said it was okay to drop her off for a few hours while I help Mrs. Fuller at the store." Rhea glanced at his untouched coffee and Bible, then back at him. "Is that alright with you?" Still timid of Josh's father, Rhea always reminded herself to watch her step with him, never certain it was safe to fully be herself around him.

"Yeah, of course, Rhea. Will you be picking her up, or will Josh?"

"Um, I'll call and let you know. I'm not sure when he gets off from Nguyen's shop." Rhea leaned in and kissed Nevaeh's cheek. "Love you, baby. Be good."

"Bye, Mommy!" Nevaeh called as she watched her leave. The moment the door closed, she looked at her grandfather and frowned. "Why you crying?"

Garrett mentally kicked himself for allowing his emotions to show. "I'm just so happy to see you, baby girl." Kissing the top of her head, he held her close and opened his Bible to the Psalms, reading softly as she snuggled against him.

JOSH

Josh glanced at the clock on the wall, elbow-deep in car grease. He had thirty minutes to finish his work on the Buick's engine before his day was through. A loud clinking sounded from his left and his eyes shot to the door where the owner had just walked through.

"Why you stand there? Work! Work!" The small man shooed Josh back to the car. Nguyen was harmless. Spunky, but harmless. Over the past month, Josh had become fond of his new boss, though he knew he was expected to mind his p's and q's with the man. It was good for him. Held him accountable and pushed him to work harder than before.

"Yes, sir." Josh nodded and ducked back under the hood of the Buick.

"You leave on time, hear? Not one minute later seven-thirty." Though the man had been in the states for years, his Vietnamese accent had never left him. "Make sure she ready to go before you leave—no minute later seven-thirty!"

"Yes, sir. She'll be ready, sir." Josh picked up a wrench and tightened a bolt, ensuring it had no give when he twisted it. By the time seven-ten rolled around, the Buick was purring. Josh quickly cleaned any grease off the car and drove her out to the lot, ready for the owner to claim her. Heading back inside, he picked up all the tools he'd accessed and placed them back in their respective spots for the next day. He clocked out at exactly seven-thirty—not a minute past—and headed for his car, eager to see the girls he loved. Rhea's text an hour before he'd gotten off had let him know he needed to pick Nevaeh up before heading home, so he took a left on Maple instead of his normal right and headed for his parents' house.

As he pulled into the driveway, his mouth drooled at the thought that his mom might have some leftover dinner in the fridge. There was no spaghetti like his mama's spaghetti. Josh walked up the steps and knocked on the door. When no one answered, he tested the knob and went in. "Mom? Dad? Nevaeh?" he called, hearing no signs of life from the house. He stepped into the kitchen, intent on heading to the backyard. His hip caught the edge of the table and knocked his father's Bible and a stack of papers to the floor. Bending, Josh picked them up and placed them back on the table. He was just about to head for the door when his eyes fell on the contents of the papers, and he froze.

"...grounds for immediate disbarment...forbidden to practice law in the state of California..."

Josh's finger touched the words as he read, his mind whirling. Disbarred? His father, unable to practice law? Because of his confessions about his past? He swallowed hard. His father had consciously decided to confess his past in court, knowing the stakes, to free him from jail. Law was his dad's life—without it, who was he? His eyes moved to the window where his parents sat in lounge chairs while Nevaeh ran through the yard. Slowly, he made his way outside, closing the patio door softly behind him.

"Josh, honey!" Elysia jumped up and gave him a hug as Nevaeh raced for his legs and wrapped herself around them.

"Daddy, take me for a ride! Take me, take me!" Nevaeh begged.

The last thing Josh felt like doing was running around his parents' yard with his daughter wrapped around his leg, but he couldn't bear to disappoint. Placing a kiss on his mother's brow, he forced a grin for Nevaeh. "Hang tight, squirt." He took off, Nevaeh's squeals of laughter propelling him forward.

"I'm going to grab him some dinner," Elysia voiced to Garrett as she headed for the door. "Poor thing looks exhausted."

Garrett watched his wife disappear inside and turned his

attention back to Josh, his heart swelling with love for his boy. He waved to Nevaeh as she clung to her father's leg, blond curls flying around her.

"Again, again!" she pleaded when Josh stopped in front of the patio.

"Nah, baby, you're gonna kill Daddy," Josh wheezed as he doubled over and fell to the ground with her in his arms. He tickled her until she screeched and wriggled free, laughing as she ran. Glancing at Garrett, Josh lay back on the grass, exhaustion pulling. He couldn't give in. There was something he had to discuss with his father. Pulling himself up, he walked to the lounge chair beside his dad and sat down.

"How was your day, son?" Garrett asked.

Josh studied his face beneath the porch lights, noting the sorrow in his eyes. "They disbarred you because of me."

Garrett's smile dropped, the corners of his mouth twitching. "No. They disbarred me because of me."

Josh glanced at the concrete. "You didn't have to tell them all that stuff, you know."

"Yes, I did." Garrett's words were quiet, pained. "I owed that to you—and to your mom. You both deserved justice in the public eye."

"I was just fine before you did that, Dad." Josh's voice had turned testy, irritated.

"Josh, for your entire life I've been your enemy. Never fought for you. Always tossed you into the flames. It's not like that anymore, son. When that woman came after you like she did, I—" He stopped, choking on the tears in his throat. "I just couldn't let her do that to you, Josh. I knew she had all this blackmail on me, ready to lay before the judge. If she had done that and been successful at convincing the judge of my guilt, there would be no more representing you and fighting for your freedom. You would have lost and been tossed in a jail cell for years to come while Nevaeh grew up without a daddy. I just couldn't let it happen, son. I couldn't."

"But your practice...it's...everything to you, Dad." Josh looked at him, confusion in his eyes. "Why would you give all that up for me? I didn't even wanna be around you. I hated you. I still can't figure out how I feel about you, but you chose to give up law for me. Why, Dad?"

"Josh, I was a real prick of a father. I did everything wrong. Everything. I pushed you out of every aspect of my life. Never included you. Me giving up my practice for the son I'd abandoned for all these years is nothing. My practice isn't everything, son. You are everything." Garrett's vision clouded through his tears as he waited for his words to sink in.

Josh sniffed and wiped a hand across his face. "I gotta go, man." He stood, his gaze following his daughter as she slid down the slide. "Nevaeh, time to go. Tell Grandpa bye."

"Bye, Grandpa!" She raced for him and squeezed him before stepping back, eyes serious. "No more crying, okay? We're okay. We're all okay."

"Yeah." He laughed. "We're all okay, baby. Bye now."

Josh led Nevaeh into the kitchen, all smiles when his mom shoved a container of spaghetti at him.

"Promise me you'll eat tonight, son." She stared, sternly.

"Promise, Mama." He kissed her cheek. "Love you."

"Love you back. Bye, Nevaeh!" Elysia smiled as they walked through the door.

Rhea sat on the couch in Josh and Jordan's living room, her sleeping daughter stretched across hers and Josh's legs as they watched their favorite show. She knew something was off with him—she could feel it. He'd been quiet ever since he'd come in and showered. "Babe, what is it?" She kept her voice low, so she didn't wake Nevaeh.

Josh glanced at her; his eyes troubled. He'd been unable to get the letter out of his head—his father's face when he'd talked to him about being disbarred. "I, uh, I need to go make a call." Carefully, he shifted Nevaeh off his lap and onto her mother's before kissing Rhea on the lips. "I love you. I'll be back in a bit, okay?"

"Sure." Rhea's smile lacked confidence as she watched him disappear into his room and close the door.

On his bed, Josh pulled out his phone and dialed Titus' number, holding his breath as the line rang four times before his voice sounded over the wires.

"Hey, hey, how's my favorite fighter?" Titus quipped playfully.

"Why'd you say you were 'a murderer on the run', if your grandpa took the charges?" Josh asked, his pulse pounding.

"Say what?" Caught off guard, Titus took a second to mull over the question.

"In the Bible you gave me. You said you're a murderer—a murderer on the run. But you told me your grandpa took the charges. So why were you on the run?"

Titus sighed. "Ah. Well, son, I was free from the court's charges, but not from the charges in my heart. I knew what I had done. I knew it was me who'd killed that mother. Knew it was me who'd let my grandpa take the fall for my sins. So, you see, I was free, but I wasn't free. Not even a little."

Josh thought on this, tears clouding his vision. "Titus?"

"Yeah, son?"

"They disbarred my dad."

"I see."

"They disbarred him because of me. If he hadn't confessed his past, the judge would never have known, and he would still be free to practice law. But he told them, Titus. He told the whole court what he did to me, and now he can't be a lawyer."

"Your dad did the right thing, Josh."

"Okay, maybe? But why? Why would he do that for the son he didn't even care about?"

"Grace."

Josh yelled and threw his sneaker across the room before he considered Rhea and Nevaeh in the next room.

"I hate that word! Everyone says that word to me, but I hate it! I don't understand it. It makes no sense to me!"

Titus took a deep breath and silently prayed for wisdom. "You hate the word because you feel grace all around you. You fear it because you do not understand it. Grace is favor we have not earned. Your dad confessed to his sins because God demonstrated grace to him in his own life. When you walked back into his life, that was God showing your dad favor he hadn't earned. Your father did not deserve another chance with you, Josh, yet God brought you back into his life and offered him one, and he took it. He took the chance, son, and that is why your father abandoned his right to practice law to save you. Because of God's unmerited favor."

"But...but...I feel like crap because of what he did. Like...I'm not happy with him giving up law, Titus. What is wrong with me? I should be happy he was disbarred—he deserved to be disbarred! But I don't feel happy. Instead, I'm miserable. Why?"

"Josh, a month ago you were freed from prison, right?"

"Yeah, okay."

"You're free from the law, son, but you are not free."

"Speak English, man!" Josh pleaded, desperate to understand this riddle.

"You're a slave to your past, son. A slave to your sins. A slave to all this mess that traps you and holds you back from living life to its fullest. You will never be free unless you accept God's grace for yourself. Your dad has already embraced God's grace. You're an outsider looking in, scratching your head in wonder at it all. But it doesn't have to be that way. You can experience God's grace on your own, Josh."

"How?" Josh's voice cracked.

"Well, the first step is realizing you're a sinner. Remember we talked about what that means? Sin is the bad stuff we do—lying, stealing, cheating, all that mess. It's anything that doesn't honor God. We're all sinners—every last one of us—but only those who recognize and admit it can see Christ. Where do you stand in all that?"

Josh thought for a minute before replying. There was no denying the truth. "Uh, yeah. That's definitely me."

"Well good, you understand the first step. The second thing is to realize that you can't save yourself. Your sin condemns you to a life without God—without His grace to cover you, you're straight out of luck. You cannot be your own hero in this story, son. You need someone to save you."

Josh took a shaky breath. "God knows I've tried to save myself for way too long. I give up, man."

"Good." Titus laughed. "Then you're ready to hear step three. The only One Who can save you is Christ. That's it. He's the only Way. The same way that your daddy sacrificed his career to set you free, that's kinda how it was with God and His Son, Jesus. God gave up His only Son so that you could go free. So instead of you receiving punishment for your sins, Jesus took that punishment on the cross. Remember reading that story and telling me there's no way they would have crucified a man as good as He? Well, son...they did. For you. He let them crucify Him so you wouldn't have to pay the price of your sins. The only thing keeping you from God's grace is believing that Jesus did that for you so that you could be saved. That's it. The sin of unbelief. Think about it–you had two towns ready to throw you away for rape, though you were innocent of that crime. Now, you may have been innocent of raping that girl, but there are a whole lot of crimes you're guilty of, correct?"

"Yes," Josh mumbled, feeling the weight in his soul.

"Jesus was hung on a cross for the sins of the entire world. He was a perfect Man. Infallible. He could not do wrong. And they beat him within an inch of His life and hung Him up on a cross for all to see. Why? So you–the one who is guilty and deserves a consequence–could go free."

"But I...I don't deserve to have someone die for me...I'm not worth it, Titus!" Josh cried.

"No, you're not. And neither am I. But that's where grace comes in. Unmerited favor. God loves you so much that He didn't want you to die without him. So, he sent Jesus. Jesus is how this story ends, son. He began it, and He'll end it, whether we agree with that or not. Do you believe Jesus died for you, Josh?"

Josh sniffed and wiped his eyes. "Yes. I just don't see why He'd do it, knowing what He knows about me."

"Love. God is love, son. He loves you too much to let you die without Him. Accept his grace and watch Him work. Read that Bible I gave you. Get in a pew on Sunday. Take any questions straight to Zeke, and don't leave until you have every question satisfied. Hear me?"

"Yeah. Yeah, I hear you. Thanks, man."

"Anytime. You call me—I'll be right here, Josh."

"Yeah." Josh hung up the phone and grabbed his Bible. Turning to Matthew, he flipped to the portion highlighted in yellow and read about Christ's crucifixion, tears streaming down his face as he finally understood the meaning of grace.

EPILOGUE

"For you formed my inward parts; you knitted me together in my mother's."
~Psalm 129:13~

JORDAN

The knocking grew louder, escalating into harsh bangs. Jordan rushed to pull a shirt over his bare chest as he raced for the door, his heart in his throat. Another bang sounded as he neared, and he jumped, reaching for the knob without even bothering to see who was on the other side. He yanked the door open and stared, mouth agape, right into the eyes of Cali Bristol. In her arms was a bundle, and the bundle was crying.

Cali cursed; her face flushed against the afternoon heat. "How long does it take you to answer a door, Jordan?" Jordan's mind raced, piecing together the last time he'd seen her.
Josh's trial.

What was she doing here? And what was she carrying? She thrust the bundle into his arms, along with a piece of paper, and took three steps back. There was no shawl wrapped around her shoulders today. Jordan gaped at her, then at the baby in his arms, shock gripping his body. "Cali, wha—?"

"There's your son." She crossed her arms and raised her chin. "Either man up and raise him, or pay for his adoption fees, 'cause I'm not done livin' life yet. I want nothing to do with either of you, so don't bother me with him. Ever. Have fun being a dad, Jordan. Hope it was worth it." She laughed as she turned and walked away.

Jordan stared at the infant in his arms before coming to his senses. "Cali! Wait! Cali!" He followed her to the parking lot, reaching her before she stepped behind the wheel of her car. "How old is he?"

"Three weeks."

"What's his name?" Jordan asked, panicked.

"Name him yourself!" She climbed inside the car and shut the door, locking it behind her. Casting the distraught father one last look, she shoved the car into reverse and peeled out onto the street, leaving them both behind.

THE END

Coming Soon from Author Elizabeth Morquecho

Novels
The Highshore Series Continues

Book Two – "Jordan's Bargain"
Book Three – "Heartbreak Promise"

Picture Book
"The Boy with the Yellow Boots"

Updates
www.crossroadspublishingllc.com

About the Author

Elizabeth lives in Houston and serves alongside her husband and children at a small Baptist church. She homeschools her three girls and enjoys bringing them up in the ways of the Lord. She has been writing since she was a child and honed her craft as she grew older. Her passion is for writing Christian fiction dealing with hard life issues and the redemption that only God can bring. Elizabeth is also an editor for Crossroads Publishing, LLC, as well as a freelance editor for writers who need a helping hand. When editing, she loves sharing her art for bringing a story to life with others and enjoys watching a writer when they catch the flame of passionate writing. she isn't writing or editing, Elizabeth can be found at the church with her family or teaching piano lessons to those with a longing to use their talent for Christ. She also enjoys puzzles and playing with her kids and the dog, Django. And she is majorly addicted to all things coffee.

https://linktr.ee/authorelizabethmorquecho

www.ingramcontent.com/pod-product-compliance
Lightning Source LLC
Chambersburg PA
CBHW050511170426
43201CB00013B/1915